A History of Women
IN THE WEST

Georges Duby and Michelle Perrot, General Editors

III. Renaissance and Enlightenment Paradoxes

D0043581

A HISTORY
OF WOMEN
IN THE WEST

III. Renaissance and Enlightenment Paradoxes

Natalie Zemon Davis
and Arlette Farge, Editors

The Belknap Press of
Harvard University Press
Cambridge, Massachusetts
London, England

Copyright © 1993 by the President and Fellows
of Harvard College
ALL RIGHTS RESERVED
Printed in the United States of America
Fourth printing, 2000

Originally published as *Storia delle donne in Occidente,* vol. III,
Dal Rinascimento all'età moderna, © Gius. Laterza & Figli Spa,
Rome and Bari, 1991.

Text design by Lisa Diercks

Library of Congress Cataloging-in-Publication Data
(Revised for volume 3)

A history of women in the West.

   Translation of: Storia delle donne in Occidente.
   Spine title: A history of women.
   Includes bibliographical references and index.
   Contents: 1. From ancient goddesses to Christian
saints / Pauline Schmitt Pantel, editor
3. Renaissance and Enlightenment Paradoxes / Natalie
Zemon Davis and Arlette Farge, editors.
   1. Women—History. 2. Women—Europe—History.
I. Duby, Georges. II. Perrot, Michelle. III. Pantel,
Pauline Schmitt. IV. History of Women.
HQ1121.S79513 1992   305.4'094   91-34134
ISBN 0-674-40372-X (acid-free paper) (cloth)
ISBN 0-674-40367-3 (pbk.)

Contents

Writing the History of Women

Georges Duby and Michelle Perrot

WOMEN WERE LONG RELEGATED to the shadows of history. The development of anthropology and the new emphasis on the family, on a history of *mentalités* centered on everyday life, on what was private and individual, have helped to dispel those shadows. The women's movement and the questions it has raised have done even more. "Where have we come from? Where are we going?" These are questions that women have begun asking themselves. Both inside and outside the university they have set out in search of their forebears and attempted to understand the roots of their domination and changes in male-female relations across space and time.

"The History of Women" is a convenient and attractive title, but the idea that women in themselves are an object of history must be rejected firmly. What we want to understand is the place of women, the "condition" of women, women's roles and powers. We want to investigate how women acted. We want to examine their words and their silences. We want to look at their many images: goddess, madonna, whore, witch. Our history is fundamentally relational; because we look at society as a whole, our history of women is necessarily also a history of men.

It is a history of the *longue durée*: five volumes cover the history of the West from antiquity to the present. And our history covers only the West, from the Mediterranean to the Atlantic. Histories of the women of the Orient, Latin America, and Africa are sorely needed, and we hope that one day the women and men of those regions will write them.

Our history is "feminist" in that its outlook is egalitarian. Our intention is to be open to the spectrum of interpretations. We want to raise questions, but we have no formulaic answers. Ours is a plural history: a history of *women* as seen from many different points of view.

It is also the work of a team. Georges Duby and Michelle Perrot are responsible for the overall coordination. Each volume has one or two editors: Pauline Schmitt Pantel (antiquity), Christiane Klapisch-Zuber (Middle Ages), Natalie Zemon Davis and Arlette Farge (early modern period), Geneviève Fraisse and Michelle Perrot (nineteenth century), and Françoise Thébaud (twentieth century) have chosen their own collaborators—some sixty-eight scholars in all, and we hope a representative sample of those working in this field in Europe and the United States.

We see this series as a provisional summary of the results achieved to date and as a guide to further research. We also hope that it will bring the pleasures of history to new readers and act as a stimulus to memory.

A History of Women

IN THE WEST

Renaissance and Enlightenment Paradoxes

Women as Historical Actors

Natalie Zemon Davis and Arlette Farge

WHEREVER ONE TURNS, they were present, infinitely present: from the sixteenth through the eighteenth centuries, at home, in the economy, in the intellectual arena, in the public sphere, in social conflict, at play, women were there. In normal times they were taken up with everyday tasks, but they also played a part in the events that constructed and transformed society or that tore it apart. From the top to the bottom of the social hierarchy women were everywhere save perhaps in war, and even there they were sometimes present in disguise. Their presence, moreover, was constantly discussed by those who observed and sometimes were frightened by it.

Apart from the real presence of women in everyday life, they also figured to an extraordinary degree in the realm of discourse and representation, myth and sermon, science and philosophy. Paradoxically, the abundant and repetitious discourse on women was part of a strategy to establish order in the universe. It was shaped by a need to hold them in check, by a barely concealed desire to turn their presence into a kind of absence or at any rate a discreet presence within narrowly defined boundaries, rather like a walled garden.

Clearly, what men said and wrote about them did not capture the reality of women's presence. They perceived women only by way of an image, that of Woman, potentially dangerous in her extravagance though necessary for one essential function, motherhood. Woman was not revealed but invented, defined by means of a learned gaze that inevitably robbed her of her substance. Given that these centuries were turbulent ones, during which nation-states consolidated their power and transformed social and political relations despite fierce internal dissension (such as the Wars of Religion), it is not surprising that historians of the early modern period also long neglected the presence of women. Writing history in the masculine gender, they did not allow sexual difference to inflect their narrative, nor were they interested in describing a society in which men and women made their own history through distinct roles and specific desires and conflicts, and through issues that at various times brought them together, drove them apart, or forced them to confront one another.

If we wish now to write a different history of women, we must first let go of a certain vision of the past and take a fresh look at the sources: rather than take contemporary testimonies and representations at face value, we must try to relate what knowledge we have of the reality of women's lives to the texts that discuss women, knowing full well that the two are complementary and intertwined. There is no point in writing a history of women that is concerned only with women's actions and modes of life and not with the way in which discourse influenced behavior, or vice versa. Taking women seriously involves reconstructing their actions within the context of the relations that men and women instituted between themselves. It involves viewing relations between the sexes as a social construct whose history can and should be an object of study.

There was lively debate between men and women in the early modern period. It was a debate that developed against a background of social and political instability and disorientation, as the established church fragmented in the violence and controversy of Reformation and Counter-Reformation and as states turned to mercantilist economic policies. Simultaneously there was talk of the "woman question" and of "the war between the sexes." The theme of male-female conflict crops up in numerous sources, including popular literature (exemplified by the so-called Bibliothèque Bleue, or Blue Library, of cheap editions sold by hawkers). The persistent conflict between men and women constitutes a historical constant whose forms changed in response to changing times and circumstances. Texts, images, and archives take us to the heart of the dispute: women were said to be malicious, imperfect, extravagant, devilish, lethal, and deceitful. Of course they were also gentle and submissive, but cruelty and sexual excess soon loomed larger than these qualities in most descriptions of the sex. In France in 1622 Mlle. de Gournay replied to detractors of the female sex; a few decades later the Précieuses made claims for women's intellectual and literary independence despite the mocking laughter of Molière; in the 1670s, François Poullain de La Barre used Descartes's separation of mind and body to argue that "the mind has no sex." The eighteenth century, which some would later call the century of woman, began with a very animated debate on the nature of female reason and its implications for sexual equality.

The examples just mentioned are French. Yet all of Europe was caught up in the turbulence of events and in the vigorous debate on the woman question. These three centuries of economic, political, cultural, and religious upheaval changed the status of women and redefined their relation to the world. Protestant and Catholic women approached culture and learning in distinctive ways that affected their relation to the family and the community. Epidemic, famine, and war drove many women into one form or another of resistance or transgression and thus brought them into the public arena. Relations between men and women, between the "masculine" and the "feminine," changed as the world changed, sometimes making the balance of power more symmetrical, sometimes not.

Our decision to focus on such historical problems as the social construction of gender difference and the shifting forms of male-female tension makes it imperative to say a few words about the meaning of the word *tension*. It should be understood in a broad sense. When a wire joining two objects is said to be "under tension," it is understood that the objects themselves play a part in maintaining the tension in the wire. This is the sense in which we will be looking at relations between the sexes—as a fragile equilibrium between two worlds made to understand but also to devour each other. This tension gives rise to conflicts but also to divisions of labor and to systems of compensation, to official powers and unofficial but sometimes equally clear-cut counter-powers. This realm "between the sexes" is a world unto itself, whose history over three crucial centuries this volume will recount.

The text that follows is not, however, a chronological narrative of events. Instead, it looks at the history of women from a variety of angles in an attempt to explode the standard myth that women were always dominated and men always oppressors. The reality was much more complex. There was inequality, to be sure, but there was also a shifting zone in which women found and used a multitude of strategies outside the roles of inevitable victims or exceptional heroines to make themselves active agents in history. The difference between the sexes is a space: a place where inequality is rationalized in order to be transcended, a place where events shape reality, an imaginary and imagined place that pictures, fictions, and documents describe in very different ways.

This volume, then, is not an exhaustive compilation of data and events but an exploration of certain problems and thematic interconnections designed to bring to life an abstract notion such as the social construction of gender roles. The process was by no means linear; sudden advances were interspersed with difficult setbacks and reverses.

The space in which women lived, appeared, and worked, whether they were princesses or peasants (and notwithstanding the considerable differences between the two), was one staked out by norms, prohibitions, and controls; but women devised ways of living within these constraints and even ways to escape from them. To stress this range of activity, we open our volume with the "works and days" of women, then turn to images of the sexes, only to show the further limits on this normative discourse by ending with "forms of dissidence" and voices of women themselves.

"Works and Days" explores how women grappled with life's vicissitudes and the religious and cultural activities and aspirations through which they expressed their hopes and dreams. To be sure, in their daily lives women constantly encountered limits on their bodies, on their desire to learn, and on their choice of a future. In every chapter in this first section we inevitably come upon the collection of rules that defined and circumscribed women's roles, both rules of gender and of the social hierarchy in which each woman had her place. The contours of woman's status emerge in Part One, but even more the many different ways in which that status was negotiated and experienced.

Everyday life for women is defined broadly to include not only work, marriage, and family, but also politics. For those whose birth or alliance allowed them access to the court—queens, princesses, and royal favorites—the struggle for power and issues of policy were a daily affair. Women's part in political life in this period can be understood only by recognizing the character of ancien régime politics and by removing the history of queens and women at court from the seeming triviality of spiteful anecdote and bedroom tattle. Of course, the distance between the working woman and the queen encompasses an entire society, but in both cases the woman's condition can be given social and political analysis.

Between the milking stool and the throne come several other aspects of female reality. First, a woman's physical appearance and her sexual nature made her both attractive and dangerous. While remaining obedient to norms and fashions, women were also alert to their own desires. Their situation was not always an easy one, for the whole aesthetic system was so highly codified that a poor but beautiful young woman was at great risk while a poor but ugly one had no identity at all. Beauty is here treated as a social and historical issue for women, not just a "natural" one. Second, in their efforts to gain knowledge, women made slow progress as education was simultaneously furthered by necessity and held back by mistrust. Learning was stingily meted out to them so as not to encourage a perilous rivalry between the sexes over the possession of reason. Finally, in matters of spirituality, some women, confronting the major division created by the Reformation and Counter-Reformation, chose to devote themselves to God, to consecrate themselves body and soul to the love of their neighbor and of Christ. The sensibility of these mystics was sometimes worrisome to both church and state.

The second part of the book is devoted to discourses and representations. The material from which to draw is abundant in these three centuries, from simple woodcuts and popular literature to the works of well-known painters and noted scholars. An iconographer, Françoise Borin, has put together a series of images that show women both as ornaments in their unspoiled beauty and as monsters in all the hideousness of their alleged faults. The debate about woman, both acrimonious and funny, is then examined in letters, theater, philosophy, and medicine. The participants in these fervid discussions embarked on a futile search for the mysterious female "nature," which somehow eluded even the physicians. Some of these images turn out to have considerable give and ambiguity.

Through an increasingly wide range of activities, women found ways to escape both oppressive realities and stifling discourses on female nature. Yet, as the chapters in the third section of this volume show, the space available for transgression was very different depending on whether one was rich or poor. The rich could challenge order usually without violating the law, whereas the poor threatened both law and order, invariably with serious consequences. Well-to-do women developed individual ways of breaking out of confining roles. Happy to take their intelligence in forbidden directions, they used their minds to understand the world. In salons, as Précieuses, as journalists, these women not only staked out a claim to reason but insisted on contributing to philosophy, science, and new political thinking. Some of them paid dearly for doing so.

Among the women of the popular classes dissidence, deviancy, and even public and political rebellion were more mass phenomena and less individual ones, as well as more somber, possibly more audacious, and certainly less freely chosen. For poor women to escape was generally to become marginal. Helpless and frightened young women ran the risk of becoming prostitutes, affirming the virility of bands of youths in the sixteenth century, offering libertines quick and refined pleasures in the eighteenth. Enclosed in family life, some women dreamed of making love elsewhere, of not being continual baby-makers: adultery, abortion, and infanticide, along with domestic theft and family disputes, were bitter symptoms of the desire to be elsewhere. In the sixteenth and seventeenth centuries, witches became the target of the judges. With their multiple forms of magical knowledge, they occupied a space somewhere between Christian religion and belief in the earth's restorative powers. Meanwhile, all through the early modern period women were active participants in riots and other forms of popular violence, alongside the men whom they encouraged and incited to join them. Putting their bodies on the line, they illuminated with their presence the battlefield of collective emancipation.

Prostitute, criminal, witch, rioter. Different types though they were, these dissidents sparked fears while revealing hidden forms of opposition and hope.

The structure of the volume reflects a deliberate design. The analysis of discourse about the sexes is framed by a section on everyday activities and beliefs and a section on women departing from the mainstream. The female voices that conclude this book—those of a Jewish merchant and a Parisian artisan—suggest this range of positions. We hope to reinforce a way of thinking about the behavior of women in terms of conformity, of maneuverability, and of resistance.

A.F.–N.Z.D.

one

Works and Days

The Horizons of Everyday Life

Daily life unfolded within the frame of enduring gender and social hierarchies. It also translated the trends that set apart the
sixteenth through the eighteenth centuries as "early modern": a
surge in population in the sixteenth century, which was leveled
off by recurrent plague and famine only to rise again with the
more productive harvests of the late eighteenth century; an increase in trade, craft manufacture, and city dwelling in societies
that nevertheless remained profoundly agricultural; an expansion
of Europe's commercial capitalism and religious fervor into empires, colonies, and religious dominion overseas; an elaboration
of political institutions, often contested, in centralizing monarchies and republics; and an increase in the rural and urban poor
at the bottom of society and in the families of prosperous lawyers, officers, and great merchants nearer its top.

Olwen Hufton's essay takes us into the fields, craftshops,
fairs, and households where many of these changes were realized. Work and family were a seamless web for women, their
domestic and economic duties adjusted to each move through
the life cycle as daughter, unmarried girl, wife, mother, and
widow. Defined by their relation to men and scarcely able to
survive outside the limits of the marital family, these women
turn out to be surprisingly resourceful, as they save money from
their servants' wages toward a dowry, take on multiple jobs to
support their children, and teach their daughters skills for the
next generation.

Appearance was important to women of all estates. Sara
Matthews Grieco describes how the paths to cleanliness and the
criteria for beauty changed from the sixteenth to the eighteenth
century. The powdering and whitening that were preferred to
water before the eighteenth century were much easier to attain
for well-off women than for peasants. The sixteenth century
liked its women round; the eighteenth century admired the cor-

seted figure. Here again there was a difference between rich and poor, although by the eighteenth century shopgirls in London and Paris tried to emulate the style-setters in their choice of colors and fabrics. Throughout, women's sexuality remained threatening any place outside the marriage bed and the generation of children. Here farming couples had an easier start than highborn ones, for rural custom allowed some exploration of each other's bodies in courtship. Matthews Grieco documents the interplay between prudery and pleasure in marital intercourse and reviews the evidence for reproved heterosexual encounters outside marriage.

Véronique Nahoum-Grappe analyzes the quest for beauty as an aesthetic-social system. Imprisoned by its criteria, some women used them to arrest the male gaze and impose their own views. A seventeenth-century wit told of men who would have liked nothing better than to be a beautiful young woman from the age of thirteen to twenty-two, after which they would revert to their own sex. But this challenge to hierarchy was short-lived, its claim to power ephemeral, as eighteenth-century feminists pointed out.

Literacy and schooling increased significantly at all levels in the early modern period, impelled by the new printing industry, family hopes for social mobility, political concerns for order, and religious devotion and controversy. Martine Sonnet describes these changes as they affected women to a lesser degree than men. Women's instruction was to make them good domestic servants or household managers, dutiful wives, committed mothers, and believing Christians, but nothing more. Still, by the eighteenth century, the new Catholic teaching orders and the expanded Protestant schools had led to a fully developed role of women as teachers—indeed, a role that might allow them to survive outside the marital system. And there were now projects on the books for the advanced education of women. Not realized until the last half of the nineteenth century, these "modest proposals" show what can happen when women take charge of a classroom.

Religious life changed dramatically in the early modern period, and if women never became priests and rabbis, and virtually never Protestant pastors, they had access to almost as many new forms of religious action as men. In Jewish communities, where rabbinical Judaism and the Lurianic Kabbala were strictly for men, the spread of printed religious literature in Yiddish inspired women to create new domestic prayers. In the Catholic world, women's charitable confraternities multiplied, and new orders, both contemplative and activistic, attracted women outside the elite families whose daughters had peopled the medieval religious houses. For those few who could not bear the enclosed life that the Counter-Reformation enforced on the women's convents, there was the pull of the New World, where Ursulines hoped to persuade the Huron and Iroquois women of the truth of the Christian religion. Meanwhile, in the Protestant churches, the priest's concubine was replaced by the pastor's wife, and Bible reading was encouraged for women even if husbands presided over family prayers and biblical interpretation. The Protestant attack on monasticism eliminated single-sex religious institutions in favor of marriage, but by the eighteenth century Protestant women were maintaining that religion and charity were more "natural" to women's sensibilities than to men's. Among the radical sects claims were even made that women had the right to speak openly in church, and the Methodist movement of the eighteenth century shocked the established church with its women preachers.

Within this proliferation of religious activity, Elisja Schulte van Kessel has focused on the spirituality of the Catholic woman mystic—its metaphors, originality, and intensity. Carried on within the convent or outside of it, this quest for union with Christ provided models for religious aspiration more generally, even while confessors and ecclesiastics tried to contain it.

In politics, considered the masculine sphere par excellence, women were present as ruling queens, favorites, observers, pamphleteers, and street rioters. Natalie Zemon Davis examines the gender style adopted by women rulers to accommodate to authority and the success and ambiguities of political actions carried on informally through female "influence." For eighteenth-century feminists of a republican stamp, the character of women's power in monarchies illustrated what was worst about royal government and aristocratic society. Could women share fully in the "manly virtue" of citizenship in a republic? In the last years of the ancien régime, a few women and men would answer this question in the affirmative, even while others were arguing that it was only in religion that women could find their rightful place.

N.Z.D.—A.F.

1

Women, Work, and Family

Olwen Hufton

WHEN THE ESSAYIST Richard Steele sought in
1710 to define woman, he did so in a terse but,
by the standards of the day, fully acceptable manner: "A woman is a daughter, a sister, a wife and
a mother, a mere appendage of the human race
. . ." (*The Tatler*, no. 172).

A good woman, one such as to merit the praise
of men, might find herself commemorated as did
the Elizabethan noblewoman Marie Dudley on her
funeral monument in St. Margaret's Westminster:

> Here lyeth entombed Marie Dudley, daughter
> of William Howard of Effingham, in his time
> Lord High Admiral of England, Lord Cham-
> berlain and Lord Privy Seal. She was grand-
> child to Thomas Duke of Norfolk . . . and
> Sister to Charles Howard, Earl of Not-
> tingham, High Admiral of England by whose
> prosperous direction through the goodness of
> God in defending his lady Queen Elizabeth,
> the whole fleet of Spain was defeated and
> discomforted. She was first married to Ed-
> ward Sutton, Lord Dudley and after to Rich-
> ard Monpesson Esquire who in memory of
> his love erected this monument to her.

From the moment a girl was born in lawful
wedlock, irrespective of her social origins she was

defined by her relationship to a man. She was in turn the legal responsibility of her father and her husband, both of whom, it was recommended, she should honor and obey. Father or husband, it was assumed, served as a buffer between her and the harsh realities of the violent outside world. She was expected to be the economic dependent of the man who controlled her life. The duty of a father, according to the model, was to provide for his child until her marriage, when he, or someone on his behalf, negotiated a settlement for his daughter with a groom. A husband expected to be compensated at the outset of marriage for taking a particular woman to wife. Thereafter he was responsible for her well-being, but her contribution at the moment of marriage was critical in the establishment of the new household.

This model had rigorous application in upper- and middle-class society throughout the early modern period. Marriage settlements for children were interpreted, in the language of the day, as "the weightiest business" a family could undertake. Ideally, the money and resources that a female child took from her family purchased her future well-being and enhanced the standing of her kin through the new alliance. A woman's dependency was a closely negotiated item.

For most women, the model could not be so completely applied. Women of the working classes were expected to work to support themselves both when single and when married. "Consider, my dear girl," runs *A Present for a Serving Maid* (1741), a work aimed at the adolescent, "that you have no portions and endeavour to supply the deficiencies of fortune by mind. You cannot expect to marry in such a manner as neither of you shall have occasion to work and none but a fool will take a wife whose bread must be earned solely by his labour and who will contribute nothing towards it herself." In short, the notion of the totally dependent daughter and wife was called into question by the limited resources of both her father and the man she could hope to marry.

Notwithstanding the obligation to labor in their own support, society did not envisage that women could or should live in total independence. Indeed, the independent woman was seen as unnatural and abhorrent. It was assumed that father and husband would provide her with a home and hence contribute in some degree to her maintenance. This assumption was reflected in customary female wages: a woman could be paid less for her labors because a man put a roof above her head. If a woman could not find work to keep her in her own home before marriage, a substitute protective environment must be sought for her. She must enter her employer's home. He would assume the role of protective male figure and be responsible for the costs of feeding and sheltering her and would stand *in loco parentis* until she left to work elsewhere, to return home, or to marry. The wages he paid her would reflect the fact that she was fed and sheltered. Ideally, she would spend as little of these wages as possible, and her employer would save them for her and place them in her hands when she left his home.

Working Life

The target of the single woman's working life was thus explicit: while sparing her own family the cost of feeding her, she was in the business of accumulating a dowry and work skills to attract a husband. When no more than a child, she was taught by her family and the society in which she lived that life was a struggle against grinding poverty and that for long-term survival she needed a husband to provide shelter and aid. Such realizations were what impelled about 80 percent of country girls to leave home at about age twelve—two years before their brothers did so—to begin equipping themselves for the time when they might hope to marry. From the moment of her departure, the average European girl began a ten- or twelve-year phase of her working life, upon the success of which her future depended. The prospect may have been daunting and frightening, and the pitfalls were known to be many. Childhood was brief for the daughters of the poor.

Agricultural Labor

The female children of smallholders, agricultural laborers, or odd-job men commanded few skills beyond those transmitted by their mothers—perhaps no more than the ability to sew, spin, perform simple farm tasks, or care for younger children. Demand for work as a residential farm servant was very high, far outstripping the supply. Residential work for women in the agricultural sector was limited to large establishments, especially dairy farms, where milking and cheese and butter making were the work of women. There was great competition for farm jobs because they offered servant girls the chance to remain near their families and to avoid an abrupt change in their way of life. Sometimes, however, help was hired only year by year or even for part of a year. In Britain, some hiring was done at fairs. A body of statutes mandated that the unemployed proceed at Martinmas (November 11) to the nearest market town, implements in hand, and offer themselves for work. On such days servant girls and male farm workers, dressed in distinctive garb, bore the tools of their trade and tried to catch the eye of a would-be employer: the experienced cook carried a spoon in her apron, the dairymaid a stool. They bartered their services with a prospective employer, and once work had been secured, the day was turned into a festival. Daniel Defoe, depicting the hiring fairs in the early eighteenth century, described female workers as "eminently impudent" in drawing attention to their talents, and a substantial body of literature bemoaned the cost of agricultural labor as a result of the bartering techniques employed at the hiring fairs.[1] These sources, however, probably exaggerate the importance of the fairs in determining the value of labor and in introducing workers to employers. Memoirs and diaries suggest that family contacts and acquaintances served to recommend most servant girls to their employers and that, once the girls were hired, the two parties rubbed along together for years.

Throughout Europe, family contacts accounted for most placements in farm jobs. In some regions of France, such as Champagne, the spread of cottage industry led to an increase in the number of farm servants because it made possible ancillary industrial labor that contributed to a girl's keep during the dead season. The availability of farm work thus varied from region to region. But overall, by the end of the eighteenth century this kind of work became increasingly scarce, in part as a result of demographic growth, in part as a result of the emergence of larger commercial farms and greater regional specialization. In other areas the overproliferation of smallholdings as a result of population growth reduced the keeping of livestock and the ability to maintain a female servant. When the cow was missing from the landscape, there were few female farm workers.

Domestic Service

The girl who could not find farm work near home looked townward, although she did not necessarily have to go very far; the nearest town of five or six thousand might afford her work as a maidservant, ranging from the lowest resident drudge, who carried heavy loads of laundry to and from the local washplace or loads of vegetables from the market and emptied privies, to cook and cleaner. The demand for urban domestic service appears to have increased considerably throughout the early modern period, reflecting both growing affluence in some sectors of urban society and the cheapness of the labor on offer. Again, the best jobs came through family and village contacts.

The potential for local jobs was usually exhausted before a young girl ventured farther afield. When she did so, it was usually along a well-established route, and at her destination she would find neighbors' daughters and kinsfolk in the vicinity. In short, young girls were rarely pioneers. Sometimes they followed an established migratory flow set up by male seasonal migrants, like the girls of the Massif Central who went down to Montpellier or Béziers to work as servants and whose brothers came down every year to the region to pick grapes; or those of South Wales who stayed in the London area as maidservants after accompanying their male relatives to work in the market gardens of Kent and who made contacts while ferrying fruit and vegetables to Covent Garden.

Female servants constituted the largest occupational group in urban society, accounting for about 12 percent of the total population of any European town or city throughout the seventeenth and eighteenth centuries. Patrick Colquhoun speculated in 1806 that London had as many as 200,000 servants of both sexes but that there were twice as many women as men.[2] Seventeenth-century censuses such as those taken in Wurzburg and Amsterdam show that the influx of young female adolescents gave a distinctive shape to the age distribution of the population. Some of these migrants then left in their twenties, perhaps to return home with their savings and marry in their villages. Contemporary observers believed that smallholding societies produced the greatest number of temporary expatriates because the prospect of setting up on a small farm lured the young back to their native villages. Young people from areas of large farms were likely to leave forever, and adolescent girls from these regions to bloom into townswomen. Probably a great deal depended upon whom one met in the town as well as upon the prospects back in one's native village.

Types and conditions of service must have varied widely. Much depended upon the status of the employer. Servants were an indicator of social standing, and since female labor was cheap and abundant, it was one of the first luxuries even a modest family permitted itself. But although certain ducal families such as the House of Orleans or the Dukes of Marlborough counted their household servants in hundreds, it was unusual for even the most extensive aristocratic household to employ more than thirty servants of both sexes. The gentry and affluent merchants in the great cities might have six or seven. Indeed, one definition of a poor noble throughout the period was someone who had only three servants. In seventeenth-century Amsterdam, however, which had more than its share of wealthy merchants, one or two servants was the norm; and this was perhaps the commonest urban model. The fewer the number of servants, the likelier it was that all the servants would be women.

In the hierarchy of employees of both sexes maintained by an aristocratic household—cooks, coachmen, footmen, butlers, ladies' maids, chambermaids, laundrymaids, grooms, scullery maids, and so on—women held many of the jobs at the bottom. Modest households employed a maid of all work—for which there is an equally cumbersome phrase in most European languages. Tradesmen might employ a girl both to work in the shop and to run errands delivering and picking up work; tavernkeepers employed girls as barmaids, waitresses, and washers up; busy housewives helping in family businesses such as cookshops and bakeries employed girls to do anything from turning a hand in commercial food production to taking the family's washing to the washplace, carrying or pumping water, or lighting and maintaining ovens and fires.

The best jobs were gained through contacts and by ascending the servant hierarchy as one acquired experience and skill. However, a great deal depended upon good fortune and the kind of qualifications one had at the outset. Employers were concerned that a girl have an honest background and would not open the door to a pack of thieving relatives or disappear into the night with the family silver. Aristocratic households traditionally staffed their urban residences with girls from the country estate of the owner. In some parts of France, notably Brittany and the Cotentin, the seigneur's wife, who usually served as godmother to all village girls, was expected to provide a reference, or the priest would be called upon to vouch for a girl. Others looked to relatives living in towns who were or had themselves been in service and who would accompany a girl when she presented herself for the first time to an employer or the housekeeper. The relatives would stress, as Deborah's aunt did to Mrs. Samuel Pepys, the rigorous moral upbringing of the girl and such education as she had had. In Spain throughout this period, employers satisfied themselves with inquiries about a girl's *gobernia,* which included parental formation and the inculcation of basic skills such as sewing and religious training. They did not expect literacy. But by the end of the eighteenth century in northwestern Europe, notions about what a servant girl's education should be had become more sophisticated: a girl seeking a position in a substantial household who hoped to advance beyond basic kitchen drudgery must be minimally literate and nicely spoken as well as competent with the needle.

Charity schools, village schools, and *petites écoles* (as the French called their primary schools), which arose in the mid-seventeenth century, may have been responsible for raising the educational attainments of girls who offered themselves for service. Certainly in Britain the charity school girl enjoyed some solid advantages over other seekers of posts in affluent households. Her education had vaunted the virtues of cleanliness and a neat appearance. Given the housing conditions of the poor and the difficulties of obtaining water and maintaining a change of clothing, the ideal was not easy to achieve. Thus the most persuasive weapons at a young girl's disposal when she presented herself at an employer's door were a clean dress (however darned), a starched collar and apron (however old), stockings without holes, and shoes that had been polished. In the world of domestic service, initial success could depend on the effective use of a couple of teaspoons of cornstarch. The charity school girl had also been taught deference and a respect for honesty and sobriety. In domestic service, these were attributes that counted.

The girl who entered a multiple-servant household at the bottom could expect to come by a variety of skills in kitchen service and in laundry work, tending and repairing linen. After a few years of washing dishes and scrubbing floors, lighting fires, and fetching and carrying coal, water, and slops, if she maintained a neat air and had a degree of good looks and a trim figure, she might advance to parlormaid. With a measure of good luck, which might include resisting the advances of employer or, more probably, fellow servant, she might find her way upstairs to chambermaid or lady's maid.

However, at each stage of the upward journey, she faced competition or came up against the limited demands of the household of which she was a member. If she was ambitious she must move "for her preferment." Hence the intense mobility within the world of domestic service by the end of the eighteenth century and the fading image, much bemoaned and exaggerated by the affluent, of the long-term retainer. Mobility was made possible by contact and recommendation and, in Britain, the newspaper. However, competition at the upper end of the scale was intense; one advertisement for a lady's maid would bring scores of applicants.

There were many girls, however, who could not compete in the career structure of service, and the immiseration of certain regions as a result of demographic growth in the sixteenth and eighteenth centuries brought many from the countryside into the towns. These girls were chronically poor, undernourished, rickety, pockmarked, dirty, and lice-ridden. They lacked the training that fitted them for employment in even a modest household. Girls from entire regions—and, in the case of Ireland, from an entire nation—who arrived in British cities seeking work were automatically excluded by the very poverty of their backgrounds from anything approaching a respectable situation as a servant.

Service, then, embraced a vast range of conditions. For a small minority it had a career structure, and in her mid-twenties a maidservant who had managed to become a chambermaid or lady's maid would have a respectable capital sum, the amount depending upon her ability to accumulate without cutting into her wages to help her family or to cope with periods of illness or unemployment. At the other end of the scale were the vast majority of women whose work was wretched, volatile, dependent upon the honesty of the employer and upon staying constantly in work so that they did not eat into their reserves. A maidservant who became pregnant was simply dismissed. In the middle were those who by their mid-twenties might have fifty pounds to their names, a modest sum but a personal triumph.

Industrial Labor

In some industrial areas, which relied on a reservoir of cheap female labor, the domiciled servant was in fact the resident textile worker. Cheap female labor was critical in the development of European textile industries, such as the silk industry at Lyons. Silk was a costly delicate fabric intended for the wealthy and prepared from start to finish in urban workshops under the supervision of a master. Female labor was used to empty the silk cocoons, twist the thread, wind the shuttles, and draw them through the loom to achieve patterned effects of great complexity. The work of men was to set up and pull the loom. Every workshop included a minimum of three to four girls, a male apprentice, the master, and his wife. Over the industry as a whole, female workers outnumbered males by five to one. Girls were recruited from the surrounding villages, the barren Forez, and the hilly Dauphiné into the master's dwelling, which also served as workshop. They slept in cupboards and under looms, and their wages were saved by their employers. Girls of twelve and fourteen started work in the lowest job, that of cocoon unwinder, sitting over basins of scalding water into which they plunged the cocoons to melt the sericine, the sticky substance binding the cocoon together. Their clothes were continually damp, their fingers lost sensitivity, and tuberculosis was rampant. Still, if she could survive without long periods of unemployment—during the frequent slumps, girls were unceremoniously shown the door—and advance to draw girl, then after about fourteen years a female silk worker had not only a sum of money but also a wide range of industrial skills. She was the ideal wife for the ambitious apprentice because she could provide him with the lump sum to pay for his mastership and contribute to the running of a new workshop.

The lace industry, too, could be organized on a resident basis to help young girls accumulate a dowry. From the purchase of raw thread through the actual fabrication to the sale of the finished product to the wholesaler, the lace industry tended to be entirely in the hands of women—an unusual state of affairs in European handicrafts. Lace was the costliest textile commodity in Europe. By the mid-eighteenth century silk sold at about ten shillings a yard; an equivalent amount of lace cost about twenty pounds. The value lay entirely in the handiwork, and many years were required to learn the skill. Yet the remuneration was at the lowest level of female wages: in France a day's labor might provide a couple of pounds of bread. In lace areas tens of thousands of women were involved in production. In some of these areas, notably in Flanders, where the best lace was made, and in the Pays du Velay in France, philanthropic effort achieved the seemingly impossible and converted lace production into a small dowry-raising enterprise. In

Flanders convents taught lacemaking to children for nothing and, when they were proficient, put aside a little of their wages to help them accumulate a small lump sum. When they married they could become outworkers or come to the convent workshops, where they did not have to pay lighting and heating costs. In the Velay there were no such convents, but groups of pious women called Béates, backed by some philanthropic money, ran lace dormitories in the city of Le Puy free of charge and negotiated the sale of work with the merchants to see that the lacemakers got the best price. After a small deduction for food, they held onto the proceeds of the sale to help the girls accumulate their precious dowries. After marriage these young women could work at home, and the Béates, by invitation of the villages, ran communal houses where the village women could congregate and share lighting costs and a common soup pot.

Silk and lace production were thus tailored to bring girls into the towns, teach them a craft, and help them with their dowries. By about 1600, however, women in two kinds of circumstances were beginning to break with the notion that a woman needed a dowry in money to attract a husband, regarding the acquisition of a skill, backed perhaps by a few assets such as linen and furniture, as sufficient. This perception gained ground both in villages where income from rural industry was steadily outstripping income from agriculture and in the towns among the lower artisan and service sectors.

In the industrial village, unmarried women would stay with textile production in their homes only if they believed the work could offer them long-term security. The financial rewards had to be higher and more constant than the proceeds from seasonal cottage industry, such as the spinning of wool or linen in winter. The young men and women of a parish stayed there if they were confident, first, that they could set up house or could, after marriage, live with their parents on sufficiently high industrial earnings; and, second, that they could secure any equipment they needed from a merchant or manufacturer to whom they sold their goods on completion. If the industry then took a downward turn, one or two generations might be caught in poverty, with the young couple clinging to the notion that an upward turn might reestablish them. In time, however, their progeny were forced back into domestic service or into another region with more flourishing industry. Perhaps eventually another industry might develop in their village, as in Devon, where serge production gradually died and button production took its place. But such developments were by no means inevitable. When the Languedoc woolen industry faded at Clermont de Lodève in the eighteenth century, this hive of industry became a virtual ghost village.

Industrial villages were remarkably endogamous, and when the industry was thriving marriages took place early because there was no need to wait for the accumulation of a sum to hire and stock a farm. When an industry took a downward turn, marriages were postponed, and the birthrate fell.

Except in a few industrial cities, a girl born of working-class parents in a town or city was unlikely to become either a domestic servant or a textile worker. Instead, as censuses make clear, she pursued one of a limited number of options in the garment trades (as seamstress, mantua maker, milliner, glove stitcher, embroiderer) or service trades (as washerwoman, street seller, stall operator). Or, perhaps most commonly, she contributed to a family business, working at home.

In most European towns girls' work options were limited by the restrictions of the guilds, which regulated the urban world of skilled work with varying comprehensiveness. The daughters and wives of tradesmen involved themselves in aspects of artisanal production, but most guilds resisted women's attempts to enter their specialties. Resistance to women in guild-regulated production often came less from the masters than from their workmen, who were afraid that women would work for less and hence undercut journeymen's wages. When work was plentiful and labor scarce, the guilds were relatively tolerant and turned a blind eye to women's activities in their sphere; but when times were hard, attitudes changed. Thus in the sixteenth century the tailors of Augsburg, who in easier times had tolerated women's production of outer garments, suddenly resisted their right to make anything except aprons and lingerie.

By the late eighteenth century the guilds were fast disappearing in Britain and France. Even so, women existed most easily in newer trades such as millinery and mantua making, which had no medieval antecedents. During the eighteenth century work became more plentiful, particularly in the garment trades, but as the number of women seeking such employment increased, the work became identified as "women's work," and wages fell accordingly. *Campbell's Directory of London* in 1762 placed all the garment trades practiced by women in the category of pauper work, exposing the incumbent to dire necessity and providing the recruiting ground for prostitution.

At a somewhat lower level than that of the solid artisan family the mother was more likely than the father to shape the choice of a daughter's job. The washerwoman's daughter became a washerwoman, the seamstress' daughter a seamstress, and the innkeeper's daughter stayed at home and served the beer and victuals. The tendency of urban parents to absorb their female children into a work pattern perhaps explains the relatively small number of recorded formal apprenticeships for women. Indeed, those who sought such apprenticeships were likely to be either orphans, on whose behalf orphanages sought guaranteed work and protection, or girls whose parents were in work that could not absorb them and who lacked relatives such as a seamstress aunt who could provide structured help. These two categories sought formal apprenticeship not because the training would guarantee a girl a better job but because they needed assurance of continuous training leading to regular employment. In seventeenth-century Geneva, contracts of formal apprenticeships for girls were made to lacemakers, buttonmakers, and makers of watch chains, clock keys, and small screws for clocks. Orphanages and British charity schools, however, regarded such training as uncertain even with the nominal guarantee; they considered that domestic service offered better prospects for an orphan girl. Such schools refused to put their girls into textile manufacture because the vagaries of trade could land them resourceless on the streets. In their view a woman's security was best guaranteed by a relative or, when a relative was lacking, by sturdy, honest, and structured employment as a maidservant.

Marriage

Most women in fact married as the model insisted they should. Between 1550 and 1800 the proportion of women who died above the age of 50 in the celibate state varied from 5 to 25 percent. The highest levels occurred in the mid-1600s but fell dramatically over the next century; permanent spinsters constituted something under 10 percent of the population by the end of the eighteenth century. In the seventeenth century more French women married than English women, but thereafter the number of French spinsters began to rise, and by 1789 about 14 percent of those dying over the age of 50 had never married. In the seventeenth century, English women married on average at the age of 26, but by the end of the eighteenth century at just over 23. In France, women's average age at marriage at the beginning of the seventeenth century, 22, rose gradually to 26.5 on the eve of the Revolution.[3] Demographers explain these dissimilar patterns as being determined by the behavior of the rural masses: lower ages at marriage reflected easier employment situations, better wages, and the availability of farmsteads. Falling real wages in late eighteenth-century France pushed up the age of marriage: couples had to work longer to raise the wherewithal to hire and stock a farm. Higher wage levels in Britain and steady agricultural prices in the early eighteenth century had the reverse effect, reducing the number of the permanently celibate and lowering the age at marriage. Such Dutch evidence as we have suggests that prosperity throughout much of the seventeenth century encouraged earlier marriage, whereas more difficult agrarian conditions and industrial depression in the second half of the eighteenth century led to later marriages and an increase in the permanently celibate.

Fewer aristocratic and middle-class women married than did those of the working class. By the eighteenth century more than a third of the daughters of the Scottish aristocracy and almost as many from the British peerage were permanent spinsters. The mounting cost of marriage portions explains part of this trend; to provide for more than one female child severely taxed even the wealthiest families. One or two female children were married to establish alliances and increase the family's status, but the rest were kept at home or, in later life, maintained in modest style in properties that would upon their death revert to the family. Whereas men of noble stock would marry wealthy commoners, noblewomen did not marry outside their caste. Because a wife assumed the status of her husband, such marriages would have brought dishonor upon their families and themselves. Middle-class women from large families also faced limited opportunities. The eldest daughter would find a husband, and widowed aunts might seek to help another, but resources were limited. Moreover, there was less adequate provision for those women who did not marry than for aristocratic spinsters.

In families in which women were responsible for the accumulation of their own dowries, there was little to prevent all the female children from finding partners. However, hard times, low wages, high rents, or the unavailability of farmsteads could lead to postponed or late marriages. Hence the rector of Bletchley described the plight of a young couple in his parish thus:

> Will Wood junior, wants to be married to Henry Travel's Daughter, the prettiest Girl in the Parish, being uneasy with his grandmother [who can't afford to settle him] . . . The Times are so hard, small farms so difficult to be met with, the spirit of inclosing and accumulating Farms together, making it very difficult for young people to marry, as was used; as I know by experience this parish, where several Farmers, tho' much wanting to marry and settle, for the want of proper places to settle at . . .[4]

Clearly, this young couple was forced to wait for a vacancy. In areas where rural industry was well established and young people could conceive of an existence without much capital to sustain them, age at marriage tended to fall. Even so, the couple would hope to have enough put by to purchase rudimentary furniture, bed coverings, cooking implements, chickens, and a goat or a pig. Below a certain level of society, economic considerations had no part to play in marital choice, because neither party had any ostensible reserves other than his or her potential earning power. In an English or Scandinavian village such couples might find their marriage opposed by the community (including the vicar and the justice of the peace), since such a marriage could lead only to a greater burden on the poor rate.

In the towns there was little to stand in the way of such resourceless marriages. However, the couple in question, whatever the genuineness of their affections, were hostages to fortune. Unless engaged in industrial work in a period of buoyant growth, they must inevitably become paupers. Such a prospect must have been a powerful deterrent to and perhaps the ultimate corrosive of a lasting human relationship.

Whom one married depended upon one's class, in some instances upon birth position—the oldest daughter of an upper-class family usually had priority—and upon the size of one's dowry. Most women did not marry beneath themselves. An aristocratic heiress had the pick of the market. The daughters of clergymen, doctors, and lawyers married men in the same profession as their fathers and thus cemented business connections. Farm servants married farm laborers and hoped to set up with their accumulated resources on a small farm. Sometimes girls who had gone to work in town as servants returned home with their little sums and set up as smallholders' wives. But those who had emigrated to town from an area of large farms were unlikely to return to their native villages. The children of the Beauce, for example, had little opportunity for local employment. Adolescents from the region were driven first toward Chartres (limited in its demands for labor), to Orleans (more promising), and inevitably toward Paris with its seemingly endless resources.

Of the young people who did not return home to marry, a minority of servant girls married other servants, and of these a minority may have remained in service, although demand for a resident couple was limited. The logical course for a servant girl upon marriage was to use her portion and her husband's contribution to set up in business of some kind, running a drink shop or a café bar, or for the pair to go into the catering business. Often the maidservant's main social contacts with the opposite sex had been with apprentices delivering goods to the back door. Tavern servants married construction workers. Other servants married tradesmen and opened lodginghouses. In industrial areas, spinners married carders or weavers. The large unskilled and largely urban female work force of flower sellers, peddlers of haberdashery, load carriers, and the like who had no dowry on marriage, or those who had failed to amass a dowry because of illness or unemployment, were not precluded from finding a marriage partner; but, lacking capital or a substitute skill, they could expect to marry only a man in a similar position.

The evidence everywhere points to economic considerations as the main determinant in the choice of partner, although this fact need not have precluded romantic considerations as well. Marriage was interpreted as an institution designed to furnish succor and support to both parties, and a clear perception of economic imperatives was essential to survival.

Marriage was seen not merely as woman's natural destiny but also as a metamorphic agent, transforming her into a different social and economic being as part of a new household, the primary unit upon which all society was based. The husband's role was that of provider of shelter and sustenance. He paid taxes and represented the household in the community. The role of the wife was that of helpmate and mother. At the highest levels of society, women became mistresses of houses with servants to organize, estates to manage with the help of stewards and agents, and hospitality to proffer on their husband's behalf. The appearance and dignity of the wife confirmed the status of the husband. The wives of professional men such as clergymen also had a defined complementary role. For the farmer's wife the provision of support services in the family economy could entail a wide range of obligations, depending upon the affluence of the household. Tending livestock, growing vegetables, keeping bees, sewing, mending, preserving, lending a hand at harvest, and exploiting the family's gleaning rights in the community were among the services ancillary to the holding that could fall to her.

Generally, although the labors of a wife were deemed essential for the well-being of a family and an idle wife was seen as a curse upon her husband, her work was rarely estimated in monetary terms. Even in areas where countrywomen were able to work in domestic industry, in agriculture, or even on the roads for pay, they were seen not as generators of money but as providers of largely unremunerated support services within the family.

Married countrywomen with children and encumbered with the work of a holding did not take on more paid work than they regarded as strictly necessary to the subsistence of their families. They defined need by reference to an adequate diet, warmth, and the ability to ward off debt. In short, they sought outside work only when the family was in need. Otherwise the arduous, long, and physically unpleasant work related to family and holding was paramount. Women carried water to steep mountain terraces in areas where the terrain was difficult and water scarce. In many cases the terraces themselves had been constructed from earth carried there in buckets by women. They cut and dried turf, collected kelp, firewood, weeds by the roadside to feed rabbits. They milked cows and goats, grew vegetables, collected chestnuts and herbs. The commonest source of heating for British and some Irish and Dutch farmers was animal turds, which were gathered by hand by women and received their final drying out stacked near the family fire. Haymaking and harvesting involved heavy spells of work, and weeding had to be done in all weather. Small wonder that women liked spinning: it gave them the chance to sit down for a few hours while productively occupied.

By the end of the eighteenth century the work patterns of the countrywoman had changed in many areas. One reason was population growth, which reduced the number of available subsistence units, depressed wages in the agricultural sector, pushed up prices, and inspired commercially minded landlords to curtail commons and gleaning rights. Growing numbers of married women tried to become casual daylaborers, hoeing and weeding vegetables on large properties in the appropriate season. In Britain, however, the introduction of heavier farm tools curtailed their labors as harvesters. Everywhere a potential labor force of married women seems to have been anxious to perform industrial work, leaving the running of the smallholding to husbands and perhaps abandoning the keeping of livestock or time-consuming agricultural work.

By the end of the eighteenth century, too, domestic industry increasingly reflected regional specialization. Some industries offered opportunities only to women and thus separated the work space and preoccupations of the sexes. In lacemaking communities in Buckinghamshire or in the Pays de Velay, women sat at their lacework—usually in groups in a specified house to share lighting costs—for twelve to sixteen hours a day while the men farmed their minuscule properties or tended sheep. In other cases, such as worsted production in the North Riding of Yorkshire or cotton manufacture around Barcelona, Rouen, and Troyes, both partners absorbed some industrial work, and industry gradually supplanted agriculture as the dominant source of income. Cottage rents rose to reflect not the real value of the land but the value of living in an area where the potential for industrial income existed.

There was, however, nothing inevitable about the establishment of industry in barren areas with a large reservoir of female laborers. In the Massif Central, the Pyrenees, many Alpine villages, the Welsh interior, most of southern Ireland, and the Scottish Highlands, which lacked extensive rural industry, adults were forced into significant migrations. In most cases the men left home and the women remained behind, but there were exceptions: Welsh women and their children walked to Kent and the market gardens of the Home Counties to pick fruit and vegetables and carry them into Covent Garden during the summer season; Highland women joined laboring gangs with their husbands on Lowland estates; the women of Massat in the Pyrenees walked their children into Toulouse during the winter months to beg on the steps of Saint Sernin while their husbands worked as itinerant tinsmiths in the Ebro Valley in Spain.

Generally, when farms in arid or mountainous regions could

no longer feed a family, women assumed responsibility for the farming for months or even years while their husbands worked as seasonal laborers or even emigrated for a time. Sometimes the woman ran the farm only between planting and harvest, and when the man returned from his seasonal job as, say, a chimney sweep, he performed the more difficult chores. Occasionally migration occurred in winter: peasants from Auvergne, Savoy, Tuscany, the Pyrenees, or Ireland went to the city—Paris, Bordeaux, Saragossa, Valladolid, Livorno, or London according to the traditions of their region—and looked for work on the docks or hauled coal or wood. Others went off in the summertime, like those peasants of the Massif Central who traveled south to Mediterranean regions to help with the grape harvest. Sometimes they stayed away for several years. In Corrèze and Aveyron a considerable number of married men as well as bachelors walked to Spain to offer their services in the ports. Their wives took over all farm work. Irish peasants also left for long periods, but of course potato farming was work that could easily be done by women. The men's remittances would pay the rental on holdings and the return fare across the Irish Sea, but the work of the farm was done by women. Everywhere, women's activity was deemed needful to hold a farmstead together and feed the children.

The role of married townswomen in the family economy does not lend itself to easy generalization; much depended on the town and the potential it offered. There, too, however, most married women filled roles complementary to their husbands'. In a family business, such as a printing shop or a drapery, a woman might function as an organizer, a fellow worker (mixing ink, cleaning letters, measuring cloth or ribbon), or, more often, a bookkeeper. Many mercantile houses in cities such as Amsterdam and London drew on the bookkeeping services of the merchant's wife. Even Mr. Thrale, the eighteenth-century brewer who would not allow his wife to work in the kitchen, saw nothing demeaning in letting her control the books, since she was a far more competent business manager than he.[5] Lower down the social scale, women appear to have virtually monopolized the actual sale of objects made by their husbands. Or they operated in their own right as petty traders in the market or shop or merely on street corners. In many towns, married women were prevented through borough custom, guild regulations, or municipal laws from trading in their own right. In sixteenth- and seventeenth-century Oxford, for example, only free men of the borough or their widows could do so. Nevertheless, women did the actual work of selling even though the shop or stall was leased in their husband's name. Hence the fishwives of Amsterdam, Marseilles, Paris, Glasgow, Edinburgh, and London dealt with customers in the market while the fishmongers handled the wholesale trade. While butchers were responsible for slaughtering cattle and preparing joints of meat, their wives and daughters were frequently involved in taking the money from customers and in selling tripe, sausage meat, and black puddings (blood sausages). Covent Garden and Les Halles were packed with women selling all kinds of food, from eggs and cheese to fruit. They also played a role in the sale of grain and flour. When George Morland chose to paint a "higgler"—a picturesque term for someone who drove a bargain with a farmer and then retailed the produce—he depicted a woman. In 1699 thirty-one licensed female breadsellers operated in the Terreiro de Paco in Lisbon; five of them had very large businesses and a virtual monopoly over the sale of bread in this major square. Probably their husbands were circumventing guild controls by baking outside the city.

One form of selling in which married women were preponderant and which was quite independent of the activities of their husbands was the secondhand clothes trade. The importance of this traffic in early modern Europe should not be underestimated. A substantial proportion of the population did not purchase new clothing. Children wore hand-me-downs or cut-down adult clothing. In times of hardship, the poor parted with their clothes (outerwear first) and acquired others from secondhand dealers when times improved. Paris in the 1760s had 268 registered secondhand clothes dealers, all of whom were married women or widows. The business needed little capital input and involved transactions primarily among women. Mothers exchanged children's clothing with appropriate compensation to a middlewoman; maidservants bartered employers' castoffs; the clothes of a deceased person were exchanged for money or other garments by the inheriting relatives. These businesswomen seldom encountered opposition from male guilds. However, in the difficult economic conditions of the mid-1500s the municipal council of Augsburg, under pressure from the peddlers' guild, tried to restrict door-to-door selling by women and also to exclude them from selling secondhand goods. Such measures, however, were temporary; when better times came, the limited profit margins involved in the secondhand clothes business relocated it in women's hands.

Contemporary advice literature counseled maidservants that

the best long-term use for a dowry was investment in a small business independent of a husband's, to serve as a resource to fall back on should they be widowed.[6] Typically these enterprises took the form of taverns, drink shops, or little *buveries,* the tea or coffee houses fashionable in English and Dutch towns, confectioneries, or services providing cooked meals—the last two limited in certain towns by guilds. Sometimes these businesses involved little more than preparing meals in one's own kitchen for sale to a neighboring household or making dripping or black pudding for the people in one's street.

Many married women in town and country were multioccupational, with no single aspect of their work occupying them full-time. They might operate as saleswomen only on market days, or as washerwomen by arrangement with specific families only a few times a month. Other responsibilities always waited: caring for children, shopping, carrying water, and perhaps organizing older children into some kind of remunerative activity, such as selling pies or commodities made by the parents. Frequently entire families performed one set of tasks during the day and another in the evening—like the Spitalfields silkworkers who made fireworks when they went home or the silk seamstresses of the Leicester area who supplied fine condoms for Mrs. Phelp's mail-order service.[7] In the economy of expedients that characterized the way most families lived in early modern Europe, the woman was likely to be the pivotal figure. While her husband performed the single job of agricultural laborer or casual worker she might be engaged in very different tasks at different seasons. Unlike her husband's tasks, which were clearly demarcated and began and ended (unless at harvest) at a specific time and usually permitted him some leisure to spend in the tavern or village square, "a woman's work was never done." If her man fell ill, was suddenly unemployed, failed to return from his seasonal migrations, or died, her work must expand to cover the deficit created in the family economy. In his lifetime she may have been an ancillary worker, but she was nonetheless crucial to the survival of the family unit.

Motherhood

The purpose of marriage, along with companionship and succor, was the reproduction of the species within a sheltered environment designed to ensure that a woman was not left to rear her child in isolation and that a man did not escape the responsibility of maintaining his offspring. Children represented the perpetuation of property, and the ultimate protection of aged parents in a violent and troubled world. Viewed in rational abstract, if woman had a role in adult life, it was as mother and procreator.

Oddly, we still do not have a convincing history of maternity. Traditionally, historians have asserted that in the early modern period the relationship between parent and child was not a caring one, that parents were hostile or at best indifferent to the young child, whose interests were regarded as subservient to that of the family as a whole. Motherhood has been presented as a negative state. More recently, however, the harsh prescriptive literature generated by clerics and physicians has been tested against diaries, memoirs, and ego-documents and found wanting.

A great variety of factors, such as seasonal migration, harvest failure, or epidemics, might determine family size among ordinary working people or the poor, but typically their advanced age at marriage ensured that families were small, with four to five children born at just over two-year intervals, two to three of whom would reach adulthood. Aristocratic and middle-class families were larger, owing to the lower age at marriage and the suppression of the natural depressant on reproduction in women, prolonged lactation; these two groups put their children out to nurse.

Infancy was a perilous period, but a child born healthy and nurtured on breast milk absorbed some of the mother's immunities. The next substantial risks would not occur until weaning, sometime around age two. In preparation the child's diet was supplemented by a starchy pap of boiled bread or the child was given crusts to suck upon. Many mothers agonized over this transition. Ann d'Ewes in the mid-seventeenth century lost a child already prone to fits at the weaning stage. Her husband reported their joint grief at the loss of a child she had so carefully nurtured "and whose delicate favour and bright grey eye was so deeply imprinted in our hearts, far to surpass our grief for the decease of his three elder brothers, who, dying almost as soon as they were born, were not so endeared to us as this was."[8] Popular sayings suggest that mothers were aware of the dangers of premature weaning. Infant mortality was a recurrent fear at all social levels. Catholic mothers arranged scapulars around their children's necks to ward off evil during the day and recited incantations over the infant in the cradle to avert sudden death in the night. A famous seventeenth-century Dutch print titled *Nightmare* depicts a child being snatched from the cradle by the figure of death. Diaries and memoirs recount anxieties over coughs and fevers, listlessness and croup. Herbals attest to an abundance of folk cures and rituals to cope with the maladies of childhood: gentian for thrush, goose grease for a wheezy chest, camomile to calm the overactive. The loss of a child was a painful experience, and the older the child, the greater the loss. Educated women left a testimony to their grief denied to the illiterate. "Every man knows," claimed Dorothy Leigh in the seventeenth century, that a mother's love for her child was "hardly contained within the bounds of reason."[9]

A mother's role was that of nurturer. A baby's place when not in the cradle was in her arms. It was her job to keep the child warm, fed, and clean according to the standards of the day. During our period swaddling, believed to form the child's limbs properly, was gradually abandoned. Children of all social levels were not washed or changed as frequently as their modern counterparts. Nevertheless, mothers were expected not to allow their children to lie in stinking, unchanged, or damp hay or to let their bodies become oververminous. In seventeenth-century Dutch genre painting the title "mother's work" referred unobliquely to delousing a child's hair, a gesture used to symbolize her control over the child's mind as well as its body. In the criminal courts a woman lost any chance of a good character reference if it was revealed that she had left her child dirty or unfed or had allowed it to wander.

A child cried, it was believed, to make its wants known. At birth a child cried on leaving the shelter of the womb; at baptism a bawling babe suggested the fitting renunciation of the devil as the sign of the cross was made on its brow. A baby crying in the night had been frightened in its sleep by troublesome dreams and needed the comfort of its mother.

Coroners' inquests reveal that overlying, defined as suffocation in the parents' bed, was cited as the commonest cause of infant death. In fact these were probably what today we call crib deaths, since it is now seriously questioned whether a child can be suffocated in a bed. However, clerics and medical men made impassioned pleas for children to be kept in cradles. They also blamed women for children's deformities, early death or character defects. Culpepper, the famous medical authority on childrearing, criticized women for prolonging breastfeeding, for overfeeding, and for ignoring modern medical recommendations such as bleeding in favor of ancient superstitions. Their rancorous prescriptions make clear that the survival of the species was safer with women than with these male professionals.

A contentious issue in medical and philosophical treatises, which emerged in the late seventeenth century and gained prominence over the next fifty years, was that of wetnursing. Historians have seized upon this phenomenon as an indicator of maternal indifference to the young. However, the probable motives of two of the three groups of women who put their children out to nurse contradict this view. For aristocratic women, social obligations and possibly taboos on sexual intercourse during lactation seem to have been important. Middle-class women living in cities seem to have been motivated by a belief, confirmed by mortality statistics, that the city was not a healthy environment for a child. Finally, for working women in occupations in which suckling a child was rendered impossible by the working environment, the need for the mother's full-time labor services and the hazards of an artisan's workshop for a baby were the most obvious justifications for employing a wetnurse. The number of infants put out to nurse was never more than a small fraction of the total number born. Moreover, in the course of the eighteenth century the number of babies from the first two categories who were wetnursed seems to have fallen markedly as propaganda attacking the practice as unnatural mounted. However, among working women in industries such as silk production in Lyons, where looms and dangerous vats of scalding water were part of the living and working environment and the mother was the organizer of an immigrant work force, the practice continued because the family had no real alternative. Thus use of a wetnurse seems to have reflected social or economic imperatives rather than parental indifference.

There were different categories of wetnurses. Affluent families tried to find a healthy, well-nourished woman who had recently weaned her own child and who lived on a comfortable farm. Either the baby would be sent to her to care for there, or she was paid to live in the family's household. Further down the social scale, those seeking wetnurses were obliged to use poor women. Over time—and this rather than the attacks by philosophers may have explained the decline in the practice—only women who could find no other source of income would take in a nursling. Hence the practice tended to become concentrated in the poorest areas such as the Morvan or the Cevennes. At the very bottom of the hierarchy of wetnurses were women who served the foundling hospitals, and these were much at risk from children carrying sexually transmissible diseases. Thus wetnursing became part of the economy of expedients of the poor in certain regions; aristocratic infants were increasingly maintained in the nursery of the parental home and fed, often lethally, on substitutes for mother's milk if their own mothers could not, or would not, feed them.

If her child survived infancy, a mother assumed the role of educator, although what that meant varied with social class, time, and place. A mother taught her child to negotiate the world in which they both lived. Notwithstanding the battery of servants, nannies, nurserymaids, and governesses available in aristocratic households, memoirs of aristocratic mothers frequently reveal concern for the advancement of their daughters and for equipping them for the marriage market. A daughter's success reflected upon the mother: in addition to some acquaintance with vernacular literature she needed to know how to present herself, dress, manage a household of servants, dance, embroider, play a musical instrument, and speak French. Lady Mary Wortley Montagu considered the upbringing of three daughters a full-time occupation. A middle-class girl accompanied her mother on charitable errands, learned how to keep household accounts, and knew about pickling, preserving, and other methods of food preparation appropriate to the season even if she herself was not the cook. A daughter reflected the image of the household.

A literate mother invariably had literate children, and unless she was from the highest social class, she usually taught her children their letters herself before they went to school. The availability of village schools varied enormously with the locality. The English dame school was often little more than a child-minding service in which a little reading might also be inculcated by the good lady who sat with her spinning wheel. Some seventeenth-century French schools run by teaching orders operated only during the dead season. Others regarded the teaching of reading as less important than basic needle or textilemaking skills. Whatever the quality of the local educational fare, however, a mother's educative role remained crucially important for her daughters. She taught them all she knew in the way of cooking skills. From corners of Dutch genre paintings children watch their mothers chop onions, peel carrots and apples, scour milkpans, turn cheese, make pancakes, knead dough and leave it before the fire to rise. The rituals of food production and of meals in traditional societies were extremely important. For the masses, bread and bread-based soups strengthened by a little salt pork or lard and improved by herbs and vegetables constituted the bulk of the diet. Even so, considerable ingenuity often went into food production. Growing vegetables, keeping hens, and feeding a pig (a task reserved exclusively for women and often included in a dowry) were important means of survival that female children had to acquire. Innumerable observers record mothers and daughters gathering weeds together at the side of the road for goats and rabbits, plundering hedgerows for berries, gathering mushrooms and herbs, and amassing firewood and animal turds. Christmas, Easter, and certain feast days such as that of Saint Catherine, which entailed the preparation of Cattern cakes, all demanded the making of special dishes. A legacy of kitchen knowledge appeared in unexpected sources. When the Inquisition attacked the Conversos, people of Jewish descent who had intermarried with Christians, it tried to locate their Jewishness in ritual and belief. Very often, however, it emerged that the beliefs had been lost and all that remained was a way of preparing dishes, the use of oil, or abstention from ham or sausage, all handed down from mother to daughter. The greater the range of cooking, pickling, preserving, and cheese- and butter-making skills that came her way, the better the daughter's chances of a good post in service.

Along with cooking, a mother was expected to teach her daughter needle skills. Fine needlework marked a great lady. A woman, however high her rank, was expected to produce baby bonnets and layettes and embroidered waistcoats to offer at Christmas to her husband or brother. Lower down the social scale, the emphasis was on hemming, seaming, mending, and darning. Shirts, petticoats, children's garments, and smocks were all made by women at home. Girls were also taught all tasks designated as female around the home. They assisted in the care of younger children. They helped to prepare food for their brothers and stitched their clothing.

The 1570 census for Norwich indicates that girls were much more readily absorbed into urban domestic industry than their brothers. Four-fifths of the girls, compared with less than one-third of the boys aged six to twelve, were working. Another third of boys were at school. Lacking as yet the physical strength to take on man's work and perhaps less dexterous at this age than their sisters, only a very small minority of boys were employed at spinning or knitting, which engaged the majority of girls. Similarly, the 1814 census of Bruges underscores that although girls were making lace by the age of ten, their brothers were not gainfully employed.

At the lowest levels of society the expedients for maintaining a frail livelihood involved close cooperation among family members, but the partnership between mother and daughter in the work force was perhaps the most striking. Girls learned survival skills from their mothers. Mothers and young daughters together sold milk, crockery, and vegetables in the markets; they also begged together. The economy of the poor was invariably a delicate balancing act, and those who lost their footing and fell into the ranks of the destitute were numerous. Where to turn in hard times was valuable knowledge.

Although the domestic conduct books of the sixteenth century made the inculcation of certain moral and behavioral values incumbent upon both parents, over the next two hundred years theologians and moral commentators alike became increasingly persuaded that female morality at least was a maternal inheritance. A daughter was what her mother made her. A witch could only beget a witch (referred to in English as "the witch's get"); a woman of low morality who begot bastards would produce a bastard-bearer. A virtuous woman, defined as one who impressed the virtues of chastity, cleanliness, and sobriety upon her child, would do conspicuously better in this scale of judgment.

Mothers were also critical in the transfer of popular beliefs. They told their children tales, warned them against witches and devils, taught them to leave bowls of milk for mischievous fairy folk, put them on their guard against what they perceived as evil.

Most European parents parted with their children in their early teens. How much contact was sustained between the two thereafter must have varied with literacy, proximity, or contact at second hand through immigrant connections. Perhaps the lower one was down the rural social scale the more conspicuous the severance. Nevertheless, evidence of a significant return rate among young men and women who had served an apprenticeship or been in service elsewhere, to a fragment of land in their native snowclad Pyrenees or the barren Maremma Toscana bears witness to the tug of family considerations.

Historians of the nineteenth century are now making us aware of a phenomenon they believe to be crucial to an understanding of the relationship between mother and daughter, which they label "dowry bonding." This has much deeper roots. Every mother knew that her daughter needed material assets on marriage and that the more she had, the higher her standing would be in the community and in the eyes of her husband's family. To assist in the important process of dowry accumulation, mothers put aside some of their work profits when they could, perhaps from the sale of eggs, a pot of honey, or a fattened pig that had been the runt of the litter, as a cumulative contribution. Or mother and daughter might rear rabbits on hand-picked weeds for the same purpose. Many mothers directed their young daughters' needlework toward making quilts and household articles either from scraps or from bits of raw wool picked from hedgerows and converted over the years into cloth. This collaboration in the accumulation of a dowry helped to cement the mother-daughter relationship and perhaps also helped it to survive physical distance.

Certainly modern sociologists consider the bond between mother and daughter to be commonly the strongest of those between members of the nuclear family. In the past such bonding emanated from complex considerations that may have included household management teaching, shared views on negotiating the system, continuing dependence over childbed advice and infant care, and perhaps sometimes a feeling of solidarity against the putative inadequacies of husband and father. Many upper-class women went to their mother's house for their lying-in, and mothers might well make use of their seniority, as Mme. de Sévigné did, to take to task a daughter's husband deemed unreasonable in his demands. How common such practices were at a lower social level is impossible to know. There are indications, however, that the ogre of the interfering mother-in-law of music-hall jokes has a long history among men in western European society, though not in southern Europe, where a wife upon marriage entered her husband's family's household and hence had to encounter her mother-in-law as a potential critical force.

Widowhood

Parents were aware that their chances of seeing their children reach adulthood were not high. The orphaned child, particularly the orphaned female child, was perceived as particularly at risk not only by fiction writers but also by philanthropists and writers of moral treatises. A widower's duty was to find a substitute mother for his children by remarriage, by bringing an unmarried female relative into his home, or by sending his children to a sister's home. The stepmother is traditionally a fearful figure, deemed in lore likely to prefer her own offspring to her stepchildren. Another alternative was for the father to substitute his eldest daughter in the role of mother and household manager while the role of the son remained unaltered. This may have reduced the daughter's ability to work on her own behalf to accumulate a dowry and placed upon her the expectation that as long as the father lived, she would tend to his wants. In many ways, the death of a mother was more to be feared than that of a father. On the other hand, a widowed mother also had to place new burdens upon her daughters.

The loss of a husband in a society that defined a woman in terms of her relationship to a man was obviously an event that carried immense social, economic, and psychological consequences for a woman. The higher the social standing of the family, perhaps the less the upheaval. An aristocratic woman was, at least theoretically, in command of her jointure, the income guaranteed to her when she brought her dowry into the marriage to sustain her in her lifetime in the event of her husband's death. Furthermore, the aristocratic widow was usually delegated rights in the wardship of her children. Hence she passed into a directorial capacity and became arbiter of her own destiny, unrestrained by any tutelage.

An abundance of evidence indicates that wealthy widows thrived when their husbands died. In the eighteenth century, for example, Mrs. Delaney, Lady Granville, the victim of a positively unpleasant match arranged by her family, blossomed as the doyenne of London etiquette, watching with tastefully concealed restraint the pursuit of her wealth by a string of suitors while retaining her independence.[10] There were Hester Thrale and the Duchess of Leinster, who, after less than harmonious marriages, married a second time gloriously and defiantly below their rank, according to personal choice. Mrs. Thrale lost many friends, including the sanctimonious Samuel Johnson, when she married her children's Italian tutor, Piozzi. The Duchess of Leinster was widely deemed to have married her son's tutor in unseemly haste—she waited only a month after the Duke's death—but her women friends at least were sympathetic. The letters, diaries, and tracts of the period reveal a hysterical obsession among middle- and upper-class males: In the event of their death, would their widows squander their wealth on impoverished gigolos who excited their physical interest? The best monument to the theme is in Samuel Richardson's *Familiar Letters on Important Occasions* (1740), titled "Letters from a Gentleman strenuously expostulating with an old rich widow about to marry a very young gay gentleman."

Churchmen also dwelt on the widow's follies in the advice literature of the Reformation and Counter-Reformation. Post-Tridentine reformers sought to channel widows' funds to philanthropic ends and to provide the widows themselves with a meaningful lifestyle through church-based activity. In these efforts they achieved some success. Many widows became founders of religious orders, using the wealth they had acquired through marriage. Louise de Marillac, widow of the de Gondi and foundress of the Sisters of Charity, and Jeanne de Chantal, widow and foundress of the Visitandines, are two conspicuous examples, but there were many more of lowlier origin. Other wealthy widows found occupation as *salonnières,* patrons of *philosophes,* and English blue-stockings.

Most widows, however, were left in middle age with adolescent families and insufficient means to indulge their whims. Society expected the widow to bury her husband with decorum or honor; doing so might entail expenses that she could ill afford. The Irish wake, for example, which demanded that the widow give hospitality to a mourning village in commemoration of her lost husband, was widely decried by clerics, from the Bishop of Cashel downward, for ruining many poor women. Thereafter society's expectations of the widow were limited to an exercise of fortitude and an ability to pick up the pieces so as not to become with her children a burden on the parish.

The funeral over, the widow's debts were not necessarily paid. The guilds generally allowed a widow to continue production in her husband's name, provided that she paid the dues for doing so. Crucial to her survival in business was permission from the guild to retain apprentices, who were the cheapest form of labor. Few guilds allowed a widow to take on new apprentices, but if she was also prohibited from continuing with those indentured by her husband, she would almost certainly have to close shop.

No one ever assumed that a widow could do as well as her

husband had done. Hence journeymen and servants to whom debts were due now demanded settlement, adding further to the widow's problems. Many had to default, and the most conspicuous sufferers were servant girls, who failed to realize their accumulated wages. Once debts had been paid, the widow had to decide at what scale she could continue to operate. If the business demanded male physical strength, she was obliged by the guild to employ journeymen. British and Dutch women, for example, might try to carry on a family printing business, but the rules of the Stationers' Company insisted that a journeyman pull the press. Women could continue to run an undertaker's shop but had to employ men to carry the hearse. In any case a male presence was required in the rituals of death. In Geneva, the assembling of clocks had to be a male business, but the widow could keep the manufacture on her premises and take a role in the making of parts or the engraving of cases. Taken overall, the need to make good the husband's labor by paying for a substitute probably stripped over 90 percent of artisans' widows of the ability to keep their husband's business fully functioning.

Best tailored to cope with the eventuality of a husband's death was the family economy that included a small business, especially a tavern, a café bar, a victualler's shop, cake, pie, or muffin production, or a lodginghouse. Most of these activities lay outside guild regulation. The maidservant who on marriage did exactly what advice books recommended with an eye to an uncertain future and took on a small business was best protected, since these activities fell outside guild regulation. If, in the husband's lifetime, the business was only an ancillary part of the family economy, upon the death of the male partner the widow could look to the business for support, and the children could contribute to the enterprise. Hence a large number of taverns, cabarets, and refreshment stands were run by widows, with large numbers of widows' children selling hot pies and sweetmeats from trays in the street.

The widow thrown back on the work of her hands with children to support probably sank as low as it was possible to sink in the European economic hierarchy. She was heavily represented on poor lists and records of charities, and if charity was to be had—and there was nothing automatic about this—she was the most conspicuous candidate whose claims were universally acknowledged.

Spinsterhood

Permanent spinsters were not much better off than widows unless they had family members to provide support. The low level of female wages precluded an independent existence. Many single women clustered in towns, sharing garrets and sparse lodgings and serving as support networks to one another. Their exiguous wages left them with little or nothing to buttress them during sickness, unemployment, or old age. Some might find shelter in a brother's dwelling or serve as mother substitute to a relative's orphaned family, but the prospects were bleak, even for those with more than a rudimentary education. Mary Wollstonecraft considered the opportunities to be limited to governess, housekeeper, lady's companion, or mantua maker. Like a growing number of desperate middle-class women, Wollstonecraft turned to the pen; but the number of women who succeeded in making a living from their writings, even by the end of the eighteenth century, when Fanny Burney, Mme. de Staël, and imminently Jane Austen had raised, or were transforming, the standard of female literature, can be counted on the fingers.

Outside the family and the allotted roles of daughter, wife, and mother, women existed against considerable odds. Independence, as Virginia Woolf observed much later, depended upon a private income and a room of one's own. The insistent location of "natural" woman within the family created enormous problems for women who had no family or who found the family inadequate to support them. In the long run, and increasingly by the end of the eighteenth century, it was the women who could or would not conform to the model roles imposed upon them who would force the pace of change. The happy ones or the ones who saw no alternative to their lot were not to be the history makers.

2

The Body, Appearance, and Sexuality

Sara F. Matthews Grieco

TWO CONFLICTING ATTITUDES toward the body characterize the early modern period. On the one hand, the Renaissance inherited from the Middle Ages a basic mistrust of the body, its ephemeral nature, its dangerous appetites, and its many weaknesses. This heritage of suspicion and diffidence carried over into the Protestant Reform and the Catholic Counter-Reformation; accordingly, sixteenth- and seventeenth-century Europeans were encouraged in prudery with respect to the body, its appearance, and its sexuality. On the other hand, the Renaissance also brought the rediscovery of the nude and a rehabilitation of physical beauty. The artists and humanists of the Italian peninsula disseminated throughout Europe classical ideals of physical and spiritual perfection as well as Neoplatonic justifications for earthly love and beauty that were to form the basis for the aesthetic canons and elite mores of the early modern period. But it was also from Italy that the dual scourges of plague and syphilis reached the rest of Europe, causing the closure of most public baths and brothels, the rejection of water for bodily hygiene, and the promotion of marital sexuality at the expense of all other sexual practices. Attitudes toward the body and sexuality were thus marked by an unceasing dialectic between the obsession with erotic love and the obligations of social and religious duty. This same paradoxical dialectic was to define women's bodies and their sexuality for almost three hundred years.

The Body

Women's social identity has long been conditioned by their culture's perception of their bodies. Whether they be considered "imperfect males" or "walking wombs," earthly reflections of divine beauty or lascivious lures in the service of Satan, their lives are dominated as much by their society's attitudes toward the body in general as by its more specific definitions of gender.[1] In order to understand both the social and imaginary dimensions of women's lives from the sixteenth through the eighteenth centuries, it is therefore essential to understand how the body was perceived and treated. What was considered necessary for its protection, hygiene, and maintenance? Above all, what were the criteria according to which women constructed their appearance, and what purposes did this appearance serve? Canons of feminine beauty and norms of physical hygiene underwent a series of significant changes between the end of the Middle Ages and the end of the early modern period. These evolutions in practice and taste reflected, however, more than just changes in the concept of the body and the appearance of women. In a period of chronic social instability and political and religious conflict, they also expressed a constant and overwhelming concern for order and clearly defined social boundaries in which the concept of gender played a ubiquitous and determining role.

Personal Hygiene

Cleanliness and personal hygiene are relative concepts that underwent a radical transformation from the early Renaissance through the eighteenth century. Formerly dependent on regular baths and the luxury of the steam room, bodily hygiene in the sixteenth and seventeenth centuries became a waterless affair. Clean linen replaced clean skin. A new fear of water gave rise to substitutes such as powder and perfume, which in turn created a new basis for social distinction. More than ever before, cleanliness became the prerogative of the wealthy.

The Dangers of Water. During the sixteenth and seventeenth centuries the custom of bathing, either in public establishments or in the privacy of the home, virtually disappeared. Fear of contagion (plague and syphilis) and more stringent attitudes toward prostitution (a sideline of many baths) accounted for the closure of most public bathing establishments. In private homes, growing distrust of water and the development of new, "dry," and elitist techniques of personal hygiene brought about the disappearance of the bathing tub.

The deliberate elimination of public baths constituted an act of social and moral hygiene. Far from being devoted solely to personal cleanliness, these establishments also offered services that civil authorities regarded as a threat to the moral tenor of the cities. Wine and meals were served to bathers in or out of the water, and beds were available for those who wished to rest after their ablutions, to meet their lovers, or to be entertained by a prostitute. Although many bathing facilities allocated different rooms or separate bathing pools to men and women (some even alternated men's and women's days or served one sex only), most public baths were places of pleasure, associated with brothels and taverns in the minds of contemporaries. Preachers thus inveighed against the evil habits of young men who wasted their time and their patrimony in visiting "brothels, baths and taverns." Similarly, Albrecht Dürer's careful accounts of travel expenses list his baths (often taken with friends) among the costs of other pastimes such as gambling and drinking.[2]

Moral depravity was not, however, the only ill associated with those naked or scantily clad bodies that mingled in the intimacy of the steam room, partaking of the often boisterous pleasures of the collective tub. Like taverns and brothels, baths were among the first establishments to be closed in times of plague, in accordance with the prevailing belief that any gathering of people would facilitate the spread of the dread disease. Doctors and public health officials also discouraged bathing of any sort during epidemics for fear that the naked skin, its pores dilated by hot vapors, would become more vulnerable to the pestiferous "miasmas" that were credited with carrying sickness. Throughout the sixteenth and seventeenth centuries, belief in the permeability of the skin and the threat that bathing presented for health in general continued to furnish medical texts with a variety of arguments against the evils of public baths and the dangers of water. In the sixteenth century, fear of syphilis joined that of other contagious diseases in the stock arguments against promiscuous baths, along with other, more fanciful but equally important fears such as that of "bath pregnancies," whereby women were supposedly inseminated by adventurous sperm wandering about in warm waters. By the seventeenth century the theoretically debilitating effects of hot water were universally recognized: dilated pores permitted the body's humors to escape, provoking the loss of vital forces, weakness, and even more serious ills such as dropsy, imbecility, and abortion. Postbathing precautions usually included a rest in bed, which might last several days. In 1610, Henri IV found it perfectly understandable that his minister Sully, though summoned to attend him, was unable to do so because he had to rest after taking a bath. Not only did the sovereign urge Sully to stay at home that day, but he also consulted the royal physician, who opined that any effort might be harmful to the minister's health. Sully was accordingly cautioned not to attend the king until the next day, and then only if he remained dressed in his night clothes, bonnet, and slippers.[3]

Slowly baths became a medical rather than a pleasurable or hygienic practice, accompanied by the use of cupping-glasses to draw off harmful humors and inevitably surrounded by a series of precautionary measures. The body was considered "open" and vulnerable when wet, "closed" and protected when dry; whence the development of new, waterless techniques to ensure the niceties of personal hygiene and presentability.

Wiping, Powdering, and Scenting. Scholars long believed that the disappearance of water from daily ablutions in the early modern period constituted a lapse into a universal state of grease and grime. This was not entirely true. Although the filth of the lower social orders remained, in this period, as much a characteristic of their inferior status as the dingy homespun garments on their back, those who could afford to do so tended to pay increasing attention to the care and appearance of their person, or at least to those parts visible to the public eye.

Where water disappeared, wiping and rubbing, powdering and perfuming took over. Courtesy books such as Erasmus' influential *De civilitate morum puerilium* (1530) not only described the proper way to blow one's nose or to sit at table but also mandated the cleansing of the body and its orifices, thus emphasizing new social imperatives that distinguished the elite from the "vulgar." Refined gestures, behavior, and appearance became so many signs of social rank to be appropriated by the new elites, constituting a hierarchy of manners to replace the old, medieval hierarchy of birth.[4] And it was here, in the domain of good manners and sophisticated appearance, that aristocratic and educated women assumed the role of *arbiter elegantiarum*—judges of taste and umpires of male conduct—whether as the taciturn muses of Italian court *conversazioni,* as the much-ridiculed but ultimately influential Précieuses, or as the hostesses of literary and philosophic salons. In all these milieus, a predominantly male audience paid due homage to women's authority and judgment in the increasingly important realm of manners and social propriety.[5]

In accordance with the new norms of civility, more attention was paid to the parts of the body that were not covered: the face and the hands. But whereas in the sixteenth century water was still used for morning ablutions on these two parts of the body, by the seventeenth it was considered fit only for rinsing the mouth and the hands—and only on condition that its potentially harmful effects be tempered by the addition of vinegar or wine. Courtesy books especially discouraged the use of water on the face because it was believed to harm eyesight, cause toothache and catarrh, and make the skin overly pale in winter or excessively brown in summer.[6] The head was to be vigorously rubbed with a scented towel or sponge, the hair combed, the ears wiped out, and the mouth rinsed. Powder made its initial appearance as a kind of dry shampoo. Left on the head overnight, it was combed out in the morning along with grease and other impurities. By the end of the sixteenth century, however, perfumed and tinted powders had become an integral part of the daily toilet of the well-to-do, men and women alike. This visible and olfactory accessory not only proclaimed the privilege of cleanliness enjoyed by its wearer but also his or her social standing, for fashion was also a privilege of the wealthy. By the seventeenth century, powder had so conquered the upper classes of Europe that no self-respecting aristocrat would be seen in public without it, and by the eighteenth century young and old sported white heads of hair, either wigs or their own silvered locks. An absence of powder came to signal not only a dual impropriety (hygienic and social) but also social inferiority: it was the bourgeois and their inferiors who had "black and greasy hair."[7]

Perfume was likewise credited with a number of virtues, the most important of which were the aesthetic elimination or concealment of unpleasant odors and the hygienic functions of disinfection or purification. Scented towels were used for rubbing the face and the torso, especially the armpits. Long used by the rich to disinfect houses, furniture, and textiles in times of plague, incense and exotic scents were also used in clothing chests to "cleanse" their contents. So powerful were some of these scents that the opening of a coffer could clear a room; thus in 1639, when the coffers of Queen Anne were opened in Saint Germain, both servants and spectators were forced to flee until the rooms were aired. Like powder, perfumes became a sign of social standing, and the distance between "good" and "bad" odors increased to the extent that in 1709 the French chemist Nicolas Lémery proposed three categories of scent: *parfum royal, parfum pour les bourgeois,* and a *parfum des pauvres* made of oil and soot, whose sole purpose was to disinfect the air. Whence another class privilege, for perfume not only protected the body but also ensured good health. It eliminated not only bad odors but also infectious vapors and contagious miasmas: in 1664 an Italian visitor to the Hôpital de la Charité in Paris noted that a bouquet of flowers and an incense burner were placed next to each sickbed in order to purify the air and disinfect the wards.[8]

Whiter Is Cleaner

The new rules of propriety, which dictated that the visible parts of the body be inoffensive to the eye and pleasing to the nose, were more concerned with appearance than with hygiene. A clean appearance was a guarantee of moral probity and social standing; whence the importance of white linen, whose candid surface was identified with the purity of the skin below. Body linen, this "outer envelope" or second skin, also served as a protection for the "inner envelope" or epidermis, and in this respect it progressively came to act as a substitute for all other cleansing functions. White cloth was especially valued, not only because it absorbed perspiration but also because it was supposed to attract impurities and thus preserve the health of the wearer. As of the early seventeenth century a change of shirt or chemise was an essential element of daily hygiene for both the bourgeoisie and the aristocracy—so much so that Savot, in his 1626 treatise on the construction of châteaus and townhouses, pointed out that bathing facilities were no longer necessary "because we now use linen, which helps us keep our bodies clean better than the tubs and steam baths of the ancients, who were deprived of the use and convenience of undergarments."[9]

In the late fifteenth century, shirts and chemises began to peek more and more boldly out from under the garments of men and women. By the end of the sixteenth century, touches of lace or a ruffle at neck and wrist had expanded into fanciful collars and ruffs, spreading into elegantly embroidered expanses that flowed over shoulder, breast, and forearm in the seventeenth, and turning into cascades of lace and transparent finery in the eighteenth. Throughout the Renaissance, the use of body linen thus increased significantly, in inverse proportion to the use of water and baths. When Jeanne d'Albret died in 1514, the inventory of her possessions mentioned only a few undergarments. By the end of the century, however, the notary in charge of Gabrielle d'Estrées's inventory declared that her chemises were so numerous that they "cannot be counted." Men were equally convinced of the value of body linen. In 1556 the Parisian physician Jean Lemoignon possessed thirty-two shirts at the time of his death, and in 1567 his colleague Geoffroy Granger left thirty-four. Inventories after death further testify to the triumph of body linen in the wardrobes of the upper and middle ranks of society: as of the middle of the sixteenth century, undergarments came to warrant a heading of their own.[10]

Not everyone, however, changed his or her shirt every day. In 1580 Henri III of France was considered "effeminate" because he changed his linen too often, whereas in 1649 Mme. de Montpensier felt her social rank compromised by the lack of a change of underwear. By the end of the seventeenth century, however, most of the urban population found a change of shirt every three to seven days to be more than adequate to their needs. Convents and schools insisted upon a regular (though not daily) change of body linen and imposed similar requirements regarding stockings and detachable collars. Over and above the frequency with which individuals of different social standing felt the need to change their undergarments, the fact remained that linen was not a material affordable by all, much less a change of linen. Even though students, workers, and artisans wore shirts made of hemp, which cost about one-fourth as much as a linen undergarment (excluding lace and other embellishments), even the price of these was steep for most purses. In mid-seventeenth-century Paris a hempen doublet was worth approximately two livres, the equivalent of three or four days' salary for a manual worker. Hemp also had two major drawbacks: it was both less comfortable and less white than linen. Only linen and silk could attain the snowy purity demanded by elite standards; once again, "true" cleanliness remained a privilege reserved to the noble and the wealthy.[11]

Body linen and undergarments did not become widely used until the eighteenth century, when the standards set by the ruling classes not only filtered down to servants, salaried workers, and artisans but also inspired a proliferation and diversification of undergarments in which feminine fashion played a decisive role. Whereas in 1700 only 78 percent of salaried women and 75 percent of female servants possessed a chemise, by the year 1789 these proportions had risen to 93 and 100 percent, respectively. The variety of body linen used by both men and women in the lower echelons also attained a sophistication hitherto reserved for the well-to-do. By the end of the century 75 percent of artisans and bourgeoisie possessed between ten and thirty chemises, eleven pairs of stockings, and thirty-four pairs of sleeves. Furthermore, almost all women owned petticoats and coifs, whereas only 60 percent owned corsets and nightgowns.[12] Drawers or underpants, however, remained restricted to the upper classes (and the servants who wore their mistresses' secondhand clothes) until the nineteenth century.

Drawers are reputed to have been an Italian invention, introduced to France by Catherine de Médicis in order to ride a horse *à l'amazone* (sidesaddle) without transgressing the rules of decorum. Many contemporaries approved of this feminine adaptation of a male garment insofar as it both preserved "those parts that are not for male eyes" in case of a fall from a horse and protected women from "dissolute young men, who put their hands under women's skirts." The preservation of feminine modesty was not, however, the only function of this unusual garment. Noblewomen had their *caleçons* or *calzoni* made from rich materials, thus adding yet another weapon to their intimate arsenal of suggestion and seduction.[13] That drawers were considered a rather daring addition to the panoply of feminine lingerie is further attested by the fact that courtesans were repeatedly condemned for wearing similar "masculine" articles of dress. Though popular with these ladies' admirers, pantalettes not only transgressed ecclesiastical rulings against cross-dressing but also were suspected of constituting a concession to male homosexuality in that they made their wearers look like boys.[14] Even in the eighteenth century only actresses, window-washers, prostitutes, and aristocrats wore drawers, whose primary functions remained, paradoxically, the protection of modesty and stimulation of the erotic imagination. It would take the hygienic revolution of the nineteenth century to impose underpants as a basic element of the feminine wardrobe.

The Return of Water

Although water continued to be credited with many harmful powers and regarded with much suspicion throughout the early modern period, the bath made a comeback in the eighteenth century, both as a luxurious pastime and as a means of a therapeutic exercise. In the 1740s aristocrats began to construct luxurious bathrooms in their palaces and townhouses; some were embellished with fountains and exotic plants. Although most immersions were still surrounded by precautionary measures (a purge beforehand, bedrest and a meal afterward), the practice began to catch on. In 1751 the bathtub described in the *Encyclopédie* was somewhat similar in shape to our own today. Made of copper or wooden staves, it was no longer round but oblong: 4.5 feet long and 2 feet wide.

It was the location and the temperature of the water, however, that determined both the purpose of a bath and its impact on the body. Hot baths in private homes were voluptuous events practiced by indolent women (and men), often in preparation for an amorous encounter. Elsewhere, hot baths could serve a curative function. In 1761 a bathing establishment was built on the banks of the Seine where the wealthy (a bath there cost the equivalent of a week's salary for an artisan) could be "cured" close to home by the virtues of river water.[15] Cold baths became increasingly popular after 1750, following a rash of monographs and medical studies on the value of bathing in maintaining health: a properly taken bath was believed to help the humors circulate, tone up the muscles, and stimulate the functioning of the organs. A new generation of physicians waxed enthusiastic about the tonic qualities of cold water, which contracted the body and increased its vigor. Cold baths were therefore considered useful, not because they cleansed the body, but because they strengthened it. On the whole, those who took cold baths did so as much out of a kind of ascetic morality as for health reasons. Favored by a rising bourgeoisie whose energy disdained aristocratic languor, the cold bath became the symbol of a new, "virile" class in opposition to an old, "effeminate" aristocracy whose delicacy was the proof of its decadance.[16]

Appearance: Beauty and Cosmetics

Beauty has always been just as relative a concept as personal cleanliness. From the end of the Middle Ages to the end of the early modern period the canons of feminine beauty and the ideal womanly form underwent a series of radical transformations. From svelte to plump and from fresh to painted, the female silhouette and complexion responded to changing conditions of diet, status, and fortune, creating new standards of appearance and taste, new ideals of the beautiful and the erotic.

Fat Is Beautiful

The medieval ideal of the graceful, narrow-hipped, and small-breasted aristocratic lady gave way in the sixteenth century to a plumper, wide-hipped, and full-breasted model of feminine beauty that was to remain valid until the late eighteenth century. This change in body aesthetics corresponded with a significant evolution in the alimentary habits of the elite. Cookbooks of the fourteenth and fifteenth centuries show a marked preference for sour and acid sauces, containing neither sugar nor fats, whereas those of the sixteenth and seventeenth centuries abound in butter, cream, and sweets. Were women of the ruling classes fatter than their medieval forebears, and did fashion thus adapt itself to a changing physical reality? Or did Renaissance women deliberately develop a rounded silhouette to emulate the current ideal of beauty?[17] In any case a "healthy" plumpness, like cleanliness, was generally reserved for the wealthy; thinness was considered ugly, unhealthy, and a sign of poverty. After all, the majority of women—peasants, servants, and artisans—ate less well than their menfolk, the best and the most food being reserved for the male members of the family, the children, and the women, in that order. European women also grew smaller as a result of an economic and agricultural crisis that persisted from the fourteenth through the eighteenth centuries. Another consequence of female undernourishment was a significant change in the age of puberty, which fluctuates as a function of the ratio between age and body weight. In the Middle Ages girls matured between twelve and fifteen. In the seventeenth and eighteenth centuries, however, the average age at puberty moved up to sixteen, being slightly lower for city dwellers and slightly higher for the peasantry.[18]

Rickets, scurvy, and a variety of unsightly ills followed in the path of chronic undernourishment. No wonder that women of the upper classes took care to distinguish themselves from their less fortunate sisters, cultivating vast expanses of milky flesh in contrast to the haggard, brown, and emaciated physiques of those whose hard lives made them not only ugly in the eyes of contemporaries, but also prematurely old. Well-to-do women afflicted with a high metabolism resorted to special preparations in order to avoid losing weight. Glissenti's *Discorsi morali* (1609), for example, mentions two types of marzipan eaten by Venetian and Neapolitan women in order to maintain their ideal size. Henri Estienne, on the other hand, disapproved of this practice, crediting French women with a preference for a less corpulent silhouette.[19]

Constructing Femininity

The Renaissance was not only a period in which women of the ruling classes distinguished themselves from their social inferiors by means of their well-fed physique and the pristine whiteness of their body linen; it was also a period in which it became more important that women be "different" from men in all aspects of dress, appearance, and behavior. The vestiary revolution of the late Middle Ages consisted in the differentiation of male and female clothing. Men's robes were shortened to reveal their legs, and the codpiece was invented, destined to become increasingly prominent and beribboned in the sixteenth and seventeenth centuries. Women, on the other hand, tended to remain more chastely dressed. Their long and voluminous robes revealed a waist made even more slender by the use of a busk and, more liberal mores permitting, might even disclose a pair of milky breasts, suitably powdered and rouged. Every movement, every gesture had to reflect the delicacy and tenderness now expected of women as opposed to the energetic virility of men. As Baldassare Castiglione observed in *The Book of the Courtier* (1528), "I hold that a woman should in no way resemble a man in her ways, manners, words, gestures and bearing. Thus just as it is very fitting that a man should display a certain robust and sturdy manliness, so it is well for a woman to have a certain soft and delicate tenderness, with an air of feminine sweetness in her every movement."[20]

From the fifteenth century on, treatises on the family, courtesy books, and even medical literature all insisted upon the fragility of the female sex and the duty of men to protect women from their own innate weaknesses by ruling them with a gentle, if firm, hand.[21] Gone were the courtly models of gender relations according to which the knight obeyed his mistress and served her as his sovereign. The Renaissance brought with it a desire for clearly defined social boundaries and immutable hierarchies (including gender hierarchies), a desire that became all the more important as the reality of economic and political life confused class distinctions and created new elites to challenge the old.[22] Sumptuary laws also reflected a chronic concern for issues of social status, sexual identity, and dress. Cross-dressing, for example, was universally condemned—a fact that did not prevent women from repeatedly affecting articles of male costume, much to the horror of their contemporaries.[23] Vestiary legislation also denounced the "mad expenditure" of vain women and accused them of being the cause of a spectrum of ills, from the ruin of the national economy to demographic crisis and their husbands' homosexuality. Distinctions in both clothing and behavior became increasingly important in the sixteenth and seventeenth centuries, whereas the eighteenth century was to witness a major upheaval in traditional categories of class and gender. Aristocratic males displayed their superior "sensibility" by affecting a feminization of dress. Their laces and silks were in turn rejected by a more austere and "virile" bourgeoisie for whom refinement and delicacy hardly constituted valid criteria for either social or moral worth.

Canons and Criteria of Feminine Beauty

Although clerical culture throughout the early modern period tended to fear feminine charms and the power they gave women over men,[24] Renaissance Neoplatonism specifically rehabilitated beauty by declaring it to be the outward and visible sign of an inward and invisible goodness. Beauty was no longer considered a dangerous asset, but rather a necessary attribute of moral character and social position. It became an obligation to be beautiful, for ugliness was associated not only with social inferiority but also with vice. Were not prostitutes rendered unsightly by syphilitic sores, and the degenerate poor monstrous by skin afflictions and mange? The body's outer envelope became a window through which the inner self was visible to all.

Feminine beauty was not only extolled as being a guarantee of moral probity and an inspiration for those who had the privilege of gazing upon a pretty countenance; it was also codified by a massive production of love poems, courtesy books, and collections of recipes for cosmetics. Beauty followed a formula, and women went to a great deal of trouble and expense to make their appearance conform to standards that remained virtually unaltered throughout the early modern period. In Italy, France, Spain, Germany, and England the basic aesthetic was the same: white skin, blond hair, red lips and cheeks, black eyebrows. The neck and hands had to be long and slender, the feet small, the waist supple. Breasts were to be firm, round, and white, with rosy nipples. The color of the eyes might vary (the French were fond of green; the Italians preferred black or brown), and occasional concessions might be made to dark hair; but the canon of feminine appearance remained essentially the same for some three hundred years.

An oral and literary tradition attributed to women a list of "beauties," whose number grew from three to thirty in the course of the sixteenth century. Morpurgo's list in *El costume de la donne* (1536) was even longer. His ideal woman possessed no less than thirty-three perfections:

> Three long: hair, hands, and legs
> Three short: teeth, ears, and breasts
> Three wide: forehead, chest, and hips
> Three narrow: waist, knees, and "where nature places all that is sweet"
> Three large: ("but well proportioned") height, arms, and thighs
> Three thin: eyebrows, fingers, lips
> Three round: neck, arms, and . . .
> Three small: mouth, chin, and feet
> Three white: teeth, throat, and hands
> Three red: cheeks, lips, and nipples
> Three black: eyebrows, eyes, and "what you yourself should know"[25]

During the sixteenth century there also developed a literary tradition known as the *blason,* a poem in honor of a lady's charms, described either collectively or singly. In a collection of such poems published in 1543, Clément Marot's famous *Blason du tétin* is followed by poems on the forehead, eyebrow, throat, cheek, tongue, nose, tooth, buttock, voice, foot, hair, knee, eye, hand, cunt, mouth, thigh, arm, heart, ear, and so on. Needless to say, some of these poems were relatively licentious and lewd, and many editions of *blasons* were illustrated by rough woodcuts representing the various parts of the body being praised. Paradoxically, these illustrations tended to be crudely realistic and could hardly have been considered stimuli to the erotic imagination.[26]

By the 1550s the taste for stock descriptions of feminine beauty had spread far and wide. Poems in honor of individual women tended to describe them in terms of the aesthetic norm, and women themselves turned to cosmetics, corsets, and high-heeled shoes to conform to the current canon. Defects were carefully corrected or hidden whenever possible, and, as True-Wit points out in Ben Jonson's *Epicoene* (1609), "an intelligent woman, if she know by herself the least defect, will be most curious to hide it: and it becomes her. If she be short, let her sit much, lest, when she stands, she be thought to sit. If she have an ill foot, let her wear her gown the longer, and her shoe the thinner. If a fat hand, and scald nails, let her carve the less, and act in gloves. If a sour breath, let her never discourse fasting, and always talk at her distance. If she have black and rugged teeth, let her offer the less at laughter, especially if she laugh wide and open."[27]

The Cosmetic Arts

How did women achieve the perfection required of them? With the invention of printing in the mid-fifteenth century, books of "secrets" and recipes for perfumes and cosmetics (some of which had already circulated in manuscripts in the Middle Ages) began to appear throughout Europe, reinforcing and enriching an oral tradition handed down from mother to daughter, from apothecary to son. Written mostly by men, whose criteria of beauty were thus implicitly imposed on their feminine readers, these collections were rarely restricted to beauty secrets. Their contents were eclectic, often gathering medical information, kitchen recipes, natural magic, astrological tables, and various other arts (such as physiognomy) all between the covers of one book.[28] Who read these books? Women (and men) of a certain social standing, of course, who were educated enough to know how to read. Not all, however, were necessarily members of the ruling classes. Jean Liebault's *Short Treatise on the Distillations of Waters* (1578), for example, addresses itself to the good housewife, who "should not be overly preoccupied with makeup" but should instead apply herself to the care of her household. "Nonetheless," writes Liebault, "I do not wish her to be ignorant of how one distills waters to make cosmetics—not that she should use them, but rather to profit from selling them to great lords and ladies, and to other people who like to paint themselves."[29] Given the repeated denunciations of painted women hurled from pulpits and pamphlets throughout the early modern period, however, it seems likely that more housewives used makeup than Liebault would have approved of. Outside certain elite circles, where cosmetics were as essential an accessory as powder, perfume, and body linen, paints and creams were considered to be a sign of vanity and an incitation to lust.[30] Yet women of all social classes persevered in "improving" their appearance by means of cosmetic concoctions, some of which ended up doing more harm than good. In Leon Battista Alberti's *Libri della famiglia* (1437), the newlywed Gianozzo tries to discourage his young wife from wearing makeup by describing its ill effects on one of the neighbors: "a woman who had few teeth left in her mouth, and those appeared tarnished with rust. Her eyes were sunken and always inflamed, the rest of her face withered and ashen. All her flesh looked decomposed and disgusting. Her silvery hair was the only thing about her that one might regard without displeasure."[31] He goes on to say that this haggard old woman was in fact less than thirty-two years old. A sixteenth-century *Tracte Containing the Artes of Curious Paintinge, Carvinge & Buildinge* dedicates an entire section to the nature of certain cosmetics then in daily use, since women were supposedly unaware of their ingredients and the ill effects they had on their users. The section begins with a gruesome description of the harmful effects of sublimate of mercury, which may have been partially responsible for the fast fading of youth and beauty bewailed by the ladies of Queen Elizabeth's court:

> Sublimate is called dead fier; because of his malignant, and biting nature. The compositiion whereof is of salte, quicksilver, and vitrioll, distilled together in a glassen vessell.

This the Chirugions call a corrosive. Because if it bee put upon mans flesh it burneth in a short space, mortifying the place, not without great paine to the patient. Wherfore such women as use it about their face, have always black teeth, standing far out of their gums like a Spanish mule; an offensive breath, with a face halfe scorched, and an uncleane complexion . . . So that simple women thinking to grow more beautifull, become disfigured, hastening olde age before the time, and giving occasion to their husbandes to seeke strangers insteede of their wives, with divers other inconveniences.[32]

Warnings about the long-term effects of cosmetics were not the only argument used against makeup. Women who painted themselves were also accused of "altering the face of God" (was not humanity made in the image of the Lord?). In *A Treatise against Painting and Tincturing of Men and Women* (1616), Thomas Tuke wondered how ladies were able to pray to God "with a face, which he doth not owne? How can they begge pardon, when their sinne cleaves onto their faces?"[33] Beneath many criticisms of paint also lay a masculine fear of deception. Was the youthful beauty they desired not perhaps an old hag or a disease-ridden body, artfully camouflaged? Besides which, those who made cosmetics were often suspected of dabbling in the magic arts, for many recipes contained incantations to be recited during preparation and ingredients such as earthworms, nettles, and blood.[34]

Despite repeated cautions, masculine accusations of adultery and deception, and daily examples of the untoward effects of cosmetics, women persevered in "improving" their appearance with the help of powders, creams, and paints. In sixteenth-century Italy it was said that all women in cities used makeup, "even the dish-washers." A further indication of the wide social distribution of cosmetics is furnished by collections of cosmetic recipes that indicate the cost of certain preparations. Caterina Sforza's *Esperimenti* (1490–1509), for example, gave alternate recipes for creams to make the face white and paints to make the cheeks red, reserving ingredients such as pearls, silver, and precious stones for those who could afford them and suggesting less costly components for the less wealthy.[35]

Most books on cosmetics and feminine beauty focused on the hair, the face, the neck, the breasts, and the hands—all parts of the body visible to the public eye. The recipes that filled these books generally fulfilled one of two functions: to correct existing faults or to improve upon nature. Hair, for example, was better if blond, thick, wavy, and long, whence the long hours Italian women spent bleaching their hair in the sun (their snowy complexions protected by the *solana,* a wide-brimmed sunhat without a crown), washing it in the juice of lemon or rhubarb, or applying other, more elaborate concoctions made with sulfur or saffron. Known as the *arte biondeggiante,* this fashion was so widespread that contemporaries were often heard to exclaim: "in the entire peninsula, there is not one brunette to be found."[36] Even in northern climes, where naturally blond hair was more common, raven locks could be considered a mortifying social handicap: Godelive de Bruges was said to be so humiliated by her black hair that the resignation and contrition with which she endured this defect was the first step on her path to sainthood.[37] After the hair was bleached, the hairline was carefully plucked or treated with a depilatory cream in order to create the high, domed foreheads that were still fashionable in the sixteenth century. The eyebrows were also plucked, sometimes entirely, and sometimes just enough to make two thin, wide-spaced arcs that were then blackened to contrast with the hair and make a frame for the eyes. Eyelashes, on the other hand, were considered unaesthetic and were either left unadorned or entirely pulled out, as can be seen on a number of Renaissance portraits of women from the Netherlands to Italy (mascara did not come into use until the eighteenth century).

The face, neck, breasts, and hands were supposed to be creamy white, enlivened by rosy hues in strategic places. White was the color associated with purity, chastity, and femininity. It was the color of the "female" heavenly body, the moon, as distinct from the more vibrant hues of the "masculine" sun. A white complexion was also the privilege of the leisured city dweller as distinct from the sunburnt skin of the peasant. Renaissance paintings systematically gave men a darker, more "virile" complexion because they spent more time outdoors than women, who tended to be cloistered in the home. White was more delicate, more feminine, more beautiful. Dark was more robust, more masculine, more tenebrous. Accordingly, cosmetic recipe books contained not only "secrets" for turning women's hair golden but also information for men on how to dye their beards black. The ivory complexion so prized by women was not, however, a uniform white. The cheeks, ears, chin, nipples (when displayed), and fingertips were touched with rouge to give an impression of health and attract the eye. Sometimes, however, the layers of paint so artfully applied became a veritable mask whose thickness prevented women from smiling, talking, or laughing. Castiglione, Aretino, and Piccolomini all criticize the rigidity cosmetics imposed on women, who seemed to be "wooden statues" and "could not turn their head without turning their entire body."[38]

The End of Artifice

Over and above the role played by cosmetics in the social and moral obligation women felt to look beautiful, makeup was a necessary signifier of social rank. Paint was the "clothing" of the visible parts of the body, distinguishing its wearer as much as rich materials, fine linens, and expensive ornaments revealed the wealth and status of their owner. Cosmetics were the ultimate accessory, without which an elegant woman did not feel herself dressed. In the eighteenth century, the elaborate construction of a fashionable appearance gave rise to a new social event, the *toilette,* a semiprivate affair during which a woman coquettishly revealed to a few privileged admirers fleeting glimpses of her myriad charms while permitting her hairdresser, dressmaker, and maids to fuss about her person. Artifice, invention, and the conscious construction of a seductive public personality were as much the objectives of the toilette as the actual perfection of personal appearance. A ceremony inspired as much by the *cabinet des précieuses* as by the *levée du roi,* the toilette made of every woman a queen.

Such artifice could not persist forever. After three centuries of unflagging criticism by churchmen, moralists, and physicians, the heavy makeup of the early modern period finally gave way before the rise of a censorious bourgeoisie (who identified the camouflage of cosmetics with the dishonesty attributed to the aristocracy), an elite nostalgia for bucolic simplicity, and, perhaps most important, the spread of vaccination against smallpox, whose scars had disfigured many a complexion. For the first time since the later Middle Ages, the "natural look" was back in fashion. No longer associated with puritanical austerity or saintly humility, soap-and-water freshness was (with a little help) considered the *summum* of feminine beauty under Louis XVI. The eighteenth century was to close with a new feminine aesthetic, a pre-Romantic taste for grace and simplicity that expressed itself in a large-eyed, pallid visage and a slender, languorous form, both of which were supposed to convey a delicacy of sentiment and feeling that set the tone for the early nineteenth century and the Romantic concept of femininity.[39]

Sexuality

If early modern hygienic and cosmetic practices were motivated by a variety of beliefs and concerns, ranging from an acute interest in health to the social imperatives of physical appearance, perhaps the most universal purpose to which these practices were applied was the service of Eros. In seventeenth-century Europe, the few remaining public baths still served two main purposes, and he who did not bathe for reasons of health was most probably preparing for an amorous encounter. Similarly, feminine cosmetics were universally decried for their uncanny powers of seduction, which, according to moralists and theologians alike, lured men to their perdition in the sweet throes of lust. Ever present, and increasingly policed, sexuality became one of the bugbears of both secular and religious authorities. Authorized only in the context of marriage, and then solely in the function of procreation, sex was subject to a wave of control and repression that strove to mold the mores of urban and rural populations along lines strictly defined by both church and state.

The Renaissance of Prudery

Whereas the Middle Ages had witnessed the formulation of a sexual ethic based on the refusal of pleasure and the obligation of procreation,[40] it was not until the sixteenth century that a coherent campaign was launched against all forms of nudity and extraconjugal sexuality. Between 1500 and 1700, new attitudes toward the body and new rules of behavior gave rise to a radical promotion of chastity and modesty in all areas of daily life. Brothels were closed, bathers were obliged to retain their shirts, and the nightgown replaced the birthday suit as approved sleeping apparel. The lower half of the body became a world apart, a forbidden territory that the seventeenth-century Précieuses refused to name. Under the dual influence of the Protestant Reformation and the Catholic Counter-Reformation, artists relinquished their hard-won battle to display the human form, and a multitude of accidental draperies, leaves, and fortuitous shrubs once again veiled the nude.[41] Nudity became vulgar, something only apprentices inflicted upon the public eye as they sported in the river on a hot summer's day; and even then they might find themselves in trouble, as did eight young men in Frankfurt in 1541, who ended up being condemned to a month in prison on bread and water.[42] In the seventeenth and eighteenth centuries refined Parisian ladies fainted at the sight of naked male bodies on the banks of the Seine, while even their occasional private bath was clouded with milk or a handful of bran in order to preserve their nudity from their servants' eyes. Modesty became a sign of social and moral distinction, especially dear to the middle ranks of society, who condemned both the uncouth physicality of the lower orders and the libertine nonchalance of the aristocracy.

The first victims of the new wave in social morality were women. Long decried by misogynist theologians and sexually frustrated clergy as the daughters of Eve, women were represented as insidious temptresses whose primary object in life was to seduce unsuspecting men and deliver them to Satan.[43] Medical science reinforced this voracious vision of female sexuality by declaring erotic fulfillment to be a biological necessity for women. Not only did their "hungry" wombs ever clamor to be filled, but dire disorders would attend upon those who ignored the "natural" imperative of reproduction. Hysteria, a malady whose origin lay in the uterus, was accounted responsible for delusions of diabolic possession and other forms of mental illness.[44] Another factor that strengthened the equation between women, sex, and sin was the appearance and rapid spread of syphilis in the late fifteenth century. Although the most virulent epidemics had abated by the 1550s, the disease had come to stay, indelibly imprinted on the contemporary imagination as a terrestrial punishment for the sin of lust and, above all, as a consequence of frequenting houses of ill repute.

Municipally owned or authorized brothels were a common feature of late medieval European towns and cities. Prostitution was encouraged and protected not only in order to meet the needs of growing numbers of sexually mature adolescents, unattached apprentices, and men who were marrying at a later and later age, but also to combat male homosexuality, considered to be one of the greater social ills of the time and responsible for various manifestations of divine wrath such as plague, famine, and war.[45] In the sixteenth century, however, the same municipalities that had encouraged prostitution closed their official brothels. Accused of spreading lechery and disease, fomenting brawls and other forms of civil disturbance, leading young men astray, facilitating adultery, and ruining family fortunes, prostitutes became one of the "criminal" populations (along with vagabonds and witches) destined for elimination by both secular and religious authorities.[46]

The consolidation of legislative authority and power that characterized the Renaissance was concerned not only with criminal law but also with moral offenses. As far as secular lawmakers were concerned, the body was as susceptible to "crime" as theologians held it to be susceptible to sin. New punishments were introduced for new offenses, and old crimes, if committed against new "enemies," were transmuted into minor misdeeds. Thus Ferdinand I of Austria in 1560 issued a series of edicts against moral offenses that culminated in the creation of a *Keuschheitscommission* (Chastity Committee), whereas only five years earlier, in France, the rape of a prostitute had been declared a crime so insignificant that it was no longer worthy of punishment. At the same time, Catholic and Protestant clergy mobilized public opinion against the ladies of the night: Lutheran preachers were responsible for the closing of brothels in Ulm in 1537, in Regensburg in 1553, and in Nuremberg in 1562. Predictably, an increasing number of arrests and trials in civil courts concerned sexual misdemeanors. In Geneva in 1562 no less than 20 percent of the criminal cases tried involved illicit sexual relations.[47] The seventeenth and early eighteenth centuries continued to police morals with the same fervor. From 1694 to 1717 the municipal court in Arras tried 232 cases, of which no less than 100 concerned sexual crimes: 92 cases were related to prostitution, 3 concerned rape, 4 dealt with problems of concubinage, 1 with polygamy.[48] Until the mid-eighteenth century, both church and state jealously enforced their rights over the body and its sexuality, condemning eroticism in favor of a conjugal and natalist conception of sexual relations in which sensual activity was considered a rather unfortunate means to a necessary end.

Authorized Sexuality

In the eyes of both religious and secular authorities, there existed two basic types of sexual behavior, one acceptable and the other reprehensible. The first was marital and was practiced in the service of procreation. The second was governed by amorous passion and sensual pleasure, its outcome malformed or illegitimate, its logic that of sterility. Guilty outside of wedlock, sensual passion became all the more blamable within the bounds of matrimony, where it threatened not only the controlled, contractual concept of conjugal affections and the health of offspring conceived in the heat of amorous excess, but also the couple's ability to love God, contaminated as they were by terrestrial rather than spiritual love.

Courtship and Premarital Sex. Despite the normative prescriptions of theologians, physicians, and civil officials, young people did not always wait for marriage to experiment with erotic pleasures. Since men and women married at an increasingly late age throughout the early modern period (an average of twenty-five to twenty-eight years), they were sexually mature for a good decade before being able to experience sex legitimately.[49] Historians differ as to the extent of sexual activity in these years: was Europe swept by a wave of chastity, or did erotic needs find alternative outlets? The closure of the vast majority of brothels and a record low birthrate of illegitimate children from the sixteenth to the mid-eighteenth centuries have led some historians to postulate a mass internalization resulting in widespread sexual continence.[50] Other scholars have asserted important changes in sexual behavior, ranging from an increase in masturbation to the spread of rudimentary contraception.[51] Scholars do agree, however, on the existence of one well-documented sexual practice. Under circumstances subject to various controls, young men and women of the lower social orders could indulge in a certain amount of sexual experimentation as well as "try out" potential marriage partners without suffering moral censure.

Known as "bundling" in England and *maraîchinage, albergement,* or *créantailles* in France, various forms of parentally authorized premarital flirtation, sexual experimentation, and even cohabitation were practiced throughout Europe. Bundling generally involved paying court to a girl at night, in a room apart from the rest of the family, in bed, in the dark, and half-naked. However, although it involved two young people spending the night together, talking and petting, bundling did not lead to much pregnancy. In the Vendée in France, maraîchinage was collective, with couples of lovers in the same room or even in the same bed, where they could control any one of their number who threatened to get carried away. In Savoy, the boy had to swear to respect the girl's virginity before bedding with her. In Scotland, the girl's thighs were symbolically tied together.[52] What bundling did lead to were marriages based on affection and sexual attraction. It provided an opportunity for the two parties to explore each other's minds and characters in some depth as well as to obtain sexual satisfaction in the decade between maturity and matrimony without running the risk of an unwanted pregnancy or an ill-fated marriage. A rise in premarital sexual practices in the late seventeenth and the eighteenth centuries has been attributed to the greater economic independence of young people and to a growing demand for affection as a basis for marriage. Since it was easier to earn a living and to marry early, parental control declined, girls were less jealous of their virginity, and a greater number of prenuptial pregnancies accompanied the spread of more liberal sexual mores.[53]

In a society without effective means of birth control, the most reliable indicator of premarital intercourse is the number of children who are born less than 8.5 months after marriage. Since the chances of conception from a single act of intercourse by a healthy couple fall between 2 percent and 8 percent, the pregnancy that led to marriage was most probably the result of several weeks or even several months of unprotected intercourse. However, not all prenuptial pregnancies entailed marriage with the father of the child. Although some betrothed couples anticipated the conjugal bond by cohabitation, and others, whose families obstructed their union, used pregnancy to obtain parental consent, lower-class girls kept as mistresses by rich men and servants seduced by their employers were often married off to poor men who were more than happy to lay hands on the dowry provided for this purpose. Whatever the circumstances of premarital pregnancy might have been, English baptismal records reveal premarital conception rates hovering around 20 percent for the years 1550–1749, shooting up to over 40 percent in the second half of the eighteenth century.[54]

Neither Protestant nor Catholic authorities regarded such carryings-on with an indulgent eye. In the sixteenth century, and especially after the Council of Trent (1563), the Roman church began to wage a systematic struggle against all forms of prenuptial sexual relations. Episcopal ordinances mark the progress of this battle in France. Young people in Savoy lost their right to albergement in 1609. In the Pyrenean dioceses of Bayonne and Alet, intercourse during the period of *fiançailles* remained customary until 1640, when it suddenly became grounds for excommunication. In Champagne boy-girl encounters in the *escraignes* became liable to the same penalty in 1680. Similarly, nocturnal visits were still being attacked in the Protestant county of Montbéliard by the civil magistrate, the Duke of Württemberg, in 1772.[55]

Despite numerous and repeated attempts to suppress premarital sex and cohabitation, rural areas long resisted the "approved" model of marriage, according to which all matches were to be arranged by parents. As late as the nineteenth century in France anthropologists avidly collected evidence of similar courting rituals, some of which persisted until the early twentieth century.[56] In the cities, however, where wealth weighed more heavily in the balance, parental influence in the choice of marriage partner became absolute. Sixteenth- and seventeenth-century Europe saw a rash of rulings against marriage without parental consent progressively deprive young people of the right to choose their helpmate, even if they had previously exchanged vows, given each other rings, or had sexual relations. Particularly efficient in urban areas, where marriage strategies played a key role in the social, economic, and political ambitions of the middle and upper ranks of society, the paternalist model of marriage remained unchallenged until the eighteenth century, when "anglomania" further validated a gradual movement toward a new, sentimental vision of conjugal affections within the upper classes. Aristocratic England was one step ahead of the rest of Europe in the development of a new ideology of the family in which closer, more affectionate, and more egalitarian relations between man and wife, parents and children, replaced the patriarchal hierarchy that had prevailed since the late Middle Ages.[57] However, even those who most ardently advocated the need for mutual affection in the choice of marriage partner were equally adamant in condemning the two other possible motives for marriage: desire for monetary gain, which was held to be at the root of much marital misery; and sexual or romantic passion, which created unrealistic expectations of conjugal bliss.

Conjugal Relations: Procreation versus Pleasure. There are several features of sexual behavior peculiar to early modern Europe. The first is the average interval of ten or more years between puberty and marriage. This gap, which tended to be larger among the lower social orders than among their betters, continued to widen throughout the seventeenth and eighteenth centuries. Moreover, a significant number of people never married at all, ranging from about 10 percent among the peasantry and urban poor to as much as 25 percent among the elites. A second unique feature is the superimposition of the notion of romantic love on the biological constant of sexual drive. Beginning as a purely extramarital ideology in troubadour literature of the twelfth century, the concept of romantic love spread via the printing press and the increase in literacy in the sixteenth and seventeenth centuries, inspiring poetry, plays, and novels until it finally found its way into real life in the mid-eighteenth century. The third and last feature is the predominance of Christian ideology in the legitimation and practice of sexuality. Though somewhat mitigated by humanist and Protestant efforts to replace the medieval ideal of virginity by that of holy matrimony, the dominant attitude toward sexuality remained one of suspicion and hostility.[58] Medical literature, theological treatises, and moral tracts all concurred in promoting a natalist vision of sexual activity in which pleasure was permitted only in the interests of a procreative norm.

Religious authorities considered any sexual act committed outside marriage to be a mortal sin, as well as any conjugal act not performed in the interest of reproduction. Saint Jerome had declared the husband who embraced his wife overly passionately to be an "adulterer" because he loved her for his pleasure only, as he would a mistress. Restated by Saint Thomas Aquinas and echoed endlessly by authors of confession manuals throughout the sixteenth and seventeenth centuries, the denunciation of passion in marriage condemned the amorous wife as much as the libidinous husband. Even the positions adopted by the couple were subject to strict controls. The *retro* or *more canino* position (not to be confused with sodomy) was declared to be contrary to human nature because it imitated the coupling of animals. *Mulier super virum* was equally "unnatural" insofar as it placed the woman in an active and superior position, contrary to her passive and subordinate social role. All erotic acrobatics other than the approved formula—the woman supine and the man above her—were considered suspect in that they privileged pleasure at the expense of procreation. The only position that favored the planting of the male seed was the one metaphorically associated with the plowing of the earth by the laborer.[59]

Medical texts supported theological rulings with respect to the optimum conditions for creating offspring in terms of both the moderation of passion and the most favorable position, threatening that any deviation from the norm might well result in deformed or deficient progeny. Both groups of authorities also stipulated a variety of days on which sexual intercourse was to be avoided. For the pious, fast days were also chaste days, as well as all religious holidays such as Sundays, Christmas, Good Friday, and Easter. Continence was also recommended throughout Lent, although early modern theologians no longer expected the faithful to be capable of total abstinence. Over and above the 120 to 140 days of religious observance during which sex was discouraged if not expressly forbidden, couples were urged to avoid intercourse during the hot summer months and during the wife's various periods of indisposition. Not only was intimacy during the monthly cycle or during the 40 days of "impurity" after childbirth considered potentially hazardous to the husband's health, but sexual relations during pregnancy and nursing were believed to threaten the child's chances for survival. A growing concern for the well-being of infants, whose mortality rate was extremely high in the first two years of life, led a number of physicians and religious authorities to forbid intercourse throughout the breast-feeding period. Although it was not universally recognized that closely spaced pregnancies were debilitating for the mother, a pregnant woman's milk was considered harmful; accordingly, a nursing child would be abruptly weaned and prematurely deprived of the nourishment and protection that "healthy" breast milk was known to provide.[60]

No doubt many women, worn out by numerous pregnancies and the care of many children, would willingly have availed themselves of the medieval right to refusal of the *debitum conjugale*, especially as marital chastity was considered desirable once a good-sized family had been created. Theologians in the sixteenth, seventeenth, and eighteenth centuries, however, were not so quick to permit either partner to neglect the other's sexual needs. No longer seen solely in the light of reproduction or as a second-rate solution for concupiscence, conjugal sexuality was increasingly considered to be a legitimate remedy for a natural physical drive, the refusal of which might drive the frustrated partner into the greater sins of adultery or "pollution" (masturbation).

The crime of Onan (who was struck down by God for having spilled his seed upon the ground) became one of the major obsessions of early modern religious and medical authorities. Confession manuals such as the *Instructions pour les confesseurs du Diocèse de Chalon-sur-Saône* (Lyons, 1682) waxed prolific on the topic of *mollesse* and urged priests to question their flock—especially young unmarried men—without going into so much detail as to give dangerous ideas to those who were still innocent. Along with *coitus interruptus,* homosexuality, and bestiality, masturbation was one of the four sexual sins that defied nature's reproductive imperative in the name of "perverse" pleasures. Although this solitary practice was too widespread to merit the exemplary punishments reserved for sodomy and bestiality, it caused a great deal of anxiety on the grounds that bad habits acquired in youth might continue into adulthood, either polluting the marriage bed or even replacing marriage altogether.[61] In the early eighteenth century lay authorities took up the struggle against what was by then perceived as a widespread social disease. Inspired by publications such as Bekker's *Onania, or the heinous sin of Self-Pollution, and all its frightful Consequences in both Sexes considered with Spiritual and Physical Advice to those who have already injur'd themselves by this abominable Practise* (1710), or Tissot's *Onanisme, ou dissertation physique sur les maladies produites par la masturbation* (1760), doctors, pedagogues, and parents participated in a collective delirium of repression that would reach its peak in the nineteenth century. What most tormented sixteenth- and seventeenth-century moralists and theologians, however, was the suspicion that both masturbation and withdrawal were practiced by married couples who desired sexual pleasure without the burdens of procreation.

Historians of the family and sexuality differ about the incidence of onanism and *coitus interruptus* in the early modern period. Some ascribe the fall in both premarital conceptions and illegitimate birthrates before the mid-eighteenth century to an increase in masturbation and withdrawal; others hypothesize an internalization of new moral values.[62] Whatever pre- or extramarital behavior patterns may have been, it is likely that fear of the dangers of childbirth and the economic burdens of a growing brood of children also motivated many married couples to limit the size of their families through these prohibited practices. Of course the practice of *coitus interruptus* requires a considerable amount of control on the part of the man and affords little pleasure to the woman, who is often left sexually aroused but frustrated. But even within the context of procreational sex, the male tendency to hasty ejaculation would also have left many female partners unsatisfied. If one adds to this tendency the experience of some ten years' self-manipulation and the loveless matches that characterized both the aristocracy and the bourgeoisie, the chances for mutually satisfying sexual relations within the framework of marriage must have been very low indeed.

The only form of masturbation authorized by both physicians and Catholic confessors was feminine self-manipulation, either in preparation for intercourse (to facilitate penetration) or, after the husband had prematurely ejaculated and withdrawn, in order to reach orgasm, "open" the mouth of the womb, and release the female "seed," which, according to seventeenth-century medical authorities, was as useful to the act of procreation as that released by the male.[63] Although the feminine "right to orgasm" continued to be debated in confession manuals well into the eighteenth century, the majority of theologians accepted Galenist medical theory with respect to the desirability of female satisfaction: would God have given women this source of pleasure without a purpose? A snag in this logic was the fact that women could conceive passively and without pleasure, in which case their "semen" would be wanting. Never at a loss, medical science came to the aid of doctrine and declared the function of feminine seed to be auxiliary to that of its masculine counterpart. If emitted at the same moment as the man's, it would create more beautiful offspring.[64] Filtering down from confession manuals and medical treatises, the natalist justification for feminine pleasure became a commonplace in popular household literature, such as *Aristotle's Master-piece* (London, 1690), a compilation of advice on procreation, pregnancy, and childrearing that survived, in a variety of forms and some thirty editions, well into the nineteenth century. Interweaving the earthy realism of popular culture with the more common precepts of medical knowledge and the optimistic naturalism of the Enlightenment, such publications attest to a general willingness to relax Christian inhibitions with respect to conjugal sexuality and to a growing acceptance of physical compatibility and pleasure as a basis for successful marital relations.[65]

Remarriage and Charivari. Although marriage presupposed a lifelong contract, it was often considered more a temporary union that would last only until death intervened. Few couples reached old age together, and young mothers or fathers left with a bevy of small children tended to remarry fairly quickly. In eighteenth-century rural France, for example, at least half of marriages lasted less than fifteen years, and over one-third less than ten years.[66] Women were the high-risk group: at least 10 percent of female deaths were related to postpartum infections and other complications related to childbirth during the fertile years between marriage and menopause (that is, from ages twenty-five to forty).

The younger a widow or a widower, the higher the probability of remarriage. Under age thirty, the majority of men and women contracted a second marriage. Above age forty, men tended to remarry more easily than women. At Meulan, in France, one widower out of six took a wife at this age, whereas only one widow out of fifteen found another husband. In Crulai the differences between men and women over forty were even more striking: one man out of three remarried, whereas only one woman out of twenty-five found another spouse. On the whole, remarriage tended to follow fairly quickly upon widowhood, but here too men had an advantage over women. Bereaved husbands usually took a second (or third or fourth) wife within eighteen months of the death of their helpmeet, whereas widows took up to two years to find another partner. Canon law did not impose any specific delay with respect to remarriage, although a year's mourning was considered seemly. On the other hand, some countries required widows to remain celibate for twelve months following a husband's death on pain of losing whatever inheritance they had obtained upon his demise.[67]

One out of every four or five marriages in early modern Europe was a remarriage. Once widowed, men tended to marry women younger than their deceased spouse, whose material holdings or dowry often brought a welcome boost to the family fortunes. Women, on the other hand, tended to contract second marriages with men older than their deceased husbands or with men of inferior social station. Notwithstanding these disadvantages, some of the latter unions actually permitted women to retain a certain amount of professional and financial autonomy. For example, a widow of an artisan who married one of her husband's apprentices often maintained a certain degree of control over her late husband's workshop.

Despite the obvious material and human advantages remarriage brought to the bereft, second unions were not always viewed with a benevolent eye either by church authorities or by the immediate community. First of all, the church had to deal with the implications of remarriage and resurrection. Would men who had married three or four times be resurrected as polygamists? For this reason, clergy in some dioceses of southern France refused until the early seventeenth century to perform the customary nuptial blessing for remarriages. Similarly, local youth groups often performed a charivari to protest the remarriage of an older man or woman with a younger and as yet unmarried member of the community.

Known throughout Europe by different names—*mattinata* in Italy, "skimmington ride" or "rough music" in England, *charivari* in France—these noisy processions generally attended upon marriages that deviated in some way from current norms. The causes for such demonstrations included "bad" conduct on the part of one of the spouses (widows were often guilty of prenuptial sexual relations and pregnancy); marriage of a pregnant girl dressed as a virgin; omission of one of the traditional aspects of the marriage ritual (such as the dance); nonpayment of a ritual "fee" in cash or drink; and, most frequently, a remarriage that involved a significant difference in age or fortune between husband and wife.[68]

Although the normative function of skimmington rides also occasionally extended to censorship of adulterous wives and henpecked husbands, the principal focus of the charivari was marriage, and especially the remarriage of widowers with nubile women. Various interpretations have been given to the discordant parody of music with which the youth group or other mattinata players serenaded the newlywed couple until they were given some money, food, or drink, with which fee the couple bought their right to nuptial peace. Long considered a kind of compensation, to the group of unwed men, for an older man's having "stolen" a young woman from their pool of potential brides, this sum has also been interpreted as a form of payment for having definitively "buried" the former spouse. The noise of the charivari was believed to appease the spirit of the dead wife, thus freeing the widower from any shadow of bigamy in this world or the next. The rowdy cacophony of this popular rite has also been understood as an expression of social disorder, which, juxtaposed with the music and dancing of normal marriages, helped insert the deviant union into the community by externalizing their differences.[69] On the other hand, the refusal to pay a fee to the boisterous musicians or the giving of a sum of money judged inadequate could lead to attacks on the house of the new couple and even to grievous bodily harm. Court records are full of accounts of charivaris that degenerated into pitched battles. In Modena in 1528 a widower refused to pay his brother and the rest of the mattinata participants their customary due. The irate revelers complained to the local magistrate, who agreed to remain neutral during their reprisals, which consisted in wrecking the bridegroom's home from roof to cellar.[70] In Lyons in 1668 Florie Nallo objected to a charivari organized by a neighbor on the occasion of her remarriage and retaliated by insulting him in public (she called him a cuckold). The following night this same neighbor organized a second charivari during which the new husband was shot and beaten, ostensibly for having insulted the *compagnons* by offering them only a few pennies with which to buy drink.[71]

Common in both country and city as early as the fourteenth century, in the sixteenth century the charivari became increasingly subject to controls by both civil and religious authorities. City magistrates tended to view all forms of popular justice with a jaundiced eye, whereas both Protestant and Catholic leaders considered rough music a challenge to their authorization of second marriages. Increasingly policed but destined to survive even into the twentieth century, the charivari constituted a popular, collective, and ritualized means of control with respect to marriage that reinforced current behavioral models while acknowledging, and ultimately accepting, necessary variants upon the social norm.

Unauthorized Sexuality

Outside marriage, there was no licit sexuality. The ascending scale of sexual crimes was defined in terms of the number of infractions committed against the three basic justifications for authorized physical relations, namely, the obligation to procreate, conformity to "natural" laws, and a sacramental concept of marriage. A "first-degree" infraction would be simple fornication between unmarried individuals who had not taken vows of chastity. The crime could be judged more or less severe according to the age and social station of the two parties. The rape of a virgin, for example, was generally considered worse than that of a widow. Similarly, the threat of violence or a promise of marriage by the man would constitute a mitigating circumstance in the woman's favor. The "second degree" of sexual sin was adultery. Simple adultery implied only one married person; double adultery involved two.

Incest was also considered a form of adultery, as was the seduction of a nun, "bride" of Christ.

The third and worst type of sexual infraction involved crimes "against nature," which surpassed the former two insofar as they precluded reproduction. Masturbation, homosexuality, and bestiality haunted churchmen, civil magistrates, and medical doctors throughout the early modern period. Solitary onanism became the bugbear of the eighteenth and nineteenth centuries, although conjugal onanism was also condemned for its sterility. Sodomy was "complete" if it entailed homoerotic relations, and "incomplete" if it described extravaginal heterosexual relations. Bestiality, on the other hand, was the sin "without a name." Always mentioned in Latin, even in the least prudish texts or manuals of confession, it not only reduced men to the level of animals but also was suspected of resulting in hybrid monsters.[72]

Seduced and Abandoned. Our knowledge of extraconjugal relations is based largely on historical records related to their fruit, although the actual birthrate of illegitimate children is hardly an indicator of the frequency or the quality of unauthorized sexuality. Extramarital pregnancy was, more often than not, an undesired complication, and studies of illicit relations in an age that knew neither effective contraception nor antibiotics have shown that various forms of sexual play could be preferred to coitus. Fear of venereal disease, pregnancy, and even emotional or legal entanglement was the cause of a great deal of fondling, groping, and mutual masturbation. And because a single act of intercourse had little chance of resulting in pregnancy, even relationships that did not rely upon some form of birth control (generally withdrawal; the prophylactic sheath was a rarity until the eighteenth century) stood an equally good chance of remaining undetected. The major source of information on illicit fornication during the ancien régime is formal complaints, to civil or religious authorities, made by women who had been impregnated by men who would not or could not marry them. Known in France as the *déclaration de grossesse,* these documents contain precious information on the mother and purported father of the child as well as on the circumstances of their relationship.

Three distinct patterns of illicit relationships can be discerned in the déclarations de grossesse. The first is the relationship between unequals, in which the man was generally the social and economic superior of the woman. Sometimes the seducer was the employer of his sexual partner, and in some cases he offered her a job, money, or food in exchange for her favors. Lower-class women were especially vulnerable to this sort of exploitation, not only because they earned less than men in whatever calling they practiced, but also because masters had a lingering traditional right to the bodies of the women they employed.[73] Servants were doubly vulnerable in this respect insofar as they not only depended upon the head of the household for their livelihood but also lived in daily proximity with a number of men: masters, sons, and other male servants. Women who took part in relations of inequality tended to be under twenty-five years of age, and ten to thirty years younger than the men they accused. This fact may indicate that women in their late teens or early twenties were more naive, and therefore more easily seduced. It may also indicate a preference among older men for girls. Not all of these women were innocent victims, however; calculating gold-diggers appear in all places at all times. Nor were all of the seducers heartless satyrs, but sometimes lovers or common-law husbands of long standing who promised to "take care" of their child. The keynote in relations of inequality, however, is the very different consequences they had for men and women. For men, there seems to have been little social opprobrium associated with paternity suits. For women, the consequences of an illicit affair were usually disastrous. Publicly disgraced, discharged from their job, and in some cases even sent to a house of correction, they would often be forced to choose between abandoning their child or turning to prostitution to support the two of them.[74]

The second type of relationship that appears in official declarations of pregnancy is one of equality. Most women who appeared before the courts had had relationships with men of equal social standing whom they accused of having promised them marriage. Whereas women who were involved in relationships of inequality could hardly have hoped for legitimation of them, those who had relationships with their social equals generally believed (or pretended to believe) that theirs was a prebridal pregnancy gone wrong. The pattern seems to have been one of promise of marriage (often accompanied by a betrothal present), ritual rape, sexual relations approved by the woman's family, followed by desertion. Every step but the last was probably fairly typical of prenuptial behavior in the lower social orders in both city and country up through the eighteenth century. This situation would explain why the women's versions of the relationships tended to insist upon marriage promises and presents, whereas the men's focused on the sexual promiscuity of their partners and denied any serious intentions on their own part.[75]

The third and last type of illegitimate relationship is the short-term, chance encounter. In this case the pregnancy was attributed either to an alleged rape or to the promiscuous behavior (or even prostitution) of the woman. The rapists were usually "unknown" men, identified from their clothing as soldiers or itinerant farm hands who had taken advantage of peasant girls or servants sent alone on errands. Inn servants and part-time prostitutes also had a hard time identifying the father of their child, given their tendency to have single encounters with different men. Such encounters were the exception rather than the rule. Thus in Aix-en-Provence between 1727 and 1749 they account for only 4.7 percent of all déclarations de grossesse as opposed to 66.5 percent involving relationships of equality and 28.7 percent relationships of inequality.[76]

To what extent did women take pleasure in these encounters? Even with allowances made for the voluntary censorship and manipulation of information that undoubtedly characterize such autobiographical recitals, there is little evidence of a search for sexual fulfillment in the *déclarations de grossesse*. It would seem that most sexual relations were short and frequently brutal. Men apparently made little attempt to ensure the enjoyment of their partner, and foreplay was so rare as to be practically nonexistent. The stock description, "he threw me on the ground, stuck a handkerchief in my mouth, and lifted my skirts," is a constant of both legitimate and illegitimate relations, and even if force was not used, the threat of violence was always present. For most women, it would seem that sexual relations were instrumental and manipulative rather than affective. They were a means to an end—marriage, money, or simply survival—rather than an end in themselves.[77]

The repression of concubinage and all forms of nonmarital sex in the sixteenth and seventeenth centuries had a decisive influence on the birthrate of illegitimate children, which was under 3 percent of all births until the mid-eighteenth century. This low figure almost certainly reflects, over and above a stricter observance of premarital chastity, a significant rise in contraceptive practices, abortion, and infanticide. With the decline of medieval tolerance of bastard children and concubinage, there remained only the déclaration de grossesse and the paternity suit to protect unmarried women and preserve the lives of their babies. After all, the greater the social opprobrium attached to a fault, the greater the temptation to suppress the evidence; whence the proliferation of laws against infanticide, the creation of new foundling homes, and the new obligation of pregnancy declarations by single women, which automatically assumed that the unwed mother of a stillborn child was a murderess unless she had previously declared her pregnancy.[78]

Around 1750, however, there was a sharp increase in illegitimate births among the lower classes in both rural and urban areas throughout Europe. From a legal perspective this phenomenon reflected a tightening of legislation regarding paternity suits. In the fifteenth century, a promise of marriage followed by sexual relations had been considered binding, and in the sixteenth and seventeenth centuries a pregnancy declaration would result in either a forced marriage or financial compensation for the mother and child. In the eighteenth century, however, the burden of proof was shifted to the mother's shoulders, with the result that court-order marriages became rare.

From an economic standpoint, the increase in illegitimacy was due in part to the development of cottage industry, which enabled young people to earn enough to live on at a comparably early age. They were therefore able to defy both their parents and community norms and indulge in premarital sex, secure in the knowledge that there would be no financial obstacle to an early wedding should pregnancy occur. Insofar as a liberalization of courtship rituals increased the vulnerability of young women, any increase in prenuptial conceptions also tended to encourage an increase in illegitimacy whenever suitors, evading custom for either financial or personal reasons, refused to marry the women they had seduced. In the cities, similar factors stimulated an increase in premarital relations. Landless rural males and young peasant women were drifting toward the towns to find employment. In the rootless atmosphere of the city their courtships lacked the powerful regulating forces of family, village community, and priest or pastor, which were often decisive in forcing a putative father to marry a girl. Relative independence from parental authority, a change in economic circumstances, and new attitudes on the part of women left them more willing to indulge in premarital intercourse and more exposed to seduction. The rise in illegitimacy thus tended to be higher in the cities than in the country, all the more so as unmarried mothers were often expelled from their rural community in order to give birth in the anonymity of the town, where they would be neither an economic burden to their parish nor a source of dishonor to their family.[79]

Whereas the lower classes were more governed by legal, economic, and social change, the upper classes were more influenced by changes in ideas. The eighteenth century also saw a rise in the egalitarian marriage based on mutual affection and sexual compatibility. Companionate husbands could no longer expect to be forgiven erotic peccadillos with servants and tended to confine their extramarital activity to prostitutes or mistresses. Prostitution was also on the rise, encouraged as much by the libertine morals of the Enlightenment as by an increase in the number of unemployed women, unwed mothers, and destitute poor. For those who most feared the consequences of promiscuity, which ranged from the public nature of paternity suits and the financial burden of supporting bastard children to venereal disease and legal petitions for separation, one of the safest alternatives to marital sex was adultery with a married woman, who was most likely to be free of disease and conveniently able to pass off any children as her husband's own.

Adultery. The history of adultery is the history of a double standard: the extraconjugal affairs of men were tolerated, whereas those of women were not.[80] One explanation for this disparity lies in the value attached to female chastity in the marriage market of a patriarchal and propertied society. Virginity was expected of a bride on her wedding night, and marital fidelity ever after, so as to ensure her husband of legitimate heirs. "We hang a thief for stealing sheep," Dr. Johnson remarked, "but the unchastity of a woman transfers sheep and farm and all from the right owner." On the other hand, "wise married women don't trouble themselves about infidelity in their husbands," for "complaint makes a wife much more ridiculous than the injury that provoked her to it."[81]

The view that masculine fornication and adultery were but venial sins to be overlooked by the wife was reinforced by the fact that before the eighteenth century, most middle- and upper-class marriages were arranged by parents in the interests of family economic or political strategies. Not only did neither bride nor groom have much opportunity before the wedding to get to know each other, but emotional attachment after marriage was considered inconvenient, indeed almost indecent. Male adultery with servants and lower-class women was therefore seen as normal, although some women protested the double standard and the wounds a husband's infidelity could inflict on feminine feelings.[82] By the early seventeenth century, however, both Counter-Reformation and Puritan sexual standards imposed greater secrecy on adulterous liaisons. Concubines and mistresses were not flaunted as openly as in the past, nor was the fruit of such relationships systematically provided for in wills.

A second explanation for the prevalence of the double standard lies in the fact that women were considered the sexual property of men, and their value would be diminished if they were used by anyone other than the legal owner. From this point of view, masculine honor became dependent upon female chastity. The cuckold was not only someone whose virility was in question because he was unable to "maintain" his property adequately (that is, sexually satisfy his wife), but he was also incapable of ruling his own household. In many countries, uxoricide was pardonable if committed in *delictum flagrans* and very lightly punished if motivated by adulterous conduct. This is all the more understandable if one remembers that an unfaithful wife was often considered a disqualifying factor for public office and other honors. In rural areas, village communities took matters into their own hands by subjecting cuckolded husbands and their wayward wives to public shame rituals in churches and raucous skimmington rides.[83]

Only among the aristocracy did the otherwise universal double standard not prevail. Attractive court ladies were practically pushed into their sovereign's bed in order to advance their husbands' ambitions, while others felt at liberty to take lovers once they had performed their conjugal duty by providing their husbands with a legitimate male heir. Furthermore, few men of wealth and fashion were willing to risk their lives in a duel to avenge a wife's compromised honor. In eighteenth-century England, one of the worst consequences of an adulterous liaison was the heavy compensation paid to the aggrieved husband, some of whom made a regular living out of the infidelities of their wives. Moreover, not all the ladies courted by aristocratic men were either married or noble. The end of the early modern period saw improved education of bourgeois daughters, together with a lack of career opportunities for genteel women suddenly impoverished by the economic uncertainties of their families' professional or mercantile fortunes. The result was a pool of good-looking and well-mannered mistresses who could be shown in public to the credit of their current lovers.[84]

Recognition of the affective vacuum in most aristocratic marriages and a masculine conviction of the need for at least token supervision of feminine virtue caused the development, in seventeenth- and eighteenth-century Italy, of a form of institutionalized adultery known as the *cavalier servente* or *cicisbeo*. A country famous for the severity with which the chastity of its middle-class women was guarded, Italy was equally famous for permitting its noble ladies to be constantly attended by a man of their own rank who was not their husband. This arrangement, which permitted upper-class women to appear in society with the necessary male escort, had several advantages. In the best of cases, the *cavaliere* was chosen by the husband and made it a point of honor never to compromise his charge's virtue. In many other cases, however, the *cicisbeo* was a kind of second husband who shared all his lady's favors with her legitimate consort.[85]

For most women, however, illegitimate love remained an area in which the price to be paid for disposing of their own bodies and affections was much heavier than that paid by men. Less and less protected against the consequences of seduction and concubinage, women were equally discriminated against in the long-lived double standard for adultery. As late as 1857, the Divorce Act in England permitted a wife to be divorced for simple adultery but a husband only if his infidelity was compounded by other circumstances such as cruelty, desertion, bigamy, rape, sodomy, or bestiality.[86]

Toward a Reconciliation of Love, Sex, and Marriage

In the sixteenth and seventeenth centuries two stereotypes of sexual conduct predominated: temperate, and often loveless, conjugal intercourse aimed at producing a male heir, whereas extramarital relations provided an arena for both sentimental love and sexual pleasure. In the lower classes, mutual affection, sexual compatibility, and marriage were more easily reconciled thanks to courtship practices that permitted couples to get to know each other intimately before betrothal. In the eighteenth century, however, the rise of illegitimate births in this same social bracket would seem to indicate a widening gap between love and marriage, with the penalty for aspiring to a union based on mutual inclination heavily visited upon mothers who remained unwed.[87] The pattern was just the opposite in the middle and upper classes. Although the double standard with respect to premarital chastity and conjugal fidelity persisted throughout the early modern period, the eighteenth century saw the rise of a more affective model of conjugal relations based on compatibility of sentiment and mutual sexual attraction. This change, as well as the greater autonomy accorded to young men and women in their choice of marriage partner, encouraged the reshaping of the ideal model for wifely behavior to include carnal and emotional functions previously performed by the mistress. In the realm of extramarital sensuality, more tolerant mores also encouraged the proliferation of adulterous liaisons, prostitution, and homosexuality as well as the development of a number of sexual devices and diversions such as dildoes and pornography.[88] In terms of sexual attitudes, however, the most radical change lay in an elite reconciliation of love, sex, and marriage that was to form the basis for our concept of marriage today.

3

The Beautiful Woman

Véronique Nahoum-Grappe

EARLY IN 1789 "women of the Third Estate" petitioned the king in these words:

> Here, nearly all women of the Third Estate are born without wealth. Their education is either sorely neglected or woefully deficient: it consists in sending them to a "school," where the schoolmaster himself does not know the first word of the language he is teaching. They continue to attend classes until they can read the office of the mass in French and vespers in Latin. Once the basic duties of religion are attended to, they are taught to work. When they reach the age of fifteen or sixteen, they are capable of earning five or six sous per day. If nature has denied them beauty and they are without dowry, they marry unfortunate artisans, vegetate painfully in the depths of the provinces, and give birth to children they are incapable of raising. If, on the other hand, they are born pretty, without culture, principles, or ideas of morality they fall prey to the first seducer, commit their first sin, come to Paris to bury their shame, end up losing it altogether in the city, and die victims of libertinage.[1]

For the woman without either dowry or looks there was no exit: despite her marriage, her children, and her husband's work, she was nothing. But the lot of the woman with looks but no dowry was even worse: beauty served only to accentuate what she lacked, namely, culture, principles, and morality, which might have protected her from her own good looks. "Of an ugly girl nothing is expected," according to one sixteenth-century text.[2] All ugly women were alike, so there was no point in asking whether a particular ugly woman was virtuous; she had no identity, did not figure on the urban stage. Beauty, on the other hand, made a woman visible. It put her sexual identity in jeopardy and revealed her lack of the "education" necessary to the creation of a protective virtue and environment. The all-too-apparent good looks of the impoverished beauty designated her as prey; vile seducers picked her out of the crowd. The consequences were predictable: a first misstep, the ensuing shame, flight to the anonymity of the city, a fall into shameless "libertinage," and physical ruin. Good looks were pernicious: "Handsome men end on gallows and beautiful women in brothels," according to a proverb cited in Brantôme. Beauty was pernicious for all women, but particularly for poor women. Works about women in the so-called Bibliothèque Bleue (or Blue Library, inexpensive books and pamphlets sold by hawkers) warned that beauty led to ruin and damnation.[3]

The "Petition of the Women of the Third Estate" therefore raises certain questions. What was meant by "beauty"? How effective was it in determining a woman's fate? Were men and women in the sixteenth, seventeenth, and eighteenth centuries similar in this regard or different? If different, was the difference a historical construct, and did it pertain to representations or practices?

Sources and Biases

These questions belong more to phenomenology and sociology than to history. They concern nonverbal interactions of which the people involved often were not explicitly aware and which have left no trace in the archives. Given the state of the sources it is all but impossible to arrive at an objective picture of the situation. The best we can do is speculate on the basis of a careful interpretive reading.

The documentation is extremely diverse. Information about

the aesthetics of the body is fragmentary. It turns up in surprising places (such as medical treatises) as well as all-too-predictable ones: eighteenth-century novels always contained at least a brief "physical and moral" sketch of the principal characters. We can learn something about the parameters of beauty and ugliness from letters, novels, poems, and medical and philosophical treatises. Archaeological investigation of early-modern sites and estate inventories (explored by many historians)[4] may also yield relevant data: the presence or absence of, for example, mirrors, bathing facilities, and pincers for plucking hair has a bearing on the issues we want to study.

Most of this information, however, pertains to the court and the city. The evolution of what Emmanuel Le Roy Ladurie called "village civilization," the civilization of the countryside, remains elusive. All we have to work with is the image of a "traditional society," an image constructed by folklorists and ethnologists largely on the basis of nineteenth-century evidence.

People presented themselves differently in different times, places, and social milieus. The urban/rural distinction is far too simple to capture the reality. During the period that interests us here, much of the rural population of Europe lived in towns of two thousand to five thousand inhabitants. Generally, these towns contained a large central square around which were arrayed church, tavern, cemetery, the homes of the most prominent citizens, and the smithy. People mingled in large numbers on holy days and feast days. They exchanged ideas and views. In short, rural society was complex and heterogeneous, and social and cultural interactions in the country towns were just as intense as in the city if much less frequently described. Even in the open country, where the human population was sparse, information traveled by foot and horseback. Historians know little about the details of rural social interactions, but that is not to say that the countryside had a culture all its own that left no trace in the written record. Nor did rural people submit passively to urban fashions or make do with the obsolete, cast-off ideas of the urban elite. We would do well to avoid overdrawing the contrast between city and countryside and to rely instead on what detailed local studies have shown the actual differences to be in specific circumstances.

Ethnographic and historical research has clarified the way in which rural people conceived of the body.[5] Knowledge that had once belonged to high culture was combined with certain visible attributes to create an autonomous and comprehensive system of significations. This cultural system explains, for example, why certain hair colors (such as red) were deemed attractive or repulsive. Such judgments were not incompatible with the norms of beauty prevailing in the court and the city. Our problem is to describe how the interpretation of beauty varied with time and place.

At the other extreme of the social structure, political power was increasingly associated with ostentatious display. European courts, whether sedentary or mobile, signaled power through visible signs (as did, more generally, all "corporate" embodiments of political power from the sixteenth to the late eighteenth centuries). Sumptuous dyed fabrics, precious gems, gold, and stately ceremonial dazzled and awed the public. Power, holiness, sunlight, the Beautiful Woman—all were, in one way or another, social spectacles, means of captivating the gaze and dazzling the onlooker so as to dominate the social scene. All the great courts of Europe vied with one another in ostentation and luxury as each attempted to impose its aesthetic fashions and language, as well as its social and economic order, on the "world." This pattern was characteristic of the Western conception of power as it developed in the early modern period.

Both the written and iconographic sources give disproportionate attention to the pomp and circumstance in which the dominant "corporations" of both sexes manifested themselves in public. The closer one came to the sources of political power, the more ostentatious the display and the more stately the ceremony. The awed spectator was overwhelmed by the stupefying sight of vast halls, palaces, squares, hairpieces, and trains and by the coruscating radiance of chandeliers, mirrors, jewels, and gold. In the forefront were the women, bejeweled, painted, and wrapped in finery. By the nineteenth century they held exclusive claim to the light and color renounced by their male companions.[6]

Physical Beauty: A Chance for Women?

The "Petition of the Women of the Third Estate" with which this chapter begins did not describe beauty. Mere mention of the word was enough to identify the subject as the female sex. When a poor young woman was called "beautiful" or "ugly," an image immediately leapt to mind. There was no need for an elaborate discussion of the nature of female beauty and its social consequences. A girl was either "pretty" or not. Given the indubitable nature of this judgment, the petition asserted that, in determining the fate of young women of comparable poverty, beauty was the decisive factor. This was a commonplace of the period, and as we move toward the eighteenth century it is a commonplace that occurs more and more frequently in written texts. During this period a more or less uniform urban culture spread throughout Europe. This culture produced images of itself, and those images were often feminine. Was not the city the locus of civilization, haste, decadence, folly and frivolity, effeminate (as opposed to feminine) display, and the decline of true values and virtues? And the city was of course a woman. The chroniclers, moralists, and novelists of the ancien régime portrayed the culture of the city and court as first traducing innocence in a frenzy of ostentation and then perverting it. The beauty of the young peasant girl newly arrived from the provinces, or of the street urchin prettier than the fruits she sold, foretold an all-too-predictable fate. The city was invariably a threat to beauty, which it first entrapped with cosmetics, jewels, and other seductive disguises and then transformed into its opposite: shameful disease, ugliness, death.

Beauty was a sign from which a diagnosis followed: a glimpse of a face or figure was enough to predict the future. Beauty was a gift, an identifying characteristic as objective as wealth or education. Distributed randomly at birth, wealth and beauty were strokes of fortune, facts that could not be justified but had to be taken into account. The fairy tales that had been making their way around Europe since the late Middle Ages often featured beautiful heroines. Words were inadequate to capture their perfection, which was a sign of grace, like the stroke of a fairy's magic wand above a baby's cradle. Such beauty was the formal concomitant of other tokens of good fortune such as wealth, rank, and moral purity (signified by a pure complexion). It was as if physical beauty alone was not sufficient to ensure good fortune. Beauty complemented other, truer gifts (the gifts of "birth") and gave physical evidence of their legitimacy.

Generally speaking, beauty was not as effective a determinant of good fortune as wealth. No aesthetic dowry could make up for the lack of an economic one. The gift of beauty merely supplemented other gifts of fortune—unless, caught in the city's trap, it actually hastened a fall already implicit in a young woman's poverty. The fortunate young lady already enjoyed the protection of such shields as culture and virtue, which wealth provided; for her, beauty was the halo wreathing the promise of high birth.

For the poor woman, beauty was one more threat to a vulnerable social position. Ugliness, on the other hand, offered protection from vile seducers. If beauty lent dazzle to the already brilliant woman of means, it only compounded the negative consequences of poverty. Destitution left the beautiful woman defenseless, with nothing to fall back on. What attracted (and thus defined) the vile seducer was precisely this vulnerability. Furthermore, the beautiful woman who succumbed to the seducer's blandishments thereby identified herself as a daughter of Eve: her fall, whether the result of an apple, a jewel, or a promise, was a consequence of original sin, inscribed in her very body. The destiny foretold by beauty was all the more inescapable because of this congruence with the culture's fundamental myth of sexual identity.

Female identity manifested itself as beauty, and beauty in turn, by activating the tautological association of physical presence with sexual identity, pointed up the menace to femininity. A poor and ugly woman was of no interest to the novelist, moralist, or seducer because she had no distinctive cultural or social significance.

Accordingly, it makes no sense to ask how aesthetic criteria influenced the fate of women. The social judgment that defines a woman as "beautiful" or a man as "handsome" is in any case a complex phenomenon. There is no objective standard against which to measure judgments almost always expressed in hackneyed terms. And if it is difficult to be objective about the aesthetic aspects of these judgments, it is even more difficult to analyze their sociological consequences. Specifically, it is impossible to know what effect aesthetic judgments may have had on marriage choices or on decisions to migrate or to enter a convent.

The revolutionary petition quoted above, in a sense a sort of informal sociological treatise, also raises another question: How was the notion of female beauty related to the differentiation of male and female sexual identities? The culture defined those identities in terms of "legends" that set forth the destinies of representative members of each sex, legends that made sense of what would otherwise have been unintelligible. A "true woman" was one who was both feminine and beautiful. She constituted an ideal type, in Max Weber's sense, a type rich in significations. By contrast, ugliness and femininity were incompatible. The ugly woman belonged to a more neutral, less sexually identified category, and was therefore less likely to appear in the narratives and images produced by the culture.

The Aesthetic Question: A Tactical Mask?

Historians have found that men and women presented themselves and groomed themselves in different ways. Some scholars take this to be a self-evident truth, while others regard it as a problem requiring explanation. Sexual differences in regard to literacy, political behavior, and creativity in the sciences and the arts are one thing, but when it comes to sexual differences with respect to grooming (makeup, dress, the wearing of jewelry, and so forth) women leap immediately to mind. Western scholars tend to use the paradigms of their own culture in an unreflective way, and it so happens that the culture establishes a close—too close—connection between femininity and appearance, femininity and physical beauty, femininity and sexuality. We would do better to resist the temptation of a paradigm whose purpose is none other than to associate the feminine with the very notion of temptation. The nineteenth century saw the culmination of a process of aesthetic differentiation that had been centuries in the making. Men renounced the "nonutilitarian" and "conspicuous": makeup, jewelry, long hair, brightly colored clothing, and so on. In Europe "important" men now dressed in sober, neutral garb: when they appeared in public it was in black, grey, or white. The male's social presence was thus euphemized under the aesthetic mask of the "serious." Any transgression of this code entailed a loss of credibility and effectiveness.

Centuries before the triumph of this new dress code, differences had emerged in the way men and women carried their bodies. Men had long been taught to discipline their movements, to keep their distance from one another, to stand proudly erect, to hold their tongues, and to restrain their gestures. Women could manifest their difference by talking idly, carrying themselves supply, fluttering about, laughing raucously, or letting slip a shoe, handkerchief, or lock of hair.

In Western Europe the distance between the intimate space of the body and public social space increased in the early modern period. Reserve, self-control, coldness, silence, an erect posture, moderate laughter, and a reluctance to stand out in society—all cultural products long in the making—became characteristic of one sex and not of the other. In "civilized" Western cultures powerful politicians and learned men faced society with a death mask, a mask of serious objectivity; their stiff posture scarcely set them apart from their background. Any infraction of this aesthetic code—wearing an ostentatious gem, say, or hair that hung down to the shoulders—became a suspect sign of femininity, that mélange of weakness and perversion, impotence and incompetence, inconstancy and inconsistency. By the nineteenth century, artists were the only men exempt from this strict code: "art," as opposed to "science" and far removed from "politics," always carried a taint of femininity, hence of possible perverse decadence, and this was reflected in the aesthetics of the body. Some European men adopted an "effeminate" appearance to express, consciously or unconsciously, deviation from the prevailing norms (not always sexual in nature). But the effeminate was increasingly stigmatized as male and female appearances diverged.

What happened in Europe from the sixteenth to the eighteenth century to allow this gender differentiation to occur? To answer this question we should look first at the social function of aesthetic information and then at the evolution of norms of appearance.

Aesthetic Information and the Consequences of Beauty

Many signs enter into the construction of a self-image: the choice of the colors one wears, the flash of a mirror attached to one's belt, a dab of rouge to accent a white foundation, the swish of a gown, the placement of handkerchiefs and shawls, the use of a high coif to accentuate an erect posture, the selection of hair length. Even before the nineteenth century many of these signs carried a feminine connotation. The most visible attributes, from a simple flower in the hair to attention-getting frivolities of every sort, were numbered among the "seductive" devices of the female. Why was appearance so important? Alexander Baumgarten, the eighteenth-century German who gave the word *aesthetic* one of its present-day meanings, helps provide an answer: "The more distinctive signs a perception includes, the stronger the impression it makes. That is why an obscure perception that includes more distinctive signs than a clear perception makes a stronger impression; the same for a confused perception that includes more distinctive signs than a distinct perception."[7]

Certain perceptions, in other words, possess a kind of vigor, a potency of impression. These perceptions are not "clear and distinct" like Descartes's but rather "obscure" yet "distinctive"; they make an impression even before they make sense. A "loud" color can have this effect. In general, any kind of aesthetic information can make an "obscure" impression luminous or an opaque fact "impressive" (Baumgarten's word is "emphatic"). A glimpse of an object, a color, or a fragrance can strike the senses and conjure up associated images.

The domain of aesthetics is therefore not limited to certain objects—to paintings, say, and other works of art. It is related, rather, to a specific kind of perception, to perception that yields a specific kind of information. The human face and body are particularly rich in the relevant kind of information. Wherever the human appears, whether in person, in images, or in texts, the effects of beauty and its opposite are always at issue. A beautiful woman, for example, becomes the cynosure of all eyes. Her appearance on the social scene is an intensely silent event. Consider this example from eighteenth-century Paris in an account by Louis-Sébastien Mercier:

> In order to stimulate the generosity of his parishioners the stern pastor of one church frequently resorts to an ingenious device of piety. In the morning he preaches against finery and denounces as dreadfully scandalous all the frivolous ornaments with which it is embellished. In the evening he hopes that the elegant figure and pretty face of the delightful woman he has invited to serve as alms collector will result in a more abundant harvest. She is dressed in fine clothes, and her visible breasts are embellished but not hidden by a large bouquet. She stands at the door of a church or prison and with a gracious smile appeals to the compassion of all who enter. She mildly berates those who resist. She stops them and, with a voice made interesting by her pretty teeth and with the irresistible eloquence of a bare arm and two beautiful, begging eyes, [asks them to reconsider] . . . The miser weakens, and the eyes of those in attendance turn from the altar to devour her charms.[8]

Mercier's pleasant style should not be allowed to obscure the sociological significance of this vignette. A woman's beauty is used tactically to support an institution (the church) critical of the means used to serve its own ends. The woman's presence distracts attention from its legitimate objects: the altar, the throne, the landscape. It encourages a moment of intense, vivid perception. Yet the erotic implications of this devouring of the female image cannot conceal her social function. The erotic gaze is interested in the face and body of a woman (or man) rather than in a sunset or architectural edifice. Here the eroticism is virtual, in suspense, and its energy can be diverted from its goal (to satisfy sexual desire) toward any other object (such as religion) without the complex mediation of a sublimative process. The agent of this diversion is the aesthetic perception, which is at once obvious and enigmatic. A woman's beauty is used tactically, to persuade, as if it were a kind of rhetoric. At a minimum the effect of beauty is to divert attention from one object to another. The desired end is not sexuality but social efficacy.

The aim is to attract the gaze of the person whose attention one wants. Female beauty is thus a means of attracting attention prior to any actual interaction. Holding another person's attention is one of the preconditions of social interaction, as any prostitute knows. Thus we can say that the primary purpose of physical display is more functional than aesthetic.

Women who supported the Revolution were often attacked for their looks: "Republican women who wear cockades are frightfully ugly." This was a more serious charge than it might appear. Ugliness excludes women from communication, which begins with an exchange of glances. Thus to mock the looks of the female politician, scientist, or scholar is an excuse for ignoring what she might say, do, or be.

Physical beauty offered tactical possibilities for social intervention. The effects of beauty were plastic and malleable. The captivation of a gaze, no matter how brief, opened up a space for creative interaction. The beggar, for example, knew that his only hope for survival lay in his ability to meet the gaze of passersby. The "ugly woman," doomed to remain always in the background, had to develop other tactics. The stimulus of beauty worked as quickly as a glance, and it benefited from a fruitful opacity, a readiness to be put to many uses. Beauty was a convincing argument, all the more so in that it had no intrinsic meaning. In Shakespeare's *Julius Caesar* Portia makes full use of it: "I charm you, by my once commended beauty . . . that you unfold to me, yourself, your half, why you are heavy" (II, 1, 271–274).

In other words, beauty was a tactical mask, which women more or less deliberately and elaborately chose to wear. The hours spent applying makeup went to the production of this fragile, impermanent mask, which time invariably destroyed. The goal was not simply sexual seduction, although it was usually interpreted as such. Beauty was also an unreliable but effective tool for social action, especially when women were prevented from using other tools (whether legal, cultural, economic, or political).

We may assume, therefore, that women continually diverted the gaze of male desire from themselves to other objects. Once a woman was looked at, she could at last open her mouth and speak. Moreover, this beauty, which women constructed culturally, technologically, and socially (tweezers and manual of grooming in hand), did not arouse the suspicion of men because it reinforced their ethnocentric notions of women: women were entirely taken up with concern for their appearance and with their desire to please men, or so men believed. Women were thus able to develop techniques of social intervention in which sex served only as a means to an end. Coquetry was a tactic aimed not at eliminating or destroying the other but simply at asserting one's own existence as a human being. When a woman succeeded in captivating a man's attention, she could propose her own views and assert her own way of being in and thinking about the world.

Beauty: A Strategic Goal

> I have known men who wished they had been girls, and beautiful, from the age of thirteen to the age of twenty-two, after which they might revert to being men.
>
> —Jean de La Bruyère

It is impossible to write a history of what people would have liked to have been. Are there societies in which all little girls dream of being boys up to a certain age, or vice versa? If such wishes could be studied, anthropologists and historians would know how to make good use of them. But let us take La Bruyère's comment for what it is: hearsay straight from the seventeenth century, speculation reported in a conversational tone. The conditions that underlie such imaginative speculation are interesting to explore.

What the comment makes clear is that men could imagine themselves as women during the period of adolescence, from age thirteen to twenty-two, when a woman's beauty was widely assumed to achieve its fullest flower. This male desire for identification stems from a wish not to possess but to take advantage of disguise. The assumption is that it is enviable to be a beautiful young woman because she enjoys a great deal of power and pleasure, a state as enviable as that of an adult male in a society made for adult males. Beauty is posited as the symbolic equivalent of a more real power, that of the adult male.

Beauty's power operates in the brief compass of aesthetic perception: the cynosure of all eyes, the Beautiful Woman is the rival of other embodiments of power such as the throne and the altar. In this respect physical beauty poses a threat to hierarchy, but an empty, purely formal threat that evaporates when its object disappears. If a fairy tale is a fantasy that falls between what is possible and what is necessary, the beauty of the shepherdess can exist only within the limits of narrative: she marries the prince because she already is a princess, because she was born a princess, and her ideal beauty is an all-but-magical sign of her social distinction. The order of the narrative thus restores the disruptive and unpredictable element of beauty to its proper place.

The aesthetics of the body function outside the economic realm, where everything has its exact value. The sociological effects of beauty and the economic process by which this pure, ephemeral spectacle was produced were concealed in two ways: beauty was dismissed as "feminine" and "frivolous," an instance of the vanity of appearances. Yet the production of a self-image was hard work. There was a whole technology of beauty in the seventeenth and eighteenth centuries: mirrors (which in urban interiors grew larger and more numerous), cosmetics, and hairpieces were complemented by a variety of scientific and medical techniques, a wealth of objects and practices, and a major investment of time and effort. Yet the description of beauty hid all this from view.

Beauty was described in two ways: by fragmentation and hyperbole.[9] Sixteenth-century *blasons* of the female body exemplify these techniques. Beauty was defined in circular fashion: beauty is that which pleases, and that which pleases is beautiful. Dictionaries old and new repeated this empty definition. At the center of the circle was the exclamation of amazement, the breathless "Oh!" of immediate and overwhelming perception. A deluge of words followed. Consider, for example, Gabriel de Minut's *Paulegraphie, or description of the beauties of a lady of Toulouse known as the beautiful Paule* (1587): the beauty of the most beautiful woman in Toulouse is rivaled, we learn, only by her virtues.[10] Once again, the praise takes two forms. The beautiful body is divided up into separate pieces, each of which is praised in turn; or the whole is characterized in terms of a series of familiar metaphors. Poems honoring the beauty of a beloved proceeded in similar fashion.

The question of a more theoretical definition of physical beauty remains to be addressed, however. Every culture has its idea of beauty, which no verbal or analytical account can adequately convey. Yet one has only to pronounce the word *pretty* or *beautiful* to conjure up certain images capable of producing the consequences described above.

Beauty is a unique kind of social spectacle. Aesthetic perception, which occurs in an instant, is its natural terrain. During the moment of perception everything remains in suspense: sexual tension permits a subversion that is purely social yet also virtual (it can vanish in a moment and be forgotten). The moment of beauty's appearance is always perfect, but it cannot last. Duration represents a fall from the height of the ideal. The more perfect beauty is, the more unreal it is. It can exist fully only in a caesura in time, in memory or retrospective narrative. Metaphors of light express stupefaction or bedazzlement at beauty's radiance. Working within the confines of rules of rhetoric and literary codes, these clichés represent an attempt to capture a specific type of interaction, a silent explosion that takes place in a complex strategic setting. The context in which beauty manifests itself is precarious and unreal.

Stunning Beauty

The effect of beauty is not simply a consequence of sexual desire, because beauty is always perceived in a social context. An exchange of glances raises the perhaps crucial issue of identity, of "first impression," for both parties. The world that concerns us here was one in which favor, slander, or disgrace could save and destroy lives: the will of the master determined whether or not a servant could start a family and what the servant's life would be like in old age; intellectual work required the patronage of a minister or other powerful personage, whose attention had to be attracted somehow in the antechamber. The desire to produce an "effect of beauty" was not idle, nor was it the mark of a perverse wish to seduce. It was, rather, a risky attempt to find one's way out of a predicament. This was true of both sexes, but to different degrees. When young Jean-Jacques Rousseau, a runaway adolescent with nothing to his name, sang along the roads, his beautiful voice often opened doors that saved his life. In the blink of an eye aesthetic charm could thus offer salvation, but it could also spell doom, and that was the issue raised by the women's petition of 1789. For women, beauty was often a strongly negative factor, one that could lead to what Georges Bataille would later call a "desire for defilement" and destruction, a desire most fully and infernally chronicled by the Marquis de Sade at the end of the early modern period.

Once a woman's beauty had disappeared and its powerful effect was forgotten, it became suspect. Her body was associated with death, whose grimacing, sexless skeleton, staring at her from beyond the mirror, already held her decaying but still bedizened body in its embrace. This terrifying couple appeared often in sixteenth-century iconography: the human body was all the more corporeal for being female, all the more perishable for being beautiful, pampered, and pearly white. The skeleton's embrace was absolute, far more intimate than any amorous embrace, because death and decay were the promise of a future contained within the beautiful body itself, underneath the skin.

Later, the image of the woman gazing at herself in the mirror shed its more terrifying connotations as the whole concept of female beauty was reinterpreted in the Renaissance. A woman might be shown in her bath, surrounded by fruits and flowers and gazing into a mirror as she groomed herself and combed her plaited hair, wreathed in gold. The space around her might be filled with vaporous, almost immaterial emanations: lace, veils, silk, locks of hair, shimmering light. Shapely and soft, she was often portrayed with an enigmatic smile, her head tilted as in images of the Virgin. Death was nowhere imminent; the threat was more diffuse. The occupation of pictorial space by the "beautiful" body would be one of the principal topoi of post-Renaissance European representations of female identity.

What was the reason for the water, the fountains, the vegetation, the animals, the playful little dogs in these scenes of bodily grooming? The setting was one without visible social referents. And why the fruits, the curls, the curvaceousness of the female body, all summed up in the adjective "soft"? Softness is a quality that allows attention to be shifted from the form of a smile to its expressive significance, from the shape of a shoulder to its imagined texture (soft to the touch): sight turns to touch in the imagination. Soft is the gaze that mirrors the soul, as soft as the curve of a back already bent in a posture of submission. The supple curve that implies softness is intended to work on all the senses, to suggest all the ways in which the feminine can be experienced. This set of painterly traits reflects a whole conception of what a real woman is. The female is thus a recognizable presence, more than real yet never actually encountered, except perhaps in the instant when beauty triggers that silent explosion.

In the end, the most intimate, the most intense of experiences thus runs the risk of being the most codified and therefore predictable. Aesthetic norms are not simply imposed by force or imbibed with a mother's milk or promulgated by edict. They are also the consequences of those fundamental chains of association by which a culture enables individuals to recognize and interpret the bodies of other individuals.

The beautiful woman is also the true woman, always grooming, always naked, always in proximity to water and flowers and fruits, and always remote from the unpredictability of social existence, of works and days. To practice a difficult profession or work in a strict science or exert physical force would subtract the Feminine from the feminine.

Images of "true" beauty/femininity define a limited range of possibilities. A woman's body is supposed to be childlike: round, smooth-skinned, with dimples and curls, and full of smiles; we see it set in "natural" surroundings, far from "civilized" society. But it also connotes death: its features are inexpressive, in suspense; its smile is soft but enigmatic; its presence is merely formal, devoid of "self." It is as if the woman did not inhabit her body, as if the representation of her beautiful body nullified any identity other than that of "true femininity" and pure beauty. Beauty here is contrasted with prettiness. A pretty girl could be more animated and talkative, darker and saucier, less diaphanous and distinguished: from the eighteenth century on this contrast became increasingly pronounced.

Ideal, changeless beauty was also suspected of being empty or vain or spiritless or soulless or uncultivated, silent because it had nothing to say. Or it might turn out to be cold and deceitful. Many negative images were attached to beauty in Europe from the end of the Middle Ages: cruelty, for example, and stupidity. Such social judgments influenced conversation as well as texts, through jokes and jibes that reinforced and revived ancient images (yet remain beyond the reach of historical research).

Beauty was also a useful tool, and women without other means of influencing society deliberately made use of it. Like the sun, the throne, and the altar, beauty fascinated, and it was thus the center of complex strategic maneuvers. Those in power did what they could to make use of the most "brilliant" women, brilliance being the material equivalent of beauty (achieving it required considerable means). Female beauty was circumscribed by a very narrow definition of femininity, a soft, silent curve that still connoted a variety of threats. Over the past four centuries the threat of femininity has been minimized by euphemism. Yet beauty in a woman still evokes the thought that she may be stupid, while conversely the intelligent woman ruins her looks by knitting her brows as she thinks—unless, of course, she makes up for her ugliness by provoking laughter in "the adventurer," the masculine type that Georg Simmel contrasts with the coquette; a study of his aesthetic would also be likely to pay dividends.

Translated from the French by Arthur Goldhammer

4

A Daughter to Educate

Martine Sonnet

How can you be content to be in the World
like Tulips in a Garden, to make a fine show
and be good for nothing?
— Mary Astell, *A Serious Proposal*
to the Ladies, 1694

BETWEEN 1500 AND 1800 educational aspirations of all kinds increased quite apart from the most vital needs of everyday life. Medieval education, largely limited to rote learning of prayers and manual skills, had no notion of a distinctive body of knowledge reserved for women. Later authorities, faced with the need to train officials to occupy positions in the church and state and untroubled by any assumption that the sexes were equally intelligent, made what they took to be a plausible distinction. The sons of the nobility and later of the bourgeoisie were made to study classical culture: the culture of the preparatory school and the university, a culture that could be understood only by those who knew Latin and that opened the way to important careers in the ecclesiastical or civil bureaucracy. Daughters of all strata of society were relegated to learning skills useful around the home: things that a girl could learn from her mother and that were useful in Christian households. There was rather little communication between the two cultures—the public and the private, the men's and the women's—and for many commentators that was a problem. Men of letters at any rate wanted their future wives to be educated well enough to understand and contribute to their conversation.

From the Renaissance through the Enlightenment the sexual differentiation of educational practices tended to outstrip the social differentiation. More and more people—men and women alike—were introduced to the three R's—reading, writing, and arithmetic—owing to the development of a range of educational institutions. But this relative democratization of education did not benefit boys and girls to the same degree. For the latter the road to emancipation through learning was often blocked. What girls were allowed to study was limited and closely scrutinized. Despite these obstacles, literacy rates among women increased in the seventeenth and eighteenth centuries, proof that an irreversible process had been set in motion.

Concerns about the Education of Young Girls

From the Renaissance on, proponents of women's education clashed with adversaries who considered it impossible, futile, or unwise. A few early feminist voices were heard, such as that of Christine de Pizan, and it would be an exaggeration to say that women's advocates preached in the desert. But in education, practice always lags prudently behind theory, and this truism is even truer when it comes to the education of women.

"A Subject That Has Yet to Be Treated"

When Jean-Louis Vivès published *De l'institution de la femme chrétienne* (On the Institution of the Christian Woman) in 1523, he was fully aware that he was dealing with "a subject that [had] yet to be treated" but that would interest some of the most important thinkers associated with the two chief intellectual movements of the sixteenth century: humanism and the Reformation.

A proponent of education for young girls, married women, and widows, Vivès was nevertheless quick to lay down limits—limits with which nearly everyone agreed and would continue to agree for a long time to come. Women were not to attend classes with men; domestic work should take priority over reading and writing; and the teaching of Latin, even to the cream of the elite, should be undertaken only with extreme caution. On these points Vivès concurred with any number of other educators, but he firmly rejected one widely held prejudice: "Most of the vices of the women of this and previous centuries," he insisted, "stem from lack of cultivation." This point would be made again. Erasmus, who shared many of Vivès' views, expressed himself with considerable sarcasm in several of his *Colloquia*. He defended education for young women on the grounds that it fostered understanding in marriage and in society, where men and women were expected to live together. Rabelais incorporated the principle of women's education into his version of a utopian community, the abbey of Thélème, where well-born men and women lived and pursued their studies in freedom and harmony.

Luther, who based his religious doctrine on the authority of scripture, logically hoped that everyone—men and women alike—would have the ability to imbibe religion at the source and therefore advocated universal instruction in reading. The Reformation thus fostered literacy. But even as Luther fought for new schools for girls and boys, he sought to limit the scope of women's education. The Reformation promoted a patriarchal model of the family in which women were subservient to their husbands. Furthermore, vernacular translations of the Bible undermined one argument for teaching women Latin. When England became Protestant, monastic libraries were broken up, depriving the fortunate few who had had access to them of an important intellectual resource.

A Counter-Reformation Priority

After the Council of Trent (1545–1563) Catholic reaction advanced into territory once occupied by its Protestant adversaries: religious education of the very young. The church launched a vast program of instruction, which sought to reach adults through preaching and missions into the countryside and children through catechism classes, which required a minimum level of literacy. Within a short time these efforts focused on children who had previously received little or no instruction, particularly in urban areas. In the 1560s Carlo Borromeo established doctrinal schools in his Milan diocese, where lay and ecclesiastic teachers offered lessons to children rounded up from the city's streets and alleyways. Within twenty years the Jesuits had founded Sunday schools in southern Netherlands towns to provide instruction for children who worked during the week.

These experiments, which involved the teaching of boys and girls, continued, but by the turn of the seventeenth century new initiatives aimed specifically at girls were under way. Catholic reformers had begun to see how important a role little girls might play in their efforts to regain the religious allegiance of the populace. Every little girl was a future mother, hence a future teacher capable of amplifying the good word being spread by Counter-Reformation preachers. This realization gave new impetus to efforts to teach young girls to read and to study the catechism. As new congregations of nuns dedicated to the instruction of girls proliferated, what had been the privilege of a few was extended to new segments of society. Wealthier girls attended convent boarding schools, which charged tuition, while poorer children attended charity schools. In either case the aim was to educate good Christian mothers. The mold to which schoolgirls were expected to conform was one that would remain largely unchanged for three centuries. It was, moreover, a mold conceived by the elite groups that gave the new schools their financial support and spiritual guidance. "The instruction and education of poor little girls early in life is one of the principal good works that Christians can accomplish and provide and one of the greatest missions and most necessary works of charity that they can perform for the salvation of souls," according to the founders of a charitable home for poor girls from Les Halles in Paris.[1]

From the beginning of the seventeenth century some very interesting women found employment for their talents in religious orders devoted to the education of young women. Shortly after arriving from England with her Catholic recusant family, Mary Ward, aged twenty-four, established a Christian institute in Saint-Omer and, with the aid of the Jesuits, developed it into a force for the education of women. She overcame the opposition of the papal authorities, which took a dim view of uncloistered women's giving lessons in city streets. Another strong personality was Montaigne's niece, Jeanne de Lestonnac of Bordeaux. An energetic woman, she raised five children and then, widowed when she was nearly fifty, founded in 1607 the Compagnie de Marie-Notre-Dame, whose influence extended throughout southwestern France,

Spain, and South America. In Paris Mme. Acarie and Mme. de Sainte-Beuve presided over the founding of two Ursuline convents, one in 1610, the other in 1621; while in Annecy Baroness Jeanne de Chantal, in conjunction with François de Sales, founded the Visitation in 1610. In Lorraine Alix Le Clerc and Pierre Fourier jointly founded the Congrégation Notre-Dame, which won approval in 1615. A little later, in 1633, Louise de Marillac, a staunch follower of Vincent de Paul, oversaw the expansion of the Filles de la Charité (Daughters of Charity) throughout the kingdom and beyond; the Daughters' mission was to care for sick paupers and teach little girls.

A Topic for Literary Salons

While Catholic reformers were busy dealing with the issue of educating young girls, men and women of letters approached the matter from another direction. The subject was treated in a variety of seventeenth-century literary genres: romance, comedy, letters. What women knew became a topic for brilliant conversation in the salons. Molière stirred things up with two plays: *Les précieuses ridicules* (1659) and *Les femmes savantes* (1672). Pedantic women were mocked, but properly and decently educated women found champions. Meanwhile, the idea that the faults customarily seen in women stemmed from want of education steadily gained adherents among all who were not blinded by misogyny. Influential women of letters such as Mademoiselle de Scudéry and Madame de Sévigné pleaded in favor of a well-rounded curriculum, while any number of philosophers and writers compared the intellectual qualities of the two sexes. Did women have the same faculty of understanding as men or not? Malebranche answered in the negative: women had absolutely no gift, he argued, for science, philosophy, or elevated speculation of any kind. But in 1673 François Poullain de La Barre published *De l'égalité des sexes* (On the Equality of the Sexes), a major event in the history of feminist thought. Using the Cartesian method, Poullain demonstrated rationally that men and women shared identical aptitudes and abilities and should therefore receive the same training: "If women studied in universities alongside men or in other universities set aside for them in particular, they could take degrees and aspire to the titles of Doctor and Master in Theology, Medicine, and [canon or civil] Law. And their natural talent, which fits them so advantageously for learning, would also suit them to be successful teachers."[2]

Poullain de La Barre's feminism tinged with social criticism was matched twenty years later by the Englishwoman Mary Astell, who in 1694 wrote *A Serious Proposal to the Ladies*. Influenced by Mlle. de Scudéry and Mme. Dacier, the plea on behalf of women's education attracted more attention than La Barre's work. Writing in a warm and friendly conversational manner, Astell attempted to make women, especially upper-class women, aware of possibilities that went unexplored owing to lack of education. If men's education were neglected as badly as women's, people would find as much fault with them as with their female companions. Aware of the obstacles that marriage and family placed in the way of women's intellectual work, Astell, unmarried by choice, expressed the hope that genteel women wishing to escape the constraints of domestic life might live together in "colleges," where they could devote themselves to study in convivial independence and provide a "Learned Education" to young women of high and middling rank.

First Programs

In the final two decades of the seventeenth century French thinkers influenced by the literary debates on the education of women began to reflect on the subject in a more practical way. The first comprehensive curricula, while clear about the need for women's education, excluded subjects thought to be too abstract (such as classical languages, rhetoric, and philosophy). One reason for the heightened interest in female instruction was a change in the structure of the population: widows, of whom there were a great many, needed to be able to take care of business affairs. The acknowledgment that women needed to read, write, and count even if their social role remained confined within the traditional domestic setting was the first step in opening up access to a new culture and new powers.

The thirty-sixth chapter of Claude Fleury's *Traité sur le choix et la méthode des études* (1685) dealt with "women's studies." Women, Fleury argued, might lack industry, courage, and resolve, but their lively, penetrating minds and gentle, modest attitudes made up for these deficiencies. Women needed to be better educated if only because of the "credit and consideration they enjoy in society." Fleury proposed a curriculum consisting of religion (but avoiding superstition), reading, writing, compositions on commonplace subjects, some practical arithmetic, a pharmacopoeia, home economics, and law. To learn more would be pure vanity, but "it would be still better than if they spent their leisure time reading novels, gambling, or talking of skirts and ribbons."[3] Fénelon's *De l'éducation des filles* (1687) was slightly more permissive. Fénelon was willing to accept subjects that Fleury regarded as vain, but only on condition that instruction be carefully limited and monitored. In particular, he proposed that women be allowed to study literature, history, Latin, music, and painting. For Fénelon the most important thing was that a girl's instruction should fit her for later life, whether as a wife or as a nun.

Inspired by Fénelon, Mme. de Maintenon proposed a curriculum for the royal house at Saint-Cyr, which she founded in 1686. There, 250 girls from impoverished noble families were taught to cope with their fate, which in most cases meant serving as pious mistresses of shabby country households while maintaining an aura of gentility befitting their noble origins. Pupils entered the school between the ages of seven and nineteen and proceeded through a series of four classes, each identified by a different color belt. The "reds" were under ten years of age and studied basic catechism; the "greens," who ranged in age from eleven to thirteen, discovered history, geography, and music; the "yellows," fourteen to sixteen, worked on French, drawing, and dancing; and the "blues," seventeen to nineteen, spent most of their time on moral instruction in preparation for returning to the perilous world outside the walls of Saint-Cyr. All, from the youngest to the oldest, practiced housework and needlework. The purpose of the institution, according to Mme. de Maintenon, was to send back to their families girls who were "very Christian, very reasonable, and very intelligent."[4]

An Attenuated Enlightenment

As piety ebbed and the *philosophes* stepped up their attacks on religion in the eighteenth century, education became a fashionable topic of conversation and writing, especially after 1750. The Enlightenment believed in education, which was credited with the capacity to create a new social being, devoid of old prejudices and saturated in the new reason. As long as the education of women was left to chance, however, the new world would remain insecure. Women were not only the mothers of the new men but also their first educators: if society was to be regenerated on a lasting basis, women would have to play a part. Catholic reformers had advanced a similar argument. In a century of pedagogical optimism, girls became, along with deaf-mutes and peasants, fodder for educational speculators.

Before 1760, when the debate got seriously under way, the Abbé de Saint-Pierre's *Projet pour perfectionner l'éducation des filles* (1730) was a highly innovative proposal. What the abbé described as a "Permanent Bureau of Public Education" was nothing less than a national education ministry *avant la lettre*. The bureau would be responsible for overseeing a system of preparatory schools for girls and boys. Girls were to attend classes from ages five to eighteen (thirteen grades). For each class of 15 boarding students, there were to be three teachers, and each school was to have a total of thirty-nine teachers and 195 students. In addition to these boarding schools, the abbé envisioned a system of free day schools. He proposed a curriculum that touched on all the arts and sciences in order to allow women to sustain conversation with male companions.

After 1760 the education question (for both sexes) became one of the central issues of the Enlightenment. The period 1715–1759 saw the publication of 51 works on education, compared with 161 in the years 1760–1790. In 1762 Jean-Jacques Rousseau published *Emile,* which was immediately condemned as sacrilegious by the Sorbonne censors and later by the Parlement. In the same year the expulsion of the Jesuits from France left the system of preparatory schools in disarray. Together, these two events stimulated imaginations and led to the publication of a number of curriculum reform proposals, treatises on education, and other works, many of which were submitted to prize competitions sponsored by provincial academies. The gazettes published critical reviews of these works along with letters from readers on the subject of education. In 1768 a gentleman named Leroux, the headmaster of a boarding school, began the first specialist publication in the field, the *Journal d'Education.* Another sign of the times can be seen in the fact that a practical guide such as *Le tableau de Paris,* by the lawyer Jèze, contained a section on education in a chapter on things "useful for life." All Parisian educational institutions for girls and boys were listed by *quartier.*

Once the need for reform of women's education was acknowledged, debate focused on the issue of where instruction should take place: in the home or in school. A related issue was who should teach and what should be taught. Criticism was aimed at convent schools, where it was said girls learned nothing and suffered from a lack of invigorating stimuli. It was absurd, some said, to entrust the education of future wives and mothers to nuns, who had no experience of marriage. Most eighteenth-century writers favored education in the home, but since only well-to-do families could provide it, the rest needed public schools.

In the introduction to her seven-volume *Traité de l'éducation des femmes* (1779–1789), Mme. de Miremont proposed a system of schooling for girls from ages seven to eighteen. There were to be just two classes, one for pupils aged seven to twelve, the other for ages thirteen to eighteen. As usual, the subjects to be studied included religion, dance, and music, but these were to be supplemented by classes in modern languages, literature, geography, history, and spelling. The training of teachers was a primary concern: they were to spend six years learning their trade.

Those who insisted that girls be educated only in the home drew inspiration from the writings of Rousseau. Scrupulously abiding by Rousseauist principles, some mothers elected to make the raising of their daughters their life's work. Mme. d'Epinay's daughter Emilie, for instance, was to be her mother's creative masterpiece. So that other mothers might profit from her experience she published *Les conversations d'Emilie* (1774), a series of didactic conversations between mother and daughter spanning the fifth to the tenth years of the child's life. Mme. Necker also took charge of educating her daughter Germaine, the future Mme. de Staël. Most of these Rousseauist mothers were themselves the products of extraordinary upbringings.

When Rousseau decided that his Emile needed a female companion, he created Sophie, to whom he devoted the fifth book of *Emile*. Her education was based on a simple principle: "All of a woman's education should relate to men. To please men, to be useful to them, to win their love and respect, to raise them when they are young and care for them when they are old, to advise them, to console them, to make their lives pleasant and agreeable: these have been the duties of women in all ages, which they should be taught from childhood."[5] No sooner did the question of educating women arise than it was subordinated, as Rousseau's words make abundantly clear, to the desires of men. Women were to be granted access to knowledge not for themselves but only to make themselves more agreeable to the men in their lives. Women were made not to understand but to please and care for their husbands and children.

In England a century earlier, John Locke had proposed that women be educated well enough to serve as their children's first teachers. Later, in the eighteenth century, Daniel Defoe and Jonathan Swift had argued that an educated woman made a better companion for her husband than one who was not educated. Enlightened Englishwomen—"bluestockings"—were disappointed that the need to educate young girls was being justified on the basis of the supposed boons not to the girls themselves but to their families. They voiced their displeasure in the salons, and by the end of the century growing numbers of female voices were speaking out against the occupations traditionally supposed to fill the time of young girls—occupations they denounced as vain and frivolous. Rousseau's views aroused the ire of Hannah More, Maria Edgeworth, Catharine Macaulay, and Mary Wollstonecraft. Wollstonecraft was perhaps the most vehement of all in her condemnation of men's unwillingness to admit that women could rival men in learning. Yet as late as 1773 *The Lady's Magazine,* which in theory favored reform of women's education, could still say that "we can never wish that society should be filled with doctors in petticoats to regale us with Latin and Greek."[6]

In France the revolutionary assemblies charged with establishing a system of national education were obliged to face the problem of women's education. Except for Condorcet, who advocated mixed education on the grounds of equality between the sexes, the revolutionaries continued to see the domestic sphere as the proper place for women and accordingly held that women's education ought to be confined to domestic subjects. Denied political rights and excluded from office, women were offered a primary education and nothing more. Another century would pass before there was any fundamental improvement in the situation.

Educational Locales

The proper place for an education confined to domestic matters was obviously the home. Although its educational uses evolved between 1500 and 1800, the home remained the primary site for the education of women. As the idea that girls needed more or better instruction made headway, alternatives began to be suggested: convents, elementary schools, secular boarding schools. The idea of broadening women's educational horizons went hand in hand with the development of new kinds of schools in which girls could study subjects clearly distinct from those studied by boys. Girls' schools were founded to combat the perceived dangers of mixed schooling. For many people, it was unthinkable that brothers and sisters should sit on the same classroom benches and study the same subjects. Moralists and clergymen fulminated against the "mixing of the sexes," thereby encouraging the development of schools exclusively for girls.

The House

Although for a long time the household was virtually the only school for women, there is unfortunately little record of what went on there. Few tangible traces survive of what mothers taught daughters and mistresses their serving girls generation after generation. In the sixteenth century most girls learned how to live and work simply by watching what went on around them. Yet a few cases of remarkable home schooling stand out. Thomas More's three daughters received exactly the same instruction as their brother at Bucklesbury, the family's London home. Margaret was the most gifted of the four children. Lessons were sometimes informal and practical, at other times formal and theoretical. No school for women offered greater opportunity for learning than a home to which enlightened parents invited carefully selected tutors. Families influenced by Enlightenment and Rousseauist educational principles enthusiastically transformed their homes into veritable educational laboratories.

Most girls learned at home by watching their mother go about her daily chores: cooking, child care, washing, mending, sewing, weaving. This domestic instruction, which encouraged agility in little fingers, formed the subject of countless illustrations. In rural areas women had additional work to do. Taking care of the barnyard animals was traditionally a chore for the farmer's wife. Little girls took part in the work of the family, whether it was agricultural, commercial, or artisanal. Some girls served a veritable apprenticeship in the home, and when they married they took the skills learned on the farm or in the store or workshop to their new husband's place of business: most women married men in the same walk of life as their fathers. Some adolescent girls completed their training in the home of a friend or relative. Families often took in outsiders: in sixteenth-century England it was common for boys aged fifteen to twenty-four and girls aged fifteen to nineteen to board with families other than their own, even among aristocrats and gentry. In 1546, for example, Thomas Fenton's daughter joined three female cousins and three other well-born young ladies at the home of her grandmother. In 1551 Sir Edmund Molineux's daughters were sent to live with a cousin of their father, where it was hoped they would grow up "in virtue, good manners and learning to play the gentlewomen and good housewives, to dress meet and oversee their households."[7] In the seventeenth century girls of more modest background left home and went to work in London or various spa towns as servants or shopgirls. By serving others and living in their homes, a girl was supposed to learn how to manage her own household.

From eighteenth-century autobiographies (and with due allowances for the biases inherent in the genre) we learn that some families preferred home education even when schools were available. Well-to-do parents kept their daughters at home and strictly supervised their tutoring. Those with the competence, time, and desire did the teaching themselves; others relied on professional tutors. Girls educated in this way did best when brothers were also kept home and educated along with them. They picked up odd bits of what their brothers learned and in some cases were allowed to study alongside them.

Keen on education and the humanities, the parents of young François-Auguste, Baron de Frénilly, who was born in 1768, established a veritable family academy for him, his sister, two female cousins, and Mlle. Necker. Classes were held on Sundays and combined with outdoor activities and intellectual games. After lunch the pupils were permitted to fly kites in the park. Later they were expected to expound historical texts "in the manner of Livy, Sallust, or Tacitus, whichever one pleased."[8] No school of that period would have proposed such an exercise to young ladies. Frénilly's parents then examined the work of their son and his four female classmates. They also encouraged them to stage plays.

Mme. de Chastenay, born in 1771, received a remarkable education from a female instructor, responsible for teaching history, music, and drawing, and two male assistants, one responsible for mathematics, the other for teaching Latin to all the children of the household.[9] Mme. de Boigne, born Mlle. d'Osmond in Versailles in 1781, owed her unusually extensive learning to her father, the Comte d'Osmond, a court noble who assumed full responsibility for his daughter's education. During the Revolution he immigrated to England, where he found plenty of time to devote to his daughter's studies: "During this period of retirement, my father concerned himself exclusively with my education. I regularly worked eight hours a day on the most serious subjects. I studied history and developed a passion for metaphysics. My father did not allow me to read these subjects on my own, but I could do so under his supervision . . . He included in my studies a number of works on his favorite subject, political economy, which I very much enjoyed."[10]

The education of Manon Phlipon, the future Mme. Roland, was typical of that received by other gifted Parisian children before the Revolution. Her father, an engraver, and mother paid for excellent private instruction at home, and this schooling was completed by a year in a convent school. Manon, born in 1754 and sole survivor of seven children, learned to read at age four. By the time she was seven she was taking lessons all day long from a series of tutors in writing, geography, dancing, music, and drawing. Because of her success as a student, Latin was added to her curriculum. When she entered the boarding school run by the Congrégation Notre-Dame, the sisters congratulated themselves on being sent such an accomplished young lady. Their one remaining task was to prepare their new charge for first communion, but Manon also continued to take music and drawing lessons from private tutors, who met with her in the convent parlor.[11] This use of the convent to supplement a course of home instruction was considered advanced and enlightened.

The Convent

In the sixteenth and seventeenth centuries convent schools had served a very different purpose. The standard image of that period is that girls were sent away while still very young to spend their entire childhoods behind cloister walls. The reality was quite different. In the first place, only the very wealthy could afford to send their daughters to live at convent schools, which cost fabulous

113

sums. Most girls were thus spared the cloister simply because their parents could not afford it. Far more attended primary day schools than were sent away to convent boarding schools.

In 1750 it cost between 400 and 500 livres per year to send a girl to a boarding school in Paris.[12] Combined with the cost of personal needs and private lessons, the bill could easily come to 1,000 livres a year. Such a sum represented two-thirds of the annual income of a skilled mason. As a result, students in boarding schools were a privileged minority: in 1760 the fifty-six boarding schools for girls in Paris accounted for 22 percent of the city's schools but served only 13 percent of its students. And surviving student records show that the upper classes were disproportionately represented. In a school such as that of the Ursulines on rue Sainte-Avoye, where the tuition was relatively "modest," 10 percent of the students came from the old nobility and 34 percent from the families of royal officers. The higher the tuition, the greater the share of blue-blooded pupils. In the great abbey schools (Penthémont, Abbaye-aux-Bois, and Port-Royal), and in those run by Visitandine and Benedictine sisters, the majority of students were daughters of men with titles.

Although the convent schools served relatively small numbers, their qualitative impact was great. Dating from the Middle Ages, convent education was the earliest form of instruction outside the home. The pedagogical role of convent schools evolved throughout the early modern period. Until the seventeenth century convents provided families with a place to which they could send daughters for retreat, surveillance, and initiation into the cloistered life. Many convent boarding students in the sixteenth and seventeenth centuries went on to become novices. Daughters chosen to become nuns, usually for financial reasons having to do with dowries, went straight from the boarding school to the novitiate without having a chance to breathe the air of the outside world. The women's orders thus relied on their schools as a source of new vocations.

In the early seventeenth century this situation began to change as certain orders began to specialize in teaching. Families who chose to send their daughters to schools run by these orders planned to keep them there for only a limited time. More and more girls passed through the convents as a prelude to a secular rather than a religious life. As a result, the convents became increasingly susceptible to worldly influences. They ceased to function as a closed universe in which pupils were encouraged to discover vocations at a very early age in order to replenish the nuns' ranks. Private tutors came to the cloister to give special lessons, as in the case of Manon Phlipon. The Sisters of the Calvary, who kept a school in Paris near the Jardin du Luxembourg, showed remarkable perspicacity and insight into their clientele when they issued this statement in 1789: "We have allowed ourselves to be convinced that the girls entrusted to us were born for the world, and we strive not only to instill in them a sense of their duties in society but also to teach them the knowledge and skills they will need to distinguish themselves."[13]

The transformation of the educational role of convents began during the Reformation, whose importance in fostering new interest in the education of women we saw earlier. Among the orders specializing in education, the Ursulines stand out: their schools relatively quickly covered a wide geographic area. Nuns of the order took the three traditional vows of poverty, chastity, and obedience, but they also promised to devote themselves to teaching. In France the remarkable proliferation of Ursuline schools in the seventeenth and eighteenth centuries attests to a real demand for such institutions. The order was founded in 1535 by Angela Merici in Brescia, Italy. In 1572 a convent was established in Avignon, and from there the order spread into southern France in the early seventeenth century: convents were founded at Chabreuil in Dauphiné in 1599, Aix in 1600, Arles in 1602, Toulouse in 1604, and Bordeaux in 1606. By 1620 there were sixty-five Ursuline convents in France, and on the eve of the Revolution the order had convents in some three hundred cities, with a particularly high density along the Rhone and Saône, in Brittany, and in the southwest.[14]

The organization of classes varied with the educational mission of the women's orders. Religious communities that took in boarding students not with the intention of teaching them anything in particular but because education was a source of income generally placed all pupils in the same class, with approximately thirty students of all ages mixed together. But nuns whose vocation was teaching grouped their pupils in several classes, usually three: "little," "medium," and "big." Housing a hundred or so young girls required a lot of space. While other convents made do with a classroom and a dormitory, the Ursulines and the Congrégation Notre-Dame developed more elaborate facilities. Boarding students had their own dining hall and infirmary and in some cases a parlor and kitchen. The school, no longer a mere outgrowth of the convent, boasted its own rooms and personnel.[15] In the specialized convents more of the sisters took part in the supervision of students than elsewhere.

Nonreligious Boarding Schools

Convents were not the only available resource for families that wished to send daughters to boarding school. Yet systematic inquiry is difficult, whether we are interested in English boarding schools, French *pensions,* or other private schools. What we know of these institutions comes from private correspondence, memoirs, diaries, and even the brief advertisements they placed in the press. Boarding schools were private commercial enterprises that operated independently and often went out of business or moved suddenly. Compared with the convent schools, long-lived like the church itself, nonreligious schools suffered from all the hazards and vicissitudes of ordinary business.

The boarding schools that began to appear in Protestant England in the seventeenth century were a secular extension of the convent school tradition. By 1650 any city worthy of the name boasted a boarding school whose mission was to transform the daughters of the merchant class into young ladies suitable for marriage to gentry. The primary emphasis was on grooming, comportment, and the fine arts. The first London boarding school opened its doors in 1617, and at times during the seventeenth century there were as many as fourteen such institutions in the city. The schools in the suburbs of Hackney, Putney, and Chelsea enjoyed the greatest reputation. One Sunday in 1667 Samuel Pepys chose Hackney and its boarders as the destination of one of his walks. By then the school had already become a much-sought-after institution, serving roughly one hundred students at any given time and referred to as "the ladies' university of the female arts." From the capital the vogue for boarding schools spread to other cities such as Manchester, Exeter, Oxford, and Leicester. By the end of the seventeenth century these institutions were being widely criticized for dispensing a superficial education. Most continued on their established course, but a few took steps toward offering more substantial instruction. At Tottenham High Cross in 1673 Mrs. Bathsua Makin, once a governess of young aristocrats but now specializing in the education of young women, offered an innovative curriculum including ancient and modern languages, natural science, arithmetic, astronomy, history, and geography. In the next century other schools imitated her model, including Mrs. Lorrington's school in Chelsea (around 1760) and the very prominent Abbey House School, which Jane Austen attended along with some sixty other pupils in 1796–1797.[16]

The French *maisons d'éducation* appeared somewhat later than the English boarding schools. They filled a need that arose in the second half of the eighteenth century, when the educational practices of convent schools and *collèges* came under attack. Numerous private schools for girls and boys then sprang up in the cities. These institutions offered parents a model closer to that of family life and respectful of new values, including the increasing emphasis on hygiene, nature, and privacy. The ideal of private education was patterned on the well-run household headed by a man and his wife: pupils were encouraged to exercise in the fresh air and eat well, and courses were designed to improve body, mind, and morals. A valuable source of information on these institutions is the travel diary of Henry Paulin Panon Desbassayns, a merchant from the island of Réunion, in the Indian Ocean, who came to Paris in 1790–1792 to place his two sons and two daughters in private schools.[17] He visited seven girls' schools before choosing one run by M. and Mme. Roze on rue Copeau. Madame kept an eye on everything that went on, while Monsieur taught music. Panon, who hoped that his daughters would learn quickly and well, visited them often and observed lessons in reading, writing, spelling, grammar, English, piano, dance, music theory, elocution, and drawing. But the Roze school was not all work: the families of students were regularly invited to concerts, suppers, fireworks displays, and evening dances. Education was conducted in an atmosphere of conviviality.

Elementary School

Elementary schools served by far the largest number of students, urban and rural, paying and nonpaying. At this level gender differences were probably less significant than elsewhere. Girls learned the truths of religion and the rudiments of reading and writing in much the same way as boys. Rural elementary schools frequently offered mixed classes without arousing much protest.

But in the cities repeated condemnations of mixed education and of male teachers for female students indicate that parents were unwilling to accept mixing in the classroom even when boys and girls had abundant opportunity to mingle outside. Because mixing was perceived as a threat to morality, girls' schools dotted the urban landscape.

Although we will probably never know exactly when the first such school came into existence, one thing is certain: in 1357 the cantor of Paris' Notre-Dame Cathedral also served as director of the "*petites écoles* of the city, suburbs, and environs of Paris" and employed 25 schoolmistresses to teach girls and 50 schoolmasters to teach boys. The cathedral was the only institution permitted to operate schools that charged tuition. Gradually the number of schoolmistresses increased, and by 1672, when new elementary school statutes and regulations were issued, the number of female teachers equaled the number of males. The 1672 edict listed 166 school districts in the capital, each with a schoolmistress for female pupils and a schoolmaster for male pupils. This parity was maintained as long as the cathedral continued to operate the school system; each time a new school district was added, both a male and a female teacher were hired. By 1791 there were 201 schoolmistress positions, all held by laywomen, mostly unmarried except for a few married to colleagues.

Like Paris, other episcopal cities had systems of fee-charging elementary schools run by the cathedral. Lyons's school districts were similar to those of Paris: fifty male and fifty female teachers served the city's population. In 1789 Grenoble had thirteen fee-charging girls' schools and fourteen for boys. The cathedral chapter in Amiens employed eighty schoolmistresses and eighty-two schoolmasters between 1715 and 1780. In Paris classes were held in the schoolmistress' residence; the number of students that could be accommodated was limited by the modest quarters in which a teacher could afford to live. Perhaps twenty pupils could crowd into a room that would revert to domestic use once class was over. When classes were held in a separate school building, it was possible to accommodate about fifty girls in one class.

Even though elementary schools charged fees, they were much more affordable than boarding schools. Parents in Paris in the eighteenth century paid 3 livres 10 sols per month to send a son or daughter to one of the Notre-Dame schools. Thus the annual cost of education was 38 livres 10 sols per student. Such an expense was within the relatively modest means of urban dwellers with sufficient income to forgo what the child might be able to earn if not in school. Nine out of ten female elementary school students in Paris (and probably in the chief provincial cities as well) came from the commercial and artisan classes (there were more daughters of master craftsmen than of journeymen).[18] Although one might occasionally encounter the daughter of a gardener or coalman or barrister or royal geographer, these classes were barely represented. The geographic distribution of the fee-charging elementary schools corroborates this assertion: most were located in the center of the city and its working suburbs where shopkeepers and artisans lived and worked.

In the wake of the Catholic missionary effort pushed by the Council of Trent, free elementary schools proliferated in France in the seventeenth century, giving young girls new opportunities to obtain an education. Teaching orders dedicated to the education of women opened charitable day schools alongside their boarding schools; some devoted themselves exclusively to teaching the poor. Other free schools came into being after 1650, founded by a new generation of priests, better trained than their predecessors, in conjunction with parish-based charitable organizations. The new institutions greatly expanded the network of urban girls' schools. Each charity school class comprised from 40 to 100 pupils. The largest day schools in Paris served as many as 500. The free schools were financed by rents, gifts, and bequests made available by wealthy Christians looking for a way to reconcile their material well-being with their spiritual concerns. Some schools financed themselves in part with the proceeds from the sale of students' needlework.

To respect the laws of competition and not insult the mistresses of the fee-charging schools, the free schools were theoretically reserved for girls whose parents could not afford to pay tuition. In reality, however, free tuition was not enough to spur interest in education among people whose more vital needs were not yet assured. The people who paid for their daughters' education and those who received charity were more alike than one might think. People from both groups were stable residents of urban parishes who lived on the fruits of their labor. The most notable difference was that among the parents of charity students there were proportionately more wage earners and journeymen and fewer master craftsmen than among the parents of tuition-paying students. The promoters of free schools were aware that their student bodies were less homogeneous than they professed. The Ursulines ordered mistresses of free classes to "take care not to place children of the better sort next to the poorest and dirtiest pupils so as not to disgust them. This should be done with discretion, however, so that the poor do not feel despised."[19] The Daughters of Saint-Anne in Paris' Saint-Roch parish in principle taught only indigent pupils, but only one of its seven classes, called the "transient class," was reserved for "poor girls who, forced by their parents and by the necessities of life to work, cannot attend school regularly but come when they can."[20] It thus appears that parents who could afford to pay tuition sent their children to schools not intended for them. The enduring conflict between administrators of free and nonfree schools shows that the student population could not be increased indefinitely even with the offer of free schooling.

Nearly a century later than in France, through the efforts of the Society for the Propagation of Christian Knowledge, founded in May 1699, charity schools for both boys and girls sprang up in towns throughout England, Ireland, and Wales. The Society's pious philanthropists, concerned to instill discipline in children running loose in city streets, enabled youngsters to attend school long enough to learn their ABC's and to receive a dose of religious and moral instruction before being sent out to work as apprentices or domestics. The Society encouraged the founding of new schools and helped administer them. In 1729 some 5,225 students attended 132 London schools, and in 1733 it was estimated that more than 20,000 students were attending charity schools throughout the country. In London the feminist Mary Astell joined theory with practice by persuading the governors of the Chelsea Royal Hospital to establish a school for 30 indigent girls in 1709. This school differed from other charity schools in that the bulk of class time was not devoted to exercises of piety; nor were students required to pay their way by working for outside employers.[21]

Everywhere girls in the countryside fared less well than those in the city, where families had a choice between charity or fee-charging schools. Villages that could barely afford the expense of one school tolerated mixed classes. Nicolas Restif de la Bretonne, who attended primary school in rural Auxerre, later described classes of boys and girls together. The smaller the village, the more tolerant the ecclesiastical authorities, although bishops continued to recommend that classes for boys and girls be held at different times or be separated by partitions, or else that girls be excluded from schooling after the age of nine. For country girls mixed classes were often the only educational opportunity available. If a bishop with puritanical Jansenist leanings or a parish priest anxious about the morals of his flock decided that it was best to avoid mixed classes, the almost inevitable result was that girls received no education. Just such a sequence occurred at Montigny-les-Arsures in Franche-Comté in 1784. The villagers adamantly refused to open a second school, pointing out that "everybody knows that in the country girls rarely attend school after the age of ten. It is not necessary for them to learn to write," and in any case "there is far more danger to morality in sending girls to tend livestock in the heath . . . with adolescent boys."[22]

Although villages commonly hired lay schoolmasters to teach boys' classes, they seldom hired schoolmistresses for the girls. The 390 rural parishes of Doubs employed 3,000 schoolmasters in the eighteenth century but only 66 schoolmistresses. Nearly all rural girls' schools were religious schools run by the regional or national teaching orders, some of which established seminars to train mistresses for rural schools. The Filles de la Charité, founded by Vincent de Paul in Paris in 1633, served as a model for other orders. Sisters of the order wore a characteristic white winged hat that soon became a common sight throughout the country as they fanned out into rural areas to teach poor girls and care for the sick. In 1678 the Dames de Saint-Maur also established a seminar in Paris to train teachers for provincial schools, especially in the Protestant south.

The example of the Filles de la Charité was imitated in countless dioceses and regions. After 1630, and in large numbers between 1660 and 1730, religious organizations dedicated to the training of teachers, many of them secular and limited to a particular locality, sprang up in many places. The great disparities between rural girls' schools in different regions can be attributed to the influence of such groups. Wherever such teaching congregations were active, girls' schools were found even in small villages. The Vatelotes, for example, founded by Canon Vatelot in Toul in 1725, staffed 124 schools in Lorraine in 1789. In western France the Filles de la Sagesse, founded by Grignion de Montfort in 1719, operated 66 schools in lower Normandy and Saintonge on the eve of the Revolution. The Auvergne and Velay regions were served by the Béates, the Demoiselles de l'Instruction, and the Soeurs de

Saint-Joseph. The Lyons region was home to the Soeurs de Saint-Charles, founded by Charles Démia. And Carmelite tertiaries taught in nearly all the parishes of the Vannes diocese in Brittany in the eighteenth century. Despite all these efforts, however, some areas went unserved.

It is interesting to consider the ratio of educational supply to educational demand in prerevolutionary France. In Paris, the city with the most cultural advantages, there were places for 11,200 female students in 265 schools: 2,700 in 153 fee-charging schools, 7,000 in 56 free grammar schools, and 1,500 in 56 convent boarding schools. The population of Paris at the time was between 600,000 and 800,000, and there were anywhere from 49,500 to 66,000 school-age girls (ages seven to fourteen). Given the number who did not attend school or who attended school elsewhere, together with the fact that students spent at most two or three years in school, it follows that there was room in the capital's schools for one in three potential students.[23] This was the educational situation—at its best—before the Revolution.

Learning and Manners

Although the quantity of education for women increased between 1500 and 1800, the quality did not. By the beginning of the nineteenth century, more girls were attending school than ever before, but they were not learning any more than in the past. No matter what school a girl went to, there was little danger that she would emerge a scholar. Convent schools and elementary schools offered a limited curriculum and devoted little time to academic subjects. Only rigorous home schooling could produce women as well educated as boys who attended preparatory schools. The average girl was not to be overburdened with academic curiosities. It was enough that her head be filled with pious notions and needlework.

An Incomplete Education

Even convents dedicated to teaching found that the first obstacle to the acquisition of knowledge lay in the established habits of their students' families. Families that paid dearly to send a child to boarding school expected their wishes to be respected. Students could be removed from school at the family's discretion, no matter what the educational consequences. Teachers had a hard time planning curricula for classes in which students could range in age from four to eighteen and for which there was no notion of a school year. School schedules and calendars from the period are revealing:[24] boys generally returned to boarding school each fall and spring, but their sisters might enter or leave school at any time. Only the Ursulines imposed something like a preparatory school calendar. Most girls, moreover, remained in boarding school only a year or two, whereas their brothers were sent away for from three to eight years. With educational careers so brief, no real curriculum could be followed. Like the future Madame Roland, the girls who were sent to convent schools in the years just before the Revolution attended classes for at most two years and for the purpose of preparing themselves for communion.[25] Later, Mme. Campan would write that after 1760 "nearly all girls spent only a year in the monasteries, and that year was devoted to in-depth study of the catechism, to retreat, and to first communion . . . The custom of leaving girls behind convent gates until the age of eighteen had long since been abandoned."[26] The number of students in the convent schools gradually declined; in the capital few were full after 1750. At the same time the number of preparatory school students also declined. The enlightened families of the social elite had clearly become disaffected with the boarding-school formula.

Most convents placed greater emphasis on obedience to the monastic rule than on education, and the result was less time available for instruction. Girls were required to rise, depending on the convent, between 4:00 and 7:00 and to go to bed between 7:45 and 9:30. At most they had only five or six hours to devote to their schoolwork. The more imbued a convent was with the spirit of the rule or, like Port-Royal, marked with Jansenist rigor, the greater the amount of time devoted to the liturgy and the less to learning. In the strictest establishments profane learning was a mere filler between religious services, prayer meetings, meditation, and hours devoted to pious reading. General education in the convent was constantly interrupted by the pealing of bells calling nuns and pupils to prayer.

The daily schedule in an elementary school was very different, even if daily attendance at mass was part of the regular school day. Schools that charged little or no tuition could impose their calendars on their pupils' families, which lacked the influence enjoyed by parents who paid high tuitions to convent schools. In schools that charged tuition girls commonly spent three to four years in class between the ages of six and ten; in free community schools the duration of schooling was three years; and in free parish schools it was two years. For financial reasons teachers in schools that charged tuition could not afford to be too strict about the ages of their pupils or the number of years it took them to learn to read. In contrast, the charity schools were concerned to educate the largest possible number of students and therefore always rushed students through so as to make room for others. In some cases a girl had to wait until she turned eight before she could be admitted to a free school. The sponsors of charity schools were always interested in yield, measured in numbers of saved souls. Students were therefore grouped into two or three sections, based on their ability to read (and, where applicable, to write).

Day school students enjoyed three to four weeks' vacation in the fall, but, depending on the need for children's help with the harvest, rural schools often recessed for longer periods in late summer. Rather than regular school vacations during the school year, numerous religious holidays were observed, and in the middle of every week there was a day or day and a half of rest. In schools devoted to work training, the pupils' day went well beyond the six to seven hours of religious and general classes. The girls of Saint Agnes' School in Paris worked from 7:00 to 11:00 in the morning and from 12:30 to 6:00 in the afternoon. For them, already workers though still students, class time was already regulated by the hours of the marketplace. The time devoted to learning needlework and to prayer infringed on other class time, so that girls just touched on subjects their brothers were free to study in depth. People were still fearful of teaching girls too much, of overwhelming them with vain and superfluous knowledge. Evidence that suspicion still surrounded the instruction of women can be seen in the brevity of the treatment of certain subjects, the curtailment of the curriculum to the bare essentials, and a general attitude of toleration rather than encouragement.

Strict Supervision

The curriculum of girls' schools in prerevolutionary France had three main components: religion with a strong dose of morality, the three R's, and needlework and sewing. This basic program was modified in various ways by the different types of schools and, in convent schools, occasionally supplemented (at least for those pupils who could afford to pay for private tutors).

What little girls learned at school was first and foremost to "love, know, and serve God." Religious instruction far outweighed all other subjects, which seemed, in comparison, peripheral. When the priest of Saint-Louis-en-l'Ile parish in Paris went looking for a schoolmistress in 1716, he sent the mother superior of the Filles de la Charité a job description that ended: "I do not mention catechism and Christian subjects because these, as you know, must take priority over everything else."[27] Lay as well as religious teachers were under orders to devote most of their energy, authority, ambition, and concern to this part of the curriculum.

Religious instruction centered on learning prayers, introductory study of sacred texts, and preparation for confirmation and first communion, bolstered by daily attendance at mass. Indeed, school life was imbued with piety. The daily schedule was punctuated by prayer before and after each class and recess period. Nine out of ten titles in the book cabinet could be classified as "works of piety," and classroom walls were covered with edifying images. Nor was the presence of religion limited to these outward signs: audible, visible, memorizable. It was also implicit in the very gestures and comportment of the students, whose spontaneous, childlike expressions were strictly repressed. It was not easy to distinguish between instruction in morality and polite behavior and instruction in religion proper: in the education of young girls, the three were intimately associated. One manual, *Conduite chrétienne, ou formulaire de prières à l'usage des pensionnaires des religieuses Ursulines* (Christian Conduct, or a Formulary of Prayers for Pupils of the Ursulines), enjoyed remarkable success. It was used in many secular as well as religious institutions and was reissued in countless editions in the eighteenth and nineteenth centuries, including an 800-page edition in 1868. The book instructs students how to act and what to think when waking in the morning, going to bed at night, and even during bouts of insomnia. In short, it reflects the omnipresence of religion in the school day and curriculum.

Religious instruction even encroached on time theoretically set aside for secular learning. Children were taught to read by scanning prayers syllable by syllable and practiced writing by copying out pious proverbs. Reading, writing, and arithmetic were really secondary concerns, inducements to children to continue in school.

Many school programs described the religious curriculum at great length with a laconic addendum: "The students will also be taught to read and write."

Reading was above all a tool of religious instruction: it helped out when memory failed and kept students from stammering incomprehensible, misshapen verses. Girls were therefore taught to read. Reading reinforced the Christian teaching they received from their mothers. Reading for other purposes was suspect, however, and educators frequently warned against misuse of the skill. When novels for young girls first appeared around 1750, they found champions among private governesses and enlightened mothers but not in the schools. Pious books were one thing, but novels were possibly licentious, and both secular and convent schools kept a close watch on student reading. Any new book that came into the cloister had to be submitted to the scrutiny of the mother superior.

An innovation introduced in girls' classes at Port-Royal around 1650 and soon widely adopted was to teach reading from French rather than Latin texts. Logic won out: since girls did not stay in school long, it made no sense to teach them to read any language but the mother tongue. Although "French and Latin" programs continued to exist on paper, few girls completed them. The Ursulines, an exception, continued to give priority to reading in Latin because of their interest in classical culture, the culture of the preparatory schools.

Although schools were supposed to teach both reading and writing, the latter sometimes fell by the wayside. For one thing, some teachers were not sufficiently masters of the art to teach it to others. For another, writing was the second phase of the curriculum, to be commenced after reading was fully mastered, and some students never got that far. The methods for teaching writing varied according to the uses that pupils were expected to make of the skill. Pupils of the Ursulines were taught to write individually and with great care by a trained specialist, whereas pupils in charity schools learned as best they could by imitating examples of letters written on posters. They never received the kind of training that was available to students of Notre-Dame, which included copying "the formulas of promissory notes, receipts, acknowledgments of merchandise delivered, and other such acts as may be useful for them to know in different walks of life."[28]

In most cases the brief introduction to reading, writing, and arithmetic that a girl received in class had to be supplemented outside or the skill learned would be quickly forgotten. True mastery came only with frequent practice and help from a more advanced companion. Without the opportunity for such practice and help, the time spent in class might easily prove to be wasted effort.

By the time a girl left grammar school she was supposed to have acquired a taste for work. In class work took concrete form: there were always needles, thread, and fabric around, and students practiced embroidery, lacework, tapestry, sewing, knitting, mending, and every other form of needlework. The meaning attached to such work varied, however, with the nature of the school. In the case of well-born girls at convent boarding schools, work with needle and thread was valued as a healthy occupation, a substitute for the work the devil might otherwise find for idle hands. The work was redemptive. In the charity schools, the skills learned in class were supposed to help a girl to find a trade, hence to lead a respectable life. The spiritual and moral salvation of poor girls depended on their finding a livelihood.

"To enable girls to earn a respectable living" is a constant theme in the writings of charity school founders. Pupils were taught, in the words of the sisters of Saint-Maur, "minor trades in keeping with their capabilities," or, in the formula preferred by Orphanage of Baby Jesus in Paris, "the minor branches of learning appropriate to girls." From these minor trades girls could expect to earn modest incomes after leaving school, but there was no danger that they would rise above their original station in life. Former pupils might become working girls, but they could not afford to purchase a costly certification as mistress of a craft. Furthermore, since skill in a trade was acquired gradually, a girl's level depended on the length of time she stayed in school. Many pupils never got beyond the most elementary skills, which were also the least remunerated. The occupational training afforded to poor girls thus left charity school sponsors with clear consciences yet did not interfere with the laws of strict social reproduction. Furthermore, as there was strong demand for textiles and clothing in the cities, training students to enter that sector of the economy satisfied the growing need for labor.

The girl who boarded at a convent school was not expected to earn her living by needlework; if all went well, she could hope to marry well and take charge of a substantial household. For this she required a more diverse preparation, and the boarding schools

127

attempted to fill this need. In a prestigious school such as Abbaye-aux-Bois, young ladies who would never be expected to dirty their hands at home learned from lay sisters what running a household entailed. Thus Hélène Massalska, the future Princess de Ligne, worked successively in the abbey's nine different "obediences": the church, the sacristy, the parlor, the apothecary, the laundry, the library, the dining hall, the kitchen, and the sisterhood.[29] The duties of the mistress of a noble household were likely to be just as varied. While charity school students prepared for working life, convent school girls prepared for a life of managerial responsibility.

Convent school girls supplemented their regular lessons with private instruction in the arts and other subjects. The parents paid for these extra lessons out of pocket, thus bringing aristocratic educational methods into the cloister. Convent rules reflect suspicion of these subjects, which were regarded as frivolous and unnecessary, but parental wishes were respected. Even in an institution as strict as Port-Royal, seven private instructors gave lessons in the parlor in 1773: five male teachers taught dance, music, harpsichord, harp, and guitar; and two women taught geography and drawing. Counting both regular and private lessons, Hélène Massalska and her classmates in the "blue class" (ages seven to ten) at the Abbaye-aux-Bois attended classes in catechism, reading, music, drawing, history and geography, writing, arithmetic, dance, and harp or harpsichord one after the other, with each class lasting from thirty minutes to an hour. Students also performed plays regularly. After its success at Saint-Cyr, Jean Racine's *Athalie* made the rounds of other prominent girls' schools. The arts, especially music, were prized everywhere. Some musicians derived a regular income from the convent schools, and much of their effort went to composing collections of pieces "for the use of young ladies brought up in houses of religion." From inventories of property seized from convent schools in Paris during the Revolution we know that the harpsichord and the pianoforte were the favorite instruments.

Measuring Knowledge: Signatures

One way of evaluating how much female students retained of what they learned at school is to examine signatures on notarized documents. It is of course a delicate matter to say just how much the ability to sign a document can tell us about the ability to comprehend its contents or to read and write in general, but a signature indicates at least some ability to wield a pen. We have figures from throughout France for two periods a century apart: 1686–1690 and 1786–1790. And the first lesson to be drawn from them is to beware of statistics, which are always misleading. Any attempt to arrive at a mean conceals important disparities between regions, between urban and rural areas, and between men and women.

The figures reveal, first of all, that northern France—broadly speaking, the section of the country lying north of an imaginary line drawn between Saint-Malo and Geneva—was more literate than southern France. In 1786–1790, 71 percent of the men and 44 percent of the women residing north of this line signed their marriage licenses, compared with only 27 percent and 12 percent in the south. A century earlier, literacy had reached the 20-percent level almost everywhere in the north but in few places in the south. In both of these regions, however, two other differences stand out: literacy was invariably higher in urban than in rural areas, and the literacy rate for men was always higher than that for women, at all times and in all segments of society.

If the men were everywhere ahead of the women, nonetheless the literacy rate for women increased more rapidly than that for men in the seventeenth and eighteenth centuries. In the eighteenth century particularly, women made significant advances. In enlightened northern France, where men had begun to write in the seventeenth century, women made up for their handicap by advancing more rapidly than their mates. In southern France, where economic and cultural conditions were less favorable, the rate of increase of women's literacy matched that of men's. Male literacy was invariably a precondition for women to begin improving their reading and writing skills. François Furet and Jacques Ozouf rightly observe that it took "several generations for literacy to pass from one sex to the other."[30]

Thus the development of a system of girls' schools obviously had an impact on the increased literacy rate for women in the eighteenth century, although it has been estimated that roughly 20 percent of those counted as literate acquired the ability to read, to write, or both, outside the schools. In Paris, where we know when girls' schools opened and where signatures on estate inventory documents have been counted, the benefits of schooling (available to some 11,200 female students annually) are strikingly apparent.[31] During the reign of Louis XIV, 61 percent of working-class men were able to sign their spouses' estate inventories, compared with only 34 percent of women. Under Louis XVI the comparable figures are 66 percent and 62 percent. This spectacular advance for women reflects the efforts of the capital's schoolmistresses. Neighborhood schools proved beneficial, particularly to those groups that had some cultural background. Knowing how to read made life easier in a city such as Paris. But despite the capital's cultural advantages, some dark spots remained: only 16 percent of the female delinquents who appeared before the judges of the Châtelet were able to sign their depositions.

The tendency to higher literacy in urban than in rural areas and in the capital than elsewhere was not unique to France. In seventeenth- and eighteenth-century England, where literacy on the whole came sooner and with less pronounced regional variations than in France, the same trend obtains. By the end of the eighteenth century 60 percent of English men and 40 percent of English women could sign their names, compared with 47 and 27 percent respectively in France. As early as 1690, 48 percent of Londoners could sign their names, compared with only 20 percent in the rest of the country.

There is no need to multiply dry statistics to explain why female literacy always lagged behind male literacy: society considered education for women less important than education for men. Child mortality was still a serious problem in this society, and the reproductive role of women, vital for survival, inevitably influenced the way the issue of women's education was approached. It was imperative that young women grow up to be mothers, and since their destiny was to raise children it made sense to instill in them, so that they might in turn teach their children, society's fundamental religious and moral values. In the end girls were taught to read because reading was a way of reinforcing the lessons of religion, and that was as far as society's requirement went. The need for more advanced instruction was evident to a few farsighted individuals but was not widely accepted. By the end of the eighteenth century the mortality rate had declined, the influence of the church had been reduced, and the Enlightenment had done its work. Only then did increasing numbers of parents begin to re-think their daughters' futures. But as long as equality between the sexes remained an illusion, not even the most talented teachers could open full access for women to learning.

TRANSLATED FROM THE FRENCH BY ARTHUR GOLDHAMMER

5

Virgins and Mothers between Heaven and Earth

Elisja Schulte van Kessel

AS WINDS OF REFORM swept through the West, early modern reformers returned to the sources of Christianity, invoking Christ and his earliest disciples. They believed that they could recover Christ's message in its original intention by following the lead of the Church Fathers, precursors on the arduous path of orthodoxy. Their quest, obviously, was very different from ours. Of course, in the light of so many centuries of paternal authority, from Saint Paul to Leopold von Ranke, from Saint Augustine to Fernand Braudel, any attempt to achieve a feminist consciousness of these issues must seem forbiddingly daring.

Love, the Mother, and the Virgin

It all began with Jesus of Nazareth. A man, Jesus not surprisingly chose other men as his closest collaborators. On matters of social relations he did not preach love of women specifically but advocated love of one's neighbor without distinction as to social class, race, kinship, or sex.

This revolutionary ideal was conceived as a prelude to eternal salvation in the kingdom of God, the true life after death. It may have been intended to encourage greater respect for women, but this is not clear. The way Jesus treated his mother, repudiating his ties to her, might suggest the opposite. As a mother, Mary of course enjoyed the distinction of transmitting her Jewish heritage to her child; but this, her only social prestige, her son repudiated.

Charity and Piety

In the eyes of the Romans it was not love of one's neighbor but hatred of the human race that characterized the first Christians. So said Tacitus (*Annals* 15.44), and many works of ecclesiastical history rely on his account of the first known persecution of the Christians, following the fire in A.D. 64 that destroyed ten of Rome's fourteen districts. In light of this widespread anti-Christian sentiment, the pyromaniac emperor Nero was able to divert the wrath of the population onto the allegedly misanthropic sect even though Christians were absolved of responsibility for the fire itself. The hostility to Christianity is all the more surprising in that the young Christian community was of little importance at the time and Romans were still fairly tolerant. Yet Christians, and especially female Christians, seem to have inspired fear.

What was so troubling then about Christians, and particularly Christian women? During the last quarter of the first century Pope Clement I noted that Christian women were not only compelled to play the Danaïdes and Dirce on the stage but were actually put to death after the performance (1 Clement 6). (Archetypal man-killers, the chaste Danaïdes murdered the men they were forced to marry on their wedding night; Dirce was the quintessential degenerate mother.) This story of Clement's may well tell us more than all the fathers of the church. In Rome's hierarchical society, Christian charity not only posed a threat to the state but also conflicted with the first duty of every Roman. That duty, implicit in the concept of *pietas,* involved loyal dedication to one's ancestors and offspring. For women, it meant willingly accepting a subordinate role, that of the obedient, loving wife dedicated to the perpetuation of the race. Because the Christian concept of love failed to make distinctions on the basis of kinship or sex, it was seen as an inhuman affront to ineluctable destiny.

Reproduction and Marital Love

Fifteen centuries later, on the eve of the Reformation, love of one's neighbor was still a troubling message. Though attractive to idealists and meliorists as well as to the poor and oppressed, it was far less appealing to other citizens. Hence this noble ideal was forever being watered down, only to appear again and again on reformers' agendas. It was cherished by the elect who looked forward to a new world: men and women, individuals or groups of kindred spirits, often gathered around a couple linked by spiritual friendship after the well-known model of Jerome and Paula. Preachers continually praised this ideal to crowds of the poor assembled in churches and town squares; meanwhile, a concern to maintain law and order drew the wealthy together. Love of one's neighbor was a favorite theme of iconography in churches and other public buildings, offering consolation to all and satisfaction to patrons and their progeny.

Procreation was of course still a crucial matter, just as it had been in Nero's Rome. But in early modern times there was far less reason to be anxious about the message of Jesus of Nazareth. Many things had changed in the relation between the Christian faith and the secular world. For example, the Christian family had become a mainstay of the social structure after centuries of struggle between the nobility and the clergy for social supremacy and thus control over marriage. One of the results of this struggle was that, in regard to sexuality, different requirements applied to different social groups. The clergy, even outside the monasteries, were obliged to abstain from sexual relations. Clerical celibacy thus became one way of marking the difference between clergy and laity and of increasing the wealth and power of the church.

It was therefore left to the laity to ensure the perpetuation of the race through contractual unions based on a promise of monogamous fidelity. In order to bring marriage into the realm of the sacred, the Council of Trent stipulated in 1563 that the marriage vow required divine confirmation and clerical supervision. Such a requirement was hardly compatible with the interests or principles of the nobility and its allies. It was therefore not until well after the Council of Trent that the bulk of the European population—Christian in name only—accepted the sacrament of marriage as a condition of procreation. These were the people who inhabited the countryside: nobles, peasants, and lifelong vagabonds—paupers, brigands, preachers (purified or degenerate), and hermits—who, taken together, accounted for no less than 80 percent of the population down to the end of the eighteenth century.

Meanwhile, to the town-dwelling minority, eager to improve

its social standing vis-à-vis the feudal nobility and the tax-exempt clergy, Christian marriage offered a better model than the aristocratic ideal of chivalrous love, which exalted the libertine proclivities of the nobility. Postfeudal marriage became the new model in terms of which townspeople defined their sexual roles and formulated their material and spiritual aspirations.[1]

The urban ethos of the late Middle Ages was remarkably similar to that of late antiquity. In the ancient world too the ethos of an aggressively dissolute ruling class—a product of violent interclan rivalries—had been eclipsed by the more temperate mores of a new elite: the servants of an ever-expanding state apparatus. Social distinctions were clarified, moderation was encouraged, and sexual relations were transformed. New prohibitions were imposed: traditional bisexuality was forcibly repressed and henceforth only heterosexual relations were approved. Affection and fidelity in marriage, once rare, now became a conjugal duty for all: "philogamy" (the positive attitude toward marriage encouraged by the church) thus promoted procreation.[2]

It is generally supposed that early Christian communities adopted the prevailing ethos of late antiquity. Temperance and philogamy were in fact characteristic of the Christian families on which the new church depended for its very survival. Yet the ideals of the most radical early Christians reflected a deep aversion to marriage, a radical "misogamy," which also had pagan roots. Not even Paul was able to resolve this social and religious dilemma. It was not until the second and third centuries that a solution was found: as a religious leadership distinct from the laity began to emerge, sexual abstinence became the chief distinguishing feature of the clergy.[3]

Sexual Abstinence and Freedom

It may seem rather odd to base an analysis of the spiritual influence of Christian women in the early modern period on a mistaken notion of how Christian marriage ethics developed. To gain further insight into the question, however, we must dispel the almost universal conviction that chastity and philogamy were in essence and *ab antiquo* Christian ideals. This idea, largely a legacy of the nineteenth century, obscures what was so disturbing in the original, and radical, Christian anthropology. It also blocks out what was ambivalent and problematic in early modern Christian images of man and conceals the growing divergence between a Mediterranean, and primarily Catholic, model and a northern, primarily Protestant, one.

It took more than a thousand years for Christianity to develop a new, internally consistent marriage ethic, which, moreover, was distinguished from the pagan ethic by its sacred content. The proto-Christian ideal of sexual abstinence remained, however, a source of great tension. Admittedly, the new ideal of love of one's neighbor was the defining characteristic of the earliest Christians, but as their identity evolved, the persistent notion of sexual abstinence played a decisive role.

In a highly conventional, bureaucratic, and hierarchical society, sexual abstinence opened the way toward achieving the dream of transcendent cosmopolitanism: to be united, through love of one's neighbor, with others, no matter how different—foreigners, inferiors, strangers, members of the opposite sex.[4] To the most radical proto-Christians, the reproductive role of woman—the obligation to submit to sexual relations and to give birth in pain—symbolized slavery, whereas virginity represented freedom. This symbolism was not unrelated to ancient depictions of virgins as mediators between natural and supernatural, inside and outside, selfness and otherness, manhood and womanhood.[5] If martyrs were heroic, virgin martyrs were still more so. The virgin, symbolizing freedom no matter what the price, including even the sacrifice of her own life, represented humanity's deepest dream: that everyone, male and female alike, should be comrades, fighters for freedom, united and equal.

Alive and Disquieting

As the urban marriage ethos gained ground, ecclesiastical and civic authorities intervened to strengthen the emerging social order by restricting and regulating virginity (and the potential for transcendence inherent in it). Protestantism found a radical solution to the problem, which of course was inextricably intertwined with another key issue, the accumulation of wealth by the church: the Protestant answer was to abolish clerical celibacy while attacking the "diabolical superstition" that prolonged sexual abstinence could give rise to superhuman powers. By contrast, the Catholic church reaffirmed absolute celibacy for priests and tightened the rules governing monastic life, including strict adherence to the vow of perpetual chastity. By continuing to insist on sexual abstinence for the clergy the church sought to underscore the distinction between the ecclesiastical and lay conditions. At the same time, moreover, the church reinforced its long-standing opposition to the choice of sexual abstinence or virginity by laypersons.

Semireligious Women

This opposition became evident in response to what might be called the "religious women's movement" of the Middle Ages. The expression is somewhat misleading in that the "movement" was really a matter of increasing participation by more and more segments of the population in a spiritual culture once limited to monks and prince-bishops. One of the most surprising aspects of this "democratization" of religious life was a marked increase in the number of women who consecrated their lives to God. Attempts to control this increase focused primarily on eliminating the semireligious way of life practiced by men and women who dedicated themselves to the Lord without taking solemn vows and who therefore were not members of the clergy. Most of those who fell into this category were women: *beguines, pinzocchere,* Sisters of Common Life, *beatas,* tertiaries, and other consecrated females. In the eyes of their champions, these women were the true devotees of God because, like the proto-Christian virgins, they did not merely pay lip service to religion but lived it in their daily lives.[6]

Nevertheless, civic and ecclesiastic authorities and even ordinary folk frowned on this semireligious way of life: it blurred the distinction between the clerical and the lay condition and often created legal confusion, especially with respect to rights of inheritance. These semireligious women were often ridiculed or attacked publicly. Their voluntary choice of sexual abstinence was particularly disturbing. They are therefore a useful touchstone for historians interested in religious tolerance.

Was the increase in the number of semireligious women simply a side effect of the democratization of religious life, or was spiritual culture in some sense "feminized"? Though often raised, this question has never really been answered, even though it seems to me fundamental to any serious research into early modern culture, gender relations, and sexuality. Before we can offer a possible answer, however, we must delve more deeply into the problematic status of the consecrated woman, whether religious or semireligious.[7]

Women could neither be ordained as priests nor become members of the secular clergy. Male ecclesiastics could choose between two essentially different ways of life: that of the monk (regular clergy) and that of the priest (secular clergy). Only women who became fully professed nuns could enter the ecclesiastical world, and even they did not join the highest rank, the so-called First Order, but only the inferior Second Order. Women who consecrated their lives to God in the lay world, thereby following the model of the secular clergy, automatically became semireligious. Taking simple vows allowed them to enter the so-called Third Order, but these "tertiaries," as they were known, did not acquire ecclesiastical status. That honor was accorded only to groups of tertiaries who affiliated themselves with a monastic community and agreed to abide by an established rule; this move entitled them to promotion to the status of "regular tertiary," equivalent to the Second Order.

By the early modern era nearly all communities of consecrated women had been institutionalized by affiliation with a religious order. But this fact by no means halted the increase in the number of semireligious women living in the world, whether alone or in groups. Many women, despite the obstacles put in their way, continued to live in this halfway state, if often only temporarily. Since they had no right to exist, most later historians either neglect them altogether or conflate them with fully professed nuns. But there is reason to believe that their numbers were large. Together with regular tertiaries and fully professed nuns, they formed an immense group of women dedicated to God—far more numerous than the male clergy. In the northern provinces of the Netherlands alone, for example, the number of consecrated women (nuns and semireligious) was one and a half times as large as the number of male clergy, both regular and secular.[8]

On the eve of the Reformation, the issue remained one of controlling the participation of women in spiritual life. Impressive examples of female spirituality had already exerted a profound influence on religious sensibility and were solidly imprinted on the collective memory. What role did these consecrated women play in subsequent events? Many questions remain unanswered.

Living Saints

Considerable research into the "religious women's movement" in Italy, however, has shed some light on the problem. Investigation of heretical trends, reformist campaigns, and a wide range of oppositional tendencies has revealed a fair amount about the influence of consecrated women on the eve of the Reformation and Counter-Reformation. Recently it has emerged that a fundamental change took place not long before the final tide of Reformation swept the country: the prestige of consecrated women, on the rise from 1500 until around 1530, suddenly suffered a reversal. This change was associated with an abrupt decline in the authority of female religious leaders, women endowed with charismatic powers such as prophetesses and visionaries, who until then had been venerated as living saints and even "divine mothers" *(divine madri)*. People from all levels of society had sought their advice on all sorts of problems, and their influence had been felt in the social and political as well as religious spheres, often well beyond the local level.[9]

It is generally assumed that the prestige once enjoyed by such women stemmed from a revival of religious feeling in Italy in reaction to various calamities that befell the country in early modern times. In particular, infamous invasions by French and German "barbarians" had wreaked havoc on crops, decimated the population, and contributed to the spread of venereal disease. The religious revival enjoyed the support of a conspicuously large number of women, most of them semireligious. They harkened to the call of the great preacher Girolamo Savonarola, but their true inspiration was Saint Catherine of Siena (died 1380), who—more than a century before the events in question—had shown a degenerate pope the path of righteousness. The "new Catherines" and other so-called spiritualists wanted to do precisely the same thing: they were men and women consecrated to God who preached a purified religion of the spirit aimed at radical reform. Amid the clatter of arms a real attempt was made, with help from France, to reform the heart of Christendom in the hope of salvaging the unity of the church. There was also widespread anticipation of divine intervention, including the prophesied appearance of a "Papa Angelicus," a saving angel who would stand guard at Saint Peter's muddied doorstep.[10]

It was a vain hope. Failure brought profound disillusionment, which in turn paved the way for a change in the tactics of reform. Dashed hopes and misplaced trust in prophets and visionaries of both sexes strengthened the authority of government and church officials and of businessmen and men of letters. More and more people turned to such authorities to solve their earthly problems rather than to divine mediators. By the end of the "Italian Wars" the charismatics were on the run. They appear to have become scapegoats for the looming schism in the church, the consequences of which were as yet incalculable. By midcentury nearly all of them had vanished from the public eye. Among the last was the *divina madre* Antonia Negri (died 1555), one of the founders of the Barnabite Order. Despite her divine mission she ended her days in prison.[11]

These developments affected men and women in different ways. Women had long been supposed to possess special faculties for communicating with the unseen, and female charismatics alleged to be in contact with the divine were heeded with at least as much attention, if also with as much skepticism, as their male counterparts. But when it came to putting God's word into practice or reforming the church, attitudes were very different: this was men's work. After the Protestant schism this was even more true: any reform, any attempt to divine the Lord's design, was for men only. Although it proved impossible to suppress female charismatics entirely, they were ruthlessly excluded from public life. Their attention consequently turned away from what was actually happening in the world or in particular communities and focused increasingly on such supernatural phenomena as heaven, hell, and purgatory as well as on various questions of faith.

Thus Antonia Negri can be seen as one of the last exemplars of the religious women's movement, which had given a small number of women with charismatic gifts spiritual authority not without social relevance. The democratization of spiritual life had shown, among other things, that women could move mountains with their faith. If the reforms aimed at healing Christianity's wounds were to succeed, this potential power of women would have to be contained.

Connivance between Literate and Illiterate Women

How was all this related to other developments in Italy and elsewhere? The question is not easy to answer, because the study of women and gender relations in the early modern period has until now focused on specific topics and avoided more general approaches.[12] Researchers, moreover, have divided their attention in an anachronistic way: they study *either* the Reformation *or* the Counter-Reformation. Until well into the sixteenth century, however, an inclination in favor of *reformatio* did not necessarily involve a choice between the old and the new church. In addition to the social and political reasons for this, many people took the view that the "new church" was truly the "old," that is, a return to the one and only true mother church in its original character. This was true of the majority of upper-class Italian women who played a role in the evangelical movement inside and outside Italy: women such as Vittoria Colonna, Julia and Eleanora Gonzaga, Renata di Francia, Catherine Cybo, and Veronica Gambara, to name a few.

Late-nineteenth-century historians dubbed these women's reform efforts the "religious women's movement" because they thought it was a movement of emancipation.[13] More recently, however, doubts have been cast on the status of women in Protestant movements. It has become clear, too, that the profoundly internalized faith of the "living saints" who aspired to recover the authenticity of early Christianity raised the possibility that the whole ecclesiastical hierarchy might be unnecessary.[14] Furthermore, although many of these women were illiterate, their "popular culture" turns out to have had a great deal in common with the "elitist culture" of the nobility. The elite often exploited the political influence of these visionaries, who, certain of their divine mission, demanded blind trust of their followers. This transaction between the sacred and the profane enabled charismatics to extend their influence beyond their native towns and villages.

Only charismatics belonging to the dominant classes could avail themselves of a wider network of social contacts. In keeping with the humanist ideal of the perfect matron, one of the most important of a literate upper-class woman's tasks was to cultivate people who might prove useful to her family or her husband's career. Through strategic marriages the aristocracy had forged social networks that stretched across Europe, creating solid ties between families in, for example, Italy and France. Reformers exploited these connections to the full, Ignatius of Loyola no less than Calvin. These two men, incidentally, shared not only a low estimate of women's intellectual abilities but also a fear of allowing women to play any role in church affairs.

Exemplary Deaths

What better way to illustrate the difference between the Catholic and Protestant faiths than to examine how the living managed communication with the heroes and heroines of the afterlife? The issue was a problem for both churches: Catholics maintained communication but with modifications, whereas Protestants discontinued it altogether. Statues and icons were banished from Protestant churches; the tangible presence of the saints faded: their bodies, their clothing, their blood, their tears. Communication with God became an entirely personal matter for each believer, with no alternate route via intermediaries. The universal priesthood of the faithful made consecrated mediators superfluous. The vast system that had been established over fifteen centuries to mediate between creator and creation was cast aside like so much flimsy scenery. Whereas the walls and ceilings of Catholic churches were filled with ascending saints and descending angels, Reformed churches became sober meetinghouses reminiscent of the earliest days of the faith.

The Resurrection of Virgins

In the first Christian assemblies women played a heroic and unforgettable role: virgins wholly devoted to God were ready to lay down their lives for their faith. Proto-Christian *virgines,* like their male counterparts, the *continentes,* lived not in communities but at home with their families like all other believers. What distinguished them (and the semireligious women of a later period) from the rest was sexual abstinence. Surprisingly, there is a great deal of information about *virgines* but very little on the *continentes,* although their numbers were probably just as large.[15]

Indeed, no category of women has ever been held in such high esteem as early Christian virgins: they were the very model of perfect Christian women. If male saints stood out for their profession of the faith in word and deed, chastity became the *sine qua non* of female sanctity. In the taxonomy of sainthood there never was a female "confessor," just as there never was a male "virgin." Among those who made the supreme sacrifice, paying for their religious zeal with their lives, only the women are described as either "virgins" or "nonvirgins." Martyrs of both sexes pleased God, but the most pleasing of all was a virgin martyr. For women, the most appropriate way to propagate the true religion and the only sure way of achieving personal sanctity was not profession of the faith but unconditional sacrifice.

My purpose here is not to reconstitute the daily life of women in the early church, nor is it to gauge the extent to which women were able to influence the development of their own image. I want instead to examine how Catholic reformers tried to polish that image, to make it more resplendent than ever. It is hardly surprising that they wished to do so, given the epoch's assiduous search for fundamental principles, for criteria with which to distinguish between orthodoxy and heterodoxy, true and false Christianity. In this search early Christendom became a new source of inspiration. The first historical studies of proto-Christian virgin martyrs were published. Their supposed burial places, often in small, dilapidated churches, were excavated; and if the search turned up sacred bones, the modest old chapel was transformed into a baroque extravaganza. Bernini's first commission in Rome followed the discovery of the bones of the martyr Bibiana. And one of his chief rivals, Pietro da Cortona, owed it to the discovery of the virgin martyr Martina's remains that he was able to build what remains the purest example of his architectural theology.[16]

Both Bibiana and Martina were all but forgotten saints of legend, but their tangible presence provided much sought-after confirmation of ancient traditions. Such discoveries invariably led to cult revivals because men in authority, eager to centralize ecclesiastical power, knew how to make shrewd use of religious symbolism. Intuitively the popes recognized that nothing appealed to the popular imagination like the image of the virgin martyr. Urban VIII composed a *Carmina* in honor of the resurrected virgin Saint Martina. The triumph of the one and only true church, whose seat was in Rome, was made manifest by the growing crowd of martyrs around Saint Peter's tomb. Unlike later cults in honor of local saints, the cult of the early Christian martyrs represented the universal community of the faithful.

Models of Sanctity

Reformed Catholicism's new models of sanctity were thus fashioned, as always, from the common beliefs of the community as molded by the rationalizing force of power relations. Not only were ecclesiastical and lay authorities competing for power, but ecclesiastics, especially those of different religious orders, vied with one another. Although women rarely played a part in these contests, they did share crucially in the collective experience of faith. In remodeling sanctity, therefore, it was necessary to strike a delicate balance: the basic criterion for recognition of sainthood had always been the existence of a popular following. As reform gradually cleansed "popular religion," and especially "female religion," of heterodox tendencies, it became easier to impose new models of sanctity, thereby bridging the gap between spontaneous faith and orthodox religion. Sanctity was no longer so much a form of protest as a matter of church politics.

The new models of sanctity reflected the ecclesiastical authorities' reactions to developments that began long before the Reformation. The democratization of spirituality even changed God's image: whereas he had been seen as a distant and inaccessible Lord presiding over the Last Judgment, he now became the Savior, the Word made flesh. At the same time saints were humanized. Where once they had been miracle-workers, to be approached with the utmost reverence and awe, now they became protectors, to be greeted with affection and trust. The patron saints of local communities were increasingly consulted by the faithful of all classes. Thus began the tradition of confiding in one's favorite saint before making any important decision.

There were dangers in all this, however, particularly when a new cult was born or a new living saint appeared. Church authorities tried in various ways to minimize the risks, as can be seen in the evolution of canonization procedures (first introduced in the tenth century). As it became increasingly difficult to distinguish between authentic and counterfeit sanctity, the hierarchy stressed virtue and orthodoxy over such other criteria as authenticity of miracles. The problem was only compounded by the fact that God all too often chose to speak through women.

The ecclesiastical reaction attained its height during the Counter-Reformation, partly owing to the negative image of "papist idolatry." The increased emphasis on exceptional virtue and pure orthodoxy, symbolizing the triumph over evil and over the "diabolical heresy" of Protestantism, turned saints into heroic captains in the *ecclesia militans* (the "church militant"). Thus "heroic sanctity" came to be the label used for the Counter-Reformation model. Downgrading miracles and miracle-working charisma and emphasizing heroic virtue and orthodoxy meant that identifying true saints became a matter for theologians and canonists in the service of an absolutist pope. Accordingly, canonization procedures became increasingly elaborate until finally codified in 1638.[17]

The consequences were numerous. In canonization hearings eyewitness testimony no longer counted for much, and traditionally the only role women had been allowed to play in these affairs was that of witness. Hence the new models of sanctity were defined mainly by men. They were disseminated through preaching, devotional literature produced by priests and monks, and holy images subject to ecclesiastical censorship. As a result, the gap widened between the "elite" saints recognized by the pope and the throngs of uncanonized saints. Female sainthood lost much of its prestige. Women, a conspicuous minority among uncanonized saints, constituted an even smaller minority of the canonized.

The End of the Living Saint

From the sixteenth century on sainthood was awarded almost exclusively to the clergy, in particular to monks and founders of religious orders. This trend further reduced the number of new female saints, for a relatively high proportion of lay (that is, nonecclesiastic) saints had been women. Of course most of those women were semireligious: women consecrated to God who, in their own view and that of their followers, no longer belonged to the world, so that the institutional distinction between clergy and laity (respected not only by the church but also by most historians) failed to capture their true situation.

A similar situation pertained to another group of saints: married women who in later life, often after a husband's death, took up a semireligious life. It is no accident that we do not know what proportion of canonized laywomen was married. It was only after women had thrown off the bonds of worldly life that they were able to embark on the path to sainthood.[18] A woman's first duty, after all, was to accept her destiny and condition by making a sacrificial gift of her own life. For married women, required to obey even blasphemous and cruel husbands, the sacrifice was often dramatic, as many medieval saints' lives attest.

In the early modern era, however, traditional Christian misogamy was increasingly supplanted by a characteristically philogynous urban ethos. In secular terms it was impossible to make sense of the paradoxical relation between marriage and devotion, fertility and sanctity, *pietas* in its pagan sense and Christian perfection. Therefore the "living saints" who had been so prominent a feature of the spiritual landscape before the Reformation gave way to a new type of saint, one oriented more explicitly to the hereafter, a development paralleled by the widening gulf between the sacred and the profane.

Perfection and "Matronage"

The quest for perfection was the primary task of every believer. In reality, however, it was a duty imposed on women more than on men, and a girl's education placed greater emphasis on virtue than did a boy's. Moreover, women were scrutinized far more closely than men, because Eve, the prime instigator of evil, lurked in every member of her sex. Yet one sign suggested that women surpassed men in the virtue that was supposed to come before all others, namely, faith: women were more loyal to the church. When their enlightened husbands began to turn their backs on religion in the eighteenth century, women did not follow suit. Why not?[19]

The Fidelity of Women

The answer usually given by historians runs like this: the church had always offered women more than the state did. Above all, it had offered a community of believers who shared the belief that God was the creator of every thing and every person. Hence all of life—seasonal change, good and bad harvests, birth, illness, education, marriage, death—became a shared experience. After the Reformation this sense of community was further reinforced: in Protestant churches and reformed Catholic parishes there was room for every believer.

This community placed a high priority on the quest for personal perfection. Even if women were excluded by the standards of intellectual and professional success that applied in the ordinary world, they could still pursue ethical ideals. For many women, it was the only area not determined by gender in which they could equal if not surpass the achievement of their male counterparts. As nondomestic skills were increasingly professionalized, the gulf between the moral aspirations of women and the professional ambitions of men widened. Virtue and piety were increasingly associated with the church's sphere, the world of ministers, monks, and women.

In the church personal virtue was always linked to the afterlife.

For many men and women the hope of eternal salvation was the only light at the end of a long tunnel, the daily struggle to survive. Given the dependence of women, they, more than men, lived under the shadow of injustice and poverty. What is more, their primary function, procreation, increased their risk of premature death but at the same time gave them an intense feeling for the relation between life and the afterlife. Women were in contact with the kingdom of death: the children they brought into the world were bound to die sooner or later, and many were stillborn or nonviable.[20] Last but not least, life after death offered equality between the sexes, which—in the view of most people, men and women alike—was something that could not be achieved on earth. Some of the more radical Protestant sects had offered at least the prospect of greater equality in life, but the few practical steps in this direction were soon thwarted by pressure to conform to prevailing norms.[21]

The speculative remarks that follow remain to be corroborated by further research. Whatever motivated women's devotion to the church, it is simply a fact that daily religious practice occupied a far greater place in their lives than in the lives of men. Catholicism, which preserved its colorful ritual, lent itself to such daily communal experience more than Protestantism, which stressed individual devotion, the reading of scripture, and the private conscience. It would be interesting to learn more about how women experienced such activities as private prayer, Bible reading, participation in the Lord's Supper or Mass, receiving the sacraments, making pilgrimages, handling relics, and fasting. All these things were experienced in different ways by the many poor and the few rich, by the majority of rural women and the minority of urban ones, by the illiterate masses and the literate elite.

Leaving aside social and economic considerations, it remains unclear how religious experience influenced the choice—if one can call it choice—of confession. For obvious reasons, it was long believed that learned women were inclined to choose Protestantism, but we now know that this was not so. Women of letters were more apt to remain faithful to the Catholic church, as the philo-Protestant Marguerite d'Angoulême did (to cite only the most famous example). It is pointless, moreover, to try to discover whether Protestants or Catholics were more misogynist and more oppressive to women: even if we could answer the question, it would shed little light on the sensibilities of early modern women themselves. What we really want to know is how women experienced their faith, what they desired from it, and what they discovered in it.[22]

Collaborators of the Clergy

One useful approach to this subject is a survey of early modern "matronage," acts of generosity and gift-giving by upper-class married women: the patronage of matrons, in other words.[23] Such an approach complements the more common economic and sociocultural approaches by introducing anthropological and socioreligious perspectives, providing new insight into both the actual experience of women and the ambivalence of their position.

Charity and matronage were the only activities in which a wealthy woman could decently engage outside the home. Her motives were generally a complex mixture of the personal, the social, and the religious. The relations between benefactor and beneficiary were far more complex than those between a superior and an inferior. Until recently, historians tended to focus exclusively on the social and economic aspects of such relationships, overlooking the importance of the mutual dependence and affection typically found in them. Charity forged a bond between the rich and the poor, the strong and the weak, the healthy and the unhealthy—a bond rooted in a radical reading of the commandment "Love thy neighbor." Owing to the symbiosis between chivalry and *imitatio Christi,* courtly love and mendicancy, embodied by new apostles such as Francis of Assisi, it became an article of faith among Christians that Jesus was most likely to be found among the indigent. To help the needy was to love and to serve Christ. A woman's duty was thus transformed into an act of compassionate mercy: she now served not only her own family but Christ himself, whom every believer encountered in the guise of suffering neighbors clad in tattered rags. Thus *pietas* became *pietà.*

Wherever loving service to God became conflated with service to one's neighbor, the redemptive potential of suffering revealed itself. The poor rewarded generosity with prayers for the patron's salvation—and of course everyone knew that it was easier for a camel to pass through the eye of a needle than for a rich man to enter the kingdom of heaven. This reciprocity not only confirmed the hierarchy of earthly status but also demonstrated that from the standpoint of eternity it was merely provisional. The donor-recipient transaction took on a dual significance: it had an immediate, visible effect within the "order of creation," but it also produced an invisible yet incomparably greater effect within the "order of salvation." Both parties reaped benefits from their relationship, partly social and economic, partly political.

Women played a remarkable role on both sides. Those receiving charity were given preferential treatment, especially when protection of either their chastity or their fertility was involved. In Italy and elsewhere, dowry funds were established to promote prosperity by helping poor girls to marry; these funds survived well into the nineteenth century.[24] Poor girls had no more choice than their wealthy benefactresses: they either married or became nuns. Any woman left without a husband in either this world or the next relinquished all hope of achieving a prestigious position in society. Only a small minority of women—courtesans and the semireligious—found ways to sustain themselves outside marriage, thereby escaping the prevailing value system: such women were either greatly venerated or deeply despised. Thus charity was mainly the work of married women, often widowed, aided by a very small number of the unmarried.

Family interests and the duty to procreate weighed heavily on the women of the elite. Charity work offered respectable reasons for evading certain family obligations. As the Catholic Counter-Reformation proceeded, the clergy increasingly asserted its control over charity. It was the very essence of the policy of church reform to impose a new discipline on pastoral work and charity. Because of their subordinate position in the family, wealthy women were only too pleased to collaborate with the church. As the clergy's authority waxed, that of husbands waned, thereby indirectly increasing the independence of wives.

These women played an important part in the reform policies of the clergy, which had every reason to want to sabotage the all-powerful kinship system. In fact, "the great obstacle to Tridentine uniformity was not individual backsliding or Protestant resistance but the internal articulations of a society in which kinship was a most important bond."[25] In the prevailing kinship system women played a secondary role. A woman was expected to act in the interest of her husband's family, not her father's. Hence there was an ambiguity about the very idea of family, and acts of charity often were performed anonymously. Women were more likely than men to seek relief from family duties in works of piety and renunciation of the world. This should come as no surprise, because *pietà* and renunciation opened up far more opportunities, even in this world, than *pietas* generally did.[26]

Middle-class women were much less involved in charity work than were wealthy women. There were also fewer of them in convents.

Perfection and Profession

Monasteries had always formed the backbone of universal Christianity. In the Catholic church they continued to expand, but in the Protestant church they were abolished. It has yet to be proved that the astonishing increase in the number of women entering convents toward the end of the Middle Ages was a phenomenon throughout Europe. Nor do we know with certainty that the subsequent desertion of the nunneries, which began before the Reformation in many places such as England, the northern Netherlands, and northern Italy, was a universal phenomenon.[27] Such monographs as we have do not warrant general conclusions. A first step would be to map the locations of all European nunneries, and a project to do just that for the medieval period is already under way; it is to be hoped that the work will continue beyond the Middle Ages to explore more recent periods as well.[28]

Nunneries

One issue that has received a great deal of attention is the relation between the number of women entering nunneries and the politics of marriage. In the early modern period, marked by violent wars not just on a local but on a continental scale, the "marriage market" was hit by a depression: the demand for women decreased, and so did the purchasing power of men. Economic uncertainty made marriage a risky business for the wealthy; there were no guarantees that hefty investments in dowries would ever pay off. Many women never married, and men tended to marry later in life, so that the number of widows (only the richest of whom would ever remarry) also rose. The Protestant policy of encouraging marriage did little to slow the resulting increase in the number of single women.

In Catholic countries nunneries continued to play an institutional role: they were a form of "social security," especially for wealthier urban women. A "marriage" with Christ required a much smaller dowry than an ordinary marriage. A man who sent his daughter to a nunnery also purchased a say in how the convent would be run, and if he had the influence to secure an administrative post for the girl he might also acquire an income. Most nunneries were safely located either inside or just outside city walls. They enjoyed tax exemptions and other privileges. In return, the nuns prayed every day for the salvation of their relatives and cities.

If the ecclesiastical authorities—a bishop, say—failed to impose discipline, powerful families were quick to intervene in spiritual matters, which were not always easy to distinguish from matters of pecuniary interest. The local elite profited not only economically but also spiritually: those who devoted their energies to worldly affairs could rest assured that others would occupy themselves with prayers for their salvation.

Nuns and citizens thus engaged in animated dialogue. Within the religious community, moreover, class distinctions were marked. Wealthy nuns tended especially to maintain ties to their families. How a nun lived depended on her social background. Those from wealthy families lived in comfortably furnished cells. They received inheritances from and made bequests to family members. A widow might share her living quarters with a daughter. The better-off nuns took meals privately in their rooms and kept their own hens and vegetable gardens. Their relatively luxurious circumstances were often the source of envy among poor members of the community.

Of course many convents, particularly those in the countryside, endured the harshest poverty. The greatest threat faced by nuns was not loss of chastity but impoverishment. Nunneries, moreover, were all too often victims of interminable power struggles between local and central governments and between lay and regular clergy; the consequences for their material and spiritual welfare were frequently disastrous.[29]

Institutions of Perfection

The Council of Trent (1545–1563) initiated radical changes. Convents were increasingly exploited in the interests of central church policy and at the expense of local communities and families. The Tridentine reform institutionalized and professionalized the personal vocation of the nun, who felt called to perfect her virtue. Convents became nothing less than "institutions of perfection," sharply differentiated from secular institutions and claiming a monopoly on canonized sanctity.

Discipline was tightened so as to strengthen the sense of community. Family factions within the convents were broken up, with the effect of reducing the influence of families outside. Steps were also taken to root out libertine and heretical tendencies and to ensure that no dangerous influences leaked to the outside world. Much was said and written about overworldly convents, from which later historians inferred that "lust" and "laxity" were a major problem. In fact the opposite was true: the preachers were really afraid of excessively ardent devotion. Because the faithful of all ranks, from the most exalted to the humblest, frequently turned to consecrated women, and especially charismatics, in search of solace, care, or advice, the church felt a need to protect itself against these breeding grounds of local cults. Furthermore, many nuns, especially in rural areas but also in the towns, lived on alms. Church and civil authorities frowned on this practice and attempted to curb it and to isolate potentially dangerous elements. In fact many Tridentine regulations, especially those relating to the cloistering of consecrated women, were designed to achieve the same results as reforms undertaken by the secular authorities.[30]

There was considerable opposition to cloistering, not only from nuns and their relatives but also from the clergy and urban communities. The clergy argued that many women lived in convents not out of devotion but because their families had sent them there. Even in the diocese of Milan, where Carlo Borromeo directed a zealous program of reform, older nunneries clung to their established ways. Newer convents were able to implement the Tridentine model more effectively, enforcing the new discipline from the start and above all adapting their facilities to the new way of thinking. Magical or sacred associations were no longer considered essential in the choice of a site. What mattered most was the distance from the bustle of the city and from monasteries. There had to be sufficient room to allow cloistered nuns a little air. High walls, heavy gates, innumerable locks, and iron bars left no doubt that Christ's brides had bidden the world a final farewell.

Cloistering radically changed the social connections of nuns, especially those of elite background. Previously, each nun had had her own circle of contacts and relationships; now the most important distinction was internal, between nuns and so-called lay sisters, or *conversae*. Lay sisters did the convent housework; they were not allowed to participate in canonical hours and had no role in administrative decisions concerning the institution. Most were country girls, illiterate and impecunious, but they still had to pay the convent a dowry, though a much smaller one than those brought by professed sisters. Whereas nunneries had once been comfortable, homey places, particularly in the wealthier nuns' quarters, reformed convents had a very different look. Nuns were required to sleep either alone or in dormitories; prohibiting two nuns from sharing a room put an end to the possibility of intimate or affectionate relationships. Not surprisingly, many felt emptiness, which one nun in Bologna expressed in these terms: "As for me, I wish things could be as they were before, that we could keep a niece with us or some other girl who was fond of us."[31]

A nun's most personal relationships were with her confessor, who was chosen for her, and her spiritual director, whom she chose herself. There were obvious risks in such relationships. Unlike monks, nuns could not escape the influence of members of the opposite sex, chiefly male members of the same order to which they themselves belonged. Priests celebrated mass, administered the sacraments, and provided individual and collective spiritual guidance.

The emphasis on the inner life was in keeping with the late medieval tendency toward internalized spirituality, evident in female mysticism and Christian humanism. This inwardness found its fullest manifestation in the Devotio Moderna movement, as the unparalleled success of Thomas Hemerken van Kempen's *Imitatio Christi* attests.[32] Individuals began to seek perfection through direct experience of God, the *summum* of human perfection, to be achieved through a combination of intellect, feeling, and imagination, developed through methodical spiritual exercise. Simplicity was the goal, but often the result was the opposite. An expert spiritual guide, a professional of the sort typical of the early modern period, became all but essential. The old textbooks were no longer good enough, and hundreds of new manuals examined every possible eventuality in exhaustive detail.

Confessors and spiritual directors needed consummate skill to deal with women. The very form of the confessional was modified:

owing to the dangers inherent in hearing women's confessions, a dividing screen was placed between penitent and confessor in order to prevent eye contact.[33] Confessors of consecrated women faced other dangers, for these women were thought to be more susceptible to erroneous ideas, immoderate passions, exaggerated scruples, and demonic passions of all sorts, including witchcraft, feigned mystical experiences, black magic, ascetic extravagance, and possession.[34]

Yet the brides of Christ were considered lucky: they had made the right choice, it was felt, even though it was well known that few of them actually chose their condition. One of the changes instituted at Trent was to insist that women entering convents do so of their own free will. The council also raised the minimum age to sixteen. Yet men such as Galileo Galilei saw no way for their daughters to survive other than to commit them to a poor nunnery before they had reached that age.[35] Some of the Tridentine reforms were intended to reduce poverty in the convents, but cloistering often made the situation worse rather than better. Why did nuns resist the Tridentine reforms so vigorously? The most convincing explanation is that they feared, with good reason, the loss of vital income from alms.

It is hard to gauge how widespread the resistance was, because all traces of it were later carefully covered up. In various places nuns quite simply ran away. When inspectors came to check on the application of the new rules, refractory sisters reportedly threw chairs at them, raising such a ruckus that the police had to be called in. Some Roman nuns saw no way out but suicide. Others preferred to take up illegal semireligious status, living at home or in small groups, often as tertiaries affiliated with an official order (generally the Franciscans).[36] Some semireligious women, however, cultivated ties with the Jesuits, so that the label "Jesuitess" became synonymous with "semireligious" throughout Europe. At times the term carried a pejorative connotation, because some of the original "Jesuitesses" were wealthy women who provided substantial financial backing to the order, in return for which they received preferential treatment.[37]

Nuns and Married Women

Were early modern convents really as dreadful as contemporary writers claimed? Yes and no. The negative image of convent life developed a life of its own over the years, aided by a pro-marriage ideology according to which the decline of convents was a sign of progress. The famous Venetian Benedictine Angela Tarabotti (died 1652) wrote a parody of Dante in three parts: the *Paradiso monacale* (Nun's Paradise, ms. 1643), the *Inferno monacale* (Nun's Inferno), and the *Purgatorio delle mal maritate* (Purgatory of the Badly Married). Material for the last came straight from victims of domestic abuse, for whom the convent parlor was the only place where they could speak freely. Perhaps it is no accident that of these three texts, only the *Purgatorio* remains lost.[38] Be that as it may, in the late seventeenth century a Protestant woman in England published a proposal to create a semireligious community for women that offered further evidence of the almost unbearable conditions under which some married women suffered. The community, which was to require no religious oaths, was conceived as a "Monastery" to provide "Religious Retirement" (in the sense of decent accommodation) for unmarried women and to serve as a refuge for married ones.[39]

Indeed, many women may have seen a vital need for communication between the world of the married and that of the religious. Shortly before the Council of Trent met, the "living saint" Angela Merici (died 1540) gave new impetus to the relationship between nuns and married women. Defying the spirit of the times, she preached unconditional, unlimited love of one's neighbor. Her followers lived in the world with families whose children they helped to educate. Angela herself made several pilgrimages, one all the way to the Holy Land. Though illiterate, she was supremely self-confident and convinced that her first obedience was to God. Ultimately she became a tertiary affiliated with the Franciscans, and it was only in the final years of her life that she decided to organize the Company of Saint Ursula, a community of women without oaths, habit, or rule. She was not canonized until the beginning of the nineteenth century, by which time memory of her living sainthood had faded, to be supplanted by the more reassuring image of her as the wise founder of a religious order, something she had never actually been.[40]

The women's congregations of the nineteenth century are generally thought of as having descended from these early open communities, but this idea is misleading. The women who founded religious orders in the early modern period, many of them widows with several children—Ludovica Torelli, Jeanne de Lestonnac,

Jeanne de Chantal, Luise de Marillac—exemplified a female spirituality with a rich past but little future.[41]

Compassion and Ambition

The Power of Female Mystics

Caterina Fieschi, a well-born aristocrat, had her first vision after ten years of marriage: it was of Christ on the cross, the blood flowing from his wounds flooding her palace. Her ascent to love began at the feet of the Lord, who pulled her up to his burning breast, then to his mouth, "and there she was given a kiss . . . and there she lost her whole self."[42] Following this experience she went out into the world to heal the sick, fortifying herself by sucking pus from wounds and eating scabies and lice.

Better known as Saint Catherine of Genoa (died 1510), this matron became an important inspiration for seventeenth-century French mystics. Her behavior contrasted in every way with the emerging ideals of urban civilization: temperance, modesty, repression. Social control in a variety of forms promoted more uniform patterns of behavior. Moralists and physicians preached a similar message. Intemperance was harmful to both body and soul. Unbridled intercourse, for example, was as damaging as abstaining from sexual activity altogether. Even the Catholic church condemned sexual abstinence unless it was justified by the choice of a superior, spiritual way of life, that of the clergy. Catholic moralists shared the widespread fear that radical sexual restraint in women (who were also thought to lose seed during intercourse) could lead to willfulness and arrogance.[43] This age-old fear fed on even older ideas about virginity as a source of freedom and of superhuman powers.

The nonconformist behavior of women such as Catherine of Genoa was proof that such fears were well founded. The result was a systematic stand against any public expression, written or spoken, of the "divine wisdom" of female charismatics. By the time the tide turned in the 1530s, Catherine had been dead for twenty years. But her spiritual legacy, embodied in writing by her followers, overcame all opposition and would continue to influence the spiritual development of the West for the next two centuries. Clearly, something in her teaching gratified needs urgently felt even by men in power. The appeal of her example was strong enough to vanquish even the resistance it aroused, and the same was true of the legacy of female mystics generally. In no other area of Western spiritual culture has the role of women been as indisputable as it was in mysticism, just as women have excelled in "divine science" as in no other branch of learning.

Was there something unique about the contribution of women? Was their mysticism different from the male variety? Suffice it to say that many works by female mystics passed for having been written by men or were deemed better left anonymous (as was often the case with women's creations). Concealing the author's name and sex, some believed, might diminish the reader's prejudice. This appears to have been the case with *Margarita Evangelica* (Cologne, 1545), the Latin edition of the *Evangelische Peerle* (Utrecht, 1535), by Reinalda van Eymeren (died 1540), who lived in a convent in Arnhem, in the northern part of the Netherlands. Along with the legacy of Catherine of Genoa, this work was among the most important precursors of French mysticism.[44]

The French *Perle évangélique* (Paris, 1602) proved the perfect vehicle for the charismatic influence of that key spiritual figure, Pierre de Bérulle, who would later found the French Oratory. The work became known through the fashionable salon of the mystic Barbe Avrillot, also known as Mme. Acarie, a mother of six and one of the spiritual forebears of Saint Francis of Sales. Barbe Avrillot (died 1618) followed the path traced out by that giant among early modern mystics, Teresa of Avila (1582). Avrillot founded the first convent of Discalced Carmelites in France and later, after her husband's death, went to live there herself. Before that her Paris salon became for a time a women's spiritual center, spreading the influence of three women from different parts of the continent: one from Genoa, another from Arnhem, and Teresa herself, from Avila. Their thought was powerful enough to cross borders, and indeed it was deemed so important that it was transcribed, published, and translated into many languages.[45]

Spiritual Love and Physical Love

What drives mystics of either gender is an unquenchable desire to forge as intense as possible a relationship not with their fellow man but with the divine. For Christian mystics this meant a direct experience of love with a personal God: God the Other, but also Partner and Equal, experienced ultimately as one's own self. Putting aside inevitable individual differences, late medieval and early modern mysticism exhibited two distinct tendencies, often combined in a single person: ontological and Platonic on the one hand, Christ-centered and nuptial on the other—or, if you will, literate elitist mysticism and illiterate popular mysticism.

In a moment of ecstasy, of total fusion of the purified self with the beloved One, mystics experienced the ultimate perfection. In metaphorical terms they celebrated, in that supreme moment, their marriage to a heavenly spouse. But the similarity to earthly marriage ended there: mystical marriage was an erotic and amorous union free of the constraints of civil and ecclesiastical regulation.[46]

How did women experience this rather abstract form of love? The democratization of spiritual life, to which women had so largely contributed, and the increasingly widespread influence of the matrimonial model undoubtedly made it easier to think of the divine lover as a husband. Tradition also helped: the very prototype of the consecrated woman, the early Christian virgin, had after all been not only the handmaiden (ancilla) but also the bride of Christ (sponsa Christi). The church itself was a bride of Christ, and so was every consecrated virgin. From the earliest days of Christianity virgins had been brides of the Son of Man, and in the ancient church the ceremony celebrating the commitment to virginity was the same as the marriage ceremony. This nuptial aspect of the original image of the consecrated woman clearly conformed to prevailing cultural models.

Of course women found it more difficult than men to rebel against these models because of their second-class status in the social and religious order. Inwardly, however, they found it easier to overcome the models' influence owing to their relatively limited education. Female mystics, whether literate or illiterate, enjoyed unprecedented freedom to explore the "inner world." There they were no longer subject to civil or ecclesiastical regulations, and nothing could impede their imaginative flights. In God, anything was possible, even the height of folly: in their imaginations mystics actually saw themselves achieving oneness with God and saw the Savior become a Mother: "Thus Jesus Christ . . . is our very Mother. We have our being of him, there, where the ground of Motherhood beginneth; with all the sweet keeping of love that endlessly followeth. As truly as God is our Father, so truly is God our Mother."[47] These words, written by a late medieval recluse, expressed desires she shared with many other women. Timeless images welled up from the depths of collective memory. Not surprisingly, Tridentine reformers had great difficulty persuading the faithful that the idea of divine bisexuality was simply unacceptable: God, the reformers insisted, had come to earth only in the form of a man and never as a woman.[48]

Mystics attached great value to the imagination and sensory perception. In this respect too they ran counter to the general tendency of the "civilizing process," although they were closely attuned to the libertine proto-psychology of learned Renaissance shamans and Neoplatonist philosophers.[49] In the quest for mystic love libidinous feelings and erotic fantasies were so many signs pointing inward to the deepest recesses of the soul. The path inward was a tortuous one of self-punishment and mortification, a rigorous trial to be faced in all its obstacles and pitfalls. This ascetic Calvary ultimately led to hard-won union with the Divine Lover, a union that female mystics seem to have experienced more intimately and spontaneously yet with less shame than their male counterparts. Again, women were less inhibited by culturally determined models, so much so that male colleagues both envied and disapproved of their radical approach.

Women very likely achieved ecstasy as much through the body as through the mind. Hence their mystical experiences were more complete, more unalloyed, than those of men. Women were able to achieve total union with God more directly and more frequently than men because they were more involved with life's corporeal dimension: with birth and death; with nurturing, care, and compassion; with milk, blood, and tears. Their Christ-centered compassion focused on the body of the Redeemer. Women were the first to venerate the Pietà: the Mater Dolorosa cradling Christ's not-yet-resurrected body in her lap, tenderly exhibiting it like a newborn babe, symbolizing the rebirth of humanity. Women were also the first to venerate the Eucharist in a ritual reenacting the sacrifice of the body of Christ. So intense was their experience of transubstantiation (bread into flesh, wine and water into blood) that when the communion wafer was placed on their tongues it triggered an intimate "imitation of Christ." In eating the divine body these women became Christ. His body was theirs, his passion theirs as well—and they repeated the experience time and time again.[50]

Opposition

As the secular world became more rational and the sacred world more clerical, it was inevitable that this kind of religious experience—all-encompassing, body and soul—would change. The gap between "sacred" and "profane" widened, and civil and ecclesiastical authorities alike took an increasingly dim view of public manifestations of mysticism, particularly those involving women. The wings that sustained flights of the mystical imagination were thus clipped. In the lives of female mystics who led semireligious existences, passionate union with the heavenly lover was often inextricably intertwined with love of one's neighbor. Henceforth, therefore, mystics were not only carefully isolated from the community but also closely watched by their spiritual directors and confessors. The fact that a woman's spiritual director often became her peer, her friend, even her pupil, inevitably compounded the problem.[51]

Consider, for example, the case of Isabella Berinzaga (died 1624), an Italian mystic who, like Catherine of Genoa, exerted a profound influence on French mysticism. Illiterate, Isabella refused either to marry or to live in a convent and adopted a semireligious way of life in her birthplace, Milan. In close contact with the Jesuits, she was a devoutly pious woman with a vast number of ideas for church reform. In collaboration with the Jesuit Achille Gagliardi, who was supposed to be her spiritual guide but succumbed to his pupil's influence, she developed a well-received plan for reforming the Company of Jesus. Out of conversations between the pair came the *Breve compendio di perfezione cristiana* (Brief Compendium of Christian Perfection), a true jewel of simplicity, clarity, and concision.[52]

The two soon became objects of suspicion and slander and were condemned to silence by the church; Gagliardi abjured their ideas, and Berinzaga slipped into permanent obscurity. Meanwhile, however, their little manual had already been published in Paris in a translation by Pierre de Bérulle (1597). Thus despite fierce opposition the fruit of their spiritual friendship gained a wide following.[53] Once again Mme. Acarie's circle played an important role in winning an audience for the work. Although such groupings of male disciples around a charismatic woman had become rare in clerical circles, they were increasingly common in the secular form known as the salon.

Spirit, Reason, and the Virgin Mother

The Berinzaga-Gagliardi doctrine regarding the path to perfection was not without danger: it inspired contempt for the world so profound that adepts were reduced to total passivity, to pure suffering, "like martyrs . . . in fact, like little lambs."[54] Their central concept, "passive quietude," excluded all activity, quite in the spirit of one of the most feared, if inexpungeable, of mystical tracts, the so-called *Mirror of Simple Souls* (ms. circa 1300) by the semireligious Marguerite Porete, which became the "Bible" of the Movement of the Free Spirit before being burned in Paris along with its author in 1310.[55] But the *Breve compendio,* unlike the *Mirror,* described the path to perfection and the total experience of God in words anyone could understand. To hardheaded realists it was only too clear that the same path could all too easily lead not to perfection but to anarchy and libertinage, anticlericalism, and rejection of all the virtues, including obedience.

Toward a Rational Piety

After centuries of democratization of religious experience, this danger was well known. The ascetic contempt for the world *(contemptus mundi)* inherent in the religious practice of a small number of medieval monks threatened to degenerate into a much more widespread phenomenon. The authorities were well aware of this threat for having had to deal with it repeatedly: arrogant consecrated women, immune to influence, challenged priests and state officials and jeopardized law and order. If there was to be democratization of *contemptus mundi,* the authorities felt, there should also be democratization of *pietas* as well as piety, that is, of virtue in its social as well as its religious sense.[56]

Such a dual democratization did in fact occur: upwardly mobile burghers, merchants, and peasants aspired to combine rigor and pragmatism in an ultimately reasonable way, and that aspiration had a remarkable impact on the mental climate of Europe at the beginning of the early modern period. This was particularly true in the largely Protestant north, especially in the Netherlands, owing to the profound and lasting influence of the "Modern Devotion" among Protestants and Catholics. Piety thus came to connote resistance to every extravagance; internalized spirituality, moreover, was combined with concrete realism. One example: in the earliest semireligious communities to embrace the Modern Devotion, namely, the Sisters of Common Life, spiritual marriage was celebrated only on the point of death, as a sister was about to embark on her eternal life.[57]

In this kind of climate, manifestations of extreme devotion were generally greeted with skepticism. This fact may explain why female mystics and saints in northern Europe, despite their large numbers in the southernmost provinces of the Netherlands, never enjoyed as much social influence as their Mediterranean counterparts and certainly had no chance of being considered prophetesses. It was not that they were less perfect, but their saintliness was perceived in a different way. It was society's response and the place it allowed women to occupy in public life that made the difference between these women and Italy's mystics and "living saints."[58]

Spiritual Virgins

After the Reformation both Catholics and Protestants regarded excessive spiritualism of any kind with circumspection, while any intervention by women in religious affairs met with mistrust. In the northern Netherlands a shortage of priests temporarily created an opening for semireligious women to do pastoral work. Official documents referred to them as *geestelijke maagden,* or spiritual virgins. In colloquial language, however, they were known as *kloppen,* a pejorative term that probably meant "castrated persons." In Catholic areas the diminutive *klopjies* softened the blow. Unlike the *beguines,* whose numbers declined dramatically after the country turned Protestant, the ranks of spiritual virgins swelled rapidly, and soon they outnumbered the remaining priests. Like semireligious women elsewhere in Europe, they lived as laywomen, alone or in groups, with families or on their own, and often were affiliated as tertiaries with mendicant orders, especially the Franciscans, or with the Jesuits and secular clergy, these affiliations being the source of considerable tension.

The activities of the spiritual virgins were dictated almost entirely by circumstance. They included tending clandestine churches; providing housing and aid to underground priests; assisting the poor, sick, and needy; and giving religious instruction. They were soon accused of being too quick with their own tongues: they sinned, in other words, by giving public sermons and acting as missionaries. So successful were they as pastors, moreover, that in the middle of the seventeenth century Calvinists raised charges against them not unlike the gossip that one heard in Catholic circles: the *kloppen,* it was said, were overbearing and impertinent; their public activities and unaccompanied travel were outrageous; and they were involved in scandalous relations with priests, who robbed them not only of their good names but of their fortunes as well.

Reactions were contradictory. Sometimes the *kloppen* were misunderstood or neglected. There was little interest in what they did and still less in what they had experienced or believed. This was Rome's reaction to alarming news about intolerable conditions on the periphery of the Catholic world. Prelates of the Curia merely issued instructions concerning relations between priests and their servants and warned against provoking outrage among Protestants. But priests actually working on the periphery proudly compared their female collaborators to early Christian deaconesses and virgins, the heroines of persecuted Christianity. The assistance of spiritual virgins was a valued asset, as can be gauged from the fact that the regular and secular clergy accused each other of giving free rein to lust and greed in their respective relations with these women.

Protestants were frightened by the *kloppen*'s extraordinary energy. Some documents give the impression that Dutch towns were literally overrun by hordes of them, zealous to convert to "papist superstition" any unfortunate passerby who fell into their clutches. Their thirst for learning provoked not fear but mirth, however, reminding Catholics as well as Protestants of the jokes about Précieuses and *savantes,* women who affected all the latest in refinement and learning. On the Catholic side, however, one particularly serious charge was raised: spiritual virgins were apt to fall into excessive piety, heretical opinions, and false mysticism. Hence it was recommended that they curb their passion for literature and read only the edifying works produced for them by their spiritual directors.

It appears, then, that Catholics and Protestants agreed about at least one thing: in matters of faith and pastoral practice, it was playing with fire to sanction close collaboration between men and women. Inspired by the example of the adventurer Jerome and his companion, the matron Paula, too many women invested all they had, material as well as spiritual, in false prophets, only to end in disappointments.[59]

Piety and Fecundity

Reactions to itinerant preaching couples (common in quietist Catholic and pietist Protestant milieus) can be used as a yardstick for measuring the established churches' opposition to male-female collaboration. Consider, for example, the controversy that arose when the well-known scholar Anna Maria van Schurman (died 1678) joined the sect or "family" of Jean Labadie, a former Jesuit, then ex-Calvinist preacher, and indefatigable traveler in the quest for truth. The two were compared to Jerome and Paula, and Anna Maria was criticized, like Paula before her, for abandoning the established order. Internationally renowned for her defense of the right of women to study, Schurman later came to rank love of one's neighbor, contempt for the world, and service to God above learning (*Eucleria*, 1673). She chose communion in love (in the ancient Christian tradition) over earthly glory. Schurman herself never abandoned her studies, but others considered her decision to join Labadie's community in Friesland a betrayal of learning inspired by an irrational passion.[60]

The condemnation of Labadie and his followers was similar to the reproaches leveled against the *kloppen*. They were admonished for abandoning parents and relatives, although many were middle-aged single women, often widows. The criticism was in fact directed against the way they chose to live: their break with family tradition seemed to imply a neglect of the piety due to one's kin, living and dead. It was further argued that women, with their irrational proclivity for generosity, then poured everything they possessed into the common fund of the Labadie "family." Not unintentionally, this argument gave the false impression that all Labadie's followers were women. The intent was not only to discourage other women from joining the sect but also to discredit Labadie and his community. A prophet who attracted mainly women, it was implied, had to be a wolf in sheep's clothing, out to satisfy his greed and lust.

The seventeenth century saw growing tension between spiritual and rationalist tendencies in Catholicism. The Inquisition began hunting quietists in the early 1680s. Trial accounts reveal bizarre accusations of false mysticism combined with sexual aberration;

they tell us more about the overheated fantasies of the prosecution than about the actual behavior of the defendants. For example, one of the most notorious of the quietists, Miguel de Molinos, was initially protected by Pope Innocent XI but was later accused of celebrating black masses in Roman nunneries. The scenes described resemble a cross between a holy mass and a fertility rite: the goblet used in the consecration contained not wine and water but the sperm of the celebrant and the vaginal effluvia of the women present. Molinos, it was said, began by bringing one nun, stretched naked on the altar, to orgasm with his consecrated hand, after which he continued collecting female "seed" from the others one by one.[61]

These traces of ancient ritual that survived in the minds of celibate church functionaries, though symptomatic of mental confusion, must be seen within their larger contemporary context, which combined worship of reason with veneration of the Virgin Mother. Indeed, the Virgin was an essential element of official Counter-Reformation theology, since Mary's unusual role in the divine birth had fundamental significance in the Catholic idea of the church and the mediating function of its ministers (which Protestants rejected). All Catholic reformers promoted veneration of Mary, and with it came increased emphasis on the paradoxical connection between piety and fecundity, priesthood and incarnation, priestly mediation and the mediatrix of all grace. Combining the procreational power of motherhood with the divine freedom (or transcendental power) of virgins, "fertile virgin" priests forged an unnatural pact with the Virgin Mother and wielded it as a mighty weapon against enemies old and new. The old enemy was a magical representation of the world in which pagan figures such as mother goddesses, *Matres* or *Matronae,* and Sibyls constituted the ineradicable source of all things, the link between darkness and light, between death and life—the Morning Star. And the new enemy was the forward march of "civilization," which was moving toward a scientific representation that allowed no room for mystery as the sign of a substantial unity between the natural and the supernatural.[62]

The Virgin Mother—that most venerated of all women, the Morning Star, the Seat of Knowledge, the Mystic Rose, the Queen of all saints—more than anything else embodies the difference between Protestant and Catholic culture. The two cultures that dominated Western society in this period developed in similar ways, but the Virgin Mother remains the symbol of discord, standing firm atop the rock where there is room for only one church.

North and South: An Epilogue

It will by now be clear that this brief exploration of two centuries of history has been conducted by someone familiar primarily with the Catholic landscape, particularly in Italy and the Netherlands. This reconnaissance mission incorporates the preliminary results of a vast cartographic project whose purpose is to map hitherto-uncharted paths, caves, and springs. Guiding this effort is a new view of the landscape, a different way of experiencing space, a different idea of the world, born of a modified concept of what human beings—male and female—are. More and more investigators have begun to contribute to this work, so that there are many new leads to follow, some of them touching on the religious sphere. These leads are so divergent that only a few of them could be taken into account here.

Much remains to be done before any new synthesis can be attempted. We still lack sufficient information about the religious experience of early modern women to add anything to the continuing debate about medieval religion. Since Natalie Zemon Davis's seminal essay "City Women and Religious Change" (1975), progress has been slow, particularly with regard to Catholic culture.[63] One reason for this is the notion, not yet as fully discredited as it deserves to be, that the Counter-Reformation put a brake on all progress.

Today we have our doubts even about progress, but we can hope for a debate in the not-too-distant future about the development of Catholic and Protestant cultures in the West with regard to gender relations, the role of women, and the female experience.

TRANSLATED FROM THE ITALIAN BY CLARISSA BOTSFORD

6

Women in Politics

Natalie Zemon Davis

IN 1586, IN THE LATIN edition of his celebrated *Six livres de la République,* Jean Bodin reflected on the various orders and degrees of citizens
in a republic and said as an afterthought:

> Now as for the order and degree of women,
> I meddle not with it; only I think it meet
> them to be kept far off from all magistracies,
> places of command, judgments, public assem-
> blies, and counsels: so to be attentive only
> unto their womanly and domestical busi-
> ness. (*The Six Bookes of a Commonweale,*
> 1606)

In 1632 an English jurist made a similar distinction
in introducing a book on laws and statutes relating
to the female sex:

> Women have nothing to do in constituting
> Lawes, or consenting to them, in interpreting
> of Lawes or in hearing them interpreted at
> lectures, leets or charges, and yet they stand
> strictly tied to men's establishments, little or
> nothing excused by ignorance. (T. E., *The
> Lawes Resolution of Womens Rights,* 1632)

In fact these men of the law somewhat overstate
the difference between the sexes. During the ancien
régime, there were many men denied full partici-

pation in political activity by reason of property, wealth, or standing, while some women had political authority by reason of birth and inheritance or at least informal access to political influence. Still, the sphere of politics contained marked asymmetries between women and men, and transgressions within it seemed especially troubling to the practice and symbolism of rightly ordered hierarchical societies. Faced with Mary Tudor, Mary Stuart, and Catherine de Médicis in 1558, the Scottish Calvinist John Knox termed their rule "the monstrous"—that is, unnatural—"regimen of women."

Armies, Lawcourts, Administration

It seemed "natural" and also prescribed by divine law that women should not bear arms in battle. The early modern armies gradually being formed out of mercenaries and recruits and what was left of feudal levies were to be male. Not that all men had to prove their masculinity by fighting: Catholic priests were forbidden to shed blood, an action that made them "impure" and "irregular"; and in the sixteenth and seventeenth centuries men of the radical Protestant sects renounced their swords, arguing that the highest masculine courage consisted in pacifism. Nor was there a lack of images of the armed female: Amazons were part of the literary landscape of western Europe, while accounts of Jeanne d'Arc with her banner reminded the French of what a woman could achieve in leading men to battle.

Jeanne never concealed her sex even while dressing as a soldier, and she may have been the inspiration for the few French women who went publicly to battle in the seventeenth century. The usual stratagem for women who wanted to join an army or a navy in England, France, and the Netherlands was to hide their identity and cross-dress as a man. The numerous women who traveled openly with every early modern army were cooks (sometimes wives preparing food for their husbands), servants, provisioners, and prostitutes.

The growing world of lawcourts, offices, and recordkeeping revealed a like asymmetry. Women made contracts and were the subject of contracts but could never swear witness to one. No matter how fine their hand, they were never notaries or secretaries for the chancellery. No matter how skilled at peacemaking in their neighborhoods or in their network of spiritual kinship (commé-

rage), they were not judges in even the pettiest of royal jurisdictions in France, or justices of the peace in England (though a very few aristocratic women had held that post in medieval times), or called to an English grand jury or trial jury. An heiress or a widow possessed of some form of high or low justice in a manorial court named an agent to judge and arbitrate in her stead, as indeed did many male seigneurs. (Anne Clifford, sheriff of Westmoreland as heir to the third Earl of Cumberland, was unusual in seventeenth-century England in convening the local courts in her own female person.) Apart from formal positions in the household of queen and princess, women were never granted any of the offices that were so central to the growth of the early modern state, from chancellor down to royal sergeant or jailer. Instead, they might try to influence appointments to office, if they had property and connections in their own right; and in any case they enjoyed the prestige, income, and connections that came to them from the official dignities of their menfolk.

What it meant to be a "citizen" of a kingdom, city-state, or town in early modern Europe was not very clear for either men or women. "Rights," "privileges," "freedoms," and "immunities" varied from place to place, as did the terminology and marks of political and legal status. But most men within the walls of an early modern city could be categorized as burgher, resident, or foreigner, with differential rights and duties, while for women these distinctions, when made at all, did not involve political activity. As a citizen, a woman was entitled to protection by the law of her town; as a widow, she might be expected to provide a man from her household (or a payment) for the urban militia; but she was rarely called to a consultative or voting assembly and never invited to sit on a town council. The one place in urban administration where women might find a niche was in hospital supervision: seventeenth-century group portraits of the regentesses of the charitable hospitals of Amsterdam and Haarlem present women who look as authoritative as male regents. But on the whole, city government was a matter for men—husbands, fathers, and widowers—who knew what was best for their families.

Monarchies and the Power of Queens

The two kinds of early modern political regimes—republics and monarchies—gave different scope to the political role of women.

The oligarchical republics, such as Florence of the early Renaissance, Venice, the Swiss cantons, and the German imperial cities, afforded the fewest settings in which women could enjoy political power publicly. Here women's political influence could be wielded only informally, such as through their husbands, sons, and wider kin networks.

In contrast, those polities organized as kingdoms—France, England, Spain, the German principalities, and ducal Florence of the later Renaissance—had places formally reserved for women and arenas for public and semipublic female action. Where power was acquired by dynastic succession rather than by election or cooptation, women were anointed as queens, and birth and marriage became matters of high politics. The brilliant courts so important to the prestige of the royal person and to the whole system of monarchical governance required women and men both. Although women never actually sat in the sovereign's privy council, they took part in the conversation—political and personal—that filled the halls, chambers, and bedrooms of the royal palace.

In England, queens could rule fully in their own right in the absence of a male heir in the direct line. The reign of Elizabeth I, like those of Henry VIII and Edward VI, has long been examined for its policies regarding religion, civil order, economic change, and foreign expansion. To such topics we can now add that of the "gender style" adopted by both kings and queens and the implications of that style for contemporary political culture and stability. Thus when Elizabeth acceded to the throne in 1558, she had to face not only the usual suspicions about female rule—that women would be subject to male favorites and would be changeable and irrational—but also the immediate legacy of her half-sister, Mary Tudor, who had in fact been dominated by her husband, the Spanish Philip II, and had delivered nothing from her royal body but a false pregnancy.

Elizabeth's stratagems were multiple, played out in the royal progress from one city to another after coronation, in the widely disseminated royal portrait, and in the smaller theater of the court. Even while using a possible royal marriage as a diplomatic ploy, she was ever the Virgin Queen to her people. Dressed in stiff ornate garments and laden with pearls, her body was as inaccessible as if it were under armor; the Virgin Queen seemed, when necessary, a manly figure, able to give courage to her soldiers; and she was also an iconic figure, a worthy replacement for the Catholic image of the Virgin Mary. (That Elizabeth's birthday fell on the feast day of the nativity of Mary surely helped.) As Virgin Queen, she could also claim to be mistress, wife, and mother to the people of England and to her courtiers, to speak to them and be sought after by them in the language of love.

Elizabeth's reign was not without its discontents and opposition, including gossip alleging that the Virgin Queen had lovers and illegitimate children or, on the contrary, that she was physically malformed. But on the whole, Elizabeth developed a style of female self-mastery that sustained her royal authority within the framework of sixteenth-century hierarchical thought.

Across the Channel, French queens had less scope. In the fourteenth century the old Salic law of inheritance had been invoked for the first time to justify excluding women from succession to the throne; by the sixteenth century jurists were claiming that the exclusion dated back to the time of the ancient Franks. As a result one of the "fundamental laws" of the kingdom, one of the few "constitutional" limits placed on royal sovereignty during the ancien régime, rested on notions of female instability and on fears of foreign domination if the crown fell to the weak distaff side. The coronation of French queens highlighted the difference between kingship and queenship. Kings were consecrated in Reims, queens in Saint-Denis. Kings were anointed with a heaven-sent balm, which brought the miraculous power to cure scrofula; queens were anointed with consecrated oil, which guaranteed fertility. The queen's scepter and throne were smaller than the king's; and whereas the king's crown was held by peers of the realm, hers was supported only by barons.

And yet the queen was also given a ring, which betokened not only the Trinity but also her duty to fight heresy and to attend to the needs of the poor. There were political roles to which the French queen was summoned, others that she could assume as regent when so named, and others that she could take on informally as royal wife and mother. Catherine de Médicis is a supreme example of action in all these capacities, with her family goal of maintaining her sons in rightful authority, her political goal of keeping a Gallican Catholic monarchy dominant over the Huguenots and the ultra-Catholic Leaguers alike, and her imperial goal of trying to keep peace between warring religious parties. Although she ultimately failed in these efforts, along the way she made expert use of the whole political arsenal, from court pageants and royal entries into cities to regional peasant dances, from pacification edicts to orders for Protestant exclusion from office, from marriage alliances to complicity in bloodshed.

Was the gender style she created implicated at all in the failure? Catherine presented herself as a pious widow like the classical Artemisia, commissioning a monumental tomb for her husband; as such she could not be seductive toward her people, but at least she could be devoted to their late king. She presented herself as a woman who had given kings to France, a mother who had been offered a golden statue of Ceres at her entry into Lyons years before; as such, she could put maternality at the heart of her queenship, making it the source of her patronage, her charity, her determined defense of her sons, and her quest for order. She presented herself as the matriarchal Juno, presiding over marriages that linked France to the Holy Roman Empire and brought peace. In the entry into Paris after the marriage of Charles IX and Elisabeth of Austria, a statue of a goddess with Catherine's face held proudly aloft a map of Gaul.

Here lay part of the difficulty, for maternality and matriarchy were images with a double potential in the sixteenth century. When murder followed in the wake of marriage, as the Saint Bartholomew's Day massacre did the wedding of Catherine's daughter to Henri de Navarre, the queen mother's enemies could readily portray her as a sorceress (and an Italian poisoner to boot), spawning weak, deceptive, and androgynous sons such as Henri III. Already in 1575, the widely read *Discours merveilleux de la vie, actions et deportemens de Catherine de Médicis* called her "the model of tyranny," ruling others "by the appetite of the passions that ruled her." She had usurped the crown, and her evil government was just what the Salic law was intended to prevent.

Queen Anne, who ruled England in her own right (1702–1714) rather than conjointly with her consort George of Denmark, affords yet a third example of monarchical style. Her gender image might be characterized as "womanly," by the gentler definitions of the early eighteenth century. Her reign was marked by war with France and by a conflict between two ideas of government: on the one hand, a sovereign with much legitimate power, who would have preferred to embody like Elizabeth the unity of England, "to keep [herself] out of the power of merciless men of both parties," and to view her ministers as personal servants; and, on the other, a postrevolutionary system of party conflict, elections, and embryonic cabinet rule intended to limit the monarch. As for war,

Anne, frequently in ill health, had none of the martial style of Elizabeth; her husband, who died in 1708, had little of it either, and the military symbolism in her reign was borne by her Captain-General, John, Duke of Marlborough. Nor was her style maternal, losing as she did all her progeny at birth or in childhood. Her manner was described as graceful but not regal, courteous but not imposing.

Anne regularly took counsel from Sidney Godolphin (sometimes moderate Tory, sometimes moderate Whig) and other men, but her closest personal-political exchange was with other women, and especially with Sarah Churchill, Duchess of Marlborough. Their connection went back to girlhood—Sarah was only a few years older than Anne—and over the years Anne took Sarah as a "friend" rather than as mere "favorite," proposing that they write to each other under the names Mrs. Morley and Mrs. Freeman. "From this time," wrote Sarah Churchill, "Mrs. Morley and Mrs. Freeman began to converse as equals, made so by affection and friendship," and indeed, the rhetoric of the letters between the two bears this out.[1] When the women became estranged in the midst of Anne's reign, Sarah was replaced by her younger cousin Abigail.

The gender style that Anne constructed for her rulership had, like Catherine de Médicis' maternality, different possibilities and uses. Though she had judgment of her own, and often a very determined one, her womanly connections and female friendships invited a perception of her as "weak" and dominated by favorites. But it could also be argued that the womanly manner was an appropriate strategy for sustaining her notion of monarchy and national unity during the period of intense party growth. A more "manly" queen might have provoked revolt, a more matriarchal one contempt.

One could extend this analysis of political role, political rhetoric, and gender style to many other royal figures and settings: to the androgynous Christine of Sweden, Catherine II of Russia, and others.

Political Action at Royal Courts: Observers and Favorites

The courts of female rulers and of their kingly counterparts encouraged women to political action within the framework of sovereign monarchy and sometimes also to political commentary. Women took part in court ceremonial and joined in the relations of patronage and faction; they petitioned for posts, pensions, and pardons for members of their families and their clients as did men. The letters of Mme. de Sévigné, like the journal of the Duc de Saint-Simon, are full of politics. Sévigné's description in 1664 of the treason trial of Nicolas Foucquet, Louis XIV's powerful minister of finance, was garnered from observers and also from participants. It shows not just her sympathy with a compatriot of her Breton husband, but also her attentiveness to issues of government and judicial procedure. Foucquet refused to take the oath at his second hearing:

> Whereupon Monsieur the Chancellor threw himself into an oration to make everyone see the legitimate power of the court, that the king had established it and that the charges had been verified by the sovereign courts. M. Foucquet responded that often things were done by authority that, after reflection, were sometimes found unjust. Monsieur the Chancellor interrupted, "What? you are saying then that the king abuses his power?" M. Foucquet responded, "It's you who are saying it, monsieur, not I. It's not my thought, and I am amazed that, in my situation, you are trying to get me into further trouble with the king. But, monsieur, you know perfectly well yourself that one can be surprised. When you sign a decree, you believe it to be just. The next day, you annul it; you see that one can change one's mind and one's opinion."

Sévigné was critical of the chancellor's conduct of the trial, sometimes referring to him by a coded name when her remarks were too pointed, and although she was relieved that Foucquet was not given a death sentence, she was still deeply disappointed that he was found guilty and sentenced to life imprisonment. "Is there anything in the world so horrible as this injustice?" Her assessments always stopped short of the Sun King, however: "Such crude and low vengeance could not come from a heart like that of our master."[2]

As for the high policies of such a royal master, women could sometimes hope to influence them through the role of "favorite." Mme. de Maintenon, first confidante then morganatic wife to Louis XIV, assumed that her views would be taken seriously by the king. As she wrote in 1695 to Louis-Antoine de Noailles, archbishop of Paris, "Make it a habit, Monseigneur, to write a separate letter about what you want me to show the king; you must not mix anything in it that suggests how often we communicate with each other, but say only that, since I am quite willing to do it, you authorize me to pass on your messages." By the time of the debate about the Spanish Succession in 1700, meetings of Louis's ministers were being held in her chambers, and diplomatic dispatches were being read in her presence. The danger of European war colored her reaction to the possibility that Louis's grandson might assume the throne of Spain ("the Spanish business is going badly," she said in a letter of November 14), and reports differed on whether she first advised for or against the succession.[3] But whichever the case may have been, the evidence is clear of the role of Mme. de Maintenon in Louis's government.

About the same time, Sarah, Duchess of Marlborough, had laid it down as a maxim that she must speak the truth to Queen Anne, "preferring the real interest of my mistress before the pleasing her fancy" (*An Account of the Conduct of the Dowager Duchess of Marlborough*, 1742). Sarah saw herself as a woman of state, collaborating with her husband Marlborough and with Godolphin. Especially she tried to warn Anne against "throwing herself and her affairs almost entirely into the hands of the Tories" with regard to church matters and appointments to the cabinet. Sometimes Anne did what the Duchess told her—as when Anne finally opposed a Tory bill that would have excluded from state or municipal office all those "who could not relish the high church nonsense of promoting religion by persecution"[4]—and sometimes she did not, even during the years when Sarah was highest in Anne's affection.

The costs of such forms of political action are those that accompany "influence" in a monarchical regime: they are hidden, they are unaccountable, and they are especially freighted with suspicion when in the hands of a woman. Thus, Mme. de Maintenon tried to shed responsibility by insisting she had no effect on royal policy, even while the Duc de Saint-Simon was portraying her as "a wicked fairy" and "a femme fatale," who dominated king and government in a "sinister" fashion.

Looking back in 1778 at the reign of Queen Anne, the radical Whig historian Catharine Sawbridge Macaulay saw it as "a glaring example" of the weaknesses of a form of government "where the welfare and prosperity of the nation depend entirely on the virtue of the Prince." However good her intentions, Anne did not understand the art of governing. She "loved power, [but was] totally incapable of exercising it independently." Instead, she was "a slave to favorites" like the Duchess of Marlborough, a woman of "fiery and imperious temperament," who used the queen's weaknesses to promote her own "private views" *(The History of England from the Revolution to the Present Time).* For Mary Wollstonecraft, republican and feminist, Marie-Antoinette represented all the evils of the French court during the reign of Louis XVI: her "voluptuous softness," "her ruinous vices," her time spent "in the most childish manner, without the appearance of any vigor of mind to palliate the wanderings of the imagination," and with all this an artfulness and beauty that brought her "unbounded sway" over the king *(An Historical and Moral View of the Origin and Progress of the French Revolution,* 1794). Acquiring power through the avenues opened at court was the stratagem of a slave.

Consultative Assemblies

But there were other arenas for women's political action, some of them systemically related to monarchical governance and its institutions, some with the potential to change them. On the whole, women were rarely direct participants in assemblies and representative institutions. Their presence at assemblies of "all the inhabitants" in villages in the Dunois, Saintonge, and other rural regions was more exceptional in the seventeenth century than it had been in the medieval period. Meanwhile, village councils of elders and parish vestries, which never extended to the men among the rural poor, excluded women even if they were widowed proprietors or freeholders. When a widow was included in the convocation to a meeting by an urban government, it would be only to listen to announcements about some new regulation or requisition, not to voice an opinion or vote.

In France, women were entitled in principle to be present at local assemblies to choose deputies to the Estates-General in their capacity as abbesses in the First Estate, as feudal heiresses in the Second, and as heads of households and officers of female guilds in the Third, but for the important Estates of the sixteenth century they seem to have named agents in their stead. How could a woman's voice be heard in such a setting? The committees that drew up *cahiers de doléances* (registers of grievances) all over

France for the Estates of 1614 had no female members; women might be the subject of some complaints (such as those about non-noble women wearing silk above their station), but women did not state grievances in their own voice. When the Estates finally assembled under the anxious eye of Marie de Médicis, the danger of having a female as regent was one of the sensitive issues.

After 1614 the Estates-General ceased to meet, but regional Estates continued throughout the ancien régime. The letters of Mme. de Sévigné suggest how women of her status could connect with such institutions and deepen their understanding of political process in an "absolute" monarchy, even without the formal role of deputy. The Estates of Brittany met in August 1671 not far from the noble property that Mme. de Sévigné had inherited from her late husband. "I had never seen the Estates; it's a rather beautiful affair," she wrote her daughter, and went on to describe the Breton nobles who came to town, some of them with their wives, her dinners and other entertainments with them, and their visits to her lands. Some of the sessions of the Estates she may have attended ("It's a great joy to see myself at the Estates") and she commented:

> The Estates don't have to take long. One has only to ask what the king wants. No one says a word; and that's it, everything is done. As for the governor, he has, by some means I don't know, more than forty thousand crowns coming to him. Any number of other gifts, pensions, road repairs and town construction, fifteen or twenty banquets, continual gaming, theater three times a week, magnificent display: that's the Estates.

She ended with an account of the toasts drunk to the king by the Breton nobles because he was returning to the province 100,000 crowns of its "present" to him. Four years later, when the king moved the parlement of Brittany from the city of Rennes to Vannes, she commented astutely that if there were Estates held now, the first order of business would be to buy back the Parlement for Rennes and purchase for a second time the royal edicts for which 2,500,000 pounds had been laid out only two years before.[5]

Conceivably, the Estates of Languedoc, which bargained every year with the king over his "free gift" (*don gratuit*), stimulated political reflection like that of Madame de Sévigné among the wives of deputies and members, even though only the ceremonial sessions were open to the public.

In Protestant England, the few women who succeeded to peerages did not sit in the House of Lords, and women never stood for election to the Commons. Nonetheless, aristocratic ladies might well throw their support behind one of the candidates, and especially after the party system was in place at the end of the seventeenth century, the wives of candidates were often much involved in their husbands' campaigns, winning male votes by being hospitable to the wives of influential constituents. As for the less notable women, they were found standing on the fringes of the election crowds being harangued and wooed by Tory or Whig.

Pamphlets and Political Writers

The limited political experience provided women by representative and consultative institutions was expanded through the development of the periodical and pamphlet press and the increase in female literacy. They could read (or hear read aloud) the abundant pamphlet literature that came out of the French Religious Wars and the religious-political struggles of seventeenth-century England. And a few of them could write it: the female opinions that might be dismissed as "gossip" when offered orally took on more substance when they appeared in print. Thus in 1536 Marie Dentière gave an anonymous account of the Protestant deliverance of Geneva from the tyranny of Catholics and Savoyards; in 1665 the Quaker Margaret Fell Fox brought out *Women's Speaking Justified,* an anonymous defense of female preachers that, in the context of Restoration England, was not only religiously daring but also politically challenging. From 1681 to 1715 Elinor James, the wife of a London printer, published thirty tracts and broadsides under her own name in defense of the Church of England and James II. "Oh, that I were but a Man," she said in introducing one of them, "I should study Night and Day, and I do not doubt I should be more than a Conqueror, and so I hope to be nevertheless" (*A Vindication of the Church of England,* 1687).

By the early eighteenth century, women's political publications had multiplied in both France and England.[6] Confined to no one political stance, the writings might support tradition or urge change. Indeed, the impulse could move beyond specific issues to utopian hopes, as in Sarah Scott's *Description of Millennium Hall* (1762), where a community of gentlewomen reforms the educational, economic, marital, and medical practice of their parish in a humane direction, in telling contrast to the cruel hunter-landlords nearby.

Catharine Sawbridge Macaulay's output in the next decades shows the range of a woman's political concerns. Her brother was in Parliament; she acted with her pen. Apart from her multivolume *History of England from the Accession of James I* (1763–1778), with its defense of the liberty-loving Commonwealth tradition against despotic or incompetent monarchs and the usurping tyrant Cromwell, she published tracts defending author's copyright; arguing against Thomas Hobbes in favor of a "democratical system" of government and against Edmund Burke in favor of frequently elected Parliaments; and condemning repressive acts against the American colonies. In the last years of her life she visited and corresponded with George Washington in the United States of America, rejoicing in its new constitution but warning him that the centralized powers given to the president might lead to an abuse of trust and that the bicameral legislature might "in length of time [become] the grounds of political inequality."[7]

Rioters, Rebels, Revolutionaries

Catharine Macaulay singled out one group of women for praise in her *History:* the petitioners to the Long Parliament during the English Revolution of 1640–1660. Early modern women were also mobilized to action during momentous political change. Women of the lower orders had long been accustomed to take part in and even initiate riots in town or village when rightful claims had been violated and the authorities were failing in their duty: when grain or bread prices were too high, taxes unjust, open fields enclosed, religious outrages committed, and the like.[8] During the Fronde (1648–1652), women's local rioting became part of a French national event. They were noted in the 1644 street tax protest in Paris, which triggered the first opposition of the Parlement to Cardinal Mazarin and the regent, Anne of Austria; and they were active in the demonstrations, bread riots, and pillaging that accompanied the escalation of the Fronde into violent resistance.

But the expansion of women's action in the Fronde was especially the work of high aristocrats, energized by family loyalty, a belief in monarchy limited by princely councils and regional institutions, and a taste for power. The Duchesse de Longueville, wife of the governor of Normandy and sister of two princes of the blood (le Grand Condé and the Prince de Conti), was a Frondeuse from the beginning, helping win her brothers to the cause. She supported the resistance of the Rouen and Paris Parlements against the regent and Mazarin; escaped from Paris when her brothers and husband were imprisoned and joined other noble leaders in a Belgian border town to scheme further action (including a treaty with Spain); returned in triumph when the princes were released and spent the last months of the civil war—when her husband, now estranged, had returned to Mazarin's camp—protecting the radical Ormée movement in Bordeaux. Along the way, the government accused her of high treason, a tribute to her importance. Undeterred, she coauthored a major pamphlet, *Apologie pour Messieurs les Princes* (1650), in which she said she must defend "the liberty to speak, which is the only thing that remains to me." In 1652 Mlle. de Montpensier—la Grande Mademoiselle—led troops against the government of her cousin Louis XIV and was borne in triumph into Orléans, events recorded in her *Mémoires* with a sense of heroism and delight. The Fronde left behind it competing images of women in politics: that of the queen regent, who once again showed the danger that arose when "the crown falls to the distaff" ("la couronne tombe en quenouille") and that of the *femme forte,* the vigorous woman acting for the good of France.

Across the Channel in the English Civil War, some women—though none with the eminence of la Grande Mademoiselle—fought as soldiers for Royalists and Roundheads, and women performed the more usual tasks of tending the wounded and helping with fortifications. They were in street demonstrations in London to put pressure on Parliament, and they were pamphleteers, especially for the Good Old Cause of Parliament and for Independency, that is, tolerance for Protestant congregations and the end to an established church.

Petitioners and the Woman's Interest

Most innovative during the English Civil War, however, was women's role as petitioners to Parliament on public matters. In 1642 "a company of women" submitted petitions against "Popish Lords and superstitious Bishops." The next year, among other efforts, "about two or three thousand Women, most of them of the inferior sort," gathered at Westminster to present Commons and Lords with a petition for the end of civil war and the return of peace.[9] After the defeat and execution of Charles I, the petitions came from women among the Levellers, the followers of John Lilburne who translated the democratic ideas of the religious sects into the sphere of politics. Wearing green ribbons as their sign, they petitioned for the freeing of Lilburne and other imprisoned leaders, the ending of imprisonment for debt, the lowering of taxes, attention to the food supply and unemployment, and more.

"Tumultuous" is how the members of the Long Parliament described the Leveller women, telling them in 1649 "that the matter you petition about is of an higher concernment than you understand, that the House gave an answer to your Husbands; and therefore that you are desired to goe home, and looke after your owne businesse, and meddle with your huswifery." The women's justifications for their petitions strikingly combined the traditional language of "the weaker sex" needing redress with novel claims about their political rights. First of all, the Lord was on their side: since God was "ever ready to receive the Petitions of all, making no difference of persons," then Parliament should do the same. More important, they said to Parliament in the spring of 1649:

> Have we not an equal interest with the men of this Nation, in those liberties and securities contained in the Petition of Right, and other good Laws of the Land? Are any of our lives, limbs, liberties or goods to be taken from us more than from Men? . . . And must we keep at home in our houses, as if we, our lives and liberties and all, were not concerned? . . . Therefore again, we entreat you to review our last petition . . . For we are no whit satisfied with the answer you gave unto our Husbands and Friends.[10]

With this response, the Leveller women challenged the central tenet of patriarchal law, that women's interests were subsumed under those of their fathers and husbands, and asserted that women had an equal and perhaps even a separate interest of their own to defend.

The Right to Vote?

The remarkableness of this position, advanced in the heat of political combat, is all the more evident when we compare it with

181

those advanced in the debates about voting rights carried on in 1647 at Putney among the men in the General Council of Cromwell's army. Cromwell and General Ireton argued that those who were to have a share in deciding the affairs of England must have "a permanent fixed interest" in it, founded not merely on having been born in England but also on having substantial property there. The Levellers and other men maintained, on the contrary, that the vote should be open to every man who had not lost his birthright: "I do think the poorest man in England is not at all bound in a strict sense to that Government that he hath not had a voice to put himself under." The generals warned that this would mean the end of property; the men wondered bitterly whether the soldiers had been fighting not for liberty, but to give power to "men of riches and estates" to enslave them. Still, there was overall agreement that one class of men should be excluded from the vote: apprentices, servants, and those taking alms "because they depend upon the will of other men and should be afraid to displease [them] . . . They are included in their masters."[11]

The debates at Putney did not touch on women, but it is clear that they would have been a troubling case on either of the grounds considered there. It would have been argued that they should be denied the vote both because they were dependent on the will of their husbands and included in them and because, if they had it, they might vote against their dependency.

In fact the idea that women lacked a rightful separate interest survived intact in the political assumptions of the Restoration. The voting franchise remained the same for men as it had been in the fifteenth century—limited to burgesses and to freeholders with property worth forty shillings a year—and the exceptional female propertyholders who had voted (or had tried to vote) in elections as late as 1640 effectively disappeared. During the Glorious Revolution of 1688–1689, women were busy again, from Princess Anne, who maneuvered successfully against her father, James II, down to London women who rioted against the papists—though this time there were no "Petticoat Petitioners." In 1690 a treatise on parliamentary law explicitly stated for the first time that women were not eligible to vote, an assertion suggesting that the question had at least been in the air. The same year John Locke's *Two Treatises of Government* constitutionalized relations within the family on the same lines as relations within civil society and government. Wives shared with husbands a parental power over their children during their years of minority, and the powers of husband and wife over each other were limited by contract. Nonetheless, "the husband and wife, though they have but one common concern, yet having different understandings, will unavoidably sometimes have different wills, too; it therefore being necessary that the last determination—i.e., the rule—should be placed somewhere, it naturally falls to the man's share, as the abler and the stronger."[12] Locke did not discuss women's votes and citizenship, but he seems to have assumed that the "people" who make known their consent to government are men, those who have "the last determination."

It remained for innovators in the eighteenth century to draw lessons from women's political past and, using new categories, apply Locke's ideas and other formulations of natural right to women's citizenship. For the radical republican Mary Wollstonecraft, the example of queens, favorites, courts, aristocratic influence, or anything that brought sexuality, frivolity, or weakness to bear on politics was negative. Nor, by her rational standards, was a disorderly female street riot much better ("strictly a mob," she was to write of the market women who marched to Versailles). Women had the capacity to be educated to "manly virtue," and men to peaceable responsibility; both had the right to participate in government and should be full citizens acting by the lights of reason (*A Vindication of the Rights of Woman*, 1792). The hierarchy within marriage would be effaced as well, even though women were to sustain their distinctive tasks of motherhood. With this middle-class vision of a new kind of polity and transformed women and men, Wollstonecraft hoped to end the seeming inconsistency, so important throughout the ancien régime, between republican and egalitarian forms of government, on the one hand, and women's full participation in politics, on the other. The female publicists and petitioners of the past she would have readily recognized as paving the way to this republican ideal. But the other forms of women's political action, from using influence to rioting, had a long life ahead of them, and may have contributed more than she could have anticipated to women's understanding of the nature of power.

Intermezzo

7

Judging by Images

Françoise Borin

TO ASK AN ICONOGRAPHER to write about
images is to accept a different kind of reading; it
is to sense that an eye instructed by "visual archives" is apt to look at pictures from a different
angle. To look to images for an answer to questions about women is to examine, out of context,
sources chosen on the basis of necessarily subjective criteria, and it is not only to focus attention
on an isolated, and for that reason distorted, object
but also to see that object with contemporary eyes,
because "the figurative image is fixed, but perception is variable."[1]

The iconography is certainly problematic. It is
difficult to separate the real from the imaginary,
and the traditional distinction between the work
of art and the historical document is useless. Thus
the peasant women, perverted or otherwise, whose
images illustrate the work of Restif de la Bretonne
are more idealized than those in the paintings of
Le Nain, for example. The illustrations found in
medical texts, scandal sheets, and political car-
toons, richly inventive though they may be, are
highly unreliable witnesses to historical reality.
Moreover, images were not always well matched
to their accompanying texts. The meaning of an
engraving may change depending on how it is cap-
tioned (moralistically or otherwise) or what text it

illustrates. Finally, most of the authors of images were men. Few women of the period had access to the means of visual expression, and works by women of so-called popular art adorned relatively fragile materials: fabrics, embroidery, and pastry were highly perishable objects by comparison with wood, china, or clay.

The number of images that could be included in this survey being limited, the selection had to be strict, and a logical, coherent arrangement had to be found. One criterion was a desire to surprise so as to stimulate the reader's interest. In the end intuition was my principal guide.

The material also had to be classified and arranged in some fashion. The images presented here side by side were not intended to be seen by a single audience. Different social groups did not have the same means of expression or access to the same works, although the barriers between them were never completely rigid and became less so over the centuries. In the sixteenth century prints were the common medium for a variety of ideologies and audiences. Frequently a theme was "covered" by more than one image, and an image could refer to more than one theme: in other words, images exploded in all directions; as Pierre Francastel has observed, "every art object is the point of convergence of a variable, possibly large, number of different views of man and of the world."[2]

This iconographic survey takes the form of a leisurely promenade. Its point of departure is the symbolic image of the couple, followed by representations of woman as influenced by the medieval heritage and by Renaissance humanism (figs. 1–3). Next come portrayals of the female body and its distinctive characteristics (figs. 4–17), culminating in the male representation of the female head, where the nature/culture dilemma comes to the fore (figs. 18–23). Stemming from this representation is a series of images depicting the sexual

1. *The Metamorphosis of Hermaphrodite and the Nymph Salmacis,* painting, Jan Gossaert, Flemish School, circa 1517. Rotterdam, Boymans-Van Beuningen Museum.

division of roles, its dangers and its concerns (figs. 24–34). There follow several attempts at female autonomy: painters, writers, mystics, and protesters all seeking escape from the confinement in which women were aware of being held (figs. 35–46). Completing our tour are images portraying the dilemma that arose on the eve of the French Revolution and that later centuries would be left to resolve (figs. 47–48): the sixteenth century's Eve-Mary-Pandora had begun to clamor for political power.

To make images our starting point is to grant them a leading, guiding role: the text follows the pictures. Just as even the most abstract of painters must refer constantly to a motif and the historian to archives, our constant referents will be the images, which are the archives here.

To begin our iconographic series with the image of an intertwined couple (fig. 1) is to underscore the fundamental question we wish to explore: the relation between the male world and the female world. At first glance the painting appears to portray Adam and Eve at the moment of the original sin. Surprisingly, however, Adam's raised arm (lifted toward the apple?) is restrained by Eve's hand. What is more, there is no serpent and no apple tree. And what is the meaning of the two hands on the man's throat, on Adam's apple? This is not the biblical couple at all. Rather, it is the imaginary primordial couple, with no predominance by either sex, the pair being at once differentiated and undifferentiated, two in one, one in two: the hermaphrodite.

Jan Gossaert's *Metamorphosis of Hermaphrodite and the Nymph Salmacis* of 1517 illustrates a story from Ovid's *Metamorphoses*. As the poet tells it, Salmacis fell in love with the handsome Hermaphrodite while he was bathing, and when he spurned her advances she asked the gods to join their two bodies into one. One might interpret this as a myth in which the strength of a woman's passion makes her redoubtable and a man is the victim, but can such a one-sided reading be sustained, given the symmetry of the image and what we know about the painter? Jan Gossaert, considered to be the first painter of the Netherlands to adopt the Italian style, chose his subjects from mythology, biblical history, and the New Testament. That he should have found himself at the crossroads of different painterly and religious cultures is indicative of the complexity of the social and cultural fabric at the dawn of the modern age. The overlapping of legs, the joined, upraised arms, and the man's effort to breathe with the woman's help (or is it hindrance?) illustrate a desire for union and separation, for fusion and autonomy, as well as an alchemist's dream of primitive androgyny. What kind of woman is this, mysterious enough that one can ask whether she is helping or hindering? Above all she is a daughter of Eve.

Medieval representations of women persisted after the dawn of the Renaissance. Berthold Furtmayr painted the miniature *Tree of Life and Death* (fig. 2) for the *Salzburger Missale,* the official missal used by celebrants of the Roman Catholic Church and thus a primary instrument for the transmission of knowledge. Mary and Eve clearly embody the dichotomy of Good and Evil, of Salvation and Mother of All Evils. The Virgin, on the left, plucks from a place on the tree close to a small crucifix the antidote to mortal sin, the host, which she passes on to a cortège of the elect, followed by an angel carrying a scroll bearing the inscription: "Look, this is the bread of angels, the food of pilgrims." On the right, Eve, stunningly nude and the cynosure of all eyes, hands the forbidden fruit, plucked from a spot on the tree close to a death's head, to a cortège of paupers: "She feeds evil." Accompanying those who eat of the forbidden fruit, a skeleton carries a scroll that

reads: "From this tree comes the evil of death and the good of life." Two images of death thus frame the universal mother. Everything in this image is round: the scenic space, the medallions, the tree, the host and the apple, Eve's breasts and stomach—a graphic homage to femininity. Eve's place on the right side of the composition emphasizes her importance and situates her chronologically after the Virgin, as if the figure of Mary did not totally efface the original sin. In this drama of damnation, man is relegated to the background: Christ, the vanquisher of death, appears only as a small figure in the tree; and Adam, the first man, is half hidden. The scene is entirely dominated by the two female presences, with the negative view appearing to outweigh the positive.

Did humanism contribute to an improvement in the status and role of women? The answer is unclear, as the interpretation of Jean Cousin's *Eva prima Pandora* (fig. 3) will show. In this major

2. *The Tree of Life and Death,* miniature from the *Salzburger Missale,* Berthold Furtmayr, Danube School, circa 1481. Munich, Bayerische Staatsbibliothek.

3. *Eva prima Pandora,* painting, Jean Cousin, circa 1540. Paris, Louvre.

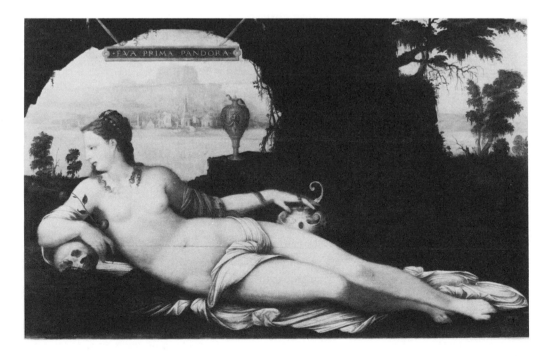

sixteenth-century painting, which is sometimes said to be the first Renaissance nude, an impassive, idealized body is shown along with a death's head, an apple branch, Pandora's vase, and a serpent. The perfect nude is thus accompanied by a number of negative images taken from mythology, the Bible, and ancient as well as contemporary history, all on the theme of the *femme fatale*. The painting is an intricate web of metaphysical, moral, and political allegories.

On the first level the ancient figure of Pandora is superimposed on the biblical figure of Eve. In both traditions woman is the root of all evil. The theme of Eve is medieval; that of Pandora, forgotten in the Middle Ages, was rediscovered and enjoyed great popularity in the sixteenth century. To link the two was not unprecedented, but Cousin's originality was to fuse them in a single figure.

The mystery of the painting is not explained, however. Why is there an ancient city in the background, and why is the serpent in so unusual a position, coiled around Eve's arm? Research by Jean Guillaume, backed by laboratory analyses that reveal the presence of other serpents, has turned up yet a third female image: that of Cleopatra dying from the bite of an asp.[3] The pose of *Eva prima Pandora,* identical with that of the queen of Egypt in several previous engravings (including a celebrated frontispiece by Holbein), enables us to identify Cleopatra, who attracted renewed interest in the sixteenth century as "an avaricious, cruel, lustful woman." Why was the message presented so discreetly? Cautiously, Guillaume suggests an allusion to the royal favorite, the *femme fatale* of the day and one with the most deleterious influence on the central power. Jean Cousin's Eve is formally similar to Cellini's nymph, who, transported to the Château d'Anet, symbolized the mistress of the premises, Diane de Poitiers, vanquisher of the royal stag. Thus, presumably, one more negative heroine was added to the other three. The paradoxical discrepancy between this idealized body and the dangers it concealed cast doubt on the Neoplatonic conception of the Beautiful as a means of access to the Good and betokened a tragic view of existence. In both of these images it is the woman's body that attracts attention. Testimony to the divine by its beauty, it is close to the animal kingdom by virtue of its capacity for reproduction. Curiously, the body's beauty is seen as a danger, whereas its "animal" function is cast in a positive light.

A Terrifying Body

The troubling strangeness of two engravings, one by Martin Heemskerck (fig. 4), the other by Abraham Bosse (fig. 5), is one index of their ambiguity. These "allegories" suggest more or less explicit conceptions of nature, woman, culture, and the earth. *Natura* (fig. 4) shows a woman with many breasts, modeled after the fertility symbols Cybele and Isis, suckling a child in a bucolic landscape, opposite a globe covered with a full panoply of scientific and technological instruments, including a sundial, a beaker, a square, and an hourglass. Nature is the feminine principle of the universe: she is like a good mother, nurturing humankind and the cosmos with her milk, the source of life.

This benevolent nature has another side, however: the savage, destabilizing force of modern science since the scientific revolution.[4] Answering to this new image of nature we have the malefic woman, embodied in the image of a headless female, a leafy vagina, in an engraving by Bosse (fig. 5). The plant is a mandrake, which was used by midwives for its power to make women fertile but also, according to innumerable texts and illustrations, by witches. (Dürer's celebrated *Four Witches* appear beneath a mandrake.)

Ambivalent nature, ambivalent woman. Heems-

Ales, et à primis producit in æra nidis
Iam iam plumantis certo modulamine fœtus,
Hortaturque sequi, breuibusque insurgere pennis;

Sic genus humanum rerum Natura nouatrix
Mollibus è cunis, grauidaq parentis ab aluo,
Ducit ad ærumnas, et duros cauta labores.

4. *Natura,* engraving,
Martin Heemskerck, Dutch
School, circa 1572. Paris,
Bibliothèque Nationale.

5. *Mandragora,* engraving,
Abraham Bosse, French
School, seventeenth
century. Paris, Bibliothèque
Nationale.

kerck opposes woman/nature to the world of technology and culture; Bosse uses a mandrake to symbolize the female sex organ as both boon and
curse, miracle-worker and harbinger of death.

This dualism coloring the view of the female
body is omnipresent in Nicholas Deutsch's *Judgment of Paris* (fig. 6). Ambiguous is the word for
this early precursor of Manet's *Déjeuner sur
l'herbe.* The clothing in the picture is extravagantly
fanciful: Paris wears the garb of a noble German
knight of the period, in contrast to the Botticellian
transparency of Venus. Juno's rich bourgeois costume contrasts with Minerva's erotic parapherna-

Mandragora mas.
Mandragore.

Bosse sculp.

lia. There is also ambiguity in the importance attached to the moralistic content of the "Judgment of Paris" theme, which was linked by long tradition to the theme of original sin, Venus receiving the golden apple being juxtaposed with Eve plucking the apple from the tree. There are numerous painterly allusions: Paris' attitude is the reverse of Adam's in Cranach's woodcut *The Original Sin;* Venus' profile is reminiscent of that of Dürer's *Fortuna,* with the huge wings reduced to a coif, although Venus is standing not precariously but with her feet firmly planted on the ground; and, finally, Minerva's pose is modeled after one of Dürer's *Four Witches.*[5] All these formal allusions attest to the circulation of ideas among artists and show that these themes were not absent from Deutsch's thought; but the only visible trace of the moralistic interpretation that he allows to stand is the relatively insignificant one of the inscription on the tree: "Paris von Troy der Torecht" (Paris of Troy, the Fool). The final ambiguity of the painting lies in the true subject of this gently ironic scene: despite the moralistic and mythological allusions and keys, such as the figure of Paris being perhaps a self-portrait and Venus the likeness of an admired wench, what the painter shows us is an amorous encounter between a man and a woman. Whereas most engravings show Paris with his eyes shut, dreaming his judgment under the influence of Hermes (here transformed into Cupid), Deutsch gives us a Paris with his eyes open and thus able to exchange glances with Venus. The meeting of their hands on the round surface of Venus' belly seals the couple's engagement with a promise of fertility.

The German midwife's sign (fig. 7) is of another order entirely: the woman, because pregnant, is the focus of all available care. In the center of the image the woman's belly is framed by the orna-

6. *The Judgment of Paris,* painting, Nicholas Manuel Deutsch, German School, between 1516 and 1524. Basel, Offentliche Kunstsammlung, Kunstmuseum.

7. German midwife's sign, painting, sixteenth century. Château de Gué-Péan, Loir-et-Cher (France).

mental bands of her gown and surrounded by rigid lines formed by her hair, the arm of the chair, and, most important of all, the midwife's three finger-scissors, which symbolize the three precepts to be followed for a good delivery.

The power of the female belly stemmed from pregnancy and its mystery, and the images in the next few pages show just what a subject of stupor and fear pregnancy was for the society of this period.

Following this moralistic view of the pregnant woman listening to the advice of the midwife, we encounter a more scientific image: the child in its mother's womb, published in the physician Adrian Van Spiegel's *De formatio foetu* in 1631 (fig. 8). In this visual translation of the text, the physician's image of woman as uterus has become the

8. *De formatio foetu,* by Adrian Van Spiegel, plate engraved by Matthieu Merlan, Swiss School, 1631. Paris, Bibliothèque Nationale.

9. *Women Who Have Given Birth to Many Children,* woodcut from the *Almanach for the Year of Grace 1677.* Paris, Bibliothèque de l'Arsenal.

engraver-poet's vision of woman as the bearer of fruit.

In addition to these relatively "reasonable" images, there were innumerable fantastic illustrations. In figure 9, taken from a French almanac for 1677, we see a woman with an external womb and a strangely flat chest. Titled *Women Who Have Given Birth to Many Children,* the woodcut actually refers to a case study published by Ambroise Paré and taken up in pamphlet literature: a woman by the name of Dorothea allegedly gave birth to twenty children in two pregnancies. She was so heavy that her belly dragged on the ground and had to be held up by a sling hung from her neck. Women too fat to give birth otherwise were told to assume incredibly contorted positions, according to one seventeenth-century physician (fig. 10). In 1726 an illiterate peasant named Mary Toft claimed that after being frightened by the sight of one rabbit she had given birth to fifteen (fig. 11).

10. *La comare o riccoglitrice,* woodcut, Scipio Mercurialis, Milan, gynecological treatise, 1618. Paris, Bibliothèque de l'Ancienne Faculté de Médecine.

11. Frontispiece to *A Short Narrative of an Extraordinary Delivery of Rabbits,* engraving, 1727. London, British Library, Harry Price Collection.

The attending physician asked for advice, and the story reached the ears of George I, who dispatched his own physicians to the woman's bedside. A year later, the fraud was uncovered. In the meantime a flood of pamphlets and depositions had divided London into two camps. Almost forty years later Hogarth alluded to the incident in his engraving *Credulity, Superstition, and Fanaticism.*

Like the belly, the breasts served a dual function: as erotic objects they were the primary focus of male fantasy; as sources of nutrition they were the subject of a normative discourse.

The figure of Salomé occupies a small place in *The Feast of Herodias and the Beheading of Saint John the Baptist* (fig. 12), an immense painting (9.52 by 2.8 meters) recently attributed to Bartholomeus Ströbel.[6] The work has given rise to a variety of interpretations: a dazzling fresco of Europe in the early decades of the seventeenth century; a

12. *The Feast of Herodias and the Beheading of Saint John the Baptist* (detail), painting, Bartholomeus Ströbel, Polish School, circa 1630. Madrid, Prado Museum.

204

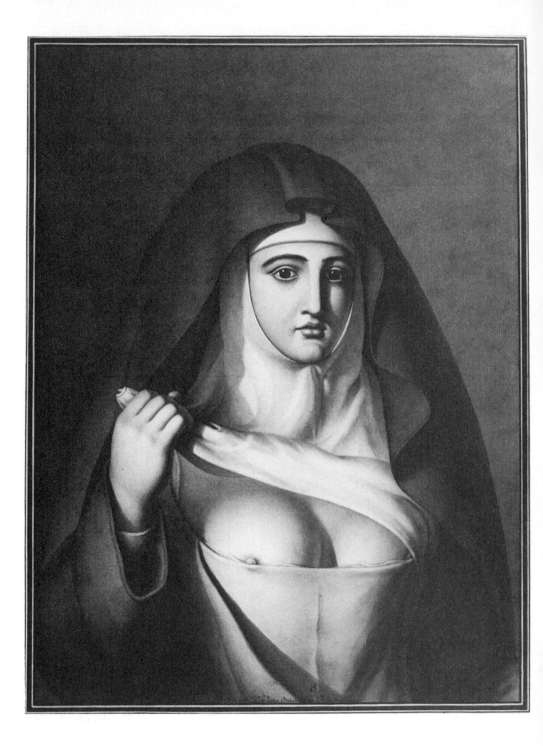

206

political satire on the balance-of-powers policy in-
augurated by Cardinal Richelieu; an allegory of
European follies in the time of the Thirty Years'
War; an allusion to the journey undertaken by the
Prince of Wales and Buckingham to Madrid in
1632 for the purpose of arranging a marriage. But
none of these interpretations matters much by
comparison with Salomé's protruding breasts and
the erotic charge in this extraordinary presentation
of her bosom together with the head of Saint John.
The whiteness of her bare breasts is heightened by
juxtaposition with the bloody red of the severed
head: red and white were the very hues of beauty.
Salomé exhibits her "two little breasts pushed up
high . . . [and] so round that they looked less like
parts of her body than like fruits that happened to
have ripened there."[7] Simultaneously, on a platter,
she offers the fruit of her labor, of her dance. Two
venomous offerings; and this resounding homage
to seduction and perversity is addressed to one of
the most negative of the female figures in the painting. The Church Fathers treated Salomé (whose
name means the Peaceful One, the Pacifier) as the
prototype of the demon-inspired woman, and in
many medieval legends she appears as the queen
of witches and organizer of nocturnal sabbaths.

Contrast the subtle eroticism of mannerist art
with the sensuality of Jean-Jacques Le Queu's sib-
ylline engraving (fig. 13). In the previous image,
Salomé, wearing a damask gown, studded with
jewelry, her doll's face framed by abundant tresses
and crowned with a diadem, appears in the midst
of a crowd of historical figures. In Le Queu's engraving large, round breasts, grazed by a phallus-
like veil, spill out of the austere habit of a solitary
nun whose sensual, determined face is imprisoned
within her cowl. The work is a monochrome sym-
phony in black, grey, and white, a grave, mysterious image of carnal desire in the female, its sexual
and maternal character underscored by the legend:
"And we too shall be mothers, because . . . !"

13. *Et nous aussi nous
serons mères, car . . . !*
(And we too shall be
mothers, because . . . !),
engraving, Jean-Jacques
Le Queu, French School,
1793–94. Paris,
Bibliothèque Nationale.

14. *Allegory of the Power of Women,* drawing, Martin De Voss (?), Flemish School, late sixteenth century. Charles Fairfax Murray collection.

Can this be read as anything other than an allusion to the Civil Constitution of the Clergy, which abolished convents, monasteries, and monastic vows? The year is 1792, and the furor raised by this issue must have influenced the visionary architect, who was fascinated by female sexuality. His nun is as disturbing as Ströbel's Salomé.

The real function of the breast, however, is to feed the newborn. This was a genuine source of power, according to a drawing attributed to Martin De Voss (fig. 14), which is interesting because it admits of two possible interpretations. It can be read as a masculine critique: the woman uses the sovereignty conferred on her by lactation to persuade man to worship idols (the Solomon episode in the upper right corner) or to deprive him of his strength (the allusion to Delilah in the upper left).[8] But it can also be read as a glorification: the nurturing mother redeems the wickedness of the women in the background, and the picture suggests that there is a power more important than any temporal power, the emblems of which lie broken at the mother's feet.

In the eighteenth century the writings of Rousseau and Diderot and the paintings of Jean-Baptiste Greuze contributed to a positive attitude toward breastfeeding. *The Good Mother* (fig. 15), a German porcelain group based on a Greuze painting, attests to the popularity of this new way of

15. *The Good Mother,* porcelain group, Karl Gottlieb Lück, German School, circa 1770. Nuremberg, Germanisches National Museum.

209

16. *La paysanne pervertie,*
by Restif de la Bretonne,
engraving by Louis Binet,
French School, 1784. Paris,
Bibliothèque Nationale.

17. Austrian ex-voto,
1775. Vienna,
Osterreichische Museum
für Volksunde.

JUDGING BY IMAGES

thinking. Now associated with motherhood, the
female breasts and womb were glorified.

Woman's true role was to bring children into
the world, and her offspring were her ornaments.
Louis Binet's engraving (fig. 16) shows Edmé Restif, the father of writer Nicolas Restif de la Bretonne, seated beneath a portrait of his own father
and surrounded by his second wife and fourteen
surviving children. In this well-to-do household it
took two women to produce a family this large.
The scene affords testimony of the degree to which
the ultimate purpose of a woman's life furnished
encounters with death. Women died in childbirth,
and children died in infancy. A votive object from
Austria (fig. 17) shows a peasant couple kneeling
beside eight small bodies, all stillborn, and im-

ploring God: "Dear God, eight children are with you, so send me the ninth." Although the prayer is addressed to God, the intercessor is the Virgin of Seven Dolors with the dead Christ on her knees. The *mater dolorosa* presides over the scene because the suffering woman can identify with her. A "familiar danger, inevitable companion," death hovered over women throughout their lives.

Women's bodies of course had heads on their shoulders, but the question was whether those heads were for thinking. The several images collected here exhibit various positions on this question. All were in wide circulation, with the exception of the frontispiece to Charles Sorel's *Extravagant Shepherd,* which was engraved by Crispin de Passe and known only to the elite. *The Housewife* (fig. 18) offers a down-to-earth view of a woman's chores. All the tools of women's work are present here, from the thimble to the casserole

18. *The Housewife,*
anonymous engraving,
seventeenth century. Paris,
Bibliothèque Nationale.

212

La belle Charite

M. Van Lochom fecit

19. *La belle Charité,*
frontispiece to *Le berger
extravagant* by Charles
Sorel, designed by M. Van
Lochom, engraved by
Crispin De Passe, 1628.
Paris, Bibliothèque
Nationale.

to the inevitable distaff, indicating what the "little
sparrow" could look forward to after her marriage. The face in the masculine counterpart of this
engraving is also made of tools, in the style of
Arcimboldo, but they are for outdoor work,
whereas the woman's tools are for work in the
home and its annex, the barnyard. The tone is
gentle, without bitterness or acrimony. Reigning

213

L'INFLVANCE DE LA LVNE SVR LA TESTE DES FEMMES

Din bon Iour de bon Coeur ma Comere Marguite
Bonne vie et bon an Nicolle au gros Couguiau
Aaga vessi Aghes et Fanne Mine frite.
He hee, et barbe itou auec son gros Muriau
Vramique rauons pretoutes, la lune sur la teste
Buuons et Rigallons puis quil est nostre feste
Haqe, valentin dict barbe que faict dan la notre hôme
Il cherche de la lune vn morcian qui est chu
Car sil la peut trouuer, il aura bonne somme
Mais il ne voit pas Clair il a vn peu trop bu
Lucas en est aussi et sont tous deux si beste
Qu'on ne leur peut montrer quilz sont dessus noz teste

20. *The Influence of the Moon on the Heads of Women,* anonymous engraving, seventeenth century. Paris, Bibliothèque Nationale.

21. *The True Woman,* anonymous engraving, seventeenth century. Paris, Bibliothèque Nationale.

alongside the old housewife with her bun, spectacles, and pipe is *La belle Charité* (fig. 19), a woman whose face is a garden and whose breasts are globes. In Sorel's parody of pastoral fiction the shepherd Lysis is in love with the shepherdess Catherine, whose name he replaces with its near anagram, Charité. He enthusiastically sings the praises of his beloved's beauty to Anselm, a painter friend, who proposes to paint a portrait of Charité based on his description. But the dumbfounded Lysis fails to see the likeness, and Anselm must explain that he painted Charité according to Lysis'

Ce Monstre horrible a double teste,   Considere ce Monstre jnfame
  Passant ne t'effraye il point :   Qui n'entend aucune raison
  Et toutes-fois ô grosse beste   Tu verras que c'est vne femme,
  Tu l'as a tes costes asses souuent conjoint.   Qui est Ange en l'Eglise et diable en la maison

own exact words: a complexion of lily and rose, teeth of coral, radiant suns for eyes, hair like a net bristling with lines and hooks for snaring hearts, and the biggest of all, Lysis', next to her ear, recounting its pain. The satire is interesting not only for its startling visual effect but for its attack, not on the literary women known as Précieuses per se, but on precious language: Sorel was not a precursor of Molière.

Women's heads, whether symbols of common birth or of membership in the intellectual elite, were said to be subject to the influence of the moon, and on this theme the iconography was nearly as vast as that associated with the fight over which sex wears the pants, but far more varied. In figure 20 the moon illuminates a nocturnal scene, its light and its crescents falling on the heads of five pert urban lasses, who decide that "the moon is on our heads. Let's drink and celebrate, because the feast is ours." At first glance the print seems to make gentle fun of women's whims, but a more serious concern underlies the uneasiness that such an image of dancing women evoked: a slight change in the picture—undress the women, place them in a less urban setting—would be enough to turn it into a witches' dance. The association of women with the moon readily conjures up images of nocturnal witchcraft.

The True Woman (fig. 21), an anonymous seventeenth-century engraving, portrays a "horrible two-headed monster . . . an angel in Church and a devil at home." The devil and the woman are perfectly symmetrical, Siamese sisters. The picture suggests no mere change of mood but a simultaneous dual nature: angel and demon.

If not the devil, woman's other double was death (fig. 22). In the realm of the imagination woman was the cause of death, the daughter of Eve, who by her vulnerability to temptation had brought death to humankind (figs. 2, 3). Her sexuality and her beauty, ephemeral and false, made

Mondains qui faictes cas des beautez d'un visage,
Scachez que les aymer, ce n'est pas estre Sage,
Puis que le temps enfin les doibt faire petir,
Nous n'auons icy bas chose aucune asseurée,
Tout change et nostre vie à si peu de durée,
Quen commencent à viure on commence à mourir.

217

her a source of death: the engraving and its legend warn against this danger.

For a woman, moreover, death was doubly terrifying. Not only was she part of the order of nature, but there was even doubt about the existence of her soul; hence the death of her body might mean eternal death.

23. *Si tu la cherches, la voicy,* woodcut, frontispiece to *The Imperfection of Women,* seventeenth century. Paris, Musée des Arts et Traditions Populaires.

The simplest response to the diabolical and death-dealing duplicity of woman was to portray her as a headless monster. The great enigma of the feminine *ratio* was resolved by capital punishment, and woman was finally reduced to her function: decapitated, she reigned over her domain. The woodcut in figure 23 served as a frontispiece to a pamphlet on *The Imperfection of Women,* whose text consists of a series of images each more negative than the last.[9] Woman is "the most imperfect of creatures . . . the scum of Nature . . . the vexation of angels." Headless and therefore good, woman reverts to her true rank as keeper of the flocks and spinner of wool. The wool-spinner was the quintessence of womanhood. A long series of mythical heroines from Penelope to Ariadne, Arachne, and the all-too-well-known Fates made the distaff the fundamental symbol of the feminine condition, its characteristic sign.

Doubt about women's mental powers influenced the sexual division of roles, the partition of space, and the way men and women lived together on a daily basis.

Living Together

"Living together," portrayed in such subjects as the tree of love, the struggle over power between wife and husband, the need for equality, and the world turned upside down, is a theme that transcended national borders, historical eras, and so-

219

24. *The Tree of Love,* earthenware salad bowl, René Legros, 1781. Paris, Musée des Arts et Traditions Populaires.

cial classes and appeared in all forms of art from the most elitist to the most popular. This universality reflects the important moral and social function of marriage. Before a man and woman could live together they had to meet, and meeting is the subject of the illustration on the salad bowl by René Legros (fig. 24).[10] The rural setting suggests a freedom in love that was presumably greater in the country than in the city. Trees of love were more or less the same from the fifteenth to the eighteenth centuries, but in some the men were in the tree, while in others the women were. When the men were on the ground, they used wine, music, and trinkets to seduce the women. Patient cajolers, they refrained from the use of force to dislodge their beautiful prey. Women, on the other hand, displayed aggressive behavior: while they sometimes offered gifts, they also brandished axes and saws, climbed ladders, and tried to lasso their men. Did the inversion of traditional roles require this recourse to violence? If so, what is the identity of the anonymous voice in the bowl's circular legend, which advises the women to attack the tree and stop offering presents? Who is speaking? The women resort to violence not on their own initiative but at someone's suggestion.

Female violence is also at issue when the question is who will wear the pants in the family. The long series of images on this theme can also be divided into two main groups. In the images of the first group (for example, fig. 25) space is divided horizontally. The man and the woman, possibly surrounded by objects associated with gender

25. *Who Will Wear the Pants?* wooden stall, mid-sixteenth century. Hoogstralten, Collegiate Church of Saint Catherine.

221

(trousers/dress, musket/distaff, spade/broom, and so on), fight over something that does not belong to either one. In the second group the man is absent, and all that remains is an emblem of his virility, a phallic pair of trousers, over which women fight, tear one another's hair out, and bite one another amid a whirl of clothing, bare thighs, and exposed breasts. The image stems more from fear of female sexuality than from the question of power as such, and this explains its violence. Here, the pants have become a sexual symbol, whereas in the other set of images the trousers are a symbol of power. If the woman wins, the worst happens: roles are reversed. One popular image of the eighteenth century (fig. 26) shows the husband seated, wearing a headpiece of some sort, holding a distaff, and cradling a child, while his wife, standing, wears a helmet and carries a sword at her side and a musket on her shoulder. The world has been turned upside down. The repetitive nature of these

26. *Woman with Musket, Husband with Distaff,* popular image, seventeenth century. Paris, Musée Carnavalet.

27. *The Housewife and the Hunter,* woodcut from the *Roxburghe Ballads,* 1500–1700. London, British Museum.

images and their lack of pictorial imagination make one wonder if role change could be conceived only in terms of inversion rather than in more inventive forms.

These symbolic images were inspired by everyday life. In reality certain occupations created spaces in which the sexes could mingle to one degree or another. The diagonal division of space in the woodcut from the *Roxburghe Ballads* (fig. 27) separates sexes, social groups, activities, and areas.[11] The nobleman has a mount, mobility, a stretch of forest, and hunting for an occupation, whereas the housewife sits immobile on her stool with her spinning wheel in front of her doorway. The action is also dual: seeing and being seen. The same "panoptic" composition can also be found in urban scenes.

Diagonal composition also characterizes *Fam-*

28. *Family Evening,*
engraving by Claudine-
Françoise Bouzonnet after
a drawing by Jacques
Stella, 1667. Paris,
Bibliothèque Nationale.

ily Evening, an engraving based on a drawing by
Jacques Stella (fig. 28), in which the staircase ban-
isters seem to govern the distribution of light and
darkness. The drawing can be read as revealing a
symbolic frontier separating masculine and feminine spaces. A young man on the women's side of
the composition, probably with his future wife,
provides the only real mingling of the sexes. The
engraving is interesting for other reasons as well.
For one thing, it was executed by a woman, Clau-
dine-Françoise Bouzonnet, Stella's niece (and also
known as Stella-Bouzonnet), who learned a craft
practiced by few others of her sex and earned her
living by it. For another, it shows how an image
could contribute to the diffusion of different ideologies. In the two other extant versions of the drawing, the engravers (Bonnart and Dewismes) added

29. *The Perplexities of Paris,* engraving, François Guérard, French School, circa 1720. Paris, Bibliothèque Nationale.

prescriptive legends that transformed what was only a genre scene into a lesson in accepting the social or cosmic order.[12]

If rural women escaped the limits of their world in fieldwork and at the market, in the cities the streets were the chief place where the sexes

225

30. *Man Cloaked in Malice,* engraving, Abraham Bosse, French School, seventeenth century. Paris, Bibliothèque Nationale.

mingled. The streets were alive not only with people but with news and rumor. *The Perplexities of Paris* (fig. 29) draws on an inexhaustible theme of literature and iconography, illustrating the kinds of behavior and conflict that grow out of inescapable proximity. All the prints on this theme portray the energy and quickness to react characteristic of the common folk of the cities. The animated little figures are shouting things like, "You'll pay for my husband's shop, and for the job you've ruined," "Stop the thief who's stolen my headdress!" and "The *grande Picarde* is going to the poor hospital."

Since this sexual division of roles was not self-evidently justifiable, it was a source of anxiety and worry. Abraham Bosse shows us a worried man, "the sex in mourning," in his *Man Cloaked in Malice* (fig. 30). A century later, this bowed head supported by a bent arm would reappear as a mark of defeat in Goya's *The Sleep of Reason Engenders Monsters.* The monkey seated beside the man in a similar position, the pose of melancholy, is emblematic of the universal artist and a symbol of human folly and passion (also signified, perhaps, by the women's faces on the lining of the cloak). This image is worth dwelling on for a moment: note the magnitude of the man's chagrin. Did the dominant role exonerate him from all worry, from all remorse, from all regret over the failure of "what would all the same be so beautiful, to be two in harmony"? Did it preclude awareness of the injustice done to the other sex? The legend, however, takes us from the ontological and metaphysical sphere to the historical one: the cause of man's woes lies where "those dangerous, malicious animals" nest, namely, in the women's faces in his cloak.

Woman is wicked and dangerous. Her moods must be held in check, her flow of verbiage stanched, her vagina and mouth stopped up. For the vagina the chastity belt was the preferred in-

Je ne vois point que le Graueur   Car s'il est tout chargé de maux,   Tout ce qu'il a de vicieux
Ait pour raison que son caprice,   D'où procedent ils que de testes   Ne vient donc pas de sa nature,
Quand il appelle ce Resueur.   De ces dangereux Animaux,   Ou bien s'il est malicieux,
Vn homme fourré de malice—   Qui trompent les plus fines bestes: Il s'en faut prendre a sa fourrure.

Bosse inuen et sc   le Blond excud auec Priuilege.

31. Saint Babille, wooden stall, sixteenth century. Pont-de-Cé, Sainte-Maurille Church.

strument: although myth attributed its invention to Vulcan, it was actually invented by a man in Padua toward the end of the fourteenth century. As for speech, a misericord underneath a choir stall (fig. 31) bears the image of a woman with a padlocked tongue: this nun or peasant woman also wears a phallic belt that occupies the place of the virile member and calls attention to its absence, the perfect counterpart to the padlocked mouth. Whereas Bosse's engraving was widely circulated, this misericord underneath a stall in Sainte-Maurille Church was all but unknown, being invisible most of the time to ecclesiastics and laymen alike. Who could see this Saint Babille, to whom husbands prayed for a padlock to silence their wives?[13] In women logorrhea was as ineluctable as infidelity, and husbands despaired over this meager compensation for their wives' lack of power. This theme of iconography and literature found increasingly harsh expression, such as Thomas Rowlandson's sadistic drawing of a shoemaker with an awl in his mouth energetically sewing together the lips of a grumpy old woman.

To deny women the right to speak was to judge them to be minors and thus to assume the right to educate them and control their appearance: "Fashion is the name for the way clothes are made at the present time. One must conform to it."[14] What should have been a matter of pleasure and fancy became one of duty and conformity and therefore, before long, of sin and reprehensible excess. The boundaries of sex and rank had to be respected. The frontispiece of *Hic Mulier, or the Man-Woman* (fig. 32) shows clearly that a woman was supposed to respect her sexual nature. The drawing depicts a young woman transformed into a man by cut of hair, a plumed hat, and a dagger, while the barber prepares to do to her companion what Delilah did to Samson. The book was pub-

32. *Hic Mulier, or the Man-Woman,* frontispiece, woodcut, 1620. San Marino, California, The Huntington Library.

229

33. *Universal Masquerade,*
designed by Bonnart,
engraved by Nicolas
Guérard, French School,
seventeenth century. Paris,
Bibliothèque Nationale.

lished in the climactic phase of a long controversy over the impudence of women in copying men's dress. In 1620 James I urged the clergy to do something about this scandalous state of affairs, and his call was also heeded by certain writers: *Hic Mulier* appeared at a time when the masculinization of women in all walks of life was being denounced.[15] A century and a half later anxiety persisted on this score, and Louis-Sébastien Mercier could write in his *Tableau de Paris* that "a woman's clothing ought to have a sex. A woman ought to be a woman from her head to her toes."

Failing to respect the boundaries of rank was the other major taboo. Countless engravings differentiate as sharply between a peasant and a bourgeoise or an aristocrat as between a Turk and a German. There was fear of an unintelligible society. In this sense fashion was violence: conformism compelled the individual not to disturb the divinely (or royally) ordained social order. The system of fashion was also based on elitism, and in this too there was violence: the beauty spots that the seventeenth-century Précieuses applied to their faces constituted a system of signs, a secret language that could be understood only by initiates, a system of exclusion for those not belonging to the same world. There was violence, too, in the luxury of fashion and its association with the ruling class. Some seventeenth-century engravings expressed outrage at the wasteful use of flour for powdering faces: "It's because of your floured noggin that bread costs so much," read the legend of one. Fashion was complex: it was the visible manifestation of a range of economic interests, religious and political imperatives, and social and cultural systems of reference. It governed not only dress but also manners and behavior, transforming the emotions and domesticating the passions. It would find its fullest expression in court society, and the reign of etiquette would prove to be its finest flower. It was this society, in which "the face dis-

appears behind tightly fitted masks,"[16] that Bonnart denounced in the *Universal Masquerade* (fig. 33), which portrays two figures in profile, a man and a woman, each with an array of bizarre masks and wearing wooden shoes and clothing reflecting a composite of the garb of magistrate, bourgeois, and aristocrat; lifting the masks of both figures is "Time, which reveals all." In this "perpetual carnival" the artist shows us the endless variety of fixed and fraudulent masks that both men and women were obliged to wear in high society. The Enlightenment ideal, perhaps unattainable, was that of a transparent, visible society.

Women needed to learn not only how to present themselves but also how to think. The engraving in figure 34, taken from a printed book, sums up the state of education at the end of the ancien régime. The boys learn reading, writing, geometry, and the art of war, while the girls study sewing. Was this image critical or supportive of the ideology it embodies? Without attribution it is impossible to say.

The Emergence of Women

Given these norms, what did women do, or try to do, in order to assert their presence? The next series of images will focus on the emergence of distinctive categories of women.

To single out the works of Artemisia Gentileschi and Clara Peeters (figs. 35 and 36) among those by female artists is to call attention to the means of self-assertion available to minorities: violence and ruse. *Judith and Holophernes* (fig. 35) is a portrait of butchery in amorous poses, of bloody brutality attenuated by the black-and-white reproduction: it is the exorcistic representation of a rape. Artemisia, the daughter of a well-known painter and an artist in her own right, was the victim of a rape that resulted in a five-month

34. Engraving on education, seventeenth century. Paris, Bibliothèque des Arts Décoratifs, Maclet Collection.

35. *Judith and Holophernes,* painting, Artemisia Gentileschi, Italian School, circa 1617. Florence, Galleria Uffizi.

trial and damaged her reputation. Judith, with whom Artemisia identifies, is the opposite of Salomé: she is the "good," virtuous woman who cuts off a man's head. The violent arrangement of limbs suggests several kinds of action. A birth, for one:

Holophernes' head emerges from a space between two arms that can be mistaken for two thighs on a bloody bed, as if snatched from a mother's entrails by two "midwives." A rape, for another: a man is violated by two women. And a ritual sacrifice, for a third. Roland Barthes has called attention to the abrupt reversal of roles and the assertion of female power, and no doubt he is right; but even more the picture suggests the neutralization of one violence by another: the painting is a form of exorcism. It has, moreover, attracted abundant commentary. Daniel Buren, for example, claims that it is all but impossible to interpret. The painting's vision "is definitively lacking, and just as cruelly as Holophernes lacks his head."[17] Is it a matter of too much female violence?

In contrast, let us turn to a tranquil still life

36. *Still Life with Vases, Goblets, and Shells,* painting, Clara Peeters, Flemish School, 1612. Karlsruhe, Staatlische Kunsthalle.

(fig. 36), to another world and another way of life. Clara Peeters occupies an important place in the history of the still life. One, painted in Karlsruhe in 1612, remains her masterpiece: the goblets and shells in the painting reflect the contemporary taste for chambers of marvels, collections of *curiosa* created by man or nature. The greatest of these marvels, and the one that makes the painting interesting to us, is the self-portrait reflected in each of the seven spherical bosses of the goblet. At first glance we see a sumptuous still life, but if we look again we see the painter calmly asserting "I am here" in seven tiny portraits, each less than half an inch high. Artemisia Gentileschi made her name known with a violent composition, Clara Peeters with a quiet artifice.

Knowing how to read and write was another kind of independence. Figures 37 and 38 offer two images of women writing, two presentations of the woman of letters. The first, painted about 1555, is of Lady Dacre, her face austere, her mouth tight, her stare vacant. Her imposing black bulk signifies that she is a widow. Her hands are occupied with writing. In the upper left corner of the composition is a portrait of her late husband, painted by Holbein in 1540. She is struggling with a difficult fate: her husband, accused of having killed one of his guards one night in April 1541, was hanged in June of that year. Since then she had worked for the rehabilitation of her husband's memory, which she would finally obtain in 1558. It is no accident that she was painted in the act of writing: as a widow she enjoyed full civil and legal rights and could act as a responsible party.

The second image is also of a woman writing under the watchful gaze of her husband's portrait, but she wears domestic clothing and writes in the intimacy of a library-study filled with personal objects—the very image of eighteenth-century pri-

37. *Lady Dacre,* painting, Hans Eworth, Flemish School, circa 1555. Ottawa, National Gallery of Canada.

vacy. The woman is Countess Ulla von Tessin, wife of Sweden's special ambassador to France and a great collector of French art. She is shown at work on her *Portraits of Illustrious Men,* and this watercolor by Olaf Fridsberg exemplifies another type of relation between men and women, one of intellectual and emotional understanding. These two portraits are separated by two centuries, but the need to portray the woman beneath her husband's gaze remains unchanged.

Another kind of writing beneath the gaze of another kind of Husband was that of the mystics. While the biblical position of women remained unchanged, the grammar of gestures by means of which spiritual joy was dramatized through bodily poses changed considerably: ecstasy, love, and even childbirth all served as metaphors. Some women were shown with their eyes closed, fas-

38. *Countess Ulla Tessin in Her Study,* watercolor, Olaf Fridsberg, Swedish School, eighteenth century. Stockholm, National Museum.

tened on an inner vision, others with their eyes open and raised heavenward. The body expressed the inexpressible. The relation to the divine took two forms. One involved the ecclesiastic and social hierarchy: this was the path of religion. The other involved a direct, immediate relation to the divine word: this was the path of mysticism, a "reaction against the appropriation of the truth by clerics . . . It gave priority to the illumination of the illiterate, the experience of women, the wisdom of lunatics, the silence of children."[18] A dialogue of love was established: "In the future you will be responsible for my honor like my true wife. My honor is yours and yours is mine," Christ is supposed to have said to Theresa.[19] "If that is love, then I am familiar with it," the writer Charles de Brosses exclaimed at the sight of Bernini's statue of Theresa of Avila (fig. 39), thereby obliterating the spiritual reality of the vision and its impact on Theresa's life, for what she felt was a compulsion to act and write that made her the focal point of apparently contradictory impulses: a mystic and a realist, a contemplative and a "businesswoman," a woman and a man. Theresa was the only female

39. *The Ecstasy of Saint Theresa,* sculpture, Bernini, Italian School, 1641–1651. Rome, Church of Santa Maria della Vittoria.

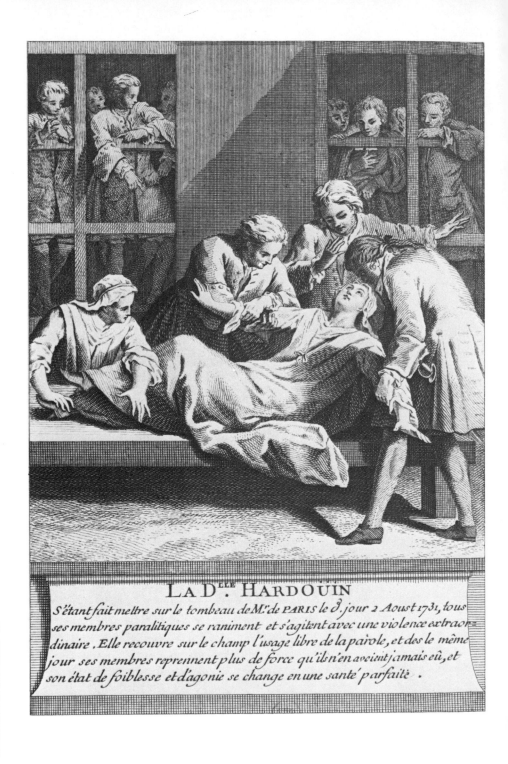

LA D.^{ELLE}. HARDOUIN

S'étant fait mettre sur le tombeau de Mr de PARIS le 8. jour 2 Aoust 1731, tous ses membres paralitiques se raniment et s'agitent avec une violence extraordinaire. Elle recouvre sur le champ l'usage libre de la parole, et dès le même jour ses membres reprennent plus de force qu'ils n'en avoient jamais eû, et son état de foiblesse et d'agonie se change en une santé parfaite.

"doctor of the Church," and her body continued to play a role after her death in the form of relics that revealed a "hunger for messages direct from heaven."[20]

Another message direct from heaven was the strange spectacle that unfolded from 1728 to 1732 in Paris' Saint-Médard cemetery (fig. 40). It all stemmed from the papal bull *Unigenitus* of September 1713, which condemned Jansenism. This led to protests by the working people of the Saint-Médard parish; alleged miracles and miraculous cures occurred around the grave of the deacon François de Pâris, who died in 1727. The cemetery was turned into something resembling both a hospital and a theater, in which the majority of actors were women of the lower classes. In 1731 one Louise Hardouin gave the first public account of healing convulsions accompanied by "frightful pains and movements so violent that those present believed I had succumbed to the *haut mal*." As Hardouin and others testified to their experiences, their response to the loss of God and to the lack of support for their cause from priests and political authorities could be read in marks on their bodies, which were like parchments bearing the textual evidence for a Christian God who had chosen the Incarnation to attest to his existence.

At the opposite extreme from these dispossessed and excluded women were those whose power derived from their rank: queens. Royal imagery took two diametrically opposed forms: allegory and satire. Consider, by way of example, two queens different in every possible way—country, period, religion, iconography, and destiny: Elizabeth I of England, a queen in the full sense of the word, born in the country she ruled and creator of her own iconography, of court-commissioned paintings destined to be seen only by an elite; and Marie-Antoinette, a queen-consort, a foreigner who fell victim to the mocking prints of her that circulated among the populace.

40. *La demoiselle Hardouin,* engraving, Restout, 1731, in *The Truth of Miracles Challenged,* by Carré de Montgeron, Cologne, 1745–1747. Paris, Bibliothèque Nationale.

41. *Queen Elizabeth I and the Three Goddesses* (detail), painting, Hans Eworth (?), 1569. Hampton Court Palace.

The painting attributed to Hans Eworth in figure 41 points up the distance between the eye of the sixteenth century and that of the twentieth. To us, the central figure, the only one in motion in an otherwise static composition, appears to be fleeing. To the cultivated elite of the sixteenth century for whom the picture was intended, the true theme was immediately recognizable because the spectators understood the painting's emblematic language: it was of course the Judgment of Paris. Elizabeth appears in the canvas as a veritable icon. The background, full of roses and Tudor coats of arms, glorifies her. Merely by appearing with the insignia of power (the scepter, crown, and orb), she routs the three powerful goddesses. The queen awards herself the role of Paris, but standing: she is a woman by her appearance but a man by her

Les deux ne font qu'un

role. Queen and virgin, Elizabeth is seen to be of another essence, different from the common run of mortal women.

In contrast to an Olympian setting, at the other extreme of royal imagery we have animals in a sty; instead of the English royal virgin, we have the French royal couple portrayed as a hybrid beast. In *The Two Add Up to Just One* (fig. 42), Louis XVI is a goat attached to the rear of his dominating wife, Marie-Antoinette, a female hyena with her head covered by snakes. Although the two monarchs appear to have equal parts in the makeup of this hybrid monster, which is impotent because it has two heads and because its two parts are pulling in opposite directions, the caricature is not impartial. Louis XVI, described in the text accompanying the picture as a "domestic pig," is

42. *The Two Add Up to Just One,* caricature of Louis XVI and Marie-Antoinette after the flight to Varennes, June 22, 1791. Paris, Bibliothèque Nationale.

243

43. *The Discovery of
Witches,* woodcut,
Matthew Hopkins,
London, 1647. Paris,
Bibliothèque Nationale.

blamed for stupidity, passivity, and ineptitude. His wife, however, who as a woman and a foreigner remained the favorite target of caricaturists, is credited with the usual litany of female vices. The cuckold horns that Louis wears symbolize her alleged lustfulness and sexual insatiability. Her pride and vanity are signaled by the peacock feathers on her head (perhaps also an allusion to the strange hats worn by the women of the period). Her thirst for blood is indicated by her portrayal as a hyena, a scavenger that feeds on carcasses (the paupers who starved to feed her extravagant tastes). She is a harbinger of death, symbolized by the serpents on her head, "so many phalluses,"[21] which link the queen to Medusa, whose fate—decapitation—she will also share.

Such zoomorphic representations were also extended to another class of women: witches. The iconography of witches is extensive, owing to their mythical and historical dimensions. Images of witchcraft reached audiences of all levels in all countries in all periods, even in places where the peculiar practice of witch hunting was unknown. Goya is an excellent example of the pervasiveness of the myth. When history and myth combined, iconography was at its richest. The woodcut in figure 43, which appeared in Matthew Hopkins' famous *Discovery of Witches* (1647), gives us a full-length portrait of the celebrated "Witch Finder Generall" (as Hopkins called himself) in the course of interrogating two witches and is as literal a rendering of the two old women's stories as the portrait of La Belle Charité was of her lover's description. Elizabeth Clark, an old, one-legged beggar, speaks of her "imps" (incarnations of the devil), which are images of the hybrid and incomplete. The other old woman gives her imps names, Hopkins tells us, "that no mortal could invent." English depictions of witches generally included a great array of fauna, whereas German and French engravings often showed the witch turning into an animal herself. Here, the two old women are seated in a room, in the static pose and indoor setting customary for women, whereas witches were usually associated with marshes or other wastelands and were generally itinerant. The inversion was typical. Traditional female objects were put to deviant uses: brooms were used to escape from domestic space; healing ointments became balms to attract demons; caldrons were used for cooking fetuses or simmering diabolical concoctions. But this inverted world was not merely symbolic: hundreds of women paid with their lives for the disorder they had supposedly sown.

Similar to a witch, Brueghel's celebrated *Dulle Griet* (fig. 44) introduces us to the world of warfare. A gigantic woman advances through a hellish landscape full of symbols taken from alchemy and from the paintings of Hieronymus Bosch. She wears a caldron for a crown, brandishes a sword, sports an iron gauntlet on her left hand, carries a gold chest under her armpit, and is laden with pots and baskets filled with absurd booty. She stares fixedly ahead, heedless of the disorder all around, and is a central element of the composition owing to the place she occupies, her outlandish size, and the extensive areas of color in her clothing.

Is she the proverbial "enraged woman going to hell sword in hand," a sort of Don Quixote of greed, a prefiguration of *Mother Courage,* or is she merely a symbol for implacable War, which destroys everything in its path? Behind Margot the Wicked or the Unfortunate, a small form clad in white, the good Margaret (Saint Margaret of Antioch) triumphs over the devil, whom she binds to a cushion, while around her a troop of little women fights valiantly with a band of demonic spirits. In fact the scene is full of women, and the only male figures are infernal or allegorical. Might this be Brueghel's recognition of the good and bad sides of women? The allegory may be more ambiguous than it seems. Is she good? Is she wicked?

Dulle Griet is "the irruption of feminine violence in the collective consciousness of turbulent sixteenth-century Europe."[22]

44. *Dulle Griet,* painting, Pieter Brueghel, Dutch School, circa 1563–64. Antwerp, Mayer Van der Bergh Museum.

Urs Graf's drawing *Lancer and Girl* (fig. 45) is the most realistic of the images assembled here. Like Jacques Callot's drawings it is taken from life, a sketch undistorted by moralism, symbolism, or propaganda. Graf was ideally placed to observe the military life. His young wench, with her purse and dagger attached to her petticoat, is one of the countless vagabonds who joined armies, usually as soldiers' slatterns, and participated publicly in battles, raids, and the division of the spoils.

Women also entered the public arena through riots. Bread riots were the best-known occasions, but women also participated in religious protest,

248

particularly in the sixteenth century, as well as in political disturbances. Lucas Cranach's drawing (fig. 46) is a sketch for a propaganda tract in favor of the Protestant Reformation. Women—both townswomen and peasants, young and old—attack monks and priests with flails and pitchforks. There is nothing surprising about their choice of victim: ecclesiastics were a favorite target of Lutherans and women alike and had long been seen as the root of all evil, the embodiment of lust, and a permanent temptation. On the other hand, even allowing for Cranach's well-known fascination with female cruelty, the fact that a man would call for female violence is in some ways surprising, especially at a time when such violence was widely denounced in both word and image.

Spreading rumors around the city, the young English propagandist in figure 47 wears her convictions on her bodice. Dominating the composition by her placement and size, she is accompanied

45. *Lancer and Girl,* quill drawing, Urs Graf (circa 1485–1527?), Swiss School. Berlin, Archiv für Kunst und Geschichte.

46. *Five Monks Beaten by Women,* Lucas Cranach the Elder, German School, circa 1537. Berlin-Dalhem, Preussischer Kulturbesitz.

47. *The Wilkes Riots,*
designed by John Collet,
engraved by Okey, English
School, 1768. London,
British Museum.

by two other women, who distribute tracts to prisoners and attempt to press them on the soldiers,
as well as by a little girl with a suffragist doll. This
woman supports the liberation of John Wilkes, the
friend of Diderot and d'Holbach who was sentenced to prison in 1768 for his progressive ideas.
The scene is set outside a London prison some
twenty years before the French Revolution.

What Louis Boilly shows us in *The Triumph
of Marat* (fig. 48) is the acme of the "good" revolution, the one in which women took part. The
date is April 24, 1793. The Friend of the People
(Marat) is being carried in triumph to the hall
where the Convention is meeting. This was an
example of a spontaneous revolutionary celebration, before the codification of such events as civic
festivals. Among the people acclaiming Marat, one

face, the only one turned toward the spectator, intrigues us. The figure is hard to make out: wearing the bonnet of a sans-culotte and a revolutionary cockade, it could be a young woman dressed as a man or a young man with an effeminate face. Is it perhaps Boilly, as comparison with other portraits suggests, or is it the revolutionary woman leader Théroigne de Méricourt, as tradition has it? Boilly, his republican sentiments questioned by a jealous rival, painted this work to confound his detractors; it was completed in 1794. Was the painter paying homage to a heroine in disgrace, one who was not present at the scene any more than he was? Or was he more tempted to portray himself? For women, in any case, this was a turning point in the Revolution: three months later Marat was murdered by Charlotte Corday, a "fe-

48. *The Triumph of Marat,* painting, Louis Boilly, French School, 1794. Lille, Musée des Beaux-Arts.

251

49. *Das Schweigen,* painting, Johann Heinrich Füssli, Swiss School, circa 1799. Zurich, Kunsthaus.

male Judas," and in November 1793 a decree ordered all women's clubs and societies closed, stifling women's speech for a long time to come.

Comparison of Boilly's painting with Johann Heinrich Füssli's (fig. 49) highlights the gravity of what was at stake at the end of the eighteenth century: would women be allowed to participate in public life or sent back to live in silence? *Das Schweigen,* the title of Füssli's painting, means silence, muteness, keeping one's peace. Given Füssli's usual fascination with curls and waves of hair, the lightness and mobility of his Shakespearean heroines, and his interest in faces, the absence of all these attributes here makes it clear how desolate he wished to make this woman appear: seated, her face hidden and shoulders drooping, she presents herself to us in a starkly frontal pose. Her attitude is one of total abandonment, of complete alienation from public life—a woman huddled around her inner self. A hundred years later Edvard Munch would use a similar frontal pose to express fear and anguish in the face of the world.

At the conclusion of this iconographic survey, it is clear that the "mirror of women" reflects some constant features despite the variety of possible interpretations and the meanings imposed in some cases by captions. Noteworthy first of all is the dichotomy of the female image: angel/devil, goddess/animal, life/death, Eve/Mary. Woman is nearly always denied an average, "normal" position. Certain themes are constant and ubiquitous: the association of woman with the moon, the struggle over who will wear the pants, the effeminate man, the Judgment of Paris, the headless woman (from Neolithic statuettes to Marcel Duchamp's last painting or Max Ernst's *Femmes cent têtes,* men persisted in showing women without heads), hysteria in the female body. Finally, sexual transgression was a major taboo: women were

dangerous if they spoke out or adopted men's clothing or characteristics. To do so was to turn the world upside down. Woman's privileges were turned against her. Her many visions of the world, depending on her "menstrual moods," the total satisfaction she felt in bringing children into the world, her ability to give life—all these things made her both an object and a subject of fear and led to doubts about her ability to think, hence to her exclusion from all the realms of *ratio* (reason).

I write as an iconographer among historians. My particular way of seeing things has of course influenced my findings. Some of the images that generally excite historians are not highly valued as art, whereas others are emphasized.[23] Is my choice of images perhaps too subjective? Has some sort of unconscious anorexia banished all images of the kitchen, the center of woman's power?

My text has yielded precedence to the image, and the reader has had to pay an inevitable price: The conventions of textual discourse, the transitions expected in academic writing, are hard to accommodate to the immediacy of visual interrelationships. I therefore end this visual promenade with these words of Roger Caillois: "I regret more and more the offensive brevity of this text. The bolder pages can scarcely do more than set the reader dreaming, or at best serve as a point of departure for reflection."[24]

TRANSLATED FROM THE FRENCH
BY ARTHUR GOLDHAMMER

two

So Much Is Said
about Her

What Are *Women Anyway?*

Gender was talked about and women were pictured throughout
early modern Europe, but certain themes and structures were
common to most of the representations. Whether likened to
males or limned as different, women were somehow inferior to
men. The habit of hierarchical thinking remained strong with
regard to the sexes, a foretaste of European conceptions of
New World peoples and Africans. That the well-ordered father-
dominated family was considered both a foundation and a metaphor for the well-ordered state surely reinforced the hierarchical
mode. Even when the heavens lost their distinctive ethereal qualities for the natural philosophers, and aristocratic birth was challenged as a claim to superior status, reasons were found to con-
strain women much more than men on the basis of alleged
sexual traits.

Not that all women were identical in their disabilities. They
came either very bad or very good, as Françoise Borin has
shown in her essay on artistic representations: Eve and Mary
(Eve more sinful than Adam, Mary less sacred than Jesus), the
whore and the chaste wife, the benevolent figure of charity and
the terrifying emblem of war and destruction. Even at their best,
they were deemed to lack full powers of reason.

Much of this imaging was done by men for male spectators
or readers. It drew upon ancient traditions, current conventions,
and professional rivalries; upon experience with women, intimate and remote; and upon male hopes, fantasies, and fears.
The resulting portraits and prescriptions were not as monovalent
as these broad strokes may suggest. Authors such as Rabelais
left loopholes for contrary interpretation (who is more blame-
worthy in his *Tiers livre:* the wife who will always cuckold her
husband or the obsessive Panurge who wants guarantees of a
kind that no one has the right to expect from another person?).
Comic genres turned gender hierarchies upside down: controver-

sies among naturalists and moralists invited readers to take their pick among different positions. Even Rousseau had some second thoughts.

Jean-Paul Desaive employs the term *feminine counterculture* in his description of the play of gender in early modern literature. As women became readers and then authors of literary works, the writings took on meanings and brought pleasures that male creators had not imagined. For the men, women served as a pretext for writing (a beloved or a muse), as readers in need of moral instruction, and as vessels for the author's dreams. More flesh-and-blood people emerge when Desaive turns to writers working outside poetry and the novel: the sixteenth-century Etienne Pasquier softening hierarchy by an image of companionate marriage, Mme. de Sévigné exuding the joys of independence, James Boswell charming his female conquests while confining his friendships to men.

The theatrical world described by Eric Nicholson also had its ambiguities. Even after women were allowed to be present as spectators and actors, the stage was both a witty and a dangerous place, where stereotypes of patriarchal marriage were called into question even if their foundation was never undermined. Plots worked themselves out and actors, often cross-dressed, played their roles in such a way that the transgressive prostitute or adulteress might come off better than the prudish maiden, and tyrannical husbands might be mocked more than disobedient wives. When women such as Aphra Behn began to write plays, the resulting attack on enforced marriage was even stronger than Molière's.

There were no Aphra Behns among those setting the Enlightenment discourse about women and gender. Michèle Crampe-Casnabet's essay shows the eighteenth-century philosophers making free adult men the model for universal Man. "Woman" was a special case, assumed by most of the *philosophes* to be endowed with a reason more concrete and less abstract than Man's. Limited by their sexuality and their bodies, women were at their worst in Montesquieu, using their charm to dominate men, and at their best in Rousseau, living to please men, and in Kant, guiding men toward higher morality. A few thinkers refused this compromise with universality: Helvétius insisted on equal education and Condorcet on equal access to citizenship for women. Women could also use Enlightenment arguments to different ends, as when Mary Wollstonecraft reasoned against Rousseau in her *Vindication of the Rights of Woman.*

Women's bodies were what supposedly caused them all this trouble, as Evelyne Berriot-Salvadore shows in her essay on medicine and science. Controversy persisted throughout our three centuries as male physicians tried to learn more about women's mysterious orifices and insatiable sexual appetite. Was the female an incomplete and inferior male, as Aristotle and Galen had asserted, her sexual organs those of the man turned inside out? Or was she rather a fully formed physical being, possessed (in another of Galen's views) of that singular organ, the uterus, source of motherhood and the "furies" of hysteria? Did she contribute seed to conception along with the male, or just food for the fetus? When the microscope revealed eggs and sperms, the argument then became which was more important. Throughout, whether the physician was working within the older doctrine of resemblances between body and nature or the newer mechanistic philosophy of the late seventeenth century, medical description was used to ground women's roles and to account for alleged female instability. At least there was some space in the controversy for concern about women's health and for attention to women's pleasure, believed to be required for or to facilitate conception. And when midwives began to write about their art, they used this discourse in similar ways (an angry womb leads to sterility), but also turned it to their own interests, claiming against the male surgeons interloping into their domain that modest women required healers of their own sex.

By the late eighteenth century, a competing image of woman was emerging, complete with her own organs, fragile rather than furious, educated enough to be a pleasing companion to her husband and a proper mother for her children. But the cases presented here suggest that it, too, was overdetermined, linked to other cultural practices, and available for mixed interpretation by men and women both.

N.Z.D.–A.F.

8

The Ambiguities
of Literature

Jean-Paul Desaive

Women as Pretext

LITERARY TEXTS THREATENED women in
many ways, not least by celebrating their femininity at the expense of their individuality. Women
were present in sixteenth-century French poetry
for only one reason: to enable the poet to demonstrate his talent. Fatal glances, pink-and-white
complexions, and lethal charms served to emphasize the merits of the male martyr; women themselves were reduced to mere appearances. Among
the three or four sixteenth-century poems that,
owing to the mysterious alchemy of time and textbooks, people educated in France can still recite
today is this sonnet by Ronsard:

> Quand vous serez bien vieille, au soir, à la
>   chandelle,
> Assise auprès du feu, dévidant et filant,
> Direz, chantant mes vers, en vous
>   émerveillant:
> "Ronsard me célébrait, du temps que j'étais
>   belle!"
>
> Lors, vous n'aurez servante oyant telle
>   nouvelle,
> Déja sous le labeur à demi sommeillant,

Qui au bruit de Ronsard ne s'aille réveillant,
Bénissant votre nom de louange immortelle.

Je serai sous la terre, et, fantôme sans os,
Par les ombres myrteux je prendrai mon repos:
Vous serez au foyer une vieille accroupie,

Regrettant mon amour et votre fier dédain.
Vivez, si m'en croyez, n'attendez à demain:
Cueillez dès aujourd'hui les roses de la vie.

You will become old. You will learn to knit
And read by candlelight when you are sleepless
The poems here, that made you marvelous.
You were beautiful.

                  Already drowsy with firelight
And the tedious march of words, you catch
And start. The book makes blessings on you.
It is my name—Ronsard—against your fingers;
A name you have heard spoken with real sound.

I will be tangled in the roots of myrtle.
A boneless ghost, a shadow hovering
Below the skin of earth. You, crippled

With age, will find bare
Memory in your arms—my love, your proud refusal,
And the stripped stem from which the rose has fallen,
And its leaves; unless you take me, living, now.[1]

It is of some significance that this magnificent and menacing text comes to us from a poet who achieved sufficient glory in his lifetime that he could count on it long afterward to awaken the obscure but necessary servant who is the companion of this old Helen, described first as "seated" and later as "squatting." We have here two images of woman's dependence and inferiority: fatiguing toil and degrading old age. We also have an image of solitude and abandonment, which takes Helen from today's triumph among the queen's maids of honor to the ignoble (and unlikely) companionship of a single servant. All that is durable in this woman comes to her from the poet, but as a pure reflection of his own glory: without Ronsard there would be no "immortal praise," and without immortal praise there would be no Helen. Q.E.D.

It would be one thing if there were only this one sonnet and this one Helen. We admire this poem for its admirable unity of idea and form, but these qualities are somewhat diluted when the poem is read in the context of the 136 other poems to Hélène that seem to be either drafts or reprises of the same theme of needless regret. And the poet's *Amours de Cassandre* and *Marie* take a similar line. Another poet of the time, Philippe Desportes, turned out no fewer than 155 sonnets on the *Amours de Diane*, 88 on the *Amours d'Hippolyte*, 104 on *Cléonice*, and forty more in *Diverses amours*, to say nothing of chansons, stanzas, elegies, *plaintes*, and *complaintes*. "Here is the record of my woes!" he proclaimed. What was the good of so many rhymes, of "paying with regrets, sighs, works, flames, and tears / for rejection, my sole reward?"[2] The answer is simple: the reward lay not in cruel beauty's arms but in the literary glory that inclined the prince to generosity. Desportes, for his part, was rewarded with several abbeys, one, it is said, in payment for a single sonnet. There was also reward in the interest of a broad audience in a form of cultural recreation not unrelated to today's advertising: this poetry, like our advertisements, purveyed an image of woman distorted by male fantasy, an image that women, like it or not, were obliged to reckon with. The mute goddesses perched on pedestals above clouds of incense could scarcely decline the poets' homage.

The Renaissance celebrated beauty as a perceptible manifestation of the divine and praised woman as the exaltation of this divine essence.[3] Maurice Scève's *Délie* is perhaps the most highly polished of these Neoplatonic monuments to Love: the "original force that creates the harmony of the world is a precondition of spiritual asceticism . . . from which carnal possession is excluded."[4] Sir Philip Sidney's unhappy loves in *Astrophel and Stella* are similarly purified and metaphorical. In all the 108 sonnets and 11 songs dedicated to his beloved, Sir Philip ventures to steal just one kiss from her while she sleeps.[5]

The torrent of verse that inundated Europe in the sixteenth century was filled with miracles of emotion and beauty and accompanied by a harmonious hodgepodge of high-flown rhetoric and learned references to mythology. Invariably, however, the poet sang of his own transports, his sempiternal wounds, his thousand deaths: a narcissistic one-man show in which women served as a pretext but not as a genuine presence. Sometimes, tired of endlessly repeating the same message, the benumbed lover changes his tone: the ever-inventive Ronsard, for example, dedicated a rather risqué ode to chambermaids, who could be far less fussy than high-born ladies:

> L'amour des riches Princesses
> Est un masque de tristesse:
> Qui veut avoir ses esbas
> Il faut aimer en lieu bas.

The love of rich princesses is a mask of sadness: he who wants to have a romp must love in low places.[6]

But beware: this is still a literary commonplace. Is there no escape from cliché? Rarely; as for example in this poem by a woman who does not play games, Louise Labé:

> Je vis, je meurs: je me brûle et me noye
> J'ay chaut estrème en endurant froidure.

I live, I die: I burn and drown. Though enduring cold I feel extreme heat.

Or, once again, Ronsard: in the midst of the highly conventional *Bocage royal* we find a surprising "discours," which describes a young man's thwarted love for his cousin with all the vehemence and bitterness of actual experience. In this case the impediment to true love comes not from the beautiful beloved but from the obstinate refusal of the young man's mother to permit a marriage that everyone else wants. The lover's father sympathizes with his son's distress but can do nothing about it:

> . . . pour autant que vieillesse m'a fait
> Par maladie impotent et desfait
> Je ne sçaurois à ton vouloir complaire,
> Car désormais ce n'est plus mon affaire
> De me mesler de noces, ni de rien:
> Le seul vouloir de ta mère est le mien.

Because old age and illness have left me weak and helpless, I cannot grant your wish. It is no longer my business to get involved in weddings or anything else. Your mother's wish is mine.[7]

The unexpected interference of this omnipotent and despotic mother by itself underscores all that is artificial in the thousands of lines of poetry surrounding this strange "discours." In the remainder of this chapter I shall explore, in a variety of examples, the relations among authors, works, readers, and the times.

The Edified Woman

The scene is sixteenth- and seventeenth-century England and France: the heart of Christendom in a time of conflict and controversy, Reformation against Counter-Reformation, Jesuit against Jansenist, Puritan against libertine. Politics and theology were inextricably intertwined in a turmoil that was at once fervent and violent. Women were caught up in the turbulence along with everyone else. What place did they have in the outpouring of literature on questions of faith, salvation, and religious practice?

Catholic literature ascribed certain duties to women by virtue of their sex. "Each vocation needs to practice its own specific virtue: different from one another are the virtues of a Prelate, a Prince, a Soldier, a married woman, a widow . . . Each person must subscribe particularly to those [virtues] required by the way of life to which he [or she] is called."[8] Gentleness, compassion, and maternal love are among the innate virtues of the female sex. Thus works of mercy and charity fall naturally to women: the care of the sick, the poor, and the elderly. Women make children; hence they are responsible for the early upbringing of their offspring, including religious instruction and training in manners. Moreover, since women are confined to the home and given charge over domestic arrangements, they are also responsible for household management and maintenance and for overseeing the servants. Obedience and chastity make them first dutiful daughters, then loyal wives. Protestant discourse, at once more egalitarian and more demanding, cast the wife as virtually her spouse's alter ego but from very early on also required her to breastfeed the children and to oversee their education and moral development; she was also expected to be a partner with her husband in the management of the family's wealth, and if the husband left home or died, his wife assumed responsibility for worship at home and for arranging the marriage of her children—in other words, for the family honor: "For the propagandists of the Reformation, a woman's life—the life of a wife, housekeeper, and mother—was an individual enterprise as well as a form of personal asceticism, indeed almost of heroism, and in any case the fulfillment of a promise."[9] The steady marginalization of the Huguenots in France allowed the circulation to a broad public of works intended not so much to persuade readers of the benefits of orthodoxy as to reconcile religion with civility.

Saint Francis of Sales was perhaps asking a great deal of women exposed to worldly temptations when he admonished them in 1608. Sympathetic followers tried to convey his message, modified to suit the times, to the respectable ladies they heard in the confessional and frequented in the salons. The Franciscan Jacques du Bosc reveals interesting things about the realities of life in the mid-seventeenth century.[10] Addressing "the Ladies" to persuade them "that there is no need to be unsociable in order to be virtuous," he begins his book *L'honneste femme* with an apologia for reading, conversation, and reverie, "the soul's noblest occupations": "Through Reading, we entertain the dead; through Conversation, the living; and through Reverie, ourselves. Reading enriches memory, Conversation polishes wit, and Reverie shapes judgment." In giving priority to reading as being "necessary to all Ladies," the author defines his public: it is urban (or aristocratic), select, "respectable," and idle. What books ought to be read? Surely he had religious works in mind, but for some reason he does not mention any but the *Introduction à la vie dévote,* to which *L'honneste femme* was intended as a kind of introduction. Besides this work, women ought to read history, philosophy, and the poets, because "examples from myth are more amusing than examples from history." Never mind that the authors were pagan (since they belong to antiquity): better to read their good precepts than to pervert oneself by reading novels. Not surprisingly, Father du Bosc advises women to take better care of their reputations than of their appearance: they should be chaste, constant, faithful, prudent, and gracious and not too flirtatious, slanderous, jealous, or licentious. In a chapter titled "On Learned Women" he portrays himself as a staunch feminist, unafraid of offending "ignorant and stupid people who think . . . that a woman can neither study nor read without becoming vicious or at least making herself suspect." To the contrary, "the support of letters fortifies the better inclinations," and as for intellectual capabilities, "their [women's] temperament being more delicate than ours, it is also more favorably disposed to the study of the arts and sciences." But when the question is what place these activities ought to have in daily life, the reigning social code is reaffirmed: the *honneste femme* must "devote herself to the household, by occupation, and to study, for recreation. This is [her] lot, according to Saint Paul," to say nothing of Aristotle and other philosophers. The sages all agree "that the care of married persons ought to be divided so that the woman is employed in domestic affairs and the man in outside affairs . . . There is no occupation more suitable to women than that which obliges them to leave home least." But this does not mean that they are to remain idle at home. "Upon considering closely what women do, might not one say that half of the human race is crippled and that only a part of our species is occupied? While men spend their lives fighting, studying, governing, and traveling, if one asks what most women do, the answer is nothing, unless it is that they spend their time grooming or strolling or gossiping or playing. Were they not born for this role?" Let them therefore divide their time among useful occupations, instruction, prayer, and wholesome recreations.

In England the Puritans placed great emphasis on marriage and the wifely role. In Puritan writings the wife is expected to be above all "a mistress of the household, no matter how well born or fortunate she may be. For such must be the estate of woman: this is her destiny, for which she was created."[11] Du Bosc's modest work can thus be seen as representative of a new current of thought in both England and France, one that increasingly recognized women's capabilities and rights as well as duties, especially in marriage. Many works have been devoted to the difficulty of achieving this consensus on the new status of the married woman (whether Catholic or Protestant) and to the literature in which the change was manifested.[12] However, whereas the English "conduct books" were intended for couples, the Franciscan wrote exclusively for women (married or widowed), thereby deliberately or otherwise assuming the role of a spiritual guide. A major figure of post-Tridentine Catholicism, the confessor virtually replaced the husband in all matters touching on the spiritual realm—and before long, if Jean de La Bruyère is to be believed, on the temporal as well: "He takes care of their business, inquires after their court cases, sees their judges. He gives them his physician, his purveyor, his workers. He takes care of finding them lodging and furniture and of organizing their retinue . . . He began by winning esteem;

he ends by inspiring fear."[13] *L'honneste femme* reminds us that, whether married, celibate, widowed, or cloistered, the Catholic woman was never supposed to be free of male tutelage (although she might terrorize or seduce her confessor, lover, or husband, as Saint-Simon shows us repeatedly). But it is unjust to read this and other naively moralistic books schematically. Absorbed in his catechism, du Bosc gives us, beyond his prescriptive propositions, a great deal of information about female society. From his way of describing its rituals, difficulties, and fashions we can see that, to his male eyes, this society is a world apart, a sort of republic unto itself, a state within a state. His largely unliterary text, with its ponderous, metaphorical prose, provides useful background to the more vivid portraits of the age provided by Tallemant, Mme. de Sévigné, and La Bruyère.

The Dream Woman

We are scarcely capable today of imagining the impact of the theater on the societies of the past, rural as well as urban. On both sides of the English Channel theater was the entertainment preferred by people in all walks of life: everyone went to the theater, and the theater, with its itinerant troupes, went everywhere. That is why it attracted such violent polemics: proponents of the established order saw it as much more harmful than pernicious books, which chiefly (though not exclusively) damaged those who knew how to read. A fierce struggle erupted in England in the 1580s between theater lovers and members of the middle class increasingly under the sway of Puritan ideals. Fortunately for Ben Jonson, Shakespeare, and us, the court, the aristocracy, and the common folk shared a love of spectacle.[14] Theaters closed under Cromwell's Puritan dictatorship reopened under Charles II. France avoided such abrupt reversals despite the tenacious hostility of elements within the church (non-Italian actors were excommunicated).

In the seventeenth century Charles de Saint-Evremond had some interesting things to say about the theater of his day. Forced to spend a long exile in England, yet familiar, as a cultivated Frenchman, with Italian, Spanish, and of course Latin literature, he was quick to compare works from different countries. In his view, "there is no Comedy more like that of the Ancients than the

English, so far as morals are concerned. This is not pure gallantry, full of adventures and romantic speeches, as in Spain and France. It is the representation of ordinary life, reflecting the variety of men's humors and characters."[15] In other words, English comedy resembled the English themselves. Furthermore, the authors of Spanish comedies struck him as "more fertile in inventions than ours . . . The reason for this is that in Spain, where women almost never allow themselves to be seen, the imagination of the Poet is consumed by ingenious means of bringing the Lovers together in the same place. And in France, where freedom of commerce is established, the Author's great delicacy is employed in the tender and amorous expression of feeling."[16] Saint-Evremond saw a close correspondence between works of fiction and the milieu in which they were produced and "consumed." Thus in France, where men and women were free to meet, concern focused more on "the function of a Charge, or the purpose of an Employment," while others became "more gallant than passionate" and used gallantry "to enter into intrigues." The novelty of such a situation is in the symmetry. In the sixteenth century the woman, as pretext for the artist's performance, listened while the poet sang of his suffering. In the seventeenth century men and women deliberately engaged in fashionable if conventional flirtation, or *galanterie:* "What is called love in France is in fact only talking about love."[17] And love was indeed talked about in every possible tone and even sung about in opera, as if the passions could now survive only by proxy.

The "noble" literary genres—theology, philosophy, history, and law—either ignored women or reminded them of their duties. In contrast tragedy, comedy, and opera, because they exalted the passions, gave women leading roles. Often this role was proclaimed in the very title of the work, a sign that the plot centered on the character of the heroine and the conflicts in which she would become involved.

This was particularly true of Racine: think of *Andromaque, Athalie, Esther, Iphigénie,* and *Phèdre.* Each name is the embodiment of a female type, an ideal of purity or depravity. And while Shakespeare named his plays either for male heroes or for couples (*Romeo and Juliet, Troilus and Cressida, Antony and Cleopatra*), he created any number of unforgettable female characters, from Desdemona, unjustly murdered, to Ophelia, with her long hair spread upon the water, and Lady Macbeth, forever rubbing hands red with invisible blood. From the end of the sixteenth to the end of the seventeenth centuries a rich array of exemplary women entered the collective imagination: in Racine's own lifetime Mme. de Sévigné used the term "une Andromaque" to refer to a widow.[18] Plays, with their frequent interludes of song and dance, and operas were experienced as festivals, as the celebration of a secular ritual of recognition: iridescent women and men in powdered wigs and gold braid greeted one another in packed theater lobbies or visited in their boxes. Shows began amid a hubbub of gossip and laughter, among the shouts of a crowd pleased with itself and glad to participate in the spectacle. It was no mean feat to keep a cool head and avoid sins of the spirit or senses. Boileau, a conservative wit, addressed these lines to the husband of a young and virtuous woman:

> Par toi-même bientôt conduite à l'Opéra
> De quel air penses-tu que ta Sainte verra
> D'un spectacle enchanteur la pompe harmonieuse,
> Ces danses, ces Héros à voix luxurieuse;
> Entendra ces discours sur l'Amour seul roulans,
> Ces doucereux Renauds, ces insensez Rolans;
> Sçaura d'eux qu'à l'Amour, comme au seul Dieu suprème,
> On doit immoler tout, jusqu'à la Vertu même:
> Qu'on ne sçauroit trop tôt se laisser enflammer;
> Qu'on n'a reçu du Ciel un coeur que pour aimer;
> Et tous ces Lieux communs de Morale lubrique,
> Que Lulli réchauffa des sons de sa Musique?
> Mais de quels movemens, dans son coeur excitez,
> Sentira-t-elle alors tous ses sens agitez?

When, before long, you take your Saint to the Opera, how do you think she will look when she casts her eyes on the harmonious pomp of an enchanting spectacle, those dances, those Heroes with lustful voices? She will hear those sonorous speeches about Love, those gentle Renauds, those mad Rolands; she will learn from them that one must sacrifice everything, even Virtue, to Love, as to the one supreme God; that to burn with love too soon is impossible; that Heaven has given her a heart only in order to love; and all these Commonplaces of lubricious Morals will be warmed by the sounds of Lully's music. But when her senses have been stirred this way, what tremors will she feel in her excited heart?[19]

It would be impossible to give a better summary of the various ingredients that went to make a play or an opera in the age of Louis XIV a total spectacle, a literally intoxicating occasion, that could hardly leave a girl or young woman unmoved. In the theater women discovered not only the amorous pleasures of triumphant mentors and graybeards but also endless allusions to the pleasures of the flesh (spoken of onstage by footmen and serving girls who served no other purpose). And they saw how women behaved when acting on their own. As for the loose morals and salty language of the actresses and dancers, women in the audience who would not have dreamed of joining in such scandalous behavior may nevertheless have found the inhibited manners and dull routine of their own daily lives wanting by comparison with the gay abandon they witnessed onstage.

Novels, though consumed in private, were no less pernicious than public spectacles. In theaters and opera houses women participated in spectacles that "flattered the senses," but in a time and place set apart from daily life, as if in a festive interlude. With novels it was possible to dream at home, alone or together with a small group; and in such circumstances one naturally dreamed different dreams. In the period that interests us thousands of novels were written: roughly twelve hundred in France in the seventeenth century, and nearly a thousand in the first half of the eighteenth century (the number for the second half of the century is much smaller).[20] Some of these books could not be read at one sitting. Many were composed as a series of episodes whose only logic was to run on and on. The first serial novel was *Astrée* (1607–1628), and its method was universally adopted in novels until well into the eighteenth century. Perhaps it was the sheer abundance of such fiction that caused everyone, proponents and foes alike, to speak as if all novels were more or less equivalent. The quality of a particular work or author mattered less than the genre, which was considered frivolous and ephemeral. As such, novels would hardly have merited so much attention except that women, being "frivolous" and "uncultivated," constituted the genre's natural audience and were apt to fall under the sway of pernicious works. In her letters Mme. de Sévigné mentions only about twenty novels, usually not by title but simply to say that a character in one of them resembles a person she knows. Mentioned most often is *Don Quixote* (24 times), followed by the *Princesse de Clèves,* a work by Mme. de Sévigné's close friend Mme. de La Fayette (21 times), *Amadis des Gaules,* an old-fashioned work of chivalry found in an armoire (17 times),[21] and the perennial *Astrée* (9 times). The works of Gautier de La Calprenède (*Cassandre* and *Pharamond*) and Mlle. de Scudéry (*Clélie, Le Grand Cyrus*) are mentioned 4 to 7 times each, and Paul Scarron's *Roman comique* and Jean Desmarets de Saint-Sorlin's *Visionnaires* are mentioned 4 times. The rest get no more than 1 or 2 mentions. It is clear that to a great reader like Mme. de Sévigné novels were far less important than Italian and French poetry (*Gerusalemme liberata* is mentioned 40 times, *Orlando furioso* 29 times, and La Fontaine 70 times for twenty-nine different fables). She drew abundantly on her contemporaries Corneille, Racine, and Molière (there are forty-three quotations from the *Médecin malgré lui*), on the operas of Quinault and Lully, on histories, and on a small number of ancient authors. But nothing comes close to the Bible, which is cited 121 times, and the moralizing and edifying works of the Jansenists Antoine Arnauld and Pierre Nicole (the latter is cited 95 times), to say nothing of such occasional pieces as funeral orations. Like her contemporaries she was sensitive to the delightful improbability of fictional plots, "which enchanted her like a little girl."[22] But she never took "such foolishness" seriously, and it was no more important to her than romance novels or mysteries are to us: aristocratic, intelligent, and cultivated, she could make fun of herself just as she did of ignorant priests and rote prayer. But du Bosc wrote for a less well-informed, less independent audience: "Since Mothers cannot look at certain paintings without affecting their children, why should we not think that lascivious Histories and Novels may have the same effect on our imagination and always leave some stains on our soul?" Worse still, novels not only "make some women bold, they make them clever as well. They discover subtlety as well as confidence, and they learn not only about evil things they should not know about but also about the most delicate ways of doing wrong . . . Such books often portray women like the one who left her homeland and her kin to run after a foreigner with whom she fell in love at first sight. We often read how this woman received letters from her suitors or how another gave assignations. All these are lessons in artifice that teach how to sin subtly."[23] In the end, woman's ultimate enemy, the devil's eternal disguise, is love, which novels, comedies, and operas "ingeniously portray as the sweetest, most charming thing in the world . . . That is all it takes to lend great impetus to this unfortunate passion."[24]

The anxiety of these morose spirits and the vehemence of their criticisms suggest that literature, theater, and music fueled a kind of feminine counterculture. The specific qualities of a work made no difference, nor did the rank or delicacy of the author. Take, for example, Mlle. de Scudéry's *Clélie:* as Nicolas Boileau said, "It is not a question, Sir, of the merit of the Person who composed Clélie, or of the esteem with which this Work has been received . . . Call it, if you like, the most beautiful of all Novels; it is still a Novel, and that is all there is to say."[25] Indeed, this literature of which women were the prime audience (or target) was part of the frivolous, dissolute world in which women were trapped by their nature, a world in which everything was of a piece: reading novels, using makeup, wearing fine clothes, capitalizing on one's physical attractions, and (as we shall see later) dancing—to the moralist, these were all equivalent. Works of fiction were important not because of their literary quality but because of the way they were used. There is abundant evidence that, with the exception of a few extraordinarily strict moralists, laymen and laywomen in France behaved as if the condemnation of sensual pleasure and respect for religious (and marital) duties was primarily a matter of age and perhaps also of social rank. Once youth had passed, a concern for one's salvation would naturally emerge. Wisdom came with maturity, and with luck one could avoid hypocritical affectations of piety that fooled no one. Saint-Simon summed up the life of Miss Hamilton, who was brought up at Port-Royal: she "had preserved all its taste and goodness through the divagations of youth, beauty, high society, and a few amorous encounters."[26] He also wrote an extremely warm funeral oration of several pages for Ninon de l'Enclos, one of the most celebrated courtesans of his day: "Her conversation was charming, disinterested, faithful, private, reliable to the utmost degree, and it can be said that, but for weakness, she was virtuous and honest."[27] It is no accident that a man of the court should have exhibited such understanding of the lapses of youth, beauty, and high society. Pierre de Brantôme made similar remarks about the court of the Valois. It may be that the "counterculture" mentioned above derived its strength from a kind of legitimacy and its legitimacy from the example set by the court.

Once again, the censors were right: the court was "where all the ways of luxury, vanity, ambition, and tact are learned; where the passions that move all the other passions are formed . . . Since vice is contagious, it spreads through the lower regions of the Kingdoms. These unruly ways are taken as models, and the unfortunate but understandable consequence is that the very sins of the great became the fashions of the people, and the corruption of the Court at last becomes established as politeness in the Provinces."[28]

The English court under James II and Charles II offered a spectacle even more licentious and carefree than that of Versailles, which was straitjacketed by etiquette. A very vivid description can be found in the memoirs of the Count de Gramont.[29] There is no doubt that the court's licentiousness served as an example. Lawrence Stone is quick to seize on the image of contamination in writing of Samuel Pepys, a middle-class Londoner who began a brilliant career in the Admiralty while writing the famous *Diary:* "The spread of the sexual habits of Charles II's court by rumor, observation, and example downward through the social scale of London life is very clearly evidenced by Pepys's diary . . . He continued to express shock and disgust, but also prurient interest and envy, at the goings-on at court. And while carefully preserving his own wife from temptation from others and from knowledge of his own extramarital activities, he slowly succumbed to the temptation to imitate—in a far more modest and guilt-ridden way—the sexual behavior of his social superiors."[30]

The circumspect approach I have adopted thus far has taken us from sixteenth-century poetry to the edifying literature of the seventeenth and eighteenth centuries. Three figures of the eternal feminine have emerged: woman as pretext, edified woman, and the dream woman. Looking at women collectively has of course made it necessary to emphasize outward appearances and behavior, especially since most of those who wrote about women were men. In the "woman as pretext" and the "edified woman" it is not difficult to recognize masculine ideals of beauty and virtue, ideals that men imposed on the object of their passion or reprobation. The "dream woman," who was also the invention of novelists and librettists, at least offered real women, who also dreamed, a refuge in the imagination.

Three Writers, Three Testimonies

With Pepys we come upon the notion of guilt and thus enter the realm of the inner life, about which it is risky to generalize. It thus becomes desirable as well as necessary to change our angle of view and compare literature with life. To do this, I propose looking at three writers, one from each of the three centuries under examination. Their testimony will corroborate, refute, or supplement what we have learned thus far. Why choose just three writers, when so many others also wrote about women? Because one can delve a little more deeply into the work of a small number. In choosing which three to include, I decided to exclude partisan literature, apologias, and specialized works as well as fiction and to consider only memoirs and letters. The author should have lived long enough to have witnessed change in people and things, and should have been sufficiently original, intelligent, and cultivated to give an account that seems distinctive as well as true. By these stringent criteria one must rule out Montaigne and Voltaire as too universal; the Norman sire de Gouberville as too provincial and unworldly; Brantôme and Saint-Simon as too close to the court; Samuel Pepys and Jonathan Swift for having kept their diaries over too short a period; Tobias Smollett as too bilious; Jane Austen as too late; and so on. A good many names remain, however, and from these I have chosen, for the sixteenth century, Etienne Pasquier; for the seventeenth, Mme. de Sévigné; and for the eighteenth, James Boswell.

Etienne Pasquier (1529–1615)

A celebrated jurist, staunch supporter of the last Valois monarchs and then of Henri IV, a great humanist, on occasion a playful poet, and, as author of *Recherches de la France,* the father of French historical science, Etienne Pasquier was one of those men who stand as rocks through the tempests of their time. After resigning from his post as *avocat général* at the Chambre des Comptes, he withdrew to his country house at Argenteuil to enjoy a life of studious leisure, and there, well past eighty years of age, he died. His collected works, including letters from his younger son, Nicolas, also a jurist, were published in Amsterdam in 1723.[31]

It may be that the example of his friend Montaigne, whom he revered both as a person and as the author of the *Essais,* encouraged Pasquier to paint an accurate portrait of himself in a voluminous and diverse series of works. Among his many books is a full-fledged treatise on male-female relations, the *Monophile* (1556), which takes the form of a fictional dialogue between a "well-educated Damsel" named Charilée and "three young Gentlemen of the elite." With the sexes so unequally represented, it is not surprising that the damsel's words are overwhelmed by the gentlemen's. She is almost constantly on the defensive, among other things about "oddness of dress." But one of her three interlocutors, Philopole, turns the discussion to more important matters, beginning with freedom, which women enjoy to a far smaller degree than men. Not only are they "excluded from the administration of Republics, the bearing of arms, [and the] exercises of political estates . . . [but] our forebears also desired a certain chastity in them . . . which was not so requisite in men because they are neither as fragile nor as lubricious as women." The outraged Charilée responds by describing queens and notable women warriors of the past (from Semiramis to the Amazons), the poetry of Sappho and of Marguerite de Valois, and the Roman eloquence of Cornelia and Hortensia. Above all she deplores "the tedious law of men, which, aware of the great mental capacity of women who are nevertheless without physical strength," prevents them from pleading cases and holding public office and even prohibits them from selling or donating property "without the express consent of their husbands." Are not "the good and great houses daily declining and falling into ruin owing to men's stupidity and profligacy? And by contrast, does not the increase and maintenance of those houses depend on women's good housekeeping and wisdom?" And if it were "legitimate for them to apply their minds to the same kinds of business" as men, "they would be capable of using the same means to guide and discipline a city's affairs." Those listening are astonished to hear her plead the case so well. She responds that "although you men still prohibit us from reading good Authors," she spends "most of her time" doing just that. As for chastity, she asks why it should be required of women and not of men when divine law "equally abhors" lasciviousness in either sex, whereas the "human statute" imposed by men makes them both "judge and party" to the case. A natural decency encourages women to "restrain and inhibit [their] carnal concupiscences," while men "boast openly of lending their hearts on credit" and have "always been in a position to allow [their] desires free rein with the first woman who happens by." Harking back to the sources of courtly love, in which the lady is mistress and the man is her servant, Charilée nevertheless deplores that "in love one can or should have more power than the other. All desiring is to be mutual and reciprocal. Once it ceases to be so, love is already beginning to wane."

Having shown, in theory, that woman is potentially man's equal and is deliberately kept in a position of inferiority ("as we see regularly the little fish devoured by the big"), Pasquier turned his attention to actual human institutions, especially marriage. In the background lies the old nature-versus-culture debate: nature drives male and female to mate, but culture distorts this spontaneous, egalitarian relation by introducing the dowry, or inequality by virtue of wealth. This perversion is so well established that "the populace" approves of a man who, for money, marries a woman he does not love yet brands as mad a man who, for love, marries "a girl made of low substance." As a result, both husband and wife seek compensations for these shaky relationships, and men (who make the laws) oblige women to obey by imposing stringent penalties for adultery. But the dowry and the return dower given the widow exist and have their benefits: children exist because of marriage, but they prosper because of the dowry and dower. People who marry must live, and to live is "to maintain oneself as is normal for one's estate, to feed oneself and [one's] children and family, to cure one's ills . . . Such burdens are enough to overwhelm the husband if he must bear them alone." At the risk of speaking "to the detriment of her sex," Charilée considers it unjust "that this double weight and burden (that you both supply your effort and furnish your coin)" should fall on the husband's shoulders, "and that the woman alone is left the contentment and pleasure with no care other than what she is willing voluntarily to take upon herself."

Pasquier, of course, can put his thoughts into a lady's mouth and have things pretty much his own way. But we must beware lest we trip ourselves on an anachronism. Society in Pasquier's time was far more radically divided than in our own between a small number of wealthy people and a large number of poor ones. And while the poor earned their daily bread in the sweat of their brow (or died of hunger), rich men either did nothing (except make love or war) or devoted themselves to noble occupations such as theology, jurisprudence, or literature, which did not dirty the hands. Their wives remained home overseeing domestic chores or participating in social diversions or other idle activities appropriate to their station. Charilée's contention that the dowry was justified as payment for services rendered stemmed from the concrete reality of contemporary marriage. A woman whose dowry was constituted by her father or kin purchased, if not "contentment and pleasure," then at least the invaluable security of a position. The daughter of a gentleman or a notable could not provide for her own needs (unless she entered a convent or sacrificed her morals), because work was incompatible with her rank. Someone had to take care of her unless she was fortunate enough to be an heiress or a widow capable of living, like a man, on the income from her property—or if she fell into the much-talked-about but little-known category of *pauvres honteux,* shamefaced poor.

Pasquier's *Letters* describe a life divided between his work as a lawyer, the management of his estates, writing, and correspondence. He writes at length of various memorable events that he witnessed firsthand. He also offers frequent advice to friends, women of his acquaintance, and his own grown children. What does he have to say about women, and particularly about his wife?

In 1558, while returning with his wife from a pleasant grape harvest in Brie, he is taken ill after eating mushrooms and nearly dies, after which he is confined to bed for a lengthy period. The next eighteen months are taken up with convalescence and travels in the provinces. Upon returning to Paris the novice attorney discovers that everyone at the courthouse has forgotten him. He spends two months hanging about without doing a thing, and the "heartache" is so great that he decides to "banish himself altogether." His wife sees him "withering on the vine," but he is reluctant to talk things over with her. As a widow, in fact, "she had married me in the belief that one day I would rank among the prominent attorneys, and with this new turn of events she found her hopes suddenly frustrated. But seeing that what I was suffering was an affliction of the mind or the great heart, she behaved, not like a besotted Parisian woman, who would have rolled her eyes and shed copious tears, but rather, with admirable even temper, told me that she found my resolution quite correct, that we had a mule and a packhorse in the stable and means enough to live comfortably." In another version of the same story it is Mme. Pasquier herself, a "true *viragine* [stalwart woman]," who perceives her husband's distress at his lack of work and urges him to leave the courthouse, "preferring that I should lose my profession rather than my life." In both versions the lady, whether *viragine* or not, displays her firmness of character in circumstances in which the couple's future is at stake and, with it, her own prominence or obscurity. She had further opportunities to demonstrate her mettle at the time of the League, and when she died in 1590 Pasquier wept for her to the point, he said, that "I would be ashamed if anyone saw me." We are a long way from the mawkish silliness of much sixteenth-century literature (including Pasquier's own writing), but the elderly man who wept for his wife in 1590 knew what he wanted before he married. In a letter to another lawyer, Le Picart, he set forth in two pages ideas that he would develop at much greater length in *Monophile:* "I, for one, shall always be in favor of marriage and against the celibate life, not only because this is, in general, the way to perpetuate ourselves in this human society but also, in particular, because when we have tired of women, we have tired of life. I mean that, to sustain us in the infirmity and weakness of old age, we would not dare rely so much on others, [no matter] how closely related, as we do on our wives, with whom we have vowed lives that are indivisible." Marriage should be based on "compatibility of habits and banishment of necessity." It should be egalitarian, with the wife obeying her husband *or* the husband obeying his wife. And as for sexual pleasure, "there is no woman, however beautiful, to whom a man is not indifferent after they have slept together for a year, nor is there any moderate ugliness that does not become tolerable with time." Pasquier is even skeptical about the traditional concern with perpetuating one's line: "To procreate is a great boon to the world, but not to have children is not, for that reason, a misfortune."

The woman Pasquier wants is not an object or a womb but a companion. Husband and wife each have their own sphere. The man works and bears the burden of a profession or official position. For relaxation he engages in "noble pursuits" (scholarship, poetry, reading the classics) and may even divert himself with a game of pall-mall or skittles in the yard or backgammon by the fire. The woman is in charge of the household, including the education of young children (later, boys will go to preparatory school and girls to the convent). Her leisure is shared with her husband: trips with friends (like the one to Brie in 1558), visits, and musical recitals at home (Mme. Pasquier played the lute and spinet). We gain a vivid and concrete impression of these activities from a letter: already elderly, Pasquier was confined with his books to a bedroom in his country home in Châtelet and left his wife to worry about the grape harvest. These circumstances provided the pretext for declining the invitation of a nearby nobleman: "My wife has completed only half of what she has to do: her grapes are in barrels, ready to be pressed, while mine age in my head." With the passage of time a man grew old, his health failed, he perhaps fell into a second childhood: how sweet it was to be coddled then by a wife who resumed her maternal role, a wife who often was younger and therefore more vigorous than her husband and less forgetful of her duties than his ungrateful offspring.

As sententious as Pasquier, Sir Francis Bacon summed up the situation: "Wives are Young Men's Mistresses; Companions for middle Age, and old Men's Nurses."[32] Other seventeenth-century English texts also attest to a gradual rehabilitation of marriage. John Donne's poems, for example, reflect the anxiety of man losing his traditional bearings in a society that was evolving too rapidly. What had become of the great houses of yesteryear, houses in which poets could find not only food and a bed but favor and protection? "Connected with this sense of contemporary change, and inseparable from it, is a deep and very characteristic sense of instability in personal relationships. It is a sense coexistent with an equally characteristic sense of the preeminence of love between men and women. In fact, the two work to intensify each other."[33] This mutual love is naturally a part of the institution of marriage, which was at once hierarchical and egalitarian, as Pasquier wished, along with Shakespeare and even John Donne, who long suffered in disgrace for his "romantic" marriage to the niece of an easily offended patron.

Mme. de Sévigné (1626–1696)

Absence, my daughter, opens many fine prospects.

It is only by a series of accidents, surreptitiously as it were, that we know of the private life of this passionate woman who, when she wrote her now famous letters, believed that she was revealing her passions only to her daughter and a few close friends. The free tone of her correspondence stems in part from her sense of being able to speak her mind openly, but it has other sources as well. An orphan from an early age, Marie de Rabutin-Chantal was brought up in Paris by her mother's kin, the Coulanges, a wealthy and cultivated family only recently elevated to the nobility. She thus escaped "the Rabutins and the cloister" and the rigors of a too-strict upbringing.[34] In 1644, at the age of eighteen, she married a Breton nobleman, Henri de Sévigné, who had a reputation as a lady's man and fast liver and who was soon killed in a duel (1651). At twenty-five his widow found herself with two children, some property, and debts. Witty, attractive, familiar with the best society, she did not lack for suitors, but she sent them all packing in order to preserve her precious freedom. In 1687 she wrote that she would just as soon forget the date of her birth and put in its place the date she was widowed, "which was quite a nice and quite a fortunate thing."[35] Later she felt sorrow for mothers who had lost sons in the battle of Fleurus, but "the young widows are scarcely to be pitied. They will be quite happy to be their own mistresses or to change masters."[36] Bussy-Rabutin went her one better in a lighthearted reply: "I know three young widows of this battle whose husbands' deaths are grounds for rejoicing, as well as two ladies who deserve consolation because their husbands escaped with their wounds and live to fight another day. The gods of hymen have long been incompatible with the gods of love."[37] Reading these letters, we can comprehend why the scandalous joy of widowhood was denounced by so many preachers and celebrated in so many comedies: "A woman has but a forlorn hope of becoming a widow. This heavenly favor always comes too late, and by then our best days are done."[38] In a world in which all marriages were compelled, freedom began with the death of the husband. A century later the system of matrimony remained much the same, and Choderlos de Laclos was able to show how Mme. de Merteuil took advantage of her widowhood.[39] In England divorce by act of Parliament existed in the eighteenth century, but the procedure was unusual and costly.

Mme. de Sévigné, meanwhile, was learning independence: she was learning how to manage a tidy fortune in real estate encumbered by substantial debts (her uncle Coulanges would help rescue her from financial disaster); how to divide her time between Paris, where society was amusing, and Brittany, where it cost nothing to live; and how to set her children up in life. She made a good marriage for her daughter, which cost a great deal, and she bought an army post for her son and much later arranged a marriage for him as well. Her behavior was thus fully compatible with the customs of her time, and as a widow she was "free" to see whomever she wished and to travel wherever she wanted to go; she could also cut back on expenditures she deemed superfluous and use the savings to do things that pleased her (such as giving gifts to her daughter and fixing up her estate at Les Rochers). She learned to protect this valuable independence even from overzealous friends. In the fall of 1689 three of her friends tried to persuade her to return to Paris from Brittany so as to avoid "the horror of a winter in the country": "They were afraid I would become bored or fall ill or that my mind would shrink or even that I might die. They wanted to see me, keep me, control me."[40] But she stubbornly refused to budge, and a month later, content with her minor victory, she wrote her daughter: "Sometimes I laugh, and I say to myself, 'So that's what they mean by spending the winter in the woods' . . . These woods are filled with sunshine at the moment . . . And when it rains, [I have] a good room with a large fire and often, as now, two gaming tables. There is lots of company, but it doesn't disturb me in the least. I do as I please. And when no one comes, we are sometimes even better off, for we then read with a pleasure that delights us more than anything else."[41]

Along with her independence she also displayed a very tolerant spirit—yet another way of demonstrating her respect for freedom. This encouraged her son, Charles, to confide in her about his various adventures, including amorous ones. When Charles become one of Mme. de Champmeslé's lovers, Mme. de Sévigné referred to her son's mistress as "my daughter-in-law." After he failed to perform in the bed of Ninon de l'Enclos, she wrote: "His thing stayed short at Lerida . . . We had a good laugh. I told him that I was delighted that he was punished where he had sinned."[42]

Attentive to the education of her grandchildren, particularly of Pauline de Grignan, she was constantly giving advice to their mother (her daughter) that she should keep her children with her and be gentle, flexible, and understanding toward them. Early childhood was the critical phase, however, and later on it was best not to become too attached but rather to "enjoy" the children (*s'en amuser:* the phrase recurs frequently). When Pauline grew older and her mother sent her away several times to a convent (a decision in which the girl's father apparently took no part), Madame de Sévigné was hesitant: "I am surprised that she did not become silly and sarcastic at the convent. You did well, daughter, to take her back home. Keep her."[43] Ten years later she wrote: "You must not think that a convent can correct an upbringing, whether in regard to religion, about which our sisters [the nuns] know very little, or in other matters. You will do much better at Grignan, where you will have time to apply yourself."[44] Pauline stayed at Grignan, where she educated herself in many ways, most notably by serving as secretary to her mother, who wrote a great deal. This was an excellent opportunity "to learn the French language, which most women do not know." Refusing, as one foolish confessor attempted, to allow this girl of fifteen to read "Corneille's beautiful comedies" was "to take refuge in piety without coming to it by God's grace." Did not the Pomponnes have their daughter learn Italian "and anything that serves to form the mind?" That did not prevent them from giving her an excellent Christian education. Not sure what books to recommend to Pauline, her grandmother first advised her to read Italian poetry: "Tasso, the *Aminta,* the *Pastor fido,* the *Filli di Sciro.*" She also told her to cultivate a taste for history, "which can console in idle hours for a long time to come."[45] In the next letter she returns to the subject of education, which was very close to her heart, and offers her daughter a splendid lesson in educating children at home:

> For Pauline, who devours books, I would rather see her gobble up bad ones than not like to read at all. Novels, comedies, the Voitures, the Sarasins—none of them lasts long. Has she tried Lucian? Are the *Petites lettres* within her grasp? Later she must read history. If you have to hold her nose to make her swallow it, I feel sorry for her. If she does not like beautiful works of piety, it's too bad, because we know only too well that even those without piety find them charming. As for ethics . . . I wouldn't at all like to see her stick her little nose into Montaigne or Charron or other writers of that ilk. It's very early for her. At her age the true morality is what one learns in good conversation, in myth, and in the examples of history. That is enough, I think. If you give her some time to talk with you, surely that would be the most useful thing.[46]

Thanks to Pauline and her little nose, we are back to the subject of literature. But do we ever leave it through all the correspondence? Literature truly had a central place in the obligatorily idle daily life of educated nobles, tonsured love poets, and women who filled the gaps in their convent schooling by reading and going to theater (activities that Mme. du Deffand considered equally important for the acquisition of knowledge).[47] In reading the letters of Mme. de Sévigné one is constantly astonished (and delighted) by the way in which quotations fit naturally into the flow of the prose. Always apt, they enliven the letters and underscore important points. Mother and daughter do not simply know the classics by heart; they hold them in the depths of their hearts. "We reread the death of Clorinda [in Tasso's *Gerusalemme liberata*]. Darling, do not say, 'I know it by heart.' Read it again."[48] The text served as omnipresent mediation between self and reality, transcending the banal, heightening happiness or setting it in context, and dispelling sorrow. In 1680, a dark year filled with mourning and anxiety, Mme. de Sévigné visited a family estate near Nantes and discovered that her son, short of cash, had ordered the forests cut down. She did not express her feelings directly but poured out her soul in the form of a bravura exercise, which begins with a long passage in which "distressed dryads," "old sylvan gods," and "venerable crows" lament the loss of their refuge and ends by asking "if some of those old oaks did not speak as did the one Clorinda was in. This place was a *luogo d'incanto* if ever there was one."[49] What better example of symbolic compensation could there be than to transform a ravaged forest into a place of enchantment?

At the time, Western culture in general depended on the authority of texts, but different people invoked different authorities. Permanently marked by their years in preparatory school, the *honnête homme* and the "gentleman" filled their letters with Latin quotations, tokens of shared experience (the letters of James Boswell and William Temple are typical in this regard). The minor clergy, the devout, and many Protestants, especially Puritans, quoted almost nothing other than the Bible. Only women, owing to their inadequate education, enjoyed the privilege of *negligence,* that is, of being natural.[50] Sévigné's manner of drawing freely and indiscriminately on any type of literature that pleased her was thus typically feminine. Leaving her luminous prose for the somber diaries of a Scottish family, one has the impression of jumping into a cold bath. The Scottish wife thinks she has "sinned unto death" because one Sunday night the family is afflicted with an irresistible desire to laugh. Her husband becomes sick with internalized guilt: "My body was sore brocken by a winde in my stomock yrby my spirit was oftn discomposed." Their daughter begins her own diary with these words: "I was a blasphemer, but I obtained mercy."[51] This contrast is perhaps somewhat overdrawn. The French equivalents of these unfortunates, however hypocritical, like Molière's Tartuffe, were not far from the solid and not at all prudish piety of people such as Mme. de Sévigné, Saint-Simon, and Dorine, the servant who makes fun of Tartuffe. Nevertheless, at a time when a number of excellent works have done much to rehabilitate Puritan culture and especially to draw attention to Puritanism's positive contributions in regard to sexuality and marriage, it may not be out of place to point out that, as the English themselves admit, the Puritan outlook did put an end to "Merry Old England," to the robust vitality still so evident in the time of Shakespeare. It is as if the tolerance and skepticism of a Pasquier or a Sévigné could be sustained only by a wide range of sources of knowledge, whereas intolerance and pessimism could thrive on the endless repetition of a single authoritative gospel.

James Boswell (1740–1795)

> I am a singular man. I have the whim of an Englishman to make me think and act extravagantly, and yet I have the coolness and good sense of a Scotsman to make me sensible of it.
>
> Boswell, *Memorabilia*

There will probably never be a source of information about a man of the Enlightenment to rival the thousands of published letters, notes, and diary pages we have from the hand of James Boswell.[52] The son of a Scottish magistrate and a strict Calvinist mother, Boswell was himself a lawyer, but it was his books that made him famous: a plea on behalf of Corsica published in 1768, an account of his journey to the Highlands with Samuel Johnson in 1785, and his *Life of Johnson,* "the most celebrated biography in the English language," in 1791.[53]

Boswell was undeniably a man of the Enlightenment by virtue of his humanity, his championing of great causes, his enormous intellectual curiosity, and his fascination with men of ideas: he met Voltaire and Rousseau and was a friend of Hume, Goldsmith,

Edmund Malone, and many others. Of course he also had a taste for travel and a voracious capacity for conversation. Friendship undoubtedly played a larger role in his intellectual life than did love, for he had a great tendency to confuse desire with love and, in his youth at least, to mistake any woman he lusted after for the love of his life. But he was also charming and much given to drink, so that he had countless amorous adventures ranging from harmless flirtation to drunken debauch. This might seem to make him an odd choice as an informant about eighteenth-century women. But Boswell had a passion for sincerity, a passion compounded of an appetite for both life and knowledge, and, unwilling to allow the least iota of his experience to be lost, he also had a mania for writing things down. His penchant for self-mortification, his horror of sin, and his constant sense of guilt compelled him to confess his most private sins and to call upon his friends and his wife to judge his actions. Many similar traits, including ambivalence toward women, can be found in another Protestant, Jean-Jacques Rousseau, but the sexual behavior revealing that ambivalence differed markedly in the two cases.[54]

The letters and diaries of James Boswell tell us a great deal about the specific nature of English civilization. His French contemporaries—Diderot or Crébillon, Voltaire or Beaumarchais—lived in a thoroughly mixed society, in which men and women lived in close, constant, and natural proximity (not to say promiscuity). Of course proximity was by no means incompatible with inequality and with a kind of muted war between the sexes.[55] By contrast, Boswell lived in an insular, fundamentally masculine society: men frequented women, of course, but the important relationships, those involving true intellectual exchange and full mutual confidence, invariably existed between individuals of the same sex. Travelers naturally observe the differences between customs abroad and at home. Thus men as different as Smollett and Sterne both registered, albeit in different ways, the intimacy that they saw in France between men and women. One was outraged, the other delighted. Smollett wrote:

A Frenchman, in consequence of his mingling with the females from his infancy, not only becomes acquainted with all their customs and humors but grows wonderfully alert in performing a thousand little offices which are overlooked by other men, whose time hath been spent in making more valuable acquisitions. He enters without ceremony a lady's bed-chamber while she is in bed, reaches whatever she wants, airs her shift, and helps to put it on. He attends at her toilette, regulates the distribution of her patches, and advises where to lay on the paint.[56]

Sterne's sentimental traveler meets a beautiful stranger in Calais and longs to know who she is, where she comes from, and where she is going:

> There was no such thing as a man's asking her directly—the thing was impossible. A debonnaire little French captain, who came dancing down the street, shewed me that it was the easiest thing in the world; for popping in betwixt us . . . he introduced himself to my acquaintance, and before he had well got announced, begg'd if I would do him the honor to present him to the lady—I had not been presented myself—so turning about to her, he did just as well by asking her if she had come from Paris.

In five minutes the captain knows everything there is to know about the woman's identity and itinerary and with a gesture of farewell continues on his way. The traveler concludes: "Had I served seven years' apprenticeship to good breeding, I could not have done as much."[57]

The impression remains even today that gentlemen formed in the unique mold of the public schools look back fondly on a time of life when they awakened together to learning, to intellectual and athletic competition, to sexuality, and to politics. Even women of similar background feel radically different for not having shared this experience. Boswell is never so much himself as in the warm, enthusiastic, yet lucid letters in which he recounts his experiences and asks advice of his longtime friend, William Temple, and the same can be said of Temple in his letters to Boswell. And Samuel Johnson, Boswell's elder by thirty years, was more than just a prestigious friend; he was a sort of spiritual father whom Boswell joined every year in London, fleeing Edinburgh and the menacing shadow of his real father. And in another of the eighteenth century's great collections of letters, the correspondence of Horace Walpole, men play just as important a role, particularly the friends from Walpole's time at Eton: Gray, West, and Ashton. Walpole's platonic and public liaison with Madame du Deffand was for him (if not for her) of only secondary importance.

Boswell thus lived in a stable society of men, who continued to frequent one another throughout their lives. Many women passed through his life, and a few remained: wives, relatives, and, in a very few cases, friends. Boswell wanted to seduce every person he met and often succeeded. Only his manner changed, and his objective. On men he used his charm to obtain an interview (as with Voltaire and Rousseau) or to win lasting esteem (as with Johnson, the Corsican general Paoli, and many others). And on women who pleased him he used his charm to possess them straightaway, to beg the hand of an heiress (he failed to obtain it) or to marry a poor cousin whom he loved. The many women who crossed his path come to life fleetingly in his diaries. One of them was the daughter of his father's gardener. In April 1766 Boswell returned to the family estate in Scotland after an adventure-filled Grand Tour. While he was away the gardener's daughter had grown into a very pretty young woman, or so she seemed to Boswell, who immediately fell in love. Since he made it a principle "never to debauch an innocent girl" and since he respected the gardener, "a worthy man of uncommon abilities," he found himself "crazy enough to think of marrying her."[58] Not one to fall victim to his own whims, he recalled many a brief escapade that amounted to nothing more, but still he could not help thinking that this time it might be something else:

> She and I were in a manner brought up together. As far back as I can remember, we used to build houses and make gardens, wade in the river and play upon the sunny banks. I cannot consider her as below me . . . She has a most amiable face, the prettiest foot and ankle. She is perfectly well made and has a lively, genteel air that is irresistible.
>
> I take every opportunity of being with her when she is putting on fires or dressing a room . . . I pretend great earnestness to have the library in good order and assist her to dust it. I cut my gloves that she may mend them. I kiss her hand. I tell her what a beauty I think her. She has an entire confidence in me and has no fear of any bad design; and she has too much sense to form an idea of having me for a husband.

The lovers exchange notes (proof that the young woman knows how to write), and we know that she has read a great deal because Boswell is forever lending her books: "In short, she is better than any lady I know. What shall I do, Temple?" Flee. Three weeks later, "the beautiful chambermaid is already like an old dream," and a year later Boswell, as if to underscore his emancipation in the crudest possible terms, writes Temple that "she lights [his] fire and empties [his] chamber-pot just like any other servant." Because he did not abuse his power and the gardener's daughter nursed no illusions about the possibility of marriage, she escaped from the affair relatively unscathed. Boswell, meanwhile, immediately found another woman whom he regarded as a kindred spirit. Aware of his tendency to succumb to impetuous infatuations, he promises Temple that he will never marry without his, Temple's, approval. The kindred spirit, Mrs. Dodds, has a body that is his for the taking: "She is paradisiacal in bed." Following a scandal of some sort the young woman had separated from her husband, who retained custody of the children. Her affair with Boswell, marked by quarrels and reconciliations, a pregnancy, and the birth of a daughter, Sally, would last for two years. He provided his mistress with rooms and a servant and an allowance for the child (who appears to have died young). His friends and relatives lectured him about the need to end his affair with this married woman, whom they regarded as a dangerous enchantress (a Lais, a Circe) and whose past mischief they reminded him of in detail. To others it seemed that if Boswell stayed with her, he must be either her dupe or a slave to his passions. Brief encounters were permissible (nature must be allowed to have her say), but once the urge was satisfied, the instrument was to be forgotten. Boswell himself admitted that she lacked education and breeding. She was simply beautiful, kind, generous, and prepared to receive him at any hour of the night. Such an "instrument" is not so easily set aside. For Boswell the affair was a time of torment, remorse, breakups, and reconciliations, finally ending in a complete severing of ties. Two years later Boswell married his first cousin, Margaret Montgomerie. The couple spent several happy years together before things went sour, ending in depression and drunkenness for Boswell, loneliness and sickness for his wife.

But the work remains as an obsessive inventory of the events of a lifetime (and to some extent of two lifetimes, Johnson's as well as Boswell's). Boswell is acutely aware of the shortcomings of language: "I observe continually how imperfectly, upon most occasions, words preserve our ideas." Nevertheless, he persists in recording the least significant of his actions as if in anticipation of the Last Judgment. He is indifferent to history and concerned only to preserve the trace of his own passage through it. Yet because of his need to be exhaustive, he unwittingly tells us a great deal about the importance of women in his own life and in society generally. There are women in the inn where he stays and takes his meals but not at the places where he works (courts and prisons). As a houseguest he attends family luncheons at which women are present. They serve him tea in the drawing room. But they are absent from the bibulous male suppers that usually take place in inns and not, as in France, at the home of one of the participants. And at night, of course, there are women lining the streets, where Boswell, well pickled, can take his pick before returning home in the wee hours. Thus the kind of woman he meets depends on the place and the hour of the day. As they appear in the diaries, women are grouped into distinct classes: bargirls and chambermaids in the inns; wives of friends and relatives; society matrons in Edinburgh and London; kept women; streetwalkers. The only common denominator is Boswell himself, who moves among them at will. Each of these women knows one aspect of the man (and perhaps guesses at the rest). Yet Boswell, who records the most trivial remarks of Johnson and other famous friends, almost never reports on the conversations he has over tea with elegant ladies. Had they nothing to say? Had he nothing to say to them? He appears to have been comfortable only among prostitutes, with whom there were no ceremonies, no taboos, no constraints: it was rather like playing with childhood friends, although there was fear (often justified) of venereal disease. Toward ladies of the night he felt neither compassion nor contempt but genuine cordiality: "I was so happy with Jeanie Kinnaird . . . She looked so healthy and so honest I had no fears." To Miss Reynolds, shortly before his marriage, he bade a friendly farewell and tried to persuade her to change her line of work: "'You have not the qualifications for it, except, indeed, being very pretty and agreeable. You have not the avarice, the falseness, which is requisite. I wish to have you out of it.' She promised me she would go into the millinery business and behave properly. It was curious to see her drink. 'Sir, I wish you all happiness in your new state of life.'"

Let us leave Boswell and his lady, both warmed by alcohol and the emotion of this, their final encounter, to wish each other an improbable happiness. Boswell was a libertine given to melancholy, as Casanova was given to high spirits. Yet these men, who briefly shared the lives of so many women in distress and on the margins, were able to give them back a modicum of humanity and, by an odd twist of fate, to restore the dignity these lowly women were so long denied.

Literature and Body Language: Dance

Throughout this chapter I have kept literature at arm's length, preferring to situate women in relation to the text rather than in the text. In so doing I have avoided, among other things, the problem of the body.

"I have finally seen poor Caderousse," writes Mme. de Sévigné; "she is green and losing blood as well as her life."[59] Sick bodies and remedies and their effects are abundantly present in memoirs and letters, but healthy bodies are just as noticeably absent. When the healthy body appeared in works of fiction, it was often in terms so conventional as to be all but meaningless: the most beautiful figure in the world, the most beautiful bosom in the world, and so on. But novels and "true" reportage did abandon their reticence and move beyond stereotypical description in one area, that of dance. Brantôme often gave voice to a fascination that he shared with everyone else at court: "No one in the room could feast their eyes enough" on the sight of Henri III dancing with his sister Marguerite de Valois.[60] Ronsard was also watching:

> Comme une femme elle ne marchait pas,
> Mais en roulant divinement le pas,
> D'un pied glissant couloit à la cadence.

Like a woman she did not walk, but with a step divinely smooth, with a gliding foot she fell in with the cadence.

Along with riding, a sport reserved for the nobility, dance was the only form of body language that allowed a woman to express herself as an equal of, and in perfect symmetry with, a man. The obligatory leisure imposed on women extended even to the sports in which men participated in their presence: from tennis to jousting, men performed while women sat and watched. A ball was thus a unique occasion for women to demonstrate that they too could move gracefully, vigorously, briskly, or with abandon. Word of a ball invariably caused a stir among women, from village

Cinderellas to the beauties of the royal entourage. It is no accident that in the novel by Mme. de La Fayette the Duke de Nemours and the Princess de Clèves, who had never seen each other, should have met at a ball. The author makes a point of telling us that both of course turned out for the occasion looking their best and wearing their finest clothes. "When they began to dance, a murmur of praise welled up in the hall."[61] Not long afterward, Nemours, worried about another ball that she will attend but he will not, spitefully declares that "no woman can think about her lover when she must worry about her appearance . . . [and] that appearance is for everybody, not just for the one she loves. At a ball women want to please whoever looks at them." It would be difficult to give a better description of the pleasures of refined exhibitionism in a society of connoisseurs or of the difference between the desire to please many and the desire to please one, in love. Dance was the ultimate form of display, the fulfillment of the need to *se pavaner*, to show off, a word derived from a conflation of *se paonner*, to display oneself like a peacock *(paon)* and *pavane*, a slow and solemn dance that originated in Padua.

Mme. de Sévigné describes not only the Breton peasants "whom one would have prevented from dancing in a well-disciplined republic" but also the nobles of the region "who dance Bohemian and lower-Breton steps with charming delicacy and grace."[62] One day, touched by the sight of a young Bohemian woman dancing in a way that reminds her of her own daughter, she writes to the general in charge of galley slaves in Marseilles to beg him to ease the lot of the dancer's grandfather, who is among the prisoners. Later she is delighted by the perfect grace of a young married couple, especially the man: "Mme. de Chaulnes, who danced well in her time, was beside herself and said she had never seen anything like it."[63] "Beside herself"—the words are revealing: ancien régime society was constraining for everyone.

People escaped the constraints as best they could, men in violence (whether in war or hunting), work, study, gambling, and debauch, and women in household chores, intrigue, flirtation, and the social whirl. Novels and religion were the only avenues open to them for freeing their minds, and dance was the only avenue open to them for freeing their bodies. Nicolas Restif de la Bretonne was of the opinion that young country girls "indulged themselves [in these activities] while they were free, knowing full well that they would have to give up such amusements once they were married . . . Those who danced and had a good time would one day, with no regrets, become hardworking mothers." By contrast, "those who were prevented from dancing by foolish mothers and priests would regret it all their lives."[64] The brief freedom of carefree youth helped people to make it through the rest of life, or so Restif believed. Restif is one of the few authors who gives us a glimpse of how peasants lived, for the peasantry at that time was deemed unworthy of literature. Peasants had little access to literature themselves, since illiteracy was widespread among them, particularly the women. That is why dance was such an important release from the burden of daily life.

From Ronsard to Restif we have discovered a wide range of female types. Despite the scarcity of evidence, we have begun to glimpse a world of women, a world that existed apart from men and of which men had little understanding. We have also seen women beginning to claim a certain independence. At first this independence was largely imaginary, embodied in a "counterculture" typified by the novel. But gradually it became more and more real and embraced ever-wider segments of society. In the sixteenth century it was limited to the aristocracy along with a few wealthy widows and courtesans. In the seventeenth and eighteenth centuries it included growing numbers of women of the middle ranks as urbanization increased, knowledge diffused, and people began imitating the ways of the court. New recreational activities developed, and with the advent of new occupational categories women found it possible to live without the support of men (albeit without children, unless they were put out to a wetnurse). The largest number worked as seamstresses and merchants, but already there were businesswomen in the cities at a time when Restif in the countryside saw nothing but peasant women "bent beneath the burden of household toil or browbeaten by brutal husbands."

Eventually the day came when every woman, standing before the mirror, heard, as in the fairy tale, that she was no longer "the fairest of them all." In the mirror of literature every woman could both dream and learn about the power, and fragility, of her charms; about the infidelity of men and the benefits of marriage; about the need to be (or at least to appear) virtuous; and about guilty desires. Women learned to live with these contradictions, doing sometimes what they had to do, at other times what they were not supposed to do. Some were ingenuously libertine, others conscientiously devout.

Was literature the road to knowledge for women? The difficulty of formulating an answer shows that the question is not an easy one. Besides idealized heroines and villainesses, writers also described women who did not read and women who presumably found sufficient contentment for their lives in dancing, like the grasshoppers of fable. All society loved opera at the time, and perhaps this was because in opera, where fictional characters sang and danced, spectators saw an image of Eden, of an earthly paradise (the adjective is crucial). Every society needs to dream, and not only women but also men. *Così fan tutte, e così fan tutti.*

TRANSLATED FROM THE FRENCH BY ARTHUR GOLDHAMMER

9

The Theater

Eric A. Nicholson

ALL THE WORLD'S A STAGE, and all the stage
is a brothel: to early modern European men and
women, the latter metaphor was as appropriate as
the former. It was also equally complex. On the
one hand, the identification of playhouse with
bawdyhouse conveyed a negative moral judgment;
on the other, it embodied the sexually enticing as
well as threatening aspects of defining human relations and identities along theatrical lines. Moreover, whether condemned as a site of debauchery
or patronized as both a comprehensive and eroti-
cally charged "mirror of nature," the early modern
theater highlighted woman in all her negative, positive, and, as often as not, ambivalent guises.

To at least some degree, plays were defined as
meretricious or even pornographic, since they
made a public display of painted and costumed
women before largely male audiences. This had
been a major complaint of antitheatrical early
Christians—notably Tertullian, Saint John Chrysostom, and Saint Augustine[1]—but the sixteenth
century's increasing emphasis on female chastity,
silence, obedience, and domestic confinement reinforced the associations between the theater and
the bordello. If a woman who let herself be seen
at her own window could be accused of prostitut-
ing herself, what were the implications of seeing

women move, speak, dance, sing, embrace, kiss, and commit adultery, incest, and even murder on the stage? The fact that for much of this period these audacious female characters were played by young male actors not only complicated but reinforced the theater's links with transgressive sexuality: homoeroticism and sexual ambiguity compounded the basic provocation of bringing female characters out of the house and into a performance space. Later, professional actresses would receive censure as harlots, praise as artists, or, more rarely, advancement as royal mistresses. Thus both acting and playgoing elicited fears, desires, taboos, fantasies, and even positive aspirations regarding the open display of either women or sexuality. Theater companies in Venice, Madrid, and London both suffered and benefited from their associations with loose morals and prostitution: at various times in the sixteenth and seventeenth centuries (such as 1642 in London), theatrical activity was prohibited in these and other cities; at other times it was enthusiastically and sometimes scandalously promoted.

This connection between theatrical performance and sexually transgressive behavior illuminates the paradoxical depictions of women in the European drama of the period. While playwrights tended to represent the feminine according to the preconceptions of contemporary discourse, certain aspects of their medium enabled them to create female characters who broke, and were often broken by, the rules of gender-determined conduct. Even the more stereotypical figures, simply by coming onstage, speaking, and affecting the play's action, sometimes belied the models of inferiority or subservience they were supposed to represent. In other cases, especially in plays that exposed the tensions and contradictions of rapidly changing social orders, women were seen to obey, demystify, challenge, outwit, or fall victim to the unjust assumptions and practices of their male-dominated worlds.

Regardless of the country, period, and prevailing religious outlook, female roles distinguish both the drama and the society of these centuries. Insofar as the postmedieval and preindustrial world categorized women almost exclusively in terms of their relationship to men, both normative roles—the virginal maid, chaste wife, and celibate widow—and transgressive ones—adulteress, prostitute, courtesan, and procuress or "bawd"—gave prominence to sexuality and the female body, precisely those entities that most demanded—and most threatened—patriarchal domination. Also of interest in this period are the evolution and demise of certain male roles, in particular the cuckold or "wittol," mate to the adulterous, and often only supposedly adulterous, woman.

By the eighteenth century the professional theater involved women as both actresses and playwrights. What connections did these new options have with changes in social roles and opportunities for women? At the representational level, what were the consequences of having women play female characters? In short, what could female characters and actresses do onstage, as opposed to offstage? When translated into theatrical performance, how were women's social conditions and experiences inverted and transformed, as well as reproduced and limited? The profound and multifaceted changes arising from the rich theatrical output of this period serve as a revealing index of competing and often contradictory ideas, customs, and identities.

The Prostitute, Bawd, and Courtesan

Although the Spanish author Fernando de Rojas may not have intended his most famous work, *The Tragi-comedy of Calisto and Melibea* (1502), for performance, it soon became best known as a dramatic piece under the name of its most notable character, "La Celestina," an "old whore" who holds sway over not only the play's other characters but also its readers and audiences. Quickly translated or adapted into Italian (1515), German (1520), French (1527), and English (1530), *La Celestina* enlarged and transformed the theatrical identity of the *lena* figures found in Plautus' and Terence's Roman comedies. A procuress takes center stage, in all her wit, charm, corruption, and above all, versatility. No longer simply the cynical, money-grubbing adviser to a younger lady of pleasure, she now emerges as a complex protagonist, at once exploiting and exploited by the sexual attitudes of her society—and audience. Her very name, "the heavenly woman," is an oxymoron that also accurately evokes the practice of contemporary prostitutes to assume a glamorous pseudonym. Although she is aged, addicted to drink, and, as Rojas describes her, "a bit of a witch," in other ways Celestina does live up to her name: she is skilled in a variety of arts and crafts, including medicine; and she is literally adored by her principal client, Calisto. Like her nonfictional counterparts, she concocts her own almost mythic identity, a move that enables her to satisfy men's fantasies and at the same time drain their resources. Thus in its mixed portrayal of Celestina's demonic corruption and versatile self-determination, the play itself becomes enmeshed in the dilemma of idolizing a supposed agent of sin. As is the case with many of her theatrical descendants, Celestina's lack of feminine virtue offsets, indeed liberates, her masculine *virtù*.

Whether intentionally or not, numerous plays would confront audiences with the choice of condoning the illicit views and actions of a "fallen woman" or of reviling her courage, talents, and intelligence. Examples of such characters include the go-between Alvigia in Aretino's *La Cortigiana* (1533), the ducal mistress Vittoria Corombona in John Webster's *The White Devil* (1612), and the scheming widow Livia of Thomas Middleton's *Women Beware Women* (ca. 1621). For if there was inevitable "corruption" in a bawd, or something "monstrous" about a vocal, independent, and "masculine" woman, there was also something fascinating about her. Thus the theater, with its capacity to give these unsettling female figures voice, costume, and movement, functioned not only as a witness but also as a vehicle of such contradictions in early modern gender roles.

There is a revealing distinction, for example, between Ariosto's *La lena* (1528), written for a carnival performance at the Este court in Ferrara, and Shakerley Marmion's *Holland's Leaguer,* a play presented at London's Salisbury Court theater a century later, in 1631. Marmion's defiant "Bawd" character embodies the stereotype of her occupation and takes little part in the play's action. In contrast, Ariosto's title character goes beyond even La Celestina, not only in attaining a distinctive identity, but also in expressing a critique of contemporary society. Lena, sold by her husband into prostitution, underpaid and mistreated by her wealthy lover, nonetheless eloquently defends learning and education, attains her practical goals, and emerges as the play's leading character. Despite her name, she is anything but a stock comic figure, whereas Marmion's Bawd is a caricature of the already caricatured Amazonian, a threat to be watched and contained, rather than a woman allowed to voice her own challenging opinions.

The prominence and evident appeal of such provocative women of ill fame also brought uneasiness, as evidenced by the censorship efforts of both civic and religious authorities. The theater-as-brothel identification becomes especially pertinent, given formal edicts' consistent denunciations of the "lascivious" and even "unnatural" words and actions spoken and performed in plays. Such is the emphasis in the Venetian Council of Ten's decree of December 1508, prohibiting all theatrical productions, but especially those at private parties and wedding celebrations. The contemporary diarist Marino Sanudo observed that prostitutes sometimes performed at these festive occasions, at least as dancers.[2] In this case, the theatrical event is literally pornographic, and the audience therefore suspect as willing patrons of harlots. The view that plays were occasions or at least stimuli for sexual licence persisted throughout the next three centuries. For example, actors and especially actresses during Spain's golden age (late sixteenth and seventeenth centuries) were vilified as lewd blasphemers and corrupters of public virtue; in France, the sixteenth-century Ritual of Paris associated actors with "whoremasters" and "women of ill life," thus denying them communion and Christian burial (Molière was the most famous victim of this stigma); in England, finally, a series of Puritans and moralists wrote lengthy and often impassioned treatises against the theater, among them John Rainolds' *The Overthrow of Stage-Plays* (1599), William Prynne's *Histriomastix* (1633), and Jeremy Collier's *Short View of the Immorality and Profaneness of the English Stage* (1698). While the prolix and nearly lunatic Prynne labels theatergoers as "adulterers, adulteresses, whore-masters, whores, bawdes, panders," it is Jean-Jacques Rousseau who most succinctly expresses the antitheatrical polemicists' misogyny, arguing that independent women "dishonor their sex. When, as in the theater, they display themselves publicly for money, they become little better than prostitutes."[3]

Fittingly enough, Rousseau's statement echoes the lines of paranoically suspicious stage-husbands who accuse their wives of infidelity, and therefore of prostitution. In Ben Jonson's *Volpone* (1605), for instance, the possessive Corvino sees his wife, Celia, drop a handkerchief from her window to the mountebank "Scoto" (Volpone in disguise), an action that he interprets in terms of the actress/harlot paradigm. "You were an actor with your handkerchief," he cries, having already called Celia a "whore" and told her, "Get you a cittern [a guitar], Lady Vanity [the name of a morality-play character], / And be a dealer [a prostitute] with the virtuous man" (II, iii, 20–21). Corvino's words thus convey the notion that women who appeared alone in public were inviting the attentions of an audience and, being women, were inevitably soliciting sexual encounters.

At the same time, his false accusation is itself an audience response: by projecting the supposed qualities of an actress/courtesan onto his wife, the jealous husband reveals his desire for her to succeed in playing such a role. In short, the line between wife and whore could be a fine one. As there were few other roles for their real-life models to play, married women in seventeenth-century English drama are often seen to suffer, whether they follow such typecasting or seek to defy it. Although she is valiantly chaste and steadfast, Desdemona in Shakespeare's *Othello* (ca. 1604) is branded as a "whore" and "strumpet" and murdered by the man who loves her. Even when the wife survives, she does so only by counteracting her husband's degradation of her, sometimes through patience and "magic," like Hermione in Shakespeare's *The Winter's Tale* (circa 1610), sometimes through wit and dexterity, like Margery Pinchwife in William Wycherley's *The Country Wife* (1675). When he threatens that he "will write 'whore' with this penknife in your face" (IV, ii, 87), Margery's husband Mr. Pinchwife expresses the violent—and in this case self-defeating—male obsession with a wife's subjection and fidelity, which also serves to drive both comic and tragic dramatic plots.

Although it would be misleading to call Wycherley's presentation feminist, his portrayal of the cruel and absurd Mr. Pinchwife invites sympathy for the adulterous Margery: her justifiable dalliance catches the audience in a dilemma of moral judgment. Several full-fledged prostitute characters in seventeenth-century English drama pose similar dilemmas. For instance, in more didactic but no less popular plays, such as Thomas Heywood's *How a Man May Choose a Good Wife from a Bad* (1602) and John Marston's *The Dutch Courtesan* (1605), the prostitute figure undergoes some kind of punishment as part of a moralistic scheme to exalt a virtuous woman's contrasting chastity. The corrupt woman's prominence in the play, however, coupled with the folly or treachery of the male characters, qualifies the ostensibly negative image that the male playwrights aim to give her. At least in part, these mixed treatments indicate how the contemporary theatrical medium's own pandering image worked against its denigrations of "bawdry."

In this regard, Dol Common of Jonson's *The Alchemist* (1610) and Angellica-Bianca of Behn's *The Rover* (1677) provide contrasting yet equally self-aware critiques of the attempt to regulate either morality, sexuality, or the theatrical treatment thereof. As her name implies, Dol may be a common "punk" or whore, but her actions are quite often extraordinary. She opens the play by disarming her quarreling accomplices Face and Subtle and reminding them of their "venture tripartite," in which they will hold "all things in common." She thus redeems the otherwise debased value of her own name and inspires her partners to call her "Dol Singular," "Royal Dol," and "Claridiana." Her most flamboyant metamorphosis, however, revives the mythical iconography of Elizabeth I, when she appears as the "Queen of Faery" and thus swindles the credulous clerk Dapper. Within the play's governing theme of alchemy, Dol appears as one of the leading theatrical alchemists, pretending to change her commonplace identity by means of grand illusions of romance, learning, royalty, and divinity. The theatricality of her profession is made explicit, and hence her role becomes doubly transgressive as she thrives on the self-deceptions that govern her audiences' thoughts, words, and actions.

In contrast, Behn's Angellica-Bianca is depicted as the most famous of all Italian courtesans, a woman who charges a thousand crowns a month for her favors, and whose portraits and songs from her balcony attract a host of suitors. She therefore resembles the alluring but wicked stage courtesans of pre-Restoration plays; however, given the libertine theatrical culture of 1670s London and the perspective of a female author, she emerges as a sympathetic individual. For example, it is she, not her virginal young rival, Hellena, who speaks for higher spiritual love between man and woman. As her love has transformed her from an artful courtesan to a constant lover, so she expects her inconstant beloved to go through a similar transformation. When she resorts to the cliché prostitute's action of attempting a murder, she fails to do the deed, and exits to an uncertain future. Behn thus shows that Angellica cannot fully escape the stereotypes associated with her courtesan role; nonetheless, she succeeds in retaining her personal autonomy.

When, however, the prostitute Jenny Diver of John Gay's *Beggar's Opera* (1728) strips Macheath of his pistols, she does so in the service of the entrepreneurial Mr. Peachum: the prostitute is no longer self-employed, but an employee. By the later eighteenth century, English authors followed continental decorum in removing such women from plays altogether. The career of the early modern stage prostitute thus parallels that of her real-life counterpart, who went from being not only tolerated but sometimes officially sanctioned in the late fifteenth century, to being outlawed and frequently driven into the shadows from the late sixteenth to the eighteenth centuries.[4]

Maid, Wife, or Widow?

Both on and off early modern stages, "honorable" women were also stereotyped. Whereas Shakespeare's Jaques explains that a man has "seven ages," Duke Vincentio of Vienna in *Measure for Measure* confirms the predominant view that a respectable woman could have but three: when Mariana denies being a maid, a wife, or a widow, the Duke declares that she is "nothing." Aptly enough, the scurrilous Lucio then interjects that "she may be a punk; for many of them are neither maid, widow, nor wife" (V, i, 178–180). These lines directly transmit the conventional view of women's three social identities, which, unlike the seven ages of man, are confined to their sexual roles; that is, they are dependent on their relationship to a male partner. Yet the same final scene from *Measure for Measure,* as well as others written by Shakespeare and his contemporaries, manages to embarrass this gender-determined categorization. Although Mariana is reunited with her faithless husband, Angelo, the maid and novice Isabella makes no answer to the Duke's offer of marriage. This indeterminate ending confounds the expected compliance with conventional female roles.

In other words, female characters could be transgressive, even when they did not transgress the basic sexual and legal restrictions placed on the three "estates of woman." Various plays feature women who preserve their virginity or sexual honor yet at the same time assert their ability to play roles usually reserved to men. In such cases, the objectification of a young woman as an ideal maid, wife, or widow is disrupted: instead of upholding the supposed correspondence between female chastity and silent obedience, the play's heroine takes the opposite course, assuming masculine prerogatives for her independent conduct. Appropriately, this process of becoming a female subject often involves self-conscious theatricality. Calderón's Doña Angela, a chaste widow, turns herself into *La dama duende* (The Phantom Lady, 1629) in order to pursue her love for Don Manuel and escape the suspicions of her jealous brothers, Don Luis and Don Juan. Confined to her room by these honor-obsessed men, she employs artful theatrics to escape their incestuous tyranny and fulfill her own romantic designs: at various points she becomes a set designer, a director, and an actress-magician. Although her end is tragic, the title character of Webster's *The Duchess of Malfi* (1614) is also a heroic widow, who stage-manages a secret but legal wedding with her steward, Antonio. Like Doña Angela, the Duchess simultaneously accepts and defies the patriarchal guidelines for her role: on the one hand, she breaks no law or sacrament, while on the other, she disobeys her brothers by marrying the man of her choice and maintaining an exemplary marriage in the face of violent threats and tortures.

Through their wit, bravery, and versatility, these two female protagonists reveal contradictions in the formula for secluded, celibate widowhood prescribed by the men who try to control them. A similar pattern, enacted in an even greater number of plays, involves the device of chaste maids and wives who disguise themselves as boys or men. Again, these characters employ theatrical techniques to solve the problem of how to slip past a constrictive role model while appearing to obey it. In a broader societal context in which self-effacement was the ideal toward which women were taught to aspire, these characters efface themselves to the point where they have no apparent female identity at all. The joke is on the male characters, who cannot anticipate such a complete reversal of gender-determination, and hence rarely see through the "masculine" exterior. At another level, the joke is on members of the audience who would similarly judge identity on the basis of gender roles, and gender on the basis of clothing. Thus, both presentation and representation mock the gender-determined boundaries of dress and public behavior, as laid down by ecclesiastical and civic authorities in accordance with the scriptural law against cross-dressing (Deuteronomy 22:5).

How these boundaries were defined in popular mentalities is harder to determine, but there is sufficient evidence to affirm that they were a topic of both fascination and lively debate. As far as deviant sexual identity was concerned, both its defenders and attackers could refer to mythic paradigms, primarily of the "androgyne," the "hermaphrodite," and the "virago." These sexually ambiguous and often threatening figures could be turned to positive account (as witness the biblical Judith, Ariosto's Bradamante, Spenser's Britomart): at least at the level of fantasy, a maid could behave like a man and still retain her maidenly virtue.

However, neither mythical nor even elevated status distin-

303

guishes the transvestite Santilla, or "Lidio Femina," in Bernardo Dovizi da Bibbiena's *La Calandria* (1513). Instead, her distinguishing traits are an exact resemblance to her twin brother, Lidio, and a fortuitous skill in substituting for him at just the right moments. In devising this scenario, Bibbiena brings the myth of ideal androgyny into the realm of comic intrigue, deception, and lowlife characters. Nevertheless, the identical-twins device, which complicates and sustains the main plot of Lidio's illicit affair with Calandro's wife, Fulvia, resolves itself into a concluding happy reunion and promise of a double wedding. Her brother is adulterous, but Santilla remains chaste, though Fulvia twice brings her into bed with her. Operating at once as farce and romance, the play's confusion of identities also prevents a final identification of its main female character as either a virago who aids and abets ribaldry or an embodiment of virginal innocence.

La Calandria influenced a number of later European comedies, among them the Accademici Intronati di Siena's *Gl'ingannati* (The Deceived Ones, 1531) and Wycherley's *The Plain Dealer* (1676). Each of these plays features a heroine who cross-dresses in order to serve and win the hand of a disloyal, self-centered, or brutal male love-object, and each in its own way dramatizes the severe obstacles to performing the ideal "maid" role. Were Lelia, the daughter of Virginio in *Gl'ingannati,* to obey her father's wishes, she would have to stay in a convent until the day of her enforced wedding to the old and decrepit Gherardo. She therefore turns to cross-dressing as an escape, only to meet further hazards and complications. For although she defends her wearing of men's clothing as a self-liberation and a way to be in her beloved's company and confidence, cross-dressing is also construed as a notorious practice of prostitutes, a cause for public shame and family dishonor, a temptation to both male and female homosexuality, and a sign and cause of madness. Throughout the play, however, Lelia retains those very qualities of virtue that her costume supposedly vitiates.

Like Lelia, *The Plain Dealer*'s cross-dressing heroine, Fidelia, arouses desire in the woman whom her beloved master loves; she is also forced to be a pimp, assaulted first by an unfaithful wife and then by the same woman's husband, undressed, nearly raped, wounded, and by happy chance betrothed in the play's dénouement to her master, the misogynist and misanthropic Manly. Fidelia, however, has no brother of any kind, and she acts within the context of the English Restoration's heavily mercantile economy and sexually audacious lifestyles. Rather than enjoying any magical self-transformation, she suffers being the instrument of both her employer's and assailants' drive for sexual gratification at all costs. Instead of arbitrarily providing a look-alike sibling, Wycherley just as arbitrarily provides a two-thousand-pound dowry for his heroine: money lies at the heart of the play's analysis of contemporary sexual politics.

In early modern drama, the device of transvestism is thus far more than a mere opportunity for comically mistaken identities and romantic plot entanglements. Especially in regard to the plays' own alleged use of sexual provocation, cross-dressing becomes both the actual and symbolic means of a critique of male sexual greed and violence, female sexual duplicity, and the system of buying and selling brides that governs such erotic crimes and deceptions.

Adulteress and Cuckold

These cross-dressing heroines come into full, provocative focus when compared with several other theatrical role models for young women. Chaste, silent, and obedient maids and wives, such as "Patient Griselda," do appear in a number of dramatic pieces, in which they are praised and rewarded for their conduct. On the other hand, the transgressive role of the adulteress was an equally familiar and often more complex stage figure.

Part of this complexity involved a close connection between fictional dramatizations of female adultery and contemporary ritual shamings of remarrying widows or unruly wives and their husbands. Called *mattinate* in Italy, *charivaris* in France, and "skimmington rides" or "rough music" in England, these rituals often ridiculed their victims by employing noisy and conspicuously theatrical devices, such as obscene verse, discordant songs, lewd props, and transvestism. Charivaris conspicuously inverted the apparatus and procedure of the wedding ceremony, substituting horns for rings, "rough" for harmonious music, and cross-dressing for conventional attire.[5] The exact form and motives of these rites differed with time and place, but they consistently assumed at least potential adultery and insubordination on the part of the wife. Charivaris, however, could operate in a paradoxical way, since their loud, disruptive, and disordering mockery of sexual offenses often came across as further offense. Moreover, there was a close link between these events and comedies, farces, and other skits that derided old, impotent, or unfaithful spouses. For example, Angelo Beolco "il Ruzante"'s epic, farcical sex-comedy *Betía* (1524–1527) was greeted by scandalized audience reaction, apparently to the play's explicit sexual language and indecorous scenarios, such as a concluding four-person communal marriage and a fourth-act mattinata featuring the return of the supposedly dead Nale to his already "unfaithful widow" Tamia.

As this plot description shows, Ruzante's drama gives prominence to adultery, but it neither stereotypes the adulteress nor condemns her actions. Similarly, in a drama showing peasants acting under pressure from particular social and economic circumstances, the *Parlamento de Ruzante che iera vegnù de campo* (ca. 1526), the character Ruzante's wife, Gnua, flees to Venice and a life of prostitution for the sake of sheer economic survival. Confronted by her ragged and destitute husband, she convincingly explains the necessity of her actions, and the two remain separated, refugees from their war-torn fields. Ruzante the character's frustrations derive from his own attempts to play such caricatures as the jilted Petrarchan lover or betrayed doting husband. In the context of Ruzante the playwright's "real-life" drama, adultery becomes an inevitable economic reality for his pragmatic female characters, and a paradoxical raison d'être for his tormented but also self-tormenting protagonist. Ruzante thus diagnosed how both the economics and psychopathology of adultery depended on the notions of woman as property, woman as weak and submissive, and woman as sexually erratic. In the patriarchal microcosm of the individual family, all these assumptions dictated that the husband (= sovereign lord) was obliged to maintain control over his wife's body and sexuality, especially since it was widely held that women could not do so themselves.[6]

In practice, however, this patriarchal theory of the husband's absolute authority and the wife's dutiful submission met with inevitable adjustments and compromises, and it is within this conflict between theory and practice that theatrical renditions of the adulteress and cuckold often appear. The squabbling couples of fifteenth- and sixteenth-century French farces can almost be defined in terms of their "fights for the breeches," or contests for domestic preeminence. For example, the farce or *débat* of *Les deux maris et leurs deux femmes* (circa 1500) develops a contrast between two wives: Alice, who is chaste but insubordinate; and Jeanne, who is docile but promiscuous. In arguing over which leads the preferable life, the women's husbands reveal the horns of their dilemma: fear of domination and fear of cuckoldry. The women then state their views on marital relations, Alice boasting of her unsullied reputation, Jeanne citing first her discretion in pleasing "well-off gentlemen" in "hiding-places," and second her piety in fulfilling the biblical decree to multiply. Finally, the audience sees vignettes of the two couples' respective lifestyles: Alice and her inebriated husband, Colin, hit and insult each other, and Colin eventually complains about being a man underneath a woman on top; Jeanne and her equally drunken spouse, Mathieu, attempt to make love but fail because of his impotence. The code of honor yields to the image of authority, and thus to a satire not so much on women as on rigid models of chastity and obedience.

These women, however, like their later English equivalents in plays such as Middleton's *A Chaste Maid in Cheapside* (1613) and Jonson's *Bartholomew Fair* (1614), are primarily objects of other characters' manipulation and the playwright's satire. In short, they are less than heroic figures. Heroism or at least subjectivity more often belongs to tragic female protagonists, who suffer mortal punishments for their infidelities. For example, Alice Arden, in the anonymous *Arden of Faversham* (1592), engineers the murder of her husband for the sake of her lover, Mosby. Although the title page of the original quarto claims that the play will show "the great malice and dissimulation of a wicked woman," it shows instead her tragic crisis of conscience, caught between desire for a man who is mainly after her money, and her sense of marital duty to a financial profiteer and jealous misogynist. At the play's end, sentenced to burning, she decries her lover's hypocrisy in calling her "strumpet," as well as the false pretenses of male romantic discourse: "Ah, but for thee I had never been strumpet. / What cannot oaths and protestations do / When men have opportunity to woo?" (scene 18, lines 15–17).

In the context of a system of patriarchal, often arranged marriages (especially among the aristocracy), adultery is sometimes portrayed as a liberation, or at least as a means of revelation. While the genre of tragedy demands that the unfaithful wife be punished and the system of honor upheld, several tragic plays dramatize the tyrannies not only of this demand but also of the

307

masculine prerogatives on which it is predicated. Hence the recurring "revenge tragedy" critique of the debauched hypocrisies of kings, dukes, cardinals, and decadent courtiers. Appropriately enough, the corrupting act of adultery can empower the previously subordinate woman, by allowing her first to defy her partner's dominion and then to decry and sometimes take revenge on an iniquitous court society. This pattern applies to the courtesan Evadne in Beaumont and Fletcher's *The Maid's Tragedy* (1611), as well as to the purchased bride/duchess Cassandra in Lope de Vega's *Castigo sin venganza* (1631). Each protests and bravely rebels against her exploitation, though she cannot escape the price of death exacted for her adultery.

This cruelty of the double standard, along with its attendant misogyny and basis in male rivalry, is even more severely criticized in plays such as Calderón's *El Médico de su honra* (1629) and Shakespeare's *Othello, Cymbeline,* and *The Winter's Tale.* In each, the wronged woman heroically defends her innocence only to meet with death, either real or symbolic. As Webster's Vittoria Corombona observes, patriarchal justice is itself deaf and blind, hearing what it wants to hear and seeing what it wants to see. In *Cymbeline,* Posthumus fantasizes killing his wife, Imogen, as soon as he hears of her supposed adultery; he then reveals how this violent urge involves a fear of his own possible femininity:

> Could I find out
> The woman's part in me—for there's no motion
> That tends to vice in man, but I affirm
> It is the woman's part: be it lying, note it,
> The woman's; flattering, hers; deceiving, hers;
> Lust and rank thoughts, hers, hers; revenges, hers;
> Ambitions, covetings, change of prides, disdain,
> Nice longing, slanders, mutability,
> All faults that name, nay, that hell knows,
> Why, hers, in part or all; but rather, all.   (II, v, 19–28)

It is an understatement to say that this tirade epitomizes projected sexual guilt, stemming from doubts and insecurities regarding the fixity of gender.

Moreover, Posthumus' psychosis is not merely personal, but cultural. However extremist he is, he speaks for the widely held view that women were of a melancholic humour, governed by Saturn and therefore prone to vice, deceit, and instability. It was therefore imperative for husbands to offset and control these "womanish" inclinations. In England, where the courts tended toward leniency in adultery cases, jurisdiction and public humiliation often took place at the unofficial level of "rough music," mocking rhymes, and "skimmington rides." Inherently theatrical, these customs could escalate into full-blown dramatization, as at Salisbury in 1614, where Alice Mustian staged an impromptu satire on her neighbors' adultery. The common motif of the cuckold's horns provided elements of monstrosity and mock fertility, as well as countless references in the contemporary theater. The insanely jealous Leontes in *The Winter's Tale* feels them growing on his forehead, to proclaim him a cuckold: the external device is internalized, showing that Leontes has so greatly succumbed to the fear of scandal that he becomes his own self-caricature. As the play's recurrent theatrical metaphors confirm, Leontes writes and performs his own misguided, violent, and tragic shaming ritual, as if to forestall anyone else from doing so.

Thus the adulteress and cuckold appeared in a variety of manifestations in early modern plays, with their one major constant being the risk for wives in seeking their desires or asserting their views. The adulterous husband or male lover faced lesser or deferred penalties, often in the form of revenge. By the eighteenth century, disloyal men, and even Don Juan and his counterparts on the French and English stages, had been demoted to would-be rather than actual "horners"; and the adulteress was no longer a potentially heroic or even leading figure: she, like the equally transgressive and insubordinate figures of the prostitute and witch, had been removed from theatrical exposure.

Women as Actresses and Playwrights

One of the main distinguishing features of accused witches, as well as of "scolds" and "shrews," was their volubility, most often in public. Not coincidentally, this verbal issue helped to keep actual women off the stage. According to many male writers, speaking parts gave a positive license to women whose supposedly loquacious natures should have been muzzled, and made them even more likely to prostitute themselves. Throughout medieval and sixteenth-century Europe, almost all mentions of women as performers cite them as dancers, tumblers, silent allegorical figures, and at most singers. In early Stuart England, royal and aristocratic ladies often performed in court masques and pageants, but they almost never uttered a line of dialogue. Under such pressure either to answer or to run counter to stereotypes of silence or excessive speech, women struggled for centuries to establish themselves as legitimate actresses. The few who wrote or produced plays encountered even stronger opposition, not only from moralists but also from rival male playwrights and impresarios.

The assumption that actresses were but a step removed from prostitutes, and vice versa, continually beset women both before and after they had won the right to work in the theatrical profession. In Spain in the 1590s and the early seventeenth century, the Council of Castile, under the influence of both Jesuit critics and influential patrons of the theater, alternately banned and reinstated professional actresses. It was alleged that these women were promiscuous, and thus openly desecrated the Virgin Mary whenever they portrayed her. In 1574 an Italian troupe performed in England, where actresses were not licensed until the reopening of the theaters in 1660, and were denigrated for their "unchaste, shameless, and unnatural tumbling."[7] In 1592 Thomas Nashe commended English players for being morally superior to their Italian counterparts: the latter were "bawdy comedians" who let "whores" play women's roles.[8]

Yet there were precedents, if often scandalous ones, for women to perform in public, and although authorities might censure them and audiences assault them—as happened to a group of touring French actresses in London in 1629—they eventually became popular enough to establish themselves as legitimate professionals. Their acceptance in Italy, France, and Spain coincided with the professionalization of theater in these countries, especially with the advent of the *commedia dell'arte* companies during the middle and late sixteenth century; indeed, women were crucial to the development of the *commedia dell'arte*'s improvisational comic techniques. Although acting was a precarious and embattled profession—a situation that remains unchanged—the most talented and fortunate could make a successful career of it. For example, Isabella Andreini owned the leading role of *prima donna innamorata* in the leading *commedia* company of the day, the Gelosi, and with her husband, Francesco, and the author Flaminio Scala wrote and perfected the intricate scenarios that came to constitute the standard repertoire of her art form. She so refined her own role of the young female lover that it was eventually endowed with her own first name, and in playing it she used not only slapstick techniques but also transvestite disguise, philosophical debate, Petrarchan parody, and passages from Boccaccio and her own writings. She is credited as the author of her most famous piece, *La pazzia,* which featured her ability to play all the other major parts or *maschere* of the *commedia,* both male and female: *pantalone, graziano, zanni,* Pedrolino, Franceschina, and so on. In addition, she was known for playing tragic and pastoral parts, and for being a dancer. Her exemplary marriage absolved her from the slur of harlot, and she was granted a church burial. In short, Isabella Andreini demonstrated that women could pursue a career outside the home that was artistic rather than sexual.

She could not, however, ensure that general public opinion would see acting as a respectable trade. In the century following Andreini's death in 1604, even such highly talented and established actresses as Madeleine and Armande Béjart, who created many of Molière's finest female roles, found themselves the targets of gossip and defamation. The well-documented English Restoration stage provides further evidence of the public's mixed attitude of adulation and disdain toward actresses. The very novelty of female performers attracted large audiences, who enjoyed seeing women in sexually provocative male disguise and also in all-female casts, as in Congreve's classic *Love for Love* (1705 and 1706). A select group of actresses, such as Nell Gwynn and Anne Bracegirdle, gained renown for their exceptional acting ability; they often concluded performances by addressing the audience directly in topical epilogues, further testimony to their high status and popularity.

On the other hand, even the most successful Restoration actresses had to contend with prejudice, discrimination, and sexual harassment. It was commonly assumed that actresses led immoral lives, and they were likened to prostitutes or made the targets of unwanted sexual advances. There were resentments and outcries over liaisons between noblemen and lowborn actresses, even when, as in the famous case of Prince Rupert and Margaret Hughes, the relationship ended in a recognized, long-term match.[9] Finally, as in today's entertainment industry, actresses were usually paid less than their male colleagues and rarely attained the privileged literary and social status accorded to some actors. Discontent with these sexist attitudes and practices informs the work of contemporary female dramatists, among them Mary de la Rivière Manley,

Aphra Behn, and Susannah Centlivre, all of whom wrote plays between the 1670s and 1720s. Despite having friends and advocates in the male theatrical community, they recognized that simply by being women who wrote for the stage, they were facing an enormous obstacle of prejudice. Behn, the most accomplished of the so-called female wits, and indeed one of the four or five outstanding playwrights of her period, was also the most outspoken and eloquent in defending women authors against sexist discrimination. She specialized in comedies of sexual intrigue, bawdy dialogue, and adulterous adventure. After both female and male audience members had protested at the frankness of her *Sir Patient Fancy* (1678), Behn asserted in a preface that discrimination against her female authorship was the cause of the criticism. In the epilogue to the same play, the author even more scathingly indicts her audience, and even more explicitly defends female authorship. This poem in rhymed couplets, spoken by the actress Mrs. Gwin, is worth quoting at length:

> I here and there o'erheard a coxcomb cry,
> "Ah, rot it, 'tis a woman's comedy,
> One, who because she lately chanced to please us,
> With her damned stuff will never cease to tease us."
> What has poor woman done that she must be
> Debarred from sense and sacred poetry?
> Why in this age has Heaven allowed you more,
> And women less of wit than heretofore?
> We once were famed in story, and could write
> Equal to men; could govern, nay, could fight.
> We still have passive valour, and can show,
> Would custom give us leave, the active too . . .
> We'll let you see, whate'er besides we do,
> How artfully we copy some of you:
> And if you're drawn to th'life, pray tell me then,
> Why women should not write as well as men.

Behn thus demands no less than full equality between male and female writers, defending a woman's right to active self-assertion against the patriarchal code for her submissive conduct.

Behn put her feminist arguments into action both in her plays and in her own life, though often in more subtle and idiosyncratic ways. Her experiences before becoming the first professional woman writer in English history were in themselves exceptional:

she had spent almost a year on or near a plantation in Suriname, had worked as a spy and intelligence agent in the Low Countries, and had done time in debtors' prison. It was to free herself from debt that she took up writing and publication, refusing the conventional avenue of finding a husband and settling down to domestic life. Although she had several love affairs with both men and women, she never remarried after her husband's death in 1665, and she remained independent until her own in 1689.[10]

Many of Behn's plays concern enforced marriage and the attempts of women to break free from the control of their fathers, brothers, and husbands. Her heroines' campaigns for self-determination sometimes provide the occasion for another of Behn's favored comic motifs, disguise as either a man or a worldly type of woman. Thus in *The Rover* Florinda and her sister, Hellena, rove the streets of Naples as gypsies. In Hellena's case, this tactic is also a complete about-face, since her brother has been trying to keep her as a nun in a convent. Again, Behn dramatizes the patriarchal tactic of confining female sexuality, which in turn provokes superior feminine stratagems of self-liberation. Announcing her intention to outwit her brother and find herself a lover of her own choosing, Hellena is emphatic: "I don't intend every he that likes me shall have me, but he that I like" (III, i, 40–41). She goes on to attract the aggressively promiscuous Willmore, cross-dressing in the process. Meanwhile, the common prostitute Lucetta entices the boorish Englishman Blunt into her bedroom, where she swindles him and sends him down a trapdoor: again, a clever and independent woman deflates the pretensions of machismo. There is also poetic justice here, since Behn consistently viewed the male-dominated institution of marriage as equivalent to prostitution, especially if financial gain was its primary goal. Her sympathetic portrayals of prostitutes and adulterous wives conspicuously feature protests against the economic constraints faced by most women in a male-dominated economy of venture capitalism. Finally, Behn's scenes of sexual role reversal, in which women actively court and enchant the men they desire, are but one theatrical realization of her alternative vision of eros.

Although actresses, despite setbacks, continued to thrive, the brief era of the female dramatist was passing. After the 1730s, when in England the censorious Licensing Act was passed, women ceased to write for the stage and instead concentrated their efforts on the more polite genre of the novel. Female roles, though now played by women, became increasingly limited in scope and complexity, and dramatized transgressions of any kind were either avoided or vastly diminished. The revision or removal of Shakespeare's more ribald or lurid passages is a revealing example of this trend. In continental Europe and the New World there were few successors to the Mexican nun Sor Juana Inés de la Cruz (1651–1695), an eloquent lyric poet who also wrote one full-length Calderonian comedy, *Los empeños de una casa,* performed in 1683. This drama by a champion of women's literary endeavors and educational rights includes a scene in which the Spanish nobleman Don Pedro woos the cross-dressed native Mexican Castaño: the class and gender confusion satirize aristocratic as well as masculine fantasies of seduction. By the play's end, Don Pedro has failed to win the hand of his beloved, Doña Leonor. Sor Juana thus demystifies machismo ideology from her own standpoint.

In the next century, however, it was left primarily to male playwrights, such as Goldoni in *La Locandiera* (1752) and Beaumarchais in *The Marriage of Figaro* (1784), to ridicule the attempts of upper-class men to seduce working women. Goldoni's Florentine innkeeper Mirandolina repeatedly announces her determination to preserve her cherished "libertà" and not to marry. Ultimately, however, the play dramatizes the problem of her desire to maintain her independence in a context of male romantic pretensions: when her absurd aristocratic suitors resolve to fight a duel over her, she quickly engages herself to her employee, Fabrizio, as the only way out of an imbalanced marriage to an outmoded world of honor, titles, and affected social airs. Her lower-middle-class marriage, like Susanna and Figaro's, promises a life of companionate stability and common sense. In Beaumarchais's play, the foiling and embarrassment of the would-be adulterer, Count Almaviva, by his wife and her maid provide a comic resolution, as well as emphasizing women's approved function as peacemakers in domestic conflicts and disputes.

With this exaltation of the bourgeois model of marital loyalty and togetherness, *The Marriage of Figaro* foreshadows both a social revolution and a major shift in public expectations about drama and female dramatic characters. No longer would the theater be regarded as a brothel or even as a comprehensive mirror of nature, but as a school for civilized virtues and sexual decorum: the reigns of the Victorian ingenue and redeemed fallen woman were on their way.

10

A Sampling of Eighteenth-Century Philosophy

Michèle Crampe-Casnabet

A REPRESENTATION IS THAT which is *present* to the mind. This presence can be more or less adequate to the reality of the thing or person represented. It may even figuratively distort that reality, in which case the distinction between representations and pure products of the imagination or fancy is blurred. The thing or person represented is always secondary, mediated by the subject who is the site of representation.

With this definition in mind, it is clear that "woman" is a representation constituted by an alien subject, man, who substitutes himself for female subjectivity. Ever since there have been men, the reduction of woman to representation has proved an effective strategy. Naturally that strategy continued to be employed in the eighteenth century, but confidence in it appears to have been shaken.

As drawn by the *philosophes,* the eighteenth century was an Age of Enlightenment even in those aspects of the period that seem least enlightened: domestic servitude and political despotism. Enlightened discourse was a discourse about man, that is, about reason as embodied in the human race, the bipedal species. Although races and sexes retained certain unique characteristics, the distinctions between them faded. Anyone entitled to claim the name "man" could attain enlightenment. But who was so entitled? What was enlightenment?

In 1784 Kant published a brief article in the *Berlinische Monats-Schrift:* "An answer to the question, 'What is Enlightenment?'" A crucial idea runs through this text: man attains enlightenment when he ceases to see himself as belonging to a minority to which he has been condemned throughout history by forces beyond his understanding: the soldier who commands obedience, the financier who demands payment, the priest who insists on belief.

To attain enlightenment is nothing other than to achieve adulthood. The age of majority is the age at which a person finally dares to use the natural faculty that defines him as man: his understanding. "Dare to know" *(sapere aude)* is a motto, not a fact. To the unenlightened powers-that-be, such audacity is exorbitant, but in fact it is a dictate of nature. Every man has a duty to uncover nature's commandments, which history has obscured. The name for such audacity, which is identical with the public use of reason, is freedom. Freedom, whose initial exercise is intimately associated with thought, rightfully belongs to all reasonable beings. Kant thus provides a theory of the contents of the enlightened mind: free rationality defines humanity in its essence (which is the logical status of a definition) and in its history (which is the status of a species "in the process of becoming").

If enlightened discourse speaks to all men, it must be couched in universal terms. From this inevitable consequence arise equally inevitable difficulties. Who, ultimately, has a right to the universal? The answer, in principle, is all human beings and indeed, more generally, all reasonable beings, including those that may exist outside the human species. All men by nature enjoy equal rights; because history has obscured this principle, it was necessary to proclaim it publicly in 1789 in the form of a "declaration" (of the Rights of Man). This concern with the universal is the ground of Kant's practical philosophy. All humanity must be treated in my own person as in any other person, always as an end, never merely as a means. The respect that each owes to all and all to each is based on a fact of reason: every human being is a free, autonomous being and therefore cannot be subjugated to the will of another *(Foundations of the Metaphysics of Morals)*. In the *Discourse on the Origin and Foundations of Inequality among Men* Rousseau argued that what distinguished man from the animals was not so much the understanding as man's character of free agent. An animal merely obeys; a man can voluntarily acquiesce or resist. If man, "born free," is today everywhere "in chains," it is the tragic consequence of a degradation of society; yet even this cannot extirpate man's freedom, which is his by nature, a fundamental component of his very essence.

It must be recognized, however, that the universal is internally contradictory. Supposedly valid for all, it is in fact the privilege of a few. It is coherent only insofar as it remains abstract, and, as Hegel would emphasize in his vehement critique of Enlightenment thought, an abstract universal is a universal without differences, hence empty.

Kant's formulation of the categorical imperative—that one must always treat others as an end and never simply as a means—is already suspect. What does it mean to treat a person as a means? Are not some human beings more likely to be treated as means than others? No doubt Kant's statement is concerned essentially with equality before the moral law, which commands every man to do his duty. But is not the inescapable requirement to do one's duty threatened if duties differ?

In the Age of Enlightenment it was commonplace to say that women constituted one-half of the human race. In the address to the Republic of Geneva that opens Rousseau's *Discourse on Inequality* we read: "Could I forget that precious half of the Republic that is the source of the other half's happiness and whose gentleness and wisdom preserve the peace and protect morality?" Condorcet, too, used the phrase "half of the human race," but the expression is not to be understood in a quantitative sense: whether women were in fact more or less numerous than men in different countries and climates and under various political regimes was a question raised at the time from various angles. The term "half" should rather be understood in a functional sense: women participated in the reproduction of the species; they were wives and mothers, daughters and sisters; they had a place in the family and in society. The expression "half of the human race" is in fact ambiguous because, oddly enough, it was not reciprocal: men were never said to constitute the other half of the species. A subtle sophism was at work: women were a "half" without an "other half." The female half existed only in relation to the male half, which was its ground and defining reference. This asymmetrical relation allowed contradictory assertions that assigned positive or negative content to woman's status. To cite just two examples: for Rousseau the feminine half did not share the same values as the masculine half, whereas Condorcet attempted to conceive of at least presumptive equality between the two. Condorcet was alone, however, among *philosophes* who took an interest in women. Most eighteenth-century writers fell well short of Poullain de la Barre, who, in *De l'égalité des sexes* (1673) and *De l'éducation des dames* (1674, dedicated to the Grande Mademoiselle), championed the idea of equality between women and men in a Cartesian manner, in the name of clear and distinct ideas and rational evidence against prejudice of all kinds. The unity of mind as it was conceived in Descartes's philosophy guaranteed strict equality between the sexes. Hence one of the most noxious of prejudices was that which took male discourse about women to be the objective truth, whereas in reality the men who produced that discourse were in effect judge and party in the same case.

Enlightenment writers on the whole were less audacious. The persistence of prejudices concerning the "fair sex" (as if beauty belonged to one sex only) is all the more paradoxical in that the Enlightenment openly attacked any opinion not based on reason and any system of thought that failed to justify its premises. It was paradoxical, too, for Enlightenment thinkers to maintain that women were intellectually inferior to men at a time when the very salons that propagated the philosophic spirit and contributed to the prestige of literature and science were hosted by women (of high social rank to be sure). The Marquise du Châtelet translated Newton's *Principia Mathematica;* Madame Lepaute, a member of the Academy of Sciences of Béziers, was the author of *Mémoires d'astronomie* and of a *Table des longueurs de pendules* (Table of Lengths of Pendula). A list of intellectual works by women would be a lengthy one.

Did women really ask to be *declared* equal? To judge by what some males wrote, women did not ask for equality because it was not to their advantage. Listen, for example, to Montesquieu (in *Mes pensées*): "Note that, except in cases brought about by a combination of unusual circumstances, women have never been wont to lay claim to equality, for they have so many other natural advantages that for them equality of power is always a situation for the worse."

Masculine Discourse

Male *philosophes* elaborated a dual discourse: man on man and man on woman. Two manners of speaking, describing, and defining thus emerged, one for each of the two unequal halves of the human race. The subject of this discourse is of course man, who can, without abandoning his subjective stance, also take himself as object of his own discourse. Woman is simply an object of a discourse that subsumes her while maintaining an external vantage point. Generally (if not invariably), unconscious ideological processes shape these pronouncements and texts in order to justify and defend the treatment of the "other half."

"Neutral" discourses about human beings did exist, in the form of texts on natural history, which studied the human species by comparing it with animal species in order to identify common and distinctive features. Such comparative investigation was concerned more with distinguishing between the human and the animal than between the male and the female except in regard to sexual difference, which was treated in anatomical and physiological terms. Thus in his *Histoire naturelle générale et particulière,* Buffon studied man from a naturalist's point of view: man is an animal that feels, thinks, speaks, and so on. A material body coupled with an organ of understanding, the soul, man is organizationally the same as woman. It was in this capacity as a naturalist that Buffon lent support to an idea that had taken shape at the time and that Rousseau would attempt to justify in *Emile,* namely that the best nourishment for an infant was mother's milk: "When mothers feed their children, it appears that the children grow stronger and more vigorous. The milk of the mother must suit them better than the milk of another woman. The physiology of the embryo suggests that it is accustomed to its mother's milk prior to birth, whereas the milk of another woman is a novel nourishment" *(Histoire naturelle de l'homme).*

Masculine discourse that treats woman as its object generally speaks in the first-person plural: *we,* meaning men as a group, who propose to set forth a theory of the other half. Examples of the non-neutral center of masculine language abound. The "we" of the masculine community is contrasted with the community of women, which is "theirs." Our sex, our virtues, our morals, our roles are not theirs. Rousseau may serve as a typical case. His

Emile, subtitled "or On Education," consists of five books. The first four outline a theory of education in the form of a history of the education of an orphaned boy raised by a philosophical tutor who is by definition enlightened in regard to nature, childhood, and man. These four books have no distinctive subtitle. But the fifth book, in which we are introduced to Sophie, whose education is entirely directed toward making her a fit companion for Emile and capable of making him happy, is titled "Sophie, or Woman." The difference in the treatment of the two sexes is thus already apparent in the organization of the text, even before we begin to examine its content. Furthermore, the third book, from which Sophie is absent, contains the long "Profession of Faith of the Savoyard Vicar," which is supposed to raise Emile's soul up to intuitive, sensuous comprehension of the supreme author of nature, the good and just God who guarantees the order of the world and the virtues of human beings. This discourse of reason is not for Sophie's ears. She must make do with an elementary catechism consisting of a series of questions put to her by her maid together with a list of very brief responses. This catechism drives home a useful if rather banal message: everyone grows, reproduces, ages, and dies.

Rousseau's idea of woman's nature was complex and perhaps even contradictory. I shall have more to say about these complexities later on. But the form of his discourse is clear. The *Discourse on Inequality* begins with these words: "It is about man that I have to speak, and the question I shall be examining teaches me that I shall be speaking to men." Similarly, in *Emile* Rousseau is speaking as a man to men *on the subject* of woman. Book five begins: "Let us begin, then, by examining the similarities and differences between her sex and ours." Rousseau goes on to say that "in every respect that does not touch on sex, woman is man." Has she not the same needs and the same faculties? The question is not as clearly formulated as it might appear, but still one must concede that there is some similarity between woman and man, if only in regard to faculties, for otherwise—and the thought is threatening—how could she be the mother of *our* children? But woman is what she is, and she must not pretend to be man. Her uniqueness stands out when measured against the masculine norm, and it would be absurd for the object of measurement to take hold of the yardstick. Women therefore should not cultivate male qualities. Mothers should raise their daughters to be decent women, not gentlemen: "It will be better for her and for us." It follows that "in this respect the system of her education should be the contrary of ours."

Someone may object that women are allowed to speak within male discourse. Montesquieu, for example, allows women of the harem to write letters in *The Persian Letters,* and Rousseau has Julie write letters in *La Nouvelle Héloïse.* But what we actually have in these instances is not a female discourse but one that is doubly male: it merely dons the mask of the other sex. Julie is nothing other than Rousseau's dream woman, a woman so perfect that she redeems her creator's lack of transparency. The bloody revolt that Roxane organizes in the sultan's harem may only reflect Montesquieu's horrified fascination with despotism's inevitable fate.

The typical form of male discourse (conventional wisdom, as it were) may be found in the article titled "Woman" in Denis Diderot and Jean d'Alembert's *Encyclopédie.* In fact this typical example reveals a whole host of theoretical difficulties: Who can define woman if she is not allowed to define herself? How is she to be defined? From what point of view?

Three authors, reflecting three different approaches, were asked to contribute to the article. The first was abbé Mallet, whose text defines the "concept" of woman in terms of a series of references. In the *Encyclopédie* as a general rule each article refers to other articles that are supposed to illuminate, develop, or explain its fundamental terms of reference. Thus Mallet's text refers to articles on "man," "female," and "sex." Woman is defined in the most obvious way: "the female of man." The article "Man" also contains references to terms presumably valid for the entire species. If, for example, one is interested in the human being before birth, one is directed to articles on a number of topics: fetus, embryo, labor, conception, pregnancy, and so on. The article on man consists of four parts. The first, signed by Diderot, gives a very general definition that appears to apply to the entire species: man is a being that feels, reflects, and thinks, is provided with a body and a soul, is capable of good and evil (hence a moral being), and, finally, lives in society, makes laws, and sometimes subjects itself to rulers (hence a political being). The second part of the article, also written by Diderot, comes under the head of natural history and consists of an anatomical and physiological description of man and woman. Based almost entirely on Buffon and Daubenton, the text enumerates the natural differences between men and women with respect to sexuality, strength, longevity, and so on. The discourse here is neutral but still written from the male point of view: "At all ages the anterior portion of the woman is higher than ours." The third part of the article, written by Charles-Georges Le Roy, deals with man as a moral species. The term *moral species* refers to humankind insofar as it is distinguished from the animal kingdom by its faculty of understanding, by labor, and by its ability to rise above instinct and subject its behavior to moral rules. The article thus reveals the power of education to shape and alter human beings. Like man, woman is formed by the education she receives. But the sexes are educated in different ways. The male order in fact governs the upbringing of women— a fact, the author emphasizes, that is harmful to men themselves.

In the fourth and final part of the article, Diderot deals with man as a political being. Among the topics covered are economic activity, prosperity, social well-being, and population. "Children become *men*. Steps must therefore be taken to protect children by devoting special attention to fathers, mothers, and nurses."

Let us return now to the article "Woman." Its three parts are concerned with anthropology (abbé Mallet), natural law (Louis de Jaucourt), and morals (Corsambleu Desmahis). Despite the apparently haphazard references to Galen, the Hebrews, and Daubenton, Mallet's text is concerned with examining the natural and cultural reasons for woman's inferiority. Philosophers such as Marsilio Ficino and anatomists had argued that a woman is an incomplete man. Natural causes were invoked to explain what was in fact a male judgment. Was female inferiority incompatible with sexual equality? Mallet naively revealed the contradiction in the guise of resolving it: "The various prejudices concerning the relation of man's excellence to woman's were produced by the customs of ancient peoples and by the political systems and religions that successively modified those customs. I except the Christian religion, which established . . . a real superiority in man while yet retaining woman's rights of equality."

Jaucourt examined the status of woman—the female of man— from the standpoint of natural law, which basically defined a woman as a possession of her husband. The purpose of forming societies is to perpetuate and preserve the species. Although both fathers and mothers contribute to that natural end, "it is essential that authority of government be vested in one or the other." In the histories of the civilized nations one finds abundant evidence to prove that woman ought to be subject to her husband's authority. Nevertheless, Jaucourt points out that the subjection of women "is not beyond all appeal." He notes, correctly, that the natural principle of equal rights is violated by the assertion of the superiority of one sex over the other in marriage, which is based on a contract, that is, a reciprocal, voluntary agreement. It might well be the case that the subordination of women was based solely on civil conventions established by men without women's consent. Be that as it may, however, a woman in marrying accepted that convention and therefore submitted to her husband's authority. Jaucourt's complex argument thus reflected the contradictions inherent in the idea of natural equality, and in the end his conception of marriage was one of voluntary domestic servitude.

Desmahis's article was supposed to treat woman from a moral standpoint, but it was in fact a compendium of conventional wisdom concerning "this half of the human race." The text appears to aim not at theoretical coherence but rather at a *mise en scène* of woman, who is conceived in terms of looks, imagination, artifice, the art of giving pleasure, a desire for domination and authority that she can achieve only in roundabout ways, and the supreme art of coquetry, which is apparently taken as a primary datum. This is of course stock material. The "argument" is dramatized in the person of Chloé, a Cretan coquette, who defines herself in terms of love and whose only concern is her often unrequited quest for one or more lovers. Chloé is the unhappy side of the amorous female. The other, discreet and all but silent, is the virtuous woman: the submissive wife, gentle mother, and kind household mistress. She reigns over a single place: the home. Yet this theatrical presentation of contrasting female types cannot conceal Desmahis's simplistic certitudes—as well as a few of his anxieties. Nature, he says, has granted man the right to govern, and woman can emancipate herself only by means of art (or artifice). But is art part of nature? Beauty, the exclusive possession of the female sex, apparently excludes the use of the noble faculties: "Praise for a woman's character or mind is almost always proof of her ugliness. It appears that feeling and reason are but supplements to beauty." Woman's character is not constant; it is a mixture of temperaments, a compromise, unstable. That is what makes woman so hard to define, for to define a thing is to identify, beyond all accidental variations, an immutable essence. "Who can define *women?* In truth, everything speaks in them, but it speaks an equivocal language." By contrast, masculine discourse speaks with one voice and can therefore claim exclusive possession of the dignity of true language. Hence it is up to men to speak of women.

If women were allowed a discourse of their own, what would they talk about, and in what manner would they speak? Diderot proposed one answer in *Les bijoux indiscrets:* "'Where in God's name will they speak from?' Mangoul shouted. 'Through the most candid part they possess.'" He is referring, of course, to the vagina: that indiscreet jewel that is the female body's intrinsic embellishment, at once artifice and natural organ. But did not all human beings speak through their heads? Of course, but a woman's head was strangely inhabited. It was the seat not so much of reason as of the agitated senses. Was not woman completely dominated, body and soul, by her mobile uterus? In woman, "the senses govern, not the mind. She contains within herself an indomitable organ, susceptible to terrible spasms . . . Her head continues to speak the language of her senses even when they are dead" (Diderot, *Critique de l'essai sur les femmes*).

Men thus spoke of women in asymmetrical, depreciative terms, perhaps most depreciative when they spoke in praise of the feminine virtues. Those virtues in fact defined the limits of a difference that could never be overcome. In some ways masculine discourse functioned as divine discourse: the creator reflected in theological terms, and not without astonishment, on his own creation, woman.

The Nature of Woman

In the eighteenth century nature was not only an object of research (in natural history, physics, chemistry, and other disciplines) but also a normative principle. Hence the question whether woman's nature was the same as man's or different was inevitable. Obviously women's bodies differed from men's in terms of physical structure. But was the intellectual, moral, social, and political condition of women based on and justified by nature, or was it related in some way to women's education? If there was such a thing as a feminine nature, then it must be that nature wanted it that way (assuming that nature pursues goals and cannot be reduced to a pure mechanical operation). Of course the most important discourse on the nature of woman stemmed from the meditations of men.

It would be an endless task to list every occurrence in eighteenth-century philosophical texts of phrases such as "nature wanted," "nature ensured," or "woman by nature is." As both order and norm, teleological nature was identified with reason. The invocation of nature was thus a way of working toward a rational theory of the feminine. It was implicitly assumed that woman in some way stands in an immediate relation to nature. Of course men are also natural beings, but their relation to nature is invariably mediated. The *philosophes* of the Enlightenment reasoned for the most part in the categories of what Claude Lévi-Strauss has called "savage thought": woman is nature, man is culture. So strong was the relation between woman and nature that nature was considered, metaphorically speaking, to be female. (Rousseau argued in his *Essay on the Origin of Languages* that metaphor comes first and words acquire their proper sense only later.) In *The Interpretation of Nature* (XII) Diderot marveled at the extraordinary fecundity of the natural power that multiplies forms yet always remains hidden from view: "She is a woman who loves to wear costumes and whose many disguises, revealing sometimes one part, sometimes another, give some hope to those who follow her assiduously that one day they will know the whole person." But what is a woman? First and foremost, a being with a sex organ that is unusual in that it is not like a man's. Sexual difference, which was studied by anatomists, physicians, and others, gave rise to a fundamental question: Was there not originally a single, undifferentiated sex, a common organ from which both masculine and feminine organs derived? Perhaps, as Galen believed, the male organ was simply a transformation of the female. Perhaps God was both male and female. One place to begin exploring these matters is Mallet's article "Woman" in the *Encyclopédie,* which reveals an anxious curiosity on the subject of the hermaphrodite.

It was not clear how the female sex ought to be approached. After marveling at women's beauty, charm, and attractiveness to men, the texts emphasized their weakness, timorousness, and flirtatiousness (conflating moral with physical characteristics). Foremost among the shortcomings of the sex was the fact that women, so long as they remained fertile, were slaves to physiology. This is what Voltaire had to say in his article "Women" in the *Philo-*

sophical Dictionary: "In physique, woman is weaker than man on account of her physiology. The periodic emissions of blood that enfeeble women and the maladies that result from their suppression, the duration of pregnancy, the need to suckle infants and watch over them, and the delicacy of women's limbs render them ill suited to any type of labor or occupation that requires strength or endurance."

Female sexuality is a kind of curse. The inferiority of women was justified on natural grounds having to do with sex. In the fifth book of *Emile* Rousseau argues that all human traits except those having to do with sex are common to the species but that in woman sex is paramount: "There is no parity between the two sexes as to the consequences of sex. The male is male only at certain moments; the female is female all her life, or at any rate throughout her youth. Everything brings her back to her sex." In the sexual act, according to Rousseau (and on this point his opinion was widely shared), the man is active and strong, the woman passive and weak; the man must have the capacity and the will to perform, whereas the woman can merely lessen her resistance. The sexualized couple is reminiscent of another couple that figured in certain epistemological theories: the understanding, an active faculty, shapes and structures the passive sensibility. For the man—in this case Emile, carefully raised by his tutor in accordance with the laws of nature—sexual need is not a physical need, hence not a true need. Sex does not define the nature of man, but it does define that of woman.

Female sexuality is thus the source of woman's subjugation. But it is important to note the series of contradictions that have accumulated under the head of "nature." In female sexuality nature is guilty of certain excesses. The so-called weaker sex suffers from limitless desires. In some climates female sexuality becomes all-devouring, to the point where men, all the more exhausted for being polygamous, must place women under lock and key for the sake of tranquillity. Montesquieu describes without justifying certain customs apparently required by the perpetual danger of an unbridling of female passion.

Rousseau also says that sexual relations are characterized by violence. Although the man plays the active role with a consenting woman, the woman is constantly provoking him. Flirtatiousness is everywhere, and man is constantly (if charmingly) threatened.

Nature, however, has provided ways to stem the natural excesses of women. She has endowed women with a sentiment that is not only natural but may also be the tenderest fruit of social existence: shame or modesty. Modesty is that ladylike restraint that stems from woman's consciousness of her own imperfections, a consciousness that curbs her excesses. "All nations agree," writes Montesquieu in *The Spirit of Laws,* "in condemning female intemperateness. This is because nature has spoken to them all. It set up the defense, just as it set up the attack."[1] In *Emile* Rousseau makes a similar statement, clearly inspired by Montesquieu.

Curbing female furies is not the only function of modesty. It also protects women from assaults by males while subtly allowing them to dominate men. By nature (in this context virtually synonymous with instinct) woman uses her gifts for apparently incompatible ends. This forms the subject of Rousseau's lengthy philosophical exposition on woman's (natural?) ability to *please* and thus to subjugate and dominate the male. Man, on the other hand, has no need to please: the law of nature is that he gives pleasure simply by existing. Woman, according to Rousseau (who once again may be taken as representative of many other writers), is fond of dressing up virtually from birth. Even young girls have their "little airs." If woman desires to please by the necessity of her nature, then she exists only through being looked at by men. She is a creature of the judgment and opinion of others. She thus fits Rousseau's definition of man as distorted by social existence to the point of being nothing more than an appearance, a thin mask, a being no longer in immediate contact with itself. This alienated being, which Rousseau describes and deplores in the case of man, is in his eyes the natural (and not social) status of woman, and for Jean-Jacques this is a good thing.

Montesquieu, who in *The Spirit of Laws* wants to explain without justifying the variety of the world's customs, also concedes that the desire to please is intrinsic to female nature but sees it as having a certain social utility because this desire "secures a place for elegant dress," which in turn encourages commerce. Although women may have a harmful effect on morals, women foster taste. Elegance of dress is an inherent part of life in society.[2]

Kant, in his *Anthropology from a Pragmatic Point of View,* examines certain characteristics of the female sex. Woman, he says, is a fit subject for anthropology because she is more difficult to analyze than man. He goes on to advance certain familiar arguments: those traits normally ascribed to feminine weakness are in fact instruments for manipulating men, and the desire to please is in fact a means of domination. The desire to dominate is not peculiar to women, however; it is a characteristic of human beings generally rather than a distinctive trait of either sex.

Kant incorporated his reflections on women into his general theory of the acquisition of culture. Culture is a state that nature pursues by apparently contradictory means. Man comes to reason by way of certain forms of madness and becomes a social being by way of certain asocial forms of aggression. It is noteworthy that for Kant, the role of woman is not only to perpetuate the species but also, child though she may be, to guide man toward morality. Woman does indeed belong to nature, but to a nature whose end is culture. Without woman the delicate but necessary transition from nature to culture would be impossible: "Because nature wished to inspire the more refined sentiments that belong to the domain of culture, sentiments of sociability and propriety, she gave the female sex mastery over men through morality and elegance of speech and expression."[3]

Women's Reason

The inferiority of the female sex, being rooted in sexual difference, naturally extended to all aspects of a woman's being, including in particular her intellectual faculties. Was she truly endowed with a mind, with powers of rationality? If she was indeed a human being, then the answer in theory ought to have been yes. But in fact the principle of intellectual equality between the sexes was challenged by the all-but-unanimous opinion of men. If woman possesses the privilege of beauty, and if reason is not a gift but something to be cultivated, then woman cannot simultaneously possess beauty (which is fleeting) and reason (which takes time to acquire). Thus Montesquieu argues in *The Spirit of Laws* that, at least in the south, where woman's sexual precocity is a consequence of the warm climate, the two sexes are unequal by nature. This inequality inevitably results in woman's dependence on man: "Reason is never found . . . among those with beauty. When beauty asks to rule, reason sees to it that the request is denied. When reason is at last in a position to govern, beauty is no longer. Women must be dependent." In temperate climates, where women become nubile later than their sisters from warmer countries, beauty lasts longer and can coexist with a measure of reason. That is why monogamy prevails in the temperate north, polygamy in the warmer south. Yet what one has in temperate countries is only a "kind of equality in the two sexes."[4]

To most Enlightenment philosophers it was reassuringly obvious that women either lacked reason altogether or possessed a faculty of reason inferior to that of men, yet they pretended to provide empirical evidence for their belief. Among the "facts" most often adduced was the claim that women are incapable of invention and devoid of genius, although it was conceded that some women had distinguished themselves in literature and certain branches of science. "Natural psychology"—woman is a creature of passion and imagination but not capable of forming concepts—seemed to provide an explanation. Rousseau carried to almost caricatural extremes the conviction that, while woman might not be utterly incapable of reasoning, her faculty of reason was nevertheless simpler than the male's, hence she ought to cultivate it only to the extent required to carry out her natural duties (to obey her husband, be a faithful wife, and take care of the children). Women, Rousseau argued, always remain children. They are incapable of seeing beyond the walls of the household, which is their natural sphere. Hence they have no capacity for the "exact sciences." The only knowledge a woman needs beyond that of her duties (which she knows intuitively) is a knowledge, based on sentiment, of the men in her life, and primarily her husband. The world, Rousseau asserts, is the only book a woman needs. In short, woman's only relation is to the concrete. Woman's role is intuitively to read the hearts of men (plural), whereas man's role is to philosophize about the human heart (in general). Woman's inability to reason like a man reveals itself in any number of ways, among them her inability to understand reasons for religious belief. That is why every girl must take up her mother's religion and every woman her husband's. The argument is perfectly clear: the female mind does not form concepts, and female reason is not a theoretical reason. As Rousseau explains in *Emile*, "The search for abstract and speculative truths, principles, axioms in the sciences, and everything that tends to generalize ideas is not within the compass of women: all their studies must deal with the practical. Their job is to apply the principles that men discover and to make the observations that lead men to establish principles."

Rousseau was simply restating in rigorous terms a paradox

that runs through the empiricist-sensualist theory of knowledge that he, along with most other eighteenth-century English and French philosophers, borrowed from Locke and Condillac. In contrast to Descartes and Leibniz, who believed that ideas were innate in the human mind and not the product of experience, these thinkers held that ideas arise out of the raw material of perception through the operations of comparison and association. These "sensualist" theories of knowledge came in many varieties and cannot be reduced to a single set of principles. Some thinkers, like Condillac, even asserted that all ideas begin with perception yet denied that we can be sure of the existence of any object outside our minds. Others, like Diderot, attempted to give a systematic materialist account of empiricism. Still others, like Rousseau, continued to believe in the spirituality of the soul (and in the consequent duality of substance). Yet despite these differences, all these philosophers shared a common goal: to describe how complex ideas originate in perception. The description of this genetic process took two forms: an analysis of the content of thought in order to trace ideas back to their sources, and an account of the mechanisms of mental representation. Memory and imagination played a key role in the process. Remembering and imagining were both ways of rendering present in the mind the impression of an object without the presence of the object that originally caused that impression. Comparing such "representations" with one another and associating them with the signs of language were the operations that made judgment possible. To judge was to establish a relation between terms represented by signs, or abstract representations. To abstract, to generalize, was the distinctive operation of reason. This process of generalization, from concrete perception to abstract idea, is, we are told, characteristic of the whole human species. All individuals, regardless of sex, race, or culture, develop psychologically and intellectually by developing this ability.

That, at any rate, was the theory. But in fact the dominant discourse of Enlightenment philosophy proceeded as if the female mind were incapable of carrying this genetic process through all the way from perception to abstract idea. To deny that women were capable of abstraction and generalization and therefore, strictly speaking, of thought was to affirm that only men are capable of generating ideas. Woman apparently remained stuck at the stage of imagination. But what kind of imagination? Not the kind that contributes genetically to knowledge, but the misleading kind that causes us to mistake desires for realities, that inspires fantasies and leads us astray. This imagination, the mother of error and untruth, bears the stamp of childhood. An excess of imagination could cause a person to fall ill, go mad, or die. Because the female mind remained stuck at the stage of imagination, it was childish, vulnerable, and unpredictable. Thus a kind of "madness" was always latent in women, and one indispensable, if inadequate, means of countering that madness was to forbid women to read novels, works of fiction fit only for the stalwart male mind.

Yet the argument that women's faculties remained stuck at a level that men were destined to surpass seriously undermined the coherence of the genetic account of the origin of our ideas, an account that implied a *historicity* of human beings as individuals and as a species. The history of the species was conceived in two ways: as a gradual, unsteady, yet ultimately teleological progress toward perfection; or, alternatively, as a loss of natural equality, which it was up to the social contract to restore on a new foundation. To say that woman's intellectual development ended at the stage of sense perception and undisciplined imagination unless subjected to somber, virile discipline was to assert that woman had no history. Always the same in her function and duties, she remained what she had always been: "To please [men], to be useful to them, to be loved and honored by them, to raise them when they are young, to care for them when they are old, to counsel them, console them, and make their lives pleasant and comfortable—these are the duties of women in all times, which should be taught to them from early childhood." On this score Rousseau is as radical as ever. Thus the "other half" of the human race could be said to typify those "savage" societies that Lévi-Strauss characterizes as "cold," in contrast to the "hot," or civilized, societies that have chosen to understand themselves in historical terms.

A "Naturally Natural" Role

Combining the sexual and intellectual inferiority of woman with her natural role in the reproduction of the species and the care of children leads "naturally" to a definition of her function and role. For Enlightenment thinkers, woman was essentially wife and mother. And since the Enlightenment was anticlerical, these same thinkers were able to criticize convent life as unnatural, particularly since the daughters of certain segments of society were educated in convents by nuns incapable of understanding the meaning of the terms *mother* or *wife* (except in the context of spiritual marriage to Jesus Christ). Countless texts reminded women of their neglected duties: to bear and suckle children in accordance with nature's dictates. It was difficult to imagine why a woman would choose not to marry and have children. This insistence on woman's reproductive role accorded well with her status of domestic servitude: taking care of husband, children, and household subjected women to so many duties that it would have been cruel to burden them with other concerns. Montesquieu, again hiding behind the veil of an Oriental woman, maintained that the burden of a woman's duties was so great that she should be prevented from taking on any others. That is why locking up the women of the harem worked so well. Rousseau drew his inspiration from quite a different culture, that of Sparta, but the idea was similar. In Sparta young brides were confined to their homes and forced to occupy their time with household and family duties: "This is the way of life that nature and reason prescribe for the sex." The Enlightenment shared this Oriental and Spartan ideal of a sexual division of labor, in which women were segregated from men, who occupied themselves with public affairs, with the business of government and state, and confined to a tranquil realm troubled only by storms stirred up by women themselves.

To be sure, many philosophers protested the high-handedness of marriages not based on mutual consent, not founded on the will of both husband and wife as required by the very notion of contract (although Rousseau, to judge by what Julie's father says in *La Nouvelle Héloïse,* believed that a father was more likely than his daughter to make a wise judgment about her choice of mate). But except for isolated instances, marriages were highly inegalitarian. The husband was the head of the family and guardian of his wife, children, and servants (if he had any). Rousseau has the tutor offer Sophie the following advice: "In becoming your husband, Emile became your master. Your place is to obey, as nature intended. When a woman is like Sophie, however, it is good for the man to be guided by her. This, too, is a law of nature." The law of nature is involved in a very subtle dialectic of domination and submission. But Sophie is able to guide her man only because she was designed and manufactured expressly to serve him.

The formal argument for inequality in marriage that can be found in so many Enlightenment texts is based on the unexamined idea that for a union to be indissoluble, one party must be superior to the other. Equality might lead to rapid dissolution. Marriage was apparently incompatible with democracy between husband and wife. The paradox is striking: marriage was conceived of as a voluntary contract but in fact based on a contract of submission. An age that rejected the idea that a man could voluntarily contract to become a slave nevertheless believed that there could be a contract of servitude between a man and his wife. Listen to Kant: "In the progress of civilization, superiority derives from heterogeneous sources: man must be superior to woman in physical strength and courage and woman must be superior to man in her natural faculty of submitting to man's attachment to her. By contrast, in a state that has not yet reached the level of civilization, superiority resides exclusively with the man."[5]

Apart from her duties as wife, mother, and housekeeper, a married woman was expected to be faithful to her husband. Although much was written on this point, the fundamental argument was simple. A woman's infidelity was a threat to the very foundations of the family and therefore of society because a man could no longer be sure that his wife's child was his own. It was impossible for a man to act as family head if he could not be certain of his rights of paternity/property over his children. Infidelity by the husband was not condemned with equal severity. One can ask why. Did not the man who had sexual relations with a married woman pose a threat to the rights of the deceived husband? Male discourse was unabashedly asymmetrical: what a man said about *his* wife could be said without regard to the fact that other men also had wives. Emile's greatest misfortune is not that he is deceived by Sophie but that she is pregnant by another man. Which is more seriously aggrieved: the husband or the father and family head?

In *La Nouvelle Héloïse* (part 3, letter 18) Rousseau has Julie defend marital fidelity, especially on the part of the wife. Anyone who believes in the existence of God and the immortality of the soul cannot tolerate the slightest infraction that might jeopardize the sacred, indestructible marital bond. Sexual freedom for married men and women was, in Rousseau's eyes, one of the most disastrous consequences of materialist philosophy. The voice of nature spoke out against this perverse doctrine: no father could accept a child not of his own blood. Julie takes up cudgels on behalf of her sex against the philosophers. With supreme, if naive, subtlety Rousseau attributes to a woman an argument that is in fact dictated by the interests of men: "If I consider my sex in particular," Julie writes, "how many evils I see in this disorder, which, they say, does no harm. The abasement of a guilty woman is a terrible thing, for the loss of honor soon deprives her of all the other virtues."

Captive

In the *Treatise on Human Nature* David Hume considers the chastity and fidelity of women in the context of a theory of passion. In the course of a genetic analysis of human nature he finds that no appetite is truly innate, that all result from a combination of sense impressions. The mechanism by which beauty attracts one sex to the other is no more complicated than that by which a good meal attracts a hungry man. Man and woman are by nature susceptible to the same desires. But naked nature can scarcely be described. Our nature is a fabric of relations woven primarily by social forces. These shape what we take to be the female "nature." It is a *fact*—no more—that an unfaithful woman experiences feelings of shame. But why is a woman's violation of her marital vows considered worse than a man's? There is no objective basis for such a judgment. In the absence of a theory, the judgment must be based in the final analysis on practice, on custom. Chastity and fidelity are justified not by nature but by social necessity. Total sexual freedom for men is not good for civil society; sexual freedom for women is even worse. What man in such a society could be sure of being any child's father? Hume offers no justification for the way things are. He claims simply to describe what has become established in custom at the end of a long evolutionary process. To be sure, this custom has become part of human nature, but that nature is merely an *inscription* of custom over a long period. The concept of nature is therefore fully intelligible only if seen in the context of a relativizing process.

Montesquieu elaborates a plausible theory of such a process in *The Spirit of Laws*. In defining the general spirit that governs men, he mentions a number of factors (climate, religion, laws, principles of government, customs, manners) that influence and affect one another in various ways. What does this theory have to say about whether or not there is such a thing as female nature? The definition of woman, like that of man, depends on the climate, government, legislation, and customs prevailing where she happens to live. At first sight the nature of woman thus seems to depend on the conditions of her existence, particularly the form of government under which she lives, which in turn is determined by the climate. But regardless of the form of government (whether ancient republic, whose principal is virtue; monarchy, whose principle is honor; or despotism, whose principle is fear), woman is never as free as man. In one sense she is always captive. This is a fact, not a justification, in keeping with Montesquieu's "objective" method. In ancient republics, women "are free by law and captives by custom." They are kept segregated in the gynaeceum, and what men feel toward them has more to do with friendship than with love, which is practiced among men. In monarchies (where Montesquieu discusses only women of rank high enough to be received at court), women are among the best instruments available to men for advancing their fortunes. As economic objects as well as subjects, women encourage the development of luxury. Finally, under despotism, woman is fundamentally an object. Is despotism really a form of government? It is rather the negation of government, an extreme case of radical equality: all are slaves—eunuchs, women, viziers, even the sultan himself, who is the slave of desires that remain forever unslaked. The nefarious influence of the hot climate is to blame. Despotism is a system for governing vast empires in which all is desert waste: the land is as barren as the hearts of the tyrant's subjects, who know nothing but fear. In this type of state "women do not introduce luxury, but they are themselves an object of luxury. They must be extremely slavish."[6] Under despotism women are feared because they are always ready to engage in intrigue; hence they must be kept under lock and key in the seraglio. Fear of women is dread of woman's freedom. In fact it is the unthinking fear that freedom of any kind inspires in the despot. Despotic government is monstrous. It can perish only by its own instruments: violence and unbridled pleasure that ends in death. Roxane's final letter to her husband, the absent sultan, in the *Persian Letters* paints a picture of the ultimate catastrophe: Roxane has seduced the eunuchs, transformed the seraglio into a pleasure palace, and proclaimed her freedom in the name of the laws of nature against the subjugating law of the male. After availing herself of this new language, she dies of a self-administered dose of poison. Of course one can object that this disaster is a fiction made up by a man from the temperate zone. Still, for Montesquieu, the specter of despotism and its women, who can escape their slavery only by swimming in an ocean of blood, is one that haunts any government that fails to establish a balance of powers, that neglects to develop a system of checks and balances to curb the tendency, inherent in all power, to abuse.

Deliberation and moderation are the politician's most important principles. Montesquieu, examining the administration of women from this point of view, states, rather oddly, that "it is contrary to reason and nature that women are mistresses in the household . . . but not that they should rule an empire." The traditional idea of woman as mistress in the home but excluded from politics is thus stood on its head. The reason for this reversal is simple: woman is weak, and the head of a family must be strong. But this same weakness is a guarantee of moderation in the realm of political power: "Their very weakness gives them more power and moderation, which are more apt to create a good government than the harsh, fierce virtues."[7]

Beyond the variety of conditions that shaped diverse feminine natures, was there some set of essential traits characteristic of *woman* as such? Man was characterized by strength and reason and woman by charm, which was the source of her power. But charm could take different forms in different circumstances. For the relativist, woman's distinguishing traits were immutable yet capable of modulation depending on circumstances. Here we touch on one of the crucial theoretical difficulties of *The Spirit of Laws,* namely, the equivocal definition of nature. Montesquieu's scientific project implied that nature both was and was not simply a principle of causal explanation. Everything that exists exists in nature and can be rationally understood. Thus there are reasons why certain peoples are immodest or polygamous and others not. But Montesquieu also uses "nature" to refer to a system of basic laws against which one can measure and judge positive laws, particularly when he wants to argue that positive law is in need of reform.

Reform is necessary to the extent that human beings are free to vary from some norm. Only beings intended to be free by nature (or by God—in this context the difference is unimportant) can depart from natural law. Primitive natural reason may take different historical forms yet remain constant, unaffected by the passage of time. From this normative standpoint Montesquieu is capable of rendering negative judgments on such phenomena as polygamy, despotism, and slavery even as he provides "objective" explanations for them.

Montesquieu's position is ambiguous because he holds both that we must try to understand the primitive laws of reason and that we can understand history in terms of laws. The variety of feminine natures can be explained in terms of women's historical experience. But the history of women cannot explain the fundamental difference between woman and man, which is not simply a matter of sex. Nevertheless, "objective" discourse about women consists essentially in a description of the various causes that have made them what they are. In *Mes pensées* Montesquieu writes: "Women are deceptive. This is a result of their dependency. With them it is the same as with the king's tariffs: the higher you raise them, the more contraband you create."

A Necessary Education

Once the formative or deformative effects of education are brought into the picture, human nature can no longer be defined in terms of essence; account must be taken of history and institutions. What is true of man is even truer of girls and women, whose education was directed toward different ends from that of the male sex. A girl's education was supposed to prepare her to assume her "natural" role as wife and mother. Countless treatises on education were written in the eighteenth century (some of them by women), and in general they insisted on the need for *practical* training for girls. The difference in the roles of men and women was frequently stressed, usually with the best of intentions. It was of course possible to believe in the natural inequality of the sexes and still denounce the unfortunate effects of traditional forms of education (such as convent schools) on fragile and malleable female natures. Though sincere and generous, such criticism was essentially moralistic. There was no notion that education might in large part be responsible for women's character and behavior, for it was easier and more comforting to blame nature.

Those philosophers who insisted on the equality of the sexes took a different line. To believe in equality it was necessary to disregard the facts, which invariably demonstrated inequality. But the facts proved nothing, it was argued, because they were a consequence of existing social arrangements. Equality was thus assumed a priori. But what sort of equality was it?

Let us look first at Helvétius' approach to the question in *De l'esprit* (On Mind, first published anonymously in 1758). He claims to be taking a Baconian approach, reasoning from facts to causes in his effort to describe the nature of mind. But what does he mean by facts? A fact is something that can be observed, in this case a human faculty, action, or passion. But observation is guided by a theory of knowledge and custom based on a radical version of sensualist empiricism: all our representations and actions are rooted in the senses. Helvétius assumes that nothing in man is naturally innate, that everything is acquired except, of course, the constitution of a sentient being capable of acquiring everything. It follows that all human beings are created equal, regardless of sexual or ethnic differences. For Helvétius, this equality is a consequence not of natural rights but of identity of mind. Under normal circumstances all men and women have the same brains and therefore the physical capacity to attain the highest levels of thought. The driving force of all human behavior is self-interest, individual utility, which is not incompatible with the general interest if the proper laws are in force. Where, then, does inequality arise? The question applies not only to inequality between the sexes but also to inequality between men. It is not, Helvétius argues, a consequence of physical, climatic, or other, similar conditions. It is solely a product of "moral" factors, by which he means the social and political factors that have shaped the human race through its history. Sociohistorical development has given rise to differences among men and in particular to certain "vices" peculiar to one sex or the other. One such vice is sexual license among women. But was this really a vice? The luxury that permitted and even encouraged such license was in fact useful to society, for it provided work for people in many walks of life.

In any event, what good laws achieved bad laws could undo, assuming, as Helvétius did, that nations as well as individuals are shaped solely by the force of law. The fundamental purpose of legislation, he insisted, is education: "We owe everything to education."[8]

Helvétius argued that the inequality of women and the differences of "nature" and "behavior" that philosophers were pleased to expound actually stemmed from deficiencies in women's education, which prevented them from making the progress of which they were capable in science and the arts. Woman was made in such a way that her virtues seemed to justify a prejudice against her. Prejudice by definition is not capable of providing reasons for its judgments: the obligation of women to remain chaste cannot be justified any more than the practices of Indian fakirs. To a theologian, libertinage might well appear to be a form of corruption. But a philosopher was under no obligation to see things the same way. Helvétius observed that libertinage was well accepted in certain countries and by certain religions and far from incompatible with a nation's happiness.

Since the brains of men and women were of equal size, the two sexes ought to receive equal education. Helvétius gave no detailed description of the sort of educational system he had in mind, but he did say that no subject that men studied should be forbidden to women. In addition, education ought to be public and run by the state. Only good laws could foster a good educational system, and it might well be necessary to reform the government in order to have one: "The art of molding men is everywhere so closely associated with the form of government that it may not be possible to make a significant change in public education without making one in the very constitution of the state."[9] In 1759 Pope Clement XIII condemned *De l'esprit,* and the book was burned on order of the Paris Parlement and later by the Sorbonne's faculty of theology.

Citizens?

If the sexes are equal and if equality requires that they be educated in the same way, then women ought to enjoy full rights of citizenship and be allowed to take part in political life. This is not the place to examine what rights women of various social groups actually enjoyed under the ancien régime. In any case the term *citizenship* came to be closely correlated with the notion of republic, despite the fact that republican government could take many forms. Geneva, for example, was a republic to which Rousseau paid tribute in the *Discourse on Inequality* (although later, after the banning of *Emile,* he would claim that he had been deluded about its virtues). He believed his native city to be a land of freedom governed by laws to which its citizens gave their consent.

But what was the situation of the women to whom Rousseau referred as lovable and virtuous citizens? They enjoyed citizenship only as wives of citizens, and as such their only rights were to contribute to purity in morals and harmony among families. In other words, women's citizenship was confined to the private sphere and cut off from the realities of politics. Sophie's situation is similar: she is not included in the political instruction (on the nature of government, contract, and citizenship) that the tutor offers Emile as an initiation into civic life before his marriage. For a woman, citizenship was passive, a mere accompaniment to the active citizenship of her husband and guardian. Rousseau's thinking is stubbornly consistent: woman is not man's equal, she does not receive the same education, and she is not entitled to citizenship in name or deed except in a metaphorical sense.

The case for granting women political rights depended on the assumption of natural equality between the sexes. Being equal by nature, women deserved equal rights and equal education and should therefore enjoy equal political rights under a republic. Condorcet was undoubtedly the philosopher of the last quarter of the eighteenth century who took the Enlightenment spirit most seriously. Let a single individual be deprived of his or her rights, he argued, and the universal principal of human equality collapsed.

In July 1790 Condorcet published an article "On Granting Civil Rights to Women" in the *Journal de la Société de '89* (no. 5).[10] He began by pointing out that philosophers and lawmakers had repeatedly violated the natural right to equality "by coolly depriving half of the human race of the right to participate in the making of laws by denying women their civil rights." He is dismissive of the idea that women are inferior because they are physically weaker than men. While it is true that menstruation, pregnancy, and the like are difficulties that women must face because of their sex, these no more incapacitate them for civic life than an attack of gout or a cold would incapacitate a man. Nor is Condorcet convinced by the other common argument against women: that they have failed to distinguish themselves in the arts and sciences. What if the right to vote were granted only to men of genius? It would then be difficult indeed to find a reasonable number of citizens. In places where the form of government allowed women to demonstrate their political abilities, they rose to the challenge. There had been and still were great queens and great empresses: Elizabeth I of England, Catherine of Russia, Maria

Theresa of Austria. Women were capable of philosophy, literature, and science, as the Age of Enlightenment convincingly proved. Condorcet was a habitué of any number of salons, including the eminent one hosted by his wife, Sophie de Grouchy, and believed that the women who organized these gatherings in which enlightened thought circulated deserved credit for one of the highest achievements of the age.

Condorcet analyzed the reasons underlying the various prejudices against women. What people mistook for the female nature was in fact the product of a long history, of an insidious accumulation of customs. Women were no more frivolous, false, deceitful, or underhanded than Negro slaves were cowardly, cringing, or shiftless. Condorcet consistently championed women and Negroes, human beings deprived of their rights by a tyrannical, irrational order. The Negro more than likely received no education. He was subject to the brute force of his master. Women were educated but to their own detriment and primarily by priests, who, by subjecting women's sexual behavior and intelligence to an authority they were not expected to understand, thereby subjected the entire human race (via its female half) to that same authority. The authority of father and husband perpetuated female servitude. But this authority was irresponsible because it applied to subjects brought up blindly to obey. In opposition to the notion that women are inferior to men in reason, Condorcet, convinced that reason is either universal or nonexistent, objected that women "are, it is true, not guided by the reason of men, but they are guided by a reason of their own." Does this imply that the two forms of reason are by nature heterogeneous? In all human beings reason is based on self-interest. If there is a difference between the two sexes, the reason is that women have their own interests. But women's interests are shaped by men's laws. Women wear makeup only because men have reduced them to a position in which only their appearance matters. Women can thus support themselves only by a "dressed-up reason."

Would granting women civil rights threaten the cohesiveness of the family? Would women leave their natural place in the home (frequently symbolized by needlework) and abandon the private sphere in favor of the public? This argument was the last resort of those who held that sexual inequality ought to be perpetuated in the name of public utility. Condorcet challenged this misleading use of the concept of utility: "In the name of utility commerce and industry groan in chains and the African is still destined for slavery. In the name of public utility the Bastille was filled with prisoners, books were censored, trials were held in secret, and torture was administered." Condorcet argued not only that a public role for women would not be harmful to the family but also that a woman who was also a member of the National Assembly would make a better mother to her children.

In 1790 and 1791 Condorcet published his *Five Memoirs on Public Education.* The Assembly assigned him the task of proposing a plan for education, which he submitted in April 1792, but it was not accepted. This far-reaching proposal is nevertheless a monument of the Enlightenment spirit. Education has a clear political purpose: ignorance has always encouraged tyranny, and the only way to protect freedom and equality is to educate the people. Education is to be public, secular, and free of charge. Such a conception of education is inseparable from a form of government based on equality before the law and on the principle that citizens are obliged to obey the law only if they are permitted to take part in its formulation: in other words, the republic. Education contributes to the perfection of the human race and hastens its irreversible progress toward freedom and rationality. The road to perfection passes through crisis and revolution on the way to universal happiness. Concerned to establish a secular, public school system, Condorcet carefully distinguishes between education and upbringing. Education is the job of a public school system, the only guarantee of equality of instruction. Upbringing is the job of families. The details of the argument are important. Families differ in social and economic status and therefore contribute to inequality. They also hold different opinions. If the schools were to interfere with the child's upbringing, they would inevitably come into conflict with the family. Condorcet is not advocating that a "private" sphere be carved out within the public sphere, a sort of state within a state. He leaves upbringing to families because he is convinced that as enlightenment progresses, opinions not based on reason will disappear. He was deluded, apparently, but it was a delusion shared by many Enlightenment thinkers.

In the "First Memoir" Condorcet argues that men and women should be educated in the same way: "Since all education is limited to imparting truths and developing proofs, it is hard to see how the difference of sexes would require a different selection of truths or a different manner of proving them."[11]

Condorcet's argument for equality of education is easily summarized. All human beings have equal rights; hence women have a right to be educated as men are. There is also a pragmatic component to the argument: equal education is a matter of public utility. An educated woman is capable of overseeing the education of her children. The woman with intellectual attainments to match those of her husband makes for a happier family and helps her husband not to forget what he learned in his youth. Above all, if inequality is perpetuated for women, it will be impossible to abolish it among men. In other words, men cannot be free and equal if half of the human race is not freed from the chains in which it has been kept for ages. Enlightenment is not for men only. To believe that it is is to hold the irrational view that one sex is the final cause of the other, a view that Condorcet sees as exemplifying a medieval form of argument. "The pride of the stronger sex allows it to be easily convinced that the weaker sex was created for its benefit. But that is not the philosophy of either reason or justice."[12]

In his *Socialist History of the French Revolution* Jean Jaurès held that Condorcet's imposing philosophy pointed the way to the future. Yet Condorcet's grandiose theory of the progress of the human spirit was not so radical as to eliminate all vestiges of older ways of thinking. Women, he argued, should have the same civil rights as men. But in order to enjoy the specific right to elect representatives (and to stand for office) citizens, whether men or women, had to meet certain conditions, the first and fifth of which call for special notice: electors must be property owners, and they must not be dependent on any other individual or corporate body. Thus not everyone was entitled to full civil rights, contrary to what might seem to follow from the assertion of a natural equality of rights. Of course during the Revolution many people believed that a proper suffrage included only those "active citizens" who paid enough in taxes to qualify. This suffrage was limited to men; women were excluded. Condorcet opposed this arrangement on the grounds that gender should play no part in the granting of civil rights: a woman should have the right to vote, provided she owned property. The old feudal right that permitted female fiefholders to participate in the election, say, of members of local assemblies ought not to be eliminated, Condorcet argued, but rather extended to all female property owners who headed households.

Condorcet hoped that common education of men and women

would lead to a withering away of the prejudices that sustained belief in woman's intellectual inferiority. Underneath the generous grandeur of the principle of equality between the sexes a difference was in fact maintained: certain occupations were reserved for men, others for women. Women, for example, were supposed to be better at writing elementary school textbooks and at using their powers of observation to further scientific knowledge. Woman was by nature and taste a sedentary being. That is why home teaching suited her so well. Women were comfortable at home. The enlightened woman received guests in her salon.

A difference thus remained between the sexes, but Condorcet refused to see this difference as a form of inequality. He even went so far as to suggest that because of this sexual difference, women might well be in a position to attain kinds of knowledge not accessible to men. "Who knows if, when a different kind of upbringing will have enabled women to develop their reason to its fullest natural extent, the intimate relationship between the mother or nurse and the child, a relationship that does not exist for men, may enable them to make discoveries more important and necessary than many believe to the knowledge of the human spirit, to the art of its perfection, and to the hastening and facilitating of its progress?"[13] Was this not a return to a definition of woman in terms of her "natural" reproductive role? Perhaps. But what seems to be neglected here as insignificant is the function of the wife.

The Troubled Universal

Despite nature's declaration of freedom and equality for all members of the species, the masculine discourses of Enlightenment philosophers, whatever differences may have existed among them, inevitably envisioned the other half of the human race as somehow irreducible and unassimilable, a troubling affront to reason's serene claim of universality. The formidable (and triumphant) idea of equal rights threatened to disrupt the established social equilibrium. That subjects should become equals was not such a terrifying idea. But what was to be done about women if the principle of equality applied to all human beings? (And what about the Negroes if they were set free?) The calamity, it seems, was that there were two sexes and several "races." Of course there was always the dream of a single sex, capable of reproducing itself despite the absence of sexual differentiation, as in Aristophanes' myth, recounted in Plato's *Symposium,* of the spherical beings that Zeus split into two parts as a punishment. And there was also the dream of autochthonous humans all of one color.

But differences did exist regardless of efforts to heighten or diminish them. The possibility of contradiction insinuated itself into masculine discourse more or less surreptitiously. One apparent way of resolving the theoretical difficulty that sexual difference raised for the Enlightenment mind was to ascribe a dual status to women. Kant was probably the philosopher who explored this avenue most fully, and not without risk.

Woman, like man, is an ethical subject, that is, an autonomous being equal before the moral law universally constituted by free will. In this sense every human being is a citizen in the ethical community that Kant called the "realm of ends." But can such equality be maintained in the juridical order? Law, according to Kant, is defined by a system of constraints: each person's freedom is limited by others' exercise of their freedom. Yet purely interior ethical freedom must be capable of realizing itself in acts, of externalizing itself, if it does not wish to remain at the level of mere intention. Now, the externalization of freedom implies its "incarnation" in a *thing.* This thing is a property (essentially, according to Kant, that of the ground, which has "substantial" value). This takes us into the realm of private law. Private law is distinct from public or political law in that it governs only relations between individuals and things (real law) and relations between individuals as property owners (personal law, contractual law). In itself this kind of law implies no supraindividual or state authority, yet it must invoke such authority if only the state is capable of guaranteeing property rights and enforcing contracts. Juridical personhood is restricted to those individuals who have the capacity to externalize their freedom in property. Similarly, in the political order, only property owners enjoy the right to vote under a republican government, which Kant says has nothing to do with any form of democracy. If a woman owns property, is she entitled to the same rights as the male property owner? No, for a fundamental reason: in order to deal with the status of women (as well as servants and other workers dependent on a master and therefore not autonomous individuals) Kant introduced a novel element into the firmament of the law: personal law of the real kind. Here is his definition, provided in *The Doctrine of Virtue:* "Man may possess another person as if that person's self were his own." This doctrine justified the legal and social inequality not just of half the human race but of any individual who received a servant's or a worker's wages. Power is vested in the male owner, be he husband, father, or master of a household. A person can be treated as a thing *(res)*. If a woman or servant flees (and Kant does not examine the reasons for this obsession with flight), the owner enjoys a right of pursuit. The only purpose of Kant's strange innovation is to attempt to provide a legal basis for a de facto domination. An examination of marriage reveals the true nature of this new right. The purpose of the institution was procreation (although sterility was not grounds for divorce). Each partner was entitled to use and take pleasure from the body of the other. Natural sexuality always contained an element of bestiality: "Sexual pleasure is in principle (if not always in fact) something *cannibalistic*. The woman allows herself to be consumed in pregnancy and maternity (which could have fatal consequences); the man allows himself to be *exhausted* by the woman's excessive demands on his sexual capacities. The only difference is in the manner of taking pleasure, and each part in this reciprocal use of the sexual organs is, in relation to the other, truly an object of consumption [*res fungibilis*]" *(The Doctrine of Virtue)*. Treating the other (in and through the body) as a thing is incompatible with every human being's right not to be treated solely as a means. But if the two parties of their own free will choose to be treated as things, reciprocity is established. Through the marriage contract each spouse agrees to be used by the other. Monogamous marriage imposes norms on the cannibalism of natural sexuality. But the marriage contract is peculiar in that it is indissoluble. According to Kant, the equality of husband and wife in physical possession neither excludes nor contradicts man's legal domination of woman, because man is naturally superior (a claim that requires no justification).

Indeed, apart from the legalized cannibalism of marriage and the moral dignity that allows a woman to do her duty, woman remains inferior. Here the categorical imperative comes up against its most troubling limitation: though valid for all human beings, it holds sway only in the order of pure practical reason, of moral autonomy.

Enlightenment philosophers attempted to conceptualize the difference between man and woman. To some degree women were invariably branded with the mark of inferiority, yet an effort was made to reconcile this inferiority with the principle of equality, based on natural law. Philosophers also sought to define the social role of women: wife, mother, and so on. It was by assuming a natural function of some kind that woman became a citizen. There was no straightforward recognition of woman's political role (except perhaps by Condorcet). The most widely shared ideology of the eighteenth century held that man was the final cause of woman. The most radical version of this view can be found in Rousseau's *Emile,* where Sophie's education is predicated entirely on the need to maximize Emile's happiness. But by radicalizing the dominant ideology of the age Rousseau destroyed it. No one taught Sophie about the realm of necessity. Her education consists of a gentle and flexible system of constraints, but she is given no way to understand that there are things beyond our control. Thus she cannot resign herself to the death of her parents or, even more, to the death of her daughter. Emile takes the inconsolable Sophie to Paris/Babylon, capital of vices that Sophie will not be able to resist (because no one has taught her how).

In *Emile et Sophie, ou les solitaires,* Rousseau demolishes the educational system responsible for the fate of Emile and Sophie. Emile leaves his unfaithful wife, finds work, abandons his family and fatherland, is made a slave in Algiers, experiences the harshness of irrational servitude, organizes a rebellion, and, if the text had not been left unfinished, no doubt would have ended with a speech to the slave master on the nature of enlightenment. In ceasing to be a father and a citizen, Emile has become more of a man. Is Sophie set free? It would be anachronistic to pose the question in these terms. In misfortune Sophie discovers the inadequacy of her upbringing. She has not deceived Emile or lied to him but has ceased to belong to him alone, and it is through her that man finally comes to experience the prosaic side of existence and perhaps to attain self-consciousness.

TRANSLATED FROM THE FRENCH BY ARTHUR GOLDHAMMER

11

The Discourse
of Medicine and Science

Evelyne Berriot-Salvadore

FROM MEDIEVAL ENCYCLOPEDIAS to Renaissance anthologies, from the preachers of the Counter-Reformation to the orators of the Revolution, medical discourse was repeatedly invoked to justify the role assigned to women in the family and in society. Marie de Gournay, in *L'égalité des hommes et des femmes* (The Equality of Men and Women, 1622), protested that a certain view of female physiology served as a pretext for various exclusions, and similar prejudices were still being denounced by Constance de Theis in her *Epître aux femmes* (Epistle to women, 1797):

> Laissons l'anatomiste, aveugle en sa science,
> D'une fibre avec art calculer la puissance,
> Et du plus ou du moins inférer sans appel,
> Que sa femme lui doit un respect éternel.

> Let the anatomist, blind in his knowledge, artfully calculate the strength of a fiber and from the greater or the lesser incontrovertibly infer that his wife owes him eternal respect.

By the end of the thirteenth century the theoretical foundations of this discourse had been laid. The range of possibility extended from the doctrine of Aristotle, who saw the female as an incomplete male, to that of Galen, for whom the female was associated with that disturbingly unique organ, the uterus. From the Middle Ages to the nineteenth century women's medicine remained trapped in a dialectic between the Aristotelian thesis and the Galenist antithesis, possibly to the detriment of more rapid progress in anatomy and biology. Yet the perennial stereotypes and endless repetition mask certain ruptures, which are particularly difficult to analyze because they do not coincide with the familiar turning points of the standard history of medicine. What was at stake, perhaps, was not knowledge of the nature and function of each sex (matters in any case not fully understood until the nineteenth century) but the concept of sexual difference as it relates to the cosmic and social order.

Female Nature

Why Speak of Woman?

The subject itself is problematic. The interest of naturalists in women was part of a broader concern with human reproduction. Sexual dimorphism was a mystery for both the biologist and the anatomist. During the Middle Ages a controversy arose between disciples of Aristotle, who saw the female as a passive receptacle for the embryo, and followers of Hippocrates, who considered the mother an active participant in reproduction in two ways: she provided semen of her own, and she furnished the nutriments out of which the embryo was formed. By the fourteenth century the conflict appeared to have issued in a compromise, the nature of which emerges clearly from the views of Henri de Mondeville: since reproduction requires both a male body and a female body, Mondeville argued, there might be some point to studying female anatomy even if Galen was right that the female body was only a turning inside out of the male.

Numerous translations and glosses of the Galenic and Hippocratic texts revived the debate in the sixteenth century, however, and because medical discourse proposed itself as both *praxis* and *doxa* the controversy took on a new dimension. Thus, although no important anatomical discovery challenged a schema that had been in place since Hierophilus in the fourth century B.C., there was active research in obstetrics and gynecology, as is evident from the interest students at the major medical schools took in dissecting women and from the proliferation of anatomical treatises and practical manuals in French. Late-Renaissance specialists in female medicine had a clear sense that their art was undergoing significant evolution. In the past, Jean Liébault wrote in the *Thrésor des remèdes secrets pour les maladies des femmes* (Treasury of Secret Remedies for Women's Diseases, 1585), most treatises on pathology avoided the subject of women's diseases, which was deemed too difficult and obscure. Today, however, physicians have a better understanding of the Hippocratic teachings and, like the Hippocratics, are motivated by charitable feelings to help women in their afflictions. Most important of all, the Renaissance physician had a more complete notion of the moral and social impact of these medical theories: How could one ignore or feel contempt for a body created for the purpose of giving birth to one's fellow human beings? To practitioners in the late sixteenth century this misogynist jibe from Arnaud de Villeneuve's *Practica* would have seemed near-blasphemy: "With the help of God I shall here concern myself with matters having to do with women, and since women are most of the time vicious animals, I shall in due course consider the bite of venomous animals."[1]

When doctors sought to address not only other doctors and midwives but all persons of sound judgment, including women, what they said influenced social behavior, although for the most part this medical discourse only mirrored already widespread attitudes. Early in the seventeenth century, in the course of an investigation into the causes of sterility, the physician Louys de Serres asked himself why most men considered the birth of a daughter to be a disgrace. Not, he argued, because they detested the female, who was after all created in the image of the male, but because they had to contend with a weighty tradition going all the way back to the ancients, to Aristotle and Galen, and continued by such moderns as François Rabelais and André Tiraqueau.

Most medical texts presented a negative image of the female sex. Was this, as Serres implies, simply a reflection of cultural prejudices? The Renaissance naturalist, like his late-medieval counterpart, was in fact the prisoner of a methodology: his observations of the female were based on analogies with the male body. In deference to the supreme scientific authority, Galen, the anatomist was forever mindful of one fundamental principle: "All the generative parts of man are also found in woman." The only difference was in the disposition of the parts. Description, which failed to erase the Aristotelian image of the female as an incomplete male, was thus a serious impediment to progress in gynecology. The magnitude of that impediment can be gauged from a remark made by the Galenist physician Philippe de Flesselles, who proposed to his readers a full description of the human body yet omitted female anatomy on the grounds that "sexual difference is merely accidental."[2]

The Parisian physician's treatise was of course written in a crucial period, just before the revolution in anatomy that paved the way for advances in gynecology and obstetrics. The famous frontispiece of Vesalius' *Fabrica,* which uses a female body to illustrate a lesson in anatomy, attests to the interest the subject aroused. But the plates in the chapters on the reproductive organs show that anatomical thinking was still shaped in large part by ancient analogies; in one illustration, for example, the uterus and cervix appear to be strikingly similar to the parts of the male urogenital tract. This drawing, which has attracted a great deal of commentary in disciplines ranging from teratology to psychoanalysis, is by no means unusual, however: for three-quarters of a century it was reproduced by countless surgeons and anatomists even though anatomical observation had made considerable progress in the interim. An excellent example can be found in Scipion Mercurio's widely read *La commare o riccoglitrice,* which was reprinted and translated into many languages up to the end of the seventeenth century.[3]

In *La dissection des parties du corps humain,* published in 1546 with plates by the surgeon La Rivière, Charles Estienne was very much concerned with giving a satisfactory description of the female genital apparatus, which he explicitly distinguished from the male. His purpose was to show "by illustration everything in the female body not found in man." Nevertheless, observational rigor succumbed to another imperative: respect for Galen's authority. Having proclaimed his freedom as a man of science, the physician nevertheless insisted on his orthodoxy, contradicting what his own descriptions revealed. A foolhardy challenge to the master's authority was the furthest thing from his mind. Was Estienne unusually conformist or cautious? Perhaps, but similarly paradoxical pronouncements can be found in the work of many other authors, even those not always blindly obedient to the ancients, such as Ambroise Paré. In *De l'anatomie* the autodidact surgeon explained that the womb is a specific organ of the female, but elsewhere he was careful to recall the unshakable truth summed up in the lapidary formula that "woman is the inverse of man."

In other words, Galen's hypothesis served to limit what physicians made of what they saw, and no doubt that was why Pierre Franco still seemed to feel a need to explain why he devoted several chapters of his treatise on surgery to female anatomy: "Because the shameful parts of women are often in need of the surgical art, we felt that it was not ridiculous to write about them."[4]

If the analogical method, along with certain ambiguities in anatomical terminology, was responsible for this attitude toward the female sexual apparatus, physicians were also influenced by popular beliefs. We find evidence of those beliefs in various kinds of texts, reflecting different levels of culture. For instance, fables about girls' being transformed into men, which had graced anthologies of "curiosities" since the time of Pliny, became scientifically attested facts: when the prolific Antoine Duverdier told the story of the peasant girl who, at the age of menarche, suddenly thrust out the virile member previously hidden in her belly, did he not invoke the authority of the physician Amatus Lusitanus? Even Montaigne, in recounting similar phenomena, referred to a text by Ambroise Paré. Scientific discourse and everyday talk substantiated each other in a game of mirrors that invariably reflected one image: that of an incomplete or defective female body.

Female Imperfection

Physicians, meanwhile, were not content merely to describe the female anatomy. They somehow had to rationalize nature's peculiar mistake. The theory of temperaments, which had originated with the ancients, and especially the imposing edifice of Galenic physiology had survived the Middle Ages to provide an explanation of sexual dimorphism. Medical thinking would continue to rely on these same fundamental ideas up to the seventeenth century. In the Galenic view, woman, being of cold and humid temperament, is equipped with spermatic organs colder and softer than those found in man, and since cold causes things to contract and tighten, it followed that these organs remain internal, like a flower that never opens for want of sunlight. Thus defined in terms of impotence and debility, the female body fitted nicely into the hierarchy of creatures between the animals and man. And that is why the Galenic hypothesis endured as long as it did: it not only accounted for female anatomy but also explained one of the peculiar features of female physiology, namely, its dysfunctional nature.

The menstrual flow was the most significant symptom of this dysfunctionality. From antiquity on, scholarly treatises and encyclopedias, authoritative texts and folklore attributed a mysterious evil power to this effusion of blood. In the sixteenth century traces of such attitudes could be found not only in the Dutch physician Levin Lemne's *Occult Secrets of Nature* but also in the work of Jean Fernel, who held that the menstrual flow contained, in addition to two necessary elements (one for nourishing the fetus *in utero* and another that was subsequently transformed into milk), a third, venomous element that was eliminated during delivery. To be sure, specialists in female diseases, Jacques Sylvius foremost among them, along with Ambroise Paré, Giovanni Marinello, and Jean Liébault, opposed this view as too irrational; yet even they saw the menstrual flow as a "superfluity," the result of a temperament too moist and cold to convert all the nutriment into useful blood. To read an explanation of menstruation free of any negative a priori assumptions, one has to wait until François Mauriceau's *Traité des maladies des femmes grosses* (Treatise on the Diseases of Pregnant Women, 1668), and even then ignorance of the ovarian cycle precluded a full understanding of the phenomenon.

In fact the theory of temperaments was used in treatises on practical medicine and works on natural philosophy to justify the view that woman was by nature fragile and unstable. This view was found in the fourteenth-century work of Guy de Chauliac, which was still being published and commented on in the early seventeenth century. The controversy over sterility is very revealing in this regard. In the *Nature, Causes, Signs, and Cure of Impediments to Conception and Sterility in Women* (1625), Louys de Serres forthrightly affirmed that both sexes can suffer from sterility and denounced both his contemporaries for their behavior and his colleagues for their errors. As Serres the practitioner was no doubt well placed to observe, men generally blamed their wives when the birth of a first child was too long delayed, and some went so far as to sue for divorce. Physicians, meanwhile, continued to hold to the fundamental view that a woman was like a cold, damp field and could thus easily cause the man's seed to rot. They interpreted this defect as a sign of divine justice: it seemed that "God wished particularly to subject women to such a malady in order to chasten their pride and make them see that they are far more imperfect than man."[5] Caught up in this kind of metaphysics, medical thought had no fear of contradiction. As for the view, held by some of his colleagues, that very beautiful women were more frequently sterile than others, Louys de Serres had no difficulty showing that this assertion ignored the principles of physiology and thus made no scientific sense: sterility, arising from a defect of "complexion" (resulting from an imbalance of humors), was more likely to occur in ugly women, he argued, because their peevish character corrupted the temperament.

Despite the efforts of Louys de Serres and others, such as Laurent Joubert and Gaspard Bachot, to combat "vulgar errors and statements," physicians continued for a long time to be swayed by these popular beliefs, as did midwives, who should have been educated by the experience of their own bodies. Thus Louise Bourgeois, the celebrated midwife of Marie de Médicis, admonished women who blamed their husbands for their lack of offspring, because, she said, "ordinarily this is not the fault of men as often as it is of women."[6]

Science, in short, merely gave its sanction to popular superstitions. Famous healing saints such as Grelichon, Paterne, and Guignolet specialized in female sterility, whereas none devoted his talent to the cure of a similar affliction in men. Sterility, caused by a deficiency of heat or an imbalance of humours, was by definition a female disease.

The implications of this medical theory were not limited to the realm of physiology. Invoking the same fundamental principles, physicians described the intellectual and moral attributes of woman. According to a tradition stemming from Aristotle and others, woman was weak, quick to anger, jealous, and false, whereas man was courageous, judicious, deliberate, and efficient. Renaissance science attempted to show how these qualities were inevitable and necessary consequences of the female temperament. The most methodical demonstration was given by the Spanish writer Juan Huarte. In *Examen de ingenios para las sciencias* (Examination of Wits Suitable for the Sciences, 1580), which met with immediate and lasting success and was quickly translated into Latin and the vernacular languages of Europe, he argued that woman, immersed in damp cold, was consequently less intelligent than man and barred from success in literature and science. An airtight theory of female physiology and psychology thus implied that women were congenitally condemned to incompleteness. Giambattista della Porta's *Della fisionomia dell'uomo* (On the Physiognomy of Man) even established a close correlation between complexion, physiognomy, and morals: women who had moist flesh, narrow faces, small eyes, and straight noses were also fearful, angry, and above all deceitful. By contrast, men's broad and strong faces exhibited the qualities of their courageous and just minds. Animal analogies provided emblematic representations of sexual differentiation: woman was a panther or partridge, man a lion or eagle. To be sure, the work of the Neapolitan physician, an adept of the occult sciences, judicial astrology, and magic, was in many ways exceptional, but its success was lasting. After the publication of the first Latin edition in 1583, it appeared in various Italian editions and in Spanish, Arabic, and French translations and continued to influence physiognomists, most notably Johann Caspar Lavater, down to the end of the eighteenth century.

The scientific underpinnings of this narrow determinism were demolished by other medical theories, such as spiritualism, exemplified by Jourdain Guibelet's *Examen de l'examen des esprits* (Examination of the Examination of Wits, 1631), which attacked Juan Huarte. Yet these earlier theories continued to be influential well beyond the seventeenth century because they accorded so well with the values of society at large. The discourses of legal, theological, and scientific elites served as mutual alibis justifying the inferiority of women. For many theologians, such as Florimond de Raemond and François Garasse, the role of women was strictly limited by the natural fragility that the physicians identified.

Woman as Womb

This logic, from which stems a negative representation of half the human race, culminates in a paradox: If woman is indeed the defective creature that science describes, why was she created? Is she perhaps an error of nature? To be sure, Aristotle had made it possible to explain the existence of monsters, and Galen had placed the mutilation of women in a teleological context, but from the sixteenth century on physicians and natural philosophers no longer seemed satisfied with the arguments of the ancients. The controversy between proponents of old-fashioned Galenism and those who admired and proposed to explore the Great Work of Nature reveals a change in attitude: to assert that the female sex was in a fundamental sense imperfect was tantamount to scientific blasphemy or heresy. In *La suite de l'Académie françoise* (Sequel to the French Academy, 1580), a work intended for people curious about the marvels of creation, Pierre de La Primaudaye launched a fierce attack on the erroneous views of the natural philosophers and above all on the comparative method that had led them astray. Each sex, he argued, was perfect in its distinctiveness, as the Creator had willed. Of course this nobleman and contemporary of Henri III was no more interested in making a case for women than was the philosopher René de Cerisiers who developed the same argument at some length in the middle of the seventeenth century; his intention, rather, was to make men of learning aware of the moral and religious consequences of depreciating the female sex beyond all measure.

Certain physicians understood the warning quite well. The scientific definition of sexual difference would have to be expressed in terms compatible with the teleological credo that "nature does nothing in vain." The French adaptation of Giovanni Marinello's *Le medecine partenenti alle infermità delle donne* (The Medicine of Women's Diseases) made this concern explicit. In a chapter not present in the original text Jean Liébault made clear his determination to prove by the laws of natural philosophy that woman is not an incomplete male. Could nature's works be called imperfect merely because the species are numerous and diverse? The smallest of them, the ant species, was as admirable as the largest, the elephants, because in the order of creation the only thing that counted was the purpose for which each thing was created. This argument, which had little to do with scientific observation, drew heavily on Renaissance cosmogony. Liébault, however, drew novel conclusions from this cosmogonic vision. In attributing an intrinsic value to each species, he did away with the old scale of values, in which animals and women occupied the intermediate levels between the inferior minerals and superior man.

Woman had a place in medical ethics as well as in the discourse of philosophical physicians. The female body ceased to be seen as a defective copy of the male; women's bodies were examined as complete and distinctive entities. In order to justify sexual dimorphism, doctors were forced to question previously incontrovertible concepts. Medicine needed to bring its understanding up to date. For example, André Du Laurens and his disciple François Ranchin chose to present anything to do with female anatomy and reproduction in the form of "controversies" or "questions" so as to give full expression to the diversity of ancient and modern opinion and ultimately to show that most prejudices on the subject stemmed from ignorance of anatomy. Once the internal and external structure of the female body had been described with exactitude, it became absurd to argue that woman was a mistake of nature: "The sex organ of the female is no less the perfection of her species than that of the male of his, and woman must not be called an accidental [*occasionné*] animal, as the Barbarians called her, but a necessary creature instituted by Nature firstly and of itself."[7]

The fact that the regent of the Faculty of Paris wrote such a vigorous defense of the new view would be enough to show how firmly rooted the old one remained, but Dr. Jourdain Guibelet's attack on Juan Huarte makes the point even more strongly. In Guibelet's eyes the Spaniard was guilty of bowing down unquestioningly before Galen's authority, which progress in anatomy had made it necessary to reconsider. Now that it was known that temperament could not change the location of the organs and, furthermore, that the parts of men were not the same as those of women, all the stories of sexual transmutations had to be judged illusory. According to Guibelet and Du Laurens, most of these alleged reports probably involved cases of hermaphroditism or monstrous protuberance of the clitoris.

Nevertheless, the stubborn adherence to Juan Huarte's view was not unusual either in his own time or in the decades that followed. In 1624 Guy Patin wrote a thesis on the subject "Can woman transform herself into man?" and although his answer was negative, it implied that the question remained open. Furthermore, Saviard, chief surgeon of the Hôtel Dieu in Paris at the end of the sixteenth century, observed that certain practitioners were still confusing prolapse of the uterus with a change of sex. Louis Barles's *Nouvelles découvertes sur les organes des hommes servans à la génération* (New Discoveries about the Organs of Men Serving in Reproduction, 1675), had no other purpose than to familiarize less well-read surgeons and physicians with what anatomical treatises had already been reporting for a century.

The persistence of such errors is explained, no doubt, in part by lack of training in anatomy but also by the continuing influence of the Aristotelian principle. Simply put, it was obvious to physicians, even without the notion of a "castration complex," that the female sex was constantly striving to attain the virile perfection it lacked. When the biological possibility of transsexuality was granted, it was always conceived in terms of virilization. Thus Jacques Duval, an expert on hermaphrodites: "Men, formed as such in the maternal vulva, never shed their virile nature and never revert to the female sex, since all things tend toward perfection."[8] Moreover, this desire for completion could be observed not only in nature but also in behavior: Duval remarked that hermaphrodites were frequently baptized as males because their parents would rather raise a boy than a girl.

Despite the efforts made to escape a frame of reference that impeded anatomical observation and hindered therapeutic progress, scientific discourse was dependent on a world order in need of legitimation, and one way to legitimate that order was to demonstrate that the role of each sex was inscribed in nature. Thus for all the precursors of gynecology and obstetrics, from the German Rösslin to the Italian Marinello and the Frenchman Liébault, the best justification of, and most useful protection for, woman lay in explaining the specific nature of the organ that defined her entire being. Because the womb was the receptacle in which "a small creature of God" was formed, and because it was connected through the nervous system and the flow of blood to the other parts of the body, it was the most necessary and noble organ, indeed the organ in which the feminine quiddity resided. To be sure, the importance that physicians and anatomists attached to the womb, even apart from the late seventeenth-century discoveries concerning the role of the ovaries, demolished the negative definition taken from the Peripatetics but condemned woman to be merely the prisoner of the strange organ that dwelled within her. Hidden and protected in the secret recesses of the body, the womb possessed a potent and mysterious symbolic value as the seat of conception and gestation. In the *Buch Matricis* (Womb Book) Paracelsus defined this organ, "die Mutter," as a "kleineste Welt" (smallest world), in itself different from both the macrocosm and the microcosm. The mother-woman (*die Mutter*) is none other than this *mundus conclusus,* and that is why she possesses an anatomy, a physiology, and a pathology different from those of man. The terminological ambivalence here is significant: the vessel that conceives and protects the child is commonly referred to as "matrix" or "mother" because woman is constituted with the necessity of this organ in view—because she exists, in other words, only by virtue of her womb. A long tradition of more or less faithful interpretation of Plato's *Timaeus* and *Republic,* according to which the womb possesses its own internal power, is easily discerned in the Paracelsian theory.

This disturbing image of the female organ as a wandering animal within an unstable one lurks behind another question whose persistence suggests that it was more than a mere provocation: Is woman a truly human creature? The origin of this debate is most unclear. Allegedly it dates back to a church council held in Mâcon in 585, at which a bishop supposedly asserted that women were not to be included under the term *Man.* Whatever the truth of this legend, it proved so tenacious that in the late sixteenth century Simon Gedicus felt obliged to refute, with the utmost seriousness, a work by the German philosopher Acidalius titled *Mulieres non esse homines* (Women Are Not Men). Echoes of this debate could still be heard in the late eighteenth century: from the podiums of revolutionary clubs champions of the rights of women stigmatized the time when a society of men had questioned whether women had a soul. Beyond the comical aspects of this controversy we perceive the subtle link between a simple physiological observation—the distinctiveness of the uterus—and the segregative response, which branded women as suspiciously alien.

Ultimately the theory that the female identity was characterized by difference led to an impasse, and from that impasse we learn a great deal about the handicaps that medicine had to overcome in order to free itself from cultural presuppositions. No sooner had surgeons and anatomists begun to focus on the female body an attention previously precluded by the theory of the "incomplete male" than wariness of still misunderstood manifestations of femininity compelled them to adopt an attitude that once again placed woman within a confining typology. The myth of the incomplete woman was replaced by the myth of woman as uterus. From the sixteenth to the nineteenth centuries scientific terminology was supplanted by metaphor in countless texts that attempted to describe the strange female "animal." The verbal gifts of Dr. Rondibilis in Rabelais's *Tiers livre* (Third Book) are the author's invention, but the theories to which he alludes were indeed part of the discourse of medicine, not only for Rabelais's contemporaries, who saw the womb as an imperious organ that tormented "poor little women," but also for Rousseau's, who were in no doubt that this "active" organ possessed a "peculiar instinct,"[9] and Michelet's, who regarded the womb as a tyrannical organ encompassing "within its dominion almost the entire range of woman's actions and affections," and even our contemporaries: "If the organ of female sexuality tends to devour, to take possession, if it diverts all psychic impulses into closed, circular patterns, then we can understand the difficulties women have in escaping from themselves, in moving beyond the bounds of their emotional lives."[10]

The Female Valetudinarian

For most physicians, even those who rejected the idea that woman was radically imperfect, the organ that defined her identity also accounted for the extremely vulnerable nature of her physiology and psychology. Despite the change in its theoretical underpinnings, medical discourse remained in harmony with common opinion: irascibility of the uterus replaced humid temperament as the explanation for woman's natural inferiority. From the end of the sixteenth century on, the proliferation of vernacular works on gynecology and obstetrics gave evidence of an evolution of the function of medicine as well as of a new consciousness on the part of practitioners: woman was a valetudinarian whose complaints had to be assuaged so that she could docilely accept her disadvantageous condition. The midwife Louise Bourgeois, whose success with career and family marked a stunning contradiction of the general opinion, was nevertheless deeply influenced by it. When she asked herself why nature had apparently been so unjust toward her sex, the only answer she could find was in metaphysics: without the illnesses from which women suffered because of their wombs, they might well "equal the health of men in body and spirit, but God wished them to be lesser in this regard in order to forestall the envy that one sex might have felt toward the other."[11]

Marie de Médicis's midwife could hardly have been expected to challenge an opinion accepted by both learned and popular physicians. In the seventeenth century Philebert Guibert, the author of *Le médecin charitable* (The Charitable Physician), and François Mauriceau, the author of *Le célèbre obstétricien* (The Celebrated Obstetrician), both ratified an assertion made by Hippocrates long before: that the womb was the cause of most diseases in women. Midwives, whose training naturally did not depend on the latest scientific opinions, held to this conviction even longer. In the *Abrégé de l'art des accouchemens* (Short Course in the Art of Delivery, 1754), Madame Le Boursier du Coudray was critical of rural midwives, who she said still looked upon the womb, "which they call 'mother,'" as the source of all women's diseases.

For centuries, in fact, the treatment of women was based on an idea shared by physicians, moralists, and theologians: that woman was governed by her sexual parts. The study of hysteria is a case in point. Until the end of the seventeenth century this disorder came under the exclusive head of female pathology. More than that, it was the very symbol of femininity in medical discourse. Instead of the relatively recondite term *hysteria* (whose etymology is of course revealing), commentators preferred more evocative expressions such as "suffocation of the womb" or "uterine furors." The primary symptom, on the basis of which physicians made their diagnosis, involved unusual movements of the uterus, which, like an animal, hurled itself about in every direction in violent convulsions. Carried away by the colorfulness of the metaphor, surgeons such as Ambroise Paré and physicians such as Jean Fernel even attributed autonomous feelings and behaviors to the organ: it could be vexed by certain irritations but calmed by things it liked. Admittedly, Fernel rejected an image of the womb as independent animal that can be traced back to Plato. For him, the uterus was only an organ, like the stomach or intestine, but its physiology distinguished it from all other parts of the body. The cause of a hysterical attack was therefore always the same: a venomous vapor exuded by the womb passed through the arteries and pores of the body to affect the entire organism, including the brain.

The treatment of hysteria was naturally based on the supposed faculties of the uterus, especially its strange olfactory sense, which accounted for the efficacy of fragrant pessaries (which were supposed to attract the womb) and fetid fumigations (which were supposed to repel it). Such remedies abounded in the popular pharmacopoeia and anthologies of "women's secrets," of course, but also in the erudite medical treatises used to train new doctors.

In this realm medical discourse wavered between anatomical defects, the excesses of a language not yet disciplined by scientific norms, and fantasies tied to the myth of the devouring womb. As a result, physicians debated the best way to eradicate the disease once the acute phase of hysteria had been arrested. According to most specialists in female pathology, the venomous substance released by the uterus stemmed from the corruption of retained matter, or, in other words, from a dysfunction in the secretion of blood or semen, which dysfunction was ascribed to the patient's mode of life. The moral implications of the assumed etiology are fully evident:

> When a woman, particularly one who is young and vigorous, plump, well nourished, and well supplied with blood and seed, either becomes a nun or chooses of her own free will to remain chastely continent, or marries a man who gives himself to his wife infrequently, or is the widow of a husband much given to this pleasure, or is tempted by the desire of Venus or stimulated by the gaze of some man or by immodest and lascivious talk or by a kiss or by the touching of the nipples or the natural parts as she imagined in dreams, she discharges a large quantity of seed into the womb . . . where it becomes corrupted . . . sending up to the heart and brain certain corrupt vapors that give rise to very cruel accidents.[12]

Hysteria, then, was a disease of women without men. Indeed, the best treatment for young women afflicted with the disease was marriage. Although certain experts, especially Jean Fernel, spoke out against such simplistic therapy, popular books and scientific anthologies persisted for a long time in this alienating vision of femininity, in large part because of the convergence on this issue of the authority of science and philosophy and of folk wisdom, both of which likened the uterus to a bottomless pit, a ground that can never hold enough water. Because woman was governed by her sexual organs, it followed easily that she must be subject to man. The philosopher Scipion Dupleix, in a work that presented the principal questions of physical and medical science in a form designed to appeal to a broad public, explained the "appetite" of the uterus as a legitimate desire for completeness, the female being said to find fulfillment in coupling with the male.

In this system of thought, hysteria became a kind of allegory in which scientific description of the disease took second place to an idea of female nature. It should therefore come as no surprise that physicians were for so long incapable of imagining that men could be affected by the disease. In 1681 Thomas Sydenham's *Dissertation on the Hysterical Affection,* which showed that the womb was not the first cause of a disease that was more properly comparable to hypochondria, seemed revolutionary. It ran contrary to too many prejudices to be accepted immediately, and it was not until eighteenth-century physicians had worked out a moral etiology of the vaporous affections, which once again designated woman as their primary victim, that the tradition of hysteria as "uterine furor" was finally abandoned.

In particular, Joseph Raulin's *Traité des affections vaporeuses du sexe* (Treatise on the Vaporous Affections of the Sexual Organ, 1758) marked a milestone. Using irony to attack the prejudices of his colleagues, he demolished all the old theories concerning the strange powers of the uterus. Hysteria, which he called a "vaporous affection," was in a sense a social disease caused by the poor air in large cities and the immorality of high society. In principle, therefore, it could afflict either of the two sexes. Nevertheless, women were far more vulnerable than men to what Raulin and his contemporaries considered the disease of the century: the vapors. This greater vulnerability stemmed chiefly from the fact that women were naturally more delicate and sensitive than men, and second from the fact that they were always idle: their way of life constituted a pathogenic state. If the reign of uterocentrism and "occult qualities" was over, the Hippocratic hypothesis continued to hold sway. According to Raulin, "women's diseases outnumber those peculiar to men by more than two hundred."[13]

Even if feminine debility was to be blamed more on civilization than on nature, it nevertheless determined woman's fate in an even more constraining manner than before. For eighteenth-century physicians, the hysterical vapors were the punishment visited on women for having forgotten the role marked out for them by nature's wisdom. In the wake of his compatriot Samuel Tissot's treatise *L'onanisme*, Dr. Bienville drove home the threat by addressing his readers directly. He recognized of course that his book *De la nymphomanie* might seem scabrous, yet he felt that there would be nothing wrong if it should fall into the hands of young girls, for they would then be able to ponder the many imperfections of their sex. They would become aware of the fragility of their nature and would cherish the principles that protected the weaker sex from disaster.

In the end, a medical discourse that claimed to be new joined forces with an utterly static ideology. Bienville's sources were still ancient physicians such as Moschion, from whom he borrowed the term *satyriasis,* and Renaissance physicians, especially Jacques Sylvius, whom he contradicted by defining "erotomania" as a disorder of the nervous fibers yet copied almost word for word in describing its victims: girls overcome by love, young widows, women married to excessively cold men, female readers of lubricious novels. In this case the physician quite consciously saw himself as a moralist, and the extremely dramatic quality of his descriptions was aimed not at achieving scientific rigor but at maximizing the impact of the edifying message.

The Female Function

Earth or Seed?

In reality, physicians were not free to be either scientists devoted to pure research or philosophers exclusively preoccupied with ontological questions. Not only were the various intellectual spheres not yet clearly delineated; even more important, medical practice, no longer left solely to barber-surgeons and midwives, had evolved to the point that physicians had become important family counselors. After the sixteenth century, practitioners were invested with greater social prestige and were increasingly called upon to lend scientific support to prevailing values.

The many treatises on human reproduction that appeared in French, from Guillaume Chrestien's translations of Galen and Jacques Sylvius to the works of Ambroise Paré, were not simply works of biology. Humanist practitioners also sought to define the function of each sex in nature and in society. To be sure, the interest in embryology was not limited to Renaissance physicians. The Middle Ages had long hesitated between the Aristotelian notion of conception as an action of the male's seed on the female's menstrual blood and the two-seed theory favored by Hippocrates and Galen and diffused by eleventh-century Arab physicians. By the dawn of the Renaissance this controversy appeared to have been settled, and the encyclopedias as well as most practitioners favored Galen's theory as modified by a tinge of Aristotelianism: in reproduction the woman contributed her menstrual blood as well as a seed whose active virtue was inferior to that of the male sperm. The most celebrated sixteenth-century specialists actually looked upon generation as a "coction" (cooking) of three elements: male seed, female seed, and menstrual blood. It might therefore seem reasonable to conclude that the issue remained closed until the Dutchman Régnier de Graaf discovered the ovaries. But nothing could be further from the truth. The Aristotelian tradition, according to which the woman had no active procreative role, was still widely influential, not only among laymen, as narrative literature attests, but also among many practitioners and midwives. Thus a chapter on the usefulness of the female seed in Levin Lemnius' *Occultes merveilles et secrets de Nature* (Occult Marvels and Secrets of Nature, 1574) seeks to demolish the dangerous opinion of ignorant midwives "who try to persuade women that they play very little part in the generation of the child, and that they only bear the burden of carrying the child in their belly for nine months, almost as if they rented their womb to men as if it were a ship to which these men brought their merchandise and into which they discharged their garbage."[14]

The aggressive tone of this text is due in part to the physicians' wariness of the midwives, who in their view wielded too much power, but the charge was still plausible and was in fact confirmed by subsequent medical works; André Du Laurens, for example, was still arguing against stubborn defenders of the Aristotelian theory. In fact the controversy over the formation of the fetus was more than a dispute between schools; the moral status of women depended on its outcome. If, through the active virtue of her seed, she participated in reproduction, then in that act at least she was the equal if not the superior of man, and later, throughout the period of gestation, she alone nourished the embryo. How could a doctrine that threatened to undermine all the prejudices about the imperfection, debility, and incompleteness of women be tolerated? At stake, in effect, was man's legitimate power in the family and in society; and this fact explains why this scientific debate found its way so readily into works of literature. The function of the female seed was one of the basic arguments cited by the champions of women conjured up by the storyteller Cholières in his *Guerre des masles contre les femelles* (War of the Males against the Females), which takes up the question whether the political and legal disqualification of women is just.

Great disparity persisted between the speculations of the learned and popular beliefs in this area. Whereas medical researchers could not ignore anatomical discoveries (especially the discovery of the fallopian tubes) that corroborated the theory of women's seed, many texts continued to claim that the "passivity" of the mother was a necessary component of the world's order. In 1750, for example, in *Zoo-génésie* (Zoogenesis), Gautier-Dagoty invoked the Bible, Salic law, and morality to support his contention that only the father played an active role in reproduction.

Another cleavage was also emerging: the discourse of scientists had begun to diverge from that of practitioners, who needed the comforting certainties of medical knowledge to cope with the routine difficulties of practice. After nearly seventeen centuries of stable beliefs, a series of biological discoveries completely altered the theory of reproduction. The Dutchman Régnier de Graaf's *New Treatise on the Genital Organs of Women* (1672) propounded the ovist theory. Following on early observations by Harvey in England and further research by Stenon in Denmark, de Graaf demolished the two-seed theory by arguing that all animals, including man, derive from an egg—not an egg formed in the womb by the cooking of seeds but an egg that already exists before coitus in the woman's ovaries. This hypothesis, which aroused considerable interest among scientists all across Europe, met with strong skepticism among many physicians. Lamy, a loyal disciple of Hippocrates, published a *Dissertation contre la nouvelle opinion qui prétend que tous les animaux sont engendrez d'un oeuf* (Dissertation against the New Opinion That All Animals Are Engendered from an Egg, 1678). If the two-seed theory shook male supremacy to a degree, ovism posed a dual challenge to human dignity: man was simultaneously degraded to the rank of the oviparous beasts and stripped of his power, since woman alone carried the sacred germ of life. As late as the middle of the eighteenth century medical literature intended for a wide readership warned against a theory that "gives woman almost all the honor of generation."[15]

The discovery of spermatozoids by the German Louis de Ham and the Dutchmen Huygens and Leeuwenhoek at the height of the ovist controversy must have seemed a providential scientific revolution, for it restored man's prestige as creator. But after enjoying a brief vogue in the final years of the seventeenth century, the "animalculist" thesis, which claimed that the human being was preformed in the male sperm, also met with doubt from physicians who could not accept that humankind grew from a kind of worm. Furthermore, the very dynamic quality of scientific research itself seems to have heightened the suspicions of some practitioners, who continued to proclaim their allegiance to the Hippocratic, two-seed system up to the end of the eighteenth century. According to Pierre Roussel, this was the clearest and most plausible of all the theories and the one that best fit the bourgeois definition of Christian marriage: procreation is the fruit of three elements of unequal virtue, in accordance with the natural and divine hierarchy.

A Fragile Mold

Whatever resistance there may have been to scientific innovations, whatever attempts were made to adapt Hippocratic seminism to the established order of the genders, curiosity about the still impenetrable mystery of procreation was responsible for a change in the attitude of practitioners toward the progenitrix. The mother was responsible not only for the child's postnatal nurturing but also for the formation and development of the embryo. It was therefore important to determine the fundamental laws of heredity by studying the specific virtue of the female seed as well as the effects of uterine physiology on fetal formation. The physicians were especially vigilant because they continued to believe that most hereditary diseases were transmitted by the mother during gestation. Walter Harris' treatise on childhood diseases, which served as a reference for doctors throughout Europe in the late seventeenth century, still maintained this view.

Congenital diseases and deformities were not an essential preoccupation, however. Since the man was not alone in providing formative matter to the fetus, he was not alone in transmitting his moral fiber, character, and intelligence. The woman could influence the psychological development of the child to the same degree as the man. Given this fact, anxiety took the form of explicit or implicit resurgences of fantasies about the wickedness, imbecility, and inconstancy of women. Girolamo Cardano blamed the depraved morals of bastards on their mothers: "They are engendered by vile women without decency . . . and, since they follow the mother, they are the same and have the same morals."[16] But it was not enough for a woman to be chaste. She also needed a subtle mind, for the child could inherit its intelligence from either parent. This no doubt was a powerful argument against those who claimed that it was pointless for girls to study; Cornelius Agrippa did not neglect this medical argument when he sharpened his pen to write *De nobilitate et praexellentia foeminei sexus* (On the Nobility and

Preeminence of the Female Sex, 1529). But the physicians did not draw the same conclusion from their research. On the contrary, the role that nature accorded to feminine heredity aroused suspicion, and the doctors recommended that steps be taken to ensure that the paternal influence remained paramount.

The study of heredity thus led beyond pathology to the fundamental question of sexual dimorphism. Since "nature does nothing in vain," the generation of a male or female could not possibly be the result of chance; hence physiologists could analyze the mechanisms that governed the formation of the sexes. According to the seminist theories of Hippocrates and Galen, fertilization took the form of a battle between the two kinds of seed within the uterus. If the female seed predominated in quantity or quality, a girl was born; but if the male seed proved more potent, the child would be a boy. As was explained by Ambroise Paré, Jean Liébault, and the author of *Dialogo, il ceva overo dell'eccellenza et uso de genitali* (1598), Giuseppe Liceti, this struggle for influence also played a part in spermatogenesis, in a process that was not only reminiscent of the myth of the hermaphrodite but also prefigured, in a strange anachronism, modern theories of bisexuality. Both the male and the female contained quantities of the cold, weak female element and the warm, robust male element. One or the other dominated depending on age and lifestyle. In some cases the battle remained indecisive, resulting in one of those hermaphrodites that were of such great interest to late Renaissance physicians: variously referred to as man-woman, *semivir, gynander,* or *gunaner,* this dual-sex creature was a veritable embodiment of the polemic over the nature of sexuality.[17]

This view of things did not satisfy all physicians, however, because it assumed something that should have been impossible, namely, that in some cases the female temperament could be warmer than the male. Medical treatises were more receptive to interpretations that blamed the mother's physiology (mediocre menstrual blood or improper uterine temperature) for the birth of a girl and thus did not cast doubt on the immutable hierarchy of creatures. Ultimately a more general law was derived from anatomy. In the *Livre de la génération,* for example, Jacques Sylvius argued that the womb, a miniature model of the body itself, consisted of two parts. The right-hand part, on the side of the liver, held blood of more suitable temperature than the left-hand part. Hence seed retained in the right half of the uterus developed into a male, while seed that had the misfortune to fall into the left half could only yield a girl. This theory enjoyed success in part because it was consistent with both folklore and Hippocratic tradition. In general, everything touching the right side of the body concerned men and youth, while everything touching the left side concerned women and old age. According to Levin Lemnius, moreover, a literal interpretation of the famous Hippocratic aphorism "foetus mares dextra uteri parte, foemina sinistra magis gestatur" (A manly fetus is born on the right side of the uterus, a female on the left) could explain the shocking anomaly of unduly virile or authoritarian women: such women were conceived by mistake on the right side of the uterus.

This profusion of hypotheses was not merely the result of exuberant research guided by admiration for nature's works. The doctors' motivation was explicit: a full understanding of the mechanisms of conception would restore to human beings a power that, according to Saint Thomas Aquinas, they possessed in the state of innocence, when the child's sex depended only on the will of the parents. This freedom to choose had been a cherished dream since time immemorial, as we know from folklore's magic incantations for producing a son or a daughter. Practitioners understood this desire quite well, since they were generally convinced that to give birth to a daughter was a source of trouble. The Spaniard Huarte, for example, offered fathers no end of advice on how to avoid engendering a sex whose coldness and humidity interfered with a balanced and healthy mind.

Of course not all physicians exhibited such extreme mistrust of women, but even those least affected by everyday prejudice were sensitive to the social implications of a child's sex. In *Les erreurs populaires* (1579) Laurent Joubert devoted serious attention to the most propitious times for sexual intercourse in order to "help men who want to have males for their service and for the inheritance of their property, honors, and dignities . . . and even if this is solely for the excellence of the sex, there is good reason to wish for it."[18]

One could hardly ask for a clearer statement. If parents wanted the freedom to choose, it was to limit the number of daughters who carved up estates and forced parents to go to a great deal of trouble to protect their fragile health, to educate their frivolous minds, to cope with their extreme sensitivity, and last but not least to establish them in a marriage or convent. For several centuries physicians sought to establish what Jacques-André Millot, who attended Marie-Antoinette's deliveries, called an *Art de procréer les sexes à volonté* (Art of Procreating the Sexes at Will): from Juan Huarte's *Examen* to Michel Procope Couteau's *Art de faire des garçons* (Art of Making Boys), recommendations about the choice of partner, the right time, and the right position were all based on the conviction that proper obedience to the laws of morality and nature would be rewarded by the birth of a boy.

A Role for Women

The Rules of Harmony

Medicine's exploration of the secrets of embryology thus made it possible to deal with such important questions as heredity, the determination of sex, and the control of reproduction. Successive theories shed new light on the complex relation between the fetus and its mother. The two-seed theory, which prevailed until the middle of the seventeenth century, and the ovist theory, which gained adherents during the eighteenth century, treated the woman as a progenitrix with sacred and dangerous power. Physicians, aware of the importance of their ideas, played an ever more central role in discussions of private and public morality. From the end of the Renaissance to the eighteenth century a medical strategy took shape, a strategy that evolved considerably in accordance with the role that society wanted to see women play in the family.

Practitioners in the time of Juan Luis Vivès and Jean Bodin were not yet motivated by natalist concerns. Their primary mission was to protect the institution of marriage on which public order ultimately rested. Marriage was of interest not only to moralists and legislators but also to physicians who saw their naturalist discourse as a protest against dangerous customs and laws. Woman was of particular concern to physicians because the fertility of the couple and the harmony of the family clearly depended on her physical and moral well-being. Physicians studied the various conditions of woman as episodes that either prepared her for or ensued upon her natural vocation, which was marriage. In this respect medicine followed the humanist Juan Luis Vivès' *Institution of the Christian Woman,* which set forth rules to be followed by the maiden, the wife, and the widow. In the late sixteenth century physicians who specialized in women's medicine had no compunction about including in their treatises practical advice of the sort that one might find today in a book on childrearing. Their most urgent mission was to protest against marriages based solely on social ambition without regard to the emotional and physical compatibility of husband and wife. Ambroise Paré and Jean Liébault vigorously denounced such abuses as marriage between persons of widely different ages or incompatible temperaments. At times ignoring the views of legal specialists, who fixed the legal age of marriage at twelve for girls and fourteen for boys, physicians saw it as their professional duty to protect women from two equally harmful threats: marriage that came either too early or too late. The authors of medical treatises were no longer merely academics who dispensed theories from their ivory towers. Obstetrical practice in particular had ceased to be a monopoly of midwives, and physicians had begun to learn about the "almost unbearable [suffering] of pregnancy."[19] They knew only too well that a mere slip of an adolescent could not expose herself to such a condition without danger to her life. In addition to proscribing marriages contracted at too tender an age, they condemned parents who, in anticipation of an advantageous match, left their already "mature" daughters vulnerable to disorders stemming from unsatisfied sexual appetites. Running through these works are the obsession of the practitioner describing in frightening terms the premonitory signs of sexual frustration, paleness followed by the terrifying uterine furor; and that of the sober bourgeois raising the specter of disorder in the family: a young woman past the age of twenty will not easily tolerate her husband's admonitions, particularly since women are by nature overbearing and contrary. In any case, Jean Liébault, who was not only a physician but also the husband of the learned Nicole Estienne, the author of *Les misères de la femme mariée,* seems to have been convinced that this was how it was.

For the physicians, the best rules were the ones laid down by nature. Aristotle's authority was again invoked to prove that, since women mature more rapidly than men (becoming fertile but also sterile earlier), the ideal age of marriage was fifteen or sixteen for females and twenty-five to thirty for males. In short, nature legitimated what Christian morality and the social order required, namely, that the husband be a master for his wife.

This advice was not limited to treatises on hygiene; fathers had only to read the humanist philosophers to behave in a more enlightened way. Physicians often drew their arguments from the same sources as moralists. But physicians claimed expert authority when it came to judging the physiological compatibility of prospective mates. Juan Huarte even dreamed of a republic in which physicians would be entrusted with responsibility for arranging marriages. Consulted as experts, they could, by examining a woman's complexion and beauty, decide whether she was or was not made for the man to whom she was betrothed. Sexual union was seen in a sense as a fusion of opposites, which succeeded when positive and negative elements complemented one another. Indeed, the notion of complementarity served as the cornerstone of a discipline that one might already call sexology. Since nature assigned each sex a different role in amorous relations, the practitioner also had to consider the question of pleasure and its purpose. While everyone agreed that "women burn in one way, men in another," there was a divergence of opinion, characteristic of a science still in its infancy, on other issues. Physicians in search of answers generally adopted the ready-made solutions provided by society, custom, and of course ancient texts. Thus the question of sexual pleasure first arose in the context of cultural assumptions about the nature of woman. Many physicians were still convinced that women were more passionate in love than men. In his study *La maladie d'amour, ou mélancholie érotique* (The Disease of Love, or Erotic Melancholy, 1623) Jacques Ferrand urged this point strenuously, aided by the doctrine that love is a movement of the soul that women, being bereft of reason or strength, cannot control; this conclusion was corroborated, moreover, by experience, since the doctor treated far more female than male erotomaniacs. Furthermore, Ferrand argued, the brutality of desire and the violence of pleasure in women were a sort of compensation thoughtfully provided by nature for the pain of childbirth.

These arguments, however, which had something in common with satirical literature lampooning the lasciviousness of women, conflicted with the necessity of proving that men were superior, even in pleasure. And in any case it was difficult for scholastic physicians to believe that woman, with her cold, damp temperament, could experience more ardent pleasures than men. Hippocrates, interpreted according to the needs of the case, could be used to show that even in this domain the hierarchy of the sexes was preserved, for although woman's venereal appetites may have been imperious, they were extensive rather than intensive like man's and therefore qualitatively inferior.

Although this controversy attracted a great deal of attention and even found its way into popular works such as Scipion Dupleix's *Curiosité naturelle* (Natural Curiosity) and Théophraste Renaudot's public lectures, another question also exercised late Renaissance physicians: Why was man the only animal species for which there was no term to reproductive activity? The point was not so much to decide whether men desired sex more than women, or vice versa, as it was to gain a better understanding of an activity of such great importance to the human race. Provident nature had arranged things so that man was constantly inflamed by the enormous pleasure of intercourse in order that he need not think about the form or structure of the reproductive organs. Terrifying images of the uterine chasm haunted the discourse of surgeons such as Ambroise Paré, physicians such as André Du Laurens, and obstetricians such as François Mauriceau, who lacked sufficient colors and odors to describe the "filth" and "refuse" in "that cloaca."[20] A mask for horror and pain, sensuality could thus be seen as legitimate and necessary. Paradoxically, the vision of female voluptuousness as sinful or monstrous, indeed the fear of the devouring womb itself, paled before the naturalist's wonder at nature's marvelous ingenuity. For Paré, Joubert, and Duval, the role of each sex was determined by the need to respond to the other not as in combat but as in a game, a game in which the potential prize was a "tiny creature of God."

The Necessity of Female Pleasure

Unconcerned by moral taboos and at the risk of incurring, as Ambroise Paré and Jacques Duval did, the wrath of the medical faculty or other censure, practitioners did not shrink from delving into the most intimate aspects of sexual life in order to help couples gain a better awareness of their desires and a fuller comprehension of their bodies. Chapters on "the manner of cohabiting and making offspring" offered advice primarily to the man, who held the initiative and was therefore largely responsible for the sexual harmony of the couple. This advice, not yet couched in the neutral language of scientific objectivity, reflected the experience of the man who, in his medical practice, learned as much as a confessor. Husbands all too often knew nothing about their wives' sensual natures, so that, as Ambroise Paré, with his taste for expressive metaphors, once remarked, men were like bad farmers who plunged headlong and heedless into the field of human nature.

Behind the physicians' concern we glimpse the old question of embryology. The primacy of the two-seed thesis required physicians to approach the subject in a new way. Paré maintained that the process of emission worked in three stages: first, there was a humid excretion that came chiefly from the brain; next, the "vital spirits" caused an erection of the genitals; and finally, there was ejaculation of seed, triggered by concupiscence and pleasure. Hence it was indispensable that "the object please and be desired, as much on the man's part as on the woman's," or else their union would be infertile.[21] Steeped in this theory, vernacular treatises on human reproduction, which were intended to be of use to midwives and surgeons as well as to satisfy the literate public's curiosity about the life sciences, were highly critical of contemporary matrimonial practices. Daughters, it was alleged, were objects that families used without regard to their sensibility or state of health and, even worse, in ways likely to foment hatred and discord in the household and impede the birth of sons and daughters. The most frequent cause of sterility, as Paré and Liébault explained and Mauriceau confirmed in his treatise of 1668, was the woman's lack of pleasure during intercourse; in this situation not only did she produce no seed of her own, but also a clenching of the uterine orifice caused her to reject the seed of the male. Fathers who ignored the warnings of science and experience and forced daughters to marry against their will were guilty in the eyes of nature itself.

Natalists' concerns were not the only motivation for the physicians' warnings. François Mauriceau no more regarded sterility as a stigma than did Jean Liébault or Louys de Serres, and he could be mordantly ironic about "the powerful passion that can be seen in some people, who have no greater regret than to die childless or, worse yet, without male progeny."[22] The study of reproduction and the discovery of how closely connected psychology is to organic functions transformed the body into a complex machine, admirable in its very intricacy. For the physicist, the contemplator of nature's works, each bodily function was a manifestation of the soul within. Once scientists began to think of sexual pleasure as compensation for disgust with copulation, they began to praise the genital organs and the sexual act (even if it produced no offspring) as sublime evidence of God's ingenuity.

Medical discourse introduced a false note into the concert of voices raised against clandestine marriages, made only at the desire of the young couple and counter to family interests. If harmonious union between the sexes depended on the physical and spiritual compatibility of husband and wife, the woman could not be looked upon as merely the passive instrument of the man's pleasure. The naturalist granted her the right, indeed the duty, to take an active part in shaping her future. To a society that denied women decisionmaking power, this protest by medical practitioners at first seemed a mere pious wish or idle theoretical speculation. Such liberating advice no doubt had little real effect on a society in which young women remained commodities, tokens of exchange in a trade based on economic power and social prestige. Nevertheless, the physicians' opinion was important because it lent scientific backing to those who argued in the name of Christian marriage or renascent naturalism in favor of emotional equality between husband and wife. Already Marguerite de Navarre had implicitly invoked the seminist theory in the *Heptaméron* to describe the failure of a loveless marriage: "How was it that she was a very beautiful woman, and he a man of fine complexion and very powerful, yet she never had a child by him because her heart was always seven leagues from her body" (novella 61). By the end of the Renaissance a substantial number of literary texts denounced "soulless unions" and gave wide currency to the medical arguments. But the medical authorities' reaction to the publication of certain texts in the vernacular attests to a fear that such writings might pose a threat to morality. The avowed motive for the trial of Ambroise Paré in 1575 was the lack of authorization for the publication of his complete works, but the surgeon's plea in his own behalf leaves no doubt about the real reasons for his censure: the professors were particularly shocked by the chapters on techniques of reproduction, sterility, and the "membrane known as the hymen," which, owing to the free manner in which they were written, might "incite youth to lascivious behavior."[23] A few years later Laurent Joubert faced similar difficulties: in order to appease his critics, who accused him of having dedicated a medical work of this type to Marguerite de Valois, the queen of Navarre, and of having revealed "lubricious" secrets to girls who might better have been kept in ignorance, he was forced to revise the second edition of his *Erreurs populaires*.

The medical faculty had its reasons for attempting to impose controls on a medical discourse that had begun to intervene more and more frequently in matters of custom and morals. Practitioners were called upon to serve as experts in cases involving marriage and sexuality generally, so that the social consequences of medical theories may well have outstripped their scientific interest. Sixteenth- and seventeenth-century physicians who were called to testify in rape cases naturally invoked the two-seed theory, according to which the emission was an indication of pleasure experienced in coitus. When Jean Liébault warned judges against women who claimed to have conceived a child without experiencing pleasure, he implicitly rejected the claims of any woman who asked compensation for a rape that resulted in pregnancy. Yet the same theory enabled Jacques Duval to restore honor and integrity to the victim of rape, for where there was no pleasure the womb remained closed and where there was no consent the woman's moral virginity remained intact. For physicians, then, rape was a simple assault in which the woman was not the guilty party but the victim. We know from case law that this was not always the opinion of the magistrates.

A Gentler, More Pitiful Voice

By the late Renaissance physicians had begun to look upon each vital function as a complex interaction between a "faculty" or "spirit" and an organ that served as its instrument, and they therefore attached particular importance to psychophysiology. This is especially evident in suits for annulment of a marriage on grounds of impotence. In 1620 Ambroise Paré's disciple, Charles Guillemeau, took up his pen to denounce the *Abus qui se commettent sur les procédures de l'impuissance des hommes et des femmes* (Abuses Committed in Examining for Impotence in Men and Women) because he could not accept the brutal test of consummation that jurists had adopted in defiance of decency as well as science. The physiologist knew full well that a man and a woman who had already separated in heart and mind would never be able to demonstrate their sexual vigor in the presence of expert witnesses (surgeons and midwives) and in the glare of public disgrace. It was therefore profoundly illogical to rely on the results of such an examination to approve the dissolution of a marriage. On this point the physician was more inflexible than the jurist, who saw sufficient grounds for annulment in the failure to respect a clause of the marriage contract, the *debitum conjugalis* (marriage debt). Guillemeau and other critics of dissolution on grounds of impotence were opposed to a procedure designed to ensure not the happiness of the couple but the interests of the families involved. Not only were the laws of separation based on erroneous anatomical notions (inadequate knowledge of female anatomy left doubt as to the marks of defloration) and on complete ignorance of the principles of physiology; canon law stated that if the impotence were somehow to disappear after the marriage had been dissolved, the couple would be required to live together again even if they had remarried in the meantime. From the standpoint of science this was a terrible error, since impotence, when it was not the result of physical mutilation, was often an effect of antipathy between husband and wife. These annulment trials, which of course concerned only the upper strata of society, contributed nothing to the liberation of women, who were treated in these affairs as nothing but causes of scandal.

When consulted as family advisers or expert witnesses, physicians frequently recommended reconciliation in order to protect the body from insulting examination. The institution of marriage was founded upon the fragile equilibrium of female physiology. Ignoring the woman's desires or forcing her to act against her will could threaten the harmony of the couple. The precepts of medicine thus recommended a policy of moderation: moderation in pleasure, moderation in the husband's marital demands, moderation in the wife's behavior. Here, too, nature was invoked to justify medical discourse. Ambroise Paré explained the differences between the sexuality of men and women as a wise precaution of the Creator, who intended that the two sexes should not both become inflamed at the same time or with the same intensity, for otherwise couples might find themselves vulnerable to the assaults of immoderate and dangerous lusts. On this point practitioners and moralists were in agreement, both being concerned to establish an ethics of private life in support of the social order. But whereas bourgeois morality reduced the wife to nothing more than a mirror of her husband's personality and rank, a symbol of the family's conservative virtues, the physician fastened on the image of female individuality, troubling in its fragility and occult disorders but also fascinating in its fertile beauty.

If Cornelius Agrippa's *De incertitudine et vanitate omnium scientarium et artium* (On the Uncertainty and Vanity of All the Arts and Sciences) is to be believed, no art contributed more to debauchery than medicine, which provided the public with many ways of embellishing the face and body. No doubt the anthologies of "women's secrets" were a very old tradition, out of which grew a certain pseudomedical literature that has not entirely disappeared even today. But even the most scientific medicine contributed to the genre, at times in paradoxical ways: the Italian Leonardo Fioravanti, for example, severely condemned the use of cosmetics in his *Specchio di scientia universale* (Mirror of Universal Science, 1564), but some years earlier he had published the *Capricci medicinale* (Medicinal Fancies), a book filled with formulas assuring women of eternal beauty and numerous lovers. In the end, wasn't the physician drawn by that diabolical beauty, the lovely body described by Cornelius Agrippa, whose appearance gives such pleasure, and which one cannot touch without enjoyable feelings?[24]

These contradictory recommendations reflect above all the ambivalent role of the physician, who spoke sometimes as a moralist but at other times as a naturalist. As moralist he repeated and gave his blessing to his contemporaries' mistrust of female otherness. As naturalist he expressed amazement at a body that existed through and for its fertile beauty. The role of the physician was therefore not only to protect woman from her own disorders but also to preserve the aesthetic harmony that was the sign of her perfection. Faithful to this mission, Giovanni Marinello followed his important work on women's diseases with a treatise *Degli ornamenti delle donne* (On Women's Ornaments), in which he claimed only to be reestablishing nature's beautiful equilibrium. What was still something of an embarrassment to the moralistic physicians of the sixteenth century vanished, moreover, as women's medicine was redefined. Once science had recognized the distinctive nature of female anatomy, physiology, and pathology, it seemed legitimate that women should have their own hygiene and aesthetics as well. This medical strategy is set forth in a forthright manner in Abraham de La Framboisière's *Du gouvernement des dames,* which he dedicated to a great lady in the early years of the seventeenth century: "Just as men surpass women in strength, so do women excel men most of the time in beauty. Hence there is nothing strange in that they should be curious about preserving what seems to belong to them by natural right . . . Since what I have been commissioned to discuss here is that which is proper to the female sex, I shall first state how ladies must govern themselves in order to preserve their beauty."[25]

Torn between social functionalism and occasionally unorthodox naturalism, medicine's theoretical concepts may have been ambivalent, but in practice the profession sometimes found itself allied with women against society's prejudices. The fact that men had begun to practice obstetrics, hitherto the exclusive domain of midwives, probably played an important part in changing attitudes. In reading the works that had the greatest impact on obstetrics, such as those of the German Rösslin, the Frenchman Paré, and the Portuguese Castro, one cannot help being struck by the repeated images of suffering, as if the doctors themselves were frightened by these ills, by the terrible anguish they could not yet control, indeed as if men felt themselves responsible for women's "passion." Louys Guyon fairly explicitly acknowledges this in his *Miroir de la beauté et santé corporelle* (Mirror of Physical Beauty and Health): "Of course reason and charity command us to give special assistance to persons in anguish or need or [in the wake of] such accidents as may befall them for serving and loving us. I say this because woman, in order to give us happiness, pleasure, satisfaction, and progeny, in order to make man's species immortal, lends her body freely to man, apprehending none of the labors, pains, griefs, and dangers to which she will subject herself when she becomes pregnant by his actions."[26]

Even when pregnancy proceeded without any particular complications, physicians saw it as a pathogenic condition that violently disrupted the system of humours and interfered with psychological equilibrium. Rational description of syndromes (dark spots on the face, swollen breasts, anxiety) was overwhelmed by fantasies about pregnancy, including the most outlandish accounts of "desires," "depraved appetites," and monstrous births. Ultimately the pregnant woman was said, in Louys de Serres's phrase, to be a "third reasoning sex," subject to all the ills of a disturbed physiology. Obstetricians expressed compassion by recommending procedures to limit the disruption, which was deemed dangerous to the fetus, and to make the crisis of delivery more bearable, neglecting nothing that might increase the comfort of the mother or calm her fears. In this respect medical discourse appears to have been at odds with Christian morality, which condemned women to give birth in pain. In *De universo muliebrium morborum* (On the World of Women's Maladies, 1620) Rodrigo de Castro spoke out against a belief that encouraged the obstetrician to stand by and do nothing, and later François Mauriceau made a similar point. Speaking as practitioners of medicine, both men refuted the theological justification for suffering: women suffer because the head of the human fetus is larger than that of other animals and also because civilized ladies are no longer used to hard labor. Thus their arguments were based on anatomy, ways of life, and custom rather than religion.

Physicians, whose overriding concern was to preserve the female body from a serious threat to its beauty and equilibrium, sometimes transgressed the boundaries of conscientious morality and became accomplices of women's "subterfuges." In their discussions of "churching"—the ceremony by which mothers are received back at Catholic mass several weeks after childbirth—Laurent Joubert and Ambroise Paré reveal the male revulsion against the deformation of the body by pregnancy, the violence of childbirth, and the stigmata that bearing children left on the mother. Both men claimed to be good husbands and good fathers yet agreed that men, generally frightened by delivery and vexed by the newborn's tears, would prefer not to be initiated into the revolting realities of female physiology. Doctors therefore did well to put their fears aside and draw upon the traditional "secrets" that midwives had passed on from generation to generation, secrets that helped women regain their strength, rid themselves of their wrinkles, and once again become "maidens" their husbands could desire. Such tolerance of remedies that had more to do with the procurer's art than with the obstetrician's—remedies that can also be found in satirical texts on "The Art of Repairing Lost Maidenheads"—no doubt reflected the feelings of physicians themselves, who in certain ways shared the common belief that women remained impure for a time after giving birth and who above all wished to hide blemishes that might threaten marital harmony.

Practitioners were even more ambivalent about contraception and abortion. Most treatises on obstetrics condemned artificial abortions, in part, to be sure, on moral grounds but also for medical reasons, because attempts at abortion all too often resulted in fatal hemorrhages. In any case, the authors' prolix descriptions of the anatomical and physiological correlates of abortion had produced one effect that the faculty did not fail to note in its indictment of Ambroise Paré: enumerating the causes of miscarriage and naming drugs that could cause harm to the fetus put information into the hands of women who wished to rid themselves of their fruit. In fact most physicians were undeterred by this dilemma and after a pro forma declaration of the purity of their intentions went on to describe the three kinds of abortion: that caused by a medicinal substance, that caused by physical violence or a mechanical intervention, and that due to a psychological shock. In *Le miroir de la beauté et santé corporelle* Louys Guyon went even further: without issuing any moral disclaimers, he argued for the legitimacy of therapeutic abortion. As he saw it, moral prohibitions were of little importance in comparison with the risks that pregnancy in some cases entailed for the mother, the child, or the family. Furthermore, he maintained that a woman whose pelvis was too narrow, or who had given birth only to monsters, or whose husband threatened to kill the newborn might well wish not to conceive any more children, and he offered her the means to attain that end.

Medical ethics were based on compassion for the mother's suffering and respect for her life, standards very different from those applied by theologians and jurists. Although doctors condemned abortion as a method of birth control, they considered it a duty to take action if the mother's life was in danger. Louise Bourgeois, who, being a midwife, was in danger if she spoke out forthrightly on this issue, nevertheless adopted a similar attitude: she disapproved of midwives who used their skills to abet immoral behavior, yet she had no compunctions about teaching a technique by which the mother's body could be induced by means of manipulation to expel the fetus. The great obstetrician Mauriceau believed that surgeons should be guided solely by the diagnosis: as soon as symptoms of a condition that might prove dangerous to the mother, such as hemorrhage, were discovered, delivery should be induced without delay, even if the pregnancy had yet to reach term. The worst thing a surgeon could do was to take a prudent, self-protective course if that meant allowing a pregnant woman to die in terrible pain and despair.

Abortion, defined by Mauriceau as "the unnatural issuance from the womb of an imperfect child,"[27] remained a pragmatic issue up to the middle of the seventeenth century, with religious considerations a secondary concern. But in the eighteenth century the debate over voluntary abortion moved beyond medical circles and into the ecclesiastical realm.

In this connection the history of caesarean section is of considerable interest. For a long time the operation was performed only postmortem, and surgeons who delivered fetuses from lifeless mothers were discharging a duty that left their consciences untroubled. If a narrow pelvis prevented delivery in a living mother, the doctor had no choice but to allow nature to take its course or resort to tools—the forceps and clamp—developed by Arab physicians. In 1581, however, the French surgeon François Rousset published a *Traité nouveau de l'hysterotomotokie, ou enfantement caesarien* (New Treatise on Hysterotomotokia, or Caesarean Delivery). He was impelled to take this step, he said, "by the pitiful spectacle of anguish, shock, prayer, and plaintive looks of the poor creatures thus tortured, crying murder, and, hands joined together, pleading with us to order them whatever help we might wish."[28] Rousset claimed that it was possible to extract a child from the womb of a living mother by making a lateral incision through the belly into the uterus. This could be done without harming the mother and even without foreclosing the possibility of future pregnancies. The Montpellier physician's work immediately stirred up a sharp polemic, for although its anatomical foundation was quite rigorous, in the view of colleagues the risks of the operation were considerable and the few successful cases of intervention were offset by numerous fatalities. There was considerable interest in the procedure among French and German physicians, including Scipion Mercurio, an Italian who came to France in the 1570s, but in the end the most celebrated surgeons of the day abandoned the technique after some number of unsuccessful attempts. Ambroise Paré, Jacques Guillemeau, and Louys Guyon refused to perform an operation that was tantamount to saving the child at the cost of deliberately murdering the mother. Practitioners, faithful to the ethics of their profession and hostile on principle to remedies more violent than the disease, were concerned only about the physical consequences of their therapeutic choices.

After casuists became involved in obstetrical issues in the seventeenth century, however, the stakes of the debate were raised. In 1630 the Jesuit Théophile Raynaud made shrewd use of examples taken from François Rousset to demonstrate that the caesarean section was anatomically possible. For him the success rate was a secondary issue, the primary one being the need to save the souls of infants by baptism. Surgeons were then asked to put their scruples aside and refuse to use forceps and clamps to deliver the child and thus save the mother at the expense of her offspring. In half a century the significance of the controversy had changed. Obstetricians opposed to the caesarean were now seen not as timid spirits reluctant to experiment with a bold new technique but as

obstinate defenders of their professional autonomy. François
Mauriceau delivered a powerful diatribe against the proponents
of what he believed to be a cruel and barbarous practice that used
religion as a pretext: "I know of no Christian or civil law that
requires the mother to be martyrized and killed in order to save
the child. It is rather to satisfy the avarice of certain people who
will suffer very little if their wives die provided there is a child to
survive her."[29]

The leading obstetricians of a later period, such as Philippe
Peu, Guillaume Mauquest de La Motte, and Hermann Boerhaave,
adhered to the same principles and tried to develop surgical techniques that would spare the mother the pain of a caesarean. To
be sure, progress in surgery eventually proved them wrong, but
purely technical criteria are an inadequate basis for judging the
generosity of their intentions in the face of interference typified by
the *Embryologia sacra* of the canon Cangiamila.

Woman's Mission

A Natural Mission: The Progenitrix

The medical conscience was probably more troubled by questions
having to do with caesarean sections and the use of abortion-
inducing medications than by any other issue, as the eighteenth-
century physician and historian Daniel Le Clerc was well aware.
In a time when obstetricians had yet to master the techniques of
"unnatural" delivery, the crux of the matter was whether it was
permissible to kill the mother or the child. In the works of the
"fathers" of obstetrics such as Rösslin, Paré, and Mauriceau, pity
for the suffering mother expressed itself in the form of a call for
the practice of medicine to become more humane: with pens
soaked in the blood of women they had seen die, medical writers
described at great length the wounds, fractures, and mutilations
inflicted by unskilled midwives and "barbarous" surgeons.[30] This
compassion may have contributed to medical progress that affected women's daily lives: midwives and obstetricians discovered
the importance of psychological preparation and other means to
increase the capacity to withstand pain; improved textbooks
taught midwives the basic rules of hygiene and anatomy.

The physician's pity was a mixed blessing, however. On the
one hand it saved women from scorn and malediction, but on the

other hand it lent credence to any number of representations of female debility. As can be seen with particular clarity in the case of Jean Liébault, the practitioner's charity reflected his sense of male superiority: to him the condition of women, subject to countless diseases and to that most difficult of ordeals, childbirth, seemed miserable. And his charity was rivaled only by his mistrust: without the help of medicine, how could a creature as weak and sickly as woman hope to fulfill her vocation?

The paradox is striking: woman, regarded as physiologically and psychologically unstable, bore responsibility for perpetuating the species, a mission vital to the human race. Physicians seemed eager to exorcise the irrational forces that constantly threatened to disrupt the process. All was mystery, to begin with the female sex: medical supervision of young girls, for whom Paré and Liébault recommended a healthy diet and invigorating regimen of hygiene, was not enough to ward off the threat of uterine bestiality. Fertility, too, was mysterious: diagnosticians strove in vain to recognize the signs that pregnancy had begun, and if the beginning of pregnancy could not be identified, neither could the end be predicted, for of all the animals only the human female lacked a fixed gestational period (the duration of human pregnancy ranging anywhere from seven to as long as eleven months). Last but not least, female psychology was also a mystery: not even the most diligent of disciplines could control woman's demiurgic imagination, whose fantasies could leave their mark on the body of the fetus itself. In short, every period of a woman's life was a time of peril, not only for herself but also for society.

The physician was like a teacher always worried about the irresponsible nature of his pupil. This concern emerges clearly from the advice doctors gave mothers, for while any woman could bear children, very few were capable of real mothering. Works on obstetrics invariably pleaded for mothers to nurse their young. People believed that the child imbibed health and virtue from its nurse; therefore, a woman was not a mother in the full sense unless she breastfed her child. Laurent Joubert and Jacques Guillemeau tried to make their arguments more persuasive by describing touching scenes in which a child's playfulness and laughter rewarded a mother's virtue. Unlike moralists who regarded the custom of paying wetnurses as a sign of female depravity, physicians apparently blamed the resistance to breastfeeding on men who, less susceptible than their wives to the joys of early childhood, resented the potential disruption of their own comfort and privacy. Nevertheless, physicians were not willing to trust entirely to the maternal instinct to ensure proper care of the newborn. The nursing mother of course had to be in suitable health and of the proper temperament as well as sufficiently disciplined to watch her diet and indeed moderate all her behavior, even to the point of curbing those puzzling excesses of tenderness that mothers sometimes displayed toward their children.

Despite doubts about the imprudent love of mothers—doubts, evident even in the writings of Erasmus and Montaigne, that were certainly influenced by the moralists—the physicians of the late Renaissance who discovered the importance of the physiological interaction between the fetus and the womb saw the mother as fulfilling an indispensable nurturing role. The progenitrix was cured of her imperfections by the mission entrusted to her by nature, and women's medicine assumed a noble place within the medical art: to care for women was to help them to discharge their difficult mission and thus to fulfill nature's intentions.

A Divine Mission: Expiating Original Sin

During the Counter-Reformation medicine was called to serve as an instrument of religious edification. In what Jean Delumeau has called the "pastoral of fear," the physician was at times more effective than the priest. Were not the "libertines of both sexes" more likely to be deterred by threats to their health than by the strictures of Christian morality? The vocations of medical practitioner and priest were complementary: both reminded God's creatures of their ultimate end, especially women, each of whom was obliged to atone in her person for the original sin. Col de Vil'ars took this approach in the *Recueil alphabétique de prognostics dangéreux et mortels* (Alphabetic Anthology of Dangerous and Fatal Prognoses), a work intended for "persons having charge of souls." In a list of maladies requiring the presence of a priest childbirth came near the top, for religious and medical as well as alphabetic reasons: ever since the fatal judgment was first rendered on Eve, the threat of suffering and death had hung over all pregnant women.

Woman's redemption lay in the maternal sacrifice, which, though it redeemed her soul, did nothing to rehabilitate her body. Doubtless that is why the question of the choice between mother and child was not really an issue for the abbé Dinouart, the French editor of *L'embryologie sacrée* (The Sacred Embryology). The physician was left with no choice but to intervene in every instance for the benefit of the child, since "the mother cannot preserve her life without incurring guilt when she does so solely at the expense of her fruit."[31]

Though humanistic in outlook and determined to resist pressures from outside the field of medicine, doctors could no longer ignore the ideological implications of medical doctrine. In dealing with human reproduction and the physiology of marriage they were forced to demonstrate the moral and social utility of their work. The best example of this is the *Tableau de l'amour considéré dans l'état de mariage* (Portrait of Love, Considered in the State of Marriage, 1685), by Nicolas Venette, a physician in the city of La Rochelle. At first reading, this book by the "royal professor of anatomy" seems to belong squarely in the tradition of late Renaissance naturalist medicine. The author's intention is to restore the dignity of physical love by banishing a morality based on guilt and imposing discipline on sexuality. As in the work of Giuseppe Liceti and Jacques Duval, the genital organs come in for precise description of both their anatomy and function. No longer treated as "shameful parts," they are seen rather as instruments of "amorous indulgence between married individuals." Like Ambroise Paré, Venette offers husbands a guide to the female body's erogenous zones and shares with wives secrets for making their bodies beautiful and even for concealing a lost virginity. For both Venette and Paré, sexual compatibility is essential to a harmonious marriage. Yet although the two physicians draw on the same, by now standard, medical sources, their motives are profoundly different. Venette knows that he must answer those who will charge him with indecency, so he shrewdly situates his text in the tradition of Christian moralizing. Although the boldness of the text belies the caution of the preface, the author initially casts himself as an ally of the theologians, casuists, and jurists by demonstrating that his work, which carries a message of danger and resignation, should be useful to married men and women: "A girl may learn in advance of all the disorders that love can cause without having experienced love herself, for, since the bonds of marriage are indissoluble, it is desirable that girls should know before being married what pain and suffering awaits them."[32]

The unparalleled success of the *Tableau de l'amour,* which was translated into all the languages of Europe and reprinted as late as the nineteenth century, proves beyond any doubt that readers did not stop at the preface and listened instead to the work's tolerant, humanistic message. Yet the very disparity between the prudence of Venette's rhetoric and the audacity of his recommendations is proof enough of the new demands that impinged on medicine as it was turned into a social instrument.

A Social Mission: The Family Guardian

During the seventeenth century practicing physicians parted company with biological investigators, whose speculative work offered little help with the daily difficulties of practice. In the next century, that of the Enlightenment, physicians still found it easy to ignore the latest hypotheses of science, but they claimed to have an important contribution to make to the reforming ambitions of the *philosophes*. The human body was part of a larger system, which by this time had come to be thought of not as a macrocosm but rather as an instituted social order. Organic functions, individual physiology, and sexual dimorphism were rationalized in terms of social teleology. Physicians were no longer specialists in women's *diseases* but rather in *women* as such, that is, in the condition of the maiden, the married woman, the woman of quality. Female nature, whether it was, as Helvétius believed, a product of civilization or, as Rousseau maintained, a primary given, must in any case be understood in the context of a specific social function.

The new definition of woman, at once medical, social, and moral, is perhaps best exemplified by a work published by the philosophical physician Pierre Roussel in 1775 to immediate and lasting success: *Système physique et moral de la femme, ou tableau philosophique de la constitution, de l'état organique, du tempérament, des moeurs et des fonctions propres au sexe* (Physical and Moral System of Woman, or Philosophical Portrait of the Constitution, Organic State, Temperament, Morals, and Functions Peculiar to the Sex). Like Rousseau, Roussel thought of femininity as an essential nature defined by purposeful organic functions: "Woman is not woman only in one place but in every aspect under which she can be envisaged."[33] Woman's predestined role was revealed by certain specific physical signs: the fragility of her bones, the breadth of her pelvis, the softness of her tissues, the small size of her brain, and the overabundance of nerve fibers were all indications that maternity was woman's natural vocation and that her life was meant to be orderly and sedentary. Pathology could then be understood as the result not simply of a flawed temperament or uncontrollable divagations of the uterus but of failure to respect nature's wishes: women being much more sensitive than men, depraved morals and civilization's excesses were more apt to disturb their souls, disrupt their physiology, and indeed derange their entire body, as the etiology of vapors and hysteria showed. For Roussel and later writers who subscribed to the social mission of medical science, the problem was to prove that woman's woes, sins, and diseases all stemmed from the rejection of her normal role, of her natural functions: Raulin worried about *Les affections vaporeuses du sexe* (The Vaporous Affections of the [Female] Sex), Tissot described the horrors of onanism, Bienville raised the specter of nymphomania, and Lignac brandished the threat of a degeneration of the species if women and men forgot the role that each sex was supposed to play in *L'état de mariage*.

In the name of natural determinism medicine now defined the feminine ideal in such a way as to fit within the narrow sphere assigned to women by the social order. The happy, healthy woman was by definition the mother, the guardian of virtues and eternal values.

TRANSLATED FROM THE FRENCH BY ARTHUR GOLDHAMMER

three

Dissidences

Conversations and Publications

A public voice was authorized only for exceptional women, such as queens and prophets; but there were several settings where women could talk among themselves. Around the well, at the mill, in a spinning circle, and at the bed of the newly delivered mother, women discussed subjects from fertility to royalty. Here were exchanged the "secrets of women," so intriguing that male writers usurped that title for their books; here occurred conversations that, by the end of the sixteenth century, men were trivializing as the "cackle" *(caquet)* of light "gossips" (a pejorative use of *god-sib*). And yet there were dangers: a spinning circle might suddenly look like a witches' coven; an overly sharp critic of local family politics might be denounced by her gossips as a "scold" and dunked in the village pond.

Men and women also talked together according to established conventions at the farmhouse fireplace and in the castle great chamber. For the peasants, the gathering (*veillée,* or vigil) took place during the winter months: women were often the major storytellers as tools were repaired and the unmarried flirted under the careful eyes of their elders. For the nobles, the late medieval court of love, with its games of conversation, riddle, and gesture, occurred whenever husbands or suitors were home from military activity or other affairs.

At the end of the sixteenth century women invented a new setting and institution for conversation, the salon, which is the subject of Claude Dulong's essay. An urban gathering presided over by cultivated and well-read women of noble or ennobled families, the salon brought men and women together to talk about love, literature, politics, and anything else that struck their fancy. Dulong shows how women redesigned interior space and furniture so that conversation could be "civil" and polite, without the feel of battlefields or lawcourts, and how the Précieuses struggled, against the ridicule of Molière, to create a language that was new, spontaneous, and free of obscene reference. Unlike conversation at Fontainebleau or Versailles, salon discussion of appointments, high marriages, and other political issues could be conducted far from the king's ears. Unlike disputes and lectures at the universities or the newly forming academies, to which women had scarcely any access, salon discussion of philosophical and scientific matters brought together people unequal in formal education, but equal in their passion to know and understand. Salons were places of intellectual and social promotion where newcomers and new ideas might make their way at the permission of the hostess. Transported to the more reserved atmosphere of Protestant England, salons played the same roles as in Catholic France. Transported to late eighteenth-century Berlin, where some of the most important *salonnières* were assimilated Jewish women, they allowed Jews and Christians to mix.

The activities in a thriving salon included the reading of new manuscripts and the winning of patronage and subscription for new publications. Publishing by women was not, of course, an innovation in the seventeenth century: treatises and plays by medieval nuns had gone into print early in the sixteenth century, as had much of Christine de Pizan's prose and poetry, an inspiration to women writers looking for antecedents. By the end of the sixteenth century, women's names were on the title pages of literary and devotional works in several parts of Europe. Perhaps the most important was Marguerite de Navarre's *Heptaméron,* with lively debates following each of its tales in a reconstruction of the genre of storytelling.

In the next two centuries women published on a wide range of topics, from Hannah Woolley's recipe books to Emilie du Châtelet's dissertation on the nature of fire, from Elizabeth Carter's translation of Epictetus and Elizabeth Elstob's Anglo-Saxon grammar to Marie-Charlotte de Lézardière's study of ancient French law and political institutions. The contribution of Madeleine de Scudéry and Mme. de La Fayette to the French novel was so significant that both opponents and enthusiasts of the genre linked women to its origin. In eighteenth-century England

Frances Burney's *Eveline* and other novels were published in large editions and won her renown and a good income to support herself and her children.

Claude Dulong suggests that women writers suffered from a prudent conformism: in their publications heroines were always virtuous and modest and the structures of society remained unchallenged. It surely is true that women writers in all genres throughout the early modern period expressed concern about the ridicule that might greet the female pen. They often dedicated their books to other women for added protection. Yet licentious heroines can be found on many pages of the *Heptaméron* and the novels of Mary de la Rivière Manley; Aphra Behn's *Oroonoko* was the first novel written against the cruelties of slavery; and Sarah Scott's *Millenium Hall* and Marie Anne de Roumier Robert's *Les Ondins* were unsettling female utopias. Female writers were sometimes sly in their rebellion, as when they used the novel or the biography of a notable husband to penetrate the masculine realm of history writing; and sometimes bold, as when Catharine Macaulay talked her way into the reading room of the British Museum, built up her own research collection of almost 5,000 tracts, and pictured herself as both Clio and Liberty in a frontispiece to her *History of England*.

The female journalists described by Nina Rattner Gelbart displayed both boldness and entrepreneurial skill as they tried to win subscribers for and circumvent censorship of their periodicals. Aimed in principle at women readers, the *Female Spectator* and the *Journal des Dames* never abandoned the cause of serious intellectual endeavor for women even when articles were devoted to finding a husband or to the joys of Rousseauist mothering of their children. Mme. de Beaumer exemplifies the radical possibilities for an ancien régime woman: a supporter of feminism, republicanism, justice for the poor, Freemasonry, tolerance, and peace, she wore a sword to the censor's office when she went to defend her journal.

N.Z.D.—A.F.

12

From Conversation to Creation

Claude Dulong

BEFORE THE WRITTEN WORD, the spoken word; before creation, conversation, that is, the salon. Why? Because, the condition of women being what it was, the salon was one of the few places where women could express themselves freely. The fact that the word *salon* did not appear until the eighteenth century is of little importance. It is the phenomenon that interests us. Of course princesses had always been able to host circles, to gather around them men and women whose principal occupation was conversation and, if they were capable of it, propose subjects and guide the talk onto selected themes. Many people are familiar with medieval courts of love and Renaissance literary and philosophical circles, and there is general recognition of the importance of the groups that gathered in the sixteenth century around Marguerite d'Angoulême and Marguerite de Valois in France and Isabelle d'Este and Lucretia Borgia in Italy. (Contrary to legend, Borgia's wit was far more important than her amours.)

The tradition continued into the eighteenth century and beyond: cultivated princesses and queens such as Elizabeth of England, Christina of Sweden, and the Duchess Regent Anna-Amalia of Weimar made their courts centers of culture, and they were joined by those "queens" of the left hand, royal favorites such as the illustrious Madame Pompadour. These women, however, enjoyed many advantages, the foremost being rank, which placed them beyond criticism. The salon did not come into existence until centers of culture began to develop outside the court, the palace, and the palazzo, in cities and their private residences. This change took place during the early modern period, but not in all the countries of Europe. For the salon was a place where men and women mingled—this was one of its primary characteristics and indeed one of the reasons for its existence. Hence it could not exist where religious and social restrictions on women were most oppressive. Thus there were no Spanish salons, even though Spanish civilization, at least in the chivalric and courtly guise in which it was imagined elsewhere, exerted such great influence on the first salons in other countries.

Observers noted these differences and, if they were French, congratulated themselves on living in a country where the fair sex was not all but cloistered, where it was allowed to frequent the other sex in "respectable freedom" (honnête liberté). In countries where this was not the case, the consequences were unfortunate.

In the 1630s in Brussels, then under Spanish rule, the poet Vincent Voiture discovered that women were still forbidden to acknowledge the attention of male admirers except by appearing on their balconies at fixed times. "Decent conversation" was therefore impossible, and, worse still, when by chance or by ruse a private interview was obtained, repressed emotions came bubbling to the surface. When men have few opportunities to visit women, and then only briefly, they tend to forget the niceties and move straight to action. In England, where greater freedom was tolerated, some observers nevertheless deplored the custom that required the ladies to withdraw at the end of dinner, leaving the men to chat and drink among themselves. This custom encouraged circulation more of the brandy carafe than of ideas.

People of refinement believed that women were essential if society was to achieve a certain tone. Women expected more from a salon than the pleasure of mingling with men and perhaps an elegant flirtation. It is no doubt significant that a young woman's debut in society was for a long time referred to as her "entry into the world." The phrase originated in the early modern period, a time when the only way for women to learn what the family, school, and convent failed to teach was from contact with a certain society, which offered an entrée into the wider world of culture.

From the sixteenth through the eighteenth centuries high society served as an agent of civilization (of which it was later reduced to a mere epiphenomenon). In France, for example, fewer than 50 percent of women could sign their own names, even in large cities. In the salons, however, a minority of this minority became an elite—an elite without which it is doubtful that the vast majority of other women would have realized what they lacked and what they wanted. In a society created by and for men, where could change come from except from women themselves?

"A Coalition against Grossness"

The salons were truly schools, not only for women but also for men, whom women educated even as they educated themselves: men who sought only their own pleasure, who lived in the past and believed that the woman who could tell her husband's bed from another knew all she needed to know, as a feminist of the time remarked bluntly. It was no accident that the first salons truly worthy of the name appeared in France at the beginning of the seventeenth century.[1] Thirty-five years of civil war had wreaked havoc there. Instinct had triumphed, morals had withered, ignorance had reached tragic heights, and of all these ills women were the first victims. Redressment was called for, and the work of the salons can be seen as part of the "coalition against crudeness" that Maurice Magendie studied in his comprehensive thesis on social manners.[2] The renascent church of the Counter-Reformation, the restored central government, philosophers, and moralists all played a role in this vast effort to educate or, rather, reeducate the French. As varied as the motives and methods of this enterprise were, there is one common denominator: people had to be taught to control, or at least to moderate the expression of, their instincts. Countless didactic works inculcated moral precepts and presented a portrait of the *honnête homme* along with advice on how to please, write, and converse, arts that were also encouraged by the many treatises on "civility" that appeared in this period and indeed throughout the century. This ideal of good social manners would remain fundamental to the salons, and Voltaire, a man of letters if ever there was one, observed that "one must be a man of the world first, a man of letters second."

Respect for women was one of the rules that theorists of manners believed ought to be observed, but the salons, which thrived on romantic illusion, called for more than respect. Young women, debarred from serious study, were thrown back on works of fiction, although these were even more taboo than other books. Taste for fiction, for the marvelous, and for the fantastic was instilled in girls, unbeknownst to their families, by the ancient folktales told to them by nurses and maids. And when, as adults, they had to face the harsh realities of life—tyrannical parents, forced marriages, brutal lovers (if they dared to take a lover)— that taste remained. Some took with them to church novels disguised as books of hours. These were of course novels of amorous adventures, apt to satisfy the need to dream. Heroes from the most barbarian ages and most savage regions sighed and died for the love of inaccessible heroines, and even when one of those heroines fell into the brute's clutches she always reduced him in the end to a state of utter abjection.

These novels drew, in rather adulterated form, on a long tradition of idealism, which was reinvigorated at the very beginning of the seventeenth century by Honoré d'Urfé's *Astrée,* an escape novel that enjoyed immense international success. Featuring shepherds and shepherdesses free of all material worries, written in a style that seemed graceful and charming then even though it strikes us as wordy today, *Astrée* conveyed a Neoplatonic message: love conquers all. But not just any love will do: lust does not count. What we love in the creatures of this world is the reflection of an ideal, heavenly beauty, which our souls yearn for and vaguely aspire to rejoin. Women are intermediaries between this world of ideas and the physical world. They are men's *mistresses* (in the word's primary meaning, not its compromised secondary one), and without the help of women men cannot hope to achieve perfect love.

This idealism of course passed over the heads of most readers, few of whom became converts to Platonic love. But *Astrée* taught them more than all the treatises and textbooks about the need to please and the difficulty of doing so. In it they discovered unsuspected, or at any rate forgotten, delicacies of feeling, conduct, and language. Love offered the best kind of education. Woman became an object of conquest and not of pleasure, and this conquest had to be carried out in accordance with a ritual, whose rules were respected with varying degrees of sincerity. What the salons added to civility was *galanterie,* that flirtatious polish, the grace and charm that could be acquired only from and for women but that would quickly extend its influence to all the behavior of a certain elite. "Gallantry" (used here in its restricted sense as an English equivalent for the French *galanterie,* meaning "polite, civilized attention to the ladies") thus became the distinguishing characteristic of this elite in every encounter, so that even a clergyman such as Fénelon, whose morals were above suspicion, could be credited with having "a gallant air."

"Hostesses" and Salons

The condition of women being what it was, where did the first salon hostesses come from? What gave these women their ability to act as arbiters of morals, manners, and taste? What enabled them to dare say to men that no civilization was worthy of the name that did not put women in their proper place, that is, first? They were of course Parisians, favored by birth, fortune, or both; and their husbands were either particularly liberal or else absent or dead. Some (like Mlle. de Scudéry) were spinsters whose parents were no longer around to hold them in check. But this independence, though necessary, was not sufficient. They had to possess a minimum of culture even to think of having a salon, and the cultivated women of the sixteenth to eighteenth centuries were those who chose to become so by seizing every available opportunity, who used cunning to educate themselves as others might have used it to hide an amorous intrigue. Many had gained their first knowledge of the humanities as young girls by sitting in a corner and listening to their brothers' lessons. This was how Mme. de Brassac, the governess of young Louis XIV, learned Latin. But it was because she continued to read of her own volition that she was able to read the authors of ancient Rome in the original, and many other books as well, since all learned works were at the time written in Latin.

Protestant women had an advantage over Catholics in this regard: a Protestant might be fortunate enough to have a clergyman for a father and therefore an educated man with a knowledge of ancient languages and a library on which she might draw, with or without permission, for books to read. The number of private libraries belonging to individuals of all professions was three times higher in Protestant cities than in Catholic ones. To be sure, these libraries consisted mostly, and in some cases entirely, of works of piety and sacred texts. But the Bible, that inexhaustible source, which Protestants were obliged to read in the practice of their religion, contained a good deal besides religious matter to interest curious female readers. This phenomenon perhaps accounts for the number of educated and well-spoken young women in the England of Shakespeare's time and later. Indeed, Shakespeare's works enable us to measure the skill and audacity of such women in rhetorical contests. To be sure, the example of Elizabeth I might also have encouraged English women to make a show of their wit. After Elizabeth the situation of course changed, and it was not until the middle of the eighteenth century that English women would manage to establish salons in the French sense, salons to which people came in search of no pleasures other than those of the mind.

The model of the French salon was established by the Marquise de Rambouillet, the archetype of the society hostess. She began her career with a great many advantages, most notably an Italian mother of great intelligence and grand manners who did not neglect her daughter's education. She was therefore bilingual, and later, in order to polish her literary culture, she also learned Spanish. Along with intellect she had heart, being a true devotee of friendship. On top of these qualities she enjoyed a spotless reputation, perhaps because she also had the good fortune of a loving and admiring husband.

Her salon was to some extent a product of circumstances. She had fled the court of Henri IV because she had found it too crude, which it was. Of delicate constitution, she could not stand "the press" of court any more than the tone. Later, her husband's partial disgrace under Richelieu contributed to her semiretirement.

Having made up her mind to establish at home a court to her own taste, Mme. de Rambouillet began with the decor, to which she devoted unprecedented care and attention. Her *hôtel* had a side staircase rather than a central one, which opened onto a suite of rooms well suited to receiving guests. Her other innovation, which occasioned a great deal of talk, was the alcove. Not that Mme. de Rambouillet invented it. The houses of the time commonly had rooms that could be used for more than one purpose, and such rooms often contained, as space for a bed, an alcove concealed by a curtain; this alcove, together with the *ruelle,* or space between the bed and the wall, created a kind of private enclave in an otherwise impersonal space. This intimate area was used not only for sleeping, lovemaking, and prayer but also, with the addition of closets and sometimes strongboxes, for storing papers, books, and valuable personal items. Mme. de Rambouillet made her alcove the center of her salon because she had a strange malady (since seen as a case of thermo-anaphylaxia) that forced her to avoid both the heat of the fire and the sun's rays. The terrible coldness of homes at this time was a serious problem for a woman who could not settle by the fire as others did. Mme. de Rambouillet chose to remain in her alcove.

A remarkable number of seventeenth-century hostesses were invalids or at any rate women of delicate constitution, hypersensitive, and more susceptible than others to the discomforts of the time and to a thousand small ills incomprehensible to contemporaries of more robust health. Mme. de Sablé was as celebrated for her wit as for the precautions, deemed ridiculous, that she took to avoid illness. She was also, like her friend Mme. de Maure, an insomniac, and the two women were so terrified of contagion that even when they lived together, they used messengers to communicate from room to room if one of them suffered from even the slightest cold. Mme. de La Fayette led a semireclusive life, and some people, ignorant of the reality of her illnesses, which she had the good taste to keep to herself, judged her mad for never wanting to go out. She was among the first to fit her carriage out with glass windows because she had suffered so much in the days when the openings in carriage doors were protected against wind, cold, and rain by nothing more than curtains.

Proust's Dr. du Boulbon would have said of these women that they belonged to "that magnificent and lamentable family, which is the salt of the earth," namely, the family of neurotics, of which the world "will never know how much it owes them, still less how much they suffered to provide it." Proust was thinking of artists, creators who suffered to create. But was not the suffering of those who could not create, and who had to content themselves with a conversation as a substitute, even more acute? This may well have been the cause of the hypersensitivity, allergies, and phobias of a Mme. de Rambouillet or a Mme. de Sablé.

Spaces and Decors

Once a fashion has been launched, its origins, which often lie in necessity, are forgotten. When the *bourgeoises* of the seventeenth century took up the habit of receiving on their beds or in their

401

alcoves, they were no doubt imitating the *grandes dames* of the aristocracy rather than protecting themselves from cold and fatigue. While these beds may not have been intended for lying in state, they were monuments nonetheless, topped by canopies, draped with curtains, decorated with valances, hangings, and flounces, and in some cases equipped with pilasters capped by feathers. Before the mid-eighteenth century, however, the rest of the furniture was relatively rudimentary and undistinguished. There were tables, chests, and armoires and, in the wealthiest homes, multidrawered cabinets inlaid with precious wood or ivory. To sit on there were regular and folding chairs. Armchairs, just coming into vogue, still had straight, high backs, but these were stuffed, as were the seats, and thus a great advance over the *caquetoire,* the ancestor of the armchair, which owed its name to the fact that women used to sit on them to "cackle" (*caqueter,* as misogynists of the early seventeenth century referred to the conversation of women). This furniture gave an impression of geometric rigidity, as engravings from the period attest.

Mme. de Rambouillet had the knack of brightening up this decor. Some of her refinements are so familiar to us that we forget that someone had to invent them. She was the first, for example, to think of placing bibelots, vases, and baskets of fresh flowers on the furniture so as to "create springtime in her bedroom." These words of a contemporary reflect the bedazzlement of the happy few privileged to enjoy an atmosphere so new that they had difficulty describing it. Mme. de Rambouillet loved nature. Unable to share in its bounties, she was not content merely to look out the window and contemplate the meadow she had planted in her yard or to indulge the novel luxury of making hay in the middle of Paris. When spring came, she wanted her entire house to reflect the season. Instead of dark wainscotting or Cordovan leather, her walls were hung with tapestries whose vivid colors matched the floral bouquets: green, gold, and red abounded and, in the bedchamber of the mistress of the house, azure blue (the original "Blue Chamber"). Paintings by important artists and portraits of close friends stood out against this bright backdrop, but the pictures were not hung, as was then customary, close together in compact arrangements. All the objects were selected and matched with the sure instinct of a connoisseur: Venetian vases, porcelain from China, ancient marble, and fine gold pieces, all reflected in mirrors (a novelty) and illuminated by crystal chandeliers (another novelty) whose multiplicity of facets softened and scattered the light from many candles.

Place and Manners

Who, in such a setting, would think of behaving as in a tavern? The poetic pseudonyms that guests adopted also lent a *galant* turn to the conversation. When a person chooses to be called Arthénice, Icas, or Léonide, he or she will not converse or correspond in the same tone as a Pierre or Pierrette. Poets, who by now were familiar fixtures in the salons, where they were much more highly regarded in the early eighteenth century than they were at court, played an important role in this new fashion. It was Malherbe who came up with the name Arthénice for Mme. de Rambouillet—a name that, despite its Hellenic sound, is actually an anagram of her first name, Catherine.

Poets and men of letters in general served many other purposes as well. They acted as volunteer tutors to the ladies; they read their latest works in their homes; they furnished subjects for their conversation. But they could be banished if they failed to maintain the proper standards, and not just in their manners but also in their works, by reforming their style and, to a certain extent, their way of thinking. Malherbe, who in his youth had written obscene couplets for satirical anthologies, now condemned these verses of Philippe Desportes:

> O vent qui fais mouvoir cette divine plante,
> Te jouant, amoureux, parmis ses blanches fleurs

> O wind, which sets this divine plant in motion, playing you, lover, among its white flowers.

"Filthy!" charged Malherbe. "Everybody knows well enough what I mean." Actually it takes a mind ready to see things in the worst light to find filth in this distich. But that was just the kind of mind that Malherbe's contemporaries had, and indeed that Malherbe himself had had before expunging himself of error.

Corneille's scruples are equally revealing. The great man had never been afraid of ribaldry. Yet in the *Examen de Polyeucte* (*Polyeucte* being a play whose first reading was associated with the *hôtel* de Rambouillet) he wrote: "If I had to set forth the story of David and Bathsheba, I would not describe how he fell in love with her upon seeing her bathe in a fountain, lest the image of her nudity make too stimulating an impression on the listener's mind; I would rather portray him with his love for her without discussing how that love took hold of his heart."

To be sure, the effect of this self-censorship, coupled with the external censorship that Richelieu imposed on French theater when he banned "indecent actions and lascivious words," was not all bad, since it gave rise to so-called classical tragedy and helped the comedy of manners to triumph over farce. And this trend in turn led to women's being allowed to attend theater and thus gain access to one form of culture. But other forms of poetry suffered from these constraints. French lyric verse lost a great deal, and for a long time to come, by conforming to the dictates of the salons. When playwrights begin to be afraid of "stimulating" their audiences (and particularly the female members of their audiences) with accurate images, and when all sensuality is banished from the stage, the writing becomes disembodied and abstract and loses its credibility as poets are forced to rely on ingenious fancy to make up for the absence of strong feeling. The result is a civilization of refined wit and madrigals, a civilization symbolized by *La guirlande de Julie* (Garland for Julie), an anthology of sixteen plays given to Mme. de Rambouillet's eldest daughter, Julie d'Angennes, by Montausier, her suitor for fourteen years.

Are the salons to be blamed, however, for advocating and cultivating the art of love without lovemaking? People who had never imagined that one could put a little art into love needed these exercises. If *galanterie* meant only treating every woman like the woman one loved, it was still better than treating the woman one loved just like every other woman. The first hostesses accomplished an important feat: they took impulsive warriors, fresh from the battlefield where they had done without women for five or six months, and made them stop at the edge of the bed. They showed these men the way from the sleeping alcove to the conversational one.

The Précieuses: The Will to Know

In the second half of the seventeenth century salons proliferated, in France at least, with fashion and with the rise of the moneyed bourgeoisie. The nature of these salons did not change: they remained places where a select company of men and women could socialize, and they were still intended to serve as a kind of intellectual brokerage. But the winds of the intellect had shifted in intensity and direction. Scientific progress spurred new curiosities. As early as 1662 Jacques Bénigne Bossuet was able to write that "man has all but changed the face of the world." This feat had been accomplished by men such as Galileo, Kepler, and Descartes, to say nothing of Pascal, who was still known only for a few experiments and for his talent as a religious polemicist. Since the university, hidebound in dogmatism and pride, remained hostile to anything that contradicted the sacrosanct ancients (and therefore to all the recent discoveries), the spirit of investigation was cultivated in private circles, where the new theories were commented on and where their authors were received and offered protection. Women were drawn not only by these curiosities but also, to a degree, by the allure of forbidden fruit, since scientific subjects were ordinarily excluded from the instruction they were permitted to receive. At the end of the century Fénelon was still writing to one of the women whom he served as spiritual guide in these terms: "Do not allow yourself to be bewitched by the diabolical attractions of geometry." Geometers, too, were now received in the salons along with physicists, physicians, and astronomers. Philaminte in *Les femmes savantes* is merely succumbing to the latest fashion when she has a telescope installed in her home. The ladies were not repelled even by chemistry, and in Paris they were not afraid to venture into laboratories like that of the celebrated Nicolas Lémery, even though it was, according to Fontenelle, "less a chamber than a cellar and almost a magic cave, illuminated solely by the light of the ovens."

Nevertheless, belles lettres, fine language, and noble feelings remained the principal interest of the salons and the substance of much of the conversation. In particular, these were the dominant subjects in the salons kept by women who in 1654 were given the name *les précieuses* (the precious ones) because it was said they attached value to many things that had none, beginning with themselves. This, of course, was a masculine irony, and one that failed to take account of the circumstances.

The Fronde, which was coming to an end when the Précieuses made their appearance, had dealt some heavy blows to the idealism of the salons. Of course four years of civil war had done less damage than thirty-five years of foreign wars, so that it was not a question of starting over as it had been at the beginning of the century. But the case for civility had to be made anew because a certain cynicism had begun to be heard among the aristocracy, which had shed many of its illusions in this episode. Although women, especially noblewomen of high rank, played a major role in the Fronde, they suffered for it. They had believed—or wanted to believe and tried to make others believe—that in encouraging their men to fight against the central government and in some cases taking up arms themselves, they were acting like the heroines of novels. But they had been defending their own material or class interests against the superior interest of the state, and in many cases the skillful Mazarin had only to place a few bags of gold in their eager hands to make them change their minds and give in. Mazarin, in any case, knew that "the person who today would wisely govern a kingdom will tomorrow be a master no one would trust with governing a dozen hens." Women, it seemed, had taken advantage of the widespread disorder to indulge their instincts, trampling on decency without concern for their image. Hence that image had to be restored; woman's right to consideration, not to say adoration, and also of course to independence and learning, had to be reaffirmed. We must forget the connotations that have subsequently attached themselves to the word *preciosity*. Historically the Précieuses represented a form of feminism. In the wake of the Fronde they felt the need and the duty to react against a state of affairs and a state of mind that threatened the tenuous conquests made by their predecessors. And perhaps because women in general had become bolder and because the Précieuses in particular were drawn from more varied, hence at once more vulnerable and more pugnacious, segments of society than the high aristocracy of a Mme. de Rambouillet, this reaction was expressed with unprecedented vigor.

The social and sexual subjugation of women was the first item of concern. Thus Mlle. de Scudéry: "One marries in order to hate. Hence a true lover must never speak of marriage, because to be a lover is to want to be loved, and to be a husband is to want to be hated." Or the abbé de Pure in *La précieuse:* "I was an innocent victim sacrificed for unknown and obscure reasons, for family interests, but sacrificed like a slave, bound, strangled . . . They buried me, or rather they enshrouded me alive in the bed of Evandre's son." As for maternity, or "lover's dropsy," the Précieuses, in order to avoid it, proposed that marriage be officially ended with the birth of a first child, the child to be left in the care of the father, who should pay the mother a cash bonus. And why not, since most men married only to assure themselves of progeny, forgetting that the women who gave their children life so often risked death for themselves?

Eager to restore the idealistic attitudes that had been so beneficial to the female sex, the Précieuses placed the human heart above all other interests:

> Dans un lieu plus secret on tient la précieuse
> Occupée aux leçons de morale amoureuse,
> Là se font distinguer les fiertés des rigueurs,
> Les dédains des mépris, les tourments des langueurs;
> On y sait démêler la crainte et les alarmes,
> Discerner les attraits, les appâts et les charmes . . .
> Et toujours on ajuste à l'ordre des douleurs
> Et le temps de la plainte et la saison des pleurs.

In a more secret place the *précieuse* is kept occupied with lessons in the morality of love. Here, pride is distinguished from haughtiness, disdain from scorn, torment from yearning. One learns to tell fear from alarm, to discern attractions, allures, and charms . . . And one always adjusts to the order of pain and the time of complaint and the season of tears.

Here Saint-Evremond helps us to understand how the French made a specialty of the psychology of love. For the amorous "delabyrinthings" and "queries" that stirred the Précieuses did not culminate only in minor works such as *La carte du tendre*. Masterpieces, too, were influenced by the phenomenon of preciosity. Surely it took the genius, the lucidity, and the deep despair of a Mme. de La Fayette to write *Zaïde* and the *La Princesse de Clèves;* but it also took familiarity with the salons, which provided an opportunity to refine one's taste and sharpen one's wit. And where else could a still inexperienced female author meet the theorists, grammarians, and clever people who could help her to construct her plot and correct her syntax and style?

As for the vocabulary of the Précieuses, it is no longer possible, after so many excellent works on the subject, to believe that they ordinarily spoke in the way the satirists portrayed them. Mlle. de Scudéry, the embodiment of preciosity in literature, never called eyes "mirrors of the soul," feet "suffering dears," breasts "cushions of love," a mirror "the counselor of graces," or chairs "the comforters of conversation": some of these metaphors were used long before her time and express what they have to say rather prettily. It is true, however, that the Précieuses compaigned against words that they considered off-color or, to use an adjective they bestowed on the language, *obscene*. They condemned any word or phrase redolent of a crude physiological reality: *crotter* (to make droppings), *lavement* (enema), *être en couches* (to be in labor). They refused to apply the verb *aimer* (to like or love) to material as well as spiritual things: *on aime sa maîtresse* but *on goûte le melon* (one loves one's mistress but "savors" melon).

Although the evidence is anecdotal, there is no doubt that some *façonnières* (fusspots) went to extremes in their prudery and that some provincials (for by now there were salons in the provinces) were undiscerning in their use of an unfamiliar poetic vocabulary. In reality, what the Précieuses were criticized for was what women who concerned themselves with questions of language had long been criticized for, namely their concern: this was none of their business. But in this area, too, the quarrel heated up at the turn of the seventeenth century. The Précieuses were accused of "making war on the old style." This charge was entirely true, and they prided themselves on it, conscious as they were of acting not only as feminists but also as "moderns" in dismissing pedantic, archaic, and technical words. For this was what *jargon* meant to the true Précieuses, and not their own style or the feminine style generally, in which they found, by contrast, what they called invention and freedom, that is, a felicitous and genuine spontaneity, the very qualities that Mlle. de Scudéry was one of the first to appreciate in a writer such as Mme. de Sévigné. Where did such qualities come from? From the fact that women's minds were not "encumbered with strange notions" or "worn out by the principles of knowledge." Claude Favre de Vaugelas had precisely the same thought when he wrote in his *Remarques sur la langue française* (1647) that "in all doubts about language it is best to consult women . . . and those who have not studied . . . because they go straight to what they are accustomed to saying and hearing said." Thus in an irony of history, the misfortune of women to have been barred from learning Latin became their good fortune in a period when the "vulgar tongue," that is, the national idiom, was being raised to noble rank and Descartes wrote his *Discourse on Method* in French, he said, so that women could understand it (a remarkable innovation for a philosopher).

Such innovations, however, are the mark of great men, and the mass of petty spirits disapproved. Because Vaugelas said that women should be consulted on doubtful points of language, he was branded a fool and his thesis was subjected to vehement refutation based on the very argument that Vaugelas was disputing: how were women supposed to know the proper use of language when they were ignorant of the precepts of rhetoric, the rules of grammar, Latin, and Greek, and the fundamentals of etymology, without which it was impossible to appreciate the meaning and scope of so many words borrowed from the ancient tongues?

Clearly, this dispute went far beyond issues of language. It had a bearing on the transmission and diffusion of knowledge. Should knowledge remain a monopoly of those with university degrees? No, said the Précieuses and, with them, all women avid for culture: knowledge should and must become civilized by being passed down to polite society. To make such a claim was to demystify the pretensions of the pedants, who took the challenge very badly indeed. The criticisms that have been heaped on the Précieuses for three hundred years stem largely from the rancorous campaign that these offended pedants waged against them. Already, in 1640, François de Grenaille had devoted a considerable part of *L'honneste fille* (Respectable Girl) to ironic remarks about women who, not content to "reign in company," also sought to lord it over writers. It was bad enough, he said, that they argued about fashionable novels and comedies and expatiated on the three unities of tragedy. But they finally crossed the line when they began having "views on the most obscure subjects," which they turned into "playthings" for their circles, and when they claimed that, "no matter what was published, nothing yet done could match the value of what still could be done." And what did they want to see done? "The general politics of all peoples, a course in the philosophy of all centuries, the general history of all things in one special volume, and a compendium of all the secrets of art and nature in one book. The style should be pure and noble, the thought subtle and popular, the flow continuous yet interrupted now and then by pleasant digressions."

Vast and obviously unrealizable, this aspiration is moving for that very reason. It shows how eager women were to learn, the way in which they wished to learn, and thus the formal qualities they sought in learned works. The objective was not to put all of Roman history into madrigals, as Molière has Mascarille say in *Les précieuses ridicules,* but to encourage works written in a clear, simple style for a broad readership, perhaps even "interrupted now and then for pleasant digressions"—why not? Women lacked the background to swallow indigestible tomes or to understand the style of the savants who, even when they did not write in Latin, seemed to be translating from it. Molière's Philaminte wants "to bring together what is elsewhere kept apart, to combine fine language with high learning." The only error she makes in her neophyte's enthusiasm is to allow herself to be deceived by charlatan scholars and counterfeit stylists.

It is possible to regret that Molière contented himself with caricatures in both *Les femmes savantes* and *Les précieuses ridicules,* since he knew, from the actresses who shared his life, that women, including women from modest backgrounds, were capable of learning and of appreciating beauty. No doubt his chief objective was to make people laugh. But in doing so he joined his voice to that of the pedants and lent them his talent to make fun of women who wished to educate and emancipate themselves. For in the seventeenth century emancipation was impossible without education, and it was typical of the Précieuses and other seventeenth-century feminists that they never separated the two. This dual objective might have been more readily understood if they had been better able to get their point across. But the hard truth is that their writings failed to match their ambitions.

To Dare to Write

Indeed, much of the literary production of women before the nineteenth century was of mediocre quality. One reason for this was that certain genres remained beyond the reach of women. Even with the aid of salons there was no way for them to absorb enough science or philosophy to do original work in these fields. The few who managed to do so, such as Anna Maria van Schurmann in Utrecht, became objects of curiosity, like strange animals. It is significant, moreover, that van Schurmann was a spinster: marriage was another, in fact the principal, difficulty that women who wished to be authors had to overcome. If they were to publish, there had to be no one whose feelings they would need to spare and no social position to protect. Only grudgingly were women permitted to write even the kinds of things they were allowed to read: spiritual works and moralizing tracts. True, some women who consecrated their lives to God were able to bear witness, within the narrow latitude they were allowed, to their faith and exalted spirituality.[3] Women who lived in the world, however, could hardly have been expected to content themselves with spiritual manuals, orthodox treatises on the rearing of daughters, and compendia of moral and practical advice for other women. Yet outside this narrow area women commanded little respect. If Mlle. de Gournay had not been a spinster and, increasingly, a social outcast with nothing to lose, she would never have dared to write vigorous pamphlets attacking the injustice of the condition of women in the early seventeenth century. At the other extreme of the social hierarchy, the Duchess of Newcastle was forgiven for brandishing the banner of feminism and dabbling in philosophy because she was a duchess. And even then her forgiveness did not last long: in the end her presumptuousness was found shocking, and she was condemned to a lonely old age in her castles. Nor were men the only ones to be shocked when women dared to publish. When Sophie von La Roche, a German woman who moved in the best society, published a successful novel in 1771, Frau von Goethe, the poet's mother, declared that Sophie, an educated and intelligent woman who should have known better, had lost her mind and would bring woe upon her children.

To be sure, women wrote letters (in astonishing numbers), but these were not intended for publication. The letters of Mme. de Sévigné circulated from hand to hand, but only within a select society. It was another matter entirely for a woman to admit that she had written a work that had actually been printed. "To meet in libraries," as Sévigné said, or, worse still, in bookshops, with all the connotations of the marketplace, was not only an offense against propriety but a derogation from high birth. It is a miracle that we are able to read today the letters of Mme. de Sévigné and of the "Portuguese nun" (in Guilleragues's *Lettres portugaises*), a miracle for which we must thank their correspondents—in the former case for their good taste, in the latter for their vanity—for preserving them.[4] Other epistolary masterpieces may have been lost forever through the negligence of their recipients. And how many private diaries were burned by the very women who kept them? Lady Mary Wortley Montagu was one of the most interesting women in eighteenth-century England, but since she stated frequently that men and women of quality ought not to publish, her daughter felt justified in burning her diary after her death.

"To write is to lose half one's nobility," Mlle. de Scudéry observed, and for that reason she published her earliest novels under her brother's name. She might have continued to do so had it not been for her success and her pressing need for cash. It was almost always need that led other women in other countries to resign themselves to becoming "professionals."

Most female authors took refuge behind pseudonyms or even in anonymity. Mme. de La Fayette, who might have believed that the nobility of what she wrote justified her writing, never admitted to being the author of *La Princesse de Clèves,* except at the end of her life in veiled words and to an intimate friend. Booksellers' catalogs from this period contain countless works whose authors are identified only as "a lady of quality."

Condemned to anonymity, these women lacked even the allure of fame to support them in their work. The prospect of glory, which sustains so many authors in lieu of any more immediate reward, was more than they could hope for. Female writers took endless risks and endured countless constraints. Disease, for one thing, was everywhere rampant, and, as the Précieuses intimate without going into detail, gynecological difficulties commonly resulted from repeated pregnancies, natural and artificially induced miscarriages, and epidemic syphilis (for those fortunate enough to survive the ravages of the disease). A woman whose husband was unsuccessful or who died prematurely had to assume a responsibility for which she seldom had any preparation: managing the family property. But by dint of will, wisdom, and talent a few women managed to progress on all fronts. Mme. de La Fayette, for example, has been accused of greed because she defended her family's interests while writing her novels. Toward the end of her life she justified herself in a letter to Gilles Ménage. Left a widow and sicker than ever, she worried how much longer she would be able to bear the burden: "I sometimes admire myself in private . . . Find me another woman with a figure like mine, with a taste for wit like the one you inspired in me, who has done as well for her household."[5] In this melancholy moment of self-satisfaction we detect a tinge of regret at having sacrificed to the "household" some of the happiness promised by beauty and talent.

At least Mme. de La Fayette left a body of work behind her, and in her own lifetime she had the pleasure, though a secret one, of knowing that her work was appreciated by the finest minds of the day. How many other women gave up in exhaustion and discouragement on literature or any other form of cultural endeavor before they were able to make their mark? Consider the case of Luisa Bergalli, who lived in Venice in the mid-eighteenth century. She belonged to a relatively "liberated" circle whose members were all involved to one degree or another in literature or the arts. But in writing for the stage and founding a theater company she incurred the hostility of her brother-in-law Carlo Gozzi, a renowned playwright. She gave birth to five children, money ran short, one lawsuit followed another, and her husband, a depressive, attempted suicide. Luisa ultimately renounced all her ambitions and sank into what was called melancholy, from which she died.

Jane Austen, writing toward the end of the eighteenth century, faced difficulties of a different kind. Although the constraints on female writers were by then somewhat looser, she was so conditioned by the prejudices of her rural England that she wrote only in secret on sheets small enough to be concealed in a book in case someone interrupted. And interruptions were frequent, because she wrote in the family living room. These circumstances were not only a result of the family's relative poverty and the presence in the house of an invalid mother, whose care fell to Jane as an unmarried daughter; daughters also were denied the luxury of the "room of one's own" that Virginia Woolf considered so essential to a writer. Jane Austen thus depended on the squeaky living room door to keep her from being surprised at her guilty endeavor. To the puzzlement of other family members, she always objected when anyone proposed oiling the hinges.

A Compulsory Conformism

Yet on the whole there was nothing subversive about the work of female writers. Although many deplored the injustice of women's condition, they did not question society or the world. It took men such as Daniel Defoe in *Moll Flanders* and the abbé Prévost in *Manon Lescaut* to dare to portray women who were poor and who, things being as they were, had no alternative to prostitution if they did not wish to remain so. No female authors wrote in the vein of Rousseau, Choderlos de Laclos, or the Marquis de Sade. Even those who practiced freedom of thought and licentiousness of behavior in their lives and wrote frankly in their letters became conformists at the prospect of publication. Most women writers produced novels, but none availed themselves of the opportunity for audacity the genre provided. Their heroines respected the prevailing norms of decency, and only a rape could deprive them of their innocence. These novelists also commonly adopted the pretense that an anonymous manuscript had somehow mysteriously come into their hands and that they were merely transcribing it. In this way the few minor liberties they allowed themselves could be blamed on a fictitious third party, and another layer of anonymity was added to the (possibly penetrable) anonymity of the author.

To be sure, some English women's novels of the eighteenth century offered original settings, acute psychological observations, and sharp styles; yet even these works conformed to all the usual conventions and by no means presage later works such as *Wuthering Heights* or even *Jane Eyre*. In a penetrating study of eighteenth-century women's fiction, Katharine Rogers raises an interesting question: In choosing to portray only virtuous heroines, were these novelists not deliberately repressing their sexuality in favor of their intellectuality?[6] In other words, the liberating act, the emancipatory act, was to write, regardless of what one wrote. If these writers had stated forthrightly in print that women have desires just as men do and sometimes give in to them (a phenomenon that André Gide himself had difficulty believing early in this century),[7] the ensuing scandal in society would have prevented them not only from living a normal and honorable life but also from continuing to publish. By doing the opposite, by demonstrating through their heroines that their reason and virtue outweighed their passion, they gained impunity. Their prudence may also have had other objectives, touching on the very essence of the debate over woman. In presenting love as the dominant passion of their sex, the female novelists might somehow have betrayed the cause they were defending by placing weapons in the hands of antifeminists. They might have confirmed an old theological argument, still current, that women were objects, impure and necessarily dependent on men, because unlike all other female animals the daughters of Eve were ready to couple in any season.

The astonishing modesty, not to say prudishness, of the hero-ines of these novels and the objections (compounding the other difficulties placed in their way) they raise before giving in to love, even in marriage, should perhaps be seen as unformulated and possibly unconscious fears of subjection, as resistance to man's fatal domination. As long as a woman has not said yes, she remains an object of desire and conquest, hence sovereign; but once she says yes, whatever freedom and prestige she enjoyed disappears. And love, as only Mme. de La Fayette found the words to say, also disappears, for it cannot survive possession.

An Intellectual Desire

It would, however, be a mistake to judge the intellectual progress of women solely by the tone of the works they produced. Quantity and diversity must also be taken into consideration. Statistics com-piled for various countries indicate that in the eighteenth century women began to write more and to expand their interests into new areas. In Venice women published only 49 works in the sixteenth century and 76 in the seventeenth. From 1700 to 1750 they published 110, almost as many works as were published by men.[8] Most of these were of course novels, followed by poetry. But there were also serious works of history and philosophy, polemics, works of science and scientific popularization, transla-tions from living and dead languages, plays, and opera librettos. And we must not forget female journalists or the women who displayed their brilliance in the academies that had begun to flour-ish in many places or even a few who obtained university chairs in letters, law, and medicine. Such achievements were not easy, and not many women managed them, but still, they were a sign of things to come: women were studying more and educating themselves more than in the past. They had acquired the capacity for such study thanks to the educational system created a century earlier, a system that had taken time to bear fruit. Despite the well-known limitations of this system, controlled as it was by the Catholic and Protestant churches, it trained generations of women readers, and reading is of course a first indispensable step toward the acquisition of culture. Mme. de Maintenon's Saint-Cyr is but one example of the many educational establishments created in the second half of the seventeenth century, but this boarding school for young women is noteworthy for having brought to the stage two tragedies by the greatest playwright of the time, Jean Racine.[9]

Once young women left boarding school, there was no higher education available to them. Culture reached them mainly through the salons, which sprang up nearly everywhere in the eighteenth century. These institutions were sometimes called *conversations* (*conversazione* in Italy). Montesquieu noted that a certain lady in Milan "held a *conversation*." He added that "what is noble about the *conversations* of Milan is that they give you lots of chocolate and refreshments and you do not pay for cards." Obviously Italian hostesses did not carry purism to the extreme of prohibiting gambling, as the English "bluestockings" did. But a salon, even if one played cards, was still a "conversation." The fact that the part could stand for the whole shows what the real purpose of these gatherings was.

France was the center of the network of salons that facilitated the spread of ideas in Enlightenment Europe. France's role in the eighteenth century was as important as it had been a century earlier in establishing the model of the salon. The many reasons for this are well known, and only one of them is worth mentioning here: the French language had, as the Précieuses had hoped, developed its potential to the full. It had become a familiar tool, apt to serve every need. Even scholars no longer thought of using anything else, and French was adopted by polite society everywhere. Furthermore, eighteenth-century salons were less educational establishments and schools of gallantry than they had been in the past, owing to progress in education and changing customs and ideas. The basics had been mastered, and the salons now became sounding boards for authors, artists, and their works. Hostesses, themselves freer to demonstrate their wit and knowledge, were obliged to compete with newer meeting places such as cafés and clubs by inviting a more varied, "intellectual" assortment of guests. Diderot held court at Mme. d'Epinay's and Buffon at Mme. Necker's, while Voltaire was the idol first of Mme. du Châtelet's salon and later of Mme. du Deffand's. The Encyclopedists were brilliant if ebullient recruits, and it took all the savoir faire of the mistress of the house to ensure that they respected society's rules of propriety. Sometimes these difficult guests were assigned a special day of their own just to make sure there were no embarrassments. Even though these salons paved the way to the French Revolution, the preaching of atheism and democracy was not tolerated.

Sometimes an author was also the lover of the mistress of the house. This circumstance raised no eyebrows, because love as pleasure or habit had become an accepted custom. Love as passion was another matter entirely, because it kept the hostess out of circulation and could drive her regular guests away. Availability was foremost among the qualities needed by women who kept salons. And barring passion or other misfortune, ladies were available because they had no careers. For twelve years Mlle. de Lespinasse received every evening from five to nine o'clock. Having once served as penniless companion to Mme. du Deffand, she had learned how to make herself available to visitors while the mistress of the house rested, so she was able to take some of the regular guests and establish a salon of her own with the turncoats, Jean d'Alembert foremost among them. With salons a thing of the past, it is hard for us to imagine what an earthshaking event this secession must have been.

The fact that Mme. du Deffand was an insomniac, obliged to rest in the afternoon on account of her sleepless nights, reminds us that despite their apparent endurance many eighteenth-century hostesses were invalids like their predecessors. Many were anxious, dissatisfied women, bored because they were unable to create, who received guests to pass the time. Because these women were educated, they suffered more over what they lacked than had their seventeenth-century predecessors. "You do not and cannot know on your own," Mme. du Deffand wrote to Voltaire, "the state of those who think, who reflect, who engage in certain activities and who are nevertheless without talent, occupation, or amusement . . . I have no resources against boredom. I suffer from the misfortune of a neglected education. Ignorance makes old age that much heavier; its weight seems unbearable to me." Voltaire consoled his friend by praising "the noble pleasure of feeling oneself to be of a different nature from the fools" but above all by telling her that what she was doing, namely, leading her life in society, was the only possible remedy: "Your only choice is to continue to gather your friends around you. The comfort and security of conversation is a pleasure as real as that of a rendezvous in youth." A rendezvous of the mind was indeed the only pleasure that remained when the body ceased to be attractive. But Mme. du Deffand still was not happy. She continued to believe that the only happy people were those born with talent, because they did not need the talents of others: "They take their good fortune with them everywhere and can forgo everything." This illusion would be dispelled, much to Mme. du Deffand's dismay, by another woman.

This woman was the pure product of a salon that was itself a pure product of the eighteenth century: the salon of Mme. Necker. There one found people who could not have been found at Mme. de Rambouillet's: political and economic theorists, philosophers, scholars, polemicists, and a fair sprinkling of foreigners created a cosmopolitan atmosphere that was one of the most notable features of the age. At the Neckers' cosmopolitanism began with the master and mistress of the household. Madame was from the Swiss canton of Vaud, and her first love had been the Englishman Edward Gibbon. Monsieur was a German from Geneva who was said to be a man whose only country was an adopted one. The two spent most of their life in Paris and married their daughter to a Swede.

The daughter of a pastor (in itself a tremendous advantage), Suzanne Necker had received a fairly good education and as a young woman was already the pride of a small literary academy in Lausanne. Settling in Paris after her marriage to the young banker Necker, she found herself at sea in a capital and a social circle whose heady, brilliant, at times frivolous tone contrasted so strongly with the habits she had acquired as a young girl in Switzerland. But she adapted because she wanted to help her husband in his career. She loved him, and he loved her—a rare situation. It was the dawn of a golden age for financiers, who in fact already controlled society but who, if they hoped to win the respect that was still only grudgingly accorded them, did best to entertain guests and subsidize artists. Mme. Necker therefore devoted her energies to establishing a salon. Scrupulous to a fault, she prepared for every occasion and jotted down remarks to make during dinner: "I shall speak to the Chevalier de Chastellux about *La félicité publique* and *Agathe,* to Mme. d'Angiviller about love . . . Praise M. Thomas again for his poem on Jumonville." Mme. Necker's "day" was chosen carefully so as not to conflict with Mme. Geoffrin's Mondays and Wednesdays, Helvétius' Tuesdays, and the Baron d'Holbach's Thursdays and Sundays. That left only Friday, and it is hard to see how authors running from salon to salon ever found time to work. But in a world without radio or television, where else could they publicize their works or obtain financial backing?

Mme. Necker sat on a wooden stool, which obliged her to

hold her back straight, and at her feet often sat a little girl named Germaine, the Neckers' only child. Perhaps she was admitted at so early an age into her mother's salon because she was an only child. She kept silent, as was only proper, but when one of the regulars approached to ask about her studies or her reading, she answered with a grace that was surprising at first but gradually ceased to be so as people grasped the exceptional quality of Germaine's intelligence. "Glowworms," Mme. Necker said, "are like women. As long as they remain in the dark, one is struck by their brilliance. The minute they try to come out in broad daylight, one pours scorn on them and sees only their faults." Germaine, however, seems to have been unwilling to settle for the feeble brilliance of the glowworm. With the discreet support of her father (and this interest in his child, this complicity between father and daughter, was a sign of the times), Germaine became the central attraction of the Necker salon, outshining even her mother. She disrupted the conversations that Mme. Necker so conscientiously organized with her diligently kept notes. While the "fundamental discussion" went on among the great men in attendance, Germaine chatted with lesser personages in a corner of her own. But her talk was so interesting and witty that one after another of the great men—Buffon, Marmontel, Grimm, Diderot, Gibbon, Bernardin de Saint-Pierre—left the group they were supposed to be part of in order to be with her. Her answers to their questions drew still other guests. Not even Necker could stop himself from listening with one ear to his daughter's conversation and smiling at what she said.

Even after her marriage to the Swedish ambassador in 1786, Germaine remained a fixture of her mother's salon. The only difference was that now she was known as Mme. de Staël. Except for beauty, she possessed a combination of advantages enjoyed by few other girls: money, the affection of her parents, a place in society, a royal minister for a father, and, most important of all, education and talent. When times changed—radically, in 1789—she also had the opportunity to fall in love, to publish under her own name, and to derive fame from her work. And yet she was not happy. Mme. du Deffand and other *salonnières* died too early to read this dispiriting and hopeless sentence in *Corinne:* "Glory for a woman is but dazzling sorrow for the loss of happiness."

TRANSLATED FROM THE FRENCH BY ARTHUR GOLDHAMMER

13

Female Journalists

Nina Rattner Gelbart

FEMALE JOURNALISTS WERE rare in early
modern Europe. They needed extraordinary courage, for they meant to be career women in an age
that sanctioned no such thing. They hoped, that
is, to exercise a profession independently and with
dignity and to be taken seriously by contemporaries of both sexes. Profit was not their sole motive, although they aspired to support themselves
honorably. They were determined to prove their
capability and thus gain and maintain a following.
But at a time when society demanded that women
be merely ornamental or of service in only the
domestic and reproductive spheres, this kind of
ambition broke all the rules.

Journalism was a child of the mid-seventeenth
century, and almost from the start women had a
small but not negligible presence in the world of
the periodical press, whose power to affect public
opinion they sensed right away. Papers edited by
women appeared sporadically during the next century. Many of them had only an ephemeral existence. An exception was the *Journal des Dames,*
launched in 1759; lasting nearly two decades, it
was the longest-lived periodical by and for women
anywhere in Europe before the French Revolution.
Dutch, Italian, and German women seem to have
involved themselves relatively little in journalism

until the end of the eighteenth century. In England and France, however, journalism had a feminine component throughout the early modern period. This essay will therefore concentrate on the remarkable women in these two nations who turned to this challenging and often thankless career.

Before looking at individual cases, however, we should pose a few general questions to keep in mind throughout our survey. How gender-conscious were these uncommon journalists? Did they practice rather than preach feminism simply by living bold and unconventional lives, or did a real feminist consciousness—a recognition of and attack on female subordination—manifest itself in their writings? What sorts of strategies did they invent and deploy to placate male rivals, circumvent intransigent royal censors, woo their audiences? Do we hear a consistent female voice in these papers by women, and if so, how does it differ from that of men? What is the significance of the various ways women editors presented and defined themselves? What were their relations with their male colleagues? with other women? Of course we cannot answer all these questions in every case; we are dealing with idiosyncratic publications that tended to be short-lived and shaped by what their exceptionally colorful editors wished to say or try rather than by any true perception of what a female audience wanted. Some of these papers also included considerable reader participation, and so did not always accurately reflect editorial policy. And rarely did female journalists seem aware of their predecessors, so separated were they in time and space; consequently no real sense of solidarity, continuity, self-conscious sisterhood or professionalism developed among these women. Still, such questions challenge us to find meaning in these brave lives and to suggest lines for further inquiry.

England

During the period of strong monarchy in England from the Restoration through Queen Anne's reign, debate was animated and intense in Parliament, where neither the Whigs nor the Tories predominated for more than a few years at a time. In these years the public followed each parliamentary session with interest, unable to predict who would be more persuasive or when a particular ministry might topple. A habit of political awareness, involvement, even participation developed in listeners and readers; and the new periodical press capitalized on this notion of the audience as arbiter, as a group whose opinion was enlightened and could even affect the course of things. Both men and women were assumed to be informed and sophisticated. John Dunton, whose *Athenian Mercury* appealed to a general readership, created *The Ladies' Mercury* in 1693 to encourage the growing market of female readers. John Tipper's *Ladies' Diary* was edited by a math teacher, who filled his paper with puzzles, computations, and brain teasers to show his faith in women's clear judgments, sprightly quick wit, and penetrating genius. Richard Steele and Joseph Addison also strongly encouraged women to read their papers. The *Tatler, Spectator,* and *Guardian* meant to cultivate and polish human life for both sexes.

In this atmosphere of esteem for women as thinking beings, some soon tried their hand at editing papers in their own right. The first to do so was Mary de la Rivière Manley, whose *Female Tatler* appeared in 1709 edited by the pseudonymous Mrs. Crackenthorpe. Mrs. Manley's father had provided her with a good education, and she grew up unencumbered by the deferential attitude forced upon most girls. An ardent Tory, her satirical paper was an exposé of intrigue and scandal among the Whig leaders currently in power. Arrested and silenced for libel, Mrs. Manley reluctantly turned her paper over to a "society of modest ladies" who proceeded to render it entirely insipid. Jail, though physically painful, did not break her spirit. Upon her release from prison Jonathan Swift, who liked her politics, hired her to take over his *Examiner* and to write a number of political pamphlets. Disparaged by some as a mere "female wit," Mrs. Manley was greatly respected by Swift, who simply accepted her as a fellow writer. She resented being labeled and prosecuted as a "slanderer," for she believed her writings helped save her country from corruption. The dominant literary form of the period was satire, yet she felt hers was regarded as more threatening, coming as it did from the pen of a female. Lamenting that what was not a crime in men was considered scandalous and unpardonable in women, after Queen Anne's death and the total rout of the Tories she turned her literary talents to writing about love, claiming now that politics was no business for a woman. Such disclaimers, false modesty, and changes of topic were strategic, for she needed to earn a livelihood as a writer despite the fact that her former fierce foes, the Whigs, were now in power (and would keep it for forty years). This tactical use of self-effacement was one of the few coping devices available to intellectually ambitious women. Mrs. Manley did not devote her journalism to feminist issues, but she certainly knew how unprecedented was her undertaking and what kinds of ploys were necessary for survival.

Ann Dodd was the major distributor in 1721 of the opposition *London Journal*. A political and religious radical, she was frequently pursued by the authorities but was also adept at gaining release on the plea of illness, the dependence of her large family upon her, or even her ignorance of the contents of the papers she sold. But she knew exactly what she was about, and believed deeply that liberty and learning went hand in hand, that readers of both sexes should be told the facts, however unflattering, about their rulers, and thus develop independence of mind.

In 1737 Lady Mary Wortley Montagu, an aristocratic Whig supporter, put out a weekly political essay paper called *The Nonsense of Common Sense*. She wrote anonymously, considering it unseemly for a noble to enter a moneymaking profession. Most famous for having imported the notion of smallpox inoculation from Turkey to Europe, Lady Montagu had watched with satisfaction as that enlightened medical practice spread, and was therefore fully aware of the influential social role women could play. She was friendly with the pioneer feminist Mary Astell, who had proposed a women's college, and in her paper Lady Montagu championed female education, attacked frivolity and extravagance, and generally mixed politics with a truly feminist message. Thus she both practiced and preached the importance of educated, active women in the world.

Eliza Haywood is probably the best-known English female journalist. Her *Female Spectator* (1744–1746) enjoyed great popularity not only in England but also in other European countries and even across the Atlantic in the colonies, especially in New York, Pennsylvania, and Connecticut. It was frequently reedited in book form and was so successful that insecure male writers tried to defame their female competitor as a "stupid, infamous, scribbling woman." By the 1740s the political climate in England had changed. The Hanoverians George I and II spoke little English and relinquished much of their monarchical influence; as a result power shifted from the crown to the Whigs, who completely dominated Parliament. The once lively debate between the two parties had subsided, and journalism had become less political. The *Female Spectator,* reflecting these developments, dealt with other subject matter, including marriage, morality, philosophy, geography, history, and mathematics. The editor and three other anonymous female journalists encouraged their readers to abandon masquerading and gaming for reading and stretching their minds in other ways. Mrs. Haywood aimed, she said, to bring learning into fashion. In her next paper, *Epistles for the Ladies* (1749–50), she stressed that scientific study was wholesome and natural for women. Microscopy was particularly encouraged, on the grounds that discoveries of tiny, hitherto unseen organisms could win for women pleasure, honor, perhaps even "deathless fame." Mothers were urged to teach their daughters science as early as they taught them religious doctrine, for awareness of nature's wonders apprehended through the microscope and telescope could only enhance a young person's admiration and love for the Creator. Thus Mrs. Haywood's papers cast women in the roles of mother, teacher, and scientific amateur. The editor herself apparently did some original microscopic research. But she certainly did not advocate careers for all women. Large portions of her papers were devoted to how women could find an appropriate mate. Even here, however, the emphasis was on seriousness, on eschewing vanity and frivolity for a steady, lasting relationship built upon common interests and trust. Although their proper place was in the home, women must train themselves to think and reason responsibly.

In the *Lady's Museum* (1760–61) Charlotte Lennox, an Irish novelist and good friend of Samuel Johnson, also tried artfully to cajole fair readers into seriousness. Brains and beauty were entirely compatible in her pages. After Lennox, however, female journalists seem to have faded from the English scene. Even the women who had been active in other capacities in publishing periodicals—the hawkers who had sold unlicensed pamphlets; the "mercuries" who had bought papers wholesale and seen to their distribution; the groups who organized "congers," networks to protect multiple press enterprises too vulnerable to stand on their own—were less visible and vocal after 1760. The men who took over, with their "magazines for the ladies," were far less encouraging to women with intellectual ambitions, mocking "bluestockings" and stressing fashion first and foremost. These male papers for women represent the trivialization of womanhood that Mary Wollstonecraft, at the end of the eighteenth century, would so vociferously deplore. Female journalists in England had risked and endured surveillance by spies, harassment, pursuit by government authorities, even prison. They had always aroused suspicion for their unorthodox conduct and calling. How and why they allowed themselves to be effectively displaced and excluded after 1760 would be an interesting problem to investigate, especially as this was a period of great journalistic vigor for women in France.

France

French women entered journalism in the heady days of the Fronde, less than two decades after the first newspaper, the *Gazette de France* with its official absolutist message, had appeared in 1631. Opposition papers surfaced everywhere during that antiroyalist rebellion, and a few of these targeted women, starred female interlocutors, and were probably even written by women. The *Gazette des Halles, Le Babillard,* and the *Gazette de la Place Maubert* featured a certain "Dame Denise." Often written in patois and read aloud, these papers aimed at a broad audience meant to include the largely illiterate lower classes and especially the fishwives.

The first French woman we know of who sought to establish a paper was Marie-Jeanne L'Heritier. In 1703 she conceived a publication to be called *L'Erudition Enjouée ou Nouvelles Savantes. Satiriques et Galantes Ecrites à une Dame Française Qui Est à Madrid,* intended as a protest against pedantic "doctoral" literary criticism and as a more individualistic, subjective approach to belles lettres and other matters of taste. However, this attempt to establish a female critical tradition never materialized.

Next came Mme. Anne-Marguerite Petit Dunoyer (1663–1719), a Protestant from Nîmes who settled in Holland after the breakup of a stormy marriage to a French Catholic. Very concerned about finding good husbands for her daughters—one of whom had a liaison with the young Voltaire when he visited La Haye in 1713—she had nothing but trouble from would-be sons-in-law, who abused her daughters, squandered her assets, and even tried to assassinate her. She had especially disapproved of Voltaire, who later repaid his *belle-mère manquée* by disparaging both her character and her literary endeavors and by attempting to turn her daughter against her. Much of this was described in Mme. Dunoyer's *Mémoires* and in *Lettres Historiques et Galantes,* her first journal (1707–1717), in a style of blunt candor that attracted numerous readers. She finally found financial security as editor of a paper in La Haye called the *Quintessence des Nouvelles,* which she directed from 1711 to 1719 and which by her own account brought her honor, money, and renown.

Partly as a result of Mme. Dunoyer's resentment of Louis XIV's revocation of the Edict of Nantes, the tone of the *Quintessence* was rather anti-French and strongly advocated freedom of conscience. Appearing twice weekly, its combination of news and gossip was a highly successful confection. The government, however, accused the author of libel on several occasions, charging her among other things with having translated Mary de la Rivière Manley's scandalous 1709 work, *Secret Memoirs . . . from the New Atlantis,* into French in 1713.

Mme. Dunoyer's paper was fascinating and entirely unique. Aptly reflecting its full title *(Quintessence des Nouvelles Historiques Critiques, Politiques, Morales et Galantes),* it was a blend of many genres. It reported not only current news but also accounts of adventures, curiosities, trials, accidents, catastrophes, crimes, riots, tempests, fires, and festivals. These "human interest" features were part reality and part fiction, and in them women, particularly *grandes dames* at court, were writ large. Mme. Dunoyer's imaginative coverage focused on people rather than on abstract issues. She worked without collaborators, used a wide variety of sources, including manuscript *nouvelles à la main,* and praised herself constantly in fictitious letters to the editor.

What were her intentions? She claimed to want to feature news especially, but news was often dismal, so she compensated by concocting a more cheerful version that would both inform and amuse her readers. Combining the public and particular, the distant and the personal, she frequently transfigured much of the news and passed fiction off as fact. Thus she made politics personal, more particular than public. Her narratives were a lively, warm rearrangement and embellishment of reality, linking political events and well-known literary characters with whom her readers would be familiar. Sometimes she provided alternative outcomes to news stories from which her readers might choose. She was always personally present, and her bold use of fantasy enhanced her sense of self-importance. The freedom with which she crossed from history to literature and back again shows an almost modern sensitivity to the vast subjective component of "fact," to the many unwarranted speculations that often masquerade as truth.

Mme. Dunoyer had a free, daring, wildly original approach. She took more liberties with journalistic conventions than did any other editor, male or female. Yet she never saw herself as a spokesperson for her sex. She did not write expressly for women, and indeed seemed to wish to avoid the double jeopardy of being a female editor addressing or rallying a female audience. Mlle. Marie Anne Barbier's *Saisons Litteraires* (1714) also sought the protection of a gender-neutral title, although it had both feminist and populist inclinations. The anonymous author of *La Spectatrice* (1728–29), whom we cannot even be entirely sure was female, aspired to the objectivity of a hermaphrodite. Mme. Le Prince de Beaumont's *Nouveau Magasin Français* (1750–1752) was again addressed to a mixed audience and had no particular feminist perspective. Not until the *Journal des Dames* did a paper make a bold commitment "par et pour les dames."

The monthly *Journal des Dames* lasted on and off from 1759 to 1778 and had nine successive editors. During its lifetime the *Journal* changed profoundly, although it was always priced far lower than most of the literary monthlies, at twelve livres a year. Originally conceived by its male founder, a staunch royalist, as an innocuous bauble to amuse society ladies at their toilette, in its last years, under Louis-Sébastien Mercier, the paper was flagrantly *frondeur*. In between, from October 1761 to April 1775, a succession of three female editors transformed a politically conformist *rien délicieux* into a serious oppositional publication addressing social issues, preaching reform, and challenging its readers to think, to abandon vanity and nourish their minds. Well before it was turned over to men with revolutionary sympathies, the paper came under serious scrutiny by the censors.

The *Journal des Dames* evidently had between three hundred and a thousand subscribers over its lifetime. Subscription lists showing who its readers were have been lost because the journal changed hands so frequently. But if we interpret the occasional advertisement or letter to the editor as consumer feedback, we can conclude that the social composition of the paper's audience broadened during its twenty years, from a pampered elite to a more practical-minded readership.

The three female editors had high hopes and higher expectations for their readers. The first one, who blamed men for having kept women in bondage, printed impassioned pleas for feminine equality. Women were not galvanized into action, however; in fact, a major drop in circulation indicates that her fiery rhetoric scared away many subscribers. Her two successors were more realistic. Realizing that wide-ranging social and political change would be necessary before women could be granted agency, these editors accepted help and support from male reformers and radicals. Though forced to work within the old system, courting patrons and protectors and placating censors, they aided and abetted men who were busy fomenting its overthrow. They especially lent their support to, and accepted the help of, many *frondeurs,* men who identified strongly with the Fronde, that "revolution manquée" that raised serious constitutional challenges to French absolutism and brought together in a fleeting but explosive alliance princes and princesses of the blood, magistrates, and city mobs. The *Journal des Dames*'s *frondeur* ideology bothered the authorities as much as if not more than the paper's feminist claims.

Mme. de Beaumer, the first *journaliste des Dames,* took over the paper from its timid founders in October 1761 and initiated its nonconformist tone. She was an enigma even to her contemporaries who, unable to discover anything about her personal life, depicted her as lacking fortune, beauty, and grace but full of determination. Almost surely she was a Huguenot with a close Dutch connection. Her radical tendencies had surfaced earlier in the cryptonymous *Lettres Curieuses, Instructives et Amusantes,* a short-lived periodical launched in The Hague in 1759 in which she denounced French newspaper censors as a detestable brood of scoundrels and praised freedom of the press in Holland. Mme. de Beaumer perceived French royal censors and book police as threats to the accomplishment of her mission. For she was prime Bastille material. A champion of women's abilities, she also crusaded for the poor and oppressed, for social justice, religious toleration, Freemasonry, republican liberty, international peace, and equality before the law. Once back in France, she faced obstacles erected by the authorities; several censors refused manuscripts she proposed. Desperate to get her message to the world, she adopted a more oblique course and took over the *Journal des Dames,* which under the ownership of male royalists had acquired a reputation for tameness and was beyond political suspicion.

Knowing that the censors would muzzle her again at the earliest opportunity, Mme. de Beaumer adopted an urgent tone and a frontal, demanding, belligerent approach in the few issues she could publish before being caught. She needed to show nothing less than that the subjugation of women was a universal tragedy, that mutual respect between the sexes would lead to the same between social classes and eventually between nations, that a revolution in *moeurs* would thus result in social harmony and international peace. Even if only briefly, she now had listeners, a captive audience of subscribers.

She argued that the honor of the French nation was intimately linked to the continuation of the *Journal des Dames* now that a woman was its editor. Insisting that they could think, speak, study, analyze, and criticize as well as men, she urged women to become bold. She called for a "revolution" in female consciousness and vowed to be one of those to precipitate it. She printed challenging articles, literary criticism, *eloges* of great women, and lists of obscure female artists, merchants, artisans, and musicians from the lower classes. This abundance of capable, talented women, who were everywhere and too numerous to name, seemed to confirm all her arguments. Here was a ready, energetic social force waiting to be tapped and challenged.

Mme. de Beaumer, who may have been a Mason herself—a lodge admitting both men and women existed in The Hague, where she spent a good deal of time—embraced the Masonic vision of universal harmony vigorously and literally. Convinced that her message applied to all people in all places, she advertised a list, filling several pages, of eighty-one cities in France, the German states, Switzerland, Holland, Spain, Italy, Portugal, Russia, Sweden, and England where the *Journal des Dames* was for sale. No other paper had anything like it. In fact the list was entirely fictitious, for while the zealous Mme. de Beaumer may indeed have sent copies of her paper to the booksellers named in the list, no such market existed. But the very possibility that her journal was internationally popular troubled the authorities, who delayed some issues and eventually suspended the paper, with catastrophic financial consequences for its editor. Even her residence in the *enclos du Temple*, a protected neighborhood where police and creditors could not penetrate and where she had composed her bold copy, could no longer protect Mme. de Beaumer. Nor could the Huguenot Jaucourt family who had supported her. The censor and Malesherbes, the booktrade director, demanded that she atone by writing a *histoire militaire* glorifying soldiers to demonstrate her patriotism. The feminist pacifist fled to Holland instead.

Although Mme. de Beaumer's passionate pleas failed to galvanize women—in fact circulation dropped—a few loyal readers encouraged her feminist vision. One even urged her to reclaim the French language from the men who had ravished it. Asserting that it was a dishonor for women that such words were not in common parlance, this reader suggested that her unique position gave her the right to use and make acceptable the feminized form of *author* and *editor.* Delighted to accept the innovations of her sympathetic neologist, Mme. de Beaumer henceforth referred to herself as *autrice* and *editrice,* reminding her readers that she loved her sex and resolved to support and vindicate its honors and its rights. Evidence suggests that after leaving France she visited Lady Montagu in England, and conversations with Dutch friends further helped to persuade her that women were on the brink of a social and intellectual breakthrough. She resolved to return to Paris to reclaim her paper.

Her censor Marin, chagrined by her reappearance, at once sent a letter to Malesherbes reporting that she had shown up that morning in his chambers, a large hat on her head, a long sword at her side, her chest (where he noted there was nothing) and her behind (where he noted there was not much) covered by a worn, narrow men's habit. This levity reflected not only misogyny but also political anxiety, for Marin had come to view "the Beaumer woman" as an offense to public morality, a writer of uncommon rashness and singular indiscretion. He now tried to force her to turn the paper into a fashion magazine, to which she responded with a fierce diatribe; she could not repudiate the principles of a lifetime. Realizing that her transgressions of the codes of feminine modesty prevented her from effective operation but determined to preserve the *Journal des Dames* as an essential channel of female communication, she relinquished it before leaving permanently for Holland to another woman, one sufficiently well connected to win the authorities' blessing yet daring enough to lend her name to the increasingly *frondeur* fare of her male collaborators.

This successor, Mme. de Maisonneuve, took an altogether different but equally courageous approach. Financially well off, she had been bored with idleness until challenged to use her social station to make the *Journal des Dames* a success. Soon she and her paper became beneficiaries of monarchical largesse: she was made a *pensionnaire du roi* to the tune of a thousand livres a year, and in June 1765 Mme. de Maisonneuve had the honor of presenting the paper personally to the king at Versailles. In less than three years she quadrupled the worth of the previously moribund *Journal des Dames* and transformed it into a thriving business, sound enough to attract the canny Charles-Joseph Panckoucke, who published only successful enterprises.

The secrets of Mme. de Maisonneuve's success were a confident, measured tone, an infallible sense of timing, and the ability to treat piquant issues within fashionable limits, balancing spice and respectability. Avoiding her predecessor's pugnacious rhetoric, she produced a pleasing confection with plentiful *pièces fugitives* supplied by a band of young male writers. In 1766, however, the paper's honeymoon period ended. The *Mercure,* a government-supported periodical that was losing subscribers to the *Journal des Dames,* enforced its royal right to make its competitor less appealing by restricting its contents. At this point Mme. de Maisonneuve gave the paper over to her primary helper, Mathon de la Cour, though retaining her name on the title page and the right to continue presenting the paper to "the crowned heads of Europe." Mathon, with her blessing, abandoned the goal of pleasing the readers and used the paper far more boldly, filling it with articles praising Spartan and Roman values, featuring the republican ideas of Rousseau, attacking *le luxe* and courtly extravagance. He especially admired the writings of the young Louis-Sébastien Mercier, whom he found fresh, vigorous, gutsy, intense. Mercier's banned works, denouncing tyranny, social inequality, and the hoarding of grain for profit while peasants starved, were published in the *Journal des Dames.*

Mme. de Maisonneuve had continued to lend her name to the paper throughout Mathon's progressive rebelliousness, as he supported the parlements against the crown's "despotism." But in the late 1760s the political climate changed. The minister Choiseul, whose wife's friendship and patronage had helped Mme. de Maisonneuve advance the *Journal*'s fortunes, lost power, and the new chancellor, René-Nicolas Maupeou, was an ardent royalist determined to crush the parlements. As much for Mathon's protection as her own, Mme. de Maisonneuve allowed her paper to be suppressed without protesting. So long as Maupeou and his despotic "triumvirate" of ministers reigned, the *Journal des Dames* remained silent.

The last female editor of the *Journal,* the Baronne de Princen, later known as Mme. de Montanclos, was as ambitious and independent as Mme. de Beaumer but took a distinctly more maternal line. Familiar with court circles through her first husband, an extravagant German baron, she dedicated her *Journal des Dames* to the adolescent dauphine Marie-Antoinette. The dauphine spent her idle hours enjoying plays by Beaumarchais and Mercier, seemingly oblivious to their revolutionary potential, to the vengeful anger hidden in the comic poet's laughter and the dramatist's tears. The Baronne de Princen, a fervent fan of Mercier, found a malleable censor and relaunched the *Journal des Dames* in 1774 as Maupeou and his "triumvirate" were losing power.

At first the editor did all she could to flatter Marie Antoinette, but after she married M. de Montanclos and left Versailles to return to Paris, she gradually distanced herself from prevailing court values and focused more on issues of motherhood, directing her paper increasingly to women who were, like herself, *meres de familles*. Mme. de Montanclos's feminism was more complex, subtle, and many-sided than that of her two predecessors, who appear to have been childless. Whereas they had disliked Rousseau, for example, Mme. de Montanclos believed that he had done a great deal for feminine self-esteem, by making women feel socially useful. Although he disapproved of intellectual females, he put women in charge of the moral regeneration of society, for mothers not only cemented their families but provided the ethical backbone of the *patrie*. Through the home, the mother's sphere, she made her invaluable civic contribution.

The *Journal des Dames* now discussed children as it never had before. They were joyful, precious little beings with whom it was a pleasure, even a privilege, to spend time. Mme. de Montanclos treated motherhood as a right that women had to reclaim and show themselves worthy of exercising. It was an awesome responsibility, but not a burden. Teaching children could even be a shared delight. Much coverage was given to the education of girls.

Yet Mme. de Montanclos also upheld the very non-Rousseauist notion that women should be able to pursue careers if they so chose. She gave the example of Laura Bassi, a determined bourgeoise who earned a doctorate in physics and a teaching post at the University of Bologna. The editor hoped that soon enough women everywhere would attain scholarly recognition that their achievements would no longer be considered extraordinary. She rejoiced that at last careers were open to both sexes. This radical position went far beyond what Eliza Haywood had advocated. The four most prominent female journalists in Germany, writing nearly a decade after Mme. de Montanclos, confined even "thinking women's" goals to the home. Mme. de Montanclos agreed that motherhood was of prime importance, but considered intellectual activity and recognition necessary too. Nevertheless, her severe criticisms of their work discouraged several of her female contributors.

For many years Mme. de Montanclos was helped behind the scenes by Mercier, whose energy and politics she admired. In 1775 she sold the paper to him for a song, believing that the author of the prophetic *L'An 2440* could shape a better future for humankind. Her last issue of the *Journal des Dames,* produced jointly with Mercier, dealt head-on with such issues as the grain famine; praise for the new finance minister, Turgot; the liberties enjoyed by the English; the importance of eliminating the hated *corvée;* and expanding human freedom. Mme. de Montanclos, like her two female predecessors, had come to regard the press as an instrument to lift both men and women out of ignorance and subjection.

The fact that none of the female editors of the *Journal des Dames* held her post very long should not detract from their accomplishment. Journalism was no career for the easily daunted. Most men found it thankless, and the well-known *salonnières* and *femmes de lettres* of the day scorned it, or were perhaps afraid to attempt it. Unlike the authors of books, journalists wanted immediate, frequent, frontal, repeated, and reciprocal contact with a broad social spectrum of readers. The *editrices* of the *Journal* had lofty intentions and believed they could better the lot of women; they also hoped to show by their own example that women could manage a very public career. The range of strategies they were forced to develop to keep the paper afloat reflects the enormous difficulties they encountered.

After the *Journal des Dames,* a few more female journalists appeared briefly on the scene, but none addressed herself to creating a serious journal "par et pour les femmes." In 1778 Mme. Charlotte Chaumet, Presidente D'Ormoy, took over the *Journal de Monsieur,* but her editorship lasted only a few years. Mme. Adelaide Gillette Dufrenoy took over the *Courrier Lyrique et Amusant* in 1787. Mme. Dufrenoy and her husband helped to hide and provide asylum for many of their pursued friends during the Revolution, but the paper she edited, full of music and poems, was not permitted to treat weighty political matters. The Revolution only brought an increasingly inhospitable climate for women journalists.

How are we to evaluate the initiative of these first female editors? On the one hand, their brief tenures and failures make them appear inadequate to their task; on the other, their bold rallying cries and their attempts to use their papers to forge a link among women make them seem heroic and centuries ahead of their time. Social forces worked to keep women in their "proper" reproductive sphere. As Mary Wollstonecraft would later articulate quite boldly, men found uneducated women sexually more docile; it was in their interest to keep their playthings ignorant. Well-off women were denied meaningful activities outside the home, were not encouraged or even permitted to follow their talents and state their ambitions. The female editors rebelled against this. Nearly all of them took on their jobs as journalists to escape the emptiness and purposelessness of their former lives.

The relations between these female journalists and their male colleagues were dynamic and at times very stimulating, marked by constant play and interplay, considerable mutual respect, dissidence but also strategies to avoid arousing indignation. When necessary many adopted a deferential attitude in order to get into print. Some men envied and resented the license enjoyed by female journalists as a result of such disclaimers. Many male journalists, including Elie-Catherine Freron, assumed female identities for a time to see if the public would be more indulgent of their efforts. Few women in this period took male names—that was a later phenomenon—but some kept their true identities secret. This masking and role playing, this reversal of male and female voice in a kind of journalistic Saturnalia, certainly merits further investigation. The relations between female editors and colleagues and readers of their own sex were also complicated. Those who were not particularly indulgent of their female contributors wounded them and were resented. Mme. de Beaumer, on the other hand, who had the highest expectations and counted on her readers to join her in aggressive republicanism and sisterhood, found herself wounded and resentful when disappointed by them. These women sought to live independently in a system based on dependence, but they could never rally significant feminine support. Professionally, they inevitably found themselves having to compromise with men.

Yet in their private lives all of them seem to have had highly irregular domestic arrangements. Mrs. Manley's romantic escapades were legendary. Eliza Haywood walked away from her marriage after just a few years. Lady Montagu, at age fifty, left her ambassador husband to elope with her Italian lover, a writer and dilettante of twenty-five. Mme. Dunoyer fled Holland to escape a spouse who failed to support her. The anonymous Spectatrice looked upon marriage as the ultimate indignity and bondage and aspired to permanent celibate status. In going so far as to claim the gender-neutrality of a hermaphrodite, this editor also enjoyed the freedom won by the concealment of identity, and thus the protection of total privacy. Mme. Le Prince de Beaumont, who had six children, was rumored to have moved through a succession of three equally shiftless husbands. Mme. de Beaumer, living alone in a furnished room in the Temple, appears to have shed her mate if she had ever had one. Mme. de Maisonneuve never assumed her husband's name and lived most of her life in seemingly contented widowhood. Mme. de Montanclos, though she married again after her first husband's death, was separated almost immediately. These facts indicate an intolerance among ambitious women for the strictures of eighteenth-century marriage, which obliterated their status as legal individuals; husbands could control not only their property, assets, and person but also their ability to publish their writing. These bold, fiery women sought alternative lifestyles more suited to their unorthodox aspirations.

Here, then, was a group of women determined to have some impact on and in the public, patriarchal, political world. Mme. Le Prince de Beaumont, editor of the *Nouveau Magasin Français,* saw herself as one of an unknown number of women determined to prove that their sex had the capacity, indeed the obligation, to attain its own identity. Their efforts and struggles shed new light on the ideological, institutional, cultural, and of course sexual tensions of early modern European society.

Infractions, Transgressions, Rebellions

Women were not arrested for opinions uttered in a salon, no matter how outrageous; women who trespassed into the realms of male learning and made them their own could be dismissed as exceptional, "beyond their sex." Women who published daring proposals for reform could be simply answered or vilified in print, unless they courted arrest by straying into the dangerous areas of heresy and treason. But most women did not write books, and when those of less exalted birth, wealth, or education defied laws or flouted moral codes, they became real troublemakers. Not that husbands and brothers necessarily disapproved of their behavior: a magical healer or grain rioter was usually acting on behalf of her family. But their bodily actions, gestures, and intentions—born of need, misery, injustice, or desire—violated codes of modesty and order in fundamental ways. They were shameless and unruly, and evidence for their behavior comes mostly from the records of criminal courts.

Early modern authorities increased the chances for people, and especially for women, to be classified as troublemakers by criminalizing certain activities and treating others with new severity. Female prostitution had been legal in the medieval period, and Kathryn Norberg's essay describes its transformation in the course of the sixteenth century into a widely practiced but illicit occupation. The medieval theory had been that of the lesser evil: the imperious sexual desire of single men needed the outlet of a prostitute so they would not fall into gang rape, sodomy, or other transgressive intercourse. Prostitutes lived in regulated urban brothels under so-called abbesses, madams, or male supervisors and were marked off from respectable women by special garments; they had a formal role in civic ritual and paid special taxes to the city treasury. Prostitutes had a recognized, albeit dishonorable, place in society.

A cluster of concerns changed this arrangement, such as the

Protestant insistence that all men must marry; the Catholic
Counter-Reformation solicitude that the priests, frequent customers at bordellos, live up to their vows; family worries lest
sons squander their income; and the zeal of pious women to lift
their fallen sisters. By the end of the sixteenth century, prostitution was banned from most European cities. Norberg describes
its expansion in the next two hundred years, carried on by individual women, with or without the help of procuresses and
pimps, in their own rooms or in clandestine brothels. Vulnerable
to denunciation from neighbors and to arrest and imprisonment
in hospitals and asylums, the women plied their trade in the cities and made sorties into the countryside. Can prostitution be
looked at as a choice for women, rather than as a catastrophe?
Norberg suggests that it sometimes can. Prostitutes were part of
a sexual counterculture, especially in the medieval period, when
they were legal *filles de joie* (joyous girls) with clerics as their
customers. Overall in the seventeenth and eighteenth centuries
they were paid better for their work than were women confined
to domestic service or textile jobs. They emerge from the police
records as working women who had defied their parents and
decided to dispose of their bodies in their own way.

Fear of female sexuality was only one of the elements that
turned "witchcraft" into a demoniac heresy and a heinous crime
from the late fourteenth to the end of the seventeenth century.
Whereas in the early medieval period persons claiming occult
powers were dismissed by the clergy as having delusions, now
persons—most of them women—were accused of doing harm as
a result of a pact with the devil. Jean-Michel Sallmann describes
the shift as the work of late medieval clerics struggling with
many forms of heresy and threatened by the independence of
female spirituality and prophecy. By the end of the fifteenth century the new image had crystallized. Witches made men impotent and women infertile, destroyed crops and animals, snatched
or killed babies, and flew to the dances and orgies of the sabbath. With their disruptive anatomy and humours, their weak

wills and minds, their carnal lusts, and their Eve-like deceptiveness, women were inevitably more tempted by the devil than men. The image could fuel the envy and suspicion of villagers troubled by the population pressures and rural poverty of the late sixteenth and seventeenth centuries. And as a symbol par excellence of disorder, the female witch was a ready target for all those trying to strengthen clear-cut authority structures, political, religious, and professional.

But as Sallmann suggests, the witch hunt was more than an overdetermined pursuit of passive women and men. Witchcraft was also associated with transgression or disobedience. First, in the course of the trial itself, in the performance of accusation, confession, and possession, women made outrageous statements in public, claimed dangerous agency, and spoke with the voice of devils. They may have done this out of despair or as a result of torture, but nonetheless they were assuming a frightening capability. At these trials, unlike in ordinary criminal trials, women could not try to blame the initiative on husbands or male superiors, for in witchcraft cases women were assigned full legal responsibility for their actions.

Second, magical healing, helping, and harming and shamanistic communication with the dead had long gone on in rural Europe, performed by women and men along with more strictly Christian observances. As the image of witchcraft spread and as both Protestant and Catholic reformations turned against magical ritual as "superstition," these village practices were recast as diabolic or at least as strongly reproved. By the early seventeenth century, a woman who had been born with a caul or with some other mark of shamanistic destiny or who had been instructed by her mother in magical healing needed caution and courage to practice her art.

Sallmann reminds us that the early modern period was not only hard on witchcraft; it was also severe on homosexuality. With regard to intimate relations between persons of the same sex (what since the nineteenth century has been called "homosexuality" and "Lesbianism"), the double standard worked against the men. Already in the biblical condemnations, imperial Roman law codes, and early Christian penitentials, this asymmetry in evaluation appears: sex between men degraded the one who lowered himself to take the woman's part and would incapacitate them both for their rightful role as progenitors of children. "Unnatural" though it was, sex between women had neither of these perils, especially since to some male critics it seemed to lack the penetration that constituted the central evil of sodomy. In fact, as John Boswell has shown, in the early Middle Ages there was tolerance for the erotic relations between men (often young men or a teacher and pupil) that sprang up in monasteries and church schools; if vows of chastity were broken thus, it was less sinful, some claimed, than bringing wives to adultery or deflowering virgins.

By the late medieval period, along with attacks on lepers, heretics, Jews, and witches, this de facto tolerance came to an end even while evidence for sexual relations among men outside the clergy increased. In late fifteenth-century Florence, Savonarola inveighed against the unnatural behavior of young unmarried men with older libertines. In Henry VIII's England, "buggery" with man or beast became a felony punishable by death, and elsewhere in Europe severe penalties, from whipping and mutilation to death, were on the law books. Protestant reformers branded the Catholic clergy as sodomites when they did not brand them as fornicators, and the Catholic reformation, eager to give new sanctity to marriage and to a celibate clergy, proscribed the male lovers in their midst. Prosecution and punishment varied with time and place: the work of E. W. Monter has shown us that by the seventeenth century in Spain, the Inquisition was questioning homosexuals as often as secret Jews; in the republic of Geneva from 1555 to 1678, 50 men were tried for sodomy and half of them executed (as compared with 318 persons tried for witchcraft, three-quarters of them women, and one-fifth of them executed during roughly the same period).

Meanwhile sexual intercourse between women was the subject of ridicule and titillation, but prosecutions were infrequent and executions even more so, occurring primarily when a household with a transvestite "husband" was unmasked.

While judges and moralists were at work, the cultural organization of same-sex intercourse and love was slowly changing, as was the self-definition of practitioners. Among men homosexual customs and language had long been a variant of clerical culture. In the early modern period, homosexual action appears in Italy and beyond the Alps as a stage of life for some young men, experimenting with each other and at the beck and call of adult "sodomites." Whether sustained by gifts, favors, and festivities or by prostitution, these activities often involved both social and age domination over the young. By the early eighteenth century, in London, Amsterdam, and Paris, adult men were also seeking intimate contact with each other, and special networks, locations, and gestures were developed to that end. Most inventive were the private clubs—molly houses, as they were called in London—where men of different backgrounds, some married, some not, came together for affection, cross-dressing, play, and sex, a temporary effacement of the social and gender boundaries of the outside world.

The evolution was different among women drawn to "tribadism" or sapphic love. We get a glimpse of the clerical variant in Judith Brown's study of Sister Benedetta Carlini in early seventeenth-century Pescia: Benedetta's attentions to her sister religious Bartolomea were an extension of her spiritual expressiveness, carried out in a trance under the guise of an angel. Outside convents women concealed their distinctiveness in stable households with one of them dressed as a man; more daring women cross-dressed as soldiers or other adventurers, and had love affairs with women along the way. In the eighteenth century emerged an open sexual style based not on the hidden carnival of the molly house, but on the seemliness of married friendship. The Ladies of Llangollen, Eleanor Butler and Sarah Ponsonby, were the exemplars of the new mode: dressed somewhat androgynously but clearly women, they lived in egalitarian intimacy in a fine "cottage" in Wales, taking healthy walks, reading Rousseau aloud, and corresponding with important friends in London and abroad. Eleanor Butler was the older of the two, but there was no head of the family as in patriarchal marriage. The molly houses were subject to periodic raids and arrests; though attacked in a newspaper article titled "Extraordinary Female Affection," the Ladies remained respectable, their house a site of pilgrimage for those curious about their way of life.

If women got into less trouble than men for "unnatural" sexual behavior, Nicole Castan also shows that aside from charges involving sorcery, far fewer women than men (10 to 20 percent) were prosecuted for crimes in early modern Europe. Women's violence in the courts did not match women's potential for violence in images and discourse about gender. Most of the crimes occurred in or near women's world of family, children, sexuality, and female sociability: thefts, sometimes homicides of husbands out of jealousy, assaults on other women. Excused for theft to feed their children and diminished in their responsibility if they were under the tutelage of father or husband, women were ordinarily punished less severely than men. The law and the courts came down most harshly on women when family values were threatened: edicts in France (1557) and England (1624) made it much easier to get convictions for infanticide, and until the eighteenth century, it was punished by execution even more consistently than witchcraft. Thus the lubriciousness of unwed serving girls, on whom the blame for infanticide was laid, was used to remind families of their duty.

Arlette Farge's essay on women in public protests reveals an important realm of early modern politics. Popular riots were part of the moral economy of regimes that gave little or no voice to the lower orders, and women were in the forefront of those actions. Farge shows the adeptness with which women made their way through the city streets and dealt with royal sergeants in defense of their interests and those of their families. In street protests they displayed the same vigor and spirit as the men, fighting with bare hands and stones, leaving haunting images of female violence long after they had returned to the routine rhythms of their households. Farge concludes with the double image of blood, linking women to their bodies, to birth and to death, and connecting them in fearsome unity with men.

N.Z.D.—A.F.

14

Witches

Jean-Michel Sallmann

THE CONVICTION THAT the practice of demoniac sorcery was intimately associated with the female nature and, by extension, that every woman was potentially a witch long lay buried in the Western unconscious.[1] This stereotype came into being as best we can tell around 1400 and lasted, at least in criminal law, until the end of the seventeenth century. Nineteenth-century Romanticism revived interest in the subject through historical novels, paintings, operas, and anthologies of folk tales. The witch thus became part of the dark legend of a still little-known and largely mythical medieval period. In 1862 Jules Michelet published *La sorcière* (The Witch), a provocative book that is also an admirable hymn to womankind, in which he attacked this historical commonplace. His witch was neither ugly nor old, and she did no harm, being simply one of the incarnations of Woman, that is, the "mother, tender guardian and faithful nurse," that he made the central figure of his book—a victim and not a criminal. Yet in attempting to rehabilitate the image of the witch, Michelet shared a way of thinking whose effects he denounced and whose origins he blamed on the church, namely, the idea that there is a special connection between women and the occult powers.

Few subjects have proved as fascinating as sorcery. Over the past twenty years our understanding has been transformed, as if historians have suddenly realized that the subject constitutes a fundamental chapter in the cultural history of the West. Sorcery reveals a whole system of representation, a world view, involving the relation between humankind and supernatural forces as well as the respective roles of men and women in early modern societies. Although it would be impossible to recount such a complex history without certain necessary generalizations, we must also be careful to respect chronological and geographic differences.

"For Every Sorcerer, Ten Thousand Witches"

Statistical evidence confirms that allegations of sorcery involved mainly women. In Essex in southwestern England 91 percent of the 270 accused of sorcery in the courts of assizes between 1560 and 1680 were women. Judicial archives in what is now the Nord department of France record 288 cases of sorcery from the middle of the fourteenth to the end of the seventeenth century, and 82 percent of these involved women. Similar figures obtain for southern Germany and the Jura, where the repression of witchcraft began. In Baden-Würtemberg, for example, the authorities noted fifteen major "epidemics" of sorcery, which resulted in the execution of 1,050 sorcerers and witches between 1562 and 1684; of these, 82 percent were women. In a far-flung region that included the bishopric of Basel, the principality of Montbéliard, Franche-Comté, the Swiss cantons of Fribourg (Freiburg), Neuchâtel, Vaud, and Geneva, 1,060 of 1,365, or roughly 78 percent, of accusations of witchcraft between 1537 and 1683 involved women. In seventeenth-century New England, which can be regarded as a European outpost in the New World, there was a relatively late campaign to eradicate witchcraft. Of 355 persons accused between 1647 and 1725, 79 percent were women. The facts are clear: in the sixteenth and seventeenth centuries a woman was four times as likely as a man to be accused of and executed for witchcraft.

Inquisitors' manuals and later legal texts corroborate the association of women with the crime of sorcery. But they appear only toward the end of the fifteenth century, whereas the demonological myth—the belief in the existence of a devil-worshiping cult—dates from the very end of the fourteenth century, when the repression of sorcery began. The first mass trials of alleged witches and sorcerers took place from 1397 to 1406 at Boltinger, in the Swiss canton of Lucerne; others followed after 1428 in Valais and the Dauphiné. The intensity of the repression increased at midcentury. It was carried out at first by inquisitors, or ecclesiastical judges, joined in the sixteenth century by the secular courts. Under the terms of the papal bull *Summis desiderantes affectibus* (1484) Innocent VIII appointed two inquisitors, Jacob Sprenger and Heinrich Institoris, to stamp out sorcery in the middle Rhine Valley, thus giving papal sanction to the practice of hunting witches.

There are two schools of thought concerning the origins of the demonological myth. According to one, the myth simply reflected shamanistic traditions common to all Eurasian cultures since antiquity. According to the other, it was an intellectual construct pieced together by clerics from various commonplaces of medieval religious polemic. In any case, a major change in mental outlook occurred around the turn of the fifteenth century, resulting in the establishment of a system of representation that would persist for three centuries. People in the West became convinced that there existed within their midst a sect of sorcerers who had signed a pact with the devil. Endowed with evil powers, these sorcerers had the ability to do injury to both humankind and God. They were blamed for natural disasters that affected entire populations (epidemics, bad weather, poor harvests, plagues) as well as for misfortunes that befell certain individuals (unexplained deaths of children, sterility in women, impotence in men). Sorcerers were said to gather in nocturnal assemblies (called sabbaths or synagogues), during which they renounced the Catholic faith and worshiped the devil. Sabbaths ended with a great banquet at which children were devoured, followed by an orgy in which sorcerers coupled with demon succubi and witches with demon incubi. The existence of a sect, the apostasy toward the Christian faith, the cult of the devil, and ritual murder were all elements that contributed to making the demonological myth a heresy, indeed the most dreaded of all heresies because its aim was to overthrow the Christian religion and replace it with the religion of Satan.

In 1486 Jacob Sprenger and Heinrich Institoris (the latter being the actual sole author) published in Strasbourg the *Malleus maleficarum* (Hammer of Witches), a book destined to enjoy a remarkable success. The book established for the first time a direct connection between the heresy of witchcraft and women. In order to prove to readers what the authors' experience as inquisitors had taught them to regard as self-evident, it drew heavily on the central antifeminine tradition of the Old Testament, classical antiquity, and the Middle Ages. Though often imitated, the *Malleus maleficarum* has never been equaled. The great demonologists of the sixteenth century—the inquisitor Bernardo Rategno da Como, the Spanish Jesuit Martin Del Rio, and the French jurist Jean Bodin—appealed constantly to its authority.

The idea of woman's inferiority went back to Genesis, and more precisely to two episodes on which many theologians had commented: the creation of Eve and the Fall. God created Eve from Adam, and in the minds of many theologians this fact justified woman's submission to man. Indeed, the account of Eve's creation from Adam's rib, a curved bone, indicated that the mind of woman was inevitably twisted and perverse. The Fall proved that this was the case: Satan tempted Eve, and Eve seduced Adam and led him into sin. Woman was therefore directly responsible for the fall of man. Accordingly, the authors of the *Malleus maleficarum* saw only two things for which women were useful: they were needed for reproduction, because only they could bear children, and they were necessary to the household economy, for their loyalty and affection aided men in their work. But the sexuality of women was dangerous. For Christians, virginity remained an ideal, and marriage was simply the lesser of two evils because it helped laymen avoid the mortal sins of lust and fornication. The misogyny of the authors of the *Malleus maleficarum* was thus based on a very ancient Christian tradition. They readily accepted John Chrysostom's peremptory judgment of woman: "the enemy of friendship, the ineluctable pain, the necessary evil, the natural temptation, the desirable calamity, the domestic peril, the delectable scourge, nature's woe painted in bright colors." Such formulas were widely repeated in the Middle Ages. Institoris and Sprenger also called upon their personal experience as inquisitors and witch-hunters. They had observed that woman's rebellious nature and congenital weakness made her susceptible to devilish and evil temptations. There were three reasons why women were more likely than men to succumb to superstition. First, women were more credulous, so Satan primarily targeted them. Second, women were more impressionable and therefore more susceptible to manipulation by devilish illusions. Finally, women were garrulous and could not refrain from discussing what they knew about magic. Owing to their weakness they used this secret knowledge to avenge themselves on men by casting spells and curses.

The *Malleus maleficarum* gives the impression that witchcraft was simply a reflection of the war between the sexes, with aggressive witches on one side and men threatened in their reproductive capacities on the other. Several chapters of the book describe how witches sap the genital capacity of men and amputate their virile members; it suggests remedies against such attacks. Within a short time the image of the evil witch had taken hold throughout the West. The fear of witches was fueled by growing numbers of trials and burnings, which reinforced the popular belief that sorcery was practiced by women. But even though the Inquisition thus bears a heavy responsibility for fostering a stereotype whose consequences were so dramatic, not all inquisitors were fanatical monks. Heinrich Institoris was indeed a lifelong scourge of heretics, but Jacob Sprenger held many high posts in the Dominican order and devoted much of his energy to assisting the pope in reforming Dominican monasteries in the Rhineland; he was also a tireless promoter of the use of the rosary, especially by women. The two men simply expressed their contemporaries' anxieties and assumptions in a plausible, intellectual form influenced by their own background.

Among historians who have intensively explored the repression of witchcraft and the sudden increase of violence against women, it is generally agreed that the widespread perception of witchcraft was a manifestation of hard times and that the intensity of the repression reflected the severity of the natural disasters that befell the population. Still incapable of controlling nature, people turned to the supernatural to explain phenomena that otherwise surpassed their understanding. Epidemics, poor harvests, unexplained deaths, and other misfortunes were blamed on the devil. Historians have therefore resurrected the old scapegoat theory first developed by anthropologists in the late nineteenth century. Society needed guilty parties and found them in nonconformist and marginal groups, on which the repression took a heavy toll. Foremost among the victims were women: the oldest, the ugliest, the poorest, and the most aggressive women, those who inspired the greatest fear. Villagers discharged their tensions on the weakest elements of rural society. In 1595 the government of Philip II in the Spanish Netherlands issued a warrant stating that elderly women were to be treated as prime suspects in cases of sorcery.

The great fear that gripped the population of Europe in the late Middle Ages and after was compounded by social and economic factors. Changes in the structure of the family may have played an important role. Delays in marriage became more common after the turn of the sixteenth century, and increasingly strict sexual mores resulting from Protestant and Catholic reforms tended to frustrate young males, who were excluded from both the matrimonial market and the market for land. At the other end of the "age pyramid," widows were easy prey, encumbered as they often were with children and economic burdens; since remarriage was unlikely, they were also emotionally vulnerable. Thus in New England, in the cases of the women who composed 80 percent of those accused of witchcraft between 1647 and 1725, two-thirds of their accusers were men. Many of these alleged witches were women alone, without husbands, sons, or brothers, and their property, in default of heirs, was not subject to the usual rules of inheritance.

Another factor often cited in the proliferation of witch-hunting is the dramatic transformation of the Western European countryside that began in the late Middle Ages. The agricultural map was redrawn as small plots were combined into larger farms and certain ancient communal privileges were abolished, ushering in the era of agrarian capitalism. These changes reduced the poorest members of the rural population, especially widows, to beggary. In England and the Netherlands the repression of witchcraft can be seen as a response to the social fear aroused by the rise of rural poverty and begging. A close correlation has been observed between the enclosure movement, the poor laws, and the repression of witchcraft. Socioeconomic factors also play a part in urban witchcraft: in Salem, Massachusetts, the persecution of witches in 1692–93 grew out of a violent conflict between farmers whose fortunes were on the decline and the merchants of the port whose economic and political power in the city was growing.

Another hypothesis, put forward in the nineteenth century by Michelet, is that women, being a repository of the secret formulas of folk medicine, therefore became a prime target of inquisitors and secular judges who believed that they could have learned these secrets only from the devil. The gradual shift from white magic to black magic, or from what English-speaking historians often call witchcraft to sorcery, is clearly perceptible in treatises on demonology. If women had the power to heal by means of effigies and herbal remedies, what was to prevent them from using similar methods to do harm? Studies of judicial records have found that the proportion of midwives and healers accused of sorcery was high. The older they were and the greater their experience, the more likely they were to be suspected.

Taken together, these various hypotheses yield a model that roughly corresponds to the standard demonological definition of the witch. Yet although a combination of factors can account for local manifestations of sorcery and its repression, it cannot explain the phenomenon as a whole, nor can it account for the frequent deviations from the norm. Not everyone accused of sorcery was a woman: on the average roughly 20 percent were men, and not all of these owed their sad fate solely to the misfortune of having married witches. Furthermore, not all witches were elderly, widowed, or poor. Even if the proportion of witches who were widows was higher than the proportion of witches in the population, the majority of witches were married or marriageable women, and the high social standing of some of them was not enough to preclude their being accused or condemned.

The connection between repeated natural disasters and belief in witchcraft appears to be corroborated by the persecution of those believed responsible for "sowing the plague" after each epidemic, as in the Milan epidemic of 1630, made famous by Alessandro Manzoni's novel, *I promessi sposi*. But when the plague first struck the West in 1347–48, it was not witches but actual, specific social groups, namely, Jews and lepers, who were blamed for spreading the disease. Not until the fifteenth century did the finger of accusation begin to point toward a supposed sect of sorcerers. What is more, the West enjoyed more than a century of relative prosperity from the late fifteenth to the early seventeenth centuries, the very period during which the repression of sorcery was greatest. Finally, although rapid transformations of the economy may have played an important role in the emergence of sorcery or witchcraft in England and the Netherlands in the sixteenth century or in New England in the seventeenth century, there is little evidence of such rapid changes in Lorraine, Franche-Comté, the Alps, or the Basque territory, all regions in which the repression of witchcraft was particularly severe.

In fact the concept of sorcery is a simplification that conceals the rich anthropological diversity that still existed in late medieval and early modern Europe, a diversity that religious rivalry only served to underscore. Different European cultures assigned different roles to women, and these differences determined how important a role women were believed to play in sorcery. The underlying causes of the belief in sorcery must be sought in the religious and cultural spheres.

A Cultural Division of Labor

As soon as one throws off the ideological blinders imposed by demonology (blinders that too many historians have been willing to wear), the picture becomes more complex. The crime of sorcery never accounted for more than a small proportion of criminal prosecutions, except perhaps in southwestern Germany, where more than 3,200 individuals were executed between 1571 and 1670. Trials for sorcery were relatively infrequent. The cases occupy such a prominent place in historical memory because the publicity attached to this crime and the spectacular form of punishment it received ensured that it attracted a great deal of attention. By isolating the crime of sorcery from other crimes, historians have exaggerated its importance. Often described as a "holocaust," the persecution of witches never amounted to anything of the kind. It may even be that the increase in the number of trials in the fifteenth century was due simply to the bureaucratization of the courts and the resulting increase in the volume of judicial records. Cases involving the casting of spells and curses now came before the courts, whereas previously they had been settled by summary, customary procedures. As scholars have correctly argued, the fact that demoniac sorcery was associated with women made women the primary targets of a culturally and socially determined repression. Yet to single out sorcery in this way is to forget that it was not the only crime strongly associated with a particular sex. Sodomy, for example, was a specifically masculine crime. A witch was a woman of unbridled sexuality who, by attacking man's genitals and coupling with demons, interfered with the natural laws of procreation. A homosexual was a man who subverted the reproductive order by engaging in intercourse with other men, thereby wasting his sperm. The two crimes were prosecuted with equal severity and were often linked in official edicts calling upon judges to show greater prosecutory zeal.

Historians have expended so much effort on trying to understand witches that they have neglected their male counterparts, the sorcerers, whose numbers in some places were significant. In German-speaking parts of Luxembourg, for example, 31 percent (98 of 316) of those accused of sorcery in the late sixteenth and early seventeenth centuries were men. In the city of Luxembourg at the height of the repression (1619–1625), twenty men were accused along with twenty-one women. In Fribourg 36 percent of all cases between 1609 and 1683 involved sorcerers. In the Vaud between 1539 and 1670 the proportion was as high as 42 percent. Repression was severe in the southern German city of Würzburg under its bishop Philipp Adolf von Ehrenberg; between 1627 and 1629, 160 individuals were put to death in twenty-nine auto-da-fés. More than half of these were males, and one-fourth were children. Finally, in the jurisdiction of the Paris Parlement (which in 1600 covered nearly two-thirds of the kingdom of France), 1,094 individuals appealed death sentences for the crime of sorcery that had been handed down by lower courts in the period 1565–1640: of these, 565 (or 52 percent) were men. In France the major episodes of sorcery that most agitated the general public involved sorcerers rather than witches. In the Vauderie, as the turmoil that erupted in Arras in 1460 is known, the only woman involved was a common prostitute from Douai, but accused, convicted, and for the most part executed along with her were a number of prominent men of the city. Other cases in Aix-en-Provence (1611), Loudun (1634), and Louviers (1647) involved priests who were convicted of diabolical commerce with women, and specifically with nuns.

Historians have also failed to ponder the significance of another important fact about sorcery. Although a great deal is now known about areas in which there was repression, it is rarely noted that witch-hunting was totally unknown in much of sixteenth- and seventeenth-century Europe: Italy, Spain, Portugal, and their colonies. The only parts of these countries to be affected by very localized persecutions were remote border regions contiguous with countries in which witches were persecuted: the Alpine valleys of Lombardy in the late sixteenth century, the Basque region in 1610, and Venezia in 1625. No correct interpretation of sorcery is possible without taking account of these unaffected areas.

The first step toward a correct interpretation is to distinguish between belief in evil spells and the Satanic myth. The former could exist without the latter, but not vice versa. England persecuted witches throughout the sixteenth century without ever referring, implicitly or explicitly, to a pact with the devil. An official link between the two was not established until the passage of the Witchcraft Act of 1604. Moreover, in the English-speaking world, including even Puritan New England, where sensitivity to the devil's work was keenest, the crime of sorcery was a matter of criminal, not religious, law. Witches were hanged rather than burned. On the continent the situation was more ambiguous. In the Holy Roman Empire the Caroline Law of 1532 provided for the death penalty in cases of sorcery but did not specify the mode of execution, probably a sign that casting spells was not yet definitively associated with the Satanic myth. In prerevolutionary France accusers denounced the evils that witches were alleged to have committed, and judges reinterpreted those charges in light of the Satanic myth. The belief that women possessed evil, supernatural powers was an ancient one. In antiquity the *strix* was alleged to be a man-eating woman who flew through the air at night; there were reported sightings of such creatures in the Middle Ages and again in the sixteenth century. In the fifteenth century belief in the power of women to cast spells combined with the Satanic myth to give rise to that hybrid, the demoniac witch.

The demonological myth took shape in the context of medieval heresy. The belief in the existence of a sect of Satan-worshiping sorcerers was a creation of the inquisitors who did battle with the Waldenses and Fraticelli, heretical sects of the late Middle Ages. In the fifteenth and early sixteenth centuries the geographic distribution of sorcery coincided exactly with that of heresy: the valleys of the upper and middle Rhine, the Alps, Dauphiné, northern and central Italy, and the Basque region. The papal bulls that granted broad powers to the inquisitors in their struggle against the alleged Satanic heresy did not mention that women were to be suspected more than men. Innocent VIII's bull of 1484, like Alexander VI's later *Cum acceperimus*, which was addressed to Fra Angelo of Verona, the inquisitor general of Lombardy, invariably referred to "persons of either sex." That is why episodes like the Vauderie of Arras were still plausible: there was still no clear indication that women were more prone than men to the Satanic heresy. But acting on their own, inquisitors in certain areas established a connection between women and the cult of the devil. In doing so they made use of still extant beliefs: that women had the power to cast evil spells, for example, or that there existed a "sisterhood of Diana" consisting of women who roamed the countryside at night in pursuit of the Roman goddess Diana (or, in another variant, the Germanic goddess Perchta), women who gathered in the woods to eat animals whose carcasses they would then bring back to life. This belief, which is mentioned in the well-known tenth-century canon *Episcopi*, was still widespread in the Alps and northern Italy in the late Middle Ages.

The intellectual tradition underlying the inquisitors' views and actions can be traced back to the beginning of the fifteenth century. In the fourteenth century women, encouraged by the mendicant orders and especially by their female tertiaries, had claimed autonomy and freedom of expression within the church. The Great Schism in western Catholicism, a crisis without precedent in the history of Christendom, had permitted the emergence of female prophets such as Catherine of Siena and Bridget of Sweden. The subversive potential of this development was immediately apparent to the clergy, which rightly perceived a challenge to its spiritual monopoly. The case of Bridget of Sweden is exemplary in many respects. No fewer than three papal bulls were required to bestow on her an official sainthood that was never fully accepted by certain segments of the clergy. Adversaries of the prophetess expressed their views in various canonization proceedings. Eminent scholars such as Jean Gerson, Pierre d'Ailly, and Henry of Langenstein voiced their skepticism of prophecy by women. This controversy led to stricter rules for "discernment of spirits," rules that, by casting women as more susceptible than men to diabolical illusions, helped to establish their theological inferiority and to exclude them from official position in the church. Obsessed by the threat of Satan, the inquisitors of the late fifteenth century had only to draw on these treatises to bolster their own convictions.

In the first half of the sixteenth century the Inquisition turned its attention away from the struggle against Satanic sorcery, in which it no longer truly believed, and toward the far more urgent challenge of the Protestant heresy, which precipitated a profound crisis. At this point the demonological myth was taken over by secular judges, but sorcery and heresy were still closely linked. The great witch hunts of the sixteenth and seventeenth centuries were fiercest where Catholic and Protestant territories came together: the Netherlands, Luxembourg, Lorraine, the Rhine Valley and southern Germany, Burgundy, Franche-Comté, the Swiss cantons, the Dauphiné, Béarn, the Basque region, and various places in the Loire Valley and Normandy. Where the Protestant heresy was quickly eliminated or never took hold—that is, in southern Europe and Hispanic America—witch-hunting was unknown.

Seigneurial and royal judges adopted the whole range of anti-feminine arguments developed by the inquisitors a century before, with greater severity on the Catholic side than on the Protestant. Consider what happened in Germany. In Baden-Würtemberg there were twice as many prosecutions for sorcery in Catholic states as in Protestant ones, and the number of executions was four times greater. But fear of a Satanic plot, heightened by religious conflict, led judges, with encouragement from the various churches, to blur the distinction between demoniac sorcery and all other forms of magic. Calvin, for example, wrote a "Warning against So-Called Judicial Astrology" (1549); and in 1586 Pope Sixtus V issued the bull *Coeli et terrae Creator* condemning all forms of divination. Both looked upon any attempt to foretell the future as an offense to the power of God, such knowledge being obtainable only through an implicit or explicit pact with Satan. But the Renaissance had witnessed a veritable vogue for various learned forms of divination derived from Jewish and Arab tradition and enriched by the practice of astrology and alchemy. As a result of the broad new definition of demoniac magic, male "necromancers," learned members of the elite, were burned for sorcery in relatively large numbers, mainly in cities.

Paradoxically, it is from the countries that were spared the hunt for witches that we learn about the complexity of the beliefs that the demonological myth helped to blur and about the respective roles assigned to men and women in manipulating the supernatural powers. Toward the end of the sixteenth century the inquisitorial tribunal of Naples, responding to the general climate of opinion in western Europe, set out to prosecute the practice of magic. It was confronted with two culturally distinct types of behavior. One kind of magic was practiced by intellectuals, monks and men of letters, all men, whose chief interest was to discover hidden wealth and become rich. They were steeped in the Neoplatonic magic of the Renaissance, which had absorbed the most diverse traditions of the ancient and medieval occult arts. The apocryphal writings of the great Renaissance magus Cornelius Agrippa of Nettesheim were their bedside reading. They shared the secrets of making talismans that could make a man powerful and invulnerable and of conjuring up spirits that could foretell the future and reveal the location of hidden treasures. But there was also a magic of the people, practiced by illiterate women of humble extraction, healers and prostitutes. Their knowledge was passed on orally from mother to daughter or from neighbor to neighbor. They practiced empirical medicine, knew the secrets of various simples, and could set broken bones and dislocated joints; they also treated diseases of women and children. Theirs was the knowledge traditionally attributed to women. Inevitably they also became soothsayers, learned how to ward off the evil eye, and were naturally suspected of casting spells. The *fattuchiere* (magicians) of southern Italy and their Spanish and American counterparts constitute a type that was probably once present throughout Europe but that survived only where the repression was less blind than it was elsewhere.

The Neapolitan inquisitors knew the standard works on demonology and attempted to impose the demonological model on those who stood accused before them, but they failed. The paradigms of traditional culture stood in their way, and the authorities, who were by no means obsessed with the danger of heresy, chose not to make an issue of it. In northern Italy, for example in Friuli, which lay close to the religious boundary, the situation was more complex. The Friulian *benandanti* (literally, "those who go out to do good") dreamed of doing battle with sorcerers in the Night of the Four Ages. They were led by a young captain who raised the banner of Christ and armed themselves with fennel against sorcerers wielding sugar cane. The outcome of the battle determined the quality of the year's harvest. Such magical beliefs were very ancient; they stemmed from a body of myths known to be current in central Europe since antiquity and involving an army of wandering souls led by the god of the dead and of war. In the early Middle Ages this cycle of myths was Christianized, and it was still current in northern Italy in the sixteenth century. The *benandanti*, as it happened, were all men. The few women implicated in the affair spoke not of nocturnal battles with sorcerers but of another fertility myth involving the sisterhood of Diana. The Friulian inquisitors also interpreted these beliefs in terms of the demonological model in which they were steeped. The *benandanti*, they claimed, did not set out to do battle with sorcerers but were themselves sorcerers, and their captain was none other than the devil himself. Under inquisitorial pressure the cultural and mythical underpinnings of these magical beliefs gradually fell apart. Still, the case that the *benandanti* were in fact Satanic sorcerers was never fully convincing, and the Inquisition chose to restrain its punishments; no one went to the stake in Friuli.

The stereotype of the evil, Satanic witch was born of the crisis into which Christendom was plunged toward the end of the fourteenth century and which was aggravated by the breakdown of religious unity in the sixteenth century. Although the Satanic model became part of the dominant ideology, it imperfectly masked a great diversity of beliefs. It nevertheless contributed to a degradation of the social image of women at the end of the Middle Ages. When the crime of sorcery was dropped everywhere at the end of the seventeenth century, the cultural status of women did not improve, however. When charges of sorcery were brought, judges were henceforth required to adduce material evidence that a spell had been cast, but the existence of spells and of the devil remained unchallenged. This marked change in the penal code was accompanied by a gradual transformation of learned discourse about sorcery. The major cases that most stirred enlightened public opinion in the seventeenth century helped bring physicians to center stage. Slowly but surely the witch moved from the realm of heresy to that of illness. Once accused of having entered into a pact with the devil, the witch was now cast as a victim of her own imagination. The demonological myth gave way to the diagnosis of hysteria, whose nosography was refined in the eighteenth and above all the nineteenth centuries. In retrospect one is entitled to ask if the image of woman profited from the change. When she was a witch, the cruelty of the gallows and the stake demonstrated her full responsibility under the law. But as a victim of her imagination, driven mad by the workings of her own body, she became a legally diminished individual, one whose personal responsibility was limited.

TRANSLATED FROM THE FRENCH BY ARTHUR GOLDHAMMER

15

Prostitutes

Kathryn Norberg

PROSTITUTES WERE A common sight in early modern cities. One could not cross the Rialto in Venice without encountering them. The Spanish sailor who disembarked at Seville was greeted by their appeals. The London theatergoer was besieged by them on his way to Covent Garden. The Parisian artisan stumbled over them outside suburban taverns. Along with the cries that rang out in European cities advertising fish, used clothes, old pastry, and knife sharpening came, usually at dusk, the softer and more alluring question: "Would you like to make a pretty acquaintance?"

According to contemporary observers, prostitutes were everywhere. A census in Venice in 1526 counted 4,900 prostitutes among a population of 55,035; when pimps and procuresses are included, it appears that approximately 10 percent of the Venetian population lived off prostitution.[1] Contemporary estimates of the number of prostitutes in mid-eighteenth-century Paris run between 10,000 and 40,000, or between 10 and 15 percent of the adult female population.[2] A German traveler in London estimated that there were 50,000 harlots, without counting kept women and courtesans.[3] All these figures are grossly exaggerated. To the righteous or even not-so-righteous observer, one prostitute seemed like ten. But such fanciful estimates aside, prostitution occupied an important place in the early modern city, and mercenary sex constituted an occasional or regular occupation for many women.

How should we characterize these women, these *filles?* Were they rebels, social insurgents bent upon undermining patriarchy? Or were they victims, unwitting supporters of male domination? On the one hand, the prostitute lived in the world of men and survived only by catering to them. Her universe was that of the tavern, the gaming house, and the barracks. She was obliged to subordinate herself to men and abide by their whims. She was a vessel of male fantasy and an object of scorn, hunted and abused by the authorities. At worst, in police blotters, she was no more than a name or a number, a cipher almost always without identity or voice.

On the other hand, by disposing of her own body the prostitute challenged male domination and patriarchy at its very heart. She chose when and where she would grant her favors, and she flaunted women's sexuality. She publicly subverted the right of fathers and husbands to monopolize women's sexuality. Far from being submissive and silent, she made her cries heard throughout the city. Her story tells us a great deal about the fate of women in the years from 1500 to 1800.

Rebel or victim: the prostitute was neither in the late Middle Ages. She was a member of the urban community, a full-fledged citizen who occupied an important and honored place in city life. In medieval and Renaissance Europe, prostitution was not merely tolerated; it was accepted and institutionalized. In Florence and Venice the city fathers designated several streets—the area around the Mercato Vecchio in Florence and just off the Rialto in Venice— as official red-light districts where mercenary sex was encouraged in the hope of stemming an imagined rise in homosexuality and a decline in marriage. Honorable citizens such as the Medicis and the nobles of Venice owned the houses occupied by the prostitutes and shared in the profits without apparent embarrassment or shame. Florence encouraged prostitution by establishing a special court, the Onesta, whose police patrolled the red-light district and protected the prostitutes.

Outside Italy, towns established official bordellos in the course of the fifteenth century. In Strasbourg (1469), Munich (1433), Seville (1469), and cities of the Rhone Valley the right to administer the house was auctioned off to a *Frauernwirt,* bordello *padre,* or *abbesse*. Except in France, the owner-operators of official bordellos were men. They were entitled to charge the prostitutes for room and sometimes for board and to take a part of their earnings. In return they were obliged to observe certain rules. Most cities insisted that the municipal bordello be closed on feast days and proclaimed off-limits to priests and married men. The municipalities also levied special fines on prostitutes who lingered too long with a particular man, and they discouraged special relationships between whores and clients.

Despite similarities, the medieval bordello was no nineteenth-century *maison close*. Prostitutes came and went freely and found clients in taverns and bathhouses. Moreover, a host of *insoumises,* or unofficial prostitutes—usually younger—plied their trade outside the bordello in defiance of the municipal monopoly. Occasionally they were fined, but generally all prostitutes were accorded a place in the ritual life of their communities. In Germany they were honored guests at weddings; in Lyons they participated in municipal processions and festivals.

Like Augustine, fifteenth-century municipal officials regarded prostitution as a lesser evil than adultery or the deflowering of virgins and as the bulwark of marriage. Prostitutes provided an outlet for male sexual energy, thereby protecting the wives and daughters of honest merchants. At the same time, prostitutes encouraged "normal" sexual activity, thereby promoting marriage and legitimate procreation. By protecting prostitutes, the officials protected their wives and daughters as well as the city's population. That most of the prostitutes were "foreigners" from outside the city helped the municipal elite rationalize their policy. That most of the girls had compromised themselves somehow—or been compromised by roving bands of young men—also soothed the burghers' consciences. At very little expense did the city fathers literally make a place for male libido within the municipal fabric.

But by the mid-sixteenth century most of the official bordellos had been closed—Augsburg in 1532, Basel in 1534, Frankfurt in 1560. Seville followed suit in 1620. Measures were less dramatic in Italy; but although they never officially closed the red-light districts, authorities in Florence and Venice adopted a more stringent attitude toward prostitutes after 1511 and tried to suppress all manifestations of venal sex. Throughout Europe authorities moved to quash unofficial prostitution. A series of edicts criminalized mercenary sex. In France the ordinance of Orléans in 1560 made owning and operating a bordello illegal. In 1623 Philip IV officially banned brothels throughout Spain. By 1650 the municipal bordello was a thing of the past.

Most historians attribute the sudden criminalization of prostitution to the advent of syphilis. But in fact the bordello closings occurred some thirty years after the worst syphilis epidemics of the 1490s.[4] In one case, Seville, faced with a serious outbreak of venereal disease in 1568, city authorities were led to increase the number of official prostitutes rather than abolish the municipal bordello and its regulations.[5] The connection between syphilis and prostitution was not strong in the sixteenth century, although Europeans understood how the disease was contracted and knew that prostitutes spread it. But they did not consider syphilis the most dangerous or even the most interesting threat posed by prostitutes. Unlike their nineteenth-century predecessors, early modern men did not fear for their bodies; they feared for their souls.

Religious change appears to have been the single most important factor in changing attitudes toward prostitution. In his *Address to the German Nobility* Martin Luther complained that "Christians tolerate open and common brothels in our midst when all of us are baptized into chastity." With the Reformation, men were to be held to the same standards as women—that is, chastity outside marriage—and masculine libido was not to be accommodated by an official bordello. For Luther and other Protestant reformers, Augustine's rationalization of mercenary sex was not tenable. In a short tract titled "Thoughts concerning Brothels," Luther refuted Augustine's defense and rejected the notion that prostitution curbed a greater sin. On the contrary, he argued, it promoted fornication and the ruin of young men. In 1543 he posted a notice warning students in Wittenberg about prostitutes, whom "the devil has sent . . . to ruin some poor young men." Elsewhere he prescribed severe punishments for prostitutes in the interests of preserving men from fornication and protecting the institution of marriage.[6]

The Protestant reformers were not alone in their condemnation of mercenary sex. Catholic reformers, too, railed against whores, and moral concerns appear to have motivated the closing of the bordellos in France, Spain, and Italy. In the 1480s preachers in the Rhone Valley began to condemn prostitution and to point to the municipal bordello as a sign of moral degradation. In 1511 Florentines began to attach as much opprobrium to prostitution as to homosexuality. Moralists began to see in the whore a threat to honest women and the matrimonial order. A similar new morality, though it occurred later, led to the end of toleration in Spain. Catholic reformers in Seville publicly condemned prostitution and succeeded in closing the local bordello in 1620.

But religious fervor alone does not account for the criminalization of prostitution. Laws banning venal sex were accompanied by a rash of peculiar statutes regulating whores' appearance. Municipalities in Italy and in the Rhone Valley passed decrees penalizing whores who dressed as men and sumptuary laws prohibiting prostitutes from wearing elegant apparel. In France, Germany, and Geneva, the persecution of prostitutes coincided with witch trials and the closing of the bathhouses. These actions appear to reflect a new fear of female sexuality and a generalized anxiety over the blurring of gender and class lines. To the Florentine city fathers and the German burghers, whores dressed as men or, worse yet, as honest women threatened the sexual and the social hierarchy.

The closing of the bordellos not only stemmed from a number of anxieties; it also constituted a response to concrete changes in prostitution itself. Although our evidence is by no means conclusive, it indicates that many prostitutes had become more mobile and independent. Most apparently abandoned the municipal bordello even before it closed, and a few had become more prosperous. Municipal authorities had more and more difficulty confining mercenary sex to the official bordellos. In Spain, Italy, France, and Germany the closing of the municipal bordellos was preceded by numerous decrees seeking to contain and control prostitutes who worked outside the official houses. Authorities in Florence, Augsburg, Dijon, and Seville complained that whores were exercising their trade outside the official houses. By the 1490s many—perhaps most—prostitutes lived outside the bordellos, worked independently, and ignored municipal regulations. In Frankfurt, for example, so many prostitutes worked outside the municipal bordello that in 1501 no one could be persuaded to purchase the office of *Frauenwirt* because the local house was no longer profitable.[7]

The scanty evidence available suggests that by the early sixteenth century most or at least a large portion of prostitutes in European cities lived and worked independently. Some also moved about the town and the region. Authorities in Frankfurt complained that "foreign" prostitutes inundated the city during fairs, and in Paris the great fairs of Saint Germain and Saint Laurent were notorious for the number of whores they attracted. During this period, camp followers also became more numerous. In Strasbourg, Frankfurt, and Nuremburg, local authorities complained of the women who followed the army, sometimes camping outside the city walls and bringing with them riot and disorder. As the size of armies grew, so did the number of camp followers; thus it may be the rise of the state with its new, larger armies that entailed the criminalization of venal love. In the sixteenth century prostitution became, in the words of historian Jacques Rossiaud, "more dangerous and more shameful."[8] Camp followers and their rowdy clients came to occupy a larger place in the world of mercenary sex, and prostitution became equated with the riot, thievery, and murder typical of men at arms. Prostitution did not just seem more dangerous; it was.

It was also more expensive, at least for some. The late fifteenth and early sixteenth centuries witnessed the birth of a new kind of whore—the courtesan. Already, in the late 1400s, preachers and municipal authorities in Dijon, Venice, Florence, and elsewhere railed against the appearance of a better sort of prostitute, one who wore fine clothes and plied her trade secretly, a prostitute who risked overturning the matrimonial order because she seduced respectable men and attached them to her permanently.

Although the rise of the courtesan has yet to attract the attention of a serious historian, her appearance seems to signal a major change in the habits and the attitudes of the elite. Clearly, the rich no longer cared to frequent the municipal bordello; they preferred secret pleasures. Just as clearly, they also preferred a more refined, more intimate sexual experience. Does the birth of the courtesan mean that the elite had acquired a taste for genteel sexual relations? The great courtesans such as the Venetian poet Veronica Franco and the writer Tullia d'Aragona offered more than sex; they offered eroticism, that is, sex with an elegant and accomplished expert. It is not by chance that the first pornographic work, Pietro Aretino's *Ragionimenti* (1534), had a courtesan as its heroine. *La cortegiana* aroused fantasies, but she also raised anxieties. Unlike the diseased, disgusting bordello prostitute, the courtesan threatened to draw men away from their lawful wives and to prevent respectable youths from seeking spouses.

Courtesans enjoyed more independence and certainly more

money than their sisters who followed armies or plied their trade in bordellos. Paradoxically, these advantages in elegance and prosperity, such as they were, came in the train of criminalization. In the aftermath of the bordello closings, many prostitutes escaped regulation and operated, like most prostitutes today, as independent entrepreneurs or at least under the control of other women. With criminalization came a need for discretion, so old women who could pass as a prostitute's mother or mistress assumed the managerial role previously filled by male brothel *padres* and *Frauenwirt*. Pimps were certainly not unknown; in Venice *lenos,* or panderers, continued to dominate prostitution as they had always done. But generally elsewhere older women, often former prostitutes, functioned as intermediaries between clients and prostitutes and therefore helped themselves to most of the profits previously enjoyed by male owner-operators. By 1600 prostitution was among the few all-female trades.

Criminalization and the consequent need for discretion among both clients and whores probably account for these changes. The switch from pimps to procuresses is less easy to explain. Perhaps for the client who spent a night with a girl in her room, dealing with an old woman and a girl rather than with a man and a girl provided more assurance against disclosure of his debauchery.

Not surprisingly, criminalization brought with it as many problems as benefits. From the prostitutes' perspective, the advantages of newfound autonomy were readily offset by vulnerability and new institutions of repression. Under the old system of regulation, prostitutes had enjoyed protection by municipal authorities. Although rape was extremely common, registered prostitutes wore a distinctive token that preserved them from the gangs of youths who roamed the cities. Official prostitutes could also appeal to the municipal authorities when clients beat or cheated them. The prostitute of the early modern period had no such recourse. A criminal herself, she could hardly ask the police to protect her from landlords and tavernkeepers who overcharged her or clients who beat her or refused to pay. Such clients were all too common, and occasionally the inspectors in Paris, particularly those in the morals brigade, stepped in to help the whore. Blackmailers or extortionists were another constant plague; they slept with prostitutes and then refused to pay under the threat of revealing them to the police, or they demanded a portion of the prostitutes' wages in return for their silence. Lacking official protection and working outside the law, more and more prostitutes attached *souteneurs,* or pimps, to themselves. In Paris, for example, a former soldier or a gambler might function as the protector of a small bordello, handling unruly clients and intimidating curious neighbors. In Marseilles the *souteneur* functioned as an intermediary between the small waterfront bordellos and the officers of the ships in port. Because the police did not pursue souteneurs provided they left respectable girls alone, evidence on their number and activities remains sketchy. But like policemen, they appear to have become more numerous in the eighteenth century.

Criminalization made the prostitute vulnerable to violence and thievery; it also left her defenseless before a harsh judicial system. In France, a series of laws beginning with the edict of 20 April 1684 established severe penalties for prostitution (incarceration in a special hospital) and gave the lieutenant of police or his equivalent in the provinces absolute authority over prostitutes. In 1713, 1724, 1734, 1776, and 1777 royal edicts reiterated the stipulations of the original law and reconfirmed the powers of the police. Despite these royal decrees, power in matters of prostitution remained where it had always been, with the municipalities. In Paris the situation was somewhat special: the lieutenant of police was a royal official with sweeping powers, and maintaining order in the capital was particularly important to the crown. In the provinces, in Marseilles, Nantes, Lyons, or Montpellier, local governments were left pretty much to themselves when it came to the policing of morals, and the degree of enforcement and severity of penalties varied greatly from one town to another. In this respect little had changed since the Middle Ages; the community maintained authority over prostitutes.

What changed were the number and authority of the police. Paris stood at the forefront. There, a host of inspectors devoted themselves solely to gathering intelligence about high-toned prostitutes, mainly opera dancers and actresses. The more prosaic streetwalkers were subject to periodic sweeps that brought scores of prostitutes before the lieutenant of police each Friday for a mass sentencing. But despite greater numbers than in the past, the police in this period were by no means as effective as their counterparts today. Enforcement was haphazard and arbitrary. Sweeps and night visits by special squads were sporadic. Only those who blocked the streets or caused uproar were likely to be apprehended. Prostitutes, who were superficially respectable and discreet, however, were unlikely to be bothered by the police.

For prostitutes who were careful, there was an unwritten toleration. For those who were not or who were just unlucky, there were terrible penalties. Whores who were apprehended by the patrol or night guard were taken to the Saint Martin holding prison (later to the Hôtel de Brienne) and sometime after that were sentenced to the Salpetrière hospital for periods ranging from two to six months. In the provinces the penalties could be steeper: prostitutes in Marseilles in the first half of the eighteenth century could spend as many as five years in a *maison de force.* Once inside the dirty, crowded hospital, these women were usually proclaimed syphilitic, sometimes without examination, and subjected to the mercury "cure," which constituted a part of their punishment.

With the physical cure came a moral cure. Many of the prostitute asylums in Europe were staffed by nuns and were intended to serve spiritual as well as social ends. In the sixteenth and early seventeenth centuries, devout Catholics in Spain, France, and Italy established numerous small convents or asylums designed to shelter and reform prostitutes. In France the Order of the Refuge, founded by the visionary Elizabeth de Ranfaing, sheltered wayward girls in Nancy, Avignon, Marseilles, Lyons, and other cities. In Florence the orders of the Convertite and the Malmaritate and in Seville the convent of the Sweet Name of Jesus provided asylum to repentant and not so repentant prostitutes. By the early eighteenth century such institutions had ceased to perform their religious functions. Though still staffed by nuns, they had become penal institutions usually operated and funded by municipal authorities. In Marseilles, for example, a municipal court—usually referred to as the Refuge court—tried prostitutes and sentenced them to long periods in the Refuge convent. The city also accepted petitions from angry parents who sought to incarcerate their wayward daughters and save the family honor.

Confinement in such a *maison de force* was greatly feared, but generally a prostitute could hope to escape detection and punishment provided she placated her neighbors, the most frequent source of complaints. Records indicate that about 80 percent of the prostitutes sentenced in Marseilles had been turned in by working-class men and women living near them. The sparseness of records makes comparisons difficult, but the proportion appears to have been about the same or higher elsewhere in France.

The role of neighbors in the prosecution of whores sheds some light on popular attitudes toward prostitution. From the court records of Nantes, Paris, and Marseilles, it is clear that neighbors felt authorized to police single women's behavior and that they heartily disapproved of prostitution, especially when it brought with it noise, disorder, and the threat of bodily harm. In Marseilles and Nantes neighbors went to the police when a prostitute's clients insulted them or, worse, threatened them with bodily harm. Certainly the proprietor or manager of a building had incentives to root out prostitutes, since he was liable for heavy fines if caught harboring them. But common artisans, renters like the prostitute, also complained, and even elite madams lived in fear of being turned in by their neighbors. The hazards of venal love in the early modern period included some isolation or separation from the working-class community.

The prostitute had to fear her neighbors because she now tended to ply her trade in a rented room, usually in a respectable house, instead of a bordello. The criminalization of prostitution and with it the need for discretion led to the dispersion of whores throughout the urban landscape.

Bordellos had not, of course, disappeared, but they tended to operate at either the highest or the lowest end of the trade. In Paris and London a few luxury establishments offered unusual sex in a discreet setting to men who could afford it. For those who could not, a series of pornographic texts purported to describe accurately the activities in these elite establishments but in fact grossly exaggerated their elegance and size. According to the *Portefeuille de Madame Gourdan*, a small pamphlet about the most famous madam in Paris, Gourdan's establishment had many rooms, something like a swimming pool, and an endless supply of willing nymphs. In fact, as the Paris police reports show, most bordellos consisted of no more than four rooms and were staffed by at most three girls, a madam, and a servant. When Casanova visited one of the most famous Parisian houses, he found it only adequately appointed and the madam ugly and flagrantly greedy.

At the other end of the spectrum, the working-class bordello usually took the form of an apartment building given over entirely to streetwalkers. The Cour Guillaume adjacent to the Palais Royal was such a building, where upward of 200 prostitutes rented rooms at exorbitant rates. Whores in Marseilles occupied entire buildings near the Carmelite, and Nantes boasted a bordello with 40 inmates. The prostitutes in such houses were not subject to the discipline of a madam. They came and went as they liked and solicited clients outside the house, either on the street or in taverns. But they did pay unusually high rents and were dependent on the discretion of the owner.

The furnished rented room in a private house provided a relatively discreet setting for venal sex, but it also posed a dilemma: how was the prostitute to be discreet enough to escape imprisonment yet demonstrative enough to attract clients? Some prostitutes solved this problem by employing a go-between, a *marcheuse* or *macquerelle*. The *marcheuse* solicited clients on the public thoroughfare, most often the boulevards in Paris; the *macquerelle* or procuress contacted men less openly. She also recruited young girls, rented them rooms, forced clients to pay, loaned the girls money and clothes, and generally skimmed as much as she could (sometimes as much as half) off the prostitutes' earnings. The procuress did not contend with unruly clients; that was the role of the pimp or *souteneur*. But she nonetheless provided a service to the prostitute, albeit at a very high price.

Most prostitutes did without a macquerelle and solicited on their own in areas known for prostitution, in unofficial red-light districts. The location of these *rues chaudes* varied from city to city according to history and tradition. But in general prostitutes were to be found near important markets such as Les Halles and in abandoned areas such as construction sites. Whether in England, France, or Germany, prostitutes solicited in cabarets, and any tavern serving girl was assumed to be for sale. Some bars had *cabinets,* small rooms for sex; others rented out rooms on the first floor for private parties. Since any "trick" began or ended with the sharing of food and wine, the drink shop was an obvious site for venal love. Sometimes it was virtually the only spot. In Marseilles taverns, wine shops, and tobacco shops of the old port constituted the principal locations for prostitution.

With the advent of new forms of leisure in the eighteenth century, new sites for prostitution appeared. The pleasure gardens of the rich—Vauxhall, the Colisée, Ranelagh—were reputed to attract whores. The *guinguettes,* or suburban taverns, of the laboring poor in the outskirts of Paris and along the Rhone also drew prostitutes. In Paris prostitutes were particularly numerous in the unsavory Porcherons suburb near Montmartre. There, whores worked out of large cabarets and hired themselves out to soldiers and working men in the dancing gardens behind these taverns or in the very fields of Montmartre.

The theater also acted as a magnet for prostitutes. Whores clogged the Parisian boulevards where the laboring poor came to enjoy popular amusements.[9] They also clustered around more respectable theaters such as the Comédie Française in Paris, Covent Garden in London, and the theater in the Place des Celestins in Lyons. When the theater moved, so did the whores. In the late eighteenth century, when both Nantes and Marseilles built new operas, the whores established themselves in the surrounding streets. Prostitutes also invaded the vestibules and corridors of the theaters. At the final curtain, they rushed into the streets and accosted men leaving the Paris Opéra or Covent Garden.

Of course, actresses and singers were themselves regarded as prostitutes, and most were. The records of the Parisian police inspectors Marais and Meunsier from the 1750s are very instructive. The typical Parisian courtesan was an adolescent opera dancer, a student in the appropriately nicknamed *magasin,* or storehouse, of the Opéra, whose entry into the royal troupe had been engineered by an older lover. A place in one of the royal theaters conferred immunity from judicial pursuit for loose morals. The girl whom the *prévot des marchands* had admitted could not be confined for loose behavior by her father, and she could pursue the life of a courtesan without dreading a *lettre de cachet.* For her favors, the opera dancer could expect her lover, whether he was a banker or a prince of the blood, to give her clothes, an apartment in Saint Germain, and furniture. She could not, however, expect much in the way of ready cash. If the police records are correct, the average Parisian protector bestowed on his mistress between 200 and 500 livres a month—a princely sum by working-class standards but hardly enough to maintain the style of life a kept woman expected. To feed her horses and maintain her carriages, the kept woman supplemented her income with suppers in the Bois de Boulogne or occasional service in a chic bordello.

Often, the courtesan in question had worked for the house before: many of the actresses had begun in the lowest ranks of the trade. Mlle. Carlier, according to the police inspector, had risen from the sordid status of common camp follower to distinguished madam, proving that a career in prostitution was not always a downward spiral. We tend to assume that prostitutes are at the peak of their careers when they begin and gradually decline as their charms deteriorate. In early modern Europe, that was not always the case: prostitutes moved up and down the ladder of their profession, graduating from streetwalking to life in a bordello, returning to the independence of streetwalking only to be elevated to the rank of kept woman. Some prostitutes in old age had descended into the lowest ranks of the profession to become *pierreuses* who slept with clients in the quarries of Montmartre or the vacant construction sites around Paris. Others had become procuresses or even bordello owners, for all madams had once been common prostitutes themselves. Former whores also opened gambling and drinking establishments. We have no records to tell us what happened to those prostitutes who had to retire. Probably we may assume that they returned to the working class from which they sprang.

If the statistical data collected in France are typical of Europe as a whole, most prostitutes in the early modern period did indeed come from the laboring poor. The police did not much care about the origins of those they arrested, but they did ask them their age, address, home parish, and occupation. None of this information was verified, and it is possible that the prostitutes lied or simply told the police what they expected. Still, certain patterns emerge. Virtually all the prostitutes were between the ages of fifteen and thirty. Most were unmarried, and most were resident in the city where they were apprehended. Many were fairly recent migrants: the proportion of these in Paris was quite high (about 70 percent), but this figure is comparable to the total number of migrants to that city. In provincial towns such as Montpellier the proportion was similar.[10] In early eighteenth-century Marseilles, however, non-natives constituted only 30 percent of the prostitutes brought before the Refuge court.

Were prostitutes fresh country girls seduced by evil procuresses and corrupted by city ways, as the pictures by Hogarth and the texts by Restif de la Bretonne would have us believe? Apparently not, for most of the whores came from towns, not villages. Parisian prostitutes came from towns such as Rouen; Marseilles whores came from Aix or Aubagne. In this regard, prostitution reflects familiar patterns of migration in the eighteenth century, patterns shared with professions such as domestic service. Still, the cliché of the country servant who was seduced and "fell" into prostitution does not hold.

Certainly, many domestic servants became prostitutes. In Montpellier they constituted about 40 percent of the women confined in the Bon Pasteur asylum, but that proportion is peculiarly high. In Marseilles they accounted for no more than 25 percent of the prostitutes tried before the Refuge court in the years 1680–1750.[11] Domestics made up an even lower share of the Parisian trade; in the late eighteenth century they accounted for no more than 12 percent of the women sentenced by the lieutenant of police.[12] Because domestic service was the most common occupation of unmarried women in the ancien régime, servants appear to be grossly underrepresented among prostitutes—all the more so in that the appellation *servante* used in Marseilles covered not just housemaids but bar girls, in particular the women who worked in the taverns that lined the old port. Consequently, we may assume that the label *domestique* covered not just maids of all work, but hardened prostitutes as well. Literary clichés notwithstanding, domestic service was not an inevitable route to prostitution.

On the other hand, washing, sewing, and selling may have led women to mercenary sex. In data for both Paris and Marseilles the needle trades bulk very large. More than half of the women in Paris worked as embroiderers, seamstresses, ribbon makers, or menders in the city's large and diverse garment industry. Most of the rest sold a variety of goods in the streets or in small shops, with *revendeuses,* or secondhand dealers, occupying a special place among the prostitutes. Once local variations are taken into account, the data for Marseilles are not very different. On the shores of the Mediterranean, needlewomen and vendors were very prominent among the prostitutes, as were women who made rope, knitted caps, and purveyed food and drink.

These data are not easy to interpret. All the professions occupied by women were represented among prostitutes, but which were overrepresented? Because we have no precise evidence about the distribution of female occupations in the world of women's work, it is hard to say which professions were most conducive to prostitution.

However, a number of plausible conclusions emerge. Domestic service and venal love appear to have been virtually incompatible. The conditions of a maid's work—her hours, the close supervision by her employer, and her residence in his home—made it difficult to work as a streetwalker on the side. Street vending and linen mending, on the other hand, could easily be combined with or lead to prostitution. Indeed, they could be an easy cover for soliciting. Street vendors often took their wares into customers' homes; washerwomen and linen menders went to their customers' rooms to pick up and return linen. Contemporary authors regularly claimed that the women who sold food, drink, or clothing on the streets also sold themselves and many boutiques, especially those of *marchandes de modes,* or dealers in women's finery, were really *boutiques prétextes,* fronts for bordellos.

Much of women's honest work, such as washing and selling, shared many of the features of prostitution: personal contact, solicitation on the streets, and visits to the customer's home. Thus in early modern Europe venal sex was compatible with virtually every kind of women's work except domestic service. What was not comparable was the pay, although the exact amounts involved are impossible to determine. Data on wages in this period are notoriously hard to come by even for work that was legal. Additional complications arise from the facts that kept women and bordello inmates received part of their wages in room and board, while other prostitutes had to share a part of their pay with procuresses, tavern owners, and pimps. Moreover, the amount of money a man paid was largely up to his discretion. Fees varied enormously even within the same establishment; a bordello patron in Marseilles might pay anything between 10 livres and 25 sous for similar services.[13] Still, it is clear that prostitutes generally made more money than other working women. In Marseilles, for instance, a skilled worker in the city's Arsenal received 25 sous a day in the 1690s.[14] At the same time, a bordello prostitute received that much per trick. In Paris, literary sources and judicial records provide the best indication of the average prostitute's fee. A number of pamphlets published on the eve of the Revolution claim that 12 sous was an average sum for a streetwalker. The figure is repeated so often in prostitutes' testimony that it carries weight. At 12 sous per trick a prostitute could clear in two tricks more than the average artisan woman earned in a full day.[15] As today, prostitution paid better than most women's work and brought with it one of the advantages missing from other forms of labor: relative autonomy. It is not surprising that so many women engaged in mercenary sex.

It is clear why women became prostitutes, but less clear how. Contemporary wisdom had it that women were either seduced and abandoned or sold into prostitution by their mothers. And indeed, cases of women's selling their daughters or at least launching them in the profession are not unknown. In Marseilles there were whole dynasties of women who owned and staffed bordellos with the tacit consent of their men. Most prostitutes, however, embarked upon their careers not with the help of their mothers but in spite of them. Police records indicate that many prostitutes began as wayward adolescents who rebelled against parental authority and ran away from home. A few were confined by their parents in one of the Refuge or Bon Pasteur prostitutes' asylums. But most did not have parents well enough off to pay for their imprisonment. These girls gradually drifted into prostitution not because of a failed love affair, but because they had a girlfriend who sold herself on the side. Such friendships tended to endure among prostitutes, for most worked in pairs and shared expenses or simply a spot on the boulevards.

In general, prostitutes were not victims; they did not "fall" into a life of sin, nor were they duped by a procuress or an ungrateful lover. Most were working-class girls who had defied first their parents and then society by disposing freely of their own bodies. Nor were they victimized by pimps or dependent upon a madam. Most were independent entrepreneurs who controlled their own labor. Such independence, such unfettered female sexual energy troubled late eighteenth-century moralists. Novelists and social commentators adopted two defenses. Novelists portrayed the prostitute as a victim, a child whose innocence and modesty bore out Rousseauist notions of femininity.[16] Social commentators portrayed her as the embodiment of disease, a contagious working-class girl bent on spreading her corruption throughout an unsuspecting society. By the late eighteenth century, syphilis came to dominate the discourse on prostitution, and anxiety over the biological consequences of venal love gradually replaced dread of its moral consequences. Bernard Mandeville as early as 1724 argued that prostitution was not criminal in and of itself but dangerous only when uncontrolled. In *A Modest Defense of Public Stews* he attributed every social scourge from adulterous women to illegitimate births to unregulated prostitution and proposed its legalization and strict supervision. Later, in 1770, Restif de la Bretonne also argued for the seclusion and regulation of prostitutes in a series of Parisian whorehouses. A host of lesser-known authors joined the chorus for legalization and promoted regulation in order to protect families and save the army.

Such publications proved prophetic. In 1792 Berlin instituted a system for regulating prostitutes that required police approval before a brothel could be opened and compelled prostitutes to live in certain streets. In 1796 the Paris Commune instructed its police officials to search out and register prostitutes, who received cards. In 1798 two physicians were assigned the task of examining Parisian whores. In 1802 a physician established a dispensary where prostitutes underwent compulsory examinations. Napoleon's prefects continued the struggle to contain and control prostitution. In Lyons, Nantes, Marseilles, and other cities local officials undertook a census of prostitutes and bordellos. They also attempted to contain prostitution in a few, preselected streets and required that all bordellos be registered. By the end of Napoleon's reign the foundations of a complete regulatory system were in place, although it was not fully implemented until many years later.

With the return of the authorized bordello, Europeans appeared to have come full circle, to have returned to the status quo ante of the late Middle Ages. But despite appearances the two regulatory systems rested on very different assumptions. In Napoleonic Paris the prostitute did not belong to the community. She was by definition diseased and therefore outside the social order. Nor was authorization synonymous with approval. Late eighteenth-century moralists did not promote the registration of bordellos in order to preserve them for use by the city's youths; they registered brothels in order to control them, to see that they did not operate secretly and escape the vigilance of the police.

For eighteenth-century observers, the prostitute was, to answer the question that began this essay, a rebel. If she were not dangerous, why did she merit so much attention, so much repression? Because she defied social norms she had to be watched and controlled. Disease was but a metaphor for the real danger she posed: the overturning of patriarchal order, that is, order *tout court*. It was not by chance that nineteenth-century conservatives identified the prostitute with the threat of working-class insurrection. Uncondoned female sexuality was dangerous, and the early modern whore, be she courtesan or tavern maid, kept woman or streetwalker, challenged and upset the established order.

16

Criminals

Nicole Castan

THE PARTICIPATION OF women in criminal
activity is difficult to assess. We immediately encounter problems with definitions and sources,
which must be resolved before we can conclude
that certain types of delinquency were specific to
women, especially since women's crimes (if any)
cannot be isolated from their familial and communal contexts. At the outset, then, let us define
the term *crime* as applied to women in the broad
sense, that is, with reference to the behavioral
norms of the period. We shall therefore be looking
not only at violations of the law subject to judicial
punishment but also at various kinds of misbehav-
ior and deviancy subject only to the sanctions of
social control.

One source of evidence is of course court records, although the gaps in these remain considerable, partly as a result of neglect in the preservation of judicial archives. Additional evidence can
be found in government administrative archives,
particularly those concerning orders for imprisonment by *lettre de cachet*. But many crimes and
misdemeanors never found their way into the archives: some were cleverly covered up in ways that
discouraged the filing of charges, but there was
also a very deeply ingrained habit of dealing with
even the most serious crimes in private, often be-

fore notaries, for the purpose of obtaining reparation and restitution without the expense of the judicial process. Taken together, the sources raise the question of why the proportion of cases involving women appears to have been so low: 10 to 20 percent, depending on the jurisdiction. This low rate contrasts sharply with the usual pessimistic and derisive pronouncements about the "brutal and impulsive female nature," which drove women to lust and excess. "Eternal and sinful Eve, drunk with desire for men," was denounced by Protestants as well as Catholics, who recommended mounting "guard over the senses" and extolled the image of woman as virgin, wife, and mother and mistress of her passions, these being snares of the demon. One would expect this female weakness, which was often associated with violence, to yield high rates of certain crimes, and this expectation is indeed borne out in the case of sorcery, 80 percent of the accusations for which involved women. The rate of female involvement in ordinary crimes, however, is far lower than one might expect.

The Point of Honor and Everyday Violence

Women's activities were concentrated in certain specific areas, most obviously the household, where women of all stations were the veritable rulers of a space at the intersection of the public and private spheres. Woman's bailiwick was the house and everything connected with it—neighbors, streets, merchants. This was where behavioral norms were most commonly violated and where frequent but minor types of crime occurred. The average Western European family consisted of four to six related individuals and a variable number of servants. The wife was responsible for the family's material needs (cooking, health care, childrearing, burial of the dead). Her daily routine brought her into contact with filth and coarseness (from which she took her very realistic diction) and at times led to her being suspected of witchcraft and poisoning. But she was also charged with an important moral mission, one summed up rather well by the word *honor*, the surest guarantee of virtue: the burden of honor was every woman's to bear. Honor of course meant chastity and fidelity, but it also involved protecting one's own reputation and the reputation of one's family. Eventually a rather flexible code of conduct took shape, one that made allowances for families of different stations and women of different conditions (daughter, wife, or widow) as it gradually extended its insistence on respectability over the middle and even lower classes, excluding only the "rabble." This code was as strict in Catholic as in Protestant countries, and it was enforced everywhere by patriarchal authority backed up in the sixteenth century by the modern state. To challenge or violate the code was risky. An insolent or guilty woman was subject to judgment by the courts or to imprisonment by *lettre de cachet,* or she might be punished instead by the agents of social control (consistories, communities, youth groups) through such rituals of denunciation as defamatory songs or the noisy demonstrations known as charivaris. Of course family discretion concealed a great deal, and servants were taught that to talk out of turn was to be guilty of disloyalty. But people, and especially women, were insatiably curious about and interested in one another's business, and it was impossible to conceal the deviancy and violence that made the family, of necessity bound to its patrimony, not only a haven and refuge but also a source of criminal behavior in which women, like it or not, played an essential role.

The primary focus was on acts destructive of the family order because they violated the sexual morality over which church and state kept a close watch. Daughters and widows were the first to feel the effects of institutional repression when public scandal threatened. Paternal authority and family rank were then crucial: a daughter of the English gentry or the French provincial nobility who became pregnant out of wedlock might be whispered about in private yet spared public disgrace. Often the affair ended with an arranged marriage, abetted by financial inducements to the groom, or with the unwed mother's discreet departure to a place where she might deliver her child in seclusion. For young women of more modest background the government took a different approach: an edict issued by Henri II required that all out-of-wedlock pregnancies be declared to the authorities, failing which the mother could be charged with illegal concealment. Under a similar English statute of 1624, failure to declare an illegitimate pregnancy became presumptive evidence of intent to commit infanticide. These laws affected mainly urban women: in the eighteenth century more than 55 percent of pregnancy declarations were filed in cities, and the annual number increased steadily throughout the century in cities everywhere. Did this trend reflect the fact that urban morals were corrupt, as was often charged at the time? Or does it reflect a greater zeal on the part of urban authorities to prosecute offenders, many of whom may have been rural women fleeing their family's wrath and unable to go on living in their native villages? These efforts to discipline the population showed results in the sixteenth and seventeenth centuries, when the rate of illegitimate births declined in France and England. In the eighteenth century this rate remained at a very low level in rural areas but rose rapidly in the cities, where penniless, disgraced young women often ended in hospital prison wards in France and Italy or in houses of correction in England, the United Provinces, and Germany.

In societies predicated on the principle of legitimacy, adultery was the quintessential subversive act because it threatened to disrupt the orderly transmission of names and fortunes. It was therefore made a criminal offense, and in the sixteenth century the punishment for it was increased, but only in cases in which the wife was the guilty party. The few cases that actually went to court were generally those that involved the wife's murder by an outraged husband or the husband's murder by the wife (often with the complicity of her lover, acting under orders in the case of a domestic or man of inferior rank or on his own in the case of a man eager to take his rival's place). In ordinary cases the most common punishment was imprisonment for life in a convent at the guilty woman's own expense, unless she persuaded her husband to grant her a pardon or obtained a letter of remission, as did one woman from a family of prominent Parisian jurists in the sixteenth century. Suspicious husbands were more likely, however, to rely on royal *lettres de cachet* for both preventive and punitive purposes. It was not difficult for a woman to incur suspicion. Take, for example, the case of one woman from a town in rural Aquitaine who not only managed her own household affairs but was allowed to make excursions on horseback accompanied by her maid. Her familiar relations with an abbé exceeded what her husband took to be the bounds of propriety. His suspicions increased as he began to suffer digestive troubles and witnessed the death of a cat that had been fed a *confit* prepared by his wife. He promptly accused her of adultery and attempted poisoning. Going to court, however, would have required presenting evidence that might have exposed the family to public scandal. The husband therefore chose the more discreet course of obtaining a royal order and dispatched his wife to an Ursuline convent in a nearby town.

Another notorious inducement to crime was the remarriage of

a widower, a common occurrence in this period. As in Perrault's tales stepmothers sometimes terrorized their husband's children for their own ends. The trial of Catherine Estinès aroused passionate interest throughout France shortly before the Revolution. Her father's wife, a greedy woman, intolerant of children not of her own blood, and determined to gain control of all her husband's property—the very image of the wicked stepmother—had reduced poor Catherine to servitude. When the father, a wealthy tavern-keeper and notorious alcoholic, died after drinking too much at a local fair, Catherine's stepmother immediately accused her of having poisoned him. What made the charge plausible was that the girl had purchased arsenic to protect the household provisions from rodents, a common practice. That night, after serving her father his soup, she had departed from her usual custom and immediately poured out the leftover soup and washed the pot. On the basis of "expert" testimony by ignorant surgeons Catherine was found guilty after a hasty trial and sentenced first to have her hand cut off and then to be burned at the stake, the usual punishment for parricides. On appeal the parlement fortunately dismissed the verdict.

This famous case shows how difficult it could be to get to the bottom of family disputes, which often smoldered for a long time before erupting suddenly, perhaps after lengthy premeditation. In such conflicts women were likely to get the blame owing to their "perfidy and feebleness of nature," which so often led to their being charged with poisoning. But few of these dramatic cases went to court. Only four appeared in the edicts of the parlement of Toulouse in the eighteenth century, and the Châtelet of Paris assumed jurisdiction in all four. The accused or convicted women seeking letters of remission justified their behavior by adducing "the anger that seized them" or claiming legitimate self-defense in view of how they and their children had been treated. In seventeenth-century England, in the county of Essex, domestic violence was recorded only when it resulted in a corpse, and not surprisingly the guilty party was usually a man: of seven cases heard by the criminal courts between 1620 and 1680, wives were victims in five. Women were more likely to be accused of negligence, possibly aggravated by brutality, in cases involving children and servants. But in eighteenth-century Surrey (with a population of around 80,000) nine women were charged with murdering their husbands, compared with only six men charged with murdering their wives. The motive was usually jealousy, long-term resentment of brutal treatment, or rejection of the children from a first marriage. In plain language that was meant to convince, the testimony reveals how neglect and inattention could cause hatred and resentment to fester. Petitions for the detention of family members in France confirm this bleak picture. The number of such petitions rose sharply in the eighteenth century (from 20 to 30 percent of all petitions for royal intervention), and in Paris fully one-third of the cases involved a husband or wife. In the *généralité* of Caen the grounds cited in requesting the detention of a woman were as follows: licentious behavior or embezzlement, 52.6 percent; madness, 18.1 percent; danger of a misalliance, 15.8 percent. These petitions were generally signed by a father, mother, husband, or wife and stemmed from all classes of society, from the aristocracy on down to merchants, artisans, and farmers. The fact that their number increased in the eighteenth century may reflect either an increase in domestic "delinquency" or a decline in the effectiveness of familial authority in dealing with corrupting and destructive acts for which, things being as they were, women were so often blamed.

An Aggressive Sociability

Social relations among women might cast doubt on the progress of "civility," given the degree to which they fostered a climate of petty crime, insulting language, and even physical violence—the staple diet of nineteenth-century courts. Although such intemperate behavior occasionally occurred among middle-class women, during the ancien régime it was more routine among the lower classes and more common in urban than in rural settings. Cases involving this kind of behavior accounted for more than half the caseload of urban courts, and 20 to 25 percent of them involved women. Penalties included reparations and monetary damages. But altercations also occurred at higher levels of society, almost always as the result of some offense to honor. One bourgeoise of southwestern France defended tooth and nail the reputation of a son destined for a career in the military: "How can my son possibly return to his regiment with his head held high?" Why were women, and particularly women of the lower classes, so quick to anger?

To the reasons that are already well known must be added the effects of freedom. Women were not confined to their homes; they met friends and acquaintances in the street on their way to work, the washhouse, or the shops. They thus became the bearers of news and gossip, a role they assumed with gusto and grandiloquence in a world where everyone knew everyone else. Living at close quarters, they knew everything and made sure that others knew. And there was always plenty to report: the frictions of daily life, conflicts over the use of common facilities (such as wells, garbage piles, and gates), and the problems of unruly children were of universal interest.

In Paris the streets were a primary battleground, where women hurled insults at one another.[1] "F—— slut, whore, filth," shouted a woman who rented carriages when accused by a busybody of stealing six livres, and her words were accompanied by slaps, stabs with a broom, and horse dung hurled at her adversary's face. Despite the efforts of the churches to promote peace and charity, violence was clearly part of popular culture, although the fact that stabbings gave way to obscene words and gestures may indicate a degree of moderation. To some extent these customs reflected an alacrity on the part of women excluded from public office and from the church hierarchy to settle their own disputes, and to do so in the presence of an appreciative audience. In one dispute over who would be served first in a bakery in the Gard, for example, the mayor's daughter tangled with the wife of an artisan who had no intention of allowing herself to be shouldered aside by such a parvenue. Nasty insults about the social background and reputation of the mayor's family were followed by a shoving match in which the bourgeoise ended up in the batter. But the mayor's daughter, having lost the battle but not the war, organized a group of her friends, who came "clubs in hand, jumping and dancing and shouting, 'We've given her a thrashing, now she can go get herself bandaged up.'" If such an encounter ended badly, with a death, say, then self-defense could always be invoked as grounds for seeking a letter of remission. But murder was the exception: from the thirteenth through the eighteenth centuries in France and England the percentage of homicide cases heard by the courts in which the murder was committed by a woman rose from only 7.3 percent to only 11.7 percent, and in the sixteenth century a mere 1 percent of letters of remission involved such cases.[2] Female violence was more a matter of sound and fury than of mortal physical violence, and men, who knew how to turn the situation to their own advantage, looked on with ironic indulgence.

Crimes of Poverty

In the early modern period, crimes that today would be judged in the lower criminal courts could result in loss of civil rights and serious, even capital, punishment. Fewer than 10 percent of cases involving women fell into this category, and the percentage is even lower if one counts only those actually sentenced. Almost all were women who had left or been driven from their family homes; half to two-thirds were unmarried daughters, one-fifth were abandoned wives, and the rest were widows. Deprived of all family support, they earned their living as domestics or textile workers and were therefore subject to the risks of the market economy and at the mercy of unemployment, illness, or widowhood. Petty crime was a constant temptation, one to which Jeanne Deschamps frequently succumbed: a native of Fribourg, she either worked as a spinner or begged for a living and stole when the opportunity presented itself. Meanwhile, in Toulouse, a woman by the name of Marion found herself abandoned when her husband went off to war and lived by washing linen and filling water jugs from the river or serving in a tavern. Rootless women such as these generally sought refuge in towns, where they fell into a life of petty crime.

One crime that women were likely to commit was far from petty. Infanticide (considered premeditated if the pregnancy was concealed) was treated as a form of parricide and an "atrocity" against "the fruits of one's entrails" that was punishable by burning or hanging. In fact it was usually an act of desperation and panic. The dishonor of an illegitimate pregnancy was catastrophic. A woman forced to choose between her job and her child did what she had to do. One mother suffocated her newborn between her thighs, according to the testimony of a surgeon, who based his conclusion on the flattening and elongation of the child's head. The incidence of such acts is difficult to evaluate, particularly in rural areas, where although women were quick to detect the signs of pregnancy and clandestine delivery they were also prepared, out of tenuous solidarity, to keep the fact secret if they decided not to testify in court. Thus infanticide accounted for fewer than

1 percent of the cases judged by the parlement of Toulouse, and during the reign of Louis XVI the Châtelet of Paris assumed jurisdiction in only three cases. In seventeenth-century Essex nearly 10 percent of those sentenced to death were women charged with infanticide, most of them unmarried or young widows. But the severity of punishment abated in the eighteenth century, and in Surrey, which averaged one accusation per year, only four women were sentenced to hang, and none was executed between 1750 and 1800. The difference had little to do with religion; Catholics and Protestants were equally concerned in the sixteenth and seventeenth centuries to combat debauchery as a threat to the family and public order. But in the eighteenth century English juries and French magistrates insisted on more substantial evidence and took account of the circumstances surrounding a child's death. Marie Guyot denied any crime even when caught in the act by neighbors as she was throwing her newborn infant out the window: "I was standing when it came out. I didn't know what it was." More commonly women accused of infanticide claimed to have delivered a stillborn child, and the state of medical knowledge was such that often it was impossible for expert witnesses to contradict them categorically. The number of death sentences therefore declined; women were sentenced instead to houses of correction or locked hospital wards. Simultaneously there was a spectacular increase in the number of abandoned children, most of them illegitimate, reflecting the growing rate of illegitimate births in cities. One effect of this trend was to reduce the number of prosecutions for infanticide, but another was to stretch hospital finances beyond the breaking point, despite the extremely high mortality rate among infants sent out to wetnurses.

Pilfering and Theft

To judge by court records alone, theft was the quintessential woman's crime. At first sight it is tempting to classify theft as the typical proletarian act of aggression, but in fact criminal records reveal the involvement of a rather broad spectrum of society, ranging from peasants to shopkeepers and artisans' wives. Women were charged with acceding to their husbands' demands or suggestions by taking part in various breaches of rural custom and offenses against the property of others. These women were not necessarily poor. Many were habitual thieves of a sort tolerated by the community, provided restitution was made whenever they were caught. Thievery could be a means of enrichment, and a wife could easily claim to be acting on orders of her husband, particularly since sordid avarice and greed were tolerated in women so long as they were acting in their roles as housekeepers and mothers. A female thief was more likely to be excused if she had children to feed. She could preserve her essential honor as a responsible mother despite her petty larceny.

On the whole, theft by women was thus a minor if common crime. The one exception was theft by servants, which was considered a more serious matter because it betrayed the trust of the masters, who could not be expected to keep watch over their possessions at all times. Suspicion of servants was common, servants being widely employed even in humble families, where the hired maid ate and shared living quarters with her employers. But the most dangerous servants were those who worked in the more affluent households, some of whom were adventuresses and many of whom had severed all ties to their own families. One such was C. Petit, the widow Boudard, aged forty-four, who worked as a cook in Paris at a salary of eighteen écus a year but also supported a timpanist in the royal guard. She robbed one household to maintain the other. Social mobility was not considered a virtue in people in service: the faithful retainer was set apart from other servants, whose greed, presumably spurred by proximity to inaccessible riches, was endlessly denounced in novels and comedies of the period. Nevertheless, the fears of the master class, which Louis-Sébastien Mercier described in the late eighteenth century, did not lead to harsh repression of servants' crimes: the Paris Parlement heard a few cases in 1782, and the provincial court of Angers heard only eighteen during the entire eighteenth century. In fact this category of crime accounted for only 5 to 8 percent of all urban thefts, and more than half the cases involved female servants, against whom masters, magistrates, and juries were reluctant to pronounce the death penalty. The preferred treatment was to search the disloyal servant's body and belongings quite rudely and then send her away to get herself in trouble elsewhere. The death penalty was reserved for dangerous recidivists or for those unfortunate enough to be arrested after a wave of complaints, like one poor seventeen-year-old in Toulouse who was hanged for stealing a handkerchief, or another in Paris who went to the gallows for the theft of a silver spoon. But the confiscation or theft of an inheritance, which could make a poor woman wealthy overnight, was severely punished. This did not often happen, because wealthy families rarely left the elderly at the mercy of servants. The ideal target was a crippled old man without close relatives. One such gentleman was rumored to have 40,000 livres in notes as well as hats full of gold and cash in his possession. A female servant made herself indispensable by performing all the tedious chores he demanded. With the help of neighbors she stripped the house clean and took advantage of the confusion following the man's death to lay hold of the notes and gold. But she was imprudent enough to make investments beyond the means of a woman of her station.

The vast majority of cases involved petty thefts, which might seem insignificant if one fails to bear in mind their frequency and their cruel consequences in a society in which consumer goods and household implements were in short supply, in which the property of the poor was the most vulnerable, and in which the loss of even small items was therefore a major frustration. Theft contributed heavily to the climate of insecurity that prevailed in the major cities, and especially in Paris, where it accounted for half to three-quarters of all crime. Of 532 accused criminals who appeared before the Paris Parlement in 1782, 98 (17 of them women) were charged with serious crimes of violence as compared with 399 (76 of them women) charged with theft or embezzlement. In other words, one in four thieves was a woman (the proportion was higher for thefts of linen and fabric, lower for thefts of silver, jewels, and coin). The frequency of theft was lower in the countryside, where seed, vegetables, fruits, and wood were the most coveted items. In the cities the most frequently stolen items included linen, utensils, and, above all, food (because of the need to feed the family). Shoplifting was also common, as thieves found irresistible the abundance of merchandise and the relative ease with which it could be taken. The profile of the female thief was much the same throughout Europe, and everywhere lawlessness moved from the countryside to the cities. Nearly all female thieves were needy workers who lived on their wages from day to day. More than half were unmarried, 45 percent were married, and 4.5 percent were widows, according to Montyon, a well-known prosecutor of the day. These proportions varied with the type of crime. Few seem to have been professional criminals, that is, members of a gang of thieves, although in 1764 the English press did report that a gang of young women was stealing from London shops. Women were, however, among the professionals in the receipt of stolen goods, dealing with experienced thieves, finding buyers for their wares, and making loans against collateral. The activities of these "fences" were well known to the police, who used them as informers.

A wave of thefts in the second half of the eighteenth century worried the authorities. The crime of theft was closely associated with poverty, and from the sixteenth century on, crime waves had often led to measures to assist the poor or to place beggars under lock and key. Poverty, begging, and vagabondage were the breeding grounds of crime, and cities and highways became particularly dangerous in bad years. It was difficult for women without roots to escape from the vicious circle of poverty and crime that made them so apt to be arrested and confined in the vast hospital-prison of Salpêtrière in Paris.

Punishment

The first step in any attempt to classify women's crimes must be to examine the ways in which society chose to punish them, because these choices are at least as significant as the crimes themselves and because only those crimes that resulted in some kind of legal action have become a part of the historical record. The perennial problem of crime statistics is particularly important in the case of women's crimes because so many of them were committed in private settings. Few women of the upper and middle classes did not enjoy the protection of their families. In the eighteenth century, moreover, courts throughout Europe tended to treat women as having diminished responsibility for crimes committed, especially in the case of mothers with children. This phenomenon accounts for the difference between the number of women charged with crimes and those actually sentenced: many were released prior to judgment because they were given the benefit of the doubt or, more commonly, because they were needed at home. Most of those detained, especially in the cities, were isolated women who had come down in the world. Thus women are generally underrepresented in crime statistics.

Women were less prone than men to serious violence. In Surrey between 1660 and 1800 only one-quarter of 7,000 assaults were committed by women. But when women did commit crimes of violence, they were punished especially severely, because those crimes involved fundamental family values: murder, infanticide, and domestic theft were all subject to the death penalty, which was still vigorously enforced in the sixteenth century. In the two years 1535 and 1545, of 18 women accused of infanticide, 13 were sentenced to death by lower courts, and 8 of these sentences were upheld on appeal to the Parlement of Paris. In subsequent centuries, although the laws either did not change much (with the criminal ordinance of 1670 in France) or were made harsher (with the addition of new capital offenses in England), the courts were more lenient, favoring terms of imprisonment over torture and capital punishment. In Neufchâtel, for example, although 103 death sentences (10.2 percent of all sentences) were handed down over the course of the eighteenth century, and 14 of these to women, only 9 people were executed, including 6 for infanticide. The most common punishment (65 percent of the total) was banishment, often combined with flogging, which was used especially to punish crimes against property. Habitual thieves and deviants were sent to the prisons. In England, meanwhile, the harshest punishments, such as death and deportation, were reserved for men. After the middle of the eighteenth century women were most likely to be sentenced to houses of correction, while those guilty of minor crimes were apt to be flogged or placed in stocks.

Female criminals were treated no more harshly in French courts. Punishment was severe in cases thought to undermine sacred family values but relatively lenient for crimes deemed to pose little or no danger to society. Even in the lower courts, where judges had always tended to be harsher, sentences became more lenient. In the final twelve years of the ancien régime, charges were dismissed against nearly half of the women whose cases came up on appeal before the parlement of Toulouse: of 462 women sentenced, 3.9 percent received the death penalty, 25.7 percent the prison ward, 22.2 banishment, and the rest flogging or the pillory. In Paris the trend was similar: capital punishment was reserved for atrocities and for serious, repeated theft. Of those sentenced to death, 15 percent were for family-related crimes, 7.7 percent for infanticide, and 6.1 percent for crimes of violence. Meanwhile, the number of death sentences diminished steadily. Thus before the Revolution women in particular benefited from a change in the focus of law enforcement.

Broadly speaking, harsh punishment was maintained only

where it was believed necessary to set an example so as to safe-guard the authority of the family to control woman's procreative powers. There was leniency toward women whose precarious economic circumstances left unfilled the basic needs that, as moral theology discreetly stated, might excuse theft. What else could one expect from a society too poor to dispense with either the fundamental discipline of the family order or minimal punishments for crimes against another person's possessions?

TRANSLATED FROM THE FRENCH BY ARTHUR GOLDHAMMER

17

Protesters Plain to See

Arlette Farge

ONE OF THE MOST PRESSING needs in European historiography is to think through the question of popular violence. The classical interpretations (Marxist and otherwise) have given way to ever more sophisticated analyses that scour the judicial archives for evidence of the actions, words, roles, and functions of the various groups and communities that erupted in anger between 1500 and 1800. Historians must therefore explain the behavior of crowds in action, and sometimes in arms, while bearing in mind that every revolution yields a multiplicity of meaning and creates a yawning gap in space and time.

All students of the subject agree that, despite singularities, popular uprisings in northwestern Europe (that is, France, Holland, England, and Germany) in the period 1500–1800 conform in essential respects to a common model. The economic demands and serious religious violence of the sixteenth century ostensibly gave way in the seventeenth to peasant movements opposing taxes, price increases, and the high cost of grain and then, in the eighteenth century, to sporadic but less severe urban and rural violence triggered by a variety of causes both social and political. In Spain the sixteenth century was marked by periodic uprisings such as the antiseigneurial revolt of the Germanías in 1519–1520 in regions belonging to the crown of Aragon and the rebellion of the Comuneros of Castille in the same period. In the seventeenth century two powerful nationalist movements were active in Spain: one in Catalonia following its annexation in 1659, and another in Portugal, which eventually triumphed. Andalusia, too, was continually shaken by a variety of movements growing out of the poverty and injustice that afflicted the region in the 1640s. And eighteenth-century Spain witnessed the emergence of a number of broad social movements, the best known being that of Motin de Esquilache.

The situation in Italy is a subject of current research. Two periods of considerable urban turmoil, one in the late Middle Ages and Renaissance, the other in the difficult period of unification, frame a long interval of frequent agrarian uprisings expressing the deep-seated resentment of the lower strata of society against those better off.

Thanks to the work of American and European historians there is general agreement about how the data are to be analyzed and interpreted and what questions ought to be asked. It has been possible, for example, to develop what Charles Tilly calls a "performance repertoire" describing the capacity of a social group in a given time and place to act collectively and change its living conditions.[1] The composition of crowds involved in riots has been examined in detail to determine the social background, occupation, and political views of those who participated. It has also proved essential to study the ideas and attitudes that led individuals to join together for the purpose of opposing one or more authorities. Social conflict can then be interpreted in all its dimensions, and popular protest can be seen in its proper symbolic, social, and political context.

Despite these scholarly advances, little has been written on one group that participated to the full in all these protest movements, namely women. Why? In the first place because female violence aroused contradictory emotions, fascination combined with a desire to stamp it out. No one can escape this contradiction, not even historians, who have been slow to consider the forms and functions of violent protest by women.

In France Albert Soboul, Robert Mandrou, and Yves-Marie Bercé were undeniably among the first to note the impressive number of women involved in the popular movements of the early modern and revolutionary period.[2] In their cautious approach they viewed the role of women as an exception and took note of only the most obvious of women's functions: females, it was argued, took part mainly in bread riots, seeking of course to protect their families from hunger. As mothers and nurses, they "instinctively" protected their children from famine, just as female animals protect their young. Since the 1970s, however, the influence of women's history has led to a more sophisticated approach: Michelle Perrot and Natalie Zemon Davis, struck by the number of female protesters encountered in their research, noted, first, that it was particularly easy for women to participate in protest movements because the law regarded them as less responsible for their actions than men, both in civic and in criminal terms; and, second, that the culture in which they lived allowed women to embody, for brief periods, the disorder of a "world turned upside down," for in so doing they merely reflected what was said about them in both popular and learned literature. Furthermore, the facts are clear: women participated in protests of nearly all types, and did not just concentrate on food riots. The pattern is uniform in studies of English protests, of German peasant movements in the period 1648–1806, of Italian uprisings such as the so-called Masaniello riot in Naples in 1647, and of popular protest in Lyons in the seventeenth and eighteenth centuries.[3] The case of Holland, which has been studied in exhaustive detail, shows that women were highly active in religious and antifiscal uprisings and, somewhat more surprisingly, in political protests (such as the Patriot Revolt of 1782–1787) throughout the seventeenth and eighteenth centuries.[4] The evidence is abundant that women do not "think only with their stomachs."

Yet despite the fact that women took part in riots and sometimes made up a majority of the crowd, the significance of this female presence has seldom been examined or interpreted. With few exceptions the works that mention women devote little space to attempting to understand what gave reason to their actions, and even less has been written about how women managed the return from protest activities to everyday routine. We must look not only at the decision to take part and at the acts and symbols of protest but also at the equally difficult problem of what came afterward.

Joining in Protest

To join a protest is to make what one believes to be a legitimate collective response to a disastrous and unacceptable state of affairs. It is to manifest one's presence in the public sphere. In legal and civic terms, however, women were totally alienated from the public sphere. Why did they periodically force their way into a realm from which they were excluded by law?

There are two different ways of explaining the forms of female protest during the period 1500–1800. Some scholars apparently believe that women were as "free" as men: there was, they argue, a real flexibility of both male and female roles, particularly among rural industrial workers. Industrialization and the advent of the capitalist system somehow disrupted a preexisting harmony.[5] This viewpoint leads to the conclusion that women were as much involved in protest as men and participated as full partners.

A different and surely more plausible perspective is that the division of labor within family groups was asymmetrical. Although men's and women's roles might appear to have been "complementary," they were nevertheless unequal in both material and symbolic aspects.[6] If this view is correct, then the participation of women in protest raises new questions that require new answers.

The extent of female dissidence (unarmed and nonviolent) should not be underestimated. A brief look at various protests and uprisings in England, France, and Holland yields a better idea of the varied and subtle ways in which women resisted the prescriptions of the civil and religious authorities. Let us look first at the English "recusants" of the period 1560–1640.[7] A minority of Catholic women resisted the Act of Uniformity of 1559, which attempted to impose one religion on everyone, and thereby revealed the nature and limits of the state's authority while at the same time demonstrating their own capacity to resist and to oppose the dogma of civil and religious obedience. These determined women refused to obey the law and bow to the will of the established church. Highly imaginative, they spoke out and justified their actions even after their husbands were asked to curb their activities. Though forced to pay fines and even sentenced to prison, they did not generally pay the ultimate price for defying the authorities: only three women were executed, compared with twenty-seven men, reflecting the prevailing principle that women bore less responsibility than men for their actions.

In making their protest recusant women used the resources available to them. They sheltered Catholic priests and arranged things so that the presence of these hidden guests remained secret from servants and merchants. If the authorities turned up despite these precautions, recusant women could plead innocence, ignorance, and helplessness (all forms of female powerlessness) in the hope of moving their enemies to pity. Aggressive, determined, and "feminine," they challenged law and order in the one sphere of activity traditionally open to them. They acted publicly by converting the private sphere into a surprisingly effective weapon of war.

Let us turn now to Paris in July 1750.[8] In that month the police decided to clear the capital's streets of juvenile delinquents, idlers, and other riffraff. The intention may have been to send those arrested to Louisiana to populate colonial settlements in need of new blood. But the people of Paris were not about to let their children be rounded up without reacting. In 1725 there had been an uprising over a similar affair, and now serious disturbances again erupted in several parts of the city. Several people would die and many would be injured before the riots were curbed and three young men were sentenced to death for their participation in the street violence.

It is hardly surprising that women were involved in this protest. What is more interesting is the way they went about looking for their children, who were held at several locations in Paris, including the Bicêtre and Fort-l'Evêque prisons. These women made use of their knowledge of how society worked. They were kept informed about the arrests and all that followed by neighborhood information networks, local contacts, and general knowledge of the social machinery. Knowing when and where the *lieutenant général de police* and his assistants made their rounds, women took up positions along the route, stopped the official carriage, and carried on discussions with the occupants. They called on policemen and influential inspectors. They went to the prison gates with food for their children, conversed with the prisoners, and even worried about their lessons. The variety of these actions indicates not only familiarity with the way the city was run and with the social habits of the police but also a ready capacity to hit upon forms of protest, thought, and expression that amount to what can only be called negotiation.

Finally, let us turn our attention to Holland and the pro-Orange uprisings of 1653, 1672, and 1745, and the so-called Patriot Revolt of 1782–1787.[9] Here women were present in greater numbers than in any of the antifiscal or grain riots of the same period. Their role in traditional neighborhood and sectional communities enabled them to take an active part in political protest movements. Though legally excluded from the public sphere, they worked in it "naturally," clearly far from indifferent to public affairs. But it would be misleading to infer that the participation of women in political protest indicates their equality with male protesters or authorities.

The Language, Signs, and Representations of Protest

Women expressed their protest differently from men. Men were aware of this and accepted it, but they also made judgments about it. Women often led the way: they took center stage and urged men to follow. Men were not shocked to see the world thus temporarily turned upside down. Drawn by the shouting and turmoil, they swelled the crowd. They knew that the women in the front ranks would impress the authorities, and they also knew that the women in the vanguard had little to fear because they were less apt to be punished than men. This willingness to subvert the usual hierarchy might well guarantee the ultimate success of the movement. But while accepting this distribution of roles, men also judged the behavior of their female comrades. Their descriptions of what they considered to be disorderly, abusive, even extreme conduct reveal a mixture of fascination and irritation.

Two complementary systems were thus socially constructed, each reflecting and feeding on the other. On the one hand women acted in concert with men yet knew that their behavior was considered extreme. On the other hand men could not rid themselves of a dualist vision of woman: she was good, gentle, and necessary yet also duplicitous, deceitful, and allied with the devil. These themes formed a staple of popular literature (the so-called Bibliothèque Bleue, or Blue Library), in which women were depicted as both angels and monsters, life and death.

The role of women in popular uprisings can be understood

only in the context of this dual system, which drew them in at certain times and excluded them at others. Symbolism was as important as concrete actions and situations.

Urban and rural domestic and neighborhood conflicts exhibited their own specific modalities. Neighborhoods, villages, and households required a certain cohesiveness in order to cope with "external dangers," and the result was the creation of a kind of space, one that Robert Muchembled has called the "territory of the ego,"[10] in which men defended collective interests by force and women by maintaining networks of surveillance and information. If, through some misfortune, a dispute erupted, women used men as a defensive shield while devising strategies to calm the situation. Women pointed fingers, brought problems to light, and then quieted overheated tempers. These local conflicts revealed a gender-based differentiation of roles in which women stood back from the front line of action.

Rioting shattered old codes and gave impetus to new forms of interaction between men and women. By a stroke of good fortune the judicial archives allow us to examine closely the moment of transition in one particular instance: in Paris on July 14, 1725, a riot broke out against the city's bakers. It all began with a dispute between a female customer and one baker in the Faubourg Saint-Antoine.[11] A woman by the name of Desjardins refused to pay the baker Radot thirty-four sous for a loaf of bread that had cost only thirty sous just that morning. The woman rallied her neighbors, and a crowd of almost eighteen hundred sacked and pillaged bakery shops in the vicinity.

When the quarrel first began, neighbors ran to find M. Desjardins, a cabinetmaker, who lived just a few doors down from Radot's bakery. When a woman became involved in an argument, the proper thing to do was to notify her husband or companion so that order could be duly restored. Desjardins was in no doubt about what to do: once on the scene, he "wanted to berate his wife [because he] wanted her to return home." In other words, what the husband wanted was an end to the public conflict and confirmation of his right as husband to chastise his wife. But he mistook the nature of the conflict. The women understood that it was a public matter and that there was no reason why it had to be settled in private: the price of bread was too high, and Mme. Desjardins was within her rights to protest. Her husband "was immediately surrounded by more than a hundred women, who told him that his wife was not wrong and that it was the baker's fault."

The dispute was not just a private altercation. The riot and ensuing pillage of bakeries constituted a legitimate protest against a public injustice, namely, an unwarranted increase in the price of bread.

From that point on women assumed the female role traditional in public protest, the opposite of their role in private conflict: speaking in a voice other than that used in running the household, they shouted for help and exhorted the mob to violence. Women were the first to force their way into nearby bakeries. They established their public identity (one they ordinarily did not possess) and became representatives of the community. This sudden passage from the private to the public domain revealed not only an understanding of the event but also a fierce determination to assert a collective identity that was normally ignored, not to say mocked.

Woman and Child

Most historians remark on the fact that large numbers of young people took part in riots. The demography of the period ensured that youth would play an important role. Puberty came early, as did the beginning of working life, but marriage was relatively late. The "young" thus constituted a large, available, and powerful group. Embodying the future of the community, they enjoyed prestige as well as innocence.

Not only adolescents but even young children participated in riots. Constables were careful to record the composition of violent mobs in their reports, which frequently mention the presence of women accompanied by their children. Children had been involved in certain episodes during the sixteenth-century Wars of Religion, but in groups of their own, which is something different. On January 1, 1589, for example, the Ligue maîtresse of Paris organized a children's march in the capital. Nearly 100,000 marchers carried candles from the Cemetery of the Innocents to the Eglise Sainte-Geneviève in the Latin Quarter. During episodes of religious violence, moreover, children had been seen attacking the wounded or helping to dismember bodies. In the Great Irish Rebellion of 1641 English pamphlets and broadsides cited the monstrous behavior of Irish children, who roamed the countryside in bands and carried whips with which to flog the English enemy.[12]

By the eighteenth century things had changed; the presence and behavior of children were no longer singled out for comment. However, descriptions of popular disturbances recurrently mention women with their children in the front ranks of rebellion. Of course one possible explanation is that women could be there only if they brought their children with them. But there may have been other reasons, too: although children were economically and culturally productive and therefore familiar with public life very early, their neighborhoods knew, recognized, and adopted them as their own. During the disturbances that followed the arrest of children in Paris in 1750, it was not only parents who went to the prisons to demand their children's release but other residents of the affected neighborhoods as well. The honor of family and neighborhood was invested in the children. That children accompanied their mothers in protest was a sign of their place between family and city—a symbol as well as a fact of life. This figure of femininity allied with youth lent gravity and legitimacy to popular uprisings, combining two subversive wills in a single image connoting a desire for innovation and for the restoration of justice.

Through the woman and child popular protest attempted to repair what was destroyed and to anticipate a future whose uncertainty was no longer tolerable. Together the woman and child symbolized the passage from the present to the future: they gave the desire for change a face.

Words, Gestures, and Attitudes

Riotous behavior is difficult to analyze. It involves various specific forms of action in which rage, anger, and violence possess a grammar and more than one logic. Through these logics the crowd sometimes discovers the meaning of what it is doing, although the men and women participating in the event may be, as it were, playing different scores. Though acting in a common cause, the participants see themselves as distinct and respond to one another's actions. The male gaze certainly influenced the course of action; the language and gestures of women were as much a creation of women as a product of their image.

From the innumerable convulsions that briefly disrupted the

life of a village, neighborhood, or trade as from broader, more emblematic uprisings we know that women had no compunctions about joining the fray. Police records and chroniclers' accounts frequently mention not only the audacity of women but also their humor and good cheer. For example, François Métra's secret correspondence concerning the Flour War of 1775, which mentions that the riot broke out "mainly among women," later observes that "the looters were street porters and other common folk and they seemed quite cheerful."[13] High spirits were also much in evidence in rural unrest from the late seventeenth through the eighteenth centuries, and memories of this time lingered long afterward, especially when women stirred things up enough to win a victory by frightening the elite into listening to their demands.

Women were not only high-spirited; they actively encouraged protest and incited others to riot. They used words to egg men on: the image became something of a stereotype. Terrified shouts and cries announced the beginning of a riot. And women's words, far from being mere insults or inarticulate utterances, as has often been charged, were shaped into sentences whose meaning propelled men forward. Although it was not uncommon to hear exhortations to death, shouts against the king, and bloody threats against the authorities issuing from women's mouths, many of their utterances went beyond pure verbal violence in the direction of social criticism. Women seized upon the issues that plunged the community into conflict. In a few words they explained the injustice, named the adversary, and gave voice to feelings of humiliation. They not only pointed out the normal price of bread, for example, but also complained about how difficult it was for women forced both to work and to raise their children. "What an outrage that women go selling greens in the streets, and then they [the authorities] come and take their children while they're not there," one woman shouted from her window in July 1750.[14] Women were articulate, proposed social explanations, and contributed to the protest in both thought and deed.

Women who went into combat barehanded had no trouble finding stones to throw or to hand to their male companions. They sounded the tocsin and sabotaged wagonloads of grain. Sometimes they hid knives or clubs beneath their skirts, and at the first sign of the authorities these weapons could be returned to their hiding places. Female rioters were likened to swarms of bees or clouds of insects, recurrent images that of course called attention to the distinctive features and sexual characteristics of the group. Zeal, collective fervor, and a readiness to repeat actions to the point of wearing down the enemy's resolve made the women's community a powerful, unified force that was hard to resist. Like the bee, the female protester was in deadly earnest; like the swarm, she was constantly abuzz: once again we recognize the perennial pair, the sober woman and the frenzied she-devil.

Just as hives of bees have a queen, so too were groups of women often led by one of their own, perhaps a particularly charismatic or imposing personality, a woman who commanded respect among her neighbors. Some of these leaders adopted or were given epithets or *noms de guerre,* like *la capitaine,* a tavern-keeper who in 1721 made speeches to a crowd that gathered in opposition to construction workers employed on royal projects.[15] Others took their names from fairy tales or noble titles, like *la princesse,* a lively, active working woman of forty-three who led disturbances in Paris in 1775 and who, after her arrest for disorderly conduct, became the object of the crowd's demands: "Leave her to us, leave her to us, she is our princess."[16] Amazon, captain, princess—such honorifics suggested a real desire to lead a group, to assert power, to join the male, and indeed the military, hierarchy. To take up arms was in fact one of the male functions most coveted by women, as *cahiers de doléances* (registers of grievances) from women's groups and manifestos of revolutionary women in 1789 make clear.

To march off to war as men did, to rebel by passing as men: cross-dressing was one of the traditional forms of popular protest. In England, Germany, and Holland women easily put on men's clothing.[17] They did so not only in riots but also in hard times when forced by economic hardship to take to the road or when they resorted to criminality, joining bands of thieves in which cross-dressing had symbolic as well as practical significance. Women also dressed as men for patriotic reasons, as when they took part in political disturbances and land and sea battles in seventeenth- and eighteenth-century Holland. When questioned by the police about their costumes, these women generally responded with pride and claimed to have been inspired by a long line of heroic women.

Men also disguised themselves as women before mingling in rebellious crowds, in the hope of protecting themselves from punishment. But there were deeper reasons for cross-dressing by both sexes.[18] Each gained something from the other: the man dressed as a woman warded off demons and avoided castration, while the out-of-place woman gained the ability to perform extraordinary acts, to enter the public arena without embarrassment. Thus cross-dressing did not generate disorder or overturn systems of values but in fact regenerated those systems by repeatedly introducing necessary innovations that subtly subverted old values. Yet this pattern, which at first sight seems egalitarian and reciprocal, was also beset by contradiction and inequality: the man who adopted the outward appearance of a woman and mimicked her behavior assumed those aspects of the traditional female role that were considered to be wild and undisciplined. Taking advantage of this license, he then denounced social injustice for the sake of the community's continued existence and prosperity. Men thereby manifested the power of women, but only the dark and detested side of that power, of woman's lustful and extravagant nature— the side that in quieter times was despised as inferior and dismissed as valueless. The man who dressed as a woman wrapped himself in a myth rather than expose its falsity.

Women not only mingled with men but also fought other women. In religious and social conflict sister fought sister fiercely and unrelentingly. In the many local conflicts that agitated early modern parishes, villages, and marketplaces, violence among women was seldom lethal, but revolt and its accompanying collective extortions led women into more forceful kinds of action and spurred a much more powerful desire to eliminate the enemy. The religious violence of the sixteenth century, for example, was all the fiercer because those involved on both sides wanted to rid themselves of the contamination that the sacrilege of their enemies introduced into their community. The "true" doctrine had to be defended and the false rejected at all costs and with the aid of ever more dramatic gestures and attitudes. Violence was not only the instrument of divine justice but a means of purification that was supposed to deliver one side from the infernal forces championed by the other. In massacres inflicted without guilt because carried out in the name of God, acts were all the more zealous because their purpose was to show that the heretic or religious enemy was not a human being but a monster. Protestants and Catholics behaved differently because the acts they perpetrated were generally borrowed from the biblical and liturgical repertoire and reflected each religion's attitudes toward the body and death and the fate of the body after death.[19] The violence of both men and women was extreme because it stemmed from each community's most fundamental values. If women played a significant role in these conflicts, even joining in battle against other women, it was because they occupied a privileged place within each community as the certain link between life and death, the central zone of creation and destruction, the carnal space in which the forces of nature and the sacred were reproduced.

In later centuries, when violent protest arose instead from nonreligious causes (high taxes, food shortages, and the like), women were no more apt to spare other women. The poor fought those richer than themselves, and their violence fed on distress and lashed out at the merest appearance of privilege. Thus in the grain riots of Ile-de-France and the urban riots of the long eighteenth century, women—particularly baker women or the wives of master bakers who worked in their husbands' shops—were targets of assault and even murder because they represented a relatively favored social group. Thus in the Paris riots of 1775 women belonging to certain specific occupational groups were attacked by other women because of their alleged shady dealing, price-gouging, and living off the hunger of the less fortunate.[20] Unity and division among women were two sides of one coin. In reacting to injuries inflicted on their communities they did not hesitate to take measures against women who seemed allied with abuses, injustice, or sacrilege.

Contemporary stories and chronicles—all written by men—describe female insurrectionists as furious, cruel, and bloodthirsty. Was the spectacle of barbarity, of a festival of death, so repellent and fascinating at the same time that perhaps men foisted it on the radically alien other, namely, woman, the bearer of children, malice, and disaster? Notwithstanding the possible exaggerations of male memory, we must attempt to provide an explanation for this cruelty. To cause blood to flow was the supreme transgression for women forbidden to bear arms or inflict death. Excluded from judicial, civil, and political decisionmaking, women found themselves momentarily empowered by the conditions of riot: the power to decide, the power to shed blood, was briefly theirs. Here their capacity to act, hence their political capacity, was greatest. The more publicly their role was recognized and the more it was sanctioned by the entire community, the crueler they could become. Actors and spectators influenced each other: perception shaped action, and action perception, inciting progressively more violent deeds.

On a symbolic level, women's shedding of blood may also have had profound transformative meaning. Blood flowed from each woman's body every month, although there were many competing theories about exactly why. The blood that flowed with each moon was man's enemy. A sign of the contamination and impurity of the female body, it periodically excluded man from access to the womb he desired. An emblem of Eve's original sin, it was both a curse and a power. Repeatedly denounced in tales and proverbs as the mark of a guilty wound, menstruation, woman's natural accomplice, became her insidious enemy. Caught between ignorance of the reason for its existence and learned disquisitions on its nature, woman internalized the menstrual taboo and experienced her monthly flow in terror and pain. It may be that she was fascinated by blood that flowed in a good cause and with the effect of purifying the community. If then, in the midst of rebellion and moved by a desire to restore justice or affirm belief in a rejected God, woman caused the blood of her enemies to flow, was she not participating in a rite of blood healing from which she was normally excluded, a rite the need for which she felt in the deepest recesses of her own body? Shed by her hand, blood became legitimate, even if her own blood was not. The spilled blood of the enemy engendered a purity denied to her menstrual flow. In this there was compensation for her taint, something to fill the void of which her absence from the political scene was one aspect.

Allegations of Extremism

Contrary to what scholars maintained only a few years ago, the presence of women in the rural and urban uprisings of early modern Europe is so obvious that it raises questions about the astonished tone of those who wrote on the subject then and now. Clearly, there was nothing extraordinary about women's participation in these tumultuous events. Despite the elaborate symbolic code involved in the description of female rioters, perhaps the whole subject is a nonissue. Indeed, to anyone studying the role of women in rebellion, only women's lack of participation should be surprising. Thus to ask why women should have been absent when rebellion threatened would raise new questions for historiography and might shed new light on the relations between the masculine and the feminine.

It is probably still a bit too soon to begin asking these new questions, but we can at least try to understand how the ordinary process by which women became involved in violence came to be seen by others as an extraordinary process, one that made the behavior of those women seem more audacious than it was. On this subject I offer a few briefly sketched points.

1. When women participated in violent protest, they did so in a variety of roles and socially acknowledged guises. As mothers with children they moved to the front ranks of rebellion. As instigators they exhorted others from windows and doorways. As members of a group, they lent support to their companions. As concerned parties, they spoke to the authorities and negotiated with them. In high dudgeon they attacked those whom they took to be the enemy, even if they were women. Certain of the justice of their cause and determined to see it triumph, they spilled blood with abandon. Interested in the community, they revitalized its meaning.

All these roles were filled by women, along with others that were attributed to them by men and by legend, in a state of anger induced by injustice and passions stirred by riot. Women drew on all that was in them and all that was said about them, taking from the crowd the energy needed to construct a temporary collective identity. On quiet days, in the monotony of daily life, women's virtues and vices were endlessly examined and scrutinized in minute detail, and as a result it was said of the female that she was a source of benefit but also a cause of fear and disgust. By bringing women together, the riot constituted them as identical yet different. In action they acquired the power to define themselves, to take positions, and to act.

2. Sustained by the masculine gaze, women were also constrained (not to say denatured) by it. Caught between meaning and the exaggeration of meaning, they were aware of how this forced their actions to conform to collective representations of frenzy and hysteria, particularly since, being deprived of the use of traditional political language, they knew that their words and acts were pushed in the direction of nonrationality. In the eighteenth century, and particularly during the French Revolution, certain women were keenly aware of this problem, which was discussed in various places, most notably in certain *cahiers de*

doléances in which women spoke of feeling suffocated as "objects of men's continual admiration and contempt."[21]

Between admiration and contempt, however, there was room for nothing but want, which was what made women act, fight, rise up, and claim a public role at the center of events.

Curiously, every action they took reinforced rather than dispelled their frenzied image. And yet in each instance, between archaism and innovation, something changed, something new was created in the city and in communal relations.

3. "On all sides is the murmur of politics,"[22] and the late eighteenth century found ample ways to give it expression, as women called in the most modern of accents for equality, for work, and for education.

As visible participants in riots women were often accused of extremism. They operated in a narrow zone where everyone looked at them and where, under the scrutiny of others, their virtues were repeatedly transformed into devilish vices. This was woman's lot because, carrying man's fruit and his desire in the same place, she had become identified with absolute excess.

4. When the storm passed, calm would return. The riot would end, leaving dead and wounded in its wake. Law and order would be restored. Accused of sedition, certain rioters would be subjected to public torture and to the opprobrium of the crowd. The police would say it was important to make examples of those who rebelled, and that the people must never be allowed to determine their own fate even when their demands were legitimate. The price of bread would go down as calm was restored. Nothing would remain of the riot but the memory—until the next riot, and the next, when those unfortunate enough to be arrested would say that they were innocent bystanders who just happened to be there to see the "revolt" because they had been told from their youth that such a thing was not to be missed.

Men went back to work and resumed their regular activities. No one asked questions. They simply resumed their places in the city. Women did the same, but with them it was different, because they returned to customary roles without a civic or political component, unlike the roles they had assumed temporarily in rebellion.

It is hard to know what this return to everyday routine was like. Perhaps women were proud of having participated. Perhaps they accepted an order of things in which they went from last to first and back to last. Perhaps different individuals reacted in different ways. No one knows. We can guess (although perhaps this is too linear a view of history) that each revolt transformed things while maintaining the traditional consensus. This is not a very satisfactory explanation. On this point it will be necessary to reflect (as has been done for more recent periods, such as 1914–1918) on the aftermaths of crises, on the sometimes imperceptible ruptures that speeded up the pace of change, even if the crises of the period 1500–1800 seem largely repetitive and not very "revolutionary."

Even if women were said to behave in extreme ways in riots, when the riot was over they went back to their men, and very few people were surprised. It bears emphasizing that until recently the fact that women took part in the great social movements of their times was forgotten. In reaction against this, women and their rebellious activities have been singled out, sometimes at the risk of isolating them from their everyday context and of seeing them in terms of contemporary representations. By so doing, historians (male and female alike) have unwittingly contributed to the fashioning of a mythical image of woman as unbridled heroine. This is what comes of failing to think about the obvious, namely, the history jointly fabricated by man and woman—precisely that history "whose eye," in Baudelaire's phrase, "is astonishing for its candor."[23]

TRANSLATED FROM THE FRENCH BY ARTHUR GOLDHAMMER

four

Women's Voices

Glückel of Hameln, Jewish Merchant Woman

Natalie Zemon Davis

BORN INTO THE JEWISH community of Hamburg, Glückel of Hameln (1646–1724) married Chaim Hamel young and brought fourteen children into the world, most of whom lived to marry and have children of their own. While her husband was alive she helped him with his business, which took him to fairs throughout Germany. After his death in 1689, Glückel married off the rest of their children into Jewish families in central Europe and continued the family business on her own, lending money, selling pearls and other goods, and attending fairs with her elder sons. She began to write her memoirs in Yiddish in the intense "melancholy" (as she called it) that followed Chaim's death. Here she recounts why, after years of widowhood, she decided to remarry. Not long after their wedding, Hirsch Levy, a wealthy Jewish banker of Metz, went bankrupt. The passage below shows us something of the religious sensibility of a Jewish woman, of her sense of herself as a parent and of her way of constructing her past.

> Matches with the most distinguished men in the whole of Germany had been broached to me, but as long as I could support myself on what my husband, peace unto him, had left me, it did not enter my head to marry again. God, who saw my many sins, did not will that I should agree to one of the proposed matches through which I and my children would have been truly fortunate and that I in dreary old age should have comfort. Such did not suit the Lord and for my sins I was induced to the match of which I shall now tell. Yet, despite

all, I thank my Creator, who has shown me mercy in my heavy punishment, more than I, a sinner, deserve. In truth I must be grateful, even though I cannot pay for my sins with fasts and other penances, as I should do, because of my troubles and sojourn in a strange land, though to God I know this is no excuse. Therefore I write this with a trembling hand and hot, bitter tears for it is written *Thou shalt serve God with all thy heart and with all thy soul*. I beg Almighty God to strengthen me that I may serve Him only—and that I may not appear before Him in soiled garments, for, as is said in the "Ethics of the Fathers": *Repent one day before your death*. As we do not know the day of death, we must repent every day. This I must do, even though I have a feeble excuse for myself: I had thought that after first settling my fatherless children I would go to the Holy Land.

This I could have done, especially as my son Moses was betrothed, and I had only my young daughter Miriam to provide for. So I, a sinner, should not have married again but should first have seen Miriam wedded, and then done what was seemly for a good, pious Jewish woman. I should have forsaken the vanity of this world and with the little left, gone to the Holy Land and lived there, a true daughter of Israel. There all the sorrows and cares of my children and friends, and the vanity of the world, would not have troubled me and I would have served God with all my heart. But the Lord led me to other thoughts and to a decision less worthy than this.

Well, to continue. A year passed before I could attend Moses's wedding. All sorts of trouble and misfortune befell me through my children meanwhile, and it always cost me much money. But it is not necessary to write of it: they are my own dear children and I forgive them, those that have cost me much as well as those who cost me nothing. Through them my fortune grew less and less. My business was large, for I had extensive credit with Jews and non-Jews. I afflicted myself: in the heat of summer and in the snow of winter I went to fairs and stood there in my shop all day; and though I possessed less than others thought, I wished to be always held in honour and not, God forbid, dependent on my children, sitting at another's table. It would be worse to be with my children than with strangers, in case, God forbid, through me, they sinned. This would be worse than death to me.

I began to find that I could no longer stand the strain of

long journeys and going about the town. I was fearful lest any bales of goods or outstanding debts were lost and I, God forbid, became bankrupt; so that those who trusted me should be losers through me, thus disgracing me, my children and my sainted husband, who lay under the sod. I then began to regret that I had let pass so many good matches and the chances of living respected and rich in my old age, and, perhaps, of helping my children at the same time. But regret does not help me now: it is too late. God did not wish it and bad luck thrust something else in my mind, as will now follow.

It was in the year 5459 [1698–99], at the time of the delay over the marriage of my son Moses, which I have already explained, that I received a letter from my son-in-law Moses Krumbach of Metz, Sivan 5459 [June 1699], in which he mentioned that Reb Hirsch Levy had become a widower. He extolled him as a fine, upstanding Jew, very learned in Talmud, possessed of great wealth and a magnificent household. In short, he praised him highly and according to all accounts what he wrote was true. But man sees with his eyes; God looks into the heart.

This letter reached me as I meditated my woes. I was then fifty-four years of age and had endured many cares because of my children. If the circumstances were as my son-in-law related, I could in my old age join a devout community, as Metz then had the name for being, and there pass the rest of my life in peace and see to the good of my soul. I trusted, too, that my children would not advise anything that was not for my good. I therefore wrote thus in answer to my son-in-law: "I have been a widow for eleven years and had no intention of marrying again. It is generally known that I could have made one of the greatest and most distinguished marriages in the whole of Germany, had I so desired. Notwithstanding, I will agree to this match, because you urge me to it so earnestly, if my daughter Esther advises the same." On this she wrote me as much as she, poor thing, knew and had seen. There was not much argument about the dowry. I was to give my husband as much as I could and he agreed that if I died first, my heirs would receive back my dowry; if he died first, he would leave me 500 reichstaler, besides returning my dowry of 1500 reichstaler. My daughter Miriam was then a child of eleven and he bound himself to support her until her marriage. If I had more money I would have given it to him as well, for

I thought that my money would be safer nowhere than with this man. I meant this also as a benefit for my daughter Miriam; she would not need to spend any of her money, all of which was lent out on interest. Furthermore, this man had a fine reputation in business: who knew what great benefit my children could derive in business as a result? But many thoughts are in the heart of man and He Who reigns in heaven laughs.

Unfortunately, God laughed at my thoughts and plans, and had already long decided on my doom to repay me for my sins in relying on people. I should not have thought of marrying again, for I could not hope to meet another Chaim Hamel. I should have remained with my children, for good or ill, and taken all as God willed; first married off my fatherless Miriam and then later, as I had decided, spent my last days in the Holy Land.

Still, all that has happened has passed and so cannot be changed. I have now only to beg of the Lord to hear and see only good of my children. With reference to myself, I receive everything from Him with love. May God the Just give me patience as heretofore . . .[1]

Anne-Françoise Cornet, Parisian Artisan

Arlette Farge

JULY 1750: A RIOT IS TRIGGERED in Paris when overzealous police, ordered to clear the streets of urchins, arrest large numbers of children. Outraged men and women rise up in protest, some attacking the police suspected of carrying out this mission while others search for their children in nearby prisons.

What follows is the deposition of Anne-Françoise Cornet, the wife of a master watchmaker. She gives a precise account of the days of waiting before she was able to reclaim her arrested son. During that time she made endless visits to officials, using her meager knowledge of the official world in the hope of locating her son.

The deposition is remarkable in its dignity, its evidence of the resolve of a woman in great pain, and above all her astonishing use of social knowledge to obtain interviews with police officials. Anne-Françoise Cornet was an artisan typical of her time. She wanted to influence events and did not hesitate to negotiate with the authorities. Here she shows that she was no dupe of the policeman and other officials who were reluctant to accept her as an equal. We see her as a subject of history, civically and politically responsible: her narrative is as tenacious as her actions and her hopes.

Here, then, are the words of Anne-Françoise Cornet, age forty-four, wife of Pierre Millard, master watchmaker, residing in the rue Royale.

As for the disturbances, she saw nothing and knows nothing. As for the abductions of children, one Sunday toward the end of September, while returning home after visiting one of her children, who lives with a watchmaker in Saint Denis de la Chastre, she saw a crowd of children from her neighborhood, who told her that her son had been arrested and that he was in the Grand Châtelet. She went there immediately and found her child in the court, crying a lot, and he told her that it was Bruxelles who had arrested him while he was playing ha'penny with two other children from the neighborhood on the steps of the equestrian statue in the Place Royale. One of the children is named Lucas and is the son of a man who was in the watch, and the other, Toussaint, is the son of a widow who cleans houses and does mending. She returned home promptly in the hope that her husband would not find out, but he knew. Between eight and nine in the evening she was told that Bruxelles, the inspector, was on his way home to the *hôtel* de Nicolaï, and she hurried off to see him. She found him under the arcade, asked to have her child back, and offered to pay the fees. He answered that it was not yet time, that he was no longer in charge, and that neither she nor her child would die if he stayed away for two days. Later she learned that he was supposed to have supper at ten o'clock with Sieur Tobary, the wine merchant across from her house, and she went there and begged him to return her child. Bruxelles said that she must be patient, that the child would not stay away long. The next day she made efforts to get her child back, submitting several petitions to Berryer, the lieutenant general, but seeing that nothing came of this, she obtained the protection of M. Montrevaux through a Sieur de Bligny, master painter, who introduced her to M. de Montrevaux, who was kind enough to give her a letter for the royal prosecutor, which was sent to Asnières. Upon receiving no answer about her child, she returned to M. de Montrevaux, where she learned that the royal prosecutor was with him, and that the aforementioned Inspector Bruxelles was in the antechamber. When she left, she paid M. de Montrevaux, who promised to have her child back that same day. But after three more days without him, she returned to M. de Montrevaux, who was quite surprised and gave her a letter for the lieutenant general of police, Berryer. Despite this letter, four more days passed without her child, and on Sunday a fortnight after her child's arrest she finally obtained his release along with ten others. It was she who took the certificates of release for her son and the others to the clerk of court. It cost her thirty-six sols for the clerk, fifty sols for the prison, thirty-six sols for the welcome, and she gave nothing to the officer of the watch.[1]

TRANSLATED FROM THE FRENCH BY ARTHUR GOLDHAMMER

Notes

Chapter 1. Women, Work, and Family
OLWEN HUFTON

1. Daniel Defoe, *The Behaviour of Servants in England* . . . (London, 1724), pp. 1–9.

2. Patrick Colquhoun, *A Treatise on Indigence . . . with Proposals for Ameliorating the Condition of the Poor* (London, 1806), p. 253.

3. E. A. Wrigley and R. S. Schofield, *The Population History of England, 1541–1871* (London, 1981); J. Dupaquier, *Histoire de la population française* (Paris, 1975) and "Les caractères originaux de l'histoire démographique française au XVIIIe siècle," *Revue d'Histoire Moderne et Contemporaine* 23 (1976):182–202.

4. *The Bletchley Diary of the Rev. William Cole, 1765–7*, ed. F. G. Stokes (London, 1931), p. 41.

5. Mary Hyde, "'The Thrales of Streatham Park,' III. The Death of Thrale and the Remarriage of the Widow," *Harvard Library Bulletin* 25 (April 1977):193–241.

6. J. Hecht, *The Domestic Servant Class in Eighteenth-Century England* (London, 1956), p. 189.

7. Olwen Hufton, "Women without Men: Widows and Spinsters in Britain and France in the Eighteenth Century," *Journal of Family History,* Winter 1984, p. 363.

8. *The Autobiography and Correspondence of Sir Simonds d'Ewes, Bart,* ed. J. O. Halliwell (London, 1845), I:10.

9. D. Leigh, *The Mother's Blessing* (1616), 10th ed. (London, 1627), p. 25.

10. *The Autobiography and Correspondence of Mary Granville, Mrs. Delany,* 3 vols. (London, 1861), particularly vol. I.

Chapter 2. The Body, Appearance, and Sexuality
SARA F. MATTHEWS GRIECO

1. See also Gisela Bock and Giuliana Nobili, eds., *Il corpo delle donne* (Ancona and Bologna: Transeuropa, 1988); Ian MacLean, *The Renaissance*

Notion of Woman (Cambridge and New York: Cambridge University Press, 1980); Susan R. Sulieman, ed., *The Female Body in Western Culture* (Cambridge, Mass.: Harvard University Press, 1986).

2. Georges Vigarello, *Le propre et le sale* (Paris: Seuil, 1985), pp. 37–48; translated as *Concepts of Cleanliness* (Cambridge: Cambridge University Press, 1988).

3. Ibid., pp. 15–29.

4. Norbert Elias, *La civilisation des moeurs*, trans. P. Kamnitzer (Paris: Calmann-Lévy, 1973), pp. 77–120; P. Stallybrass, "Patriarchal Territories: The Body Enclosed," in Margaret N. Ferguson, Maureen Quilligan, and Nancy J. Vickers, eds., *Rewriting the Renaissance: The Discourses of Sexual Difference in Early Modern Europe* (Chicago: University of Chicago Press, 1986), pp. 123–144.

5. Renata Bridenthal, Claudia Koonz, and Susan Stuart, eds., *Becoming Visible: Women in European History* (Boston: Houghton Mifflin, 1987), pp. 251–278; Carolyn C. Lougee, *Le Paradis des Femmes: Women, Salons, and Social Stratification in Seventeenth-Century France* (Princeton: Princeton University Press, 1976).

6. Philippe Perrot, *Le travail des apparences, ou Les Transformations du corps féminin XVIIIe–XIXe siècle* (Paris: Seuil, 1984), pp. 17–19.

7. Vigarello, *Le propre et le sale*, pp. 95–96.

8. Ibid., pp. 98–101.

9. L. Savot, *L'architecture française* (Paris, 1624), pp. 102–103.

10. Vigarello, *Le propre et le sale*, pp. 76–77.

11. Ibid., pp. 78–88.

12. Daniel Roche, *La culture des apparences: Une histoire du vêtement, XVIIe–XVIIIe siècle* (Paris: Fayard, 1989), pp. 149–176.

13. Ibid., p. 175; Perrot, *Le travail des apparences*, pp. 74–76.

14. Jean-Claude Bologne, *Histoire de la pudeur* (Paris: Olivier Orban, 1986), pp. 63–65; Madeleine Lazard, "Le corps vêtu: Signification du costume à la Renaissance" (Paper delivered at the Conference Le Corps à la Renaissance, Centre d'Etudes Supérieures de la Renaissance, Université de Tours, July 2–10, 1987).

15. Vigarello, *Le propre et le sale*, pp. 105–117.

16. Ibid., pp. 125–143; Perrot, *Le travail des apparences*, pp. 19–23.

17. Jean-Louis Flandrin and Marie-Claude Phan, "Les métamorphoses de la beauté féminine," *L'Histoire* 66 (June 1984):48–57.

18. Edward Shorter, *A History of Women's Bodies* (New York: Basic Books, 1982), chap. 2.

19. Emmanuel Rodocanachi, *La femme italienne avant, pendant et après la Renaissance* (Paris: Hachette, 1922), pp. 110–111.

20. Baldassare Castiglione, *The Book of the Courtier* (Harmondsworth: Penguin, 1967), p. 211.

21. MacLean, *The Renaissance Notion of Woman*, chaps. 3–5.

22. Joan Kelley[-Gadol], "Did Women Have a Renaissance?" in *Women, History and Theory: The Essays of Joan Kelley* (Chicago: University of

Chicago Press, 1984), pp. 19–50; D. Owen Hughes, "Sumptuary Law and Social Relations in Renaissance Italy," in John Bossy, ed., *Disputes and Settlements: Law and Human Relations in the West* (Cambridge: Cambridge University Press, 1983), pp. 66–99.

23. Carroll Camden, *The Elizabethan Woman: A Panorama of English Womanhood, 1540 to 1640* (London: Cleaver-Hume, 1952), pp. 263–267; Sara F. Matthews Grieco, *"Querelle des Femmes" or "Guerre des Sexes"? Visual Representations of Women in Renaissance Europe,* exhibition catalogue (Florence: European University Institute, 1989), p. 32.

24. Jean Delumeau, *La peur en Occident, XIVe–XVIIIe siècles: Une cité assiégée* (Paris: Librairie Arthème Fayard, 1978), pp. 305–345.

25. Rodocanachi, *La femme italienne,* pp. 90–91 and n. 4.

26. Alison Saunders, "'La beaulté que femme doibt avoir': La vision du corps dans les blasons anatomiques" (Paper delivered at the conference Le Corps à la Renaissance, Centre d'Etudes Supérieures de la Renaissance, Université de Tours, July 2–10, 1987). See also note 14 above.

27. Camden, *The Elizabethan Woman,* p. 214.

28. Jean-Jacques Courtine and Claudine Haroche, *Histoire du visage. Exprimer et taire ses émotions, XVIe–début XIXe siècle* (Paris: Editions Rivages, 1988), chaps. 1, 2.

29. Jean-Louis Flandrin, "Soins de beauté et receuils de secrets," in Denis Menjot, ed., *Les soins de beauté. Moyen age, temps modernes (Centre d'Etudes Médiévales, Actes du IIIe Colloque International, Grasse, 26–28 avril 1985)* (Nice: Faculté des Lettres et Sciences Humaines, Université de Nice, 1987), pp. 13–32.

30. Sara F. Matthews Grieco, "Vice de femme est orgueil," in *Ange ou diablesse. La représentation de la femme au XVIe siècle* (Paris: Flammarion, 1991).

31. Leon Battista Alberti, *The Family in Renaissance Florence,* trans. and ed. R. N. Watkins (Columbia: University of South Carolina Press, 1969), p. 215. Alberti's *Della famiglia* was considered an authoritative text throughout the sixteenth and seventeenth centuries.

32. G. P. Lomazzo, *A Tracte Containing the Artes of Curious Paintinge Caruinge & Buildinge,* trans. R. Haydocke (Oxford, 1598), quoted in Camden, *The Elizabethan Woman,* p. 203.

33. Camden, *The Elizabethan Woman,* p. 198.

34. Rodocanachi, *La femme italienne,* p. 109.

35. Marie-Claude Phan, "Pratiques cosmétiques et idéal féminin dans l'Italie des XVème et XVIème siècles," in Menjot, *Les soins de beauté,* pp. 109–110.

36. Rodocanachi, *La femme italienne,* pp. 105–106, 111–113.

37. Ibid., p. 102.

38. Phan, "Pratiques cosmétiques et idéal féminin," pp. 116–117.

39. Perrot, *Le travail des apparences,* chaps. 2, 4.

40. Jacques Le Goff, "Le refus du Plaisir," in Georges Duby, ed., *L'amour et la sexualité,* special issue of *L'Histoire* (1984):52–59.

41. Bologne, *Histoire de la pudeur*, pp. 187–220.

42. Ibid., p. 34.

43. Delumeau, *La peur en Occident*, pp. 305–334.

44. MacLean, *The Renaissance Notion of Woman*, pp. 23–46.

45. Guido Ruggiero, *The Boundaries of Eros: Sex Crime and Sexuality in Renaissance Venice* (Oxford and New York: Oxford University Press, 1985), chaps. 4, 6.

46. Leah Otis, *Prostitution in Medieval Society: The History of an Urban Institution in Languedoc* (Chicago: University of Chicago Press, 1985), pp. 40–43. See Kathryn Norberg's essay on prostitution elsewhere in this volume.

47. Otis, *Prostitution in Medieval Society*, pp. 190–191.

48. Robert Muchembled, *Culture populaire et culture des élites dans la France moderne (XVe–XVIIIe siècles)* (Paris: Flammarion, 1978), pp. 238–239.

49. Jean-Louis Flandrin, *Le sexe et l'Occident. Évolution des attitudes et des comportements* (Paris: Seuil, 1981), pp. 280–281; Jean Gaudemet, *Le mariage en Occident: Les moeurs et le droit* (Paris: Cerf, 1987), pp. 352–354; François Lebrun, *La vie conjugale sous l'Ancien Régime* (Paris: Armand Colin, 1975), pp. 85–110.

50. Shorter, *A History of Women's Bodies*, passim.

51. Flandrin, *Le sexe et l'Occident*, p. 290.

52. Jean-Louis Flandrin, "Repression and Change in the Sexual Life of Young People in Medieval and Early Modern Times," in Robert Wheaton and Tamara Hareven, eds., *Family and Sexuality in French History* (Philadelphia: University of Pennsylvania Press, 1980), pp. 32–37.

53. Lawrence Stone, *The Family, Sex, and Marriage in England, 1500–1800* (New York: Harper & Row, 1977), pp. 607–612.

54. Ibid., pp. 607–611.

55. Flandrin, "Repression and Change in Sexual Life," pp. 32–37.

56. Flandrin, *Le sexe et l'Occident*, pp. 285–291.

57. Randolph Trumbach, *The Rise of the Egalitarian Family: Aristocratic Kinship and Domestic Relations in Eighteenth-Century England* (New York: Academic Press, 1978), passim.

58. Stone, *The Family, Sex, and Marriage*, pp. 490–491.

59. Jean-Louis Flandrin, *Familles, parenté, maison, sexualité dans l'ancienne société* (Paris: Hachette, 1976), pp. 156–161; translated by Richard Southern as *Families in Former Times: Kinship, Household, and Sexuality* (Cambridge and New York: Cambridge University Press, 1979).

60. Jean-Louis Flandrin, "La vie sexuelle des gens mariés dans l'ancienne société: De la doctrine de l'Eglise à la réalité des comportements," in Philippe Ariès and André Bejin, eds., *Sexualités occidentales*, Communications no. 35 (Paris: Seuil, 1982), pp. 125–126; translated by Anthony Forster as *Western Sexuality: Practice and Precept in Past and Present* (Oxford and New York: Basil Blackwell, 1985).

61. Flandrin, *Familles*, pp. 186–187.

62. Robert Rotberg and Theodore Rabb, eds., *Marriage and Fertility: Studies in Interdisciplinary History* (Princeton: Princeton University Press, 1980), passim.

63. Stone, *The Family, Sex, and Marriage*, pp. 489–495.

64. Shorter, *A History of Women's Bodies*, chap. 1; Lebrun, *La vie conjugale sous l'Ancien Régime*, pp. 124–125; Flandrin, *Le sexe et l'Occident*, pp. 132–135.

65. Roy Porter, "'The Secrets of Generation Display'd': Aristotle's Master-piece in Eighteenth-Century England," in R. P. Maccubin, ed., *'Tis Nature's Fault: Unauthorized Sexuality during the Enlightenment* (Cambridge: Cambridge University Press, 1987), pp. 1–22; Stone, *The Family, Sex, and Marriage*, pp. 527–529, 542–543.

66. Lebrun, *La vie conjugale sous l'Ancien Régime*, p. 48.

67. Ibid., pp. 48–51.

68. Claude Karnoouh, "Le charivari ou l'hypothèse de la monogamie," in Jacques Le Goff and Jean-Claude Schmitt, eds., *Le charivari. Actes de la table ronde organisée à Paris, 25–27 avril 1977 par L'Ecole des Hautes Etudes en Sciences Sociales et Le Centre National de Recherche Scientifique* (Paris: Mouton, 1981), p. 35.

69. Ibid., pp. 37–38.

70. Christiane Klapisch-Zuber, "La 'Mattinata' médiévale d'Italie," in Le Goff and Schmitt, *Le charivari*, p. 153.

71. Natalie Zemon Davis, "Charivari, honneur et communauté à Lyon et à Genève au XVIIe siècle," in Le Goff and Schmitt, *Le charivari*, pp. 214–216.

72. Marcel Bernos, Charles de La Roncière, Jean Guyon, and Philippe Lécrivain, *Le fruit défendu. Les chrétiens et la sexualité de l'antiquité à nos jours* (Paris: Centurion, 1985), pp. 186–188.

73. Cissie Fairchilds, *Domestic Enemies: Servants and Their Masters in Old Regime France* (Baltimore: Johns Hopkins University Press, 1984), pp. 164–192.

74. Cissie Fairchilds, "Female Sexual Attitudes and the Rise of Illegitimacy: A Case Study," in Rotberg and Rabb, *Marriage and Fertility*, pp. 170–176.

75. Arlette Farge, *La vie fragile. Violences, pouvoirs et solidarités à Paris au XVIIIe siècle* (Paris: Hachette, 1986), pp. 165–190.

76. Fairchilds, "Female Sexual Attitudes and Illegitimacy," pp. 176–185; Farge, *La vie fragile*, p. 40.

77. Farge, *La vie fragile*, pp. 165–190; Edward Shorter, "Illegitimacy, Sexual Revolution, and Social Change in Modern Europe," in Rotberg and Rabb, *Marriage and Fertility*, pp. 53–54.

78. Stone, *The Family, Sex, and Marriage*, pp. 612–613, 633–639; Flandrin, *Familles*, pp. 176–185.

79. Stone, *The Family, Sex, and Marriage*, pp. 636–646.

80. Keith Thomas, "The Double Standard," *Journal of the History of Ideas* 20 (April 1959):195–216.

81. Quoted in Stone, *The Family, Sex, and Marriage*, pp. 637, 502.

82. See also Christine de Pizan, *La cité des dames* (1405); and Marguerite de Navarre, *L'heptaméron* (1558).

83. Stone, *The Family, Sex, and Marriage*, pp. 501–504.

84. Ibid., pp. 529–534.

85. Rodocanachi, *La femme italienne*, pp. 322–327.

86. Stone, *The Family, Sex, and Marriage*, pp. 503 and n. 51.

87. Flandrin, *Le sexe et l'Occident*, pp. 95–96.

88. Stone, *The Family, Sex, and Marriage*, pp. 527–529, 542–544.

Chapter 3. The Beautiful Woman
VÉRONIQUE NAHOUM-GRAPPE

1. Anonymous, "Pétition des femmes du Tiers-Etat au Roi," January 1, 1789, quoted in P. M. Duhet, ed., *Cahiers de doléances des femmes* (Paris: Editions des Femmes, 1989), p. 25.

2. *Blasons anatomiques du corps féminin* (Paris: C. d'Angelier, 1554).

3. Pierre de Bourdeille seigneur de Brantôme, *Oeuvres complètes,* vol. II (Paris: A. Desrez, 1888), p. 268. Arlette Farge, *Le miroir des femmes: Textes de la Bibliothèque Bleue* (Paris: Montalba, 1982).

4. By Micheline Baulant, François Piponnier, and Daniel Roche.

5. Among others, Yvonne Verdier, *Façons de dire, façons de faire* (Paris: Gallimard, 1979).

6. Philippe Perrot, *Le travail des apparences, ou les transformations du corps féminin, XVIe–XIXe siècle* (Paris: Seuil, 1986).

7. Alexander Gottlieb Baumgarten, *Aesthetica* (1750; rpt., Hildesheim: Olms, 1961).

8. Louis-Sébastien Mercier, *Tableau de Paris*, vol. 2 (1782), bk. 11, chap. 132, pp. 87–89.

9. Véronique Nahoum-Grappe, *Beauté, laideur. Unessai de phénoménologie historique* (Paris: Payot, 1990).

10. Gabriel de Minut, *De la beaute, discours divers . . . Avec la Paulegraphie, ou description des beautez d'une dame tholosaine nommée La belle Paule* (Lyons: B. Honorat, 1587).

Chapter 4. A Daughter to Educate
MARTINE SONNET

1. *Règlemens pour la communauté des filles établies pour l'instruction des pauvres filles de la paroisse Saint-Roch* (Paris, 1688).

2. Poullain de La Barre, *De l'égalité des deux sexes* (1673), pp. 162–163.

3. Claude Fleury, *Traité du choix et de la méthode des études* (Paris, 1686), p. 270.

4. Mme. de Maintenon, *Lettres sur l'éducation des filles* (Paris, 1854), p. 140.

5. Jean-Jacques Rousseau, *Emile, ou de l'éducation* (Paris: Garnier-Flammarion, 1966), p. 475.

6. Quoted by Lawrence Stone, *The Family, Sex, and Marriage in England, 1500–1800* (New York: Harper & Row, 1977), p. 356.

7. Quoted in Rosemary O'Day, *Education and Society, 1500–1800: The Social Foundations of Education in Early Modern Britain* (London and New York: Longman, 1982), p. 184. See also Olwen Hufton's essay on women's work elsewhere in this volume.

8. Baron de Frénilly, *Souvenirs, 1768–1828* (Paris: Plon, 1908), p. 12.

9. Madame de Chastenay, *Mémoires, 1771–1815*, vol. I (Paris: Plon-Nourrit, 1896).

10. Comtesse de Boigne, *Mémoires* (Paris: Mercure de France, 1971), p. 99.

11. Mme. Roland, *Mémoires* (Paris: Mercure de France, 1966).

12. Martine Sonnet, *L'éducation des filles au temps des Lumières* (Paris: Cerf, 1987), pp. 44–48.

13. Quoted by Heinke Wunderlich, *Studienjahre der Grafen Salm-Reifferscheidt (1780–1791). Ein Beitrag zur Adelserziehung am Ende des Ancien Régime* (Heidelberg: Carl Winter–Universitäts Verlag, 1984), p. 311.

14. Map in Dominique Julia, ed., *Atlas de la Révolution française, vol. II: L'enseignement, 1760–1855* (Paris: Ecole des Hautes Etudes en Sciences Sociales, 1937), p. 19.

15. Sonnet, *L'éducation*, pp. 67–74.

16. O'Day, *Education and Society*, pp. 188–189.

17. Henry Paulin Panon Desbassayns, *Voyage à Paris pendant la Révolution (1790–1792), journal inédit d'un habitant de l'île Bourbon* (Paris: Librairie Académique Perrin, 1985).

18. Sonnet, *L'éducation*, pp. 87–89.

19. *Règlemens des religieuses ursulines de la congrégation de Paris* (Paris: Louis Josse, 1705).

20. *Règlemens de la communauté des filles de Sainte-Anne établies pour l'instruction des pauvres filles de la paroisse Saint-Roch à Paris*, part 2, 1698. Manuscript in the Bibliothèque Mazarine.

21. Ruth Perry, *The Celebrated Mary Astell: An Early English Feminist* (Chicago: University of Chicago Press, 1986), pp. 233–240.

22. Quoted in Bernard Grosperrin, *Les petites écoles sous l'Ancien Régime* (Rennes: Ouest-France, 1984), p. 128.

23. Sonnet, *L'éducation*, pp. 80–82.

24. Julia, *Atlas de la Révolution française*, II, 60.

25. Martine Sonnet, "Première communion et éducation au XVIIIe siècle," in Jean Delumeau, ed., *La première communion. Quatre siècles d'histoire* (Paris: Desclée de Brouwever, 1987), pp. 115–132.

26. Madame Campan, *De l'éducation* (Paris: Baubouin Frères, 1824).

27. *Etablissements desservis par les Filles de la Charité, paroisse Saint-Louis-en-Ile*, Archives Nationales S 6160.

28. *Usages des religieuses de la congrégation de Notre-Dame* (Châlons: J. Seneuse, 1690), p. 77.

29. Lucien Perey [Luce Herpin], *Histoire d'une grande dame au XVIIIe siècle: La princesse Hélène de Ligne* (Paris: Calmann-Lévy, 1887).

30. François Furet and Jacques Ozouf, *Lire et écrire: L'alphabétisation des Français de Calvin à Jules Ferry* (Paris: Editions de Minuit, 1977), I, 44; translated as *Reading and Writing: Literacy in France from Calvin to Jules Ferry* (Cambridge and New York: Cambridge University Press, 1982).

31. Daniel Roche, *Le peuple de Paris: Essai sur la culture populaire au XVIIIe siècle* (Paris: Aubier Montaigne, 1981), pp. 206–212; translated by Marie Evans as *The People of Paris: An Essay in Popular Culture in the 18th Century* (New York: Berg, 1987).

Chapter 5. Virgins and Mothers between Heaven and Earth
ELISJA SCHULTE VAN KESSEL

1. Susan Dwyer Amussen, "Féminin/masculin: Le genre dans l'Angleterre de l'époque moderne," *Annales, ESC* 40 (1985): 269–287; cf. Jeanne-Marie Noël, "Education morale des filles et des garçons dans le Pays Bas au XVIe siècle," in Elisja Schulte van Kessel, ed., *Women and Men in Spiritual Culture (XIV–XVII Centuries)* (The Hague: Staatsuitgeverij, 1986), pp. 94–98.

2. Paul Veyne, "La famille et l'amour sous le Haut-Empire Romain," *Annales ESC* 33 (1978): 35–63.

3. Peter Brown, *The Body and Society: Men, Women, and Sexual Renunciation in Early Christianity* (New York: Columbia University Press, 1988).

4. Julia Kristeva, *Etrangers à nous mêmes* (Paris: Fayard, 1989).

5. A. Blok, "Notes on the Concept of Virginity in Mediterranean Societies," in Schulte van Kessel, *Women and Men*.

6. Romana Guarnieri, "Pinzocchere," in Guerrino Pellicia and Giancarlo Rocca, eds., *Dizionario degli istituti di perfezione*, vol. VI (Rome: Paolini, 1980), cols. 1721–49. See also idem, "Beghinismo d'oltralpe e Bizzochismo italiano tra il secolo XIV e il secolo XV," in Raffaele Pazzelli and Mario Sensi, eds., *La beata Angelina da Montegiove e il movimento del terz'ordine regolare francescano femminile* (Rome: Analecta T.O.R., 1984), pp. 1–13; Anna Benvenuti Papi, "'Velut in sepulchro': Cellane e recluse nella tradizione agiografica italiana," in Sophia Boesch Gajano and Lucia Sebastiani, eds., *Culto dei santi, istituzioni e classi sociali in età preindistriale* (Rome: Japadre, 1984), pp. 365–455; Brigitte Degler-Spengler, "Die religiöse Frauenbewegung des Mittelalters," *Rothenburger Jahrbuch für Kirchengeschichte* 3 (1984): 75–88; Joyce Pennings, "Semi-Religious Women in 15th-Century Rome," *Mededelingen van het Nederlands Instituut te Rome* 47 (1987): 115–145.

7. Elisja Schulte van Kessel, "Vis noch vlees. Geestelijke maagden in de Gouden Eeuw," *Jaarboek voor Vrouwengeschiedenis* 2 (1981): 190–192.

8. Ibid., pp. 171–172.

9. Gabriella Zarri, "Le sante vive. Per una tipologia della santità fem-

minile nel primo Cinquecento," *Annali dell'Istituto Storico Italo-Germanico di Trento* 6 (1980): 371–445.

10. Adriano Prosperi, "Dalle 'divine madri' ai 'padri spirituali,'" in Schulte van Kessel, *Women and Men*, pp. 71–90.

11. Andrea Erba, "Il 'caso' di Paola Antonia Negri nel Cinquecento italiano," ibid., pp. 193–211.

12. Joyce Irwin, "Society and the Sexes," in Steven Ozment, ed., *Reformation Europe: A Guide to Research* (St. Louis, Mo.: Center for Reformation Research, 1982), pp. 343–359; Olwen Hufton, "Women in History: Early Modern Europe," *Past and Present* 101 (1983): 125–141; Els Kloek, "De Reformatie als thema van vrouwenstudies. Een histories debat over goed en kwaad," *Jaarboek voor Vrouwengeschiedenis* 4 (1983): 106–149; Sherrin Marshall, "Women and Religious Change in the Sixteenth-Century Netherlands," *Archiv für Reformationsgeschichte* 75 (1984): 276–289; idem, ed., *Women in Reformation and Counter-Reformation Europe: Private and Public Worlds* (Bloomington: Indiana University Press, 1989); Kathryn Norberg, "The Counter-Reformation and Women: Religious and Lay," in J. W. O'Malley, ed., *Catholicism in Early Modern History: A Guide to Research* (St. Louis, Mo.: Center for Reformation Research, 1988), pp. 133–146.

13. Bruto Amante, *Giulia Gonzaga, Contessa di Fondi e il movimento religioso femminile nel secolo XVI* (Bologna: Zanichelli, 1986), pp. xiv–xv, 263.

14. Zarri, "Le sante vive," pp. 376 n.22, 377, 398, 439.

15. G.-M. Colombàs, "Asceti e ascete," in Pelliccia and Rocca, *Dizionario*, I, cols. 917–924.

16. Karl Noehles, *La chiesa dei SS. Luca e Martina nell'opera di Pietro da Cortona* (Rome: Ugo Bozzi, 1970), p. 97.

17. Romeo De Maio, *Riforme e miti nella Chiesa del Cinquecento* (Naples, 1973), pp. 257–278. Cf. Zarri, "Le sante vive"; André Vauchez, *La sainteté en Occident aux derniers siècles du Moyen Age d'après les procès de canonisation et les documents hagiographiques* (Rome: Ecole Française de Rome, 1981); Donald Weinstein and Rudolph Bell, *Saints and Society: The Two Worlds of Christendom, 1100–1700* (Chicago: University of Chicago Press, 1982); Boesch Gajano and Sebastiani, *Culto del santi;* André Vauche et al., "Santità," in Pelliccia and Rocca, *Dizionario,* VIII, cols. 857–890; Anna Benvenuti Papi, "Il 'patronage' nell'agiografia femminile," in Lucia Ferrante, Maura Palazzi, and Gianna Pomata, eds., *Ragnatele di rapporti. Patronage e reti di relazione nella storia delle donne* (Turin: Rosenberg and Sellier, 1988), pp. 201–218; see also the rich introduction (pp. 7–56) and essays by Anna Scattigno and Marina Romanelli, ibid.; and Claudio Leonardi, "La santità delle donne," in Giovanni Pozzi and Claudio Leonardi, eds., *Scrittrici mistiche italiane* (Genoa: Marietti, 1988), pp. 43–57.

18. Vauchez et al., "Santità," col. 865.

19. Hufton, "Women in History," pp. 136–137; Norberg, "The Counter-Reformation," p. 142.

20. Carlo Ginzburg, *Storia notturna. Una decifrazione del sabba* (Turin:

Einaudi, 1989), p. 282; translated by Raymond Rosenthal as *Ecstasies: Deciphering the Witches' Sabbath* (New York: Pantheon, 1991).

21. Kloek, "De Reformatie"; Merry E. Wiesner, "Nuns, Wives, and Mothers: Women and the Reformation in Germany," in Sherrin Marshall, *Women in Reformation and Counter-Reformation Europe,* p. 13; see also note 12 above.

22. Natalie Zemon Davis, "City Women and Religious Change," in *Society and Culture in Early Modern France: Eight Essays* (Stanford: Stanford University Press, 1975), pp. 65–95; idem, "From 'Popular Religion' to Religious Cultures," in Ozment, *Reformation Europe,* pp. 321–341. See also Jane Dempsey Douglass, *Women, Freedom, and Calvin* (Philadelphia: Westminster Press, 1985); Merry E. Wiesner, "Beyond Women and the Family: Towards a Gender Analysis of the Reformation," *Sixteenth Century Journal* 3 (1987): 311–321.

23. Elisja Schulte van Kessel, "Gender and Spirit, *pietas et contemptus mundi:* Matron-Patrons in Early Modern Rome," in *Women and Men,* pp. 47–68; Ferrante, Palazzi, and Pomata, *Ragnatele di rapporti,* esp. Introduction.

24. Marina D'Ameglia, "La conquista di una dote. Regole del gioco e scambi femminili alla Confraternità dell'Annunziata (sec. XVII–XVIII)," in Ferrante, Palazzi, and Pomata, *Ragnatele di rapporti,* pp. 305–343.

25. John Bossy, "The Counter-Reformation and the People of Catholic Europe," *Past and Present* 47 (1970): 55.

26. Schulte van Kessel, "Gender and Spirit," pp. 57–63.

27. Gabriella Zarri, "Monasteri femminili e città (secoli XVI–XVIII)," in Giorgio Chittolini and Giovanni Miccoli, eds., *Storia d'Italia. Annali 9: La Chiesa e il potere politico dal Medioevo all'età contemporanea* (Turin: Einaudi, 1986), pp. 377–398; Sherrin Marshall, "Vrouwen en godsdienstkeus," *Jaarboek voor vrouwengeschiedenis* 4 (1983): 101–103.

28. Mary Martin McLaughlin, "Looking for Medieval Women: An Interim Report on the Project 'Women's Religious Life and Communities, A.D. 500–1500,'" *Medieval Prosopography* 8 (Spring 1987): 61–91.

29. Zarri, "Monasteri femminili," pp. 378–398.

30. Ibid., pp. 404–405; see also Marco Bescapè, "Le fondazioni francescane femminili nella diocesi di Lodi," in *Il Francescanesimo in Lombardia. Storia e arte* (Milan: Silvana, 1983), pp. 172–173.

31. Deposition of Sister Cecilia, Bologna, December 23, 1622, quoted in Zarri, "Monasteri femminili," p. 415 n.16.

32. Elisja Schulte van Kessel, "Moederschap en Navolging van Christus," in Petty Bange et al., eds., *De doorwerking van de Moderne Devotie* (Hilversum: Verloren, 1988), pp. 269–273, 281–282; Zarri, "Monasteri femminili," pp. 417–419.

33. W. de Boer, "Note sull'introduzione del confessionale, sopratutto in Italia," *Quaderni Storici* 77 (1991): 543–572.

34. Judith Brown, *Immodest Acts: The Life of a Lesbian Nun in Renaissance Italy* (Oxford and New York: Oxford University Press, 1986);

Fiamma Lussana, "Rivolta e misticismo nei chiostri femminili del Seicento," *Studi Storici* 28 (1987): 243–260; Geneviève Reynes, *Couvents de femmes. La vie des religieuses cloîtrees dans le France des XVIIe et XVIIIe siècles* (Paris: Fayard, 1987).

35. Lussana, "Rivolta," pp. 256–258; Giuliana Morandini, ed., *Suor Maria Celeste Galilei. Lettere al padre* (Turin: La Rosa, 1983).

36. Guarnieri, "Pinzocchere," cols. 1745–48; Zarri, "Monasteri femminili," p. 402; also Lussana, "Rivolta."

37. Elisja Schulte van Kessel, "Scandaleuze dienstmaagden in de zielzorg," in *Geest en Vlees in godsdienst en wetenschap. Vijf opstellen over gezagsconflicten in de 17e eeuw* (The Hague: Staatsuitgeverij, 1980), pp. 101–107; Guarnieri, "Pinzocchere," col. 1740; Matthäus Bernards, "Kölns Beitrag zum Streit um die religiöse Frauenfrage im 17. Jahrhundert," *Annalen des historischen Vereins für den Niederrhein* 177 (1975): 76–91.

38. Ginevra Conti Odorisio, *Donna e società nel Seicento. Lucrezia Marinelli e Arcangela Tarabotti* (Rome: Bulzoni, 1979), pp. 79–80; Lussana, "Rivolta," pp. 250–251.

39. Bridget Hill, "A Refuge from Men: The Idea of a Protestant Nunnery," *Past and Present* 117 (1987): 109.

40. L. Mariani, E. Tarolli, and M. Seynaeve, *Angela Merici. Contributo per una biografia* (Milan, 1986); T. Ledóchowska, "Angela Merici," in Pelliccia and Rocca, *Dizionario,* I, cols. 631–634.

41. See Ruth Liebowitz, "Virgins in the Service of Christ: The Dispute over an Active Apostolate for Women during the Counter-Reformation," in Rosemary Ruether and Eleanor McLaughlin, eds., *Women of Spirit: Female Leadership in the Jewish and Christian Traditions* (New York: Simon and Schuster, 1979), pp. 131–152.

42. "E ivi le fu dato un bacio . . . e ivi perdette tutta lei propria"; *Corpus Catherinianum,* quoted in Pozzi and Leonardi, *Scrittrici mistiche,* pp. 348–349.

43. Schulte van Kessel, *Geest en Vlees,* pp. 115, 158; idem, "Sapienza, sesso, pietas: I primi Lincei e il matrimonio. Un saggio di storia umana," *Mededelingen van het Nederlands Instituut te Rome* 46 (1985): 123–125.

44. P.-J. Begheyn, "De verspreiding van de Evangelische Peerle," *Ons Geestelijk Erf* 51 (1977): 391–421; idem, "Die Evangelische Peerle," *Spiegel Historiael* 13 (1978): 29–33; idem, "Nieuwe gegevens betreffende de 'Evangelische Peerle,'" *Ons Geestelijk Erf* 58 (1984): 30–40.

45. Benedetta Papàsogli, *Gli spirituali italiani e il "Grande Siècle"* (Rome: Edizioni di Storia e Letteratura, 1983), pp. 9–21, 56, 61–63, 91ff.

46. Caroline Walker Bynum, *Holy Feast and Holy Fast: The Religious Significance of Food to Medieval Women* (Berkeley: University of California Press, 1987); Pozzi and Leonardi, *Scrittrici mistiche;* Michel de Certeau, *La fable mystique, XVIe–XVIIe siècles* (Paris: Gallimard, 1982).

47. J. Walsh, ed., *The Revelations of Divine Love of Julian Norwich* (Wheathampstead, 1973), p. 161; quoted in Kari E. Börresen, "Christ notre Mère. La théologie de Julienne de Norwich," in Martin Bodewig, Josef

Schmitz, and Reinhold Weir, eds., *Das Menschenbild des Nikolaus von Kues und der christliche Humanismus* (Mainz: Matthias Grünewald Verlag, 1978), p. 325 n.31. See also Giovanni Pozzi, "L'alfabeto delle sante," in Pozzi and Leonardi, *Scrittrici mistiche,* pp. 40–42; Kari E. Börresen, ed., *Image of God and Gender Models in Judaeo-Christian Tradition* (Oslo: Solum Forlay, 1990).

48. Prosperi, "Dalle 'divine madri,'" p. 87.

49. Ioan P. Couliano, *Eros and Magic in the Renaissance* (Chicago: University of Chicago Press, 1987); see also Papàsogli, *Gli spirituali italiani,* p. 64; Gloria Flaherty, "Sex and Shamanism in the Eighteenth Century," in G.-S. Rousseau and Roy Porter, eds., *Sexual Underworlds in the Enlightenment* (Manchester: Manchester University Press, 1987), pp. 261–280.

50. Bynum, *Holy Feast,* pp. 55–77, 93, 256–259, 274–276; Pozzi and Leonardi, *Scrittrici mistiche,* pp. 23, 40–42.

51. Romana Guarnieri, "Nec domina nec ancilla sed socia. Tre casi di direzione spirituale tra '500 e '600," in Schulte van Kessel, *Women and Men,* pp. 111–132; Anna Scattigno, "'Carissimo figliolo in Cristo.' Direzione spirituale e mediazione sociale nell'epistolario di Caterina de' Ricci (1542–1590)," in Ferrante, Palazzi, and Pomata, *Ragnatele di rapporti,* pp. 219–239.

52. Papàsogli, *Gli spirituali italiani,* pp. 22–28, 59–69; Pozzi and Leonardi, *Scrittrici mistiche,* pp. 392–398.

53. The first known Italian edition is dated 1611; Pozzi and Leonardi, *Scrittrici mistiche,* p. 393.

54. "Come i martiri . . . come a punto un agnellino"; *Breve Compendio,* quoted by Pozzi in ibid., p. 395.

55. Romana Guarnieri, "Il movimento del Libero Spirito. Testi e documenti," *Archivio Italiano per la Storia della Pietà* 4 (1965): 353–663.

56. Jean Delumeau, *Le péché et la peur. La culpabilisation en Occident (XIIIe–XVIIIe siècles)* (Paris: Fayard, 1983), chaps. 1, 2; Schulte van Kessel, "Moederschap," pp. 283–284.

57. Paul Vandenbroeck, "Zwischen Selbsterniedrigung und Selbstvergottung. Bilderwelt und Selbstbild religiöser Frauen in den südlichen Niederlanden," *De Zeventiende Eeuw* 1 (1989): 71.

58. See Anneke Mulder-Bakker, "Concluding Remarks," in Schulte van Kessel, *Women and Men,* pp. 233–237.

59. Elisja Schulte van Kessel, "Le vergini devote nella missione olandese," in *Actes du colloque sur le jansénisme* (Louvain: Nauwelaerts, 1977), pp. 187–203; idem, *Geest en Vlees,* pp. 51–115; idem, "Vis noch vlees"; idem, "Gender and Spirit," pp. 49–50. Cf. Sherrin Marshall, "Protestant, Catholic, and Jewish Women in the Early Modern Netherlands," in *Women in Reformation and Counter-Reformation Europe,* p. 129.

60. Joyce Irwin, "Anna Maria Van Schurman: From Feminism to Pietism," *Church History* 46 (1977): 48–62; Mirjiam de Baar, "De betrokkenheid van vrouwen bij het huisgezin van Jean de Labadie (1669–1732)," *Jaarboek voor Vrouwengeschiedenis* 8 (1987): 11–43.

61. Romana Guarnieri, "Il quietismo in otto manoscritti Chigiani. Polemiche e condanne tra il 1681 e il 1703," *Archivio Italiano per la Storia della Pietà* 4 (1965): 685–708; Luigi Fiorani, "Monache e monasteri romani nell'età del quietismo," in *Ricerche per la storia religiosa di Roma,* vol. I (Rome: Edizioni di Storia e Letteratura, 1977), pp. 98–105, 106 n.123.

62. See Ginzburg, *Storia notturna,* pp. 65–118; Luisa Accati, "Simboli maschili e simboli femminili nella devozione alla Madonna della Controriforma: Appunti per una discussione," in Schulte van Kessel, *Women and Men,* pp. 35–43; idem, "Il padre naturale. Tra simboli dominanti e categorie scientifiche," *Memoria. Rivista di Storia delle Donne* 21 (1987): 79–106; Marina Warner, *Alone of All Her Sex: The Myth and the Cult of the Virgin Mary* (London: Weidenfeld & Nicolson, 1976); Roberto Zapperi, *L'uomo incinto. La donna, l'uomo e il potere* (1979), pp. 79–87 and passim.

63. See note 22 above. Some previous works are less known but equally groundbreaking. See, e.g., Nancy L. Roelker on noblewomen and Reform in France (1972); see note 12, esp. Kloek, "De Reformatie," pp. 131–134.

Chapter 6. Women in Politics
NATALIE ZEMON DAVIS

1. Sarah Churchill, *An Account of the Conduct of the Dowager Duchess of Marlborough, from her first Coming to Court to the Year 1710* (London: George Hawkins, 1742), p. 14; *Private Correspondence of Sarah, Duchess of Marlborough,* 2 vols. (London, 1838).

2. Mme. de Sévigné to Simon Arnaud de Pomponne, Paris, November 17, December 21, and December 25, 1664, in Mme. de Sévigné, *Correspondance,* ed. Roger Duchêne, 3 vols. (Paris: Bibliothèque de la Pléiade, Gallimard, 1972), I, 55–56, 80 (nos. 59, 70, 71).

3. Françoise d'Aubigné, marquise de Maintenon, *Lettres,* ed. Marcel Langlois, 5 vols. (Paris: Letouzey, 1935–1939), IV, 426 (no. 1025); V, 521 (no. 1399).

4. Churchill, *An Account . . . of the Duchess of Marlborough,* p. 140.

5. Mme. de Sévigné to Mme. de Grignan, Les Rochers, August 9, 1671, and October 20, 1675, in *Correspondance,* I, 312–314; II, 136–137 (nos. 189, 440).

6. See Nina Gelbart's essay on female journalists elsewhere in this volume.

7. Lucy Martin Donnelly, "The Celebrated Mrs. Macaulay," *William and Mary Quarterly,* 3d ser., 6 (1949): 197–198; Bridget Hill, *The Republican Virago. The Life and Times of Catharine Macaulay, Historian* (Oxford: Clarendon Press, 1992), p. 226.

8. See Arlette Farge's essay on women in riots elsewhere in this volume.

9. Patricia Higgin, "The Reactions of Women," in Brian Manning, ed., *Politics, Religion and the English Civil War* (London: Edward Arnold, 1973), pp. 185–187, 192.

10. Ibid., p. 217.

11. A. S. P. Woodhouse, ed., *Puritanism and Liberty: Being the Army*

Debates (1647–1649), 2d ed. (London: J. M. Dent, 1951), pp. 53, 71–73, 79, 83.

12. John Locke, *The Second Treatise of Government*, ed. Thomas P. Peardon (Indianapolis: Bobbs-Merrill, 1952), chap. 7, para. 82, p. 46.

Chapter 7. Judging by Images
FRANÇOISE BORIN

1. Pierre Francastel, *Etudes de sociologie de l'art, création picturale et société* (Paris: Denoël, 1974), p. 56.

2. Ibid., p. 17.

3. Jean Guillaume, "Cleopatra Nova Pandora," *Gazette des Beaux-Arts*, October 1972, pp. 185–194.

4. Carolyn Merchant, *Death of Nature: Women, Ecology, and Scientific Revolution* (San Francisco: Harper & Row, 1980).

5. Hugo Wagner, "Niklaus Manuel, Leben und Kunstlerisches Werk," in *Niklaus Manuel Deutsch, Maler, Dichter, Staatsman*, exhibition catalog (Bern, September–December 1979), p. 26.

6. Lode Seghers, "Los enigmas de un cuadro del Museo del Prado," *Goya*, no. 198 (1987): 348–357.

7. Marcel Proust, *A la recherche du temps perdu: La prisonnière* (Paris: Gallimard, 1988), III, 587.

8. Madlyn Millner Kahr, "Delilah," in Norma Broude and Mary M. Garrard, eds., *Feminism and Art History: Questioning the Litany* (New York: Harper & Row, 1982), pp. 111–145.

9. *L'imperfection des femmes . . . tirée de l'Ecriture sainte et de plusieurs auteurs, dédiée à la bonne femme. A ménage, chez Jean trop tôt marié, à l'enseigne de la femme sans tête*, quoted in Geneviève Bollème, *La Bibliothèque Bleue: Littérature populaire en France du XVIIe au XIXe siècle* (Paris: Julliard, 1971), p. 16.

10. Jean Cusenier, *L'art populaire en France. Rayonnements, modèles et sources* (Fribourg: Office du Livre; Paris: Société Française du Livre, 1979), p. 61.

11. The *Roxburghe Ballads* is an anthology of old songs on various subjects published in various editions between 1550 and 1700, in which, as in the Bibliothèque Bleue, the woodcuts are repetitive and not always directly related to the text.

12. Bonnart, *Mesnage champestre:* "Tout est content dans ce village / Père, Mère, Enfant, et Valets / L'or éclate dans les palais / Mais le repos règne au village." Dewismes, *L'hiver:* "A la fumée d'un bon repas / L'hiver n'est point désagréable / Quand on boit, qu'on rit, qu'on tient table / Toute saison a ses appâts."

13. See Claude Gaignebet and Jean-Dominique Lajoux, *Art profane et religion populaire au Moyen Age* (Paris: Presses Universitaires de France, 1985).

14. *Les règles de la bienséance et de la civilité chréstienne* (Paris: The

Widow of Nicolas Oudot, 1716), quoted in Bollême, *La Bibliothèque Bleue,* p. 136.

15. Carroll Camden, *The Elizabethan Woman: A Panorama of English Womanhood, 1540 to 1640* (London and New York: Cleaver-Hume, 1952).

16. Jean-Jacques Courtine and Claudine Haroche, *Histoire du visage. Exprimer et taire ses émotions, XVIe–début XIXe siècle* (Paris: Editions Rivages, 1988), p. 242.

17. Daniel Buren, "Autour du manque" or "Qui a vu Judith et Holpherne?" in *Artemisia,* exhibition catalog, with texts by Roland Barthes et al., Collection "Mot pour mot/Word for Word," no. 2 (Paris: Yvon Lambert, 1979), pp. 78–86.

18. Michel de Certeau, *La fable mystique XVIe–XVIIe siècles* (Paris: Gallimard, 1982).

19. "Faveurs de Dieu 555," quoted in Emmanuel Renault, *Sainte Thérèse d'Avila et l'expérience mystique* (Paris: Seuil, 1970), p. 67.

20. Marina Warner, *Alone of All Her Sex: The Myth and the Cult of the Virgin Mary* (London: Weidenfeld and Nicolson, 1976).

21. Jean Clair, *Méduse* (Paris: Gallimard, 1989).

22. Jacques Revel, "Masculin/féminin: Sur l'usage historiographique des rôles sexuels," in Michelle Perrot, ed., *Une histoire des femmes est-elle possible?* (Paris: Editions Rivages, 1984), p. 133.

23. According to Marc Abélès, *Jours tranquilles en 89, ethnologie politique d'un département français* (Paris: Odile Jacob, 1984).

24. Roger Caillois, *L'homme et le sacré,* preface 3d ed., February 1963 (Paris: Gallimard, 1988), p. 16.

Chapter 8. The Ambiguities of Literature
JEAN-PAUL DESAIVE

1. Pierre de Ronsard, Sonnet VI, in André Lagarde and Laurent Michard, eds., *XVIe siècle. Le grands auteurs français du programme* (Paris: Bordas, 1970), p. 145; translated by Nicholas Kilmer in *Poems of Pierre de Ronsard* (Berkeley: University of California Press, 1979), p. 165.

2. Philippe Desportes, *Oeuvres* (Paris: Adolphe Delahays, 1858).

3. Enea Balmas, "La Renaissance," in Antoine Adam, ed., *Littérature française* (Paris: Arthaud, 1970–1978), IV, 71.

4. Maurice Scève, *Délie objet de plus haute vertu,* ed. Françoise Charpentier (Paris: Gallimard, 1984), p. 13.

5. A. C. Hammond, *Sir Philip Sidney: A Study of His Life and Works* (Cambridge: Cambridge University Press, 1977).

6. Pierre de Ronsard, Ode III, in *Oeuvres complètes,* ed. Gustave Cohen (Paris: Gallimard, 1978), I, 462.

7. Ronsard, *Le bocage royal,* ibid., pp. 893–902.

8. Saint Francis de Sales, *Introduction à la vie dévote,* ed. Silvestre de Sacy (Paris: Techener, 1860), pt. 3, chap. 1, p. 245.

9. Janine Garrisson, *L'homme protestant* (Paris: Editions Complexe, 1986), p. 145.

10. Jacques du Bosc, *L'honneste femme, divisée en trois parties,* 4th ed. (Paris: Jean-Baptiste Loyson, 1662).

11. Thomas Gataker, *A Mariage Praier* (London, 1624); quoted in Edmund Leites, *The Puritan Conscience and Modern Sexuality* (New Haven: Yale University Press, 1986).

12. See Leites, *The Puritan Conscience;* René Pillorget, *La tige et le rameau. Familles anglaise et française XVIe–XVIIIe siècle* (Paris: Calmann-Lévy, 1979); Lawrence Stone, *The Family, Sex, and Marriage in England, 1500–1800* (New York: Harper & Row, 1977); André Burguiere, Christiane Klapisch-Zuber, Martine Segalan, and Françoise Zonabend, eds., *Histoire de la famille,* 2 vols. (Paris: Armand Colin, 1986).

13. Jean de La Bruyère, *Les caractères,* ed. A. Chassang (Paris: Garnier, 1881), p. 58.

14. A. L. Rowse, *The England of Elizabeth: The Structure of Society* (London: Macmillan, 1961), p. 206.

15. Charles Marguetel de Saint Denis, seigneur de Saint-Evremond, "De la comédie angloise," in *Oeuvres meslées* (Paris: Claude Barbin, 1693–1694), II, 260.

16. Idem, "Sur les comédies," ibid., p. 248.

17. Ibid., p. 251.

18. Marie de Rabutin-Chantal, marquise de Sévigné, letter of January 22, 1674, *Correspondance,* ed. Roger Duchêne (Paris: Gallimard, 1972–1978; hereafter cited as Sévigné), I, 679.

19. Nicolas Boileau-Despréaux, "Letter of Monsieur Arnauld, Doctor of the Sorbonne, to M. Perrault, on the Subject of My Tenth Satire," in *Oeuvres* (Amsterdam: François Changuion, 1735; hereafter cited as Boileau), IV, 136.

20. Henri Coulet, *Histoire du roman en France,* vol. I: *Le roman jusqu'à la Révolution* (Paris: Armand Colin, 1967), p. 287.

21. Sévigné, III, 1646.

22. This entire passage is indebted to the work of Roger Duchêne. The list of titles is drawn from an index in his edition of Sévigné. See also his article "Signification de romanesque: L'exemple de Madame de Sévigné," in *Ecrire au temps de Mme de Sévigné: Lettres et texte littéraire,* 2d ed. (Paris: Vrin, 1982), pp. 121–137.

23. Du Bosc, *L'honneste femme,* pt. 1, pp. 15, 17.

24. Boileau, p. 137.

25. Ibid., p. 140.

26. Louis de Rouvroy, duc de Saint-Simon, *Mémoires,* ed. Gonzague Truc (Paris: Gallimard, 1953–1961), II, 1043.

27. Ibid., p. 514.

28. Esprit Fléchier, "Oraison funèbre de Marie-Thérèse d'Autriche," in *Recueil des oraisons funèbres* (Rouen: Pierre Machuel, 1780), pp. 153–154.

29. Antoine Hamilton, *Mémoires de la vie du comte de Gramont* (1713),

in René Etiemble, ed., *Romanciers du XVIIIe siècle,* vol. I (Paris: Gallimard, 1960).

30. Stone, *The Family, Sex, and Marriage in England,* p. 349.

31. Etienne Pasquier, *Les oeuvres . . . contenant ses Recherches de la France . . . ses lettres; ses oeuvres meslées; et les lettres de Nicolas Pasquier, fils d'Estienne,* 2 vols. (Amsterdam: Compagnie des Libraires Associez, 1723).

32. Francis Bacon, *The Essayes or Counsels Civill and Morall,* ed. Michael Kiernan (Oxford: Clarendon Press, 1985), p. 26.

33. William Zunder, *The Poetry of John Donne: Literature and Culture in the Elizabethan and Jacobean Period* (Abingdon, Sussex: Harvester Press, 1982), p. 33.

34. Sévigné, I, xxiii.

35. Ibid., letter of June 17, 1687, III, 300.

36. Ibid., July 12, 1690, p. 914.

37. Ibid., July 16, 1690, p. 916.

38. Thomas Corneille, *Le galant doublé,* II, 2.

39. Pierre Choderlos de Laclos, *Les liaisons dangereuses,* letter 81. I am grateful to Mme. Martine Riga for pointing this passage out to me.

40. Sévigné, October 12, and 16, 1689, III, 723, 725.

41. Ibid., November 29, 1689, p. 768.

42. Ibid., January 15, 1672, and April 8, 1671, I, 417, 210–211.

43. Ibid., letter of October 6, 1679, II, 695.

44. Ibid., January 24, 1689, III, 482.

45. Ibid., June 1, 1689; May 1, 1689; January 11, 1690, III, 607, 592, 808.

46. Ibid., January 15, 1690, p. 810.

47. Horace Walpole, *Horace Walpole's Correspondence,* ed. W. S. Lewis, vol. 3: *Horace Walpole's Correspondence with Madame du Deffand and Wiart* (New Haven: Yale University Press, 1970), p. xxvii.

48. Sévigné, November 17, 1675, II, 166.

49. Ibid., May 27, 1680, p. 950.

50. Duchêne, *Ecrire au temps de Mme de Sévigné,* p. 72.

51. Arthur Ponsonby, *Scottish and Irish Diaries from the Sixteenth to the Nineteenth Century* (New York: Kennikat Press Scholarly Reprints, 1970), p. 10.

52. Frederick A. Pottle, *Pride and Negligence: The History of the Boswell Papers* (New York: McGraw-Hill, 1982).

53. "Boswell," in Margaret Drabble, ed., *The Oxford Companion to English Literature,* 5th ed. (Oxford: Oxford University Press, 1985), p. 120.

54. Christian Rotureau, "Jean-Jacques Rousseau et les deux visages de Tante Suzon," *L'Information Littéraire* 41, no. 3 (May–June 1989): 8–24.

55. A state of affairs attested to by *Les liaisons dangereuses* and by the vengeance of Mme. de la Pommeraye in Diderot's *Jacques le fataliste.*

56. Tobias George Smollett, *Travels through France and Italy* (Sussex: Centaur Press, 1969), p. 76 (October 12, 1763).

57. Laurence Sterne, *A Sentimental Journey through France and Italy* (1928; rpr. London: Oxford University Press, 1965), pp. 40–41.

58. This and the following quotations are from *The Yale Editions of the Private Papers of James Boswell,* vol. VI: *Boswell in Search of a Wife, 1766–1769,* ed. Frank Brady and Frederick A. Pottle (New Haven: Yale University Press, 1957).

59. Sévigné, I, 686.

60. Pierre de Bourdeilles, seigneur de Brantôme, *Oeuvres complètes accompagnées de remarques historiques et critiques* (Paris: Foucault, 1822), V, 183.

61. Marie-Madeleine Pioche de la Vergne, comtesse de La Fayette, *La Princesse de Clèves,* in Antoine Adam, ed., *Romanciers du XVIIe siècle* (Paris: Gallimard, 1958), p. 1126.

62. Sévigné, July 29 and August 5, 1671, I, 309, 313.

63. Ibid., July 1, 1671 (I, 284), and July 24, 1689 (III, 650).

64. Nicolas Restif de la Bretonne, *Monsieur Nicolas,* ed. Pierre Testud (Paris: Gallimard, 1989), I, 646.

Chapter 9. The Theater

ERIC A. NICHOLSON

1. See Tertullian, *Apology, De Spectaculis,* trans. T. R. Glover (London, 1931), and *De cultu feminarum (The Apparel of Women),* trans. Edwin A. Quain, in *Disciplinary Moral and Ascetical Works,* trans. Arbesmann, Daly, and Edwin A. Quain (New York, 1959); these texts, as well as the relevant passages from Chrysostom and Augustine, are discussed thoroughly in Jonas Barish, *The Antitheatrical Prejudice* (Berkeley: University of California Press, 1981), pp. 42–64.

2. See Marino Sanudo, *I diarii,* ed. Rinaldo Fulin et al., 58 vols. (Venice, 1879–1902), XVIII, 265. This entry, dated June 12, 1514, describes a production sponsored by the "Zardinieri" (Giardinieri), one of the city's Compagnie della Calza, festive organizations comprised mainly of aristocratic youths. The 1508 edict of the Council of Ten is reprinted in Giorgio Padoan, *La commedia rinascimentale veneta* (Vicenza: Neri Pozza, 1982), pp. 38–39.

3. See Jean-Jacques Rousseau, *Lettre à M. d'Alembert sur les spectacles* (1758), quoted in Barish, *The Antitheatrical Prejudice,* p. 282.

4. This pattern is fully discussed in several recent studies of early modern prostitution, especially Leah Otis, *Prostitution in Medieval Society: The History of an Urban Institution in Languedoc* (Chicago: University of Chicago Press, 1985); and Jacques Rossiaud, *Medieval Prostitution,* trans. Lydia Cochrane (London: Basil Blackwell, 1988). For local studies of prostitution in London, Florence, and Bologna, respectively, see E. J. Burford, *The Orrible Synne* (London, 1973) (a sensationalistic work, but with useful excerpts); Richard Trexler, "La prostitution Florentine au XVe siècle: Patronages et clientèles," *Annales ESC* 36, no. 6 (1981): 983–1015; and Lucia Ferrante, "Honor Regained: Women in the casa del Soccorso di San Paolo in Sixteenth-

Century Bologna, in Edward Muir and Guido Ruggiero, eds., *Sex and Gender in Historical Perspective* (Baltimore: Johns Hopkins University Press, 1990), pp. 46–72. Finally, see the chapter by Kathryn Norberg in this volume.

5. On charivaris and other shaming rituals, see Jacques Le Goff and Jean-Claude Schmitt, eds., *Le charivari* (Paris: Mouton, 1981), especially the essays by Carlo Ginzburg, Christiane Klapisch-Zuber, Richard Trexler, Andre Burguière, and Martin Ingram; Natalie Zemon Davis, "The Reasons of Misrule," in *Society and Culture in Early Modern France: Eight Essays* (Stanford: Stanford University Press, 1975), pp. 97–123; and Martin Ingram, "Ridings, Rough Music, and Mocking Rhymes in Early Modern England," in Barry Reay, ed., *Popular Culture in Seventeenth-Century England* (New York: St. Martin's Press, 1985), pp. 166–197.

6. See the essay by Sara Matthews Grieco elsewhere in this volume.

7. Thomas Norton, quoted in E. K. Chambers, *The Elizabethan Stage*, 4 vols. (Oxford: Clarendon Press, 1923), II, 262.

8. Thomas Nashe, "Pierce Penilesse His Supplication to the Devil," in *The Works of Thomas Nashe*, ed. R. B. McKerrow, 4 vols. (Oxford: Blackwell, 1958) I, 215.

9. On this subject see Antonia Fraser, "Actress as Honey-Pot," in *The Weaker Vessel* (New York: Alfred A. Knopf, 1984), pp. 418–439; and Jacqueline Pearson, "Women in the Theater, 1660–1737," in *The Prostituted Muse: Images of Women and Women Dramatists, 1642–1737* (New York: St. Martin's Press, 1988), pp. 25–41.

10. On Behn's life, work, and arguments for sexual freedom and equality, see Pearson, *The Prostituted Muse*, pp. 143–168; Janet Todd, *The Sign of Angellica* (New York: Columbia University Press, 1989); and Angeline Goreau, *Reconstructing Aphra: A Social Biography of Aphra Behn* (New York: Dial Press, 1980).

Chapter 10. A Sampling of Eighteenth-Century Philosophy
MICHÈLE CRAMPE-CASNABET

1. Montesquieu, *The Spirit of Laws*, bk. 16, chap. 12.

2. Ibid., bk. 19, chap. 8.

3. Emmanuel Kant, *L'anthropologie du point de vue pragmatique*, trans. Michel Foucault (Paris: Vrin, 1964), p. 150.

4. Montesquieu, *The Spirit of Laws*, bk. 16, chap. 2.

5. Kant, *L'anthropologie*, p. 148.

6. Montesquieu, *The Spirit of Laws*, bk. 7, chap. 9.

7. Ibid., bk. 7, chap. 17.

8. Claude Adrien Helvétius, *De l'esprit*, discourse 3, chap. 30.

9. Ibid., discourse 4, chap. 17.

10. The text of this article has been published by Christine Faure in *Corpus: Revue de Philosophie*, no. 2 (January 1986).

11. Condorcet, *Cinq mémoires sur l'instruction publique*, ed. Charles Coutel and Catherine Kintzler (Paris: Edilig, 1989), p. 71.

12. Condorcet, *Fragment sur l'Atlantide* (Paris: Flammarion, 1988), p. 325.

13. Ibid., p. 328.

Chapter 11. The Discourse of Medicine and Science
EVELYNE BERRIOT-SALVADORE

1. Arnauld de Villeneuve, "Compendium Medicinae Arnaldi de Villanova," in *Praxis medicinalis* (Lugduni, 1586), bk. 3, p. 111.

2. Philippe de Flesselles, *Introductoire de chirurgie rationelle* (Paris, 1547), p. 42.

3. Scipion Mercurio, "Forma della matrice," in *La commare o riccoglitrice* (Venice, 1621), bk. 1.

4. Pierre Franco, *Traité des hernies contenant une ample déclaration de toutes leurs espèces et autres excellentes parties de la chirurgie* (Lyons, 1561), p. 331.

5. Louys de Serres, *Oeuvres complètes* (Lyons, 1625), p. 1.

6. Louise Bourgeois, *Observations diverses sur la stérilité* (Paris, 1626), p. 1.

7. *Les oeuvres d'André Du Laurens,* trans. Théophile Gelée, rev. and supp. G. Sauvageon (Paris, 1646), bk. 8, chap. 1, p. 366.

8. Jacques Duval, *Traité des hermaphrodits* (Rouen, 1612), chap. 51.

9. Pierre Roussel, *Système physique et moral de la femme* (Paris, 1803; 1st ed. 1775), bk. 1, chap. 3, p. 187.

10. "Matrice" (Womb), in *Dictionnaire des sciences médicales,* ed. Dechambre (1864); *Encyclopedia universalis,* VII, 583.

11. Bourgeois, *Observations diverses sur la stérilité,* p. 74.

12. Jacques Sylvius, *Livre de la nature et utilité des moys des femmes* (Paris, 1559), p. 236.

13. Joseph Raulin, "Discours préliminaire," in *Traité des affections vaporeuses du sexe* (Paris, 1758).

14. Levin Lemnius, *Occultes merveilles et secrets de Nature* (Paris, 1574), chap. 3, p. 15.

15. Planque, *Bibliothèque de médecine de France,* (1762), I, 11.

16. Jérôme Cardan, *De la subtilité, et subtiles inventions, ensemble les causes occultes et raison d'icelles* (Paris, 1584), bk. 11, p. 309.

17. Duval, *Traité des Hermaphrodits,* chaps. 29–61.

18. Laurent Joubert, *Erreurs populaires au fait de la médecine et régime de santé* (Bourdeau, 1579), bk. 2, chap. 4, p. 170.

19. Jean Liébault, *Thrésor des remèdes,* chap. 23, p. 46.

20. Ambroise Paré, *De la génération,* ed. Malgaigne, II, 636; Du Laurens, *Oeuvres,* bk. 7, chap. 1, p. 337; François Mauriceau, *Des maladies des femmes grosses,* bk. 1, chap. 4, p. 71.

21. Paré, *De la génération,* II, 640.

22. Mauriceau, *Des maladies des femmes grosses,* p. 49.

23. "Response de Monsieur Ambroise Paré aux calomnies d'aucuns medecins touchant ses oeuvres," in Le Paulmier, *Ambroise Paré d'après de nouveaux documents* (Paris, 1887), pp. 86–93.

24. Denys Janot, ed., *De la noblesse et preexcellence du sexe foeminin* (Paris, originally published in 1527), folio c.

25. *Les oeuvres de N. Abraham de La Framboisière* (Lyons, 1644), bk. 3, chap. 1, p. 105.

26. Louys Guyon, *Miroir de la beauté et santé corporelle* (Lyons, 1625), bk. 5, chap. 23, p. 884.

27. Mauriceau, *Des maladies des femmes grosses,* bk. 1, chap. 24, p. 184.

28. François Rousset, "Epistre au lecteur," in *Traité nouveau de l'hysteroto-motocie ou enfantement caesarien* (Paris: Denys du Val, 1581).

29. Mauriceau, *Des maladies des femmes grosses,* bk. 2, chap. 33, p. 357.

30. Ibid., bk. 1, chap. 20, p. 159.

31. Abbé Dinouart, *Abrégé de l'embryologie sacrée* (Paris, 1762), bk. 1, chap. 3, p. 17.

32. Nicolas Venette, *La génération de l'homme, ou tableau de l'amour conjugal* (London, 1773), p. xii.

33. Pierre Roussel, *Système physique et moral de la femme, ou tableau philosophique de la constitution, de l'état organique, du tempérament, des moeurs et des fonctions propres au sexe* (Paris, 1803), p. 1.

Chapter 12. From Conversation to Creation

CLAUDE DULONG

1. On seventeenth-century French salons readers may wish to consult Claude Dulong, *L'amour au XVIIe siècle* (Paris: Hachette, 1969), chap. 3; and *La vie quotidienne des femmes au Grand Siècle* (Paris: Hachette, 1984), chap. 4, with bibliography.

2. Maurice Magendie, *La politesse mondaine et les théories de l'honnêteté en France au XVIIe siècle de 1600 à 1660* (Paris: Presses Universitaires de France, 1925), p. 944.

3. See the essay by Elijsa van Schulte elsewhere in this volume.

4. Assuming, of course, that the *Lettres portugaises* were in fact written by the nun and sent to Noël Bouton de Chamilly.

5. See Claude Dulong, "Mme. de La Fayette et ses placements immobiliers," *XVIIe Siècle,* no. 156 (July–September 1987): 241–266.

6. Katharine Rogers, *Feminism in Eighteenth Century England* (Urbana: University of Illinois Press, 1982), pp. 151, 215–216.

7. André Gide, *Et nunc manet in te* (Neuchâtel and Paris: Ides et Calendes, 1947), p. 23.

8. Several works published either anonymously or under male pseudonyms should undoubtedly be added to this number.

9. Mme. de Maintenon commissioned Racine to write *Esther* and *Athalie* expressly for the female students of Saint-Cyr.

Chapter 14. Witches

JEAN-MICHEL SALLMANN

1. Throughout this essay, the French *sorcellerie* is translated as either "sorcery" or "witchcraft."—*Trans.*

Chapter 15. Prostitutes

KATHRYN NORBERG

1. U. Gnoli, cited in Paul Larivaille, *La vie quotidienne des courtisanes en Italie au temps de la Renaissance* (Paris: Hachette, 1975), p. 31.

2. Erica-Marie Bénabou, *La prostitution et la police des moeurs au XVIIIe siècle* (Paris: Perrin, 1987), p. 327.

3. D'Archenholz, quoted in Fernando Henriques, *Prostitution in Europe and the Americas* (New York: Citadel Press, 1969), p. 143.

4. See Claude Quetel, *Le mal de Naples. Histoire de la syphilis* (Paris: Seghers, 1986).

5. Mary Elizabeth Perry, *Gender and Disorder in Early Modern Seville* (Princeton: Princeton University Press, 1990), pp. 137–152.

6. Martin Luther, quoted in Vern Bullogh and Bonnie Bullogh, *Women and Prostitution: A Social History* (Buffalo: Prometheus Books, 1987), p. 141.

7. Merry E. Weisner, *Working Women in Renaissance Germany* (New Brunswick, N.J.: Rutgers University Press, 1986), pp. 106–107.

8. Jacques Rossiaud, *Medieval Prostitution,* trans. Lydia Cochrane (London: Basil Blackwell, 1988), p. 50.

9. Bénabou, *La prostitution et la police des moeurs,* pp. 195–199.

10. Colin Jones, "Prostitution and the Ruling Class in 18th-Century Montpellier," *History Workshop* 6 (Autumn 1978): 15.

11. This figure comes from my own research. Annick Riani has come up with a very similar figure for a slightly different period in "Pouvoirs et contestations: La prostitution à Marseille au XVIIIe siècle" (Thèse du troisième cycle, Université de Provence, 1982).

12. Bénabou, *La prostitution et police des moeurs,* pp. 300–306.

13. Archives Municipales de Marseille, FF 239.

14. Felix Tavernier, *La vie quotidienne à Marseille de Louis XIV à Louis Philippe* (Paris, 1973), p. 114.

15. Bénabou, *La prostitution et police des moeurs,* p. 326.

16. Klausse Sasse, *Die Entdeckung der "courtisane vertueuse" in der franzosischen Literatur des 18. Jahrhunderts* (Hamburg: Facultat der Universitat Hamburg, 1967).

Chapter 16. Criminals

NICOLE CASTAN

1. See the essay on rioters by Arlette Farge elsewhere in this volume.

2. Natalie Zemon Davis, *Fiction in the Archives: Pardon Tales and Their*

Tellers in Sixteenth-Century France (Stanford: Stanford University Press, 1987), p. 85.

Chapter 17. Protesters Plain to See
ARLETTE FARGE

1. Charles Tilly, *British Conflicts, 1828–1831* (Ann Arbor: Center for Research on Social Organization, University of Michigan, 1982), p. 5.

2. Robert Mandrou, "Vingt ans après ou une direction de recherches féconde: Les révoltes populaires en France au XVIIe siècle," *Revue Historique* 93 (1969):37, Yves-Marie Bercé, *Revolt and Revolution in Early Modern Europe: An Essay on the History of Political Violence,* trans. Joseph Bergin (Manchester: Manchester University Press, 1987).

3. P. Blicke, "Les communautés villageoises en Allemagne," in Charles Higounet, ed., *Les communautés villageoises en Europe occidentale du Moyen Age aux temps modernes* (1984), pp. 123–136; Peter Burke, "The Virgin of the Carmine and the Revolt of the Masaniello," *Past and Present* 99 (1983):3–21; R. Villari, "Masaniello: Contemporary and Recent Interpretations," *Past and Present* 114 (1987):197–199; C. Maurin, "Le rôle des femmes dans les émotions populaires dans les campagnes de la généralité de Lyon de 1665 à 1789," in *Révolte et société. Histoire du présent* (Paris: Sorbonne, 1989), II, 134–140.

4. Rudolf M. Dekker, "Women in Revolt: Popular Protest and Its Social Basis in Holland in the Seventeenth and Eighteenth Centuries," *Theory and Society* 16 (1987):337–362.

5. See the pioneering work of Alice Clark, *Working Life of Women in the Eighteenth Century* (London: Routledge, 1919); and Hans Medick, "The Proto-Industrial Familial Economy," in P. Kriedte, H. Medick, and J. Schlumbohm, *Industrialization before Industrialization* (Cambridge: Cambridge University Press, 1981), pp. 38–73.

6. Joan N. Scott and Louise A. Tilly, *Women, Work, and Family* (New York: Holt, Rinehart, and Winston, 1978); *Les femmes, le travail et la famille* (Paris: Rivages/Histoire, 1987); Mary Prior, "Women and the Urban Economy: Oxford, 1500–1800," in Mary Prior, ed., *Women in English Society, 1560–1800* (London and New York: Methuen, 1985), pp. 93–118.

7. M.-B. Rowlands, "Recusant Women, 1560–1640," in Prior, *Women in English Society,* pp. 149–180.

8. Arlette Farge, *La vie fragile. Violences, pouvoirs et solidarités à Paris au XVIIIe siècle* (Paris: Hachette, 1986).

9. Dekker, "Women in Revolt."

10. Robert Muchembled, *La violence au village* (Brépols, 1989).

11. Archives Nationales, Y 12571, July 14, 1725, affidavit of Commissaire Labbé.

12. P. Loupès, "Le jardin irlandais des supplices, la grande rébellion de 1641 vue à travers les pamphlets anglais" (Paper presented at the Colloque

franco-irlandais, Marseilles, September 28–October 2, 1988, "Culture et pratiques politiques en France et en Irlande, XVe–XVIIIe siècle").

13. François Métra, *Correspondance secrète, politique et littéraire ou mémoires pour servir à l'histoire des cours, des sociétés et de la littérature en France depuis la mort de Louis XV* (London, 1787), I, 338 ff.

14. Archives Nationales, Series X, X2B 1367, July 3, 1750.

15. Archives de la Bastille, August 9, 1721, ms. 10728.

16. Archives Nationales, Series Y, Commissaire Chénon, Affaire de 1775, Y 11441, January 1, 1775, interrogation of M. Pochet.

17. Rudolf M. Dekker and Lotte C. van de Pol, *The Tradition of Female Transvestism in Early Modern Europe* (New York: St. Martin's Press, 1989).

18. Natalie Zemon Davis, "Women on Top," in *Society and Culture in Early Modern Europe* (Stanford: Stanford University Press, 1975).

19. Natalie Zemon Davis, "The Rites of Violence," ibid.

20. C. A. Bouton, "Les victimes de la violence populaire pendant la guerre des Farines, 1775," in Jean Nicolas, ed., *Mouvements populaires et conscience sociale, XVIe–XIXe siècles. Actes du colloque de Paris 24–26 mai 1984* (Paris: Maloine, 1985), pp. 391 ff.

21. Paule-Marie Duhet, ed., *Cahiers de doléances des femmes et autres textes* (Paris: Editions des Femmes, 1981), p. 25; B. Didier, *Ecrire la Révolution, 1789–99* (Paris: Presses Universitaires de France, 1989), pp. 57–72.

22. Nicolas, *Mouvements populaires et conscience sociale*, pp. 14–20.

23. Charles Baudelaire, "Parfum exotique," in *Oeuvres complètes* (Paris: Gallimard, 1975), p. 25.

Glückel of Hameln, Jewish Merchant Woman
NATALIE ZEMON DAVIS

1. *The Life of Glückel of Hameln, 1646–1724, Written by Herself*, trans. and ed. Beth-Zion Abrahams (New York: Thomas Yoseloff, 1963), pp. 149–151.

Anne-Françoise Cornet, Parisian Artisan
ARLETTE FARGE

1. Archives Nationales, X2B 1367, June 2, 1750. Riot of May 1750 for abduction of children.

Bibliography

Abensour, Léon. *La femme et le féminisme avant la Révolution.* Geneva: Slatkine Reprints, 1977.

Accati, Luisa. "Il padre naturale. Tra simboli dominanti e categorie scientifiche," *Memoria: Rivista di Storia delle Donne* 21 (1987):79–106.

Adam, Antoine. *Histoire de la littérature française au XVIIe siècle,* 5 vols. Paris: Domat-Montchrestien, 1948–1956.

Adburgham, Alison. *Women in Print: Writing Women and Women's Magazines from the Restoration to the Accession of Victoria.* London: Allen and Unwin, 1972.

Adorno, Theodor. *Minima moralia,* trans. E. F. N. Jephcott. London: New Left Books, 1974.

Alberro, Solange. *Inquisition et société au Mexique, 1571–1700.* Mexico City: Centre d'Etudes Mexicaines et Centramericaines, 1988.

Albistur, Maïté, and Daniel Armogathe. *Histoire du féminisme français,* 2 vols. Paris: Editions des Femmes, 1978.

Amussen, Susan Dwyer. "Féminin/masculin: Le genre dans l'Angleterre de l'époque moderne," *Annales ESC* 40 (1985):269–287.

——— *An Ordered Society: Gender and Class in Early Modern England.* Oxford and New York: Basil Blackwell, 1988.

Anderson, Bonnie, and Judith Zinsser. *A History of Their Own: Women in Europe from Prehistory to the Present.* 2 vols. New York: Harper & Row, 1989.

Anderson, Michael. *Approaches to the History of the Western Family, 1500–1914.* London: Macmillan, 1980.

Andrieux, Maurice. *La vie quotidienne dans la Rome pontificale au XVIIIe siècle.* Paris: Hachette, 1962.

Arenal, Electa, and Stacey Schlau. *Untold Sisters: Hispanic Nuns in Their Own Works.* Albuquerque: University of New Mexico Press, 1989.

Ariès, Philippe. *Centuries of Childhood: A Social History of Family Life,* trans. Robert Baldick. New York: Vintage, 1962.

Ariès, Philippe, and André Bejin, eds. *Western Sexuality: Practice and Precept in Past and Present,* trans. Anthony Forster. Oxford and New York: Basil Blackwell, 1985.

Ariès, Philippe, and Georges Duby, eds. *A History of Private Life,* trans. Arthur Goldhammer. 5 vols. Cambridge, Mass.: Harvard University Press, 1987–1991.

Atkinson, Clarissa. "Precious Balsam in Fragile Glass: The Ideology of Virginity in the Later Middle Ages," *Journal of Family History* 8 (1983):131–143.

Backer, Anne Liot. *Precious Women: A Feminist Phenomenon in the Age of Louis XIV.* New York: Basic Books, 1974.

Badinter, Elisabeth. *Emilie, Emilie: L'ambition féminine au XVIIIe siècle.* Paris: Flammarion, 1983.

Bald, R. C. *John Donne: A Life.* Oxford: Clarendon Press, 1970.

Bange, Petty, et al. *Saints and She-Devils: Images of Women in the 15th and 16th Centuries.* London: Rubicon Press, 1987.

Barish, Jonas. *The Antitheatrical Prejudice.* Berkeley: University of California Press, 1981.

Barles, Louis. *Les nouvelles découvertes sur les organes des hommes servans à la generation.* Lyons: Chez Esprit Vitalis, 1675.

Barreiro, Bernardo. *Brujos y astrólogos de la Inquisición de Galicia y el famoso Libro de San Cipriano.* 1885; rpt., Madrid: Akal Editor, 1973.

Barstow, Anne. "On Studying Witchcraft as Women's History: A Historiography of the European Witch Persecutions," *Journal of Feminist Studies in Religion* 4 (1988):7–20.

Barzaghi, Antonio. *Donne o cortigiane? La prostituzione a Venezia: Documenti di costume dal XVI al XVIII secolo.* Verona: Bertani, 1980.

Baulant, Micheline. "Costume populaire et costume bourgeois à Meaux au XVIIIe siècle: Nuances ou contrastes," *L'Ethnographie* 80 (1984):269–275.

———— "Un dossier: La personne âgée dans la société briarde aux XVIIe–XVIIIe siècles," *Annales de Démographie Historique* (1985):283–302.

———— "La famille en miettes: Sur un aspect de la démographie au XVIIe siècle," *Annales ESC* 27 (1972):959–968.

———— "La femme de Brie, 1650–1750," *Pénélope* 7 (1972):21–24.

Baumgarten, Alexander. *Aesthetica.* 1750; rpt., Hildesheim: Olms, 1961.

Beasley, Faith. *Revising Memory: Women's Fiction and Memoirs in Seventeenth-Century France.* New Brunswick, N.J.: Rutgers University Press, 1990.

Beattie, J. M. *Crime and the Courts in England, 1660–1800.* Oxford: Clarendon Press, 1986.

Beik, William. *Absolutism and Society in Seventeenth-Century France: State Power and Provincial Aristocracy in Languedoc.* Cambridge: Cambridge University Press, 1985.

Belsey, Catherine. *The Subject of Tragedy: Identity and Difference in Renaissance Drama.* New York and London: Methuen, 1985.

Bénabou, Erica-Marie. *La prostitution et la police des moeurs au XVIIIe siècle.* Paris: Perrin, 1987.

Bercé, Yves-Marie. *Revolt and Revolution in Early Modern Europe: An Essay* on the History of Political Violence, trans. Joseph Bergin. Manchester: Manchester University Press, 1987.

Bernards, Matthäus. "Kölns Beitrag zum Streit um die religiöse Frauenfrage im 17. Jahrhundert," Annalen des Historischen Vereins für den Niederrhein 177 (1975):76–91.

Bernos, Marcel, Charles de La Roncière, Jean Guyon, and Philippe Lécrivain. Le fruit défendu. Les chrétiens et la sexualité de l'antiquité à nos jours. Paris: Centurion, 1985.

Berriot-Salvadore, Evelyne. Les femmes dans la société française de la Renaissance. Geneva: Droz, 1990.

—— Images de la femme dans la médicine du XVIe et au début du XVIIe siècle. Thesis, Université de Montpellier, 1979.

Berry, Philippa. Chastity and Power: Elizabethan Literature and the Unmarried Queen. London and New York: Routledge, 1989.

Bevis, Richard. English Drama: Restoration and the Eighteenth Century, 1660–1789. London and New York: Longman, 1988.

Bienville, M. D. T. La nymphomanie ou traité de la fureur uterine. 1771; rpt., Amsterdam, 1778.

Bilinkoff, Jodi. The Avila of Saint Teresa: Religious Reform in a Sixteenth-Century City. Ithaca, N.Y.: Cornell University Press, 1989.

Blaisdell, Charmarie Jenkins. "Calvin's Letters to Women: The Courting of Ladies in High Places," Sixteenth Century Journal 13 (1982):67–84.

Blasons anatomiques du corps féminin, ensemble des contreblasons. C. d'Augebie, 1554 (damaged copy): Bibliothèque National no. 5, E. Picot 811; 1570 edition (Vve. Bonnefous): Bibliothèque National Enfer 600; and a copy at the Bibliothèque de l'Arsenal, 8°H11 131 Rés. in-12. Among numerous reeditions: Pascal Quignard, ed., Blasons anatomiques du corps féminin. Paris: Gallimard, 1982.

Bock, Gisela, and Giuliana Nobili, eds. Il corpo delle donne. Ancona and Bologna: Transeuropa, 1988.

Boguet, Henri. Discours exécrable des sorciers. 1606; rpt., Marseilles: Laffitte Reprints, 1979.

Bollême, Geneviève. La Bibliothèque Bleue. Littérature populaire en France du XVIIe au XIXe siècle. Paris: Julliard, 1971.

Bologne, Jean-Claude. Histoire de la pudeur. Paris: Olivier Orban, 1986.

Bonomo, Giuseppe. Caccia alle streghe. La credenza nelle streghe dal secolo XIII al XIX con particolare riferimento all'Italia. Palermo: Palumbo, 1971.

Börresen, Kari E., ed. Image of God and Gender Models in Judaeo-Christian Tradition. Oslo: Solum Forlay, 1990.

Boucher, Jacqueline. La cour de Henri III. Rennes: Ouest-France, 1986.

Bourgeois, Louise, dite Boursier. Observations diverses sur la sterilité, perte de fruict, foecondité, accouchements et maladies des femmes et enfants nouveaux naiz. 1609; rpt., Paris: Melchior Mondiere, 1626.

Bousquet, Joe. La peinture maniériste. Neuchâtel: Ides et Calendes, 1964.

Boyer, Paul, and Stephen Nissenbaum. *Salem Possessed: The Social Origins of Witchcraft.* Cambridge, Mass.: Harvard University Press, 1974.

Brantôme, Pierre de Bourdeille seigneur de. *Les dames esclaves,* ed. Maurice Rat. Paris: Garnier, 1955.

—— *Oeuvres complètes,* 2 vols. Paris: A. Desrez, 1888.

Bray, Alan. *Homosexuality in Renaissance England.* London: Gay Men's Press, 1982.

Brémond, Henri. *Histoire littéraire du sentiment religieux en France.* 11 vols. Paris: Bloud et Gay, 1920–1933.

Brink, Jean, Allison Coudert, and Maryanne Horowitz, eds. *Playing with Gender: A Renaissance Pursuit.* Urbana: University of Illinois Press, 1991.

Broude, Norma, and Mary M. Garrard, eds. *Feminism and Art History: Questioning the Litany.* New York: Harper & Row, 1982.

Brown, Judith. *Immodest Acts: The Life of a Lesbian Nun in Renaissance Italy.* Oxford and New York: Oxford University Press, 1986.

Brown, Peter. *The Body and Society: Men, Women, and Sexual Renunciation in Early Christianity.* New York: Columbia University Press, 1988.

Brunel, Pierre, ed. *Dictionnaire des mythes littéraires.* Paris: Editions du Rocher, 1988.

Bugge, John. *Virginitas: An Essay on the History of a Medieval Ideal.* The Hague: Nijhoff, 1975.

Bullogh, Vern, and Bonnie Bullogh. *Women and Prostitution: A Social History.* Buffalo: Prometheus Books, 1987.

Burckhardt, Jacob. *The Civilization of the Renaissance in Italy.* 2 vols. New York: Harper, 1958.

Burgelin, Olivier, Philippe Perrot, and Marie-Thérèse Basse, eds. *Parure, pudeur, étiquette.* Special issue of *Communications* 46 (1987).

Burgelin, Pierre. "L'éducation de Sophie," *Annales de la Société Jean-Jacques Rousseau* 35 (1959–1962):113–137.

Burguiere, André, Christiane Klapisch-Zuber, Martine Segalen, and Françoise Zonabend, eds. *Histoire de la famille.* 2 vols. Paris: Armand Colin, 1986.

Burke, Janet. "Freemasonry, Friendship, and Noblewomen: The Role of the Secret Society in Bringing Enlightenment Thought to Pre-Revolutionary Women Elites," *History of European Ideas* 10 (1989):283–294.

Burke, Peter. *Historical Anthropology in Early Modern Italy.* Cambridge: Cambridge University Press, 1987.

Buxton, John. *Sir Philip Sidney and the English Renaissance.* New York: St. Martin's Press, 1966.

Bynum, Caroline Walker. *Holy Feast and Holy Fast: The Religious Significance of Food to Medieval Women.* Berkeley: University of California Press, 1987.

Camden, Carroll. *The Elizabethan Woman: A Panorama of English Womanhood, 1540 to 1640.* London and New York: Cleaver-Hume, 1952.

Camporesi, Piero. *The Incorruptible Flesh: Bodily Mutilation and Mortification in Religion and Folklore,* trans. Tania Croft-Murray. Cambridge and New York: Cambridge University Press, 1988.

———— *Le officine dei sensi*. Milan: Garzanti, 1985.

Cangiamila, Francesco Emanuele. *Embriologia sacra, overo dell'uffizio de' sacerdoti, medici, e superiori, circa l'eterna salute de' bambini racchiusi nell'utero*. Palermo, 1745.

Carlson, Susan. *Women and Comedy: Rewriting the British Theatrical Tradition*. Ann Arbor: University of Michigan Press, 1990.

Carmona, Michel. *Les diables de Loudun. Sorcellerie et politique sous Richelieu*. Paris: Fayard, 1988.

Caro Baroja, Julio. *Las brujas y su mundo*. Madrid: El Libro de Bolsill, 1966.

Castan, Nicole. *Les criminels de Languedoc. Les exigences d'ordre et les voies du ressentiment dans une société pré-révolutionnaire, 1750–1790*. Toulouse: Association des Publications de l'Université de Toulouse–Le Mirail, 1980.

———— and Yves Castan. *Vivre ensemble. Ordre et désordre en Languedoc aux XVIIe et XVIIIe siècles*. Paris: Gallimard/Julliard, 1981.

Céard, Jean, Marie-Madeleine Fontaine, and Jean-Claude Margolin, eds. *Le corps à la Renaissance: Actes du XXXe colloque de Tours 1987*. Paris: Amateurs de Livres, 1990.

Certeau, Michel de. *La fable mystique, XVIe–XVIIe siècles*. Paris: Gallimard, 1982.

———— *La possession de Loudun*. Paris: Julliard, 1970.

Charles, Lindsey, and Lorna Duffin, eds. *Women and Work in Pre-Industrial England*. London and Dover, N.H.: Croom Helm, 1985.

Chartier, Roger, ed. *Passions of the Renaissance*. Vol. 3 of Philippe Ariès and Georges Duby, eds., *History of Private Life*. Cambridge, Mass.: Harvard University Press, 1989.

Chartier, Roger, Marie-Madeleine Compère, and Dominique Julia. *L'éducation en France, XVIe–XVIIIe siècles*. Paris: CDU-SEDES, 1976.

Chartier, Roger, and Henri-Jean Martin, eds. *Histoire de l'édition française*. 3 vols. Paris: Promodis, 1983–1986.

Chartier, Roger, and Denis Richet, eds. *Représentations et vouloir politiques: Autour des Etats-Généraux de 1614*. Paris: Ecole des Hautes Etudes en Sciences Sociales, 1982.

Christian, William. *Apparitions in Late Medieval and Renaissance Spain*. Princeton: Princeton University Press, 1981.

Ciammitti, Luisa. "One Saint Less: The Story of Angela Mellini, a Bolognese Seamstress (1667–17[?])," in Edward Muir and Guido Ruggiero, eds., *Sex and Gender in Historical Perspective*. Baltimore: Johns Hopkins University Press, 1990, pp. 141–176.

Clancy, Patricia. "A French Writer and Educator in England: Madame Le Prince de Beaumont," *Studies on Voltaire and the Eighteenth Century* 201 (1982):195–208.

Clark, Alice. *The Working Life of Women in the Seventeenth Century*. London: Routledge, 1919.

Clark, Stuart. "Inversion, Misrule, and the Meaning of Witchcraft," *Past and Present* 87 (1980):98–127.

Cohen, Sherill. "Asylums for Women in Counter-Reformation Italy," in Sherrin Marshall, ed., *Women in Reformation and Counter-Reformation Europe: Private and Public Worlds*. Bloomington: Indiana University Press, 1989, pp. 166–188.

—— *The Evolution of Women's Asylums since 1500: From Refuges for Ex-Prostitutes to Shelters for Battered Women*. New York: Oxford University Press, 1992.

Cohen, Walter. *Drama of a Nation: Public Theater in Renaissance England and Spain*. Ithaca: Cornell University Press, 1985.

Cohn, Norman. *Europe's Inner Demons: An Enquiry Inspired by the Great Witch-Hunt*. London: Chatto, 1975.

Conner, Susan. "Sexual Politics and Citizenship: Women in Eighteenth-Century France," *Western Society for French History* 10 (1982):264–273.

Conti Odorisio, Ginevra. *Donna e società nel Seicento. Lucrezia Marinelli e Arcangela Tarabotti*. Rome: Bulzoni, 1979.

Couliano, Ioan. *Eros and Magic in the Renaissance*. Chicago: University of Chicago Press, 1987.

Courtine, Jean-Jacques, and Claudine Haroche. *Histoire du visage. Exprimer et taire ses émotions, XVIe–début XIXe siècle*. Paris: Editions Rivages, 1988.

Crampe-Casnabet, Michèle. *Condorcet, lecteur des Lumières*. Paris: Presses Universitaires de France, 1985.

Cressy, David. *Literacy and the Social Order: Reading and Writing in Tudor and Stuart England*. Cambridge and New York: Cambridge University Press, 1980.

Cusenier, Jean. *L'art populaire en France. Rayonnements, modèles et sources*. Fribourg: Office du Livre; Paris: Société Française du Livre, 1979.

Daenens, Francine. "Superiore perché inferiore: Il paradosso della superiorità della donna in alcuni trattati italiani del Cinquecento," in Vanna Gentili, ed., *Trasgressione tragica e norma domestica: Esemplari di tipologie femminili dalla letteratura europea*. Rome: Edizioni di Storia e Letteratura, 1983, pp. 11–50.

Dailey, Barbara Ritter. "The Visitation of Sarah Wight: Holy Carnival and the Revolution of the Saints in Civil War London," *Church History* 55 (1986):438–455.

D'Ameglia, Marina. "La conquista di un dote. Regole del gioca e scambi femminili alla Confraternita dell'Annunziata (sec. XVII–XVIII)," in Lucia Ferrante, Maura Palazzi, and Gianna Pomata, eds., *Ragnatele di rapporti: Patronage e reti di relazione nella storia delle donne*. Turin: Rosenberg & Sellier, 1988, pp. 305–343.

Darmon, Pierre. *Le mythe de la procréation à l'âge baroque*. Paris: Seuil, 1981.

—— *Mythologie de la femme dans l'ancienne France, XVIe–XIXe siècle*. Paris: Seuil, 1983.

Daumard, Adeline, and François Furet. *Structures et relations sociales à Paris au milieu du XVIIIe siècle*. Paris: Armand Colin, 1961.

Dauphin, Cécile, Arlette Farge, Geneviève Fraisse, Christiane Klapisch-Zuber, Rose-Marie Lagrave, Michelle Perrot, Pierrette Pezerat, Yannick Ripa, Pauline Schmitt-Pantel, and Danièle Voldman. "Culture et pouvoir des femmes: Essai d'historiographie," *Annales ESC* 41 (1986):271–293.

Davidoff, Leonore, and Catherine Hall. *Family Fortunes: Men and Women of the English Middle Class, 1780–1850*. London: Hutchinson, 1987.

Davidson, Caroline. *A Woman's Work Is Never Done: A History of Housework in the British Isles, 1650–1950*. London: Chatto & Windus, 1981.

Davis, John. "Joan of Kent, Lollardy and the English Reformation," *Journal of Ecclesiastical History* 33 (1982):225–233.

Davis, Natalie Zemon. *Fiction in the Archives: Pardon Tales and Their Tellers in Sixteenth-Century France*. Stanford: Stanford University Press, 1987.

———— "From 'Popular Religion' to Religious Cultures," in Steven Ozment, ed., *Reformation Europe: A Guide to Research*. St. Louis, Mo.: Center for Reformation Research, 1982, pp. 321–341.

———— "Gender and Genre: Women as Historical Writers, 1400–1820," in Patricia Labalme, ed., *Beyond Their Sex: Learned Women of the European Past*. New York: New York University Press, 1980, pp. 153–182.

———— *The Return of Martin Guerre*. Cambridge, Mass.: Harvard University Press, 1983.

———— *Society and Culture in Early Modern France: Eight Essays*. Stanford: Stanford University Press, 1975.

———— "Women in the Crafts in Sixteenth-Century Lyon," *Feminist Studies* 8 (Spring 1982):47–80.

Dawson, Ruth. "Women Communicating: Eighteenth-Century German Journals Edited by Women," *Archives et Bibliothèque de Belgique* 54 (1983):95–111.

De Baar, Mirjiam. "De betrokkenheid van vrouwen bij het huisgezin van Jean de Labadie (1669–1732)," *Jaarboek voor Vrouwengeschiedenis* 8 (1987):11–43.

De Beer, E. S., ed. *The Diary of John Evelyn*. London: Oxford University Press, 1959.

De Clementi, Andreina. "Una mistica contadina: Caterina Paluzzi di Morlupo," *Memoria* 5 (1982):23–33.

Defoe, Daniel. *Moll Flanders*. London: Dent, 1982.

Degler-Spengler, Brigitte. "Die religiöse Frauenbewegung des Mittelalters," *Rothenburger Jahrbuch für Kirchengeschichte* 3 (1984):75–88.

DeJean, Joan. *Tender Geographies: Women and the Origins of the Novel in France*. New York: Columbia University Press, 1991.

Dekker, Rudolf M. "Women in Revolt: Popular Protest and Its Social Basis in Holland in the Seventeenth and Eighteenth Centuries," *Theory and Society* 16 (1987):337–362.

———— and Lotte C. van de Pol. *The Tradition of Female Transvestism in Early Modern Europe*. New York: St. Martin's Press, 1989.

Delarue, Paul, and M.-L. Teneze. *Le conte populaire française*. 4 vols. to date. Paris: Maisonneuve et Larose, 1957–.

Delcambre, Etienne. *Le concept de la sorcellerie dans le duché de Lorraine au XVIe et au XVIIe siècle.* 3 vols. Nancy: Société d'Archéologie Lorraine, 1948–1951.

Delooz, Pierre. "Santità. II. Santità e sociologia," in Guerrino Pelliccia and Giancarlo Rocca, eds., *Dizionario degli Istituti di Perfezione,* vol. 8. Rome: Edizioni Paoline, 1988, cols. 861–873.

Delumeau, Jean. *La peur en Occident, XIVe–XVIIIe siècles. Une cité assiégée.* Paris: Librairie Arthème Fayard, 1978.

——— *Sin and Fear: The Emergence of a Western Guilt Culture, 13th–18th Centuries.* New York: St. Martin's Press, 1990.

De Maio, Romeo. *Donna e Rinascimento.* Milan: Mondadori, 1987.

Demos, John. *Entertaining Satan: Witchcraft and the Culture of Early New England.* New York: Oxford University Press, 1982.

Dickens, A. G., ed. *The Courts of Europe: Politics, Patronage, and Royalty, 1400–1800.* New York: McGraw-Hill, 1977.

Diderot, Denis. *The Nun,* trans. Leonard Tancock. Harmondsworth: Penguin Books, 1974.

Doody, Margaret. *Frances Burney: The Life in the Works.* New Brunswick, N.J.: Rutgers University Press, 1988.

Doran, Susan. "Religion and Politics at the Court of Elizabeth I: The Habsburg Marriage Negotiations of 1559–1567," *English Historical Review* 104 (1989):908–926.

Douglas, Mary, ed. *Witchcraft Confessions and Accusations.* London and New York: Tavistock, 1970.

Douglass, Jane Dempsey. "Christian Freedom: What Calvin Learned at the School of Women," *Church History* 53 (1984):155–173.

——— *Women, Freedom, and Calvin.* Philadelphia: Westminster Press, 1985.

Dowling, Maria. "Anne Boleyn and Reform," *Journal of Ecclesiastical History* 35 (1984):30–46.

Duby, Georges, ed. *L'amour et la sexualité,* special issue of *L'Histoire,* 1984.

Duchet, Michèle. *Anthropologie et histoire au siècle des Lumières.* Paris: Maspéro, 1971.

Dugaw, Dianne. *Warrior Women and Popular Balladry, 1650–1850.* Cambridge and New York: Cambridge University Press, 1989.

Duhet, Paule-Marie. *Les femmes et la Révolution, 1789–1794.* Paris: Julliard, 1971.

——— and M. Rebérioux. *Cahiers de doléances des femmes de 1789.* Paris: Editions des Femmes, 1989.

Dulong, Claude. *L'amour au XVIIe siècle.* Paris: Hachette, 1969.

——— "Mme. de La Fayette et ses placements immobiliers," *XVIIe Siècle* 156 (1987):241–266.

——— *La vie quotidienne des femmes au Grand Siècle.* Paris: Hachette, 1984.

Du Pleix, Scipion. *La curiosité naturelle redigée en questions selon l'ordre alphabétique.* 1620; rpt., Rouen: Chez Jacques Cailloue, 1648.

Dupont-Bouchat, Marie-Sylvie, Willem Frijhoff, and Robert Muchembled.

Prophètes et sorciers dans les Pays-Bas, XVIe–XVIIIe siècle. Paris: Hachette, 1978.

Duval, Jacques. *Des hermaphrodits, accouchemens des femmes et traitement qui est requis pour les relever en santé et bien elever leurs enfans.* Rouen: Chez David Geoffroy, 1612.

Elias, Norbert. *The Civilizing Process.* New York: Urizen Books, 1978.

Elliott, J. H. "Revolts in the Spanish Monarchy," in Robert Forster and Jack Greene, eds., *Preconditions of Revolution in Early Modern Europe.* Baltimore: Johns Hopkins University Press, 1970, pp. 109–130.

Epstein, Julia, and Kristina Straub, eds. *Body Guards: The Cultural Politics of Gender Ambiguity.* London and New York: Routledge, 1991.

Erlanger, Philippe. *Madame de Longueville. De la révolte au mysticisme.* Paris: Perrin, 1977.

Faderman, Lillian. *Surpassing the Love of Men: Romantic Friendship and Love between Women from the Renaissance to the Present.* New York: William Morrow, 1981.

Fagniez, Gustave. *La femme et la société française dans la première moitié du XVIIe siècle.* Paris: Gamber, 1929.

Fairchilds, Cissie. *Domestic Enemies: Servants and Their Masters in Old Regime France.* Baltimore: Johns Hopkins University Press, 1984.

——— "Female Sexuality and the Rise of Illegitimacy: A Case Study," *Journal of Interdisciplinary History* 8 (1978):627–667.

Farge, Arlette. *Dire et mal dire. L'opinion publique au XVIIIe siècle.* Paris: Seuil, 1992.

——— "Le siècle au féminin. Rôles et représentations des femmes," *Electra* (June 1987).

——— *La vie fragile. Violences, pouvoirs et solidarités à Paris au XVIIIe siècle.* Paris: Hachette, 1986.

——— "La violence, les femmes et le sang au XVIIIe siècle," *Mentalités* 1 (1988):95–111.

——— *Le vol d'aliments à Paris au XVIIIe siècle.* Paris: Plon, 1974.

———, ed. *Le miroir des femmes: Textes de la Bibliothèque Bleue.* Paris: Montalba, 1982.

——— *Vivre dans la rue à Paris au XVIIIe siècle.* Paris: Gallimard/Julliard, 1979.

——— and Michel Foucault, eds. *Le désordre des familles. Lettres de cachet des Archives de la Bastille au XVIIIe siècle.* Paris: Gallimard, 1982.

Farrell, Michèle Longino. *Performing Motherhood: The Sévigné Correspondence.* Hanover, N.H.: University Press of New England, 1991.

Fauchery, Pierre. *La destinée féminine dans le roman européen du XVIIIe siècle, 1713–1807.* Paris: Armand Colin, 1972.

Fauré, Christine. *Democracy without Women: Feminism and the Rise of Liberal Individualism in France,* trans. Claudia Gorbman and John Berks. Bloomington: Indiana University Press, 1991.

Favret-Saada, Jeanne. *Deadly Words: Witchcraft in the Bocage,* trans. Catherine Cullen. Cambridge and New York: Cambridge University Press, 1980.

Febvre, Lucien. *Autour de l'Heptaméron, amour sacré, amour profane.* Paris: Gallimard, 1944.

Ferguson, Margaret N., Maureen Quilligan, and Nancy J. Vickers, eds. *Rewriting the Renaissance: The Discourses of Sexual Difference in Early Modern Europe.* Chicago: University of Chicago Press, 1986.

Ferrand, Jacques. *De la maladie d'amour ou melancholie erotique.* Paris: Chez Denis Moreau, 1623.

Ferrante, Lucia. "Honor Regained: Women in the Casa del Soccorso di San Paolo in Sixteenth-Century Bologna," in Edward Muir and Guido Ruggiero, eds., *Sex and Gender in Historical Perspective.* Baltimore: Johns Hopkins University Press, 1990, pp. 46–72.

————— "Pro mercede carnali . . . Il giusto prezzo rivendicato in tribunale," *Memoria* 17 (1986):42–58.

Filippini, Nadia Maria. "Levatrici e ostetricanti a Venezia tra Sette e Ottocento," *Quaderni Storici* 58 (1985):149–180.

Finlayson, Iain. *The Moth and the Candle: A Life of James Boswell.* New York: St. Martin's Press, 1984.

Fiorani, Luigi. "L'esperienza religiosa nelle confraternite romane tra Cinque a Seicento," *Ricerche per la Storia Religiosa di Roma* 5 (1984):155–196.

————— "Monache e monasteri romani nell'età del quietismo," *Ricerche per la Storia Religiosa di Roma* 1 (1977):63–111.

Flandrin, Jean-Louis. *Les amours paysannes. Amour et sexualité dans les compagnes de l'ancienne France (XVIe–XIXe siècle).* Paris: Gallimard/Julliard, 1975.

————— *Families in Former Times: Kinship, Household, and Sexuality,* trans. Richard Southern. Cambridge and New York: Cambridge University Press, 1979.

————— *Le sexe et l'Occident: Evolution des attitudes et des comportements.* Paris: Seuil, 1981.

Fontenay, Elisabeth de. *Diderot ou le matérialisme enchanté.* Paris: Grasset, 1981.

Foucault, Michel. *Discipline and Punish: The Birth of the Prison,* trans. Alan Sheridan. New York: Pantheon, 1977.

————— *The History of Sexuality,* trans. Robert Hurley. 3 vols. New York: Vintage, 1988–1990.

Fouquet, Catherine, and Yvonne Knibiehler. *L'histoire des mères du Moyen Age à nos jours.* Paris: Montalba, 1980.

Fraisse, Geneviève. *Muse de la raison. La démocratie exclusive et la différence des sexes.* Aix-en-Provence: Alinea, 1989.

Francastel, Pierre. *Etudes de sociologie de l'art, création picturale et société.* Paris: Denoël, 1974.

————— *Histoire de la peinture française.* Vol. 1: *Du Moyen Age à Fragonard.* Paris: Denoël, 1984.

Fritz, Paul, and Richard Morton, eds. *Women in the 18th Century and Other Essays.* Toronto: Hakkert, 1976.

Furet, François, and Jacques Ozouf. *Reading and Writing: Literacy in France from Calvin to Jules Ferry.* Cambridge and New York: Cambridge University Press, 1982.

Gallini, Clara. *Dono e malocchio.* Palermo: S. F. Flaccovio, 1973.

Garber, Marjorie. *Vested Interests: Cross-Dressing and Cultural Anxiety.* New York: Routledge, 1991.

Garrard, Mary. *Artemisia Gentileschi: The Image of the Female Hero in Italian Baroque Art.* Princeton: Princeton University Press, 1989.

Gaudemet, Jean. *Le mariage en Occident. Les moeurs et le droit.* Paris: Cerf, 1987.

Geffriaud Rosso, Jeannette. *Montesquieu et la féminité.* Pisa: Libreria Goliardica, 1977.

Gelbart, Nina Rattner. *Feminine and Opposition Journalism in Old Regime France: Le Journal des Dames.* Berkeley: University of California Press, 1986.

———— "Frondeur Journalism in the 1770s: Theatre Criticism and Radical Politics in the Pre-Revolutionary French Press," *Eighteenth Century Studies* 17 (1984):493–514.

———— "The *Journal des Dames* and Its Female Editors: Politics, Censorship, and Feminism in the Old Regime Press," in Jack Censer and Jeremy Popkin, eds., *Press and Politics in Pre-Revolutionary France.* Berkeley: University of California Press, 1987, pp. 24–74.

Gelis, Jacques. *History of Childbirth: Fertility, Pregnancy and Birth in Early Modern Europe,* trans. Rosemary Morris. Cambridge: Polity Press, 1991.

Gentileschi, Artemisia. *Actes d'un procès en viol suivis des lettres.* Paris: Editions des Femmes, 1984.

George, Margaret. *Women in the First Capitalist Society: Experiences in Seventeenth-Century England.* Urbana: University of Illinois Press, 1988.

Georgelin, Jean. *Venise au siècle des Lumières.* Paris: Ecole des Hautes Etudes en Sciences Sociales, 1978.

Giesey, Ralph. "The Juristic Basis of Dynastic Right to the French Throne," *Transactions of the American Philosophical Society,* n.s. 51, pt. 5 (1961).

Gilder, Rosamond. *Enter the Actress: The First Women in the Theater.* Boston: Houghton Mifflin, 1931.

Ginzburg, Carlo. *Ecstasies: Deciphering the Witches' Sabbath,* trans. Raymond Rosenthal. New York: Pantheon, 1991.

———— *The Night Battles: Witchcraft and Agrarian Cults in the Sixteenth and Seventeenth Centuries,* trans. John and Anne Tedeschi. Baltimore: Johns Hopkins University Press, 1983.

Glotz, Marguerite, and Madeleine Maire. *Salons du XVIIIe siècle.* Paris: Nouvelles Editions Latines, 1949.

Goldzink, Jean. *Charles-Louis de Montesquieu, Lettres persanes.* Paris: Presses Universitaires de France, 1989.

Goncourt, Edmond, and Jules de Goncourt. *The Woman of the Eighteenth*

Century: Her Life, from Birth to Death, Her Love, and Her Philosophy in the Worlds of Salon, Shop, and Street, trans. Jacques le Clercq and Ralph Roeder. Westport, Conn.: Hyperion Press, 1982.

Goodman, Dena. "Enlightenment Salons: The Convergence of Female and Philosophic Ambitions," *Eighteenth Century Studies* 22 (Spring 1989):329–350.

Green, David. *Sarah Duchess of Marlborough.* New York: Charles Scribner's and Sons, 1967.

Gregg, Edward. *Queen Anne.* London and Boston: Routledge & Kegan Paul, 1980.

Grenaille, François de. *L'honneste fille.* 3 vols. Paris, 1640.

Grimal, Pierre, ed. *Histoire mondiale de la femme.* Vol. 2: *L'Occident, des Celtes à la Renaissance;* vol. 4: *Sociétés modernes et contemporaines.* Paris: Nouvelle Librairie de France, 1966.

Grimmelshausen, Hans. *Courage, the Adventuress and the False Messiah,* trans. Hans Speier. Princeton: Princeton University Press, 1964.

Grimmer, Claude. *La femme et le bâtard. Amours illegitimes et secretes dans l'ancienne France.* Paris: Presses de la Renaissance, 1983.

Grivelet, Michel. *Thomas Heywood et le drame domestique élisabéthain.* Paris: Didier, 1957.

Grosperrin, Bernard. *Les petites écoles sous l'Ancien Régime.* Rennes: Ouest-France, 1984.

Guarnieri, Romana. "Beghinismo d'oltralpe e Bizzochismo italiano tra il secolo XIV e il secolo XV," in Raffaele Pazzelli and Mario Sensi, eds., *La beatà Angelina da Montegiove e il movimento del terz'ordine regolare francescano femminile.* Rome: Analecta T.O.R., 1984, pp. 1–13.

——— "Pinzocchere," in Guerino Pelliccia and Giancarlo Rocca, eds., *Dizionario degli istituti di perfezione,* vol. 6. Rome: Edizioni Paoline, 1980, cols. 1721–49.

Guilhem, Claire. "L'Inquisition et la dévaluation des discours féminins," in Bartolomé Bennassar, ed., *L'Inquisition espagnole, XVe–XIXe siècle.* Paris: Hachette, 1979, pp. 193–236.

Gurr, Andrew. *Playgoing in Shakespeare's London.* Cambridge: Cambridge University Press, 1987.

Gutton, Jean-Pierre. *La société et les pauvres, l'exemple de la généralité de Lyon, 1534–1789.* Paris: Société d'Edition "Les Belles Lettres," 1971.

Guyon, Louys. *Le miroir de santé et beauté corporelle.* 1615; rpt., Lyons: Chez Antoine Chard, 1625.

Hahn, H. George, and Carl Behm III. *The Eighteenth-Century British Novel and Its Background: An Annotated Bibliography.* Methuen, N.J.: Scarecrow Press, 1985.

Hamilton, A. C. *Sir Philip Sidney: A Study of His Life and Works.* Cambridge: Cambridge University Press, 1977.

Hanawalt, Barbara, ed. *Women and Work in Preindustrial Europe.* Bloomington: Indiana University Press, 1986.

Hanley, Sarah. "Engendering the State: Family Formation and State Building in Early Modern France," *French Historical Studies* 16 (1989):4–27.

Harris, Ann Sutherland, and Linda Nochlin. *Women Artists: 1550–1950*. Los Angeles and New York: Alfred A. Knopf, 1976.

Harth, Erica. *Cartesian Women: Versions and Subversions of Rational Discourse in the Old Regime*. Ithaca: Cornell University Press, 1992.

Head, Thomas. "The Religion of the *Femmelettes*: Ideals and Experience among Women in Fifteenth- and Sixteenth-Century France," in Lynda Coon, Katherine Haldane, and Elisabeth Sommer, eds., *That Gentle Strength: Historical Perspectives on Women in Christianity*. Charlottesville: University Press of Virginia, 1990, pp. 149–175.

Henriques, Fernando. *Prostitution in Europe and the Americas*. New York: Citadel Press, 1969.

Henry, Philippe. *Crime, justice et société dans la principauté de Neuchâtel au XVIIIe siècle (1707–1806)*. Neuchâtel: Editions de la Baconnière, 1984.

Herlihy, David, and Christiane Klapisch-Zuber. *Tuscans and Their Families: A Study of the Florentine Catasto of 1427*. New Haven: Yale University Press, 1985.

Higgin, Patricia. "The Reactions of Women," in Brian Manning, ed., *Politics, Religion and the English Civil War*. London: Edward Arnold, 1973, pp. 179–222.

Hill, Bridget. "A Refuge from Men: The Idea of a Protestant Nunnery," *Past and Present* 117 (1987):107–130.

———— *The Republican Virago: The Life and Times of Catharine Macaulay, Historian*. Oxford: Clarendon Press, 1992.

———— *Women, Work and Sexual Politics in Eighteenth-Century England*. London and New York: Basil Blackwell, 1989.

Hirst, Derek. *The Representative of the People? Voters and Voting under the Early Stuarts*. Cambridge and New York: Cambridge University Press, 1975.

Hoffmann, Paul. *La femme dans la pensée des Lumières*. Paris: Ophrys, 1977.

Honig, Edwin. *Calderon and the Seizures of Honor*. Cambridge, Mass.: Harvard University Press, 1972.

Hoock-Demarle, Marie-Claire. *La femme au temps de Goethe*. Paris: Stock, 1987.

Hopkins, Lisa. *Women Who Would Be Kings: Female Rulers of the Sixteenth Century*. New York: St. Martin's Press, 1991.

Houillon, Henriette. "La femme en France aux XVIIe et XVIIIe siècles," in Pierre Grimal, ed., *Histoire mondiale de la femme*, vol. 4. Paris: Nouvelle Librairie de France, 1966, pp. 7–98.

Houlbrooke, Ralph. *The English Family, 1450–1700*. London and New York: Longman, 1984.

Howard, Jean. "Crossdressing, the Theater and Gender Struggle in Early Modern England," *Shakespeare Quarterly* 39 (1988):418–440.

Howell, Martha. "Citizenship and Gender: Women's Political Status in Northern Medieval Cities," in Mary Erler and Maryanne Kowaleski, eds., *Women and Power in the Middle Ages*. Athens: University of Georgia Press, 1988, pp. 37–60.

────── *Women, Production, and Patriarchy in Late Medieval Cities*. Chicago: University of Chicago Press, 1986.

Huarte, Juan. *The Examination of Men's Wits*, trans. M. Camillo Camilli. London, 1616. Original Spanish edition, *Examen de ingenios para la scientias*. Baeza, 1575.

Hufton, Olwen. *The Poor of Eighteenth-Century France*. Oxford: Clarendon Press, 1974.

────── "Women and the Family Economy in Eighteenth Century France," *French Historical Studies* 9 (1975):1–22.

────── "Women in History: Early Modern Europe," *Past and Present* 101 (1983):125–141.

────── "Women without Men: Widows and Spinsters in Britain and France in the Eighteenth Century," *Journal of Family History* 9 (1984):355–376.

──────, ed. "Marginalité et criminalité à l'époque moderne," *Revue d'Histoire Contemporaine* 21 (1974).

Hunt, Lynn, ed. *Eroticism and the Body Politic*. Baltimore: Johns Hopkins University Press, 1990.

Hunt, Margaret. "Hawkers, Bawlers, and Mercuries: Women and the London Press in the Early Enlightenment," *Women and History* 9 (1984):41–68.

──────, Margaret Jacob, Phyllis Mack, and Ruth Perry. *Women and the Enlightenment*. New York: Haworth Press, 1984.

Ingram, Martin. *Church Courts, Sex, and Marriage in England, 1570–1640*. Cambridge: Cambridge University Press, 1987.

────── "Ridings, Rough Music, and Mocking Rhymes in Early Modern England," in Barry Reay, ed., *Popular Culture in Seventeenth-Century England*. New York: St. Martin's Press, 1985, pp. 166–197.

Institoris, Henricus, and Jakob Sprenger. *The Malleus Maleficarum*, trans. Montague Summers. New York: Dover, 1971.

Irwin, Joyce. "Anna Maria Van Schurman: From Feminism to Pietism," *Church History* 46 (1977):48–62.

────── "Society and the Sexes," in Steven Ozment, ed., *Reformation Europe: A Guide to Research*. St. Louis, Mo.: Center for Reformation Research, 1982, pp. 343–359.

Jacquart, Danielle, and Claude Thomasset. *Sexuality and Medicine in the Middle Ages*, trans. Matthew Adamson. Cambridge: Polity, 1988.

Jardine, Lisa. *Still Harping on Daughters: Women and Drama in the Age of Shakespeare*. Abingdon, Sussex: Harvester; Totowa, N.J.: Barnes & Noble, 1983.

Joeres, Ruth-Ellen, and Mary Jo Maynes, eds. *German Women in the Eighteenth and Nineteenth Centuries: A Social and Literary History*. Bloomington: Indiana University Press, 1986.

Jonard, Norbert. *Milan au siècle des Lumières.* Dijon: Université de Dijon, 1974.

Jones, Colin. "Prostitution and the Ruling Class in 18th-Century Montpellier," *History Workshop* 6 (Autumn 1978):7–28.

—— "Sisters of Charity and the Ailing Poor," *Social History of Medicine* 2 (1989):339–348.

Jordan, Constance. *Renaissance Feminism: Literary Defenses of Women in Early Modern Europe.* Ithaca: Cornell University Press, 1990.

—— "Representing Political Androgyny: More on the Siena Portrait of Queen Elizabeth I," in Anne Haselkorn and Betty Travitsky, eds., *The Renaissance Englishwoman in Print: Counterbalancing the Canon.* Amherst: University of Massachusetts Press, 1990, pp. 157–176.

Jouhaud, Christian. "Révoltes et contestations d'Ancien Régime," in *Histoire de la France: Les conflits,* ed. Jacques Julliard. Paris: Seuil, 1990, pp. 17–99.

Julia, Dominique, ed. *Atlas de la Révolution française.* Vol. 2: *L'enseignement, 1760–1815.* Paris: Ecole des Hautes Etudes en Sciences Sociales, 1987.

Kagan, Richard L. *Lucrecia's Dreams: Politics and Prophecy in Sixteenth-Century Spain.* Berkeley: University of California Press, 1990.

Kahn, Coppelia. *Man's Estate: Masculine Identity in Shakespeare.* Berkeley: University of California Press, 1981.

Karant-Nunn, Susan. "Continuity and Change: Some Effects of the Reformation on the Women of Zwickau," *Sixteenth Century Journal* 13 (1982):17–42.

Karlsen, Carol. *The Devil in the Shape of a Woman: Witchcraft in Colonial New England.* New York: Norton, 1987.

Kieckhefer, Richard. *European Witch Trials: Their Foundation in Popular and Learned Culture, 1300–1500.* Berkeley: University of California Press, 1976.

King, Margaret. *Women of the Renaissance.* Chicago: University of Chicago Press, 1991.

Kintzler, Catherine. *Condorcet. L'instruction publique et la naissance du citoyen.* Paris: Le Sycomore, 1984.

Klapisch-Zuber, Christiane. *Women, Family, and Ritual in Renaissance Italy,* trans. Lydia Cochrane. Chicago: University of Chicago Press, 1985.

Kloek, Els. "De Reformatie als thema van vrouwenstudies. Een histories debat overgoed en Kwaad," *Jaarboeck voor vrouwengeschiedenis* 4 (1983):106–149.

Knibiehler, Yvonne, and Catherine Fouquet. *La femme et les médicins. Analyse historique.* Paris: Hachette, 1983.

Kofman, Sarah. *Le respect des femmes. Kant et Rousseau.* Paris: Galilée, 1982.

Koon, Helene. "Eliza Haywood and the *Female Spectator,*" *Huntington Library Quarterly* 42 (1978–79):43–55.

Kuhn, Annette, et al. *Frauen in der Geschichte.* 5 vols. Dusseldorf: Schwann, 1982–1985.

Kunze, Bonnelyn. "'Poore and in Necessity': Margaret Fell and Quaker Female Philanthropy in Northwest England in the Late Seventeenth Century," *Albion* 21 (1989):559–580.

Labalme, Patricia, ed. *Beyond Their Sex: Learned Women of the European Past.* New York: New York University Press, 1980.

Laqueur, Thomas. *Making Sex: Body and Gender from the Greeks to Freud.* Cambridge, Mass.: Harvard University Press, 1990.

Larivaille, Paul. *La vie quotidienne des courtisanes en Italie au temps de la Renaissance.* Paris: Hachette, 1975.

Larner, Christina. *Enemies of God: The Witchhunt in Scotland.* Baltimore: Johns Hopkins University Press, 1981.

——— "Was Witch-hunting Woman-hunting?" *New Society* 58 (1981):11–12.

——— "Witch Beliefs and Witch-Hunting in England and Scotland," *History Today* 31 (1981):32–36.

Lascault, Gilbert. *Figurées, défigurées. Petit vocabulaire de la féminité représentée.* Paris: UGE, coll. 10/18, 1977.

Laslett, Peter. *Family Life and Illicit Love in Earlier Generations: Essays in Historical Sociology.* Cambridge: Cambridge University Press, 1977.

Lathuillière, Roger. *La préciosité, étude historique et linguistique.* Geneva: Droz, 1966.

Lazard, Madeleine. *Le théâtre en France au XVIe siècle.* Paris: Presses Universitaires de France, 1980.

Le Boursier Du Coudray, Angélique-Marie. *Abrégé de l'art des accouchemens dans lequel on donne les preceptes necessaires pour le mettre en pratique.* Paris: Chez la Veuve Delaguette, 1759.

Lebrun, François. *La vie conjugale sous l'Ancien Régime.* Paris: Armand Colin, 1975.

———, Marc Vénard, and Jean Quéniart. *Histoire générale de l'enseignement et de l'éducation en France.* Vol. 2: *De Gutenberg aux Lumières.* Paris: Nouvelle Librairie de France, 1981.

Le Goff, Jacques, and Jean-Claude Schmitt, eds. *Le charivari. Actes de la table ronde organisée à Paris, 25–27 avril 1977, par l'Ecole des Hautes Etudes en Sciences Sociales et le Centre National de Recherche Scientifique.* Paris and New York: Mouton, 1981.

Levin, Carole. "Power, Politics, and Sexuality: Images of Elizabeth I," in Jean Brink, Allison Coudert, and Maryanne Horowitz, eds., *The Politics of Gender in Early Modern Europe.* Kirksville, Mo.: Sixteenth Century Journal Publishers, 1989, pp. 95–110.

——— "Women in the Book of Martyrs as Models of Behavior in Tudor England," *International Journal of Women's Studies* 4 (1981):196–207.

Lewalski, Barbara. "Rewriting Patriarchal Patronage: Margaret Clifford, Anne Clifford, and Aemilia Lanyer," *Year Book of English Studies* 21 (January 1991).

Lholest, Benoît. *L'amour enfermé. Amour et sexualité dans la France du XVIe siècle.* Paris: Olivier Orban, 1990.

Liébault, Jean. *Thresor des remedes secrets pour les maladies des femmes.* Paris: Chez Jacques Du Puys, 1585.

Liebowitz, Ruth. "Virgins in the Service of Christ: The Dispute over an Active Apostolate for Women during the Counter-Reformation," in Rosemary Ruether and Eleanor McLaughlin, eds., *Women of Spirit: Female Leadership in the Jewish and Christian Traditions.* New York: Simon and Schuster, 1979, pp. 131–152.

Lougee, Carolyn. *Le Paradis des Femmes: Women, Salons, and Social Stratification in Seventeenth-Century France.* Princeton: Princeton University Press, 1976.

Loux, Françoise. *Le corps dans la société traditionnelle.* Paris: Berger-Levrault, 1979.

——— and Philippe Richard. *Sagesse du corps. La santé et la maladie dans les proverbes français.* Paris: Maisonneuve et Larose, 1978.

Luppé, Albert, comte de. *Les jeunes filles dans l'aristocratie et la bourgeoisie à la fin du XVIIIe siècle.* Paris: Champion, 1924.

Lussana, Fiamma. "Rivolta e misticismo nei chiostri femminili del Seicento," *Studi Storici* 28 (1987):243–260.

MacFarlane, Alan. *Witchcraft in Tudor and Stuart England: A Regional and Comparative Study.* New York: Harper & Row, 1970.

MacLean, Ian. *The Renaissance Notion of Woman: A Study in the Fortunes of Scholasticism and Medical Science in European Intellectual Life.* Cambridge and New York: Cambridge University Press, 1980.

——— *Woman Triumphant: Feminism in French Literature, 1610–1652.* Oxford: Clarendon Press, 1978.

Magendie, Maurice. *La politesse mondaine et les théories de l'honnêteté en France au XVIIe siècle, de 1600 à 1660.* Paris: Presses Universitaires de France, 1925.

Magne, Emile. *Voiture et les années de gloire de l'Hôtel de Rambouillet, 1635–1648.* Paris: Emile Paul, 1930.

——— *Voiture et l'Hôtel de Rambouillet. Les origines, 1597–1635.* Paris: Emile Paul, 1929.

Maire, Catherine-Laurence. *Les convulsionnaires de Saint-Médard. Miracles, convulsions et prophéties à Paris au XVIIIe siècle.* Paris: Gallimard/Julliard, 1985.

Major, J. Russell. *The Deputies to the Estates General in the Renaissance.* Madison: University of Wisconsin Press, 1960.

Mandrou, Robert. *Magistrats et sorciers en France au XVIIe siècle. Une analyse de psychologie historique.* Paris: Plon, 1968.

——— "Vingt ans après ou une direction de recherche féconde. Les révoltes populaires en France au XVIIe siècle," *Revue Historique* 93 (1969):29–40.

Marinello, Giovanni. *De gli ornamenti delle donne.* Venice, 1572.

——— *Le medecine partenenti alle infermità delle donne.* 1563; rpt., Venice: Giovanni Valgrisio, 1574.

Marion, Michel. *Recherches sur les bibliothèques privées à Paris au milieu du XVIIIe siècle (1750–1759).* Paris: Bibliothèque Nationale, 1978.

Marshall, Sherrin. "Women and Religious Change in the Sixteenth Century Netherlands," *Archiv für Reformationsgeschichte* 75 (1984):276–289.

———, ed. *Women in Reformation and Counter-Reformation Europe: Private and Public Worlds.* Bloomington: Indiana University Press, 1989.

Martin, Henri-Jean. *Livre, pouvoirs et société à Paris au XVIIe siècle (1598–1701).* 2 vols. Geneva: Droz, 1969.

Martin, John. "Out of the Shadow: Heretical and Catholic Women in Renaissance Venice," *Journal of Family History* 10 (1985):69–90.

Martin, Ruth. *Witchcraft and the Inquisition in Venice, 1550–1650.* Oxford: Basil Blackwell, 1989.

Matthews Grieco, Sara. *Ange ou diablesse. La représentation de la femme au XVIe siècle.* Paris: Flammarion, 1991.

Mauriceau, François. *Les maladies des femmes grosses et accouchées.* Paris: Chez Jean Henault, 1668.

Mavor, Elizabeth. *The Ladies of Llangollen.* Harmondsworth: Penguin, 1971.

Maza, Sarah. *Servants and Masters in Eighteenth Century France: The Uses of Loyalty.* Princeton: Princeton University Press, 1983.

McGill, William J. "In Search of a Unicorn: Maria Theresa and the Religion of State," *The Historian* 42 (1980):304–319.

Medick, Hans, and David Sabean, eds. *Interest and Emotion: Essays on the Study of Family and Kinship.* Cambridge: Cambridge University Press, 1984.

Menjot, Denis, ed. *Les soins de beauté. Moyen age, temps modernes (Centre d'Etudes médiévales, Actes du IIIe Colloque International, Grasse, 26–28 avril 1985).* Nice: Faculté des Lettres et Sciences Humaines, Université de Nice, 1987.

Merchant, Carolyn. *Death of Nature: Women, Ecology, and Scientific Revolution.* San Francisco: Harper & Row, 1980.

Mercier, Louis-Sébastien. *Tableau de Paris.* 6 vols. Geneva: Slatkine Reprints, 1979.

Mercurio, Scipion. *La commare o riccoglitrice.* 1604; rpt., Venice, 1621.

Meyer, Gerald. *The Scientific Lady in England, 1650–1760.* Berkeley: University of California Press, 1955.

Midelfort, H. C. Erik. *Witch Hunting in Southwestern Germany, 1562–1684: The Social and Intellectual Foundations.* Stanford: Stanford University Press, 1972.

Millot, Jacques-André. *L'art de procréer les sexes à volonté ou système complet de génération.* Paris: Chez Migneret, 1800.

Minut, Gabriel de. *De la beaute, discours divers . . . Avec la Paule-graphie, ou description des beautez d'une dame tholosaine, nommée La belle Paule.* Lyons: B. Honorat, 1587.

Mish, Charles. *English Prose Fiction, 1600–1640.* Charlottesville: Bibliographical Society of the University of Virginia, 1952.

Mitchison, Rosalind, and Leah Leneman. *Sexuality and Social Control: Scotland, 1660–1780.* Oxford: Basil Blackwell, 1989.

Möbius, Helga. *Woman in the Baroque Age,* trans. Barbara Beedham. Montclair, N.J.: Allenheld & Schram, 1982.

Monter, E. William. *Witchcraft in France and Switzerland: The Borderlands during the Reformation.* Ithaca: Cornell University Press, 1976.

———— "Women in Calvinist Geneva (1550–1800)," *Signs* 6 (1980):189–208.

Montrose, Louis. "'Shaping Fantasies': Figurations of Gender and Power in Elizabethan Culture," in Stephen Greenblatt, ed., *Representing the English Renaissance.* Berkeley: University of California Press, 1988, pp. 31–64.

Morandini, Giuliana, ed. *Suor Maria Celeste Galilei: Lettere al padre.* Turin: Edizioni La Rosa, 1983.

Morgan, Fidelis. *The Female Wits: Women Playwrights of the Restoration.* London: Virago, 1981.

Muchembled, Robert. *Les derniers bûchers. Un village de Flandre et ses sorcières sous Louis XIV.* Paris: Ramsey, 1981.

———— *La sorcière au village, XVe–XVIIe siècles.* Paris: Gallimard/Julliard, 1979.

Muller, Sheila. *Charity in the Dutch Republic: Pictures of Rich and Poor for Charitable Institutions.* Ann Arbor, Mich.: UMI Research Press, 1985.

Nahoum-Grappe, Véronique. *Beauté, laideur. Un essai de phénoménologie historique.* Paris: Payot, 1990.

Needham, Gwendolyn. "Mary de la Rivière Manley, Tory Defender," *Huntington Library Quarterly* 12 (1948–49):253–288.

Nicolas, Jean, ed. *Mouvements populaires et conscience sociale, XVIe–XIXe siècles. Actes du colloque de Paris 24–26 mai 1984.* Paris: Maloine, 1985.

Norberg, Kathryn. "The Counter-Reformation and Women: Religious and Lay," in J. W. O'Malley, ed., *Catholicism in Early Modern History: A Guide to Research.* St. Louis, Mo.: Center for Reformation Research, 1988, pp. 133–146.

———— "Women, the Family, and the Counter-Reformation: Women's Confraternities in the 17th Century," *Western Society for French History* 6 (1978):55–62.

Nussbaum, Felicity. *The Autobiographical Subject: Gender and Ideology in Eighteenth-Century England.* Baltimore: Johns Hopkins University Press, 1989.

O'Day, Rosemary. *Education and Society, 1500–1800: The Social Foundations of Education in Early Modern Britain.* London and New York: Longman, 1982.

Otis, Leah. *Prostitution in Medieval Society: The History of an Urban Institution in Languedoc.* Chicago: University of Chicago Press, 1985.

Ozment, Steven. *When Fathers Ruled: Family Life in Reformation Europe.* Cambridge, Mass.: Harvard University Press, 1983.

Padoan, Giorgio. *La commedia rinascimentale veneta (1433–1565).* Vicenza: Neri Pozza, 1982.

Pagels, Elaine. *Adam, Eve, and the Serpent.* New York: Vintage, 1988.

Papàsogli, Benedetta. *Gli spirituali italiani e il "Grand Siècle."* Rome: Edizioni di Storia e Letteratura, 1983.

Paré, Ambroise. *Oeuvres complètes,* ed. Joseph Malgaigne. 1575; rpt., Geneva: Slatkine Reprints, 1970.

Pateman, Carole. *The Sexual Contract.* Cambridge: Polity Press, 1988.

Pavan, Elizabeth. "Police des moeurs, société et politique à Venise à la fin du Moyen Age," *Revue Historique* 264 (1988):241–288.

Pearson, Jacqueline. *The Prostituted Muse: Images of Women and Women Dramatists, 1642–1737.* New York: St. Martin's Press, 1988.

Pelous, Jean-Michel. *Amour précieux, amour galant: 1654–1675. Essai sur la représentation de l'amour dans la littérature et la société mondaine.* Paris: Klincksieck, 1980.

Pennings, Joyce. "Semi-Religious Women in 15th-Century Rome," *Mededelingen van het Nederlands Instituut te Rome* 47 (1987):115–145.

Perrot, Philippe. *Le travail des apparences, ou les transformations du corps féminin XVIIIe–XIXe siècle.* Paris: Seuil, 1984.

Perry, Mary Elizabeth. *Gender and Disorder in Early Modern Seville.* Princeton: Princeton University Press, 1990.

Perry, Ruth. *The Celebrated Mary Astell: An Early English Feminist.* Chicago: University of Chicago Press, 1986.

——— "Colonizing the Breast: Sexuality and Maternity in Eighteenth-Century England," *Journal of the History of Sexuality* 2 (1991):204–234.

Peter, Jean-Pierre. "Entre femmes et médecins. Violences et singularités dans les discours du corps et sur le corps," *Ethnologie Française* 6 (1976):341–348.

Petitfrère, Claude. *L'oeil du maître. Maîtres et serviteurs de l'époque classique au romantisme.* Brussels: Complexe, 1986.

Phan, Marie-Claude. *Les amours illégitimes. Histoires de séduction en Languedoc (1676–1786).* Paris: Editions du Centre Nationale de la Recherche Scientifique, 1986.

Pillorget, René. *Les mouvements insurrectionnels de Provence entre 1596 et 1715.* Paris: A. Pedone, 1975.

Piponnier, Françoise. *Costume et vie sociale. La cour d'Anjou, XIVe–XVe siècle.* Paris: Mouton, 1970.

Plaisant, Michèle, Paul Denizot, and Françoise Moreux. *Aspects du féminisme en Angleterre au XVIIIe siècle.* Paris: Editions Universitaires, 1972.

Pollock, Linda. *Forgotten Children: Parent-Child Relations from 1500 to 1900.* Cambridge and New York: Cambridge University Press, 1983.

Pomeau, René. *L'Europe des Lumières. Cosmopolitisme et unité européenne au XVIIIe siècle.* Paris: Stock, 1966.

Porchnev, Boris. *Les soulèvements populaires en France de 1623 à 1648.* Paris: SEVPEN, 1963.

Pouchelle, Marie-Christine. *The Body and Surgery in the Middle Ages,* trans. Rosemary Morris. Cambridge: Polity Press, 1990.

Pozzi, Giovanni, and Claudio Leonardi, eds. *Scrittrici mistiche italiane*. Genoa: Marietti, 1988.

Prior, Mary, ed. *Women in English Society, 1500–1800*. London and New York: Methuen, 1985.

Quetel, Claude. *De par le roy. Essai sur les lettres de cachet*. Toulouse: Privat, 1981.

—— *Le mal de Naples. Histoire de la syphilis*. Paris: Seghers, 1986.

Rapley, Elizabeth. *The Dévotes: Women and Church in Seventeenth-Century France*. Montreal and Kingston: McGill–Queen's University Press, 1990.

Raulin, Joseph. *Traité des affections vaporeuses du sexe*. Paris, 1758.

Ravoux-Rallo, Elisabeth. *La femme à Venise au temps de Casanova*. Paris: Stock, 1984.

Les religieuses enseignantes, XVIe–XXe siècles. Angers: Presses de l'Université d'Angers, 1981.

Rétat, Pierre, et al. *Le journalisme d'Ancien Régime*. Lyons: Presses Universitaires de Lyon, 1981.

Révolte et société. Actes du IVe colloque d'histoire du présent (Paris, mai 1988). 2 vols. Paris: Histoire du Présent, Publications de la Sorbonne, 1989.

Reynes, Geneviève. *Couvents de femmes. La vie des religieuses cloîtrées dans la France des XVIIe et XVIIIe siècles*. Paris: Fayard, 1987.

Reynier, Gustave. *La femme au XVIIe siècle, ses ennemis et ses défenseurs*. Paris: Tallandier, 1929.

Riani, Annick. "Pouvoir et contestations. La prostitution à Marseille au XVIIIe siècle." Thèse de troisième cycle, Université de Provence, 1982.

Richardson, Lula. *The Forerunners of Feminism in French Literature of the Renaissance from Christine de Pisan to Marie de Gournay*. Baltimore: Johns Hopkins University Press, 1929.

Riley, Philip F. "Michel Foucault, Lust, Women, and Sin in Louis XIV's Paris," *Church History* 59 (1990):35–50.

Rimbault, C. *La presse féminine de langue française au XVIIIe siècle. Place de la femme et système de la mode*. Paris: thèse E.H.E.S.S., 1981.

Roberts, David. *The Ladies: Female Patronage of Restoration Drama*. Oxford: Clarendon Press, 1988.

Roche, Daniel. *La culture des apparences: Une histoire du vêtement, XVIIe–XVIIIe siècle*. Paris: Librairie Arthème Fayard, 1989.

—— *The People of Paris: An Essay in Popular Culture in the 18th Century*, trans. Marie Evans. New York: Berg, 1987.

Rodocanachi, Emmanuel. *La femme italienne avant, pendant et après la Renaissance*. Paris: Hachette, 1922.

Roelker, Nancy. "The Appeal of Calvinism to French Noblewomen of the Sixteenth Century," *Journal of Interdisciplinary History* 4 (1972):391–418.

Roger, Jacques. *Les sciences de la vie dans la pensée française du XVIIIe siècle*. Paris: Armand Colin, 1963.

———— and Jean-Charles Payen. *Histoire de la littérature française.* Vol. 1: *Du Moyen Age à la fin du XVIIe siècle.* Paris: Armand Colin, 1969.

Rogers, Katharine. *Feminism in Eighteenth-Century England.* Urbana: University of Illinois Press, 1982.

Rohan-Chabot, Alix de. *Les écoles de campagne au XVIIIe siècle.* Nancy: Presses Universitaires de Nancy, Editions Serpenoise, 1985.

Romanello, Marina. "Il caso di Marta Fiascaris tra affettata santità e rete di solidarietà femminile," in Lucia Ferrante, Maura Palazzi, and Gianna Pomata, eds., *Ragnatele di rapporti. Patronage e reti di relazione nella storia delle donne.* Turin: Rosenberg & Sellier, 1988, pp. 240–252.

Roper, Lyndal. "Discipline and Respectability: Prostitution and Reformation in Augsburg," *History Workshop* 19 (1985):3–28.

———— *The Holy Household.* Oxford: Oxford University Press, 1989.

Rose, Mary Beth. *The Expense of Spirit: Love and Sexuality in English Renaissance Drama.* Ithaca: Cornell University Press, 1988.

————, ed. *Women in the Middle Ages and the Renaissance: Literary and Historical Perspectives.* Syracuse: Syracuse University Press, 1986.

Rossiaud, Jacques. *Medieval Prostitution,* trans. Lydia Cochrane. London: Basil Blackwell, 1988.

———— "Prostitution, jeunesse et société dans les villes du sud-est au XVe siècle," *Annales ESC* 31 (1976):289–325.

Rosslin, Euchaire. *Der schwangerenn Frauen und Hebammen Rosengarte.* 1513; rpt., Augsburg: Henri Stayner, 1537.

Rotberg, Robert, and Theodore Rabb, eds. *Marriage and Fertility: Studies in Interdisciplinary History.* Princeton: Princeton University Press, 1980.

Roudinesco, Elisabeth. *Théroigne de Méricourt: A Melancholic Woman during the French Revolution,* trans. Martin Thom. London and New York: Verso, 1991.

Rousseau, Jean-Jacques. *The Confessions,* trans. J. M. Cohen. London: Penguin, 1954.

Roussel, Pierre. *Système physique et moral de la femme ou tableau philosophique de la constitution, de l'état organique, du tempérament, des moeurs et des fonctions propres au sexe.* 1775; rpt., Paris: Chez Crapart, 1803.

Rousselot, Paul. *Histoire de l'éducation des femmes en France.* 2 vols. Paris: Didier, 1883.

————, ed. *La pédagogie féminine extraite des principaux écrivains qui ont traité de l'éducation des femmes depuis le XVIe siècle.* Paris: Delagrave, 1881.

Rousset, François. *Traitté nouveau de l'hysterotomotokie, ou enfantement caesarien.* Paris: Chez Denys du Val, 1581.

Ruggiero, Guido. *The Boundaries of Eros: Sex Crime and Sexuality in Renaissance Venice.* Oxford and New York: Oxford University Press, 1985.

Sachs, Hannelore. *The Renaissance Woman,* trans. Marianne Herzfeld. New York: McGraw-Hill, 1971.

Sallmann, Jean-Michel. *Chercheurs de trésors et jeteuses de sorts. La quête du surnaturel à Naples au XVIe siècle.* Paris: Aubier, 1986.

——— "La sainteté mystique féminine à Naples au tournant des XVIe et XVIIe siècles," in Sofia Boesch Gajano and Lucia Sebastiani, eds., *Culto dei santi, istituzioni e classi sociali in età preindustriale*. Aquila: Japadre, 1984, pp. 681–702.

——— *Les sorcières, fiancées de Satan*. Paris: Gallimard, 1989.

Sasse, Klaus. *Die Entdeckung der "courtisane vertueuse" in der franzosichen Literatur des 18. Jahrhunderts*. Hamburg: Fakultat der Universitat Hamburg, 1967.

Scattigno, Anna. "'Carissimo figliolo in Cristo.' Direzione spirituale e mediazione sociale nell'epistolario di Caterina de' Ricci (1542–1590)," in Lucia Ferrante, Maura Palazzi, and Gianna Pomata, eds., *Ragnatele di rapporti. Patronage e reti di relazione nella storia delle donne*. Turin: Rosenberg & Sellier, 1988, pp. 219–239.

Schama, Simon. *The Embarrassment of Riches: An Interpretation of Dutch Culture in the Golden Age*. New York: Alfred A. Knopf, 1987.

Schiebinger, Londa. *The Mind Has No Sex? Women in the Origins of Modern Science*. Cambridge, Mass.: Harvard University Press, 1989.

Schnapper, Bernard. "La justice criminelle rendue par le Parlement de Paris sous le règne de François Ier," *Revue Historique de Droit Français et Etranger* 52 (1974):252–284.

Schulte van Kessel, Elisja. *Geest en Vlees in godsdienst en wetenschap. Vijf opstellen over gezagsconflicten in de 17e eeuw*. The Hague: Staatsuitgeverij, 1980.

——— "Moederschap en Navolging van Christus," in Petty Bange et al., eds., *De doorwerking van de Moderne Devotie*. Hilversum: Verloren, 1988, pp. 267–285.

——— "Sapienza, sesso, pietas: I primi Lincei e il matrimonio. Un saggio di storia umana," *Mededelingen van het Nederlands Instituut te Rome* 46 (1985):121–144.

——— "Le vergini devote nelle missione olandese," in *Actes du colloque sur le jansénisme*. Louvain: Nauwelaerts, 1977, pp. 187–203.

——— "Vis noch vlees. Geestelijke maagden in de Gouden Eeuw," *Jaarboek voor Vrouwengeschiedenis* 2 (1981):167–192.

———, ed. *Women and Men in Spiritual Culture (XIV–XVII Centuries)*. The Hague: Staatsuitgeverij, 1986.

Schwoerer, Lois Green. "Women and the Glorious Revolution," *Albion* 18 (1986):195–226.

Segalen, Martine. *Love and Power in the Peasant Family: Rural France in the Nineteenth Century*, trans. Sarah Matthews. Oxford: Basil Blackwell, 1983.

Serres, Louis de. *Discours de la nature, causes, signes et curation des empeschemens de la conception et de la sterilité des femmes*. Lyons: Chez Antoine Chard, 1625.

Sgard, Jean, ed. *Dictionnaire des journalistes, 1600–1789*. Grenoble: Presses Universitaires de Grenoble, 1976 (and the 5 supplements).

Sharpe, J. A. *Crime in Seventeenth-Century England: A County Study.* Cambridge and New York: Cambridge University Press, 1983.

Sherman, Claire. "The Queen in Charles V's 'Coronation Book': Jeanne de Bourbon and the 'Ordo ad Reginam Benedicendam,'" *Viator* 8 (1977):255–298.

Shevelow, Kathryn. *Women and Print Culture: The Construction of Femininity in the Early Periodical.* London: Routledge, 1989.

Shorter, Edward. *A History of Women's Bodies.* New York: Basic Books, 1982.

——— *The Making of the Modern Family.* New York: Basic Books, 1975.

Simmel, Georg. *On Women, Sexuality, and Love,* ed. and trans. Guy Oakes. New Haven: Yale University Press, 1984.

Smith, Bonnie. *Changing Lives: Women in European History since 1700.* Lexington, Mass.: D. C. Heath, 1989.

Snyders, Georges. *La pédagogie en France aux XVIIe et XVIIIe siècles.* Paris: Presses Universitaires de France, 1965.

Solé, Jacques. *L'amour en Occident à l'époque moderne.* Paris: Albin Michel, 1976.

Soman, Alfred. "Les procès de sorcellerie au Parlement de Paris (1565–1640)," *Annales ESC* 32 (1977):790–814.

Sonnet, Martine. *L'éducation des filles au temps des Lumières.* Paris: Cerf, 1987.

Spaans, Joke. "Negenenveertig Haarlemse Mirjams over het aandeel van vrouwen in de moeilijkheden rondom de lutherse predikant Conrad Victor 1617–1620," *Nederlands Archief voor Kerkgeschiedenis* 67 (1987):1–14.

Spencer, Samia. *French Women and the Age of Enlightenment.* Bloomington: Indiana University Press, 1984.

Springer, Marlene, ed. *What Manner of Woman: Essays on English and American Life and Literature.* New York: New York University Press, 1977.

Stearns, Bertha. "Early English Periodicals for Ladies (1700–1760)," *PMLA* 48 (1933):38–60.

Steinberg, Leo. *The Sexuality of Christ in Renaissance Art and in Modern Oblivion.* New York: Pantheon, 1983.

Stenton, Doris. *The English Woman in History.* London: Allen and Unwin, 1957.

Stone, Lawrence. *The Family, Sex, and Marriage in England, 1500–1800.* New York: Harper & Row, 1977.

——— *The Road to Divorce: England, 1530–1987.* Oxford and New York: Oxford University Press, 1990.

Strong, Roy. *The Cult of Elizabeth: Elizabethan Portraiture and Pageantry.* London: Thames and Hudson, 1977.

——— *The English Icon: Elizabethan and Jacobean Portraiture.* New York: Pantheon, 1969.

Sullerot, Evelyne. *Histoire de la presse féminine en France des origines à 1848.* Paris: Armand Colin, 1966.

Sydenham, Thomas. "Epistle from Dr. Thomas Sydenham to Dr. William Cole; treating of the Small-pox and hysteric Diseases," in *The Entire Works.* London: E. Cave, 1742.

Thomas, Chantal. *La reine scélérate: Marie-Antoinette dans les pamphlets.* Paris: Seuil, 1989.

Thomas, Keith. "The Virgin in History," *New York Review of Books* 18 (November 11, 1976):10–14.

——— "Women in the Civil War Sects," *Past and Present* 13 (1958):42–62.

Thompson, E. P. "The Moral Economy of the English Crowd in the Eighteenth Century," *Past and Present* 50 (1971):76–136.

Thompson, Roger. *Women in Stuart England and America: A Comparative Study.* London: Routledge and Kegan Paul, 1974.

Tilly, Charles. *The Contentious French.* Cambridge, Mass.: The Belknap Press of Harvard University Press, 1986.

Tomizza, Fulvio. *Heavenly Supper: The Story of Maria Janis.* Chicago: University of Chicago Press, 1991.

Trexler, Richard. "La prostitution florentine au XVe siècle. Patronages et clientèles," *Annales ESC* 36 (1981):983–1015.

Trumbach, Randolph. "Sex, Gender, and Sexual Identity in Modern Culture: Male Sodomy and Female Prostitution in Enlightenment London," *Journal of the History of Sexuality* 2 (1991):186–203.

Underdown, David. *Revel, Riot, and Rebellion: Popular Politics and Culture in England, 1603–1660.* Oxford: Oxford University Press, 1987.

Vandenbroeck, Paul. "Zwischen Selbsterniedrigung und Selbstvergottung. Bilderwelt und Selbstbild religiöser Frauen in den südlichen Niederlanden," *De zeventiende eeuw* 1 (1989):67–88.

Van der Meer, Theo. "Tribades on Trial: Female Sex Offenders in Late Eighteenth-Century Amsterdam," *Journal of the History of Sexuality* 1 (1991):424–445.

Van Dijk, Suzanna. *Traces des femmes. Présence féminine dans le journalisme français du XVIIIe siècle.* Amsterdam: APA–Holland University Press, 1988.

Vauchez, André. *La sainteté en Occident aux derniers siècles du Moyen Age d'après les procès de canonisation et les documents hagiographiques.* Rome: Ecole Française de Rome, 1981.

Veith, Ilza. *Hysteria, the History of a Disease.* Chicago: University of Chicago Press, 1965.

Velay-Vallantin, Catherine. "Tales as a Mirror: Perrault in the Bibliothèque Bleue," in Roger Chartier, ed., *The Culture of Print: Power and Uses of Print in Early Modern Europe,* trans. Lydia Cochrane. Cambridge: Polity Press, 1989, pp. 92–135.

Venette, Nicolas. *La génération de l'homme ou tableau de l'amour conjugal consideré en l'état de mariage.* 1685; rpt., London, 1773.

Verdier, Yvonne. *Façons de dire, façons de faire. La laveuse, la couturière, la cuisinière.* Paris: Gallimard: 1979.

Vetere, Benedetto, and Paulo Renzi, eds. *Profili di donne: Mito, immagine, realtà fra Medioevo ed età contemporanea*. Galatina: Congedo, 1986.

Vigarello, Georges. *Concepts of Cleanliness: Changing Attitudes in France since the Middle Ages*. Cambridge and New York: Cambridge University Press, 1988.

—— *Le corps redressé*. Paris: Delarges, 1978.

Vigée-Lebrun, Louise-Elisabeth. *Memoirs*, trans. Sian Evans. London: Camden Press, 1989.

Vuarnet, Jean-Noël. *Extases féminines*. Paris: Arthaud, 1980.

Ward, A. W., and A. R. Waller, eds. *The Cambridge History of English Literature*. 15 vols. Cambridge: Cambridge University Press, 1967–1968.

Warner, Marina. *Alone of All Her Sex: The Myth and the Cult of the Virgin Mary*. London: Weidenfeld and Nicolson, 1976.

Wayne, Valerie, ed. *The Matter of Difference: Materialist Feminist Criticism of Shakespeare*. Ithaca: Cornell University Press, 1991.

Weaver, Elissa. "Spiritual Fun: A Study of Sixteenth-Century Tuscan Convent Theater," in Mary Beth Rose, ed., *Women in the Middle Ages and the Renaissance: Literary and Historical Perspectives*. Syracuse: Syracuse University Press, 1986, pp. 173–205.

Weber, Alison. *Teresa of Avila and the Rhetoric of Femininity*. Princeton: Princeton University Press, 1990.

Weil, Rachel. "The Politics of Legitimacy: Women and the Warming-Pan Scandal," in Lois Schwoerer, ed., *The Revolution of 1688–1689: Changing Perspectives*. Cambridge: Cambridge University Press, 1992, pp. 65–82.

Weinstein, Donald, and Rudolph Bell. *Saints and Society: The Two Worlds of Western Christendom, 1100–1700*. Chicago: University of Chicago Press, 1982.

Weisman, Richard. *Witchcraft, Magic, and Religion in Seventeenth-Century Massachusetts*. Amherst: University of Massachusetts Press, 1984.

White, Cynthia. *Women's Magazines, 1693–1968*. London: Michael Joseph, 1970.

Wiesner, Merry E. "Beyond Women and the Family: Towards a Gender Analysis of the Reformation," *Sixteenth Century Journal* 3 (1987):311–321.

—— "Guilds, Male Bonding, and Women's Work in Early Modern Germany," *Gender and History* 1 (1989):125–137.

—— *Working Women in Renaissance Germany*. New Brunswick, N.J.: Rutgers University Press, 1986.

Wilson, Lindsay. "*Les maladies des femmes*: Women, Charlatanry, and Professional Medicine in Eighteenth-Century France." Ph.D. diss., Stanford University, 1982.

Wiltenburg, Joy. *Disorderly Women and Female Power in the Street Literature of Early Modern Europe and Germany*. Charlottesville: University Press of Virginia, 1992.

Woodbridge, Linda. *Women and the English Renaissance: Literature and the*

Nature of Womankind, 1540–1620. Urbana: University of Illinois Press, 1984.

Yates, Frances. *Astraea: The Imperial Theme in the Sixteenth Century.* London: Routledge and Kegan Paul, 1975.

Yoder, R. Paul. "Clarissa Regained: Richardson's Redemption of Eve," *Eighteenth Century Life* 13 (1989):87–99.

Zarri, Gabriella. "L'altra Cecilia. Elena Dugliolo Dal'Olio (1472–1520)," in Sofia Boesch Gajano and Lucia Sebastiani, eds., *Culto dei santi, istituzioni e classi sociali in età preindustriale.* Aquila: Japadre, 1984, pp. 573–613.

———— "Monasteri femminili e città (secoli XVI–XVIII)," in Giorgio Chittolini and Giovanni Miccoli, eds., *Storia d'Italia. Annali IX: La Chiesa e il potere politico dal Medioevo all'età contemporanea.* Turin: Giulio Einaudi, 1986, pp. 359–429.

———— *Le sante vive. Cultura e religiosità femminile nella prima età moderna.* Turin: Rosenberg & Sellier, 1990.

———— "Le sante vive. Per una tipologia della santità femminile nel primo Cinquecento," *Annali dell'Istituto Storico Italo-Germanico di Trento* 6 (1980):371–445.

Contributors

EVELYNE BERRIOT-SALVADORE *Maître de conférences* at the University of Corsica. Her area of research covers the history of ideas and literature in the Renaissance. She is the author of *Les femmes dans la société française de la Renaissance* (Geneva, 1990) and *Un corps, un destin. La femme dans la médecine de la Renaissance* (Paris-Geneva, 1993).

FRANÇOISE BORIN An iconographer and a book designer for publishers such as Plon, Gallimard, and Payot, she also holds a *licence* in history. She is presently working on images of tears and the emotions and on writer-painters.

NICOLE CASTAN Professor of early modern history at the University of Toulouse II. Her research focuses on the study of domestic space based on judicial and notarial archives of the ancien régime and on gender differences pertaining to the judicial system. She is the author of *Les criminels de Languedoc au siècle des Lumières* (Toulouse, 1981) and, with Yves Castan, *Vivre ensemble. Ordre et désordre en Languedoc, 17e et 18e siècles* (1981).

MICHÈLE CRAMPE-CASNABET Professor of philosophy at the Ecole Normale Supérieure of Fontenay-Saint-Cloud. She is interested in the themes of religion and history in the philosophy of the Enlightenment in Germany and France. She is the author of, among other works, *Kant, une révolution philosophique* (Paris, 1989) and *Condorcet, lecteur des Lumières* (Paris, 1985).

NATALIE ZEMON DAVIS Henry Charles Lea Professor of History at Princeton University and director of the Shelby Cullom Davis Center for Historical Studies. Her primary interest is the social and cultural history of Europe in the sixteenth and seventeenth centuries. She is the author of *Society and Culture in Early Modern France* (Stanford, 1975), *The Return of Martin Guerre* (Cambridge, Mass., 1983), and *Fiction in the Archives: Pardon Tales and Their Tellers in Sixteenth-Century France* (Stanford, 1987).

JEAN-PAUL DESAIVE *Maître de conférences* at the Ecole des Hautes Etudes en Sciences Sociales. He is interested in the history of rural France in the ancien régime. His published works include "Du geste à la parole: Délits sexuels et archives judiciaires 1690–1750," *Communications*, 1987. His thesis, "La mesure du possible" (1985), deals with households, property, and farming in the Aillant Valley (Burgundy) in the eighteenth century.

CLAUDE DULONG A paleographic archivist, she is also a writer whose research focuses on the seventeenth century. Among her works are *Anne d'Autriche* (Paris, 1980) and *La Vie quotidienne des femmes au Grand Siècle* (Paris, 1984).

ARLETTE FARGE *Directeur de recherches* for the Centre National de Recherche Scientifique, she uses judicial archives to study popular behavior in the eighteenth century. Among her works are *Le désordre des familles* (with Michel Foucault; Paris, 1982); *La vie fragile: Violence, pouvoirs, et solidarités à Paris au XVIIIe siècle* (Paris, 1986); *The Vanishing Children of Paris: Rumor and Politics before the French Revolution* (with Jacques Revel; Cambridge, Mass., 1988); *Le goût de l'archive* (Paris, 1989); and *Dire et mal dire. L'opinion publique au XVIIIe siècle* (Paris, 1992).

NINA RATTNER GELBART Professor of history at Occidental College in Los Angeles, California. She is currently interested in health politics in the Enlightenment press and is completing a biography of the eighteenth-century midwife Mme. du Coudray. Among her works are *Feminine and Opposition Journalism in Old Regime France: Le Journal des Dames, 1759–1778* (Berkeley: University of California Press, 1987) and the Introduction to Fontenelle's *Conversations on the Plurality of Worlds* (Berkeley: University of California Press, 1990).

OLWEN HUFTON Professor of European history and the history of women at Harvard University. She is presently working on a comparative history of women in modern Europe. Her works include *The Poor of Eighteenth-Century France* (Oxford, 1975); *Europe, Privilege and Protest* (London, 1981); and *Women and the Limits of Citizenship in the French Revolution* (Toronto, 1992).

SARA F. MATTHEWS GRIECO   Professor of history at Syracuse University (Florence). Her specialty is the representation of women, gender ideology, and sexual roles in sixteenth-century France and Italy. Among her works are *"Querelle des Femmes" or "Guerre des Sexes"? Visual Representations of Women in Renaissance Europe* (Florence, 1989); *Ange ou diablesse. La représentation de la femme au XVIe siècle* (Paris, 1991); and *Historical Perspectives on Breastfeeding* (Florence, 1991).

VÉRONIQUE NAHOUM-GRAPPE   An instructor at the Ecole des Hautes Etudes en Sciences Sociales. Her work includes the history and phenomenology of bodily identity (beauty, ugliness). Among her works are *De l'ivresse à l'alcoolisme, essai d'ethnopsychanalyse: Histoire et anthropologie du buveur, France, XVIe–XVIIIe siècles* (Paris, 1989) and *Culture de l'ivresse, un essai de phénoménologie historique* (Paris, 1991).

ERIC A. NICHOLSON   Assistant professor of literature and drama studies, State University of New York (Purchase). He is currently working on Shakespeare, on early modern comedies and their audiences, and on the history of sixteenth-century actresses. He directs plays: for example, *A Midsummer Night's Dream* (Purchase, 1992) and *The American Mandrake,* his adaptation of Machiavelli's *La mandragola* (Purchase, 1993). He has also translated Jean Delumeau's *Le péché et la peur: Sin and Fear: The Emergence of Western Guilt Culture* (New York: St. Martin's Press, 1990).

KATHRYN NORBERG   Associate professor of history at the University of California, Los Angeles, and director of the UCLA Center for the Study of Women. She is currently working on a study of prostitution and its representation in seventeenth- and eighteenth-century France. She is the author of *Rich and Poor in Grenoble, 1600–1814* (Berkeley: University of California Press, 1985).

JEAN-MICHEL SALLMANN   *Maître de conférences* at the University of Paris X–Nanterre. He is the author of *Chercheurs de trésors et jeteuses de sorts. La quête du surnaturel à Naples au XVIe siècle* (Paris, 1986) and *Naples et les saints à l'âge baroque, 1540–1750* (Paris, 1993), and, with Serge Gruzinski, Antoinette Molinie, and Carmen Salazar, *Visions indiennes, visions baroques. Les métissages de l'inconscient* (Paris, 1992).

MARTINE SONNET   *Chargée de cours* at the Institut Catholique in Paris. Her interests include the history of the family and of education. She is the author of *L'éducation des filles au temps des Lumières* (Paris, 1987).

ELISJA SCHULTE VAN KESSEL Professor-doctor of early modern cultural history at the Netherlands Institute in Rome and codirector of the project Building Baroque Rome: Immigrants from the Netherlands in the Seventeenth Century. Her research has concerned the foundation of the Accademia dei Lincei in post-Tridentine Rome, the misogyny of early modern scholars, female spirituality in the Dutch Republic, and women as patrons in baroque Rome. Among her works are *Geest en vlees in Godsdient en wetenschap* (The Hague, 1980) and *Women and Men in Spiritual Culture, XVI–XVII Centuries* (The Hague and Rome, 1986).

Illustration Credits

Index